INDIANA

A Guide to the Hoosier State

INDIANA

A GUIDE TO THE HOOSIER STATE

✓✓

*Compiled by workers of the Writers' Program
of the Work Projects Administration
in the State of Indiana*

AMERICAN GUIDE SERIES

ILLUSTRATED

SPONSORED BY THE DEPARTMENT OF PUBLIC RELATIONS
OF INDIANA STATE TEACHERS COLLEGE

OXFORD UNIVERSITY PRESS · NEW YORK

Republished 1973
SOMERSET PUBLISHERS – a Division of Scholarly Press, Inc.
22929 Industrial Drive East, St. Clair Shores, Michigan 48080

HOUSTON PUBLIC LIBRARY

COPYRIGHT 1941 BY THE DEPARTMENT OF PUBLIC RELATIONS
OF INDIANA STATE TEACHERS COLLEGE

FIRST PUBLISHED IN SEPTEMBER 1941

DEPARTMENT OF PUBLIC RELATIONS
OF INDIANA STATE TEACHERS COLLEGE
State-wide Sponsor of the
Indiana Writers' Project

FEDERAL WORKS AGENCY
JOHN M. CARMODY, *Administrator*

WORK PROJECTS ADMINISTRATION
HOWARD O. HUNTER, *Commissioner*
FLORENCE KERR, *Assistant Commissioner*
JOHN K. JENNINGS, *State Administrator*

Library of Congress Cataloging in Publication Data

Writers Program. Indiana.
   Indiana; a guide to the Hoosier State.

   (American guide series)
   "Sponsored by the Department of Public Relations
of Indiana State Teachers College."
   Bibliography: p.
   1. Indiana. 2. Indiana--Description and
travel--Guide-books. I. Series.
F526.W93 1973   917.72'04'4   72-84471
ISBN 0-403-02165-0

Foreword

The United States is a young Nation approaching maturity. It has been a melting pot for many nationalities, and out of that melting pot has come an alloy of Old World culture tempered by New World conditions.

Now our Nation, in the consciousness of its approaching maturity, is beginning to become interested in its own cultural heritages. During the feverish period of economic, scientific, and social expansion there was little time in which Americans could look backward. They were more interested in pushing ahead than in looking back over the trail they had taken. Indeed there seemed to be a fear of looking backward lest they stumble in the headlong rush. That is a characteristic of youth.

But in late years the people of the United States have come to the realization that there has been slowly developing a heritage peculiar to themselves. Steps have been taken to probe into the sources of this heritage, and to seek to discover its component elements. The American Guide Book Series is such an attempt.

This study of the past in the light of the future is no sign of weakness. It does not mean that progress has stopped nor that our Nation has begun too early to dwell in its past. Neither is it a resting on old laurels. Rather it is a quickening of our national consciousness.

Indiana State Teachers College and other agencies of educational leadership that have sponsored the Guide Series take pride in contributing to the gathering together of a great treasure trove of historical and cultural information. The story of America is an exciting history of dynamic progress, and much of it is to be found in the individual stories of the States such as this one.

Every Hoosier believes that Indiana has made a great contribution to culture in the United States, and that the story of this peculiarly distinctive State is worthy of the closest scrutiny by all Americans.

RALPH N. TIREY
President

Indiana State Teachers College

Preface

Indiana: A Guide to the Hoosier State, like its companion volumes in the American Guide Series, goes beyond the usual limits of a guide-book and portrays Indiana in terms of its people and their background, its points of interest, natural setting and resources, and its social and economic development.

Differences in people, in topography, and in economic factors have made the compilation of this book a difficult task. Information was not always available in its entirety. Authorities often differed on selection and interpretation of facts, and at many points honest and justifiable divergence of opinion occurred. The editors, nevertheless, believe they have achieved a maximum of accuracy, but if here and there they have fallen short of this objective, they will appreciate learning of it for subsequent correction.

Hundreds of Hoosiers aided generously in compiling this book. To list all of them would require pages, but to each go the thanks of the staff. Particularly helpful were: Dr. Christopher B. Coleman, Director of both the Indiana Historical Bureau and the Indiana State Library; the entire staff of the State Library; various faculty members of Indiana State Teachers College, Indiana University, Purdue University, and the University of Notre Dame; Dr. Otho Winger, president of Manchester College; Dr. Sanford C. Yoder, president of Goshen College; Wilbur Peat, director of the John Herron Art Institute; Dr. Charles F. Voegelin of the Department of Anthropology, DePauw University, and Dr. Erminie W. Voegelin of DePauw University; officials of the Department of Conservation and the State Highway Commission; the staff of the State Planning Board of Indiana; the late Reverend James Matthew Gregoire (1880-1938), Vincennes; Mrs. Bess V. Ehrmann, Rockport; the late Clarence P. Wolfe, New Harmony; Judge Hal C. Phelps, Peru; Dr. William A. Huggard and Dr. Andrew W. Crandall of the faculty of DePauw University; Dr. Stith Thompson of the faculty of Indiana University; Charles E. Baurle, Indianapolis; Lee Burns, Indianapolis; Ross F. Lockridge, director of the New Harmony Memorial Commission and at one time State Supervisor of the Indiana Writers' Project; and

Thomas R. Johnston of Purdue University. Thanks are due to Harcourt, Brace & Company for permission to quote from *Smoke and Steel* by Carl Sandburg. Acknowledgment is also due to national, regional, and State officials of the Work Projects Administration, who have without exception been most co-operative.

Although this book has been a joint responsibility involving many workers, especial mention should be made of Rebecca E. Pitts, Charlotte Davis, Howard G. Underwood, Norbert W. Meyers, W. Clay Stearley, William A. Myers, John F. Kingsbury, Roger A. Hurst, former Assistant State Supervisor; and Dickson J. Preston and Ray Thurman, Assistant State Supervisors. Final work on the guide was done with the editorial co-operation of Stella Bloch Hanau of the WPA Writers' Program.

GORDON F. BRIGGS
State Supervisor

Contents

Part I. Indiana's Background

Part II. Principal Cities

Part III. Tours

Part IV. Appendices

Illustrations

HIGHWAYS AND BYWAYS   *Between* 438 *and* 439

Maps

General Information

Railroads: Algiers, Winslow & Western; Baltimore & Ohio; Chicago & Eastern Illinois; Chesapeake and Ohio; Cleveland, Cincinnati, Chicago & St. Louis; Chicago, Indianapolis & 'Louisville; Chicago, Milwaukee, St. Paul & Pacific; Erie; Ferdinand; Grand Trunk; Illinois Central; Indiana Harbor Belt; Indianapolis Belt; Joliet, Elgin & Eastern; Louisville & Nashville; Louisville, New Albany & Corydon; Michigan Central; New Jersey, Indiana & Illinois; New York Central; Pennsylvania; Pere Marquette; Southern; Toledo, Peoria & Western; Wabash.

Bus Lines: Major east-west transcontinental bus lines crossing Indiana include Greyhound, Swallow Coach Lines, National Trailways, and the All American Bus Lines. A network of intrastate lines connects almost all cities and towns in the State.

Highways: 15 Federal highways and State roads link almost every important town and city in the State; there is also a system of graveled county roads. North-south highways are odd numbered, east-west highways even numbered. No border inspection. Highway patrol during periods of heavy traffic. No areas in which water and gas are difficult to obtain. State gasoline tax, 4¢.

Airlines: Transcontinental & Western Air, Inc., east-west flights, stops at Indianapolis. American Airlines, east-west flights, stops at Indianapolis and South Bend. Eastern Airlines, north-south flights, stops at Indianapolis. Modern airports maintained at nearly every city.

Accommodations: The usual tourist rooms and tourist camps at frequent intervals throughout the State; good hotel facilities in all cities of 5,000 or more population. Hotel accommodations scarce in Indianapolis during last week in May because of Memorial Day 500-mile Auto Race, and Labor Day because of State Fair. Accommodations scarce at South Bend, LaFayette, and Bloomington on week-ends during the football season.

Recreational Areas: Most important are the Dunes country on the shore of Lake Michigan in LaPorte and Porter Counties, the lake region in Kosciusko, Steuben, LaGrange, and Noble Counties in the northeastern part of the State, and the State parks in the central and southern part. Fair to excellent fishing in almost all Indiana streams. State parks are: *Indiana Dunes State Park* (Porter Co.), on US 12 and State 49, near Chesterton, 142 miles northwest of Indianapolis; *Pokagon State Park* (Steuben Co.), on US 27, near Angola, 166 miles northeast of Indianapolis; *Bass Lake Beach* (Starke Co.), on State 10, near Knox, 112 miles north of Indianapolis; *Mounds State Park* (Madison Co.), on State 67 and State 32, near Anderson, 40 miles northeast of Indianapolis; *Turkey Run State Park* (Parke Co.), on US 41 and State 47, near Marshall, 70 miles west of Indianapolis; *McCormick's Creek State Park* (Owen Co.), on State 46, near Spencer, 59 miles southwest of Indianapolis; *Shakamak State Park* (Clay, Sullivan, Greene Cos.), on State 48 and State 159, near Jasonville, 86 miles southwest of Indianapolis; *Brown County State Park* on State 46 and State 135, near Nashville, 48 miles south of Indianapolis; *Muscatatuck State Park* (Jennings Co.), on State 3 and State 7, near North Vernon, 66 miles southeast of Indianapolis; *Spring Mill State Park* (Lawrence Co.), on State 60 just off State 37, near Mitchell, 85 miles southwest of Indianapolis; *Clifty Falls State Park* (Jefferson Co.), on State 256 and State 7, near Madison, 88 miles southeast of Indianapolis. Picking wild flowers, cutting or defacing trees not permitted in State parks. Fires may be built only at designated points, which are marked.

Fishing Laws: Open season on trout, May 1 to August 31. Bag limit 15, minimum size, 7 inches. Open season on all other fish, June 16 to April 30. For sunfish, bluegills, crappies, and rock bass, bag limit is 25, minimum size 5 inches. For silver or yellow bass, smallmouthed and largemouthed black bass, Kentucky bass, white or striped bass, and walleyed pike, bag limit is 6, minimum size, 10 inches. For pike and pickerel, bag limit is 6, no size limit. There is no bag or size limit on perch.

Hunting Laws: Open season, Nov. 15 to Jan. 31, on opossum, raccoon, skunk, mink, muskrat, north of US 40; Nov. 25 to Jan. 31, south of US 40. Open season, Nov. 10 to Jan. 10, on rabbits (bag limit 10). For open season on squirrel, inquire county clerk. Open season all year on gray fox. Unlawful to kill beaver or deer at any time. Open season, Nov. 10 to Dec. 20, on quail (bag limit 10) and Hungarian partridge (bag limit 5). For open season on cock pheasants inquire county clerk. Unlawful to kill prairie chickens until Oct. 15, 1942. Unlawful to kill hen pheasants, wild turkeys, ruffed grouse, chukar partridge, or doves at any time.

Hunting and Fishing Licenses: Resident hunting, fishing, trapping, $1.50; resident fishing, women, 50¢; non-resident $15.50; non-resident 10-day fishing $1. Licenses required of all persons over 18 years of age to hunt, fish, and trap. Persons under 18 may fish without licenses but must have a license to hunt and trap. It is illegal to trap or net any game birds, or to kill or catch fish by means of any gig, spear, fyke-net, trap, weir, gaff hook, snare, electric current, or by means of explosives. Licenses issued by county clerks. Consult county clerks for changes in fishing, hunting, and trapping laws.

Poisonous Snakes and Plants: Rattlesnakes and copperheads, while not common, may be encountered in the hill regions of the southern part of the State. Poison ivy is common in all wooded areas in Indiana, but the poison elder or swamp sumac is found almost wholly in bogs and swamps. Ragweed, goldenrod, and other pollen-bearing plants are prevalent in almost all parts of the State. Persons allergic to these pollens may expect difficulty from mid-summer until frost.

Climate and Equipment: Travelers should expect extremely warm weather in summer; intermittent warm and cool weather in spring and fall. Winter weather ranges from cool to extreme cold with sudden changes common. Highways are not usually blocked with snow, but this may occur in severe winters.

Information for the Motorist: Cars must not be parked with motor running. At night parked cars outside towns or cities must display both head and tail lights; elsewhere, only tail light. Drivers must stop when signaled by a person driving animals. No vehicle allowed to pass a school bus, streetcar, or bus when loading or unloading. This does not apply in cities having safety zones. Spotlights are prohibited and dimming is compulsory. Vehicles must stop at intersections that are marked with 'stop' signs. Vehicle approaching intersection from the right shall have the right of way over vehicle approaching from the left. Passing a vehicle on hills and curves is unlawful. Hand signals must be used. The speed limit in business districts of cities is 20 miles per hour, in residential districts 30 miles per hour. A speed designated as 'reasonable and prudent, in relation to traffic density and condition of highway' is permitted where limits are not marked. Heavy fine or imprisonment for drunken driving.

Driver's license issued to persons 18 years of age and over. Beginner's license issued to persons between 16 and 18 years of age, who have driven a motor vehicle for at least three months under a beginner's permit and then passed an examination. No person under the age of 16, or who is a habitual drunkard or user of narcotics, or who is idiotic, insane, or feeble-minded, or whose sight or hearing is impaired, or whose physical condition is such that would render him incapable of properly operating a motor vehicle, shall be licensed. Non-residents of Indiana who are 18 years of age or more, and who hold a driver's license from their home State, or residents of States that do not require a driver's license, may operate a motor vehicle in Indiana for a period of 60 days without obtaining a license, provided that the license plates properly issued in the non-resident's home State are attached to the car. Non-residents under the age of 18 years must obtain a beginner's license the same as residents.

In all accidents classed as more than the most minor, no person is permitted to leave the scene until State police or other officers have arrived. Not more than 15 gallons of fuel may be brought into the State in any one vehicle without payment of tax. State police barracks are located in Michigan City, Ligonier, West LaFayette, Pendleton, Rockville, Evansville, Connersville, and Seymour.

State Liquor Law: Liquor-dispensing places closed on Sundays, election days, and Christmas. Open weekdays from 6 A.M. until midnight; Saturday night closing extended to 1 A.M. Sunday. Purchasing limit 1 gallon to each customer. Persons under 18 years of age not permitted in liquor-dispensing places unless accompanied by parents. Sale of intoxicants to persons under 21 years of age is unlawful.

ィィ

Calendar of Annual Events

JANUARY

Sixth	at Vincennes	Creole King Balls
Twenty-fifth	at Bicknell	Scotch Celebration of Robert Burns's Birthday
No fixed date	at Indianapolis	Exhibit, John Herron Art Institute
No fixed date	at LaFayette	Agricultural Conference, Purdue University
Last two weeks	at Terre Haute	Wabash Valley High School Basketball Tournament
Last two weeks	at Indianapolis, South Bend, Fort Wayne, Evansville, Terre Haute	Golden Gloves Tournament, extending into February

FEBRUARY

Twelfth	at Boonville	Nancy Hanks Lincoln Memorial Service

MARCH

Fourth	at South Bend	Knute Rockne Memorial Service
No fixed date	at Indianapolis	Finals, State High School Basketball Tournament

APRIL

Sixth	at Indianapolis	Army Day, Fort Benjamin Harrison
No fixed date	at Hope	Easter Sunrise Service, Moravian Church

| No fixed date | at St. Meinrad | Easter Service, St. Meinrad's Abbey |
| No fixed date | at Indianapolis | Model Home Show |

MAY

Sixteenth to eighteenth	at St. Meinrad	Ordination Services, St. Meinrad's Abbey
Twenty-seventh	at Oldenburg	Corpus Christi Service
Thirtieth	at Lincoln City	Nancy Hanks Lincoln Memorial Service
Thirtieth	at Indianapolis	500-mile Speedway Race
Thirtieth	at Terre Haute	Opening games in Midwest Semi-pro Baseball Tournament
No fixed date	in Brown County	Apple Blossom Festival

JUNE

Fifteenth to twenty-fourth	at Anderson	International Camp Meeting, Church of God
Sixteenth		Opening, Fishing Season
Sixteenth to eighteenth	at LaFayette	4-H Club Round Up
Nineteenth to twenty-second	at Indianapolis	Arlington Horse Show
Twenty-fifth	at St. Mary-of-the-Lakes	Tulip Festival
No fixed date	at New Harmony	Festival of the Golden Rain Tree
No fixed date	at New Albany	Strawberry Festival
No fixed date	Statewide	All-Indiana Air Tour
No fixed date	in Shakamak State Park	Archery Meet

JULY

| Fourth | at Rockport | Lincoln Pioneer Village Services |

| Fifteenth | at Chesterfield | Spiritualist Convention, extending to August 31 |

AUGUST

Fifth to seventh	at Michigan City	Dunes Water Sports Carnival
No fixed date	at Elwood	State Tomato Festival
No fixed date	at Evansville	Dade Park Horse Races
No fixed date	at Plainfield	Friends Yearly Meeting
No fixed date	at Washington	Graham Farms Fair

SEPTEMBER

First Monday	at Indianapolis	Opening of State Fair Grand Circuit Horse Racing
No fixed date	at Indianapolis	Air Circus
No fixed date	at Shelbyville	Soft Ball Tourney

OCTOBER

Seventh	Statewide	James Whitcomb Riley Memorial Program
Second Saturday	at Versailles	Farmers' Fair Pumpkin Show
Sixteenth to twentieth	at Vincennes	Harvest Festival
No fixed date	Place varies	Fox Hunt, Indiana Association of Fox Hunters
No fixed date	at Oldenburg	Homecoming Bazaar
No fixed date	at Indianapolis	Saddle Club Round Up
No fixed date	at Indianapolis	State Teachers Convention

NOVEMBER

| Tenth | | Opening, Hunting Season |
| No fixed date | Place varies | State Corn Husking Contest |

No fixed date	at Indianapolis	Indianapolis Symphony Orchestra Concerts Begin
No fixed date	at Indianapolis	Automobile Show

DECEMBER

Eleventh	Statewide	Programs, Indiana's Birthday
No fixed date	at Indianapolis	Indiana History Conference
No fixed date	at Madison	Tobacco Auction

PART I
Indiana's Background

Indiana Today

DESPITE the fact that Indiana lies in Meredith Nicholson's 'Valley of Democracy,' it is not wholly a typical corn-belt State. Wide topographical variations, a close economic balance between agriculture and industry, and the fact that it is directly in the path of the Nation's greatest east-west traffic flow, combine to make it almost a microcosm of the United States.

The State is populated, except in the predominantly industrial north-west section, largely by a racially homogenous third a..1 fourth generation stock. Most Indianians are descendants of pioneers either from New England or the South—English, Scotch-Irish, and German—who transmitted to posterity all the robust traditions of these races. The isolation of the frontier for many years fostered a mingling of Southern warmth and Yankee shrewdness and eventually out of this amalgamation flowered a distinct literature and art. For example, the books of Edward Eggleston, many of Booth Tarkington's, the poems of James Whitcomb Riley, and the paintings of the Brown County and Richmond groups are wholly Hoosier in conception and feeling.

Some explanation of the word 'Hoosier' must come early in almost any discussion of Indiana. It has been used to describe Indianians for many years and, after 'Yankee,' is perhaps the best-known sobriquet applied to the people of any particular division of the country. Its origin is uncertain. As early as 1833 the term must have had an accepted meaning, for in that year John Finley printed in the Indianapolis *Journal* a poem called 'The Hoosier's Nest.' A little-known term would hardly have been used in a poem intended for popular reading. The Cincinnati *Ohio Republican* in 1833 said: 'The appellation Hooshier [*sic*] has been used in many of the western States for several years to designate in a good natured way an inhabitant of the State of Indiana.' Some students profess to find a connection with the old Saxon 'hoo,' meaning a hill dweller or rustic person (hillbilly in the modern sense), but this view is not widely held. Another theory is that the word is a

3

corruption of the pioneer's hail to newcomers at his home, 'who's yer' or 'who's yere.' Perhaps the most likely version springs from the fact that in 1825 there was a contractor on the Ohio Falls Canal at Louisville named Samuel Hoosier. He found that men from the Indiana side of the river suited him better than the immigrants usually hired for such work and gave them preference. Soon his gangs were composed largely of Indianians, with the result that they became known as 'the Hoosier men,' and later simply as 'Hoosiers.' When they returned to their homes the name naturally went with them. No matter how the term originated, Indianians are always Hoosiers everywhere.

However, the Indianian who spoke the dialect of Eggleston and Riley, who ordered his affairs to the tempo of an earlier day, and who was so largely motivated by uncompromising piety, has almost disappeared. In the scientific development of agriculture and in industrial growth the State has kept pace with the Nation. Normally about 35 per cent of the gainfully employed workers of Indiana are on manufacturing and other industrial pay rolls; agriculture absorbs 20 per cent; trade, transportation, and communication, 20 per cent; professional service, 6 per cent; and domestic, clerical, and other services, 19 per cent. Although the farmers are not in the majority, the ideals of a once purely agricultural society still largely dominate the State in politics as well as in social and cultural life. This is accounted for by the fact that the average citizen is either a small-town product or the son of a farmer who migrated to the city. Finally, Indiana's highly decentralized industrial pattern contributes to the supremacy of rural and small-town elements.

So the average Hoosier is neither a highly polished urbanite nor wholly rustic. Rather, he is something in-between. Friendly and democratic, he is little given to ostentation and is likely to agree with Riley that 'they's nothin' much patheticker 'n just a-bein' rich.' 'Neighborly' perhaps describes him better than any other word. When he and his fellows get their heads together late at night they are likely to indulge in 'barber-shop harmony' rather than current song hits. The influx of foreign-born workers into the industrial northwest of Indiana has as yet had little effect on him. In general, he has simply accepted them and made a place for them in his community.

Like other States formed from the Northwest Territory, early Indiana founded its political and social life on an economy of agriculture. The pioneers brought a political ideal of equalitarian democracy that stemmed from Thomas Jefferson and reflected the interests of the farmers and small mechanics of the Colonial period. A case is recorded in the early days of Franklin County in which a citizen collected $1,000 damages in court because a neighbor had called him a Federalist.

By 1840, the supremacy of Jacksonian democracy was challenged by the Whigs in Indiana, and the State has been 'doubtful' ever since. Following the Civil War the farmers, who still dominated the State, found themselves selling their products at wholesale, buying tariff-protected goods at retail, and attempting to pay for land bought at high prices with products sold on a falling market. In their economic discontent they looked to political parties for help and to the Grange, not a political party but largely political in its aspirations. Consequently the Mugwumps, the Greenback Party, Populism, and other minority movements long engaged their attention. As a result, the Hoosier became—and remains—peculiarly and passionately addicted to year-round politics. He is both canny in prognostication and virulent in debate.

In its physical aspects Indiana presents marked contrasts, which have to some extent influenced the lives of the people. Here the prairie starts its westward sweep, and most of the northern half of the State is flat. Northern and central Indiana are, for the most part, fertile and progressive, with more level land, better kept farms, more abundant crops, and a greater air of prosperity than much of the southern half of the State. Corn, wheat, and tomatoes are widely grown; agriculture surrounds—if it does not actually pervade—even such industrial centers as South Bend and Fort Wayne. Around the former city lies one of the Nation's greatest mint-producing areas, and onions are the dominant crop in the muck lands of the former Kankakee marsh and in the vicinity of Fort Wayne.

Northeastern Indiana is a lovely pastoral region, with gentle little hills and innumerable small, clear lakes. To the northwest are the strangely beautiful dunes with their 'singing sands' and the massive, grimy Calumet area—the incarnation of industry set down on the shores of Lake Michigan.

South of Indianapolis, the central focal point of the State, the character of the terrain changes. The tumbled hills and narrow valleys of Brown County attract thousands of visitors annually. Hamlets with such unbelievable names as Shake Rag Hollow, Bean Blossom, Gnaw Bone, and Bear Wallow are the homes of a sturdy breed of folk who carry on their affairs in a way entirely different from that of the rest of the State. Here too is a growing art colony. Farther south begins a panorama unexpected in the midlands. Extending south to the Ohio River is a country of rolling hills and narrow intervening valleys. Throughout much of this region farms are smaller than in other parts of the State, and there are long stretches in which the fields are not cultivated. In south central Indiana are quarries from which comes the oölitic limestone that goes into so many of the Nation's public buildings.

Down the southwestern edge of the State runs the extremely fertile Wabash Valley, devoted to corn and fruit raising. Adjoining the Wabash on the Indiana side are the coal fields, and on the river itself is Terre Haute, cultural hub of the valley. Also on the Wabash are romantic old Vincennes, with its cathedral more than a century old and its magnificent memorial to George Rogers Clark, and New Harmony, home of the first of several American experiments in communal living and center of much pioneering in liberal thought. Along the southern boundary of the State, marked by the winding Ohio, are such towns as Madison, New Albany, and Evansville that still retain traces of the glamorous days of river traffic on the Ohio and on the Mississippi.

And so Indiana emerges as the sum of widely differing parts: industry, both massed and scattered; large, fertile farms and farms less attractive; big towns, intermediate towns, and little towns; hills, prairies, sleepy rivers lined with sycamores; lakes and sand dunes; factory hands fresh from southeastern Europe and fourth generation descendants of the pioneers; shrewd politicians and men with the chuckling good will and kindly tolerance of 'Kin' Hubbard and 'Jim' Riley.

Natural Setting

INDIANA, thirty-seventh in size of the forty-eight States, is almost an exact parallelogram in shape, bounded on the north by Michigan, on the east by Ohio, on the south by Kentucky, and on the west by Illinois. The entire southern boundary is formed by the Ohio River, and the Wabash becomes the western boundary just south of Terre Haute. Except for these irregular river courses and the arc of Lake Michigan shore that forms part of its northwestern border, the boundary lines are straight. The length of the State from north to south is approximately 265 miles; its breadth is 160 miles. Of the total area of 36,354 square miles, 309 square miles are water surface—exclusive of that portion of Lake Michigan over which Indiana has jurisdiction. This lake area, defined by extensions of the west and north boundary lines, fills out the northwest corner of the rectangle.

Indiana lies in the heart of the east central section of the United States. The parallel of latitude approximately halfway between its northern and southern extremities passes through Indianapolis; and the north-south line bisecting the eastern half of the Nation passes just east of that city.

About two-thirds of Indiana is prevailingly level or rolling, while a smaller portion, largely in the south, is hilly. The average altitude is 700 feet above sea level. The greatest height, 1,285 feet, is in Randolph County, near the eastern border; the lowest point, 313 feet, is in Vanderburgh County on the Ohio River.

The State is divided into three great regions: the northern lake country; the central agricultural plain; and the more varied southern section, containing both hills and lowlands. The boundary of the northern region is the upper Wabash, which flows southwestward across the State to Terre Haute. This northern area consists of low plains, little modified by stream action and broken by marshes and many lakes. The northeastern section, in particular, has hundreds of small bodies of water, and is characterized by low morainal hills left by retreating

7

glaciers. Farther west, in Kosciusko County, lies Lake Wawasee, the largest lake in Indiana.

Within the lake country rises the almost imperceptible watershed separating the systems of the St. Lawrence and the Mississippi. Across the marshy area in the northwest flow the Kankakee and Iroquois Rivers, to empty into the Illinois. The Tippecanoe, long and meandering, empties into the Wabash near LaFayette; Eel River rises north of Fort Wayne and reaches the Wabash at Logansport. But the tiny tributaries of these Mississippi-seeking streams have their sources often only a few hundred feet from those that flow ultimately into the St. Lawrence. The St. Joseph of Michigan dips across northern Indiana through South Bend, flowing northward again into the lake and draining a considerable area. The St. Mary's rises in Ohio and flows northwest to Fort Wayne, there uniting with another stream, also called the St. Joseph, to form the Maumee, which flows northeastward into the St. Lawrence system. Thus, intricately winding between the sources of tiny streamlets, the watershed runs through Adams and Allen Counties, curves around Fort Wayne, passes northwest through the lake country, and skirts Lake Michigan. Only a faint ground swell in a marshy plain, it divides two great river systems, the Mississippi and St. Lawrence. In northwestern Indiana, where Lake Michigan cuts into the corner of the State, is the famous dunes region.

The central portion of Indiana is a great till plain, which owes its remarkable levelness to deep glacial deposits of soil and gravel. Next to the Wabash the most important stream is White River, the west fork of which has its source in Randolph County and wanders sluggishly southwestward across the State to reach the Wabash in Gibson County. Other important tributaries of the Wabash are the Mississinewa and the Salamonie, flowing northward through the upper part of the plain. In eastern Indiana the twin forks of the Whitewater meet and flow southward into the Ohio. In the southernmost part of this region some stream erosion has taken place and there is more topographical variety.

The southern third of Indiana consists of an east-to-west succession of seven lowlands and uplands, bounded sometimes by steep escarpments of outcropping rocks. The first three of these divisions are usually (except in highly technical descriptions) grouped together as southeastern Indiana; the next three form south central Indiana (the unglaciated, or 'driftless,' area); while the seventh is known as southwestern Indiana, or the Wabash lowland. Topographically the most interesting division is south central Indiana, which is decidedly rugged and drained by scores of little rivers meandering toward the Ohio. The Crawford Upland in this area is the most beautiful and the most inaccessible part of the State; stretching from Parke and Putnam Counties to the Ohio, it contains hills, sharp ridges, and rounded knolls, valleys and wall-like bluffs, canyon-like gorges, natural bridges, caves and waterfalls. Its best-known formations are the Wyandotte and Marengo caves in eastern Crawford County, and 'Jug Rock' and 'The Pinnacle,' remarkable pillars of rock near Shoals in Martin County. In marked contrast to this region the Wabash lowland is an alluvial plain through which the Wabash, fed now by hundreds of lesser streams, moves majestically toward the Ohio.

CLIMATE

Like much of the east central part of the United States, Indiana has strongly marked seasons. The climate is distinguished by high humidity, much rainfall, and moderate cloudiness and windiness—characteristics due to the State's position in the mid-latitudes and in the path of moisture-laden winds from the Gulf of Mexico.

Although occasionally Indiana experiences severe winters with protracted below-zero weather, normal winter temperatures hover near 28° or 30° F. Freezing night temperatures and daytime thaws are characteristic throughout the cooler part of the year. The consequent contraction and expansion of surface soil sometimes breaks the roots of winter grains; but the long periods of moderate coolness are favorable for 'stooling'—the development of multiple stalks from one seed. Indiana summers are hot, with warm nights and temperatures during the day frequently approaching 100°. The growing season averages 170 days.

The average annual precipitation throughout the State is 40 inches, distributed fairly evenly throughout the year. Some years, however, bring drought, especially in the southern hills; while others bring extremely heavy rains. Of the annual precipitation only one-fifteenth, on an average, is snow. Gales are rare, the average wind velocity being only eight miles per hour. Infrequently there are tornadoes.

GEOLOGY

Before the glaciers wrote their chapter in the long geological history of what is now Indiana, a great drama had been enacted and recorded in the rocks. All the underlying rock strata found in Indiana are sedimentary rock, formed—in the course of thousands of centuries—along the margins and at the bottom of the seas. At some time the pre-Cambrian seas covered the Indiana area, and during this earliest period the first sedimentary rocks were deposited upon the original earth crust. Rocks formed during this time are exposed at no point in the State today; but their presence has been discovered, in digging deep wells, beneath all the strata of later periods.

Except for this basic layer, all the rock strata in Indiana were deposited during the Palaeozoic era, an incalculably long period within which most of the lower orders of plant and animal life developed. There were, in order of time, six great subdivisions within the Palaeozoic: the Cambrian, Ordovician, Silurian, Devonian, Carboniferous (including the Mississippian and Pennsylvanian), and Permian periods. Rocks of these periods are identified by their plant and animal fossil remains.

During the Cambrian, Ordovician, and most of the Silurian periods, Indiana was submerged beneath the seas. In the later Silurian a mighty upheaval began; eventually most of the continent was uplifted and the great interior seas slowly receded. This was not a violent or sudden process; the earth rose only an inch, perhaps, in a century or more.

In the Indiana region the first and sharpest uplift was the formation of what is now called the Cincinnati Arch. Pressure from the earth's crust slowly forced upward the layers of rock formed in the preceding periods. These layers were pressed into a kind of long ridge, from which they sloped on either side to form flanks. As it slowly reared itself, the arch divided the sea of the Indiana region into two basins— a relatively small one to the north and a larger southwestern sea. In Indiana this ridge (or rather, the 'stubs' of its flanks, for the ridge was worn away by thousands of centuries of weathering) extends northwest from Cincinnati to Richmond, thence to Kokomo, Logansport, and Chicago.

Most of the Cincinnati Arch was formed in the late Silurian and Devonian periods; but the slow process of continental upheaval continued throughout the Palaeozoic era. In the Mississippian and Pennsylvanian epochs of the Carboniferous period, Indiana was steadily elevated; at the close of the Mississippian the whole region was above sea level. During the Pennsylvanian, a period of millions of years, Indiana was probably a rank, lush swamp—populated by amphibious creatures, and covered with fern-like plants growing in vast luxuriance.

In the Permian period the swamps dried and the climate became cooler. Seas never invaded the Indiana region again.

With this brief outline in mind, the geological formations of Indiana are easily understood. In the southeastern corner of the State the surface rocks, immediately under the topsoil, are of Ordovician age. Then in order, toward the west, appear belts of Silurian, Devonian, Mississippian, and Pennsylvanian outcroppings; a second and smaller Devonian formation to the north indicates the presence in that period of a separate northern basin. Cambrian and pre-Cambrian rocks, though not exposed anywhere in Indiana, underlie these more recent formations; there are no Permian rocks, because Indiana was above the sea level during and after this period.

Ordovician rocks are exposed only in the southeastern corner because of the uplift that began at this point to form the Cincinnati Arch. Elsewhere in the State Ordovician strata are found beneath more recent formations. Next to the Ordovician outcropping a belt of Silurian rocks is exposed. Farther west the Silurian rocks are overlapped by rocks of succeeding periods—a narrower Devonian formation, a still narrower Mississippian. Only in the southwestern part of the State are Pennsylvanian rocks found, overlying the uptilted layers of previous periods.

During the many millions of years intervening between the Permian period and the glacial epoch, Indiana experienced three major cycles of erosion. In the entire Mesozoic era, however, the region was above sea level and thus has no rocks of the Triassic, Jurassic, or Cretaceous age. For the same reason no rocks were formed in Indiana during the Tertiary period of the Cenozoic (recent life) era. At the beginning of the Pleistocene (Glacial or Ice Age) the Indiana region was elevated a fourth time. Then came the glaciers, creating by their action many of the salient physical features of present-day Indiana. In the Pleistocene about five-sixths of the whole region—all except what is now south central Indiana—was at one time or another under a massive layer of ice, sometimes 2,000 feet thick.

There were at least three ice invasions into Indiana. The earliest, or Illinoian, extended farther south than the Ohio River except in the south central part of the State. Later came the early Wisconsin, which reached a line dividing the northern two-thirds of Indiana from the southern third. The last of the glaciers, the late Wisconsin, covered only the northern half of the State. After each invasion came a warmer period lasting many thousand years, during which the glacier ebbed slowly away, and plants and animals flourished.

The glaciers modified the terrain in several important ways. Their most striking effect was the present bed of the Ohio River, channeled by the ice melting at the edges. They cut off many hills in the northern region, filling the valleys with the rocks thus removed, and smoothing and leveling the entire area. By mixing these materials and grinding them into rock flour an excellent subsoil was formed, particularly a fine clay. Over much of Indiana today the glacial subsoil, the surface of which is excellent farmland, is scores of feet deep, in marked contrast to the shallow and easily eroded surface of the unglaciated areas. Glaciers also greatly altered drainage conditions by destroying streams and valleys, melting and thus creating new ones, and leaving water in many depressions to form marshes and lakes. In melting, they left extensive deposits of sand and gravel they had picked up, and created many hills in the north by piling up soil and rocks into moraines.

The glaciers were not the last agency to alter the surface of Indiana. Wind, water, chemical action, and heat and cold are still at their ceaseless labor of lifting and breaking the soil, cutting into bedrock, and carrying away the debris thus formed. In the unglaciated section the soil is thin and easily worn away, and in the course of centuries innumerable swift streams have cut into bedrock to form deep gorges, canyons, and hills. In the northern two-thirds of the State, however, the processes of erosion proceed much more slowly. Here drainage is less rapid, for the land is level and the streams sluggish.

PLANT AND ANIMAL LIFE

In Indiana there are no clearly defined floral and faunal zones, as the climate is nearly uniform throughout the entire region, and there is no passage from mountain to lowland or from seacoast to interior. Hence, with certain exceptions, the indigenous plant and animal species are distributed fairly generally throughout the State.

The principal regions in Indiana that can be differentiated according to their characteristic plant life are the Ohio River area in the south, the northern lake and marsh region, and the dunes near Lake Michigan. Most of the plants growing in these regions can be found elsewhere in Indiana, and even in the whole north central area of the United States; but a few plants are restricted to each of these limited sections.

Only in the southern counties along the Ohio is the persimmon common; the black gum tree and the southern cypress are seldom found far north of the Ohio. Certain oaks and shrubs are likewise limited to the southern part of the State.

Many know of the northern Indiana swamps (now cleared and drained) largely through Gene Stratton Porter's novels about the great 'Limberlost.' Outstanding among the trees characteristic of marshy regions are the tamarack and the bog willow. The rarest and most exotic residents of the swamps and dune country are two carnivorous plants: the pitcher plant and the round-leafed sundew. The former has a deep-purple blossom and cylindrical leaves, or 'pitchers,' holding water, into which unwary insects are lured and absorbed. The round-leafed sundew exudes onto its leaves a sticky fluid by which its insect prey is caught and held until the leaves fold over slowly and digestion begins. Floating pondweeds, bladderwort, and water milfoil are common water plants in the swampy regions. Before the marshes were drained, crops of cranberries and blueberries were raised in this region, and peppermint is still gathered for its oil.

In the dune region, shifting hills of sand skirt Lake Michigan for miles and merge gradually into rolling prairies and marshes to the south, a juxtaposition of desertland and jungle that fosters a startling variety of plant life. Great white pines and many species of oaks thrive here; the arctic lichen moss and the jack pine, that sturdy tree of the far north, grow near the sassafras, tulip, sour gum, and pawpaw, natives of the semitropics. The same contrast is apparent everywhere. The prickly-pear cactus thrives on the sand wastes, bearing beautiful yellow blossoms; within walking distance bloom irises and orchids in shady moist places. The dune regions contain also the typical trees, shrubs, and flowers that are distributed more generally throughout the State.

In his *Trees of Indiana* (1931), Charles Deam reports 134 species. Of these, 124 are native to Indiana, the remaining ten having been successfully introduced. There are 17 species of oak; the black walnut and many species of maple are common. Especially prominent are the beech, lovingly painted by Indiana artists for its mottled trunk and rich autumn colors; the massive sycamore, gleaming white along the banks of streams; and the majestic tulip tree, or yellow poplar, the State tree. Poplars and hickories of many species are numerous, and there are several common types of fruit trees, notably the apple, cherry, peach, and pear.

Among the ten species successfully introduced are the common catalpa and the golden rain tree. The latter was brought from China by William Maclure and first planted at New Harmony; it is a small, round-topped tree producing large panicles of yellow flowers in June.

Trees of Indiana lists 163 shrubs (including vines) of which all but one, the Japanese honeysuckle, are native. Probably the commonest is the elderberry, which covers roadsides and fence rows, first with its masses of white flower clusters, and later with its dark purple fruit. The trailing, twining bittersweet is an attractive shrub in the autumn, when its bright orange berries open to reveal scarlet centers. Roses, wild berries, the prolific trumpet-creeper—adorning waste places with its large reddish-orange flower—and many species of the sumacs, flaming red in autumn, are common. The rarest shrub is the trailing arbutus, found only in Monroe County and the dune region. The Virginia creeper, or five-leaved ivy, is the most ornamental of the vines; perfectly hardy, it transplants easily, and its leaves in autumn are rich scarlet, crimson, and purple.

Pussy-willows, jack-in-the-pulpits, dainty spring beauties, and great masses of violets are among the earliest arrivals of the year in meadows and oak openings and along the streams. Blue lupine, one of the loveliest of wild flowers, covers the slopes in early May; soon the rue anemone raises its pinkish blossom from a whorl of leaves, then comes the wood anemone, with its single deep pink flower. Summer brings sweet clover and the ox-eyed daisy, with its yellow center and white petals; corncockle, with a beautiful purple-pink blossom; and the wild carrot, or Queen Anne's lace, with finely divided leaves and large umbels of white flowers. Goldenrod, asters, and sunflowers are perhaps the most striking and conspicuous of all the autumn flowers, and the late fall brings the fringed gentian, shaped like a beautiful deep blue vase, from the top of which drop four deeply fringed lobes of violet.

Of the 66 species of mammals found in pioneer Indiana, at least 14, including the bear and wild cat, no longer inhabit the region. Although timber wolves and coyotes are occasionally reported in the northern woodlands, the red fox is the only carnivorous animal thriving today in the State. Other animals frequently hunted and trapped are the rabbit, muskrat, raccoon, woodchuck, opossum, mink, and several species of squirrel. Common small animals are the mole, shrew, field mouse, chipmunk, striped gopher, weasel, skunk, and bat.

Fish are plentiful in lake and stream—catfish, pike, pickerel, bass, goggle-eye, and sunfish. Several species of blind fish, all small, inhabit the cave waters. Reptiles and other lower forms differ little from those of other States in the same faunal area.

At the turn of the century about 320 species of birds, nearly all migratory, were known to be residents of this region at some time during the year. Today more than half of them are rare or extinct.

Near Lake Michigan and the dunes, the bird-lover still finds birds from the far north, the plains, the deep woods, and the swamps. South of the dune region in the Kankakee River and swamp area, now partly drained, are many waterfowl and marsh birds, including the fish duck, the teal, the American golden-eyed duck, and the mallard (all winter residents); and the great blue heron, American bittern, and wild goose. In the prairies near these swamps are seen the yellow-winged sparrows and prairie larks. The shy wood thrush is found only in the rare densely forested areas. In the southeastern part of the State, just north of the Ohio, the forests of beech, oak, maple, sweet gum, and black gum attract the Cape May warbler, summer redbird, and black-throated blue warbler.

In the intensely farmed central section are many orchard and meadow birds: the field sparrow, yellow warbler, orchard oriole, robin, meadow lark, redheaded woodpecker, bluejay, bluebird, flicker, cardinal, wren, swallow, and many other species. Most of these birds are found to some extent throughout the rest of the State, but they are most common in this section.

In other parts of Indiana, winter residents include the junco, shore lark, tree sparrow, sapsucker, white snowbird, snowy owl, and waterfowl. In mild winters, however, a few robins, meadow larks, and woodpeckers remain all season. Among game birds, the quail is most common, although it has been wantonly destroyed; and the ruffed grouse is occasionally found.

NATURAL RESOURCES AND CONSERVATION

Indiana has great wealth in its mines and quarries, its water supply, and, in spite of waste and misuse, its soil and timber. The mineral wealth is derived largely from the sedimentary rocks consisting of limestone, sandstone, shale, and coal, with large deposits of clay and kaolin in certain parts of the State. Sand and gravel are also plentiful.

The State's best-known mineral resource is an almost unlimited supply of building stone, chiefly obtained from limestone deposits. The most dependable Indiana stone, of which there are several varieties, is quarried from the Mississippian system of rocks. All the varieties are used widely for the manufacture of lime and cement, and locally for building. The Indiana oölitic limestone (so called because of its granular structure, which suggests a mass of fish eggs) is one of the finest building stones quarried in the United States. A medium- to fine-grained stone with even texture, it is soft and easily carved when first quarried, but under the action of atmospheric agents becomes hard and durable. From the chief quarries in Monroe and Lawrence Counties, this stone is shipped all over the United States and to foreign countries.

In the area of the Pennsylvanian rocks there are extensive deposits of bituminous coal. It is estimated that the entire coal section, covering about 7,000 square miles, holds about 13,000,000,000 tons of coal suitable for mining with present-day methods. Gas, coke, and producer gas are important by-products.

Third in value among mineral resources is clay, found largely in the Pennsylvanian rocks, especially in the coal-bearing areas. Thirty years ago the clays were regarded as a detriment to coal mining; today, although not yet fully utilized, they rank in value next to coal and stone.

Because of its fine clay deposits and immense supply of limestone, Indiana ranks high in the manufacture of Portland cement. There are extensive deposits of stone in southern Indiana, at present unused, that are also suitable for cement manufacture. Huge quantities of sand and gravel are extracted from gravel pits every year and used in the manufacture of cement, plaster, and glass, and in the surfacing of roads.

In earlier periods several minerals were more important to Indiana industry than they are today. Iron ore was formerly mined, but in recent years iron of much better quality is imported. Marl, a clay-like substance found at the bottom of some lakes, was formerly an important mineral used in making cement. Immense wells of natural gas were wasted between 1890 and 1910; a little later, in the same area, oil production boomed but declined after a few years. Today another oil boom is developing in many Indiana counties. Mineral waters are still present in 22 important springs or wells in 18 counties.

Indiana has a great area of rich soil suitable for agriculture. Over most of the northern two-thirds of the State lie deep, silty, light-brown loams, weathered by glaciers from limestone and sandstone. In the 'driftless' area the soils are thinner and less fertile—heavy clay soils, brown silt loams, or yellowish soils of a silty to sandy character, weathered largely from limestone. Their fertility was depleted by an unvaried succession of corn crops during pioneer times.

Except for the Ohio there are no large rivers in the State, but a well-developed system of small streams provides potential hydroelectric power, adequate water supply for many cities, and good drainage (supplemented in the lowlands by artificial tile drainage). In its lakes Indiana has vast reservoirs of water for use in northern fields during dry weather, and abundant deposits of sand and gravel form important storage basins in many parts of the State.

A hundred years ago fully seven-eighths of the State was covered with forests. The only treeless area was the prairie land in the northwest. A century's waste of these forests, however, has meant devastation of many kinds. The trees had stored moisture in the earth, and this served the thirsty plants in time of drought. After the trees were gone, when heavy rains fell, the water (no longer held back by roots and mold) drained swiftly toward the streams and washed the soil off the hillsides. Swollen tributaries rushed into main streams, overflowing their banks and sometimes creating serious floods. In a long dry period, on the other hand, the soil dried quickly to a great depth, since water could no longer be easily retained. Streams ran dry, and moistureless winds blew away the topsoil in clouds of dust. Thus the destruction of the forests brought in its wake floods, drought, and soil erosion. At least 100,000 acres of southern Indiana land are today in serious stages of erosion.

Despite these tragic losses, the supply of hardwood timber still constitutes a valuable natural resource. Although much of it is of young trees, the remaining first-growth timber is of high quality, including such species as walnut, ash, poplar, elm, hickory, maple, and many kinds of oak, some reaching an exceptionally large size. Throughout southern Indiana and in several northern counties are vast areas that could easily be devoted principally to forests.

In the southern hills the problems of drought, flood, and soil erosion are extremely acute. A suggested solution is the retirement of most of the region from agriculture and the reforestation of the hills. Good drainage and limestone soils in certain areas would make the cultivation of fruit trees profitable, and a gigantic State forest stocked with game is contemplated in the 'driftless' area. Throughout the reforested section, tree roots would nail the soil to the slopes; water would be adequately stored; and streams would not swell toward flood proportions in rainy weather.

Northern Indiana is so low that bogs are common and storage is more than adequate. Hence there is no danger of flood, drought, and soil erosion. But even here natural resources have been misused in the clearing and drainage of submarginal land. Again a suggested solution is to retire this poor land from agriculture and plant extensive forests.

In central Indiana, agriculture is sometimes menaced by drought and flood, since rainfall, although fairly adequate, is irregular. Because of the deep, level soil, however, there is less damage from erosion here than in the south. Since the region is too valuable agriculturally for extensive reforestation, experts particularly recommend the planting of 'riverside forests'; the development of irrigation; and the increased use of the self-controlling dam, allowing an ordinary flow of water to escape but retaining the excess amount in storage ponds. Thus the water table would be lifted and maintained as a precaution against drought. During rainy weather the dams would take the crest off the floods, preventing torrents.

In 1919 the State Department of Conservation was established by legislative act, consolidating the formerly independent divisions of fish and game, entomology, geology, forestry, engineering, and parks, lands, and waters. Since its establishment this department has done much toward reclaiming worn-out soil; controlling stream pollution; conserving and propagating wild life; and guarding against drought, flood, and soil erosion.

In 1933 the General Assembly created the State Planning Board, a research agency co-operating with the National Resources Committee, now the National Resources Planning Board. The board's *Preliminary Report,* which appeared in 1934, contained not only a thorough survey of Indiana's natural resources—soil, forest, water, and minerals—but also many recommendations for their conservation and proper use. Supplementing the work of the State Planning Board are active planning commissions in several counties and most of the State's principal cities.

Aided by State-wide conservation clubs with a membership of 150,-000 and the active support of the general public, the Department of Conservation has carried out a persistent and enlightened program of public education through schools, newspapers, radio, and its own publications. It publishes *Outdoor Indiana,* a monthly magazine devoted to all phases of conservation, and provides trained speakers and motion picture films to interested groups.

The department maintains 4 game preserves and 5 major fish hatcheries, 10 State parks, 4 historical memorials, and 11 State forests. Of the State parks, the Brown County State Park in the south central part of Indiana, with an area of 3,821 acres adjoining an 11,000-acre State game preserve, is the largest and perhaps the best known. Next in size is 2,200-acre Dunes State Park, along the shore of Lake Michigan. This is an important summer playground for Indiana people and residents of Chicago and the adjoining region. Other parks, scattered over the State, range in area from 251 to 1,300 acres.

The department also maintains nurseries for reforestation purposes, sponsors an extensive forest-fire prevention campaign, and is concerned with the protection of songbirds and migratory waterfowl. It maintains an efficient game-warden service, inspects apiaries to check the spread of diseases destructive to honey bees, and supplies information to growers and property owners on control of insects and plant diseases. It compiles data on water-table levels throughout Indiana; aids in efforts to raise the water table and prevent floods by State-wide stream improvement; and has inaugurated a program for the treatment of abandoned mines to eliminate acid drainage, a continued source of stream pollution.

Since 1933, an important function of the department has been its work as the State co-ordinating agency for the Emergency Conservation Work program. With the aid of the Civilian Conservation Corps, roads have been built and trails and sanitation facilities provided for State parks and memorials; and, in the State forests, main service roads, fire trails, and administrative buildings have been constructed.

Vitally important to Indiana is the work being done by the Soil Conservation Service of the United States Department of Agriculture. In 1937 projects were set up in Henry and Lawrence Counties, and a study has been made of the special economic and soil conditions prevalent in each area. On the basis of this study long-range plans have been made, and many farmers have signed five-year agreements to operate their farms in accordance with these plans. In general, the agreements provide for crop rotation; the retirement of steeply eroded hillsides for use as pasture or woodland; and strip planting on less steeply graded slopes. In this type of planting, close-growing crops, such as small grains and grasses, alternate with cultivated crops, to slow up the runoff from the cultivated strips. Such conservation measures, if widely practiced in the next few years, may avert otherwise inevitable ruin of excellent farmland.

The Federal Government is purchasing more than half a million acres of submarginal land, chiefly in southern Indiana, to be converted into national forests or land utilization projects. In addition, it maintains recreational demonstration areas near Versailles in Ripley County and near Winamac, in Pulaski County.

Archeology

IN the valleys of the Ohio and the Mississippi once lived a prehistoric people, popularly called the Mound Builders, who left throughout the Middle West abundant traces of their material culture. They left earthen forts and embankments, the enigmatic mounds so long the subject of many theories, and the village sites which are now being discovered in connection with these mounds. Indiana is one of the regions richest in these archeological treasures.

Mounds are found throughout the Middle West, particularly in the river valleys, and they increase in number as the confluence of the Ohio and the Mississippi is approached. They are generally simple cones of earth, varying from 4 to 70 feet in height; but many are truncated and sometimes terraced. Occasionally stone mounds are also found. Enclosures and fortifications made of earthen walls of many shapes (circles, parallelograms, and other geometric forms indicating a knowledge of measurement) surround areas of from 1 to 30 acres. Mounds and the pits that may mark the former sites of dwellings are usually found within these enclosures.

Roughly about a third of Indiana's counties contain mounds or enclosures of one type or another. Most of them are found in the south, perhaps because of the Ohio and its tributaries; but there are several in La Porte County, at the northern border of the State. In the north central part of Indiana, in Howard, Tipton, and Hamilton Counties, there are numerous sites of interest; and in Madison County, four miles from Anderson, is the famous Mounds Park, presented to the State by the people of Madison County and opened as a State Park in 1931. The Fudge Mound, which has been thoroughly excavated and leveled, was in Randolph County near Winchester. The southeastern corner of the State (Franklin, Bartholomew, Ripley, Dearborn, Ohio, Switzerland, Jefferson, Scott, Clark, and Floyd Counties) is dense with mounds and fortifications of great interest. There are mounds in Fountain, Vermillion, Morgan, Owen, Greene, Vigo, and Sullivan Counties;

and in the southwestern part of the State, Knox, Posey, Vanderburgh, and Warrick Counties are known to contain many mounds.

At one time a veil of mystery hung over the Mound Builders. What was their origin? What became of them? Was theirs a civilization comparable to that of the Aztecs of Mexico, or were they primitive savages? Were the mounds built for altars of human sacrifice, for burial of the dead, for temples to the sun, or for palaces of kings? Theories were spun about a vast slave empire, with kings and priests, temples and cities, and a culture no less impressive than that of ancient Egypt. But for a century little concrete archeological knowledge was acquired in Indiana, in spite of the excavations of Charles A. LeSueur near New Harmony, and the enthusiastic work of E. T. Cox and John Collett, State geologists during the 1870's and 1880's.

In the summer of 1926 J. Arthur MacLean was the first to study an Indiana mound thoroughly and with scientific technique. Funds for the excavation were privately raised, and in July Mr. MacLean began to excavate a mound on the farm of William Albee, in Sullivan County. The task was completed in the summer of 1927. Meanwhile, in December 1926, the Archeological Section of the Indiana Historical Society was formed. In co-operation with the Historical Bureau it has raised funds to finance further expeditions. New material thus brought to light has been published in the *Indiana History Bulletin* and in the *Pre-history Research Series,* which was started in 1937. In 1928 a survey was made of Whitewater Valley; since that time Greene, Porter, Randolph, Dearborn, and Ohio Counties have been systematically surveyed, and important mounds and sites have been explored. In 1939–40, under the direction of Glenn A. Black, the Angel Mounds in Vanderburgh County were excavated. It is planned to continue with this work until the whole State is mapped and catalogued.

Largely on the basis of research done in Ohio, which completed such a task long ago, Indiana archeologists are able to allocate to one culture or another the pottery, ornaments, and stone blades found so frequently in Indiana mounds. Moreover, Indiana scientists have added new material to the existing store of knowledge. Their recent work has accumulated a modest but solid store of facts to serve as a basis for further investigation.

The Mound Builders possessed a fairly well-developed culture— either early Neolithic (New Stone) or possibly late Paleolithic. The Neolithic age was that culture period in which men made tools of polished stone; developed pottery, the bow, textiles, and basketry; domesticated a few plants and animals; and began to use copper. Prehistoric traces in America, however, show that not all the people had attained this level of culture.

Recent research has established that two sub-cultures existed among the Mound Builders of the Middle West: the Woodlands and the Mississippi. These may be easily distinguished from each other, and each contains within itself divisions that are also easily distinguished. The Woodlands culture is divided into the Algonquian, Hopewell, and Adena variants; and the Mississippi into the Upper, Middle, and Lower Mississippi. The upper Mississippi is further divided into the Iroquoian, Fort Ancient, and Tennessee-Cumberland subvariants. These cultures are named for general areas in which they have been discovered or for particular places where important artifacts have been found.

Recent excavations and research have made it clear that the Indiana area was dominated by tribes of the Woodlands culture. They built a majority of the Indiana mounds (in which they buried their dead) and threw up massive geometrical earthworks in many places. They even encroached on the territory in the southern part of the present State along the Ohio, where tribes of the Fort Ancient and Tennessee-Cumberland variants of the Upper Mississippi culture were dominant.

The Hopewell variant of this Woodlands culture is most widespread and investigators agree that it represents a high point of esthetic and economic development among the Mound Builders. Important characteristics found at Hopewell sites include: log- or stone-walled tombs within the mounds; cremation of the dead; well-prepared burial floors of stone or clay; clay altars—possibly for cremation; ceremonial pottery; obsidian blades of rare forms and ornaments of mica—implying commerce, since neither material is plentiful in Indiana; stone platform pipes, with animal and bird forms carved on the bowls; the lavish use of copper for both ornament and utility; the use of polished jawbones and freshwater pearls for ornaments; and geometrical earthworks erected around the mounds. Hopewell mounds have been found widely scattered in La Porte County in the north, in Rush, Greene, Dearborn, and Ohio Counties; and near Anderson, Newcastle, and New Harmony.

In Mounds State Park, four miles east of Anderson, near the bluffs overlooking White River, is the largest single earthwork in Indiana, a wall 9 feet high, 1,200 feet in circumference, and 50 or 60 feet wide at the base, surrounding a central mound. The mound itself is 4 feet high and 30 feet in diameter. Near this embankment are several other mounds—two of them presenting the curious and unique 'fiddle back' formation (*see Tour* 6).

The other variant of Woodlands found in Indiana is the Adena culture, regarded by some authorities as a less highly developed form of the Hopewell complex. It is widely distributed in Ohio, but for the most part found only in eastern Indiana. It is characterized (although further research in Indiana may alter this view) by the following traits: leaf-shaped blades of flint; slate gorgets of the expanded-center type; tubular pipes of clay or stone; a sparing use of copper, and for ornament only; the presence of red ocher on many artifacts; and conical mounds with log-and-bark-lined tombs beneath. These were excavated before the mounds were built and had logs over the top to prevent the earth of the mound from caving in. Franklin County contains several good Adena sites, but perhaps the most conspicuous example was the famous Fudge Mound near Winchester. In spite of such a striking variation from type as the presence of large rectangular earthworks, this was considered an Adena mound because of the artifacts discovered there.

It is evident that a good deal is known about both the Hopewell and Adena peoples; this knowledge is largely based on their arts and is derived from burial mounds, where personal ornaments and ceremonial objects were deposited. But since no objects of ordinary life—for example, kitchen utensils—were deposited in the burial mounds, only an occasional accident, such as the discovery of some chemically preserved textiles, gives the investigator any insight into the mode of life of these people. One might guess at their religion, but without assurance, and it can be assumed that they carried on some kind of primitive commerce. They wove rather coarse cloth of wood-fiber, and certain 'corncob' markings on their pottery indicate that they practiced agriculture.

Along the Ohio and in the lower Wabash Valley two aspects of the Upper Mississippi culture are dominant: the Fort Ancient and the Tennessee-Cumberland variants.

The Fort Ancient culture is largely represented in Indiana and is easy to identify. Habitation sites near the mounds are large, and the great accumulation of debris shows that the people were sedentary and agricultural. They built mounds—though not so many or so large as those of the woodlands people—in which they seem to have buried their dead accumulatively. Burials are also found in shallow earth-and-stone-lined graves. The pottery of this group is distinctive, and they were fond of working in bone—awls, needles, and flaking tools of bone and antler are found in great numbers. But they made very few stone tools except arrowheads, hammers, and knives. Perhaps their most distinctive culture trait is the fact that they built great forts, such as Fort Ancient in Ohio. Their forts, mounds, and habitation sites are found along the Ohio River, westward from the Ohio State Line to a point as yet undetermined. A striking example is Stone Fort on the Ohio, three miles from Charlestown at the mouth of Fourteen Mile Creek. Natural bluffs and strong embankments of earth and stones make this a practically impregnable military position.

The Tennessee-Cumberland variant (sometimes called Muskhogean) is found in southwestern Indiana in Posey, Sullivan, Knox, and Vanderburgh Counties. Flat-topped mounds, often elaborately terraced, and surrounded by smaller mounds both flat-topped and conical, are characteristic of this culture. Some of these mounds contain shallow earth-and-stone-lined graves for burial; and it is thought that others were foundations for the houses and temples of chieftains and priests. Prolific pottery makers, the Tennessee-Cumberland people made long-necked water bottles (sometimes in effigy of the female form, or of animals) and wide-mouthed bowls with figures of fish and frogs around the periphery. They used copper for tools as well as ornament, and made beautifully chipped blades of flint, large flint hoes and spades, and large stone pipes. They were sedentary, agricultural people, building houses of wattle work or cane and mud.

Perhaps the most interesting site of this culture is in Sullivan County: Fort Aztalan, near Merom, on the Wabash (*see Tour 20b*). This is a great, irregular, three-sided defensive enclosure, with a circumference estimated at 2,450 feet. Within are 5 mounds and 45 pits, or depressions, regarded by authorities as the foundation-sites of dwellings.

Archeological work has just begun in Indiana, and there are many questions not yet answered about the cultures and migrations of the prehistoric tribes of Indiana. Even now, however, it is possible to say that the Mound Builders were a race of Indians who had attained a level of culture not much higher than that of the Indians of the period immediately preceding the invasion by the whites. In spite of the size and geometrical form of the mounds, the tools, pottery, and ornaments found with the burials do not indicate that their makers had entered or were about to enter a period of highly developed or complex culture. They had neither a written language nor an art stamped with great beauty.

It is not yet known whether or not the Indiana Mound Builders were the direct ancestors of the Miami and other tribes living here at the time of the early settlements. If they were not, the question of their fate is still unanswered. These problems may be solved, however, by further research—by careful analysis of culture sites and of probable migrations. In any event it has been established that the Mound Builders were neither the ancestors nor the descendants of the Aztecs or any other highly civilized prehistoric nations. They were the first Indiana Indians.

Indians

IN all parts of this continent except the Ohio Valley region, early explorers, fur traders, or settlers encountered Indian tribes who lived in or claimed as hunting territories the lands under exploration. In Indiana, Kentucky, and Ohio, this was not the case. In the early eighteenth century, when the whites first began to penetrate the wilderness country west of the Alleghenies, they encountered practically no Indian groups within the Ohio Valley region who could lay certain claim to this vast territory by virtue of long and continuous occupation or use of it.

Yet Indiana, like its sister States on the east and south, is extremely rich in archeological remains that attest the fact that in prehistoric times the region supported a large or fairly large native population. What happened virtually to clear the Ohio Valley of this population prior to the advent of the whites? One explanation is that the confederated Iroquois tribes of central New York gained power after their early acquisition of guns from white traders, and sent out war parties westward. It has been suggested that they swept Ohio, Indiana and Kentucky clear of their native population during the seventeenth century. This is a possible explanation, although recent studies of the Iroquois render dubious the extent to which the Five Nations dominated the native tribes in regions as far distant from New York State as the valleys of the White and Wabash Rivers.

Many archeological, linguistic, and ethnological problems of the Great Lakes-Gulf area, which includes Indiana, are not yet solved. Only the most tenuous clues are available on what tribal or linguistic groups constituted the early historic inhabitants of the present State. One of the most positive statements concerning Indiana's early population is that made by Father Gravier who, in his description of a trip down the Mississippi River in 1700, remarked that the Wabash and lower Ohio Rivers were called the river of the Akansea (Quapaw), 'because the Akansea formerly dwelt on its banks.' If this is actually so, the Quapaw, a Siouan-speaking tribe, would be the earliest recorded group in Indiana. However, their reported occupation on the Wabash and lower Ohio had terminated before Indiana itself was explored; when Marquette and Joliet descended the Mississippi in 1673 they encountered the Quapaw on its banks, near the mouth of the Arkansas River, and in 1682 La Salle and members of his party 'established a peace' and took possession of the Quapaw villages on the Mississippi River for the French.

Beside the Quapaw, two other tribes, the Algonquian-speaking Shawnee and Miami, are often mentioned as early inhabitants of Indiana. Some scholars have suggested that southern Indiana and Kentucky was the aboriginal home of at least a part of the Shawnee tribe. The most explicit reference to the Shawnee being located on the Ohio River in the late seventeenth century is by Abbé Gallinée, in the Jesuit *Relations*. Gallinée states that, in 1668, some Seneca told La Salle 'many marvelous things concerning the Ohio River, which they claimed to be perfectly acquainted with . . . They told him that this river had its source at three days' journey from Sonnontouan [near Naples, Ontario County, western New York] and that after a month's travel he would reach the Honniasontkeronons [Andaste?] and the Chiouanons [Shawnee], and that after having passed these and a great waterfall which there was in the river [the Falls of the Ohio?] he would find the Outagame and the country of the Iskousogos . . .' In 1669 Gallinée and La Salle embarked from Montreal to explore the Ohio under the guidance of their Seneca informants, but the expedition ended disastrously and they did not even succeed in reaching the headwaters of the Ohio River.

Marquette also mentions the 'Chaouanons' or Shawnee; in his account of his trip down the Mississippi with Joliet he remarks that the Waboukigou, which was the name some of the Indian tribes gave to the Ohio below its confluence with the Wabash, 'flows from the lands of the East, where dwell the people called Chaouanons in so great numbers that in one district there are as many as twenty-three villages, and fifteen in another, quite near one another.' On Joliet's sketch maps the Shawnee are located variously, near the eastern bank of the Mississippi and south of the Wabash-Ohio.

The evidence presented by Gallinée and Marquette on the late seventeenth-century location of the Shawnee is based on hearsay, and not on any direct contacts between these explorers and the tribe in question. None of the early French explorers, as far as is known, encountered the Shawnee in their travels through the Mississippi Valley. On the other hand, definite contacts were made east of the Allegheny region with various Shawnee groups before the close of the seventeenth century by English traders and settlers, and numerous late seventeenth- and early eighteenth-century sources would seem to indicate that the Shawnee were probably situated much farther east and south than Gallinée and Marquette put them. The suggestion that the Shawnee, as a large and united tribe, were one of the early historic groups of southern Indiana is therefore questionable.

The claims of the Miami to aboriginal occupancy of Indiana were most clearly set forth by a famous leader of this tribe, Little Turtle, in a speech delivered in 1795. Little Turtle stated: 'My fathers kindled the first fire at Detroit; thence they extended their lines to the headwaters of the Scioto; thence to its mouth; thence down the Ohio to the mouth of the Wabash, and thence to Chicago over Lake Michigan.' This claim, coupled with the fact that in 1680 French explorers found Miami groups actually living on the St. Joseph River in extreme northern Indiana, gives some grounds for the assumption that the Miami were the aboriginal occupants of at least the northern half of the State.

For two reasons, however, their title is by no means clear. It has been generally believed that Little Turtle was either a fullblood Miami, or half Miami and half Mahican. But in a recently published manuscript, which was compiled and written at Fort Wayne by C. C. Trowbridge 13 years after Little Turtle's death, it is stated on the authority of Miami informants that 'The Little Turtle is not considered a Miami.' He was, it seems, the offspring of a Mahican man and an Ioway girl who 'settled among the Miamies and had a great many children, of whom the eldest was Little Turtle.' There is no doubt that Little Turtle spent his life among the Miami and rose to eminence as their most astute war leader, but whether he was qualified to speak on the past history of this tribe, or whether his reference to his 'fathers' applied particularly to the Miami, is open to question.

The second and more serious reason for not accepting the Miami as the original proprietors of Indiana lies in the fact that in 1658 some of this tribe, at least, were reported by Gabriel Druillettes as living at the mouth of Green Bay, Wisconsin. In 1670 Nicolas Perrot, a French explorer, actually visited a Miami village at the headwaters of the Fox River, in Wisconsin. Within a decade, however, these Miami had moved south from Fox River and formed settlements at Chicago and on the St. Joseph River in extreme northern Indiana. It is here, in 1680, that their history as Indiana Indians appears to begin, although it is not impossible that a few of the Miami, representing the southernmost members of the tribe, may have been living in Indiana prior to 1680.

Despite the cloud of uncertainty that shrouds the identity of the early peoples of Indiana, this region was by no means devoid of an Indian population during the early period of white penetration. In the eighteenth and early nineteenth centuries both Indiana and Ohio were refuge areas for a large number of Indian tribes, and at least a dozen different groups spent some time in Indiana. Some of these, such as the Mahican, Nanticoke, Wappinger, Delaware, Munsee, and Shawnee, were originally from the eastern seaboard region and had been pushed out of their home territories by the press of white settlement. Others, such as the Kickapoo, Potawatomi, Miami, Piankeshaw, Wea, and Huron, were from the Great Lakes area to the north. With one exception all of the groups who migrated to Indiana spoke Algonquian languages; the exception was the Huron, whose speech belonged to the Iroquois family.

A few of these intrusive groups stayed within the borders of Indiana for only a brief period. Orontony's (or Nicholas's) band of Huron, for instance, settled on the White River in April 1748, but by the end of the summer of that same year the band removed to the Illinois country on the Ohio River, near the Indiana Line. Other groups, such as the Shawnee, the Potawatomi, and the Kickapoo, lived from 25 to 60 years in Indiana, while one tribe, the Miami, remained as a group within the State for almost a century and a half, and is even today represented by about 40 individuals who live chiefly in Wabash and Miami Counties in the north central part of the State.

Of the dozen or so tribes that moved into Indiana during the historic period, the Miami and two closely related groups, the Wea and the Piankeshaw, occupy a foremost place. In 1680 the Miami were living on the St. Joseph River in northern Indiana, and in the vicinity of Chicago. During the early decades of the eighteenth century the Miami proper occupied the country north and northwest of the upper Wabash. The Wea and Piankeshaw were located farther south on the same river, the Wea around Ouiatenon (near LaFayette) and the Piankeshaw at the mouth of the Vermilion River.

From their early location northwest of the Wabash the Miami gradually moved east. Kekionga (now Fort Wayne), at the junction of the Maumee and eastern St. Joseph Rivers, became their principal town. During the middle part of the eighteenth century the Miami removed even farther eastward and established towns in northwestern Ohio, but after 1763 they deserted these Ohio settlements and moved back into northeastern Indiana, where they remained until many of them sold their lands and removed west of the Mississippi, around 1827. One band, known as Meshingomesia's band, continued to live on a reservation in Wabash County, Indiana, until 1872, when the land was divided among the 300 surviving members. The Wea and Piankeshaw removed to the west from their villages near the Wabash at intervals between 1800 and 1832; in 1820 the Wea sold their last lands in Indiana, at the mouth of Raccoon Creek, in Parke County.

The Miami, Wea, and Piankeshaw were separate tribal and possibly dialect units, but all three spoke one mutually intelligible language. In 1825 C. C. Trowbridge was told by a Miami informant that the Miami could understand perfectly the speech of the Wea and Piankeshaw, as well as that of two Illinois groups, the Kaskaskia and Peoria. The Kickapoo language was intelligible to the Miami only because the Kickapoo had 'become incorporated with the Miamies by intermarriages and [had] greatly assimilated to them in manners and language.' In other words, Kickapoo was a separate language and had to be learned as such. So also were Delaware, Shawnee, Sauk, Potawatomi, Ojibwa, and Ottawa unintelligible to the Miami.

Like all the other Indian groups who lived in Indiana in historic times, the Miami led a semisedentary life, having fixed villages but spending part of the year hunting, away from the villages. They depended upon wild game, fish, corn, wild roots, and tubers for food. Early French explorers and travelers who visited Miami villages in northern Indiana were impressed by the large amount of land under cultivation in corn, but none of these travelers gave specific details regarding the approximate acreage under cultivation. It is doubtful whether the Miami raised much more than a quarter to a half acre of corn per person a year. Trowbridge, writing of the Miami in 1825, mentions their use of every variety of wild game and fish, of all wild fowl except the raven, crow, and loon, as well as their utilization of roots and tubers for food. Roots, he observes, 'are much used . . . particularly in seasons of scarcity.' In their feasts dog flesh was not considered an essential part of the feast, as among the Kickapoo and Potawatomi, but the Miami occasionally used it as a matter of convenience.

The social organization of the Miami tribe resembled at many points that of the Potawatomi, Sauk, Fox, and other central Algonquian groups. The Miami were divided into halves, or moieties; each of these moieties was further subdivided into several gens groups in which descent was reckoned through the father. Each of the gens was named; Trowbridge enumerates five Miami groups, namely, the Raccoon, Little Turtle, Snow Thaws, Turkey, and Moon [or Sun] gentes. Lewis H. Morgan, who collected the names of Miami gentes several years later than Trowbridge, states that the Miami had ten gentes, namely, Wolf, Loon, Eagle, Buzzard, Panther(?), Turkey, Raccoon, Snow, Sun, and Water. There is little hope of reconciling the discrepancy between these two lists at the present time, but it is interesting to see that Morgan repeats four out of five of Trowbridge's gens names.

Although there is no explicit statement for the Miami, their gens groups were in all probability exogamic groups—that is, a person could not marry within his own gens, but had to take a mate from another gens. All children of a union belonged to the same gens as their father, descent being reckoned patrilineally among the Miami, as among all other central woodlands groups. Personal names, which were bestowed on infants a short time after birth, usually contained some reference to the gens to which the child belonged.

It is likely that the Miami gens groups coincided with their local village groups which, at the time the Miami were living in Indiana, were the important political units. Whether or not this was the case, it is known that each Miami village had certain definite officials, and, as among other Algonquian tribes, women, as well as men, served as village functionaries. In each settlement there is said to have been a male civil chief and a war chief, a civil chief woman and a war chief woman, and two messenger men, one for the civil chief and one for the war chief. All of these offices were hereditary in the male line, passing from the father to the eldest son, or in the case of the female officials, to the eldest daughter. If a civil or war chief died without male issue, his office descended to the eldest son of his eldest daughter; if the chief left no issue, his messenger man was likely to assume the office. Also, curiously enough, the Miami permitted a man to be a war chief, even though he was not even of Miami blood. Occasionally a Miami war chief who had been slain in battle was succeeded by a warrior from another tribe, who had been taken prisoner to avenge the slain war chief's death. The children of the dead Miami chief might, if the captive warrior possessed the requisites of a good war chief, adopt him as their father. The adopted man then assumed the dead

chief's position and the Miami accorded him all the respect and obedience previously accorded the slain Miami chief.

Among the Miami there was no group of elderly men who served as
a council group for the village, nor is any tribal or head chief mentioned for the Miami as a nation. When important matters arose which
concerned the entire Miami population, the civil and war chiefs from
all the villages met in council to debate and decide the question at
hand.

Each of the village officials had certain functions and duties to
perform for the welfare of his group. A Miami civil chief attended to
the internal regulation of the village. He was not supposed to join war
parties; in fact, the war chief could prevent his doing so. He did, however, receive peace proposals. He could also institute such for his people, acting as an ambassador to the chief of an enemy group and carrying, as the insignia of his mission, a white flag in one hand and the
grand calumet or peace pipe, ornamented with bones and feathers, in
the other.

A village war chief, on the other hand, concerned himself exclusively
with war. He could initiate war proceedings by sending his messenger
man to the war chiefs of neighboring villages with a black belt of
wampum painted red, and a message declaring his intentions. With the
machinery thus set in motion, a war party could soon be assembled;
it was then the duty of the war chief to take command and plan
the attack. He was also responsible for the safe return of all the men
in his party, or for returning a captive to the family of a warrior killed
in battle. For this reason all prisoners were under the war chief's
charge. The war chief of the Raccoon gens always acted as head of a
war party.

The two chief women had less arduous duties and far less actual
power than the male chiefs; they superintended the preparation of
food served at large feasts, and collected and prepared smoked skins,
moccasins, awls and sinews used by the members of war parties for
mending their footgear and leggings while on the march. They also kept
track of daily happenings in the village, and of the behavior of its
inhabitants.

Messenger men carried messages for their respective chiefs, and divided all treaty goods and money among the people. The war chief's
messenger also served as a cook and waiter for the members of a war
party. It was his duty to carry the kettle and cook the provisions that
each warrior carried with him, while a war party was on the march.

All officials of a village were supposed to be persons of responsibility; the office of chief, for instance, called for a man who was of an equable disposition and who never appeared to sulk, much less to become angry or fly into a rage in the presence of others. The chief, observes Trowbridge, 'is oftentimes obliged to submit to insults and losses of property which an ordinary member of the tribe would resent. His utensil for cooking, his horses and hunting apparatus, are at the mercy of the villages. On the other hand, if the nation or tribe [gens] to which he belongs esteems him as a wise and a good man, they do not fail in the spring of the year to make him presents of peltry or game and thus to compensate him for some of his losses.'

Men engaged chiefly in the more strenuous tasks connected with daily life. They hunted, trapped, and also helped their wives plant and hoe corn. Women gathered the firewood, tended the fire, cooked the food, gathered and stored the crops, dressed the game and tanned the skins, and built the bark lodges in which the Miami lived. As a man grew older he was more apt to assist his wife in cutting wood, dressing meat, and tending the fire, but during his vigorous years he left such matters to his wife, or wives, if he had more than one.

Among the Miami, as among all the other Indian groups that migrated to Indiana, intertribal warfare was motivated either for revenge, or by the desire to gain standing and prestige in the social group. Warfare, it has been suggested, was so dominantly emphasized within the pattern of the eastern tribal cultures that escape from participation in it was virtually impossible. This is illustrated by Trowbridge's observation that among the Miami the young men of a village could not refuse to go on a war party when summoned to do so by their village war chief.

At a council the war chiefs explained to their young men the motives for engaging in a war. The night before the party was to leave, all the warriors gathered at the village council house where each deposited a piece of medicine obtained by him from his guardian spirit, on a square of cloth. This cloth, with all the warriors' individual medicines, was then tied up in a bundle, and the warriors began a dance that lasted throughout the night. In the morning a *shaman* or medicine man put the war bundle in his own medicine bag and, with the latter slung across his shoulders, started a war song and led the dancers out of the council house and away from the village. The young warriors followed the leader, shouting in reply to his song. Another war bundle, duplicating the one actually carried on the warpath, was left in the village in care of two medicine men. In case a war had been begun, and the war chief of a particular village decided to join in, he and his men set out without any preparatory dance of incitement. During the ceremonies held prior to going to war women were usually conspicuously absent, but in rare instances a woman who had lost all her friends in war and had fasted and received a revelation that she was to lead a war party actually did so. In such a case the woman told the war chiefs of her dream, and was appointed to carry the war bundle for the party.

Warriors always walked in single file on the march and never passed the *shaman* carrying the medicine bag, who was at the head of the line. At night when the party was encamped, the fires were built in a west-east line; the older men of the party, 'those who are respected,' encamped on the south side of the fires, the younger men, 'those who respect,' on the north. The younger men helped the war chief's messenger cook the food for the older men, supplied the latter with firewood and water, and mended their moccasins and leggings. It was considered highly improper for anyone to step over the campfires or to hand anything across them to a person sitting on the other side.

When a victorious war party returned home there was much dancing and feasting and ceremonial procedure in connection with the war bundle. This was given into the temporary custody of two old women who sang over it; then it was taken by the *shaman* to his own home. Five or six days later the war bundle and its duplicate were carried to the council house, where six *shamans* performed various magical feats such as vomiting bones, glass, and ice and 'shooting' each other with the skins of animals. Afterward the war bundle was opened and the small bundles of medicine belonging to the various members of the war party were returned to their owners. Following this there was a general feast. Later each warrior also made a small feast at his home for his medicine, singing and praying over it before he put it away.

A not uncommon practice indulged in by victorious war parties was to send a messenger home ahead, shouting the death yell and informing the villagers that their warriors had been defeated and certain specific individuals killed. The war party then would enter the village and scenes of lamentation and mourning quickly changed to ones of rejoicing among the villagers.

Captives taken by the Miami were either presented for adoption to the families of warriors who had been killed in battle; or presented as slaves to some other tribe or to some Miami chief who had not been concerned in the war; or turned over to the local members of the Miami man-eating society to be burnt to death and their flesh boiled and eaten. Captives whose lives were to be spared were painted red; those who were to die, black. Doomed captives were made to run the gantlet between two rows of women who often clubbed them to death before they could reach the council house. The burning of captives is said to have been practiced by the Miami and Shawnee as late as 1812, but in 1825 Trowbridge was told that the custom of cooking and eating prisoners, which was common enough not only among the Miami but many other central and eastern tribes, had been discontinued by the Miami around 1789. A young Miami woman who was fasting for supernatural power was shown in a dream a large fire heaped with the bones of her ancestors, who had been members of the man-eating society and were undergoing punishment for their cannibalistic practices.

The Midewiwin or Grand Medicine society, a magico-religious-curative organization, was represented among the Miami as well as among many neighboring tribes. Membership in the society was open both to men and women. The Miami Midewiwin was divided into a number of branches. A candidate for admission in the society applied to a member of any branch; at a given time the members of this branch met with the candidate, in a sweat house distant from the village. After the new entrant had presented a pile of goods as payment for initiation he was instructed in the magical and curative practices of the society. Later, at one of the four or five meetings of the Miami medicine society as a whole, which were held throughout the year, the initiate was publicly acknowledged as a member of the Midewiwin.

Members of this society, besides being able to shoot each other with their medicine bags, also possessed considerable knowledge of plants useful as medicines and as poisons, and were believed to be able to transform themselves into animals and birds. The founder of the society had supposedly been taught all this by the culture hero and by various animals. The powers of persons in the Midewiwin were half good, half evil, and witchcraft as well as healing was practiced by them. No one was allowed to participate in Midewiwin ceremonies who did not belong to the society.

After the Miami, the Mahican of the upper Hudson River Valley came next as early entrants into Indiana. In 1721 a band of Mahican established a village on the banks of the Kankakee River. Near the close of the eighteenth century other members of this tribe also lived on the White River. One mixed Mahican group known as the Stockbridges removed from New York to Indiana under their chief, Austin E. Quinney, in the early nineteenth century, but in 1822 bought land near Green Bay, Wisconsin. Like the Miami, the Mahican were divided into several unilateral groups, but descent was matrilineal. The tribal chief inherited his office through his mother; he had as assistants councilors, called chiefs, a 'hero' or war chief, an 'owl' or speaker, and a runner.

The tribal chief had charge of the peace bundle containing belts and strings of wampum, and represented his people in all treaty arrangements. The councilors consulted with him on matters of war and peace and the welfare of the tribe. The war chiefs were in charge of war parties. The 'owl' or speaker, who had to be gifted with a good memory and a strong voice, sat beside his chief and proclaimed the latter's orders, and also arose every morning at daybreak, woke the inhabitants of the bark-house settlement, and ordered them to their daily duties. The runner carried messages and convened councils. All of the offices except that of tribal chief were based on individual merit among the Mahican; for example, councilors were elected.

The band of 119 Huron warriors and their families who lived in Indiana for a few months in 1748 was under the leadership of Orontony, or Nicholas. Like two later Indian leaders, Pontiac and Tecumseh, Orontony tried to organize his people. He proposed that several of the tribes in the Great Lakes region, including the Miami and Shawnee, league together to destroy the French posts, but his plan became known to the French and failed. In April 1748, Orontony destroyed his village and palisade on Sandusky Bay and removed with his band to the White River in Indiana. During the summer or fall of the same year he and his people removed from White River to the Illinois country, where Orontony died that same fall.

Around 1770 the Delaware and closely related Munsee, eastern seaboard groups that had been pushed west, received permission from the Miami and Piankeshaw to occupy the country between the Ohio and White Rivers. There were a few Delaware towns in southern Indiana after 1770, but the main settlements of the Delaware and Munsee were on the upper course of the west fork of the White River, northeast of Indianapolis in Hamilton, Madison, and Delaware Counties, where at one time the Delaware had as many as six towns. A 'Delaware Town' is also mapped four miles from Fort Wayne by

The Setting

SYCAMORES

TRAIL IN TURKEY RUN STATE PARK

WINTER IN NORTHERN INDIANA

DOGWOOD IN MORGAN COUNTY

FALLS IN McCORMICK'S CREEK STATE PARK

DUNES ALONG LAKE MICHIGAN

SUNSET ON SYLVAN LAKE, ROME CITY

Photograph by L. W. B

THE HILLS OF BROWN COUNTY FROM THE BLOOMINGTON ROAD

BROWN COUNTY VISTA

Photograph by L. W. B

GREASY CREEK, BROWN COUNTY

MAKING SORGHUM

INDIANA'S SOUTHERN BOUNDARY—THE OHIO RIVER

'ON THE BANKS OF THE WABASH .

Thomas Ridout (1788), and is mentioned by Henry Hay (1789), but Hay explains that this town was the wintering ground of George Girty, a Pennsylvanian who had spent practically all his life among the Delaware and Shawnee Indians.

A Moravian mission was started among the Delaware on White River in 1801, but it had to be closed in 1806. The Delaware themselves left Indiana 12 years later, releasing their lands on White River to the United States in 1818 and removing west of the Mississippi. At this date the White River Delaware numbered about 800 persons.

The Delaware had kept an account of their wanderings from very early times by means of pictographic symbols painted on sticks. A set of these painted sticks was given to a white physician by a grateful member of the White River group in 1820; later the sticks came into the possession of the naturalist Constantin Rafinesque, who obtained the 'songs' or verbal account that went with the sticks from another Indiana Delaware. The narrative, known as the Walum Olum, starts with a mythical account of primeval waters, goes on to tell of the creation of the world, of a flood caused by an evil monster, and of the re-creation of the world by Nanabush, the culture hero. It then accounts for the division of the Delaware into various groups and tells of their wanderings eastward to the seacoast from the lands of spruce fir, of their first acquisition of corn, of their numerous wars with many different enemies, and finally, of the arrival of the whites on the eastern seacoast.

At almost the same time that the Delaware and Munsee entered Indiana from the east, the Kickapoo entered from the west. After the destruction of the Illinois confederacy in 1765, the Kickapoo moved south from Wisconsin to Illinois. There the tribe split, one part gradually moving westward while the other part moved eastward into Indiana where, despite Miami and Piankeshaw opposition, the new entrants settled on the Vermilion and Wabash Rivers and became known as the Vermilion band of Kickapoo. Trowbridge comments upon the fact that these Indiana Kickapoo had intermarried with the Miami and had to a great extent been assimilated by the latter in language and culture. The Kickapoo were strongly influenced by the teachings of the Shawnee Prophet, but in 1809 they ceded their lands on the Wabash and Vermilion Rivers and removed west of the Mississippi. Previous to their division into two bands the population of the Kickapoo was estimated at 3,000.

Like the Miami, the Kickapoo were organized in paternal gens groups, and a person's name had a definite connection with the gens to which he or she belonged. The Kickapoo occupied rectangular bark houses in the summer and flagreed oval lodges in the winter. They claim to have practiced the Midewiwin far in the past, but during the period when they lived in Indiana their most important ceremonies were probably the feast dances of the various gens groups.

The Nanticoke, who were originally from Maryland, entered Indiana about 1784 and lived on the White River a short distance west of the Delaware. After 1818 the Nanticoke removed west of the Mississippi with the White River Delaware group and some Mohegan who had come west with them. The combined number of Nanticoke and Mohegan who left Indiana in 1818 is estimated at 200. Although the Nanticoke are now extinct as a group, the Delaware still recall their great ability in witchcraft and their peculiar customs connected with the disposal of their dead. The Nanticoke buried or exposed the body of a dead person until the flesh decayed, then gathered up the bones and held a skeleton dance. Afterward the bones were either reburied or kept, wrapped in skins. Whenever the Nanticoke moved to a new location they carried the bones of their dead with them.

By 1788 some Shawnee were living in northeastern Indiana, while others were beginning to roam through southern Indiana. Kakinathucca's band, probably belonging to the Pekowi division of the Shawnee tribe, was in April of that year hunting and making sugar at a winter camp in the extreme southeastern part of the State. Thomas Ridout, an English captive with this band, states that southeastern Indiana was a hunting place for this group of 'Shawanese Indians' who, up to 1787, had been living on the Scioto. After they had finished their sugar-making in the spring of 1788 the band removed westward across the southern part of the present State to a location below Vincennes, near the junction of the Wabash and White Rivers, where the Shawnee women planted their crops. From that spot Kakinathucca and his people continued their journey north along the Wabash to Fort Miami (Fort Wayne). Ridout mentions two Shawnee chiefs, Blue Jacket, a white captive who spent his life with the Shawnee, and the Great Snake, as living a mile or two distant from Fort Wayne.

Henry Hay, who was at Fort Miami a year later, also refers to Blue Jacket, the Great Snake, and a 'Chilicothe village' of Shawnee, of which 'Black Bairde' was chief. In the closing decade of the eighteenth century then, part of the Shawnee had removed from northeastern Ohio to villages in the vicinity of Fort Wayne, while other Shawnee were in southern Indiana. A third group of Shawnee also moved out of Ohio and settled on White River, south of Fort Wayne, in 1798. It was in a White River town that the Shawnee 'Prophet' had the vision that caused him to begin preaching among the central woodlands tribes for a return to their native mode of life and the espousal of the cause of his brother, Tecumseh (see History). The Prophet gained many followers, but few of the Shawnee were won over to his cause. In 1808 he removed to the Wabash after a brief stay in Greenville, Ohio, and established a town near the mouth of the Tippecanoe River. The Kickapoo and Potawatomi were then in western Indiana, and many of them became converts to the Prophet's teachings. After the battle of Tippecanoe (1811) the Prophet and his band left Indiana and removed to Fort Malden, at the mouth of the Detroit River on the Ontario side. The Shawnee at Fort Wayne and on the White River also left Indiana during the first quarter of the nineteenth century.

As a tribe, the Shawnee were divided into five divisions, Pekowi, Chalakatha (often referred to as Chillicothe in eighteenth-century references), Thawikila, Kishpoko, and Mekoche. Each of these divisions had its own peace chief, war chief, chief woman and messenger men, and its sacred bundle. At least two of the divisions, Chalakatha and Pekowi, are mentioned as having established villages in Indiana. Tecumseh and the Shawnee Prophet belonged by birth to the Kishpoko division. Shawnee tribal chiefs were chosen from either the Chalakatha or Thawikila divisions. The members of the five Shawnee subgroups were divided into a number of patrilineal gens groups; an individual's personal name referred either directly or indirectly to some characteristic of the animal from which the gens took its name. The Shawnee did not practice the Midewiwin, but each spring and fall some of the divisions, at least, held a Bread Dance to insure good crops in the spring and a successful hunting season in the fall.

The Potawatomi tribe was the last to enter Indiana. After 1765 the Potawatomi gradually spread into southern Michigan and in 1795 they notified the Miami that they intended to move farther south. This they did, in spite of Miami protests. Around the close of the century numerous bands of Potawatomi had established villages in the northern part of Indiana, from the Kankakee River region east across the State. Other groups of Potawatomi settled in Illinois. The Potawatomi bands in Indiana around the headwaters of the Tippecanoe River were known as the 'Potawatomi of the Wabash.' These bands sold their reserves in Indiana in 1836 and agreed to remove west across the Mississippi within two years. Many of the Potawatomi in Indiana refused, however, to leave their homes until they were driven out by military force in 1838 (see Tour 4). The aboriginal population of the whole Potawatomi tribe probably did not exceed 3,000 persons.

Like so many of the other Indiana groups, the Potawatomi were divided into a number of patrilineal, exogamous gentes bearing animal, bird, or fish names. Each gens possessed a sacred bundle, and ceremonies that included dancing, singing, and feasting were held periodically for the gens bundles. During a gens ceremony, infants who had recently been born into the gens were named; the names usually referred in some way to the gens to which the child belonged. At all Potawatomi gens bundle feasts, and at most of their other religious feasts, dog meat was served as a ceremonial food.

Besides being divided into gentes groups, the Potawatomi were also separated into halves or moieties, designated as Oskush and Kishko. The order of birth of children in a family determined to which moiety each child belonged; the eldest child born to a couple always became a member of the Oskush moiety, the members of which used black paint and were under obligation to carry through to the end any undertaking they had started, particularly undertakings of a warlike nature. The next child born to the same couple became a member of the Kishko moiety, which used white paint and could do as it pleased about carrying out any undertaking. Thus moiety membership alternated from one child to the next in a Potawatomi family.

With the Potawatomi the migration of Indian groups to Indiana ended, for while the Potawatomi were moving into the region white settlers were already beginning to cut down the forests and establish homes. By 1815 the issue whether whites or Indians should possess Indiana had been decided (see History). Many Indians left to take up new land west of the Mississippi. Those who remained suffered greatly from contact with white civilization. Their hunting grounds were soon destroyed; their villages were ravaged by smallpox and other diseases; and their traditional mode of life was disrupted by drunkenness and carousing. Between 1812 and 1830 it is said that 500 Miami alone were killed in drunken brawls. Continual pressure by the whites brought about a series of treaties in which the Indians gave up all claims to their Indiana lands, and by 1838, when the last

Potawatomi were forcibly removed, the State was virtually cleared of its Indian population save for a few Miami.

Indiana has erected few monuments to the Indians, whose love for the region was as deep and real as that of any later Hoosier. Except in the musical place-names they have left to a later generation, few traces of their vanished life remain. But Kokomo, Miami, and Mishawaka; Wawasee and Maxinkuckee; the Kankakee, Maumee, and Mississinewa—these are their enduring memorial. And in the name of the river most Hoosiers love rather sentimentally today, the bright Wabash of song and story, we preserve the best-loved word in the forgotten language of the Miami. It was the Wa-pe-sha for which they were willing to die.

History

THE first white men to set foot in Indiana were French Jesuits. As soon as the French colonies in the St. Lawrence Valley, founded in the first half of the seventeenth century, were firmly established, the French began to push westward into the unknown country beyond Lake Erie. In this move the Jesuits, who hoped to build missions and convert the Indians to Christianity, took the lead. At their side were representatives of the government of New France, interested in the Indian fur trade, in reported copper mines, and in the great western river of which the Indians had told them, the 'Father of Waters,' which might be the long-sought outlet to the Pacific.

However at this time neither the Jesuits nor the traders were primarily interested in the territory that became Indiana. Father Marquette may have crossed the dune country of northern Indiana in 1675. Certainly his successor, Father Allouez, followed the St. Joseph Valley in his wanderings. But the French were seeking Indian villages, and Indiana in the last half of the century was practically deserted. The English also hoped to profit from the fur trade and, to counteract French influence in the interior, they had encouraged the powerful Iroquois nation to go on the warpath against the tribes of the Great Lakes region. If there were Indians in the Indiana area before this time, they probably retreated to escape the attacks of the better-armed and better-organized Iroquois.

This Iroquois onslaught, which temporarily forced the Indiana Indians from their traditional homes, was the first move in the French-British rivalry that was to shape the development of the Northwest for 100 years. France formally took possession of 'the West' at Sault Sainte Marie on June 14, 1671, in a ceremony designed to impress the Indians. Less than three months later English explorers, in a similar ceremony on the headwaters of the Ohio, took possession of the interior in the name of Charles the Second, King of England. These ceremonies meant less than nothing, since neither nation had even a faint idea of what 'the West' was, but they symbolized the opening of a struggle that was to continue until England, at the close of the French and Indian War in 1763, gained sole title to the Mississippi Valley.

The first white man who actually explored the Indiana region was Robert Cavelier, Sieur de la Salle, a French fur trader and traveler who advocated building a series of forts from Lake Ontario to the mouth of the Mississippi. La Salle hoped thus to protect the western Indians against Iroquois raids. On December 3, 1679, La Salle and a party of explorers ascended the St. Joseph in canoes until they reached the 'south bend' of the river, where the city of South Bend now stands. The next day they portaged across to the Kankakee River and continued their journey down the Kankakee toward the Illinois.

La Salle came again to the south bend in the spring of 1681, holding a council with the Miami and Illinois Indians under the great tree known later as the Council Oak (*see South Bend*). In the next few years he explored the Indiana region extensively. Though his attempt to form an anti-Iroquois confederacy was not altogether successful, by 1700 the Iroquois joined with other tribes in signing an agreement to live at peace. Soon thereafter the Miami and other tribes reoccupied the valleys of the St. Joseph, the Maumee, and the Wabash. La Salle died in Texas in 1687, but his dream of a chain of protective forts was later carried out by the governors of New France.

After the Indians returned to Indiana, many fur traders arrived to offer trinkets, whisky, and blankets in exchange for peltry. Licensed traders, or *voyageurs,* traveled with a permit from the king; wandering smugglers, or *coureurs de bois,* also ventured into the wilds to pick up what trade they could, but when they returned to Canada they were sometimes arrested as outlaws. By 1720 there were in Indiana dozens of French traders, scattered for the most part along the Wabash and its tributaries, since here the Indian villages were most numerous. For 40 years French policy in the west was dominated by the determination to protect these traders against English competition, and to keep open the vital Wabash-Maumee line across Indiana, the all-important link between Lake Erie and the Mississippi.

To this end three principal forts were established in the Indiana region—Miami, Ouiatenon, and Vincennes. These forts were part of the chain envisioned 40 years earlier by La Salle, which stretched from Detroit to New Orleans. They were the first permanent white settlements in Indiana.

Authorities differ on which of these is oldest, for there is no conclusive evidence of the dates of their founding. However, it is likely that a military post was established on the site of the Indian village at Ouiatenon, four miles below the present city of LaFayette, in 1720. Fort Miami, at the site of Fort Wayne, may have been built even earlier; for in 1722 a 'new fort' was constructed at that point. Neither of these forts became stable white settlements with real community life, and after the French were driven out they reverted to the Indians.

Vincennes alone was a permanent community. There is considerable dispute about the date of the founding of this post, which was to flower into a beautiful town of great cultural as well as historic interest. Important church records were found by Bishop Bruté, indicating that both the town of Vincennes (not then known by that name) and the church of St. Francis Xavier were in existence as early as 1708. Perhaps if the settlement was made at an early date it was temporarily abandoned, for letters written by French commanders and traders in 1720, 1724, and 1725 indicate that no post had yet been established. But all authorities agree that settlers had arrived before 1727, and that a fort was already built by 1732. Vincennes was named for the French officer in command during the early period, François Morgane de Vincennes.

During the next 50 years, Vincennes was a trading post and a center of French life. Here lived Catholic families from Canada, some belonging to the gentry, many of them sturdy peasants, conservative and law-abiding. They lived in whitewashed log houses on narrow streets, built picket fences around their orchards and gardens, and cultivated long, narrow plots with wooden plows. Their houses were one-story, four-room cabins, with dormer windows and porches, furnished with homemade rustic furniture, Indian mats, and sacred pictures. Social as well as religious life centered largely in the Church. On feast days and Sundays after Mass there were visiting, dancing, and cards, and the priest was often present. Mardi Gras brought its feast and dancing and contests. Sugar-making time was a season for great merriment and love-making; the signing of the prenuptial contract and later the wedding called for special celebrations. There was a good deal of hard drinking at the taverns, and gambling and cockfighting were popular sports. Such characteristic French gaiety was misunderstood by English visitors; George Croghan, an Indian agent who spent many years in the region, reported that the *habitants* were a 'parcel of French renegadoes, worse than the Indians.'

Croghan's remark was probably inspired by British rivalry. Although English traders were in the region from the beginning, they were for many years outstripped by the French in the struggle for furs. They were handicapped in their dealings with the Indians by their feeling of arrogance and racial superiority, while the French laughed, played, and even intermarried with the savages, imposing upon them no racial discrimination. But by the middle of the century two important factors were tipping the scales in British favor. In the first place, the English were willing to give the Indians firearms, a practice which French policy had always opposed. Even more important was the fact that the English, because of superior manufacturing and shipping methods, could pay higher prices for furs, and charge lower prices for their whisky, cloth, and other trade goods than could the French.

The outcome of the struggle, however, was not determined in the Indiana region. On the high seas, in the remote valleys of India, on the battlefields of Canada, French and British imperialists came to blows. By the Treaty of Paris in 1763 the French agreed to give up the western territory to the English. French garrisons were to be withdrawn and the posts delivered over to the English as soon as possible.

But the conquerors had reckoned without the Indians, who hated the English and regarded the French as their friends. The arrogance of British traders soon brought Indian hostility to a head. Under Pontiac, chief of the Ottawa nation, the Senecas in the east and the Ottawa-Ojibway-Potawatomi confederacy in the west joined forces in 1763 in a mighty uprising to drive the English out of the territory forever. From May 1763 to August of the following year, the region from Canada to the Ohio was ravaged by bands of Indian warriors, who butchered garrisons at Sandusky, Fort St. Joseph, and Michilimackinac. In Indiana Pontiac's men forced Lieutenant Jenkins and the Ouiatenon garrison to surrender and destroyed the post; at Fort Miami they murdered Ensign Holmes and most of his company. But the fury of Pontiac's army dashed itself in vain against the palisades of Detroit, which received English reinforcements in August 1764. These troops were able gradually to restore peace throughout the territory. Later in the fall Colonel Bouquet set out from Fort Pitt with a strong army; by threats and a show of force he compelled the return of 206 white prisoners, many of whom had been held in Ohio and Indiana. For a time the power of the Indians was broken.

Now masters of the Northwest, the British attempted to pacify the Indians in order to secure a profitable fur trade. Even before Pontiac's war the king had issued the Proclamation of 1763, ceding to the Indians the land 'beyond the heads of the Atlantic rivers.' The Proclamation was an effort to win Indian friendship by adopting the former French policy of trading rather than settlement. Shrewdly recognizing the superior power of the new government, the Indians joined forces with British fur traders and soldiers in a common hostility toward the pioneer, the march of whose farms and towns threatened hunter and trader alike. For a time, except for an influx of lawless elements and squatters, the immigration of land-hungry settlers was checked.

Because it was considered a part of Louisiana, the post at Vincennes had not been turned over to the English. In 1765, however, General Gage sent George Croghan to conciliate the Indiana Indians. Soon, although colonization was at a standstill north of the Ohio, fur trading along the Wabash began to boom again. But the British made one mistake. They failed to establish any civil government in the territory north of the Ohio, a region not included in any of the provinces formed by the Proclamation of 1763. They even failed to send a garrison to the Wabash forts, with the result that Forts Miami and Ouiatenon ceased to exist, and the stockade posts at Vincennes rotted down and disappeared. Meanwhile Vincennes became more and more lawless, overrun with drunken Indians and arrogant traders. In those days French *habitant* and English settler suffered together, and discontent was acute.

For 10 years after 1763 the wealthy colonists of Virginia and Pennsylvania were intensely interested in the Northwest. Various land companies were formed, which vainly petitioned for land grants from the crown. Although a few British statesmen saw the need for a farming population to support the garrisons and to furnish a wider market for British manufactures, most royal governors opposed any move that would encourage settlement. Meanwhile there was unauthorized purchase of land from the Indians, unregulated fur trade, and absence of any protection for property or lives.

The Quebec Act of 1774 was an effort to bring order out of chaos. Placing the Ohio Valley under the jurisdiction of the Province of Quebec, the act promised the region a stable government and pacified the French by protecting their religion and civil law. Before it could be given a fair trial, however, the American Revolution changed the entire situation.

At the outbreak of the Revolution there was no English garrison in Indiana. Throughout the Northwest, however, the English were contending with the Americans for Indian friendship and encouraging them to make punitive raids upon pioneer settlements. In Detroit, Governor Henry Hamilton became so notorious in his bargains with the Indians for American scalps that he won the unpleasant title of 'Hair-buyer.' Early in 1777 Hamilton sent Lieutenant Governor Edward Abbot to Vincennes to rebuild the fort and organize the French and Indians for attack upon the frontier. The Indians were willing, naturally enough, since American settlement meant ruin for them; but the French had no eagerness to join their recent enemies against the friendly pioneers. Abbot returned to Canada in 1778, leaving Vincennes without a military command.

British influence succeeded in stirring the Indians into many savage outbreaks during 1777, long remembered as the 'bloody year.' Terror hung over the West, the frontier was in a fever, forts and blockhouses were hastily constructed. During that summer George Rogers Clark, a militia officer who represented the county of Kentucky in Virginia's legislature, learned through spies that the English forts at Kaskaskia and Vincennes were poorly guarded, and that the people of those towns were not devoted to the English. Seeing clearly that the colonies were unsafe as long as the English held the frontier forts, Clark hastened to lay his plans before Governor Patrick Henry. After a conference at Williamsburg he was commissioned to raise an 'army' to capture the Northwest, which Virginia claimed by her charter of 1609.

In May 1778, Clark and his little band of 175 frontiersmen started down the Ohio to the mouth of the Tennessee, and struck across country to Kaskaskia, arriving July 4, 1778. Town and fort fell without a struggle, and the French helped to take other posts along the Mississippi. Having won the good will of Pierre Gibault, an influential priest, Clark sent him to Vincennes (which was now without an English garrison) to explain the Treaty of Alliance recently made between France and the United States. Father Gibault was trusted and beloved, and the *habitants* of Vincennes soon raised the American flag, with Clark's best officer, Captain Leonard Helm, in command of the fort.

But the news of Clark's victories finally reached Detroit, and in December 1778, 'Hair-buyer' Hamilton arrived with 600 men and recaptured Vincennes. He repaired Fort Sackville and kept a small garrison, but supposing himself safe from attack during the winter dismissed most of his soldiers until spring. News of this folly would not have reached Clark but for the heroic journey of Francis Vigo, a rich trader of Vincennes who fled in a canoe to Kaskaskia with the news.

Clark was in a difficult position. The spring would undoubtedly bring revenge and victory to Hamilton, as soon as his scattered Indians and soldiers reported for duty. On the other hand the wilderness was grim and almost impassable during the winter months. Clark did not hesitate, but gathered together 170 French and American volunteers and set out on the long march of 240 miles in the dead of winter. Across icy swamps and rivers in flood they marched, to reach Warrior's Island, just out of Vincennes. Here they cleaned their rifles and sent a message to the citizens, warning them of the attack and urging those friendly to the Americans to stay quietly in their homes. By the time Clark's men had surrounded the fort in the darkness and were ready to attack, they had received dry powder and supplies from the inhabitants of the town. Wholly taken by surprise, the British were befuddled, and their cannon did no damage in the dark. The frontiersmen were deadly marksmen and with the coming of daylight rained a hail of well-aimed bullets that silenced the artillery of the fort. On February 25, 1779, the garrison surrendered. Fort Sackville became Fort Patrick Henry; protected by Virginian arms, 20,000 settlers poured into Kentucky during the following two years.

Clark's brilliant exploit seriously crippled the British rear attack upon the settlers for the rest of the war. Undoubtedly it also had much to do with England's surrender of the lands west of the mountains in 1783. For a time Virginia claimed the territory, but under the stress of revolutionary conditions proved as incapable of governing it as the British had been. In 1784, recognizing the need of stable government in what had become a lawless region, the Old Dominion relinquished its title. The backwoods empire became the 'Public Domain.'

In 1787 the Continental Congress enacted the famous 'Ordinance for the Government of the Territory Northwest of the River Ohio.' Embracing the present States of Wisconsin, Michigan, Illinois, Indiana, Ohio, and part of Minnesota, the Territory was to be ruled by a governor and three judges, who were to adopt laws and enforce them. The ordinance prohibited slavery, encouraged public education, and guaranteed religious freedom and civil rights to all the people. The first governor was General Arthur St. Clair, a veteran of the Revolution, and the seat of government was established at Marietta, Ohio.

Within a year after the Territory was organized 20,000 home-seekers came down the Ohio.

They had been coming for the past 20 years, drifting down the great river in flatboats. At first every settler built his own rude boat, a cabined raft with a long oar for rudder; but as the flow of colonizers increased, a class of professional boatmen developed. A tough and lusty breed of drinkers and brawlers, jolly and resourceful, the river boatmen had to be skilful enough to combat ice and sandbars and rapids, brave enough to fight cutthroats, robbers, and Indians. Many a pioneer family owed its safe arrival to these river guides.

After 1787 the influx of colonizers thoroughly alarmed the Indians, who still had the support of the British. In defiance of the Treaty of 1783, British traders had not given up their posts and forts and were still scattered here and there, slyly suggesting that England would continue to protect the Indians if they fought bravely against the American invasion. Every month saw a new band of painted savages take the warpath.

Thus the first task of the new government was to 'pacify' the Indians. In 1789 Congress authorized St. Clair to call out the militia of adjoining States whenever necessary, but at first he sought to quiet the Indians by peaceful means. In the spring of 1790 Antoine Gamelin, a Vincennes trader who knew the Indians well, was sent to the Wabash country with a message of friendship. The older warriors listened, but the young braves spoke of the British commander at Detroit. Gamelin returned to Vincennes, his mission a failure.

Then St. Clair determined to strike the Indians so ruthlessly that they would never dare to launch another war party. Three military expeditions were hurled rapidly against the most powerful and influential tribes in the Territory. In October 1790, General Josiah Harmar destroyed the deserted Maumee towns but suffered two severe defeats, the second at the hands of Little Turtle, the ablest war chief of the Miami. In the spring of 1791, President Washington sent General Charles Scott into the Territory to quell disorder by the destruction of the Wea towns near the present site of LaFayette. When Scott's troops returned, St. Clair sent the Kentucky militia, under General James Wilkinson, to overthrow the Eel River Miami; but the only outcome of this sally was the wanton destruction of the Indians' corn crop. All these expeditions merely enraged the Indians and provoked a campaign of murder and robbery.

So far the Indians had been definitely victorious in the conflict.

Their ruined crops and flaming villages forced them into the Wabash confederacy, led by the Miami and including even the Lake Indians. These allied tribes had already killed hundreds of settlers. Late in the autumn St. Clair himself set out with an undisciplined expeditionary army. At a snail's pace these troops crept toward Miami-town, unaware that an Indian army was stalking them. Near the headwaters of the Wabash on the morning of November 4, they paraded as usual at daybreak and broke ranks for breakfast just as the Indian war whoop signaled the attack. In spite of a stampede of the militia (many of them never stopped to eat a meal until they reached Cincinnati) the regular troops held firm, but suffered a crushing defeat by Little Turtle. St. Clair and his shattered troops reached Cincinnati on November 8, 1791.

This disaster forced President Washington to send General Anthony Wayne ('Mad Anthony,' they had called him during the Revolution) to the troubled West. Wayne realized that to end these struggles a decisive defeat had to be administered to the Indians. Therefore he drilled an army for more than a year; early in 1794 he marched boldly through the Indian country and built Forts Greenville, Defiance, and Recovery. The hostile tribes meanwhile fell back sullenly before him, watching eagerly but vainly for a chance to surprise his army.

By this time Little Turtle saw that to defeat this 'army that never sleeps' would be far more difficult than to scatter the troops of Harmar and St. Clair. Repeatedly he counseled his people to accept Wayne's offers of a peace treaty. The Wea had already concluded such a treaty, but the Miami, flushed with their victories and under British influence, remained obdurate. Had not Governor Simcoe of Canada built them a fort at the Maumee rapids and supplied them with arms and ammunition?

A short distance above this very fort was a dense forest strewn with fallen trees, an excellent spot for ambush. Here Little Turtle decided to wait for General Wayne; and here, in the battle of Fallen Timbers, the Miami confederacy met its doom. Early in the morning of August 20, 1794, the American army approached in battle formation. As soon as their scouts located Little Turtle's army, Wayne's men charged with bayonet and close rifle fire, in savage hand-to-hand conflict driving the Indians from their position and scattering them through the dense woods. The fort did the Indians no good, for the Americans got there first.

Although actually fought on the soil of what is now Ohio, this battle proved an important event in Indiana history. The allies of the Miami, worn out and convinced that further resistance was futile, went home to their own hunting grounds. After destroying all the property in the neighborhood, both Indian and English, Wayne marched up the Maumee (ravaging as he went), to the confluence of the St. Mary's and St. Joseph Rivers. Here he built Fort Wayne and then returned with his army to winter quarters in Greenville. Defeated, robbed of their grain, broken in spirit, the Indians subsisted that winter on British charity. One after another Buckongahelas, Blue Jacket, Little Turtle, and other chieftains visited Wayne and promised to come to a council to be held at Greenville the following summer.

They kept their word. In August 1795, the Treaty of Greenville, ratified by the tribal chiefs, ceded much of what is now Ohio to the settlers. Only a narrow strip of eastern Indiana was at that time opened up for settlement, but the Indians promised to cease their war parties. It now seemed certain that peace would prevail on the frontier. The British agents, for the most part, withdrew to Canada, where they continued their agitation against the United States.

Peace did prevail for about 15 years, and settlers kept pouring in. In 1800, however, there were only 50,000 whites in the whole Northwest Territory, and 45,000 of these were in Ohio alone. In that year William Henry Harrison, the Congressional delegate from the Northwest, secured the passage of a bill which split off Ohio and created Indiana Territory, embracing the present States of Wisconsin, Michigan, Illinois, and Indiana. Vincennes became the capital, and President Adams appointed Harrison as the first governor. In 1805, Michigan was separated from Indiana Territory; in 1809 Illinois Territory was formed, including all the western region. So Indiana shrank to its present area.

Although his first 10 years were peaceful enough, Governor Harrison found frontier government difficult. The settlements had to be defended, a problem solved by means of the militia, to which every able-bodied man belonged. Laws had to be adopted and enforced, at first by the governor himself and three judges, later by a council of elected delegates. (By 1804 the population had increased enough to permit the latter.) Indians had to be protected from dishonest traders; at least an effort must be made to regulate the whisky traffic. Slavery presented a knotty problem. Forbidden by the Ordinance of 1787, this institution was still approved by most of the earlier settlers. In

1803 the judges and the governor (himself a Virginian) adopted a Virginia law allowing masters who owned Negroes to make an agreement with them for lifelong slavery. Thus by rude makeshift or compromise the machinery of civil government was set in motion.

But more important than civil government was the perennial Indian problem. By a treaty in 1784 the Ohio River had become the Indian boundary, but by 1795 aggressive squatters had scattered over Ohio and penetrated Indiana. Beyond the new boundary set by the Treaty of Greenville, however, the Indians were the legal owners of most of Indiana. Only a few patches of land had been granted to the whites, small tracts at Fort Wayne, Ouiatenon, and Vincennes, and 149,000 acres at the Falls of the Ohio, known as Clark's Grant. In these areas a few hundred settlers lived, surrounded by Indians that outnumbered them many times over.

This situation was tense when Harrison arrived early in 1801. Indiana Territory looked rich and promising to many sturdy veterans of the Revolution, men not disposed to honor the land claims of a few 'miserable savages.' Hundreds of squatters were entering southern Indiana every year, mostly by flatboat, and settling on Indian land in open defiance of the Treaty. Unless a solution could speedily be found, another Indian war was inevitable.

No governor could have resisted the influx of settlers for very long. Pioneers were driven by the lure of adventure and economic need. To restrain and dam up in the East these tides of immigration, in order to preserve the wilderness empire of a few thousand primitive people, would have been a strange reversal of history. Governor Harrison therefore resolved to purchase southern Indiana from the Indians, extinguishing their ancient title by legal means. Before the close of 1809, in a series of remarkable, although doubtfully honest, triumphs, he had won peacefully most of the southern third of Indiana. The Treaty of Fort Wayne was ratified September 30, 1809, by chiefs of the Miami, Wea, and Delaware. By this last agreement Harrison bought—for only $10,000 and a small annuity—3,000,000 acres of good land between the Wabash and White River. The northern boundary of this purchase was the famous 'Ten O'Clock' line, so-called because the Indians insisted that the line be determined by the shadow cast by the sun at 10 A.M. on the day the treaty was signed.

But Indian resistance was growing. Little Turtle counseled the Indians to face the inevitable; to live amiably with the white men and learn their ways. Younger leaders were arising, however, to whom these counsels were a bitter mockery. Chief among them were the great Shawnee brothers, Tecumseh and the Prophet, who listened to the advice of the British.

Their theories were simple. If the Indians were to survive, they had to avoid the white man's whisky and degenerate ways, returning to their ancestral mode of life; they must not sell any more land, for the land belonged to all in common. The theory of 'cultural conservatism' was the contribution of one-eyed Laulewasikau, known popularly as the Prophet. A man of great physical strength and oratorical ability, with a strange mixture of savagery and gentleness, chicanery and apostolic fervor, he rekindled the ancient flame of Indian religion, thus fusing into emotional unity the scattered peoples his brother was attempting to lead. Tecumseh himself was even more remarkable, a fearless, upright, generous man, with a deep love for his troubled race and an unusual grasp of the necessity for political unity and co-operation among the scattered Algonquian tribes.

The confederation the Shawnee leaders sought to found had as its cornerstone the agreement of all the tribes not to sell any more land. But the tribal chieftains hated to give up, even in face of a common threat, their traditional rights of selling land and making treaties. The Shawnee were a refugee tribe, they argued, who had no real claim to the territories the Indians were selling. Why should the Shawnee dictate to the ancient owners of these forest lands? The Treaty of Fort Wayne was a repudiation of Tecumseh by these chieftains.

Meanwhile Laulewasikau built a village on the north bank of the Wabash, near the mouth of the Tippecanoe. Known as Prophet's Town, this village soon became a rendezvous for discontented Indians from every tribe in Indiana, warriors who were increasingly breaking away from their chieftains and joining the Shawnee leaders. It was also a center of British influence, as the Prophet himself finally admitted.

During the winter of 1809–10 feeling ran high among the Wabash Indians. Under Little Turtle the Miami maintained throughout the whole troubled era an official attitude of friendship; they had signed the Treaty of Greenville and they meant to keep the faith. The Delaware likewise remained pacific. But the Shawnee, Wyandot, Potawatomi, and bands of deserters from other tribes were in a state of angry unrest, threatening to kill the chiefs who had signed the Fort Wayne Treaty. So turbulent did their mass meetings become under the spell of the Prophet's magnificent oratory that Governor Harrison became thoroughly alarmed.

A grand council in the summer of 1810 proved futile; neither Harrison nor Tecumseh yielded on the question of land sales (*see Vincennes*). Later that year Tecumseh went South in an attempt to enlist other allies in his confederacy, and in his absence Harrison received orders from President Madison to break up the Indian rendezvous at Prophet's Town. Tecumseh had been gone a year, however, before Harrison was able to set out. With an army of less than 1,000 men, with whom he intended to establish a post farther up the Wabash, he reached the highlands at Terre Haute on October 3, 1811. Here he built Fort Harrison, which soon became a target for Indian hostilities. A sentinel was shot; frightened bands of Miami and Delaware came to protest their own friendship and to report that Prophet's Town was seething with war preparations. These reports offered Harrison the excuse he needed for what was after all a military invasion of Indian territory. On October 29 he began to march toward Prophet's Town.

As Harrison's troops neared the Prophet's stronghold on the Tippecanoe, Indian scouts began to hover threateningly on their flanks. When they were within a mile of the town, however, an Indian deputation came out and begged for a truce. After exchanging promises that no fighting should be engaged in till the next day, the Indians retired to Prophet's Town and Harrison led his army into camp. Harrison was not deceived by the Indians' promise and gave all necessary orders in anticipation of a night attack. In Indian town all was in turmoil. Women and children prepared to flee if the Prophet's counterattack should fail. According to tradition the Prophet called his warriors together and brought out the magic bowl and other talismans that would protect them against wounds and death. Then the night throbbed with the war song and savage dance, until the frenzied Indians seized their weapons and rushed out to make the attack.

The Battle of Tippecanoe was begun before dawn on November 7, 1811. A chilly drizzle had put out the campfires, and in the dim morning twilight the two armies engaged in a deadly, often hand-to-hand, struggle. After heavy losses on both sides, the Indians broke and fled soon after daylight. Harrison destroyed Prophet's Town with all its supplies and made his way back to Vincennes.

Tippecanoe was a death blow to the Prophet's prestige. He had promised his warriors a magical immunity from wounds and death, but 38 were left dead on the field and the number of fatally wounded was probably very great. His town on the Wabash was destroyed, and with it went the confidence the Indiana tribes had placed in the Shawnee confederacy. The Delaware and Miami renewed their pledge not to fight the whites, although if the Prophet had been victorious they might not have done so. When Tecumseh returned, the work of 10 years lay in ruins.

The Prophet, however, did not lightly relinquish his hope of victory. Leaving the Wabash towns, he started on a long tour among the Kickapoo, Potawatomi, and other Northern tribes. At the same time relations between the United States and Great Britain were becoming more strained. Soon bands of these Indians began to commit murders at Chicago and the remoter Indiana towns, and the settlers retreated southward into more populous regions. In April 1812, Governor Harrison gave orders for the militia to hold themselves in readiness, and a row of blockhouses was built from Vincennes to Greenville.

British influence was behind Indian activity at this time, for the British had never given up hope of an Indian buffer state to the rear of the American colonies, a state at once highly profitable to English fur traders and an effective barrier to American expansion. Although there were many other factors leading to the War of 1812, this one persistent aspect of British policy might alone have provoked armed conflict. The destiny of the hinterland had to be decided.

In the summer of 1812 war was declared. The first disaster took place at Chicago, when the commander of the fort evacuated it under orders and attempted to march to Detroit. The garrison and accompanying civilians were captured and massacred at once, and Detroit itself was surrendered the following day. The events were the signal for a general uprising among the Indiana Indians. Even the Miami took the warpath, only a few in Little Turtle's village remaining friendly to the whites. Tecumseh hurried from tribe to tribe urging unified action. To terrorize the border and if possible prevent a northward movement of troops, a small band of warriors attacked and massacred the peaceful little Pigeon Roost settlement in the northern part of what is now Scott County on September 3. Two days later an army of Indians and British attacked Fort Wayne, which held out desperately until Governor Harrison arrived with fresh troops on September 12. Meanwhile Fort Harrison was attacked and partly burned by an Indian war party. In retaliation Harrison sent troops to destroy Little Turtle's town on Eel River, the Potawatomi village on the Elkhart, and the strong Miami and Kickapoo towns at the forks of the Wabash. Their villages and granaries in flames, the Miami gathered in the towns on the Mississinewa, where in December they attacked with desperate fury another army sent to rout them.

This was the last real battle fought on Indiana soil. Except for petty raiding parties the Indians were quiet during the next year, although the settlers huddled in blockhouses until the militia had restored order. But Indiana kept 4,160 men under arms in 1813, either for home defense or duty on the northern front. Meanwhile the Indians, discouraged after their series of bitter defeats, began to leave the Territory. Many bands of Miami and Delaware who had not taken a prominent part in the fighting fled into Ohio; the Shawnee, with most of the tribes that had followed Tecumseh and the Prophet, went to Detroit to place themselves under British protection. But the British surrendered Detroit in September 1813. A few days later Harrison defeated Tecumseh and the British general, Proctor, in the Battle of the Thames. The war was over. After the Treaty of Ghent, two years later, the British gave up all hope of dominating the Northwest Territory.

With peace came the end of an era. Tecumseh, symbol of revolt, was killed at the Battle of the Thames. The Northwest was no longer a battlefield, and in Indiana's fertile river valleys an indigenous midwestern culture was destined to unfold.

In the first year of the nineteenth century there had been only about 1,000 persons in Indiana, concentrated along the Ohio River and the lower Wabash. In addition, there was a scattering of hunters and trappers. As newcomers invaded this region and found pleasing locations, they became squatters; when a land office was opened they became settlers; where a few congregated, a rude beginning of government sprang up and they became citizens. By 1813, with the exception of a finger of settlement up the Whitewater Valley, the frontier extended east from Vincennes to where Madison now stands. Farther north there were no whites except traders at Fort Wayne, Anderson, and South Bend.

From 1800 to 1813 Vincennes was the capital of Indiana Territory. By 1805 there were enough people in Indiana to elect a legislature under the terms of the Ordinance of 1787. When Harrison resigned the governorship in 1812 to take part in the war against England, the population had grown to nearly 30,000. Harrison was succeeded by John Gibson, secretary of the Territory, and in 1813 the capital was moved to Corydon, with General Thomas Posey as governor. By 1816 Indiana had reached a population of more than 60,000.

This growth was the outstanding fact of the period. The land offices at Vincennes and Jeffersonville were besieged daily by dozens of new settlers, many of whom laid claim to the same quarter-section. The difficulties of administering the sale of land and dealing with the defeated Indians were advanced as reasons why Indiana needed a strong State government.

STATEHOOD

The Territorial legislature that met in December 1815 framed a petition for statehood, and in April 1816 Congress passed the Enabling Act. This act designated May 13 as the day for an election of delegates to a constitutional convention—an election in which, for the first time in the Territory's history, no property qualification was required for voting. Under the terms of the Ordinance of 1787 slavery had been excluded, but this question was a sore one from the beginning. Most of the early pioneers came from the South and resented the restrictions of the Ordinance. It was not until 1843, in fact, that slavery disappeared in Indiana, Negroes having been held in some places until then under the fiction of 'voluntary servitude.'

The delegates met from June 10 to June 29, 1816, in the old Statehouse at Corydon, which is still standing (1941). In this short time they framed a constitution modeled closely after those in force in neighboring States. This document did contain one notable innovation, however, in Article IX, which expressly recognized the State's obligation to educate all its citizens (see Education). In the August elections Jonathan Jennings was elected governor; and on December 11, 1816, Congress formally declared Indiana a member of the Union.

At the outset the new State was beset with many difficulties. Its comparatively small population was made up of poor farmers, with a sprinkling of artisans and tradesmen in Vincennes, Jeffersonville, Brookville, Madison, and other little towns in southern Indiana. There was no important source of State revenue except the land tax, but settlers were exempt from this tax for five years after they had bought their land from the Federal Government. Two-thirds of Indiana was still a wilderness owned by the Indians; hence it was necessary to open up the central region for further settlement.

In 1818 three commissioners, including Governor Jennings, met the

Indian chieftains at St. Marys, Ohio, and bought from them the entire central portion of Indiana. This territory, long known as the 'New Purchase,' was opened in 1820 and rapidly settled. As soon as it had been surveyed, the legislature appointed 10 men to select a site for the permanent capital, for which purpose Congress had already granted Indiana four sections of government land. In June 1820, the commissioners selected a tiny squatter village where Indianapolis now stands. A city was soon laid out and settlers began to come in. By 1824 the seat of government was removed from Corydon (in four wagons) and established temporarily in the Marion County courthouse.

In 1820 the population of Indiana was nearly 150,000, and it continued to increase rapidly. Men, women, and children came into the State on foot, on horseback, or in huge, creaking wagons drawn by ox teams or horses. From the South, especially the North Carolina Piedmont, poured a stream of pioneers largely of English and Scotch-Irish origin—prosperous Quakers, wandering prospectors, and riflemen with coonskin caps. Between 1820 and 1840 many immigrants arrived from England, a band of Swiss founded Vevay on the Ohio, and a number of Irish laborers came to work on the Wabash & Erie Canal. Into northern Indiana scattered thrifty farmers and small traders from New England, of English and Scotch-Irish ancestry. For 30 years these tides flowed into Indiana, until the frontier had passed.

For many years transportation was so costly and difficult that the pioneer family was forced to manufacture most of its necessities at home. Clothing at first was made almost entirely of skins and furs, neat and comfortable in dry weather but ill-smelling, clammy, and shrunken when it rained. Soon linsey cloth took the place of skins, and by the 1830's homemade woolen garments were plentiful. Women wore plain, homespun dresses with petticoats, and woolen shawls instead of coats. Sunbonnets in summer and knitted hoods in winter took the place of hats. Shoepacks were worn in winter, but in summer many went barefoot—men, women, and children. By 1822 Indianapolis stores were advertising Eastern broadcloth, muslins, calico, hats, bonnets, shoes, silverware, tools, and glassware; tea, coffee, medicine, soap, tobacco, musical instruments, clocks, stoves, and plows. People who were prosperous enough to buy these products were the envy of their neighbors.

For the average farmer, however, even if his crops were abundant, such luxuries were unobtainable, although a little tea, coffee, and marmalade might be bought every year to find its way to the table when distinguished visitors arrived. Because wheat, corn, and hogs had to be transported a long way to market, they were worth little in exchange for manufactured goods. 'A yard of silk cost as much as 80 bushels of corn would sell for,' says one writer. 'Good broadcloth commanded 100 bushels of corn a yard.'

These facts determined almost all the political struggles in Indiana for nearly 20 years. Even in the so-called 'era of good feeling' between 1816 and 1824, politics in Indiana revolved largely around the need for roads and waterways, although there was also considerable agitation from the poorer settlers concerning the policy of the Federal Government toward public lands. For those who had bought their land on credit and found payments difficult to make, Congress issued due bills to be used in future land purchases if the original holdings had been lost. After 1824 internal politics continued to focus on the need for roads and canals. Opposition came from people who were already well located on navigable rivers and objected to paying taxes for the benefit of their less fortunate fellow citizens; but this opposition was inevitably overruled.

Great roads were eventually built, making wagon transportation of both immigrants and merchandise cheaper and less difficult. For many years this wagon travel made tavern-keeping profitable, and the most lively centers of social and political life were these gay and often rowdy houses of entertainment along all the principal highways. The first important road was the National Road (now US 40), which ran from Cumberland, Maryland, to Vandalia, Illinois, crossing central Indiana from Richmond to Terre Haute. It was never fully improved by the Federal Government beyond Indianapolis, and the Indiana section reverted to the State in 1839. At one time 12 stage lines operated over this road, and for two decades it was a powerful factor in binding East and West together.

The main north-south highway was the Michigan Road, extending from Michigan City through South Bend, Logansport, Indianapolis and Greensburg to Madison. The northern section of the route was obtained from the Potawatomi Indians in 1826. Poor as it was, this road carried heavy traffic in pioneer days, the inhabitants of 35 counties using it to reach Indianapolis. Other State roads were also built in this period, with money from the 3 per cent fund provided by Congress from the sale of public lands. The available money, however, permitted only the clearing of timber, and these roads were at times almost impassable. With the growth of wealth and population, State roads improved and in 1879 a system of free, tax-supported county roads was inaugurated.

Nor were the waterways neglected. In 1827 Congress granted Indiana a strip of land for the purpose of constructing a canal uniting the Maumee and the Wabash. In 1836 Governor Noble signed the Mammoth Internal Improvement Bill, which carried appropriations of $13,000,000 for three canals, two railroads, and various road improvements, and mortgaged the State for many years. Work on the Wabash and Erie Canal, which finally cost nearly $25,000,000, continued until 1852. Its total length was 460 miles, 380 of which were in Indiana and 80 in Ohio. But although this canal was eventually completed and proved an important outlet to the East for northern Indiana, most of the projects undertaken under the Mammoth Bill were failures. They were too costly for so young and poor a State, and graft and inefficiency added to the financial disaster.

All work on the canals and railroads ceased in August 1839. Contractors who had put their own money into the projects were forced to take huge losses, and the laborers upon the canals and railroads were deprived of their means of livelihood. The bondholders pressed for their money in vain; for in 1840 the State debt was more than $13,000,000, a hopeless amount for such an impoverished State. In the meantime a furious wave of litigation had arisen, as bondholders tried to realize something on their investments. Finally they grouped together and hired a New York attorney, Charles Butler, to represent them. Butler conferred with a joint committee of the General Assembly, but for a long time was unable to find a solution for his clients. Despairing of making a better deal, Butler succeeded in getting a bill through the General Assembly providing that the unfinished railroads and canals were to be turned over to the bondholders, although the State did assume some part of the debt. Even this, however, was not paid, and eventually the investors lost more than half of their money. As late as 1871, the General Assembly passed a bill forbidding any payment of the debt.

This preoccupation with internal improvements did not prevent the people of Indiana from becoming absorbed in national politics, especially after the elections of 1824. A large proportion of the early settlers were mechanics or poor farmers from the East and South, enterprising persons who desired to better themselves in a region of cheap land and greater opportunity, and who often went into debt to buy their 160 acres of uncleared forest. Naturally a majority of such people belonged to the party of Jefferson, and the circumstances of their new life gave them no reason for a shift in allegiance. But another group of settlers had also entered Indiana; prosperous Quakers who left the South partly because they objected to slavery and partly because they could buy broad acres cheaply in the new country; land speculators whose supply of ready cash enabled them to amass a fortune in a few years; all kinds of business people who saw a chance to make money in a region of rising land values. This prosperous group was small at first, but it grew as the resources of the young State were developed. It formed the backbone of the emergent Whig party in Indiana.

The first real political contest in Indiana was among supporters of Clay, Adams, and Jackson in 1824. Jackson opposed the tariff, which was already blamed for the high prices of Eastern goods; he opposed the Bank of the United States as politically controlled and undemocratic. When Adams was elected, in spite of the opposition of a majority of frontiersmen, the dissatisfied Jacksonians of Indiana were welded into the Jacksonian Democratic party. At log-rollings, boat-loadings, and especially on muster days, the Jackson agitation continued—not merely for the stalwart hero himself, but also for a wider democracy and more universal participation in government. Broadcloth was going out of politics and homespun was coming in; coonskin caps and plug tobacco were about to replace wigs and silver buckles. By 1826 the Democrats had completed county and township organizations and most offices in those units were in their hands.

For some years the Jacksonian Democrats were dominant, although the power of the Whigs grew steadily as the State's commerce and industry developed. After Jackson's smashing national victories in 1828 and 1832, the Whigs realized that their chance of political success depended on the choice of a figure who would appeal to the West as Jackson did. In 1836 they chose William Henry Harrison, a sturdy old warrior who had spent much of his life on the frontier and who was particularly dear to Indiana because of his activities in territorial days. But Jackson's influence elected Martin Van Buren, although the Whigs swept into power in Indiana. In 1840, with Van Buren and Harrison again the candidates, the Whigs scored a sweeping national success with a 'log cabin and hard cider' campaign, which had as its rallying cry 'Tippecanoe and Tyler too' (see *Newspapers and Radio*).

In this early period religion was an important factor in Indiana life. Earnest and all-engrossing, it provided in a bare, harsh environment not only moral stability but recreation and emotional release. The first preachers were circuit-riders, who held exciting camp meetings in fields encircled by tents and wagons; their sermons burned with a recital of the terrors of hell. Before long, however, rough log meeting houses were built, and stable religious communities developed. These communities founded and supported academies and colleges, and exerted a restraining influence against the turbulent laxity of the taverns.

The Baptists were the first Protestant group in the State. They held services in Knox County, near the Falls of the Ohio, in 1798, and three years later they organized a church. The Indiana Baptist convention met in 1833; in 1837 Indiana Baptist Manual Labor Institute—now Franklin College—was opened. Shortly after the Baptists came the Methodists, to develop into the most popular religious group in Indiana. In 1804 Methodist circuit-riders from Kentucky were preaching near Charlestown; in 1826 there were almost 11,000 Methodists in the State. They founded Indiana Asbury College, now DePauw University, in 1837.

Like other Protestant denominations, the Presbyterians entered Indiana from Kentucky. The Presbyterian group was small, in comparison with others, but the members were generally prosperous and the cultural level of the clergy was high. The Presbyterians, who already dominated Indiana University, founded Hanover College in 1827 and Wabash in 1832. Charges were made that they were trying to dominate higher education, and one denomination after another founded its own college to offset Presbyterian influence.

Among other fairly large religious groups the Disciples of Christ (Christians), the Society of Friends (Quakers), and the Roman Catholic Church were the most important. The first settlers in Indiana, of course, were French Catholics at Vincennes, and the first chapel was built soon after the town was founded. The present St. Francis Xavier Cathedral was begun in 1825, and with the appointment of Bishop Gabriel Bruté in 1834 Vincennes became an independent See. After the dedication of the cathedral, Bishop Bruté, with a resident priest, Lalumière, began to travel over his diocese, organizing Catholic settlers into parishes. In 1839, when Bruté died, the Church was well organized in Indiana.

The Disciples of Christ denomination grew rapidly because of its protest against the narrower creeds of other churches; by 1840 it was well organized and prosperous; in 1855 it opened Northwestern Christian University, now Butler University. The earliest Quaker meeting was organized in 1807, in a log hut where Richmond now stands; the sect spread slowly, though widely, throughout the State, which is one of the chief centers of Quakerism today. The Quakers established many schools, including Earlham College, founded in 1847 in Richmond. Mystical, devout, gentle and pacifist, rejecting ceremony and decoration in their meeting houses, the Friends brought a distinctive quality to Indiana life. When a principle they held sacred came into conflict with legality, they did not hesitate to defy the law, a fact attested by their militant struggle against slavery and their role in the operation of the Underground Railroad.

Important for the State as a whole was the outbreak of the Mexican War. Many families had relatives who had gone West to colonize still newer country and so felt a vital interest in the Texas Declaration of Independence, in the 1845 annexation, and in the actual declaration of war. Indiana sent approximately 5,000 volunteers to the scene of conflict, of whom 542 were killed.

Great economic and social changes were taking place during the 1830's and 1840's. Two years after a log cabin was built in a forest clearing, fields of corn and wheat would appear, perhaps also a young orchard. Within ten years the cabin might be replaced by a brick or white frame house, sometimes a stately and beautiful structure. Many of the brick houses built during this period are still standing. Squatters who had once cleared land gained wealth, perhaps, from pork packing or land speculation, and rose to membership in the General Assembly. Increasingly the rude hand-woven clothing of the pioneer gave way to imported goods, particularly in the larger towns. Broadcloths, brocades, gay waistcoats and ruffled shirts, taffetas, beaver hats, flounced skirts, balloon-shaped hoops, hats trimmed with veritable gardens of flowers, cutaway coats, silk stocks over hard buckram collars—these were the holiday garments of the more prosperous farmers and townsfolk in Indiana from the late thirties to the Civil War.

In the decade before the war economic factors were emerging that were to shape the future. Most important of these was the development of the railroads, as a result of which the produce of the Indiana farmer could be sent to the East, where the important markets were located. At the same time, mines and quarries were opened and mills and factories were built at favorable sites. Thus the bonds of trade and credit began to link Indiana with the North and East more strongly than with the South, while merchants, manufacturers, and bankers grew increasingly powerful.

These changes were reflected in the political realignment of the period. The party of Jefferson and Jackson—for all its great tradition—was rapidly hardening into a bulwark of the Southern planting interests, and no longer served the majority of the people. But although the Middle West was weakening in its allegiance to the Democratic party—which opposed not only the tariff, but 'free soil' as well—there was no indication that the Whig party was capable of formulating a popular platform to meet changing conditions. The time seemed ripe to form a new political party.

As the decade wore on, the somber shadow of the 'irrepressible conflict' appeared more menacing upon the horizon. A majority of Indiana's citizens had come from the South, and the approaching struggle awoke in them all sorts of partisan and sectional loyalties. A strong suspicion was abroad, moreover, that the abolitionists were at the bottom of the disagreement with the South. Thus turbulent sympathies and passions battled with economic realities, and political harshness and vituperation were the order of the day.

During this period there was a tremendous political and social awakening. Its first expression came in 1849, when the voters called for a new State constitution. In October 1850, the constitutional convention, with 150 delegates, met in Indianapolis, and remained in session for 18 weeks. The principal changes effected were that most minor governmental business was turned over to counties and the number of legislators was increased. The election, instead of the appointment, of some State officials was also provided for, and the foundation was laid for the modern school system. Robert Dale Owen (*see New Harmony*) made an effort to win equal rights for women but was only partly successful; and a clear indication that the State officially frowned on the Underground Railroad method of helping fugitive Negroes was given by the provision that no Negro should settle in the State, that any contract made with a Negro should be void, and that any person who employed or otherwise encouraged a Negro to remain in Indiana should be subject to a fine. This provision was struck out in 1881.

After the first election under the new constitution, it was apparent that the old Whig party was dying and several new parties began to bid for popular favor, including the Free-Soilers, Abolitionists, and Know-Nothings. The last-named party had a mushroom growth in the mid-fifties but although its strange platform of opposition to foreigners, Catholics, and socialism proved attractive to a reactionary element in Indiana, it soon disappeared.

In 1854 a convention of anti-Democrats made up of temperance sympathizers, antislavery men, Know-Nothings, and former Whigs was held in Indianapolis. Out of this confused coalition emerged the People's party, soon to be transformed into the Republican party on a simple three-plank platform: the non-extension of slavery, a prohibitory liquor law, and citizenship as a condition of suffrage. The passage of the Kansas-Nebraska Bill in 1854, repealing the Missouri Compromise and opening the territories to slavery, drove many hesitant elements into the Republican ranks; but the Democrats won the 1856 election.

When the National Republican Convention of 1860 was held in the famous Chicago Wigwam, Indiana was represented by a powerful uninstructed delegation headed by Henry Smith Lane. Because of Lane's unswerving devotion to Lincoln, the delegation voted as a unit for the great ex-Hoosier on every ballot; indeed some historians believe that their solidarity on the first ballot influenced many wavering States and made Lincoln's nomination possible. In the election that fall the Republicans scored a sweeping success, both in Federal and State offices, with a platform of free soil. The Assembly of 1861 sent Governor Henry Smith Lane to the United States Senate, and Oliver P. Morton, elected lieutenant governor, became governor.

From this time until April 12, when Confederate troops fired upon Fort Sumter, a pall of uncertainty hung over Indiana. Among both Republicans and Democrats there were those who held that the States who wished to secede should be allowed to do so. Any course, in their opinion, was better than coercion and bloody civil war. Most of these people were sincerely devoted to the Union; but there were many—particularly in southern Indiana—who sympathized with the South and hoped that Southern secession would eventually carry the old Northwest along with it. In sharp conflict with these waverers was Governor Morton. He led a considerable faction (and there were Democrats among them) who felt that 'coercion' was merely 'enforcement of the law'; that the President had no choice but to crush the rebellion in South Carolina before it spread farther. Yet while there was much debate upon these momentous questions, cutting sharply across party lines at many points, an atmosphere of hushed suspense seemed to prevail. For Indiana, almost as much as the Southern border States, was doomed to internal strain and division in the event of either peaceful secession or civil conflict.

But when news of the fateful attack upon Fort Sumter reached Indiana, sentiment throughout the State crystallized. The arguments for preserving the Union intact, which had been advanced in speeches for four months and had seemed to make little impression, suddenly flamed into living passion among an overwhelming majority of the people of Indiana. The simplest citizen now felt the weight of Morton's words: 'The right of secession conceded, the nation is dissolved . . . It would not be twelve months until a project for a Pacific empire would be set on foot. California and Oregon . . . would have a right to withdraw and form two separate nations . . . We should then have before us the prospect presented by the history of the petty principalities of Germany. Need I stop to argue the political, intellectual, social, and commercial death involved in this wreck and ruin?'

These clear and forceful words were a typical expression of Indiana's great war governor, one of the few commanding figures among the Northern governors during the war—a man of tremendous energy, bold executive ability, and relentless devotion to the Northern cause. He was, however, a man of bitter partisan passions, who had left the Democratic party because of its subservience to the planters; and after this decision on his own part he had no faith in the progressive elements that remained in this party. Upon the outbreak of the war, he believed, in fact, that all opposition to the Republicans should be crushed as treason. That there were in Indiana a large number of Democrats who were loyal to the North and whose criticism of his administration was not treason, but a legitimate privilege of the 'opposition,' was a principle he was never willing to admit. In spite of his uncompromising attitude, however, Morton was able to command the loyalty and support of the State to an unusual degree.

Indiana was unprepared in almost every respect to carry its part of the burden of war. The State owned very little war equipment and its credit was bad. In the emergency, merchants, banks, and others advanced funds, and the legislature, meeting in special session, authorized a $2,000,000 war loan. Indiana bonds could not be sold in large amounts, however, and finally Governor Morton induced J. F. D. Lanier, a former resident of Indiana and at that time a New York banker, to advance the State $400,000. But other difficulties soon developed. Enlistment was inadequate and desertion a common practice, especially after the volunteers had collected their bounty. Finally, to insure victory, conscription became necessary.

The election of 1862 put into office a majority hostile to Governor Morton. His vigorous prosecution of the war, together with the unpopularity of the draft and the suspension of the writ of *habeas corpus*, contributed to the defeat of the Republican party. Charging that Morton used the State militia for political purposes, the Democrats proposed to remove him as commander in chief, and in order to prevent this the opposition bolted the legislature without passing necessary appropriation bills. For two years Morton ran the State government without legislative assistance; he raised money to maintain schools and State institutions, and to finance military operations, on his own credit and that of the State. The situation was unique, since Morton's actions could be legalized only if public sentiment changed and the rebellion were defeated.

Until 1863 there was no fighting on Indiana soil, but then General John Hunt Morgan and 2,500 Confederate cavalrymen crossed the Ohio into Harrison County and raided Corydon, Salem, Dupont, and Versailles, destroying property and looting as they went (*see Corydon*). Learning that his force was in danger of being surrounded and captured, Morgan crossed the State Line into Ohio, where he and a remnant of his band were taken by Union troops.

As the war dragged on, opposition became open, resulting in resistance to the draft, attacks on newspapers, political demonstrations, and activities of secret organizations. Resistance to the draft was Statewide; violence occurred in some 30 counties, usually in isolated communities, and some enrolling officers were killed. Newspaper presses were wrecked in Terre Haute, Franklin, Richmond, Vincennes, and other towns. The most serious opposition came from the Knights of the Golden Circle. This secret organization had a fantastic program envisioning the conquest of Mexico and the setting up of a vast empire around the Gulf based on cotton and slavery. The order began to grow in 1862 and by 1863 there were in Indiana probably 50,000 members, who discouraged enlistment, opposed conscription, and otherwise aided the South. In 1864 the United States Government broke it up through the arrest and conviction of the leaders; the order disintegrated and the idea of ending the Civil War by revolution was abandoned. Despite its considerable membership the order was never a serious threat to the Northern cause.

By the close of the war, economic and social life in Indiana had changed greatly. A general dislocation of trade and industry had resulted in an increase of about 75 per cent in prices, making merchants and manufacturers wealthy, but creating hardship and misery for the majority of the people. Other changes, especially in the larger towns, were noticeable. Indianapolis had grown from a quiet town to a noisy and obtrusive city. Over half the residents were newcomers; the simple ways had almost vanished. A certain demoralization had taken place during the war, and there was an increase in crime and drunkenness.

As in the whole country, post-war politics in Indiana were dominated for a decade by the issues of Reconstruction, chief of which was the question of Negro enfranchisement. Bitterness and resentment within the Republican party were so intense that the psychology of Reconstruction resembled that of the war period. Governor Morton endorsed President Johnson's Reconstruction policy, which differed little from Lincoln's in granting a position of equality to Southern States. This policy, however, meant inevitable delay in Negro enfranchisement, and more fiery counsel was to prevail. George W. Julian—Quaker, abolitionist, and member of Congress from eastern Indiana—soon began a vigorous campaign for the point of view that was to split the country once more into two hostile camps: the enfranchisement of the Negro and punishment for the leaders of the Confederacy. Meanwhile, in Washington, Schuyler Colfax, congressman from Indiana and Speaker of the House, made a plea—the first shot fired by the radical group—for adequate protection of Negro rights.

The election of 1866 revealed that the radical Republicans had won, not only in Indiana but throughout most of the North. When the State legislature convened, Governor Morton recommended the ratification of the Fourteenth Amendment. The Democrats raised the States' rights principle and the amendment was ratified by a strictly partisan vote. In the following year Morton resigned as governor to fill the post of U. S. senator and served until his death in 1877. Owing to the attitude of the Southern States in refusing to ratify the Fourteenth Amendment, he became a leading radical in the Senate.

In 1869 Congress adopted the Fifteenth Amendment, and Morton introduced the resolution requiring the ratification by Southern States as a condition of readmission into the Union. When this amendment came before the Indiana legislature, 17 Democratic senators and 37 representatives resigned, and the measure could not be considered because of the lack of a quorum. At a special election held to fill the vacancies, the members who resigned were all re-elected. A special session of the legislature was called and the amendment came up again for consideration. Ten Democratic senators and 41 representatives resigned; but the doors of the Senate Chamber were barred, so as to maintain a quorum, and the amendment was ratified. In the House the amendment was ratified after the speaker ruled that a majority was sufficient to pass a resolution. An unsuccessful attempt was made to rescind the amendment two years later, when the Democrats had a majority in the legislature.

Feeling died down a little after the passage of the Negro Suffrage amendment; and a more friendly policy toward the South began to win favor. In 1872, although Grant carried Indiana, Thomas A. Hendricks, a Democrat, was elected governor, a definite indication of this political shift. In 1874 the Democrats were again victorious; and a number of radical Republicans led by George W. Julian, began to drift toward the Democratic party, which was recovering its peace-time role of 'popular representative of the masses.'

This trend reflected the momentous economic and social changes that were taking place in Indiana, as well as in the rest of the Nation. The rise of many diversified manufacturing enterprises, the utilization of natural resources on a larger scale, the rapid development of roads and railways—all these factors resulted in a complex industrial structure. But the transformation was a painful one, marked by unrest and maladjustments, and the creaking of the social machinery gave rise to strain and bitterness among groups with conflicting interests.

The greatest sufferer throughout the late nineteenth century was the farmer (*see Agriculture*). The development of improved farm machinery led to a self-defeating scramble to mortgage the farm in order to buy new plows and tractors—a process that merely increased agricultural production and drove down prices. Staggering under his burden of debt, unable to get good prices for his crops, the farmer was further victimized by the protective tariff, high freight rates, and profiteering middlemen. Moreover, the reclamation of swampland added several million acres to the agricultural area of Indiana—a fact that led to a further increase in production and still lower prices.

In spite of a marked population shift to the cities between 1870 and 1900, a majority of Indiana people lived on farms throughout most of this period. For many of them it was a bleak, hard life—drab and laborious for the men, even worse for the women, whose drudgery was unrelieved by labor-saving devices. The hope and excitement which had made the poverty of the pioneer period bearable were gone. Now, in his difficulty, the Indiana farmer began to turn with greater awareness to agencies that promised to improve his lot.

In the seventies the Grange was particularly important. A semipolitical fraternal order, with far-reaching social and cultural program, it did much to provide recreation, education, and political guidance. At a convention in Indianapolis in 1874, the Grange organized the Independent party with a platform advocating railroad regulation, the curtailment of land and grain monopolies, banking reforms, and the substitution of a paper currency for the gold standard. In the State election that year the party polled 19,000 votes.

Currency reform and railroad regulation were the fundamental demands of every third-party movement during this period. The fundamental cleavage between group interests was strikingly demonstrated in regard to both issues. For the farmers and other debtor groups, high freight rates worked great hardships, and 'hard money' meant only the payment of debts in money that was increasingly valuable. For the bankers and other creditors, who had invested heavily in the railroads, inflation meant simply the repudiation of honest debts. The post-war boom postponed, but could not avert, the conflict between these interests.

In 1876 the National Greenback party, having previously absorbed the Independent party in Indiana, held a convention in Indianapolis. Favoring inflation and the continued issuance of greenbacks, this party polled more than 9,000 votes that year, and nearly 40,000 votes two years later, electing one congressman. Although it lost influence in the next few years, the Greenback party influenced State politics more than its voting strength would indicate, since both Republicans and Democrats began to advocate currency reform.

The eighties and nineties brought a not inconsiderable improvement in the farmers' status in Indiana, and the State was by this time closely identified with the East in its industrial and social structure. Nevertheless, the Populist party, with its platform calling for increased Federal control of currency, free silver, a graduated income tax, and government ownership of railroads and utilities, found support among Indiana workers and farmers. By 1890 the frontier had disappeared, and the escape of the ambitious poor to free land farther west was cut off. With this safety valve for restlessness and discontent closed, and with immigrants entering the country in greater numbers, wages could no longer be kept up by a shortage of labor.

This was a period of industrial expansion, in which many county-seat towns acquired mills and factories (see Industry and Labor). In spite of the prosperity of middle classes, however, the wage-earners in these towns were finding the new conditions difficult. Hence the period was one of awakening and organization for industrial workers as well as the farmers, since the former found their interests conflicting at many points with those of the banks, the railroads, and the merchants and manufacturers.

The depression of 1893–4 caused severe suffering. Factories were closed and most of the banks suspended payments. Labor conflict developed, particularly in Sullivan, Daviess, and Lake Counties, where the National Guard was sent on strike duty. The United Mine Workers was already powerful in the coal fields, and the American and State Federations of Labor were established. Out of these labor conflicts, Eugene V. Debs began to come into national prominence and started on his career in the Labor and Socialist movements (*see Terre Haute*).

During most of the period between 1870 and 1900 Indiana was politically a doubtful State, for the strength of the Jacksonian tradition and the ferment of conflict and discontent soon enabled the Democratic party to regain its influence. Because the two major parties were so evenly divided, large sums of money were spent to win elections and political corruption was general. After the election of 1888, when vote-buying reached a high point, the Australian ballot was adopted and a statute was passed to stop vote-buying on a large scale. During this same politically doubtful period, Indianians were candidates for President and Vice President in five national elections. Thomas A. Hendricks was the Democratic candidate for Vice President in 1876, and in 1884 he was elected as Grover Cleveland's running mate. In 1880, William H. English was the candidate for the same office. Benjamin Harrison, a Republican, was elected President in 1888, but he was defeated for re-election in 1892 by Grover Cleveland.

For the relatively prosperous folk who lived in the cities and towns, the closing decades of the nineteenth century brought marked changes and, in general, social and cultural opportunities unknown before the Civil War. The physical aspect of the towns had changed. Homes were going up by the thousands every year; streets were paved and the streetcar was introduced—horse drawn at first, later run by electricity; gas lights brightened streets and homes. With the development of industry the standard of living was rising; and although it was a period of difficulty and hardship for many farmers and factory workers, an increasing number of people were beginning to have more time in which to enjoy life.

It was an era of prosperity, and a simple, leisurely mode of life that now seems remote. The age of jigsaw architecture, plush sofas, and puffed sleeves, of plumed hats, high bicycles, pompadours, and whatnots, it seems a romantic interlude between the struggles of the pioneer era and the rush of the age of automobiles. People had 'time for everything; time to think, to talk, time to read, time to wait for a lady.' The greatest event of the year was a trip to one of the larger cities for a concert or play. Social life was largely informal, consisting of church suppers, small literary clubs, or the kind of gaiety fostered by the presence of a college in the town, as Butler in Irvington, Wabash in Crawfordsville, and DePauw in Greencastle.

During this era young ladies went to college too—a notable victory for feminism—and the woman's club movement developed. Literary, musical, travel, historical, and social clubs were started in most Indiana cities. In 1875 the Indianapolis Woman's Club was founded, with May Wright Sewall one of the charter members; in a few years this remarkable woman had completed the building of the Propylaeum, the second women's clubhouse in the country. In 1890 federated club work began.

But this transition period was altered almost before it took shape. The twentieth century ushered in an innovation of great importance, and within a few years the whole tempo of life changed. In the nineties the first 'horseless carriages' appeared on the streets of Kokomo and Indianapolis; but only a few people owned them, and whole neighborhoods turned out to gape whenever one went jiggling by. But by 1910, Indianapolis was becoming an automobile metropolis, manufacturing motor cars on a mass scale. The consequent boom in heavy industry, the increased thousands of industrial employees, the sharpening of competition, the hastened pace of all business life, the penetration of the countryside, eventually, by the Ford—all these factors began to transform Indiana (*see Industry and Labor*).

At the same time, a sparsely settled region of wasteland on the shore of Lake Michigan, in the northwest corner of the State, was converted into one of the great industrial centers of the world. Standard Oil, seeking a convenient site near Chicago, constructed great refineries at the little village of Whiting; Inland Steel and other industries located plants at Hammond and East Chicago; and the United States Steel Corporation, building vast mills on the sand dunes, created Gary, which within a few years grew into the most important manufacturing city in the State (*see Cities of the Calumet*).

To provide labor for these new industries, thousands of European immigrants were brought in. Since the period of early settlement the principal immigrant groups had been Germans and Poles. After the failure of the 1848 Revolution many thrifty middle-class Germans—farmers, businessmen, and scholars—had been attracted to Indiana because it still offered the advantages of a young and rapidly expanding society. Especially in central Indiana, the heavy German migration during two decades after 1850 had left a marked influence on succeeding generations. In the latter part of the century, however, when the Nation was admitting yearly a tremendous flood of immigrants, Indiana's foreign-born population increased comparatively slowly. Lacking great centralized industries and a metropolitan city, the State offered little to the southern Europeans whom American industry was recruiting. The only foreigners to settle here in considerable numbers were Polish farmers, part of that broad migration that brought thousands of Danes, Poles, Swedes, and Norwegians into the Mississippi Valley in search of cheap land. Today an impressive number of people in northern Indiana, especially in La Porte and Kosciusko Counties, are of Polish descent. But with the development of large-scale industry, the tide of foreign immigration increased rapidly, until Hammond, East Chicago, Whiting, Gary, and South Bend all had important colonies of Hungarians, Italians, Poles, and other nationalities.

Indiana's industrialization, already proceeding at a rapid pace, was further stimulated by the first World War. Workers were scarce, and this labor shortage was increased when the United States entered the war. Within two months the Indiana National Guard was called into service. One unit was assigned to the famous Rainbow Division, eventually becoming the 115th Field Artillery and the only distinctly Hoosier outfit to serve in the war. When conscription went into effect, 255,145 men registered; of this number, 17,510 were sent to camps shortly afterward. Altogether, Indiana furnished 130,670 men, of whom more than 3,000 died either in battle or from disease.

At home men, women, and children threw themselves into the war effort. The women of the State put together countless 'comfort kits,' knitted thousands of sweaters and socks, made surgical dressings, pajamas, nightshirts, and other articles of clothing for the soldiers. Under the slogan 'Food will win the war,' they were regimented to cut down in the use of foods needed by the army. Many participated in drives to obtain money for the Red Cross and in war bond and thrift stamp sales.

To the State's farmers the war brought booming prosperity. Even before the United States entered, European demands for American agricultural products moved prices to their highest levels in history. After 1917 prices of corn, wheat, livestock, and other products skyrocketed to almost unbelievable levels, and farming suddenly became a highly profitable occupation. Land values increased with profits, and farmers began to expand their activities and modernize their equipment. They bought automobiles, new farm machinery, improved strains of livestock. They put up new barns and improved their houses. To do all this, or to add to their land holdings, they mortgaged their farms, intending to pay off the debts out of their future income.

But with the end of the war came the end of high prices for farm produce and a steep drop in land values. By 1921 Indiana and the Nation were caught in a sudden, sharp depression. Industry recovered rapidly and eased into a period of steady prosperity that was to last until 1929, but agriculture, not prosperous before the war, was in even worse shape after. Indiana's farm mortgage debt had doubled during the boom period, and many farmers now found their land mortgaged for more than its total worth. Farm prices failed to keep step with the steady increase in the cost of living; farm surpluses were a drag on the world market; and the steady development of machinery, along with the lowered productivity of Indiana's soil, made farming an increasingly expensive enterprise.

Nevertheless, the 1920's were years of prosperity for the State as a whole, since Indiana was no longer predominantly agricultural. The farmers' plight was hidden behind a great industrial and financial expansion, part of the Nation-wide prosperity of the Coolidge-Hoover period. The factories of the manufacturing cities—Indianapolis, Muncie, Anderson, Evansville, Terre Haute, Fort Wayne, Gary, Hammond, East Chicago, and South Bend—absorbed thousands of men and women who had been raised on the farms. As a result, the State's rural population dropped sharply during the decade while its urban population steadily increased.

At this time an astounding chapter was written into the pages of Indiana history by the Ku Klux Klan. Under the leadership of D. C. 'I-am-the-Law' Stephenson, this organization dictated the choosing of at least one governor, of United States senators, mayors and thousands of lesser officials. Stephenson was convicted in 1925 of the murder of an Indianapolis young woman and is (1941) serving a life term in the Indiana State Prison. Early in 1928 the Attorney General of Indiana took the offensive against the Klan in two suits asking its dissolution.

These suits were never tried, but public opinion was beginning to veer; this fact, coupled with a savage campaign waged by the Indianapolis *Times* against the Klan, for which that newspaper was awarded the Pulitzer Prize in 1928, spelled the end of this turbulent growth as a political power in the State.

During this decade, with added restrictions on the part of the Federal Government, foreign immigration decreased; but the Negro population, centered chiefly in Indianapolis and the Calumet cities, reached a new high. After the Civil War, despite legislative attempts to exclude freedmen, Indiana gradually had begun to provide economic opportunities for a steadily growing Negro population. The situation was a curious contradiction, since the United States Constitution expressly gave Negroes the franchise, while the State denied it until 1881. By 1910 there were 60,000 Negroes in Indiana, four-fifths of them in the cities. Then came the World War, with higher wages paid by factories; and from the tobacco and cotton fields of the South a steady stream of Negroes poured northward. By 1920 there were 80,000 in Indiana; by 1930 there were nearly 112,000, all but 9,000 in the larger cities.

Indiana offered the Negro comparatively favorable economic opportunities even after the war boom was over. A number found employment in barber shops, drugstores, groceries, and other small businesses. A somewhat smaller number engaged in agriculture. The professional group was perhaps the most favored, for in Indiana the Negro doctor, lawyer, or teacher was able to engage in his profession at least within his own race without molestation. The majority of the race, however, were limited by poverty and lack of training to domestic service, day labor, and unskilled industrial work. Excluded for the most part from trade unions, until the advent of the Committee for Industrial Organization, they rarely were able to win important economic gains.

Politically Indiana Negroes fared somewhat better, for they had no fear of disfranchisement. Election campaigns often found them in a strategic position to dictate terms to the major parties. More than a few Negroes were rewarded with political favors, and several have been elected to the General Assembly or to city offices. In 1936 the State constitution was finally amended to permit Negroes to serve in the militia.

Like other States, Indiana suffered in the depression that followed the financial collapse of 1929. Farm prices dropped still further and farm tenancy resumed its upward climb as mortgages, many of them dating from the World War, were foreclosed. Dozens of banks failed throughout the State; in the cities thousands were unemployed and private charities were swamped. Hardest hit of all were the southern counties, which depended on coal mining or stone quarrying for their economic welfare; both industries collapsed almost completely and in some places as much as 50 per cent of the population was without a means of support.

With this widespread suffering it became apparent that ordinary machinery for relief was entirely inadequate. Since the formation of the State, township trustees had been charged with the support of indigents in their districts. County poor farms and State institutions for the care of special groups, such as the School for the Deaf, the School for the Blind, and the Central State Hospital for the Insane, had been considered adequate for many years. In 1889 the General Assembly had created a Board of State Charities and a Board of Children's Guardians, the most important step in the field of public welfare until the 1930's. Starting in 1933, the Federal Government began to supplement the work of private charities and State-supported agencies, providing some measure of relief through the CWA and FERA, forerunners of the present WPA.

Governor Paul V. McNutt, who took office in 1933, at once took steps to effect a drastic reorganization of the State governmental structure. Under his leadership a law was passed by which the State's governmental activities were all departmentalized under the control of the governor. This placed far more power in the hands of the governor than has been exercised by any chief executive of the State, if not of any State, since the Territorial days of William Henry Harrison.

In 1936 three laws were enacted providing for a comprehensive welfare program and participation in the provisions of the Federal Social Security Act. One act set up an unemployment compensation system applicable to large numbers of urban workers; a second provided for participation in the health extension phases of the Social Security Act; and a third established the State Department of Public Welfare and County Welfare Boards, which supervise all public welfare, public assistance, and public institutional functions of the State.

Early in 1937 southern Indiana was devastated by the swirling waters of the Ohio River, which on January 31 reached the highest stage ever recorded. The flood took a heavy toll, inundating entire towns and cities, leaving thousands of people homeless, and causing millions of dollars' worth of property damage. The number of dead, which must have run into the hundreds, has never been ascertained.

Refugees from Jeffersonville, New Albany, and smaller towns were evacuated to the northern part of the State, where they were cared for in hospitals, public buildings, and private homes. A valiant fight against the water, disease, and privation was made by the National Guard, Red Cross, WPA, Salvation Army, and many other organizations. Coast Guard cutters were used in areas where no other means of transportation was available. Volunteers from all over the State hurried to the scene, many of them bringing boats to use in rescue work.

When the waters receded, the river towns began the difficult work of reconstruction, and within a few months nearly all traces of the flood had been erased. One town, Leavenworth, was moved entirely and relocated on a hill out of the reach of future floods. In other cities levees were improved and heightened; a vast government reforestation program throughout the Ohio Valley was undertaken to reduce future flood dangers.

In the summer of 1940 Indiana moved into the Nation's headlines when Wendell Willkie, a native of Elwood, received the Republican nomination for the presidency. Mr. Willkie waged a vigorous campaign and received 22,000,000 votes, but was defeated by President Roosevelt.

Indiana industries, in the summer and fall of 1940, were beginning to feel the first effects of a national drive to strengthen the defenses of the United States. Little Charlestown, a sleepy village near the Ohio River, boomed after the announcement that a giant powder plant of the E. I. du Pont de Nemours Company was to be located near by. Approximately 250 farms in La Porte County were purchased by the Federal Government for an ammunition loading plant. Nearly 300 factories in the State, headed by the important Allison Engineering Company, airplane motor manufacturers, received Government orders in the first few months of the defense program, and in more than 5,000 others preparations were being made to convert peace-time products into war essentials if necessary.

Early in 1941 the machinery of State government was brought to a standstill by a conflict between Democratic Governor Henry F. Schricker and the Republican majority in the State Legislature. The Legislature repealed the reorganization acts of 1933 and thus removed most of the governor's appointive powers. Governor Schricker immediately challenged the constitutionality of this action and the controversy is now before the State courts for decision.

Agriculture

FROM the earliest days of settlement, agriculture has been basic to the economic development and cultural progress of Indiana. In the wake of trappers and solitary riflemen came land-hungry settlers to establish relatively small family-sized farms, which for 50 years were the backbone of Indiana economy. During that time the industries of the State were in the main mere offshoots of agriculture; and even today, when manufacturing, quarrying, and mining have far outstripped farming in the number of workers they engage, Indiana is still one of the leading agricultural States.

The first settlers to enter Indiana Territory around 1800 came from Kentucky, Virginia, and the Carolinas, and made their homes in southern Indiana, along the Ohio River. Soon thereafter immigrants from the North and East bought Government land along the Wabash and Whitewater Rivers and their tributaries. A little later this dependence upon waterways was broken somewhat by the building of the National Road and the Michigan Road, paid for by the sale of near-by lands. Before long a great belt of farms extended north and south, and another east and west across the State, and by 1830 the population of Indiana was 348,000.

Because of the natural fertility of the deep glacial soil in the northern two-thirds of the State, it was possible to make a good living on a small holding. The soil on the southern hills, being thinner and subjected to heavy water runoff, was more rapidly depleted. In the early days, however, before forests had been cut off and soil erosion had occurred on a large scale, this land also was generally fairly productive.

Most of the early settlers lived in log cabins and produced most of their necessities. Pioneer farm implements were few and crude, and efforts to raise crops unsuited to the region resulted in many costly failures. Some of the farmers wasted much time and energy trying to raise cotton and tobacco; they tried to introduce grape culture on a large scale, in imitation of the Swiss settlers at Vevay. The culture of hemp, flax, and hops was also widespread in the first quarter of the century, but by 1850 all these attempts had been abandoned in favor of more adaptable crops.

One of the chief obstacles to agricultural expansion in those early days was the presence throughout most of the State of large areas of marshy land. In the north especially the marshes covered a wide area, and fevers and ague were common. Proper drainage later brought better farms and better health.

The most unfortunate feature of pioneer agriculture was the utter disregard for maintenance of soil fertility. The soil seemed infinitely rich, and after clearing a field farmers often planted 12 to 20 corn crops in succession. Especially on the southern uplands this practice was ruinous, and when part of the land eventually was turned back to pasture there was a struggle with briars, sassafras, weeds, and erosion.

In spite of these adverse conditions the farms of Indiana multiplied and the farmers prospered. Gradually they learned that hogs, corn, and wheat could be raised profitably and a swelling stream of grain and pork began pouring southward to the New Orleans market. By 1830 the most populous town in Indiana, Madison, with 2,000 inhabitants, was noted for the quantity of pork barreled there. Richmond, Indianapolis, Logansport, Terre Haute, Crawfordsville, LaFayette, and New Harmony also were stable communities rising along the principal waterways. Everywhere this general quickening of life and trade rested on the foundation of improved farming.

For the farmers of the Middle West, the period from 1825 to 1860 was one of political ascendancy and economic growth. Aided by the mechanics and factory workers of the Atlantic seaboard, they held the balance of power in the struggle between the industrial Northeast and the agricultural West and South. As a debtor class they benefited from 'cheaper money,' low-priced commodities, and the continued power of the Democratic party.

In this prosperity the railroads became an increasingly important factor in Hoosier life. The canals that linked northern Indiana to the Gulf of Mexico by way of the Ohio and Mississippi Rivers had done much to enable farmers to transport their products to market cheaply. But the railroads were faster and less dependent upon the weather, and by the 1850's this new form of transportation was welding the East and the West together. 'The stream of migration westward,' in the words of Dr. Charles A. Beard, 'became a torrent; in return the stream of wheat, corn, and bacon from the farms became an avalanche.'

In Indiana, as elsewhere during this period, there was great improvement in agricultural methods. The reaper added enormously to the efficiency and speed of harvesting grain and made farmers more independent of weather conditions. Agricultural societies were formed and farm journals appeared in many counties; and in 1850 Governor Joseph White asked for legislation looking toward the diffusion of popular and scientific knowledge about soil treatment, animal husbandry, methods of cultivation, and better seeds. The result was the State Agricultural Society and the State Board of Agriculture. The first Indiana State Fair was held in 1852, and since then this annual event has done much to popularize and spread agricultural knowledge in Indiana.

In addition to Governor White, Solon Robinson and Governor James D. 'Blue Jeans' Williams stand out among the prominent persons in early Indiana agriculture. In his *Biographical and Historical Sketches of Early Indiana*, W. W. Woollen says of Governor Williams: 'To him more than any other man, with probably the exception of the late Governor White, are the people [of Indiana] indebted for the establishment of the State Board of Agriculture.' Governor Williams was a member of the board for 16 years, during four of which he served as president.

Solon Robinson, who came to Indiana in 1830 and had a varied career as a farmer and real-estate operator, was first heard of as the organizer of the Squatters' Union in 1836. The Union had considerable success in preventing speculators from running up prices at Government auctions of lands where its members lived. After 1840 Robinson was widely known for his advocacy of a national agricultural society, and as a writer and speaker on farm problems. In 1853 he became agricultural editor of the New York *Tribune,* where he wielded a wide influence. He also conducted an experimental farm in Westchester County, New York.

By 1860 Indiana's agricultural pattern was not strikingly different, at least so far as crops were concerned, from that of the present day. Stock-raising and grain-farming were prevalent then as now. Hogs were the most important livestock; the census of 1860 gave an average of nearly 10 hogs for every family in the State. Sheep were raised more extensively then than now, and Kentucky and Virginia strains of saddle horses were numerous and of high grade. Corn was the leading grain crop, with wheat second. Hemp, flax, and such minor crops were being abandoned in favor of other crops, and a slowly increasing production of vegetables for city markets. Although the people of Indiana in 1860 numbered only about a third of the present population, there were almost as many persons living upon farms then as today.

The Morrill Act of 1862 offered Federal land grants to each State to establish agricultural and engineering colleges. This Federal aid was accepted by the Indiana General Assembly in 1865, and trustees were appointed to take charge of the grant and to found the Indiana Agricultural College. In 1869 John Purdue, of LaFayette, gave the State $150,000 and 100 acres of land, backed by $50,000 from Tippecanoe County, on condition that the agricultural school be located in Tippecanoe County and named Purdue University. The legislature accepted the gift and the university opened for its first full year on September 16, 1874, with Abram C. Shortridge as president. Its research in various fields of agriculture and its dissemination of information among farmers have done more than any other thing to elevate Indiana to its present high position among agricultural States.

Up to this time the alliance with the industrialists of the East was proving profitable to Indiana farmers. But in the 1870's the improvement of farm implements and machinery began to change the picture of agriculture throughout Indiana as well as in the rest of the Nation. Even before the Civil War, the reaper had started a revolution on the land; to prophetic minds it was already clear that the old self-sufficient farming unit was doomed. In 1868, James Oliver of South Bend invented the chilled-steel plow, which immediately became popular because of its low price, adaptability to any kind of soil, and the ease with which it scoured. In the seventies Indiana became one of the great plow-manufacturing States of the Union. Other inventions followed: automatic self-binders, improved harvesters, corn planters, improved harrows, and the two-horse cultivator. Rapidly growing industry found a vast potential market among the farmers.

As new equipment increasing the individual farmer's efficiency came into use and the westward movement to new land continued, production increased at a rapid pace. It was the common philosophy to produce more to get more money to buy more land. A large percentage of farmers following this idea of expansion plunged heavily into debt.

In Indiana between 1860 and 1890 the investment in farm implements more than doubled. During this period new acres were constantly being put to the plow as forests were cleared and swamps were drained. The acreage of tillable land in the State almost doubled in the two decades following the Civil War.

As free land in the West began to be scarce, land values in Indiana and other States rose. Taxes began to mount as improvements in roads and schools were demanded. Between 1880 and 1890 the number of mortgages on real estate increased 82 per cent, and the amount of mortgage indebtedness 73 per cent. Meanwhile, in spite of the increase in the quantity of farm products during the seventies and eighties, the price declined so that the value of agricultural products for the State in 1890 was below that of 1870 and 1880.

Thus the economic background was conducive in Indiana to various political third parties (such as the Greenback movement of the seventies and the Populists of the nineties), which swept the Nation for many years as an outgrowth of mounting agrarian discontent. There was a social background for the Grange, a rural federation of secret lodges, organized soon after the Civil War. The life of the farmer was all too often a lonely, hard-bitten existence, and the Grange was a powerful organization striving not only for economic improvement, but for a fuller social life. At the peak of its influence, the Indiana Grange had nearly 60,000 members, but it declined in numbers after a few years. It is still an effective organization, however. Among farm organizations that succeeded it were the Farmers' Alliance, the Farmers' Mutual Benefit Association, and the Populist party.

The panic of 1893 brought farm prices to a lower level than ever before, but in the subsequent revival the farmers were greatly benefited. The end of free land in the West, industrial development, the influx of immigrants, with greatly expanded urban and foreign markets, caused land values to rise. From about 1896 on, farm prices rose steadily, culminating in the high prices during the World War period. The annual value of farm products in Indiana rose from less than $200,000,000 in 1910 to nearly $500,000,000 in 1920, the latter figure largely an inflated one in keeping with the times. This increase was accompanied by an increase in the values of land and buildings, which advanced in Indiana from less than $2,000,000,000 in 1910, to $2,654,000,000 in 1920. Encouraged by the high farm commodity prices and the Federal Farm Loan Act of 1916, many farmers purchased land at exorbitant figures, and the farm mortgage debt in Indiana nearly doubled.

The boom collapsed in 1921 with the general industrial and financial crisis of that year. Farm property values in Indiana declined more than $1,000,000,000 in the next five years, as the prices of farm products dropped ruinously. The industrial and financial crisis was quickly surmounted and American business rushed forward into the glittering years of President Warren G. Harding's 'normalcy.' But the farmers did not go with it. They had not recovered from the slump. Farm prices climbed only a little and land values rose even less. The net result was that Indiana's farms, valued at $2,654,000,000 in 1920, had declined 60 per cent to $1,040,000,000 by 1932, and the average price per acre from $126 to $51. A distressing aspect of the situation was that the farmer had incurred large debts in an era of high prices for commodities and land. With lowered prices, his money was suddenly worth a great deal more but he had less of it and he found himself parting with valuable money to pay for property that had lost much of its value. Thus the prosperous 1920's were really a hindrance to agriculture.

In spite of this, Indiana is today one of the leading agricultural States in proportion to its area. Approximately a fifth of the workers of the State are engaged in agricultural work; farm products are the raw materials of many important industries; and about 91 per cent of Indiana's 23,000,000 acres of land is in farms. Of this vast farm area, only about a fifth is classified as 'unimproved,' while the remainder is cultivated or is temporarily fallow.

Since about 1890 there has been a sharp decline in the percentage of the State's farm population, and a gradual decrease in the actual number of people upon farms. At least two factors have contributed to this: a general decrease in the size of families, and the increasing use of farm machinery. Since families with no money cannot invest in machines, they try to eke out a living on small areas, selling much of their acreage to more prosperous neighbors who can make a fair living from larger farms. (In 1935 there were 200,835 farms in the State, in contrast to 220,000 in 1900.) As a result, Indiana farms are larger today and, when properly handled, more productive than they used to be, in spite of the decline in farm population from 907,295 in 1920 to 852,994 in 1935.

This increase in size per farm was accompanied by a decline in the number of farm tenants during the last 30 years. In 1900 there were nearly 65,000 tenants, operating 6,000,000 acres of Indiana farmland, the size of the average tenant-farm being less than 100 acres. In 1930, however, 55,000 tenants were operating some 7,000,000 acres—an increase of more than 27 acres in the average size of each farm. These 55,000 Indiana tenants constitute only 30 per cent of the State's farmers, while the average percentage of tenant operators for the whole country is 42 per cent.

Indiana farmers have avoided the tendency to excessive crop specialization, which is sometimes ruinous to land and always highly speculative because of the risks from weather and the economic market. The agriculture of the State is widely diversified. Indiana farming is characterized by improvement of both houses and equipment, and by local variation in land values. The most common type of farm in Indiana is still the fairly small general farm, devoted to raising a variety of crops and farm animals.

Today, as in the past, the chief crops raised in Indiana are the staple grains. From 20 to 25 per cent of the total State farm acreage is planted in corn, with a yield per acre 40 per cent higher than the average yield for the United States. Wheat is second, covering about 12 per cent of the total farm acreage. Both cereals are found everywhere except in certain hilly southern sections, with the heaviest crop harvested in the State's central plain. Oats and soy beans rank next to corn and wheat as field crops. Hay and forage, also important, are raised uniformly throughout the State.

Indiana produces also a number of important minor crops. In the 1920's it contained a fourth of the whole area in America planted to canning tomatoes; in the 1935 season it led all other States with a production of more than 350,000 tons. Only four or five States grow more onions than Indiana, and mint is extensively grown in the northern muck land of Indiana and adjacent southern Michigan. Peas, melons, celery, and other vegetables, largely for city markets, are raised throughout the State, and tobacco is quite widely grown in southern and central Indiana. Indiana exports relatively little fruit, although during favorable years large crops of melons, apples, peaches, grapes, and smaller fruits are harvested for local consumption. Dairying has gone ahead rapidly and the annual value of the returns from this phase of agriculture is estimated to be $40,000,000 to $50,000,000 a year. This business is well distributed over the State with the most intensive development naturally around the larger cities and in northwestern Indiana for the Chicago market.

Many animals are also raised in Indiana: horses, chiefly for power; hogs, sheep, and beef cattle for market. Occasionally profitable enterprises specialize in the breeding of rabbits, pigeons, guinea pigs, frogs, and goldfish. Silver fox, skunk, and raccoon are bred on several fur farms.

The average annual income for Indiana farmers now is approximately $300,000,000 a year, about where it was in 1929–30 before the depression hit agriculture with its full force. In 1932 it had dropped to the record low of $137,000,000, but since 1935 has been from $250,000,000 to $300,000,000 a year. These figures have included benefit payments that have been made by the Federal Government to Indiana farmers for participation in the crop control or the soil conservation programs of the Agricultural Adjustment Administration. These payments, however, have been a relatively small percentage of the total income—usually from $8,000,000 to $20,000,000 per year, depending upon the program and the rate of payment for participation.

Indiana is fortunate in its proximity to markets and in its network of good roads. About 60,000 of the State's 77,000 miles of roads are improved with hard surface, gravel, stone, or other material better than dirt. This means that most farmers can get to the market almost any day of the year that they have something to sell. Railroads, and truck and trailer lines give Hoosier food products unexcelled transportation facilities.

The outstanding co-operative agency for farmers in the State is the Indiana Farm Bureau. A unit of the American Farm Bureau Federation, the State division functions in the economic and educational fields. It conducts co-operative sales and marketing activities, supplies automobile insurance to its members at cost, and owns its own hog cholera serum plant at Thorntown, Indiana. Hardly less important are its educational functions. It watches all farm legislation, both national and local, and supplies farmers with information concerning this legislation and other facts vital to their interests. In addition, it conducts summer schools to develop farm leadership, broadcasts a daily radio program, and publishes monthly *The Hoosier Farmer,* official organ of the Farm Bureau. One of the most valuable of the bureau's enterprises is its present rural electrification program, carried on in co-operation with the Rural Electrification Administration of the U. S. Department of Agriculture.

In the general development of Indiana agriculture, it would be impossible to overestimate the role of Purdue University. In the 1880's the university started interesting experimental work in agriculture. Farmers were asking questions and Purdue was supplying the answers, even then giving valuable information on crop rotations, on soil fertility, on livestock feeding and management, on fruit production and marketing, on all of the farm enterprises.

In 1889 a far-seeing Purdue staff member, the late Professor W. C. Latta, was largely responsible for enactment of the Farmers' Institute Act, which legally recognized the work the university had been doing in holding farm schools throughout the State. This work led eventually to the Clore Act in 1911, which authorized expansion of this activity under the direction of the Department of Agricultural Extension. The Smith-Lever Act of 1914 provided for co-operative relations between State and Nation to aid in the far-flung program of agricultural education.

Under this joint program, boys' and girls' 4-H Clubs have been formed. In 1940 about 55,000 Indiana boys and girls between 10 and 20 years of age were enrolled in these groups, which have wielded tremendous influence for the improvement of farm life in the Hoosier State. More than 2,000,000 persons attended in one year the lectures and demonstrations that the county agents, home demonstration agents, and specialists from Purdue conducted. This work extends into every community and is available to every citizen of Indiana. The entire State has long been the Purdue University campus.

Industry and Labor

THE earliest economic effort in which white men engaged in Indiana was the fur trade. Upon the heels of the first explorers came French traders from Canada, intent upon turning into gold the numberless bales of furs the Indians were willing to trade for glass beads, whisky, blankets, and bright cloth. Some of these French traders were smugglers—that is, unlicensed by the king, but willing to risk hanging for a fortune in beaver skins. As the English began to press into the interior, rivalry grew more intense and the fur trade became a struggle often involving the crack of the rifle and the flash of the knife. Until the end of the eighteenth century the principal towns—Vincennes, Fort Miami (later Fort Wayne), and Fort Ouiatenon—were all fur-trading posts.

But by the opening of the nineteenth century the pioneers were coming in such great numbers that it was easy to foresee the end of the fur trade. With ax and flame the settlers cleared land for their first scanty crops of corn, hemp, flax, and potatoes.

Indiana's earliest industries grew out of family enterprise. At first, men ground corn in small hand mills and tanned their own leather for shoes; women made all wearing apparel, picked fowl for pillows and mattresses, and made soap and candles. Later, the itinerant cobbler and the local miller took over many of these activities. Pioneer commerce flourished as soon as agriculture began to prosper. For many years Indiana's surplus farm produce was shipped down to New Orleans, by way of the Ohio and Mississippi, on flatboats—raftlike structures laden with geese, turkeys, hogs and pork, cattle, beef, corn, flour, and venison.

During most of the period from the late 1820's to the Civil War, Indiana developed young industries that depended directly upon agriculture—milling, distilling, meat-packing, and lumbering. From the first, corn was the principal crop, and farmers distilled their surplus corn into whisky. Soon Indiana began to produce great numbers of hogs, and packing became important; by 1830 Madison was the second largest pork-packing center west of the Alleghenies, and Indianapolis and Hammond later became packing towns.

The development of the steamboat (see New Albany) accelerated the stream of farm products flowing toward the South. To aid this trend, the State began to construct canals to connect with the larger rivers. Indiana went bankrupt, however, after the panic of 1837, and before the canals were completed the projects were surrendered to private bondholders. In private hands they gave good service for some years, bringing prosperity to isolated farmers, enabling them to market their produce and move out of log cabins into better homes, stimulating the growth of cities, trade, and manufacture.

The chief factor, however, in industrial expansion was the development of the railroads. In 1839 the State let the first railroad contract to a private firm. The road was built slowly, since public opinion was apathetic at first, but in 1847 the first train from Madison puffed into Indianapolis. Town after town prospered as the road was completed northward, and soon the immense success of the Madison line started a railroad craze. In the 1850's the rail mileage of Indiana increased tenfold. After the Civil War came another period of railroad expansion, linked inseparably with the rise of modern Indiana.

The railroad, at first tolerated only as an experiment, evolved into a gigantic economic force. It linked Indiana's economic life to the industrial East, breaking the long dependence upon the South. This was in part because Eastern capital and credit were heavily involved in the construction of the railroads; in part because the industrial States, needing Midwestern corn and hogs, could ship by rail to Indiana an ever-increasing stream of manufactured goods.

An equally important outcome of the growth of the railroads was the development of coal mining in Indiana. Local blacksmiths had dug surface coal along the Wabash since the earliest days of settlement, and in 1837 a company on the Ohio River, where Cannelton now is, began to mine coal for the use of passing steamers. In 1854, when the Evansville & Terre Haute Railroad crossed Sullivan County, a coal mine was opened only three miles from the main line. With the completion of the Baltimore & Ohio Railroad in 1857, coal mining began in Daviess County on a commercial scale.

Because of the difficulty of transportation, the full development of limestone quarrying came only after the Civil War. But the State was aware of its resources long before this time. In 1837 the governor, authorized by the assembly, had appointed David Dale Owen to make a 'complete and minute geological survey of the whole State.' In two years Owen had delimited with fair accuracy the great belts of coal and limestone (*see Natural Setting*) that form the outstanding natural assets of Indiana, and found that good stone for lime and cement was present in practically every county. In 1854 and 1859 the State government authorized other geological surveys, and in 1869 the State Department of Geology was established, a division that has done much in recent years to advise and encourage Indiana industries.

In spite of many changes, Indiana was still essentially an agricultural State in the early 1860's. An overwhelming proportion of the workers were farmers, and most of the rest were either professional men, small shopkeepers, or independent craftsmen. Wage earners in mine and mill numbered only a few thousand.

The war itself accelerated the pace of industrial change. The army withdrew more than 200,000 men from active farm labor in Indiana, and their places were taken by women, children, and the aged. Because of this shortage of labor, people were compelled to buy many household commodities they formerly had made on the farm—a circumstance that stimulated the growth of factories, especially those manufacturing clothing and leather goods. Tempted by soaring agricultural prices, farmers strained every nerve to buy improved plows and other labor-saving implements. This also stimulated production. ·

The period between the Civil War and the advent of the automobile was a period of amazing expansion, of shrewd business enterprise, of the rise of scores of little cities—each dependent upon some mill or factory. An almost bewildering diversity of young industries arose in Indiana—lumber, cotton goods, glassware, farm implements, furniture, vehicles, band instruments, toys, Mason jars, pottery, and brick. Historically most important were the great Oliver Plow Company of South Bend, which helped to revolutionize agriculture throughout the world; the Rumely Company of La Porte, manufacturing threshing machines and other farm implements; and the plants of the Studebaker brothers, who came to South Bend in 1852 to begin to build fine wagons that became famous the world over.

Throughout this era Indiana was developing its natural resources aided by the post-war expansion of the railroads. With several railroads running from Terre Haute, center of the coal industry, and all of them serving the vast deposits underlying the adjacent territory, a wide market for Indiana coal was exploited. In the eighties important mines were opened up in Brazil, in Clay County, largely upon the advice of E. T. Cox, then State geologist. Meanwhile from the late seventies on, new limestone quarries were opened until the Bedford-Bloomington district became one of the world's largest quarrying centers.

Eventually businessmen and manufacturers began to utilize Indiana's other resources. The State's almost unlimited supplies of sand, clay, gravel, and soft stones became the basis for a vast output of Portland cement, glass, brick, and pottery of all sorts. In 1886 a natural-gas well was completed in Portland, and apparently inexhaustible quantities were soon tapped all over the east central part of the State. Free gas was offered to factories as an inducement for locating in towns; as a result, a number of small towns—stimulated by new industries—grew into prosperous cities. If the supply had been used carefully it might have lasted a century, but it was squandered in less than 15 years. Meanwhile, in the same type of rock, petroleum had been found; and while gas was still bubbling freely, men were exploiting the first valuable oil deposits. In 1890 Indiana's output was estimated at only 63,000 barrels; by 1904, it had jumped to 11,000,000 barrels. At the present time (1941), however, production has dwindled, although new wells are being brought in, in the southwestern part of the State.

The post-Civil War position of the working people in Indiana was difficult. Wartime expansion had lured thousands from farm to factory. When the soldiers returned, unemployment was serious and prices and rents remained high, while wages dropped because of intense competition. Then came the panic of 1873, bringing throughout the country a six-year period of industrial distress and strikes. 'The decade of the seventies in Indiana,' says Logan Esarey, historian, 'is primarily noted for the awakening of class consciousness.' Throughout the country, railroad companies were pooling their interests and raising freight rates, to the great disadvantage of the farmers. Merchants and manufacturers were demanding that State and Federal Governments meet the labor movement with military force. The great railway strike of 1877 was crushed by Federal troops. Conflict was less bitter in the Middle West than in the industrial East, yet even here people felt the growing pains of expanding industry.

Working people, defeated everywhere on the picket line, turned to political and semipolitical means of remedying their ills. The pressure of the Greenback party, which advocated progressive labor legislation as well as monetary reform, and the general industrial discontent of the seventies led to important labor legislation in Indiana. In 1879 a law was passed providing for the inspection of mines for sanitation and safety. The highlights in labor legislation during the subsequent half century may be summarized as follows: In 1893 a law was passed providing for the imprisonment of any employer who tried in any way to prevent workers from joining a labor union. Under pressure from Populists and Socialists, the mine inspection statute was broadened in 1897 to include all manufacturing establishments. At the same time a labor commission was created to investigate labor disputes. In 1911, laws were passed making employers responsible for industrial safety; two years later an investigation of working conditions of women was ordered. A workmen's compensation act followed, requiring all employers to insure their employees against injury. Workers were to wait until the 1930's, however, for legislation on wages, hours, and unemployment.

While minority parties were working for the betterment of labor conditions in the 1870's, an independent labor movement was developing in the State. By the mid-seventies, typesetters, railroad workers, and a few other crafts were organized. Then in 1878 the Knights of Labor, a national labor society founded in 1869, became powerful in Indiana. The Knights stood for one organization of skilled and unskilled workers, white and Negro; their militant program did much to aid the trend toward the industrial type of union.

In the late 1880's the Knights of Labor declined and State federations of labor rose in influence. A group of national labor leaders had met in Terre Haute in 1881 and sent out a call for the formation of a national organization differing from the Knights in objectives and structure, and in 1886 the American Federation took its present name and form. Meanwhile, in 1885, Indiana trade union delegates meeting in Indianapolis formed what was probably the first State federation of labor in America. The national federation's policy was to organize skilled workers into craft unions, to avoid militant strikes whenever possible, and to exert non-partisan legislative pressure upon whatever party was in power. This policy the Indiana State Federation has carried out from its inception to the present time—achieving notable legislative victories and taking part in the struggle for the eight-hour day. But most of the workers of Indiana—divided geographically and ineligible for membership in the craft unions of the Federation—remained unorganized until the 1930's.

Eugene V. Debs, a native of Indiana (*see Terre Haute*), was one of the first advocates of industrial unionism, the organization of all workers in a given industry not on the basis of their crafts but of the industry itself. When the panic of 1893 plunged working people into misery and unemployment, Debs organized the American Railway Union, which admitted railway workers of every type and which voted to support the Pullman strike in 1894. The strike was crushed, strike leaders were discharged throughout the country (the Erie shops at Huntington, Indiana, dismissed 60 men), and Debs served a six-months jail sentence for contempt of court.

Dramatically contrasting with this defeat, the United Mine Workers conducted a successful strike in Indiana, Illinois, Ohio, and Pennsylvania in 1897. This union had been organized by a group of Knights of Labor miners in 1890 and had almost immediately become powerful. After the 1897 strike its prestige was dominant in the bituminous coal fields.

In the following year Debs, feeling that labor must take independent political action, founded the Social Democratic party, a loose coalition of socialist and semisocialist groups not affiliated with the Socialist Labor party. Three years later a dissatisfied faction from the S.L.P. met with Debs and his party in Indianapolis, to launch the Socialist Party of the United States. Eugene Debs was chosen to lead the new party, and in 1904, 1908, 1912, and 1920 he ran for President— polling 402,312 votes in 1904, and 915,302 in 1920.

Industrial growth in Indiana since the turn of the century has followed the national trend toward corporate control and mass production. The two outstanding developments are the rise of the automobile industry, and the development of the Calumet region—Gary, Hammond, Whiting, and East Chicago.

The first clutch-driven automobile with electrical ignition was made in Kokomo by Elwood Haynes, a native Hoosier. In 1894, on an unfrequented road near Kokomo, Haynes made his first run of one mile and a half, with a 240-pound engine, at a speed of 8 miles an hour. In 1895 he began to manufacture, but it was not until after 1900 that the industry assumed mass proportions. Until the 1920's Indianapolis was one of the automobile capitals of the world, manufacturing several types of cars and various parts. Because many of the smaller firms were either driven into bankruptcy or forced to re-locate for cheaper transportation of steel and coal, Indiana lost its motor supremacy; yet large subsidiaries of national corporations sprang up in South Bend, Anderson, Indianapolis, and elsewhere to manufacture automobile bodies and parts.

The Calumet region was developed from a waste of swampland and sand dunes, with two or three small villages, into a great industrial area. This expanse of cheap, sparsely inhabited land on Lake Michigan and next door to Chicago was a convenient site for large mills, factories, and refineries, particularly the so-called 'nuisance industries.' In 1889 the Standard Oil Company invaded the region. Although vast supplies of Ohio crude oil needed an outlet near Chicago, residents of that city objected to the odor of oil and sulphur. Pipe lines, however, had already been laid and a location not far away was imperative. With the selection of the tiny hamlet of Whiting for the new site, Standard Oil began to build the world's largest refinery, which today (1941) makes oil products ranging from gasoline and fuel oil to the lightest oil for the most delicate wrist watch. Other industries soon followed. The little packing town of Hammond grew into a large city with many heavy industries, and East Chicago with its port at Indiana Harbor became not only an industrial city but one of the great shipping centers of the Nation.

The most important industry to enter the region was steel. Inland Steel had established a plant in East Chicago in 1893; and when the United States Steel Corporation decided in 1905 to erect its greatest mills on the sand dunes, the industrial future of the region was assured. Gary came into being when massive mills were built along miles of lake front and tens of thousands of workers, many of them immigrants, were brought in. With U. S. Steel firmly entrenched as a magnet, other enterprises were irresistibly drawn to the region; important subsidiaries of Republic Steel and of other smaller steel companies, now grouped together under the name 'Little Steel,' were soon established. Cities Service, Du Pont, Sinclair Oil, Carbide and Carbon, and Shell Petroleum also flourish here, as well as many independent concerns. One of 'Big Steel's' factories, in Gary, is said to be the largest cement plant in the world, employing nearly 600 persons and manufacturing annually 10,-000,000 barrels of cement.

While the Calumet cities thus became the very embodiment of twentieth-century changes, the rest of the State was also transformed. From 1900 to 1930 the population increased about 30 per cent; but the total value of manufactured products increased 600 per cent. The number of factory workers increased from 154,000 to 315,000, and there was a marked drift toward mass production and concentration of ownership.

By 1929 steel was the leading industry in Indiana, with an annual output valued at $333,000,000; motor vehicles and parts followed with $300,000,000; and electrical machinery, meat packing, and furniture were next in order. By that time also Indiana was ranking second among the States in the limestone industry; eighth in sand and gravel; and seventh in coal—the last-named industry surviving (in spite of a marked decline in output and employment) largely through the development of strip mining. The financial crisis of 1929 wiped out many small enterprises and checked the production of steel and automobiles, but by 1937—with rising prices and easier credit—Indiana industry and commerce were approaching pre-depression levels. In that year the State's population had reached an estimated 3,474,000; the total value of the manufactured products was $2,497,547,946; and there were 313,342 wage earners.

These changes could not fail to exert a profound influence upon Indiana workers. Technical advances in manufacturing and the development of mass production drove many into semiskilled categories, and the series of depressions that culminated in the crash of 1929 created widespread unemployment. Wages, moreover, in the upswing of business activity following each of these disasters, always lagged behind rising rents and the price of milk and meat.

The American Federation of Labor, though strong in certain crafts, organized only a fraction of the workers in the State's mass production industries. The slow decline of the coal industry and the development of strip mining, in which machinery replaced man power to a considerable degree, did much to weaken the United Mine Workers, Indiana's most powerful and progressive union. The scattered and diversified character of Indiana's manufacturing likewise tended to divide the working class and retard the growth of unions.

The bulwark of the open shop, in Indiana as throughout the rest of the country, was the steel industry. In 1918 (according to a report of the Interchurch World Commission) a majority of steel workers were earning less than a living wage, and unskilled laborers were working 12 hours a day and frequently in shifts of 18 to 24 hours for even less. In that year, the A..F. of L. launched a campaign to unionize the 500,-000 employees in the steel industry.

Thousands of Indiana workers were involved in the steel strike of 1919, which practically paralyzed the cities of the Calumet during October and November of that year, and was not completely ended until January 1920. Although the steel companies refused all offers of compromise and arbitration and fought the strike with every weapon at their disposal, it seems today, long after the smoke of battle has cleared, that the workers' demands were justified. The 8-hour day, union recognition, and modest wage increases for the lowest paid workers in time proved economically possible. But not in 1919. Driven by hunger, the workers went back to the mills. Steel, cornerstone of American industry, was still untouched by collective bargaining.

During the same autumn a great coal strike, involving several thousand Indiana miners, also was defeated. The effect of this defeat was immediate and unfavorable to the striking steel workers. But the upward movement of prices after the depression of 1921–2 provoked another wave of protest. In July 1922, Indiana was one of the theaters of action for a national coal strike that called 600,000 miners from the pits, and for a railway shopmen's strike that called out 500,000 workers. Twice in the same month Governor McCray sent out the militia. The railway strike was defeated and the union exterminated; but the miners, in Indiana as elsewhere, sang, 'You can't dig coal with bayonets.' The outcome, after many months, was a partial victory for the United Mine Workers.

Perhaps because of the prosperity of the Harding-Coolidge era, a prosperity in which the workers shared, there was industrial peace in Indiana from 1922 to 1929. Then came the great depression, with its mass unemployment, relief demonstrations, and depressed wages. Organized labor attempted to uphold the wage standard, but with unemployment so widespread, it was a losing fight. As the American living standard declined, the strength of the unions ebbed.

As soon as partial recovery came and prices began to move upward, a great wave of organizational enthusiasm swept over Indiana workers, many of whom spontaneously formed local unions. Brief, sporadic walkouts for higher wages were conducted by these groups, and also by the old established craft unions. Only three Indiana strikes, however, attracted national attention during 1934 and 1935. From April 6 to May 25, 1934, 1,000 workers struck in the Real Silk Hosiery Mills in Indianapolis; and 850 workers walked out of the Wayne Knitting Mills in Fort Wayne in June 1935. Most dramatic of all was the Terre Haute general strike, which filled the national headlines July 22–3, 1935, while 26,000 workers and many merchants demonstrated their disapproval of antilabor conduct on the part of the city administration (*see Terre Haute*).

The Terre Haute strike, whatever its other implications, was an impressive display of labor solidarity in a highly unionized city. Throughout most of Indiana, however, this union tradition was lacking; therefore the workers' enthusiasm for collective bargaining was easily channeled into company unionism. Meanwhile a number of labor leaders were proposing industrial unionism as the solution. Under the leadership of eight industrial or semi-industrial unions already in the A. F. of L. (including the United Mine Workers and Amalgamated Clothing Workers), the Committee for Industrial Organization was created in the autumn of 1935.

When the CIO drive got under way in Indiana late in 1936, the effect was immediate. In the Calumet region, so long the stronghold of the open shop, steel workers flocked by the tens of thousands into unions formed by the Steel Workers' Organizing Committee. After U. S. Steel had signed an agreement giving the men substantial wage guarantees, a 40-hour week, and vacations with pay, organizers claimed that 80 per cent of the steel workers in the region had joined the union. Soon the drive spread to other industries throughout the State, resulting in many union contracts, both national and local in scope.

Since then only two major breaks have occurred in the peaceable progress of collective bargaining, a progress that many employers welcomed as economically sound and workable. Early in 1937, community feeling ran high and bitter in Anderson, where employees of General Motors were involved in the Nation-wide auto strike. In June 1937, employees of 'Little Steel' struck a snag when officials of that corporation refused to bargain collectively with them. In this crisis Governor M. Clifford Townsend, operating through the Labor Division of the Indiana Department of Commerce and Industry, induced each party to the conflict to sign a separate agreement with the State of Indiana, thus assuring both that the agreement would be kept. Since this solution, widely admired as the 'Indiana Plan,' unionization of workers in the oil, textile, automobile, and steel industries has gone forward with few conflicts.

Education

THE first settlers in Indiana were sturdy, freehold farmers and small traders, believing in equalitarian democracy and individual freedom. They knew that neither democracy nor freedom was possible without universal free education; hence from the first many of them agitated for free schools. But the long, difficult delays they encountered were a reflection of the struggle of a young society. It was not because Hoosiers loved ignorance that thousands of them opposed free schools in the 1830's and 1840's; it was because they felt the lash of economic need. There were swamps to be drained, roads to be built, crops to be carried to market; and roads, canals, and railroads were a costly business. Awakened, however, to the need of public education, a majority of the people voted in 1851 to organize a State-supported school system. The economic upheaval of the Civil War temporarily prevented its development, but by the 1870's universal free education in Indiana began to be a reality. Later expansion and improvement were related to the State's growth in wealth and population.

Long before Indiana became a State, plans were laid to provide schools for the children of future settlers. In 1787 the Congress of the Confederation divided the Northwest Territory into townships, reserving Section 16 in each township for the maintenance of public schools. This same provision was incorporated in the Act that made Indiana a State in 1816; and one whole township, in addition, was reserved for a 'seminary of learning.'

Theoretically, at least, Indiana pioneered in the establishment of tax-supported public schools. Its Constitution of 1816 directed the General Assembly to organize a graduated system of schools extending from the district schools to the university, equally open to all on the basis of free instruction. No other State as yet had written such a provision into its constitution.

This idealistic program, however, was destined to exist on paper only for many years. Money was needed to put it into operation, and the poverty of pioneer life before 1850 did not permit anything so drastic as State taxation for education. During the whole period there were no free elementary schools in Indiana.

Nevertheless there were schools. Nearly every township had its log schoolhouse, where a more or less adequately prepared 'master' instructed a few children in reading, spelling, penmanship, and sometimes arithmetic. The parents helped build the log house; they paid the teacher a small sum per child; and they all took turns in boarding him. These schoolmasters were of widely varying caliber, and it was a hard task even for the best of them to govern a score or so of hardy young pioneers. Nor was it easy for either teacher or pupils to endure the sheer physical distress of attending school. Some walked miles through rain or snow to get there, and the cabin itself was dark and drafty, with log benches, dirt floor, and a roaring fire. In the towns there were sometimes private schools maintained by the teachers themselves, to which the children were sent for a regular tuition fee. These also varied in quality, but some of them were very good.

During these earliest years one interesting educational venture was begun in Indiana. In the wilderness on the Wabash River Robert Owen established a colony at New Harmony where, among other notable social experiments, the most advanced educational theories of the day were put into practice. Infant schools, manual training, and instruction by means of stimulating pupil interest, all made New Harmony a revolutionary educational center for the whole country (see *New Harmony*). There is no reason to suppose, however, that the experiment had any influence on pioneer Indiana; ultimately the ideals of the group were brought back to Indiana by way of Eastern educational methods. But two of Owen's sons, Robert and Richard Dale Owen, received their inspiration in New Harmony and contributed much to the later development of Indiana schools.

The period was characterized by the growth of seminaries, largely under church guidance. In 1818 and 1824 laws were passed providing for county seminaries and a State seminary, but inadequate funds crippled most of these institutions. Church groups here and there, however, began to shoulder responsibility for the secondary schools of Indiana. Although some church seminaries were undistinguished, the names of the Spiceland, Salem, and Bloomingdale Academies and the Friends' Boarding School at Richmond were for half a century synonymous with scholarly thoroughness.

Another feature of the period was the rise and development of church

History

THE WABASH * THROUGH WILDERNESS AND FLOOD

CLARK'S ADVANCE ON VINCENNES
Mural by Ezra Winter in George Rogers Clark Memorial, Vincennes

FORT WAYNE IN 1812.

FORT WAYNE IN 1812

TECUMSEH'S MEETING WITH GENERAL HARRISON AT VINCENNES IN 1810
Hostilities were narrowly averted at this conference between the great Shawnee and the American General, held when the whites were aroused over Tecumseh's plan for an Indian federation. This engraving by Chapin is after the drawing by W. Ridgway.

GENERAL GEORGE ROGERS CLARK

GENERAL ANTHONY WAYNE
(from an Old Lithograph)

THE BATTLE OF THE THAMES

In this decisive struggle between the American forces and the Indians, Tecumseh lost his life. This engraving was made after the original painting by A. Chappell.

CATHEDRAL OF ST. FRANCIS XAVIER, VINCENNES

GEORGE ROGERS CLARK MEMORIAL AND LINCOLN MEMORIAL BRIDGE, VINCENNES

RECONSTRUCTED LINCOLN VILLAGE, ROCKPORT

RECONSTRUCTED PIONEER VILLAGE, SPRING MILL STATE PARK

ograph by courtesy of Department of Conservation

PORTRAIT OF ROBERT OWEN

STEAMBOAT ROUND THE BEND
Mural by Henrik Mayer in Post Office at Aurora

ELWOOD HAYNES AND HIS HORSELESS CARRIAGE
Built in 1893, this was the first successful clutch-driven automobile in America

FORT WAYNE AQUEDUCT (From a painting by Ralph Dille)
This carried the Wabash and Erie Canal over the St. Mary's River

AN EARLY PICTURE OF FOUR FAMOUS HOOSIERS
(front: George Ade and Booth Tarkington; rear: James Whitcomb Riley and Meredith Nicholson)

colleges—the only really influential centers of higher learning in Indiana before the Civil War. The settlers were men and women of strong religious feeling. They made the country or village church the center of their community life, and they took sectarian rivalry very seriously. Both these facts made it hard for them to trust a nonreligious institution, such as the State University; and since they didn't trust it, they failed to support it adequately. As a result, each religious denomination felt impelled to establish its own college.

Thus the period between 1827 and 1860 saw the rise and growth of nearly all the colleges accredited today in Indiana. The first was Hanover, founded by the Presbyterians in 1827 near Madison overlooking the Ohio. Then in Crawfordsville in 1832 a group of Presbyterian ministers and laymen founded Wabash College, a nonsectarian undergraduate college for men.

Soon Catholic leaders, recognizing the importance of church colleges in the Middle West, founded Notre Dame (*see South Bend*) in 1842. An unsuccessful attempt had already been made to maintain a Catholic college in southern Indiana; hence the new school was established in the north, to attract students from Michigan and Illinois as well as Indiana. With heroic toil in what was then a wilderness, Father Sorin and a band of Brothers built the school that today ranks with Purdue and Indiana Universities as a leader in Indiana education. Known from coast to coast as the home for many years of some of the greatest football teams in America, the University of Notre Dame is also famous for its beautiful campus, its great library, its art treasures, and its scholarship.

Important Protestant colleges founded during the same period were Indiana Asbury College, now DePauw University, founded by the Methodists in Greencastle in 1837; Earlham, at Richmond, which developed from the Friends' Boarding School and attained collegiate rank in 1859; Franklin, founded at Franklin by the Baptists in 1834; and Northwestern Christian University, founded in Indianapolis in 1855, which later became Butler University. For 35 years these church colleges bore the chief burden of Indiana education. Even in the 60 years or more since then, when the State institutions have forged ahead to a position of leadership, these colleges and universities have also grown in power and usefulness, contributing scholars, libraries, liberal arts courses, and well-trained teachers to the cause of educational progress.

Meanwhile State-supported institutions were fighting for a bare existence. In 1804 Congress had set apart a township of land near Vincennes, to be used for founding a college. Vincennes University, active for only a few years because of financial difficulties, was thus a forerunner of later State institutions. The 1816 Constitution provided for a 'general system of education,' ascending from township schools to a State university; one township in Indiana, located near Bloomington, was to be used for the maintenance of the university. In May 1824, Indiana Seminary opened its doors to students. It became a college in 1828 and by legislative enactment was called Indiana University in 1838. Verbal encouragement, however, was not enough. Members of various denominations charged that the board of directors was under 'unscrupulous' Presbyterian control—a charge leading to the foundation of one church college after another. Too much reliance was placed upon land grants as a source of support, and thus no tax was levied on property for the university's maintenance. Students were warned away because the institution, secular in origin, was considered to be the source of depravity and godlessness. Hence Indiana University staggered along without aid until after the Civil War.

The pre-war era in Indiana education presents a strange picture. It was an era of earnest effort to provide educational opportunity, but the system grew from the top down. While colleges and seminaries sprang up and flourished, there prevailed among the farmers who lived in the backwoods and wrestled to clear the land a condition of appalling ignorance and even sheer illiteracy. Hundreds of devoted citizens wrote, lectured, and agitated persistently, in the name of Indiana's ideal of democracy, for free tax-supported schools. But the majority of the people were either apathetic or hostile, for misguided economic or political reasons. Many thought that free schools would be pauper schools. Others felt that parents must educate their own children, and that any State control of such matters would be an undemocratic violation of individual rights. Still others objected to taxation for such a purpose, believing that it was more important to build roads, canals, and other improvements. So, although the constitution provided for a school system, the failure of citizens to permit taxation kept one from materializing.

In the fight for education waged during the pre-war era three men were outstanding—Caleb Mills, Robert Dale Owen, and John I. Morrison. Mills was the great propagandist. In a series of six masterful and comprehensive papers Mills presented the problem to legislature and public. He showed the necessity for a sane financial basis for operation and adequate State and local supervision. So profoundly did he affect public opinion that his recommendations were all embodied in the 1851 constitution and school laws. For practical work in the constitutional convention and legislature, however, Owen and Morrison were indispensable, persuading delegates with their oratory, and hammering away, in committee and on the convention floor, until every essential point was passed.

Thus 1851 was a crucial year for Indiana education. The office of State Superintendent of Public Instruction was created, centralizing authority, supervision, and responsibility. A common school fund was established, today amounting to more than $17,000,000, the interest from which was to be allotted to schools throughout the State on a per capita basis. At the same time a State school tax of 10¢ on every $100 was voted. In 1852 the legislature passed a school law providing in detail for a State school system, creating the State Board of Education and providing for both State and local levies for school purposes.

It took several years to work out any actual educational system even after such laws were passed. Before much had been done the Civil War broke out, and the attendant disorganization of civil life deferred the orderly development of Indiana schools. But soon after the war great changes occurred in the life of the Nation, changes reflected in Indiana's educational system. Under the impetus of the protective tariff and free land in the West for farmers and railroads, business enterprise everywhere embarked upon an imperial expansion. Cities and vast industries sprang up; commerce multiplied and wealth and population increased; rural districts were linked more closely to the industrial areas by better transportation and farm machinery. These changes tended to break down Indiana's religious sectarianism, and to develop friendliness toward purely secular institutions. They also strengthened popular demands for good elementary schools in both cities and rural areas; they sharpened public awareness of the need for training teachers, farmers, and engineers.

Influenced by changing times, the legislature in 1867 characterized Indiana University as the 'crowning glory of our present great common school system' and granted funds for its support. In the same year the university opened its doors to women. From this time on its attendance grew rapidly; between 1883 and 1908 the student body increased from 156 to 2,051. The rapid growth of the common school system was responsible for part of this increase. Much of it was due, however, to the prestige the university attained through the presence of Dr. David Starr Jordan, president from 1884 to 1891.

Meanwhile in 1865 the legislature provided for the establishment of a scientific and technical university. In the Morrill Act of 1862 Congress had granted land to the States for the founding of agricultural and technical schools, which should, however, not exclude 'other scientific and classical studies.' In 1869 John Purdue of LaFayette, with other citizens of Tippecanoe County, donated $200,000 on condition that the university be established in LaFayette. Instruction was begun in 1874, and from the first, Purdue University's relation to the public schools of Indiana has been continuous and close. Its influence has vitalized high school courses in home economics, agriculture, and science. The institution has also (*see Agriculture*) done much to supply Indiana farmers with information and assistance.

In 1865 the legislature also provided for a teachers' training school. Terre Haute offered a large tract of land and $50,000, and an institution was opened there in 1870. This became the present Indiana State Teachers College. In 1918 the wealthy Ball brothers of Muncie donated buildings and nearly 100 acres of land for a similar institution, and the Ball State Teachers College was established. These are fully accredited colleges.

The post-war period was no less remarkable for the growth and evolution of the public schools of Indiana. Next to lack of funds, the school system's chief drawback had been lack of centralized leadership. The establishment of the office of State Superintendent of Public Instruction was a step in the right direction. Nevertheless, a gap remained between State and local school administration, for there was no connecting link between the superintendent and the township trustees.

This gap was bridged in 1873, when the General Assembly created the office of County Superintendent of Schools. County boards of education were soon formed and provision was made somewhat later for city and town superintendents and boards of education. From then on progress, both in urban and rural districts, was rapid and steady. The State superintendent supervised the unification of courses of study and professional standards for teachers. In 1897, for the first time, Indiana enacted a compulsory education law, requiring children between the ages of 7 and 14 to attend school for at least 12 weeks each year. Soon recognized as inadequate, this law was changed in 1901 to compel attendance of children between 7 and 16 years of age during the entire school year. Attendance officers for counties and cities are appointed by the boards of education to see that this law is enforced.

An important development was the rise of the public high schools as part of the State school system. For several years after the Civil War there were no publicly supported secondary schools in Indiana; the State Supreme Court had ruled against the right of local communities to raise taxes to meet local needs. Eventually this decision was reversed, and local communities again taxed themselves to support township or town high schools. Gradually one-room country schools were replaced by consolidated township schools, with bus service to all points in the township. In most cases today these provide at least seventh to twelfth grade opportunities for country pupils. Because standards had to be set for college entrance requirements, the State Board of Education exerted a real supervision over all these schools, accrediting those that came up to standard. At last in 1907 the legislature established the high schools as part of the State school system.

Several factors have contributed to the progressive development of Indiana education. Doubtless the greatest single influence has been exerted by the colleges and universities. Long before there was a public school system, institutions of higher learning were training the future leaders of educational and social progress. (Outstanding in the twentieth century was William Lowe Bryan, who in 1937 retired from the presidency of Indiana University, after having served in that office with distinction for 35 years.) Another important educational influence is the Indiana Historical Bureau, now part of the State Department of Education. In 1915 the Indiana Historical Society, founded as a result of a growing interest in Indiana history, organized the Historical Bureau. Devoted to the task of investigating and making available to the public all aspects of Indiana history, the bureau is making Indiana citizens aware of the heroes, struggles, and social movements of the past—an awareness of the utmost importance in the development of future citizens.

Still another progressive factor has been the teachers of Indiana themselves. Organized in State and local Teachers' Associations, they have obtained progressive school legislation and their institutes have improved professional standards. Indiana's libraries, from the New Harmony Workingmen's Library and the county, township, and Sunday school libraries of the nineteenth century, to the city and township libraries of the present, have contributed much to public education. Today (1941) the Indiana State Library serves the entire State with traveling libraries, reference works, and advice to local librarians. Finally, the Federal Government's recent appropriations have helped to expand adult education and occupational training. The National Youth Administration has helped many young people to stay in college, and Federal loans and other aid have enabled townships to build new school buildings.

Newspapers and Radio

THE first newspaper in Indiana was the *Indiana Gazette,* established in Vincennes in 1804 by Elihu Stout, a Kentuckian. In spite of a fire that nearly wrecked it in its second year, the *Gazette* lived on sturdily; later its name was changed to the *Western Sun.* In 1813 the *Western Eagle* appeared in Madison, with Seth Leavenworth and William Hendricks (who brought their press with them from Cincinnati) as owner-editors. In a few years the *Eagle* was moved to Lexington, Indiana, and the *Indiana Republican* took its place in Madison. Meanwhile John Scott, a roving printer, founded the *Enquirer and Indiana Telegraph* in Brookville; and William C. Keen, from Ohio, established the *Indiana Register* in Vevay. By 1830, one or more papers had also appeared in each of the following towns: Salem, Terre Haute, Greencastle, New Harmony, LaFayette, Logansport, New Albany, Indianapolis, Richmond, and Centerville.

Enterprising editors were frequently among the first to enter a new town. They sometimes began their county weeklies even before the population was large enough to furnish more than 100 subscribers. Indianapolis was barely a village in 1822 when the Indianapolis *Gazette* was established; South Bend was a lonely little cluster of cabins when in 1831 the *Northwestern Pioneer* was started there by John and Joseph Defrees. In the same year the Richmond *Palladium* was established, the only early Indiana newspaper to survive to the present.

Pioneer newspapers were all weeklies, except when 'circumstances beyond our control' compelled the editors to suspend publication for a longer period. Many were distinguished by their grotesque names, such as *The Coon-Skinner,* the *Whig Rifle,* and the minutely descriptive *Broad Axe of Freedom* and *Grubbing Hoe of Truth.* In some ways they resembled magazines more than newspapers, since they often published love stories and other serials on the front page. There was the time-honored poet's corner in every issue; the *Ripley County*

Index published serially all of *Pilgrim's Progress*—a not inconsiderable contribution to frontier culture in an age when books were few. Because of bad roads and slow mail coaches, it was unbelievably hard to get news. The principal source of foreign and seaboard news was the famous old *Niles' Weekly Register*, a 16-page compendium of news and history published in Baltimore from 1811 to 1849. Without *Niles' Weekly*, frontier journalism could hardly have existed.

But whatever news these early papers did print was sure to be largely political—national party speeches, reports of congressional debates, and the like. There was almost no local news and very little of State-wide interest. Almost nothing can be found in the files of the period concerning the admission of Indiana to the Union; nor is there any notable mention of the Constitutional Convention at Corydon, although the public might well have been interested in both events. The startling earthquake shocks of 1811–12 and the star showers of 1833 are dismissed with the merest mention, while local items (which would enrich greatly our knowledge of the period) are scarce.

There were several reasons why Indiana editors emphasized national political news. It interested their readers more than anything else, particularly after the election of Jackson, a Western man himself and dear to the frontier. Then, too, almost every editor was politically ambitious. By printing political news and championing a political party, he was in a strategic position to win political favors. Even more important was the fact that there was a great deal of public printing to be done—Federal, State, and local. The average editor of that day was owner, business manager, reporter, and printer of his paper; and in most cases he had to depend for his livelihood upon job printing. In order to get important Government orders he had to join a political party, fight its battles, and claim the reward if victory resulted.

It is therefore not surprising that much bitter rivalry, personal and political, existed among the Indiana editors of that period. They devoted a surprising amount of space in every issue to acrimonious debate and mud-slinging, and not until after the Civil War were impersonality and urbanity considered newspaper virtues. Modern newspapers have their faults, but the worst of them today would not publish such a diatribe as appeared in the Indianapolis *Journal* of November 3, 1836, addressed to 'the Lying, Hireling Scoundrels who do the dirty work as Editors of the *Democrat.*'

Until the late 1840's Indiana journalism survived only under very difficult conditions. It was hard to move presses into frontier towns, and to repair them when necessary. In 1823 the *Western Register* came to Terre Haute by wagon over primitive roads, and the whole kit (press, type, and paper for the first issue) was upset in fording a stream.

It was also hard to get paper. In 1828 there was only one paper mill, in Madison; by 1840 there were but two others, in Richmond and Brookville. Editors constantly apologized for their lack of supplies. It is recorded that the *Dog-Fennel Gazette,* Rushville's first paper, was distributed in single sheets printed on one side; the subscribers returned it after reading, to be printed on the other side for the next issue.

Finally, it was almost impossible to keep afloat financially. Only by supplementing his income by printing jobs, and by accepting kindling, pork, and flour in place of cash, could the average editor exist at all. The Bloomington *Post* of October 26, 1838, advertised that 'persons expecting to pay for their papers in produce must do so soon, or the cash will be exacted. Pork, Flour, Corn, and Meal will be taken at the market prices. Also, those who expect to pay us in firewood must do so immediately—we must have our wood laid in for the winter before the roads get bad.' More pathetic is the wail of the Madison *Indiana Republican* for July 26, 1817, which says: 'Mr. Clerk, I wish you to discontinue my dunning advertisement. My debtors pay no attention to it. Be so good as to inform the Sheriff that I wish to see him. Yours truly, B. Young.'

With these handicaps the high death rate among pioneer newspapers is not surprising. In the words of one writer:

The early history of newspaper enterprise in small towns is usually a record of lives as brief as those allotted to the angels of Rabbi Jehosha:

> Whose only office is to cry
> Hosanna once and then to die.

From a journalistic standpoint, the most picturesque political campaign ever waged in the State began in 1834 and ended in November 1840. In this campaign the Whig newspapers of Indiana, uniting behind General William Henry Harrison, broke the power of Jacksonian Democracy, which had carried Indiana since 1824, and then helped their hero sweep onward to the presidency of the United States.

Almost before the cheering that attended Jackson's second inauguration died down, the Nation's politicians were quarreling over who was to be his successor. Martin Van Buren, Jackson's own choice, was a New Yorker, and Western leaders saw an opportunity to maintain their national dominance if only they could find a vital, heroic figure to succeed Jackson in the public fancy. The most likely candidate appeared to be Colonel R. M. Johnson, a Kentucky Democrat who had served in the Indian campaigns of the War of 1812. In newspaper accounts Johnson grew from one of the mounted Kentuckians who took part in the Battle of the Thames, to the 'dashing Colonel Johnson who had killed Tecumseh,' and finally to the 'glorious General Richard M. Johnson, who won the battle of the Thames.'

The Whigs, however, also had a soldier candidate—General William Henry Harrison, who had governed Indiana Territory for many years, had personally negotiated the treaties by which the entire region was opened up to settlement, and had been in supreme command of the forces that crushed the Tecumseh confederacy. Harrison resented bitterly the publicity given Johnson as the hero of the Thames, although he had no fault to find with the colonel's ability as a soldier. When, in September 1834, a committee of Indianapolis citizens invited him to come to Indianapolis and help celebrate the anniversary of the victory that he had 'helped' Colonel Johnson win, the old general issued a fiery reply which was printed in nearly every Whig newspaper in the Midwest:

> If I had an associate in the Command of the forces it was unquestionably Governor Shelby [a Kentucky Whig] and not Colonel Johnson. But Gentlemen, I had no associate in the command of the army. I was as completely clothed with the character of 'commander of the forces,' . . . as was General Brown or General Jackson in their respective districts . . . In the most celebrated of the distinguished battles won by the former, [that of Niagara] the contest was decided by a most desperate charge on the enemies' batteries, by the gallant Colonel James Miller. Have you ever seen, Gentlemen, a reference to the victory as having been gained by the forces under General Brown and Colonel Miller? You have no doubt, been often, gentlemen, engaged in celebrating the battle of [New] Orleans:—would it have been tolerated by any company assembled for that purpose, to have said that the command of the army which achieved that glorious victory, was a copartnership affair between General Jackson and one of his Colonels?

This letter was like a trumpet to the old hero's admirers, and they flocked to his support by the thousands. Harrison was induced to make a speaking tour down the Ohio River; odes were read in his honor at monster mass meetings; he was nominated for the presidency in Pennsylvania, Ohio, Indiana, and elsewhere, and became the Whig candidate in 1836. But Martin Van Buren, with Colonel Johnson as his running mate, won the election, although Harrison carried Indiana and other Middle Western States that had gone Democratic for 12 years.

General Harrison remained a potent political figure in the West. Stalwart, simple, and rugged, he made the right kind of political copy, especially since his 'glorious' achievements were mellowed by 20 years of telling and retelling. In Indiana such newspapers as the *Indiana Journal*, the Crawfordsville *Record*, the Vincennes *Gazette* (formerly a Jacksonian organ), the LaFayette *Free Press*, the Richmond *Palladium*, and many others, kept Harrison's name alive. When the 'hard cider' campaign got under way in 1840—to the strains of 'For Tippecanoe and Tyler too,' and 'with them we'll beat little Van, Van, Van is a used up man'—the Midwestern newspapers had done their work. Harrison was elected by a comfortable majority, carrying every State but two north of the Mason-Dixon Line.

When advertising began to be an increasing source of revenue in the fifties, editors at first knew little about professional ethics. They advertised medicines like 'Radway's Ready Remedies,' three in number, which were supposed to be so 'prepared as to harmonize and act in unison with each other' and when taken separately or together would instantly stop pain. In that era of little medical knowledge, patent medicines brought fortunes to their manufacturers and fat sums to the newspapers in which they were advertised. Other merchants gradually learned the value of advertising, and before the Civil War legitimate businesses were putting newspapers on a sound financial basis.

Greater financial security brought a number of progressive changes to Indiana journalism. In the larger cities newspapers began to appear every day. With the daily came the demand for more news, and especially news of a local, nonpolitical character. The first venture in the local field, however, was a little weekly called *The Locomotive*, launched in 1845 by three apprentices in the *Indiana Journal* offices in Indianapolis. Wholly local and literary, it played up the society-column interest and after a trying period proved a financial success. It was said to be the 'first paper in the State that women and girls wanted to read regularly.' Other papers from this time on devoted more space to local features.

The pioneer period in Indiana journalism may be said to have ended with the increased advertising of the fifties and the appearance of the daily newspaper in the larger cities. By 1850 there were in the State 107 newspapers, of which 84 were political; in 1860 Indiana had 154 political weeklies and 13 dailies. Perhaps because of the social and political strain preceding the Civil War, this decade was alive with controversy and intellectual combat and saw the rise in Indiana of several forceful and interesting journalists. There was J. B. Norman of the New Albany *Ledger*, whose description of Jenny Lind's concert in the Madison pork house became a classic example of reporting. Another noted journalist was William J. Brown, editor of the Indianapolis *Sentinel* and a congressman for several terms. Outstanding among many Indiana editors who were politically successful was Schuyler Colfax, who established the *St. Joseph Valley Register* in 1845 and edited it for ten years. He was very influential in the 1851 Constitutional Convention and was elected to Congress in 1854, serving until 1868. During his last two terms he was Speaker of the House; in 1868 he was elected Vice President under Grant.

Colfax's rather stuffy political success may be contrasted with the vital political influence of a younger man, Columbus Stebbins. Shortly after 1848 a little Whig paper was founded in Columbus, Indiana, called the *Spirit of the West*. Soon W. C. Statelar got hold of it and acquired as his co-proprietor the young, fearless, and radical Columbus Stebbins. Stebbins gave the *Spirit* an aggressively prohibitionist and antislavery tone, in sharp contrast to a majority of Indiana papers at that time. In 1854 the name of the sheet was changed to the Columbus *Independent*. Meanwhile the old Whig party was dying for lack of a popular program (it was too much the party of the rich in its essential proposals); for a brief period a strange jumble of prejudice, reaction, and conspiracy, called Know-Nothingism, swept over Indiana. Most of the 'Whig' papers were inclined to sympathize with Know-Nothingism, but not the *Independent*, which fought it courageously and alone. In 1856 there was a convention of anti-Democratic editors in Indianapolis, most of them Know-Nothing sympathizers. Stebbins was one of the committee on resolutions, which submitted a majority report favoring the Know-Nothings. Stebbins, however, submitted a minority report, forcefully and clearly setting forth the main principles on which the Republican party was being founded. This minority report was accepted after a stormy session, and the next day, when the first State Convention of the Republican party was held in Indianapolis, Stebbins's already famous document was embodied in the platform. At a crucial moment in party realignments an Indiana journalist had crystallized a new program.

Larger, more resourceful and influential, the journals of the fifties were a great improvement over those of pioneer time, but they were still a far cry from today's press standards. They were printed on poor paper, with large type and unattractive make up. The editor's name was invariably at the head of the editorial column; there was no anonymous shirking the consequences of one's opinions. The editorial style was far more personal then than now, and the editorial 'we' was often comically abused. 'We took a ride yesterday,' or 'We have been sick,' or 'We shall be out of the office tomorrow,' were not uncommon expressions. Local and general news were mixed. The telegraph was sparingly employed for only a half column or so of market news and the most important foreign or political dispatches.

In invective and mutual recrimination news writers of the fifties had lost little if any of their ancient venom. The principal Indianapolis papers were the *Journal* and the *Sentinel,* both of which became dailies in 1851. When the former became sharply Republican and antislavery, the Democratic *Sentinel* frequently indulged in descriptive passages calling the *Journal* writers 'Negro Lovers,' 'Black Republicans,' and 'Disunionists.' The *Journal,* in reply, could give no kinder name to the *Sentinel* than 'Doughface.' Both papers, firmly established at this time, were destined to be State party organs for many years. The *Journal* was descended from the *Western Censor,* started in 1823; the *Sentinel* had been the old Indianapolis *Gazette* and later the *Democrat.* In 1904 the *Journal* became the Indianapolis *Star.*

The Civil War period in Indiana was extremely disastrous to journalism. Newspapers reached their lowest ebb in 1865; the long struggle had depleted the resources of the people, and since the Government was the main buyer of produce, advertising was no longer necessary. Many of the ablest editors, furthermore, were with the army and the papers suffered accordingly.

But with the Reconstruction period and subsequent economic development, the modern era of journalism in the State may be said to have begun. Within 25 years a dynamic sweep of forces created factories, opened mines, introduced machinery to the farmer, and laid the base for modern commerce. These changes brought a considerable increase in Indiana's per capita wealth, creating simultaneously great enterprises seeking a market and a population rapidly seeking a higher standard of living. Thus modern advertising evolved from crude beginnings into a mainspring of economic life. Meanwhile the development of telegraphic service, the invention of the linotype, and the improvement of the printing press made it possible to get news from anywhere in the world and publish it a few hours later.

But Indiana journalism did not assume its modern form suddenly. Until the nineties the typical paper was the intimate, rural county-seat weekly; and oddly enough one of the leading journalistic figures of the day was not a journalist at all, but a poet, who won his reputation largely in the columns of such weekly papers as the Anderson *Democrat* and the Kokomo *Dispatch*. Undoubtedly the poems and whimsical sketches of James Whitcomb Riley, which had wide currency through Midwestern exchanges, gave a distinctive flavor to these rural newspapers.

In the summer of 1877 Riley, who was conducting a weekly column for the Anderson *Democrat*, created a storm of controversy that reached Nation-wide proportions when he wrote a poem that was published as a hitherto undiscovered manuscript by Edgar Allan Poe. In a literary discussion with some Anderson friends Riley had contended that editors bought poetry on the reputation of its author rather than on its merits. Thinking it over later, he decided to prove his point with a practical example.

Occasional pieces of his own poetry were being published at this time, but for the most part editors were turning them down. So he wrote 'Leonainie' in imitation of Poe's style and sent it to the editor of the Kokomo *Dispatch*, explaining what he hoped to do. With a lurid tale of its discovery in an old book belonging to an illiterate Kokomo laborer, the poem was published on the front page of the *Dispatch* and copies were mailed to every literary editor in the Nation.

'Leonainie' became an overnight sensation. Many editors printed it, affirming their belief that the work was genuine. Others were more cautious—William Cullen Bryant, editor of the New York *Post* and a famous poet himself, denounced the poem as a hoax and the Boston *Evening Transcript* remarked, 'if Poe really did write it, it is consolation to think he is dead.'

Soon the skeptics were rallying around one very embarrassing question—where was the original manuscript? There was none, of course, but two of Riley's friends, using a facsimile of the original manuscript of 'The Bells' as a model, copied the lines on the flyleaf of an old dictionary. Riley himself boarded a train to take the book, carefully wrapped in newspapers, to Kokomo. 'Thirty-five miles,' he said later, 'and every inch a torment . . . I was so fearful of detection a shadow scared me.'

He arrived safely, however, and with an 'original' manuscript on the scene the conspirators felt safe. They were ready now to let the experts come and examine their evidence. But just as it seemed the hoax would succeed, someone whispered the true story to the editor of an opposition paper, and the Kokomo *Tribune* told the world the name of the real author of 'Leonainie.'

The result was an even more violent journalistic explosion. The Nation's critics, furious at having been deluded, attacked Riley angrily. They lamented the injustice to Poe, the 'chief victim, who was powerless to avenge the wrong done his name and honor.' Saucy weeklies talked volubly about 'a great fraud,' 'insufferable nonsense,' the 'unscrupulous young man,' and 'an exceedingly foolish piece of criminality.' 'The poem,' said a New York paper, 'effectually sets at rest whatever suspicion there may have been that the author had the material out of which a poet is made.' A Detroit daily regretted quite solemnly that the American people had been deluded into the notion that there really did exist a place by the name of Kokomo.

Heartsick in the face of such biting criticism, Riley resigned from the staff of the *Democrat* and went home to reflect dismally on the unexpected outcome of his practical joke. A few weeks later, however, he wrote a public apology that was printed in the Indianapolis *Journal,* and the incident was soon forgotten.

Another important journalistic figure of this period was Berry Sulgrove (1827–90), a man whose reputation and influence in his own day were great and well deserved. He was born in Indianapolis and as a young man studied law. For several years before he became a professional newspaperman, he enlivened his legal routine by contributing sketches and articles to various papers under the pseudonym of Timothy Tugmutton. In 1854 he became an editor of the Indianapolis *Journal,* doing work now divided among many departments—writing leaders and general news items, reporting on conventions, copying telegraphic news. He inaugurated the system of covering the night's news for the paper of the following morning (a startling innovation in the fifties), and introduced the first verbatim reports ever used by local papers.

Sulgrove wrote gracefully, even brilliantly, at all times; but qualities that perhaps earned him more prestige were his steady political wisdom and his vast and versatile erudition. Many stories have been told of his ability to write entertainingly and instructively, at a moment's notice, on any subject. A publisher, for example, once had a cut representing a covey of quail. Sulgrove was shown the engraving and asked if he could write something to accompany it. He immediately wrote an essay upon the quail and its habits, with a number of diverting anecdotes about the bird, that would have done credit to an authority on the subject. The piece was reprinted and widely read for many years.

Less spectacular but more important was Sulgrove's political maturity and influence. A Whig in his youth, he became a Republican upon the founding of that party and during the Civil War exerted a great influence upon both the Indiana public and Governor Morton himself. In later years his articles and editorials were an important factor in molding Republican thought in Indiana. Except for a short time during the war, Sulgrove remained with the *Journal* nearly 20 years. Then he joined the staff of a vigorous new paper—the Indianapolis *News,* established in 1869 by John Holliday.

The *News,* outstanding among State newspapers for its innovations, originally appeared as a 2¢ daily, the first paper west of the Alleghenies, outside of Chicago, to be issued at so low a price. Like Sulgrove, Holliday exerted a powerful influence on Indiana journalism. He openly declared his complete political independence; and because day labor was easier to get than night, he issued his paper in the afternoon.

Following Holliday's lead, the larger city papers began to lower their price to win more subscribers. With an assured income from advertising, the number of dailies increased steadily and rapidly; by the end of the century nearly every county-seat paper was issued daily. Some cut away from political affiliations and dared to call themselves 'independent.' All increasingly took advantage of news syndicates, beginning also to use syndicated feature columns as these developed in the early years of the twentieth century.

Today (1941) there are 392 newspapers in Indiana, 98 of them dailies. Most of the dailies are county-seat political organs, limited in circulation but deriving solid revenues from legal and political advertising. Some, however, have a circulation of several thousand, printing the same domestic and foreign news and syndicated features that appear in the metropolitan dailies. Outstanding among Negro newspapers are two weeklies, the Indianapolis *Recorder* and the Gary *American.* The *Goniec Polski* (Polish) and the *Varosi Elet* (Hungarian) are published in South Bend.

Indiana newspapers, large and small, have preserved a distinctly Hoosier character. Strongly partisan in State and national politics, active in every political campaign, they are still uniformly loyal to Indiana and zealous to preserve their local flavor. Their most popular features have been those that employed the native idiom and humor. Perhaps in this regard the Indianapolis *News* led the State for a good many years, with Gaar Williams's cartoons and Kin Hubbard's 'Abe Martin' sketches (*see Literature*). Other Hoosier features were Chic Jackson's *Roger Bean*, the ballads of William Herschell, and in another field the pungent political column of Frederick Landis. Thus modern newspapers have continued the task of Riley in raising to self-consciousness the home-grown qualities of the people of the State.

Two of Indiana's dailies have won the Pulitzer Prize in recent years. The Indianapolis *News* received it in 1931 for distinguished service in tax reform, and the Indianapolis *Times,* a Scripps-Howard publication, won the award in 1928 for its crusade against the Ku Klux Klan and for its championship of liberalism.

RADIO

Because stations in Cincinnati and Chicago reach large areas of the State, radio development in Indiana has taken the form of small broadcasting plants specializing in programs of local interest. Indiana's most powerful station, WOWO in Fort Wayne, has a full strength of only 10,000 watts and few others have a power of more than 1,000; but in 13 cities throughout the State one or more stations are located.

Indiana's part in the development of radio broadcasting began in 1910, when Purdue University students and staff members undertook experimental work on code equipment. Class instruction in radio was started in 1918 at Purdue, and a year later a code station, 9YB, was licensed. WBAA, the noncommercial broadcasting plant now owned and operated by Purdue University, was licensed in April 1922, and is the oldest station now operating in the State. By 1927 most of Indiana's present commercial studios were established, some of them under call letters that were later changed.

At present (1941) 11 of the State's 19 licensed broadcasting units are members of national networks. Nevertheless, even the larger stations still give much of their time to local programs. Farmers find the radio a convenient source of recreation and a valuable medium for getting market reports. Many Hoosier farms that lack electricity, plumbing, or central heating are equipped with radios; as a result, most studios maintain special programs designed primarily for agricultural areas. Outstanding in this field is the 'Indiana Farm and Home Hour,' a daily feature of WIRE in Indianapolis, which is carried twice weekly over a coast-to-coast network. This program includes livestock reports direct from the Indianapolis stockyards, reports from grain and produce markets elsewhere in the United States, comprehensive Government weather forecasts, bulletins of the State Highway Department, talks on topics of interest to farmers, and music. Other stations present programs of a similar nature.

Radio is becoming increasingly important as a means of education, and several State colleges and universities sponsor daily programs. Nearly half of WBAA's time is given over to educational broadcasts, some of them for use in public school classrooms and others for general adult education. Indiana University's programs, released through WIRE, include round-table discussions, classroom broadcasts, and descriptions of athletic contests. Indiana State Teachers College at Terre Haute maintains daily programs over WBOW with a student staff, as does Ball State Teachers College at Muncie over WLBC.

Folklore and Folkways

W E lived the same as Indians 'ceptin we took an interest in politics and religion,' Dennis Hanks, cousin of Abraham Lincoln, said of the Indiana of 1817, the year after the State was admitted to the Union. And Lincoln described his boyhood home as a 'wild region with bears and other wild animals still in the woods.' All about was unbroken forest where 'the clearing away of surplus wood was the great task ahead.'

In such a frontier region it was inevitable that the folk life would express itself in terms of the backwoods. Folklore and folkways were conditioned by the scenes and customs of the locality where they had originated or had taken root after having been transplanted. Most Indiana folkways were not indigenous but, in common with those of other Midwestern States, had survived migrations over trails such as the one made into the western country by Daniel Boone. Many migrants followed this trail into Indiana, where they became integral parts of a variegated backwoods pattern.

The pioneer necessarily was hard-working and practical. This new country offered a challenge to muscle rather than to mind, and the early settler contented himself with the limited culture he had brought with him. The family Bible and sometimes another book or two were the extent of his cultural tools.

With all these limitations, however, there has come down from the frontier a lore composed of beliefs, customs, crafts, anecdotes, both true and untrue, bearing in its content and terminology the unmistakable stamp of the backwoods. The daily round of living yielded its natural by-product of stories about eccentric members of the community; exaggerated tales of prowess in hunting, fishing, and working; tales of giant reptiles and beasts with more than ordinary intelligence; stories about freaks of the weather, floods and great droughts.

Good or bad luck to crops and to members of the family was indicated by certain infallible signs. Evil luck was presaged by the flight of a bird past the window, by the breath of a horse on a child's head, by a dog crossing the hunter's path. It was considered better to cut fence rails in the light of the moon and to plant crops that ripened above ground in the full moon and root crops in the dark of the moon. Soap should be made in the light of the moon and stirred one way by one person. Butchering had to be done before the full moon if the meat was not to 'fry hard and leave only lard.' A waning moon was good for shingling because it pulled the shingles flat. These and many more were sincere beliefs among almost all the early settlers. Some went further in their faith in signs and portents, and believed in ghosts and witches and in the efficacy of the silver bullet to exorcise the witch.

Today the imprint of the frontier is found on all the traditional tales, beginning with those about the Indians and continuing through the French settlement and the various waves of American migration into the Indiana wilderness. By the light of the fireplace in the pioneer cabin, in the crossroads store, in the wake of the circuit-riding preacher, there has grown up a wealth of stories and anecdotes telling of the early days of a people. For the most part they form no body of myth around supernatural beings. They probably do not offer a close parallel to European or Oriental folklores, but they do reflect the life, customs, and beliefs of the frontier. This body of material has been transmuted by some strange alchemy of soil, climate, and varied personalities into something that we can label Indiana folklore and that reflects in an infinite variety of ways that indefinable entity called Hoosierdom.

The first need of the pioneer was water, so cabins were usually built along creeks or rivers. Those who pushed farther inland commonly made use of the willow divining rod to locate underground springs. It was believed that since the willow was accustomed to wet ground it would dip, in seeking its favorite element. The earliest settlers were of necessity hunters, not farmers. After the ax, the rifle was the most essential tool. A little land, enough to provide some corn, wheat, and a few vegetables, was cleared. It was partly tended by the womenfolk while the men hunted and fished to provide meat. However, this promised land turned out to be a land of plenty and, as George Ade once said, 'The pioneer had gumption enough to unpack once he had arrived.'

The women of the family did with very little in the way of household equipment. An iron skillet was all that most of them had for their cooking; an iron pot or kettle made a woman an aristocrat. A homemade, unglazed clay pot was often the only one in the cabin. The lamp was fashioned of the same material in the shape of a deep saucer with a lip on one side. Bear grease was the most common illuminating oil.

The social life of these first comers also drew its inspiration from their environment and was expressed in log-rolling, house-raising, and other tasks that could best be accomplished and celebrated co-operatively. During these affairs the women of the family, with the wives and sweethearts of the visiting helpers, quilted, sewed, and talked. Recipes and zodiacal signs for weaning babies, planting seeds, and curing meat were freely exchanged. Children should never be weaned when the sign was in the stomach, but when the sign was in the feet. A good way to remove freckles was to wash in dew or stump water before sunrise the first of May. A girl should never marry until she could pick clothes out of boiling water with her fingers. If she sat on a table, she would never marry.

If a person killed a toad, his cow would give bloody milk. One must never move a broom or a cat from one home to another. Children were measured by 'string doctors' for short growth; the string was buried and when it began to rot the child began to grow. The rite was most effective if performed by the seventh daughter of a seventh daughter. Incantations were said for rickets and fits. When Venus went into ascendancy as the evening star, it was 'Mary going over the mountain.' If it rained on that day, it would rain for six weeks; if it was fair, the weather would be fair for six weeks.

The time to plant corn was when elm tree leaves were the size of a squirrel's ear. When the corn reached the roasting-ear stage, the ears were cooked in hot ashes. Some of the kernels were grated and water added; the liquid was then strained and allowed to stand overnight. The result was a supply of starch for laundering the men's 'biled' shirts.

Whisky was a cure-all, and it was a poor occasion that did not call for it. It was used to keep off heat strokes in the summer and to keep one warm in the winter; for chills, fever, ague, snake bites, and toothache; and as a partial anesthetic during the performance of the crude surgery of the day. Bleeding was freely practiced, and many varieties of 'yarb tea' were much used.

Tongues wagged as fingers flew and turned scraps of calico into beautiful quilts. Elaborate quilt patterns were the Prairie Rose, Log

Cabin, Lone Star, Irish Chain, and Flower Garden. Four Patch and Nine Patch were simpler designs for everyday use.

Cooking for these gatherings taxed the housewives' cupboards to the utmost. Corn bread was baked in a spider over a pile of coals or on a hoe. (From this comes the present word 'hoecake.') Wild berries, plums, and apples, dried or preserved, were the fruits. Turnips, potatoes, dried corn, all sorts of wild game and fish, and sometimes chicken and dumplings filled the table. Spreads were maple syrup, pumpkin butter, and wild plum preserves.

Children stood around the table to 'strengthen their legs.' After supper they went to bed in the loft to sleep on straw ticks exposed to winter snows that came through chinks in the logs.

The by-products of the pioneer's recreation were almost as useful as the products of his regular work. Sugar making, bee hunting, husking bees, and apple cuttings were standard amusements. Shooting matches, cockfighting, 'rassling,' and foot racing were the main sporting events.

Shooting matches were always an accompaniment of Thanksgiving and Christmas. The match began early in the day and lasted until darkness made the target—a live chicken or turkey—invisible. There were rules, of course. Should the target be struck above the knee by a bullet, it became the property of the marksman who had hit it. If the ball struck below the knee, the wounded fowl was left tied and the firing continued.

Cockfighting usually took place on a Sunday when the settlers would gather with their favorite birds. A ring was cleared, and the owners of two cocks, matched evenly for fighting weight, would bind steel spurs or gaffs upon each bird's leg over its sawed-off natural spurs. The cocks would then be held close and allowed to pick at each other. Then they were taken to opposite sides of the ring and released. They would meet high above the center of the ring in a whirring kaleidoscope of brilliant feathers and flashing steel. Feinting, leaping, slashing, they fought until one was dead or ran away—which seldom happened. They were blooded birds whose ancestors had been brought from England or Ireland and purity of strain was jealously guarded.

Customs relating to courtship and marriage were definitely conditioned by distance and poor transportation facilities. Courtship was a serious business for the reason that everybody knew when a young couple began to 'set up' with each other. They could tell by the sparks flying from the chimney late at night.

Wedding presents were such utilitarian articles as homemade blankets and other forms of bedding, toweling, a bucket of sorghum, a bag of dried apples, a supply of candles, or a rag carpet. The bride's mother usually presented a feather bed and a pair of pillows; her father, a heifer and a start of chickens or a sow. After the wedding all the finery was wrapped in linen sheets and carefully put away in a chest of drawers or a trunk.

The pioneer was an assertive, talkative individual ready to 'rassle,' shoot, or lie against any competition. Perhaps the most robust examples of these traits were the river boatmen of the flatboat era who, as a rule, characterized themselves as 'half alligator and half horse, with a tech of wildcat.' Tales of their prowess were legion, one of the most modest being that they never were bothered by rapids or sand bars—they simply picked the loaded boat up and carried it around the obstruction. These tales of the clans of Fink, Girty, Colonel Plug and his spouse 'Pluggy' have never been entirely forgotten along the Ohio and the Wabash. Certain it is that the boatmen were denounced by the godly as a breed whose 'habits and education seem to comprehend every vice.'

So from the earliest times an endless crop of tall stories has sprouted among those who gather at the country store or at the Liar's Bench. The listener is likely to hear about the man who tied two cats together by their tails and threw them over the clothesline, whereupon they ate each other up completely; about the summer that was so hot that popcorn popped in the fields, and the mule that saw such a field and froze to death because to him it looked like snow; of hunters saving themselves from bears by reaching down their throats and turning the animals wrong side out; and of iron soap kettles being turned wrong side out by the Indiana breezes. Or he may hear about Bill Stafford in Morgan County who, picking raspberries in the woods one day in June, encountered a bear. Being unarmed, Bill turned and ran with the bear in hot pursuit. On and on they went until, Bill says, 'we come to White River and I crossed it on the ice but the bear broke through and I got away.' To the usual inquiry as to how he could have crossed White River on the ice in June, Bill replies: 'Well you see, we'd done a heap of runnin' and by the time I got to White River it was December.'

Almost every locality has its haunted house or ghost story. About 12 miles north of Williamsport in Warren County stands a two-story frame house, from which, it is asserted, Harrison's army can be heard on favorable nights, marching to Tippecanoe. People tell how the troops come up from the South, drums rolling and steps reverberating. The sounds increase as the soldiers approach and fade as they march into the distance. Many former tenants of this house will vouch for the tale.

In central and southern Indiana in the early days the play-party was a common form of amusement. Its origin was both simple and logical. Most of the inhabitants of this region were deeply religious and drew the line at dancing. They saw no wrong, however, in 'playing games.' In the most religious of these communities there was no musical instrument, not even a parlor organ, because, as one old-timer said, 'a music-box would spile the gals and a stuckup woman wud make no man a good helpmate.' In less strict communities a fiddler was usually found. The games played were accompanied by rhythmic movements performed to the generally nonsensical lines of the song. Typical of the songs, which probably numbered a hundred, were 'Old Dan Tucker,' 'Skip to My Lou,' and 'Weevily Wheat.' Also surviving in Indiana are many ballads (about 135 have been recorded) distinctly English in origin, such as 'Barbara Allen,' 'Lord Lovell,' and 'The Two Brothers.'

In a class by themselves are the religious songs of the 'brush-arbor' and other camp meetings—'white spirituals,' which have been brought across the Ohio River from Virginia, the Carolinas, and other Southern States (*see Music and the Theater*).

Many times across Indiana, finally to rest among its people, strode one of the strangest figures that the American scene has ever known. John Chapman, destined always to be known as Johnny Appleseed, was born in Massachusetts in 1774. He early became a disciple of Swedenborg and for a time was a Swedenborgian missionary in Virginia. After he had been kicked in the head by a horse, he had a vision of heaven in which it appeared as a vast place filled endlessly with rows of apple trees in bloom. He decided that 'fruit is next to religion,' began to collect apple seeds, and, until his death near Fort Wayne in 1845, he wandered from Massachusetts to Missouri (although mostly west of the Alleghenies), planting apple orchards and preaching a weird interpretation of the Scriptures. It has been estimated that he tramped over 100,000 square miles. Barefoot most of the time, even in winter, attired only in the roughest clothes, wearing an iron cooking pot on his head for a hat, and subsisting on the most meager fare, this strange character was unique in the Middle West. However, orchards of his planting still bloom in Hoosier valleys, and towns had an almost uncanny way of springing up wherever he selected an orchard site.

The most distinctive national group of Indiana was the early French Creoles who settled along the Wabash River. To the pioneer making his way along the river highways into the wilderness, the wide savannah at Post Vincennes presented a novel picture as it lay spread out before him. Each thatched white cottage was surrounded by its own garden, where the family raised enough food to last the year around. Surplus food was shipped by flatboat to New Orleans. Produce from outlying gardens was brought to the market in the *calèche,* a two-wheeled cart made entirely of wood, the first vehicle in the old Northwest Territory.

Flatboatmen returning semiannually from New Orleans were welcomed with great joy. It was then that all the new songs learned by the men during their voyage were sung. The songs were long, so each man learned a line of the verse and all learned the chorus. Instead of singing the song through, each man sang his line, and after each line, all joined in the chorus. On these occasions, people stayed up all night learning the songs. These trips to New Orleans were the settlement's only contact with the outside world.

During the holiday balls and at the singings held in the homes, the Creoles sang all their songs. Some of the popular favorites were 'Au Clair de la Lune,' 'Mon Amour,' and 'La Belle Françoise.' After the sad strains of 'La Belle Françoise,' they paused in silence. 'Kersie,' also called 'The False Lover,' was the last song sung at the traditional Christmas King Ball of Old Vincennes. Lovers who had quarreled then made up and walked home together.

New Year was the great Creole holiday. Festivities began with New Year's Eve. The following day masqueraders went from house to house singing and playing old songs and dramas. Early New Year's morning each Creole went to visit the oldest member of his family, and the older people in turn were hosts throughout the day. Each visitor kissed all members of the family.

Many folksongs had a special meaning and use. 'L'Alouette' was sung when the French women prepared chickens for the feast. Other songs were 'Rose d'Amour' and 'Mon Berger.' 'La Gui Année,' or the 'Beggar's Song,' thought to be of Druid origin, referred to the New Year mistletoe.

In the folk tales handed down by the early French the *Loup Garou* is a favorite character. He was a bewitched person who took the form of an animal. When the animal was injured to the extent that blood was drawn, the charm vanished and the human form reappeared. Traces of both the 'cape of invisibility' and Siegfried legends appear in the Creole lore of Vincennes. Idle tales perhaps, but each a definite link with Greek, Roman, Celtic, Teutonic, and Scandinavian mythology.

Many foreign groups have enriched Indiana with the lore and ways of their homelands, particularly in the industrial northern portion of the State. In South Bend, Hungarians celebrate their harvest festival to the music of the age-old *czardas*. Farmers annually bring their seed wheat to the priests on March 24 to be blessed so that the harvest may be good. A Polish rite still observed is the *dyngus,* in which the men switch the women on Easter Monday. Corpus Christi is celebrated with an elaborate ceremony every year at Oldenburg. Belgians in Mishawaka wear wooden shoes as they work in their neat gardens, and are as intent on breeding and flying homing pigeons as they were in the old country. Croats, Slovaks, Poles, Syrians and many other races have brought their religious and domestic customs to the Calumet region. A visitor fortunate enough to eat with them in their homes will taste many a dish that is the more delightful for being entirely unknown to the American palate.

The Negro also has his folk heritage. A sincere belief in ghosts, spirits, hoodoo, charms, and spells accompanied the slave here from the South, and even today much of it persists among Indiana Negroes. They have an infinite variety of remedies for common ills, such as parching and grinding a pig's hoof and making a tea of the powder for chills and fever, and making a tea of silkweed root for dropsy. Charms and potions are in common use, and in Indianapolis there are some 15 'conjure' doctors who make a living selling powders and ointments that will cast or break spells. Others prepare and sell love charms, good-luck pieces, and all manner of similar devices. In most of its essentials the folklore of the Negro parallels that of the whites.

Deep and simple faith is reflected in the epitaphs found in old Hoosier churchyards where the story of the pioneer is cut in enduring stone. Many young wives of early settlers lie in these churchyards. Some were buried in their early twenties, worn out by privation and toil. Their story is told in inscriptions such as this one from Benton County:

> Thirteen years I was a virgin,
> Two years I was a wife.
> One year I was a mother,
> The next year took my life.

Sincere belief in immortality is shown by the following from St. Joseph and Clay Counties, respectively:

No pain nor grief shall touch him
No harm shall come near
No earthly voice shall reach him
For he sleeps beneath this stone here.

.   .   .   .

Go home, my friends, dry up your tears
I will arise when Christ appears.

In the folklore and folkways of Indiana is the best history of the State and its people. In the work of Eggleston and Riley especially, the local scene and tradition, with their distinctive characters, customs, and speech, have entered into literature, both realistically and romantically. And if folklore, as one authority maintains, 'is anything that is traditional rather than logical,' much of the real essence of Indiana folklore influences the life of its people today.

Arts and Crafts

LIFE in the Northwest Territory was no more conducive to art activity than that of any other frontier region. However, with the steady growth of certain communities in the years following the entrance of Indiana into the Union, life became sufficiently stable to offer certain inducements to the artists and artisans who were adventurous enough to follow the stream of migration into this part of the country. Their commissions at first were as humble as they were scarce, but judging from extant works, this scarcity of employment was not out of line with the deficiency of talent among the artists themselves. The decoration of carriages, lettering of shop signs, and painting of family portraits constituted their main activity, while the limited number of patrons in each community forced many artists to move constantly from one place to another.

The names of several pioneer painters are mentioned in early chronicles, but the lack of signatures on old paintings makes it difficult to identify their work now. Chester Harding, whose phenomenal success in Boston as a fashionable portraitist is a well-known chapter in the story of American art, is recorded as having been in Vincennes in 1820, but no pictures painted by him in Indiana can be found.

The early educational and social experiments that were so significant to Indiana's cultural development also gave to the art movement an initial impetus. Men and women of varied intellectual interests came from the East to fill the new teaching positions, and they formed small circles of sympathetic persons who not only fostered the enjoyment of art in their communities by sharing books and pictures with their neighbors but also gave encouragement and inspiration to the younger men and women who wanted to follow an artistic trade. New Harmony was one of the most important of these settlements. It reached the height of its influence as an educational center under the guidance of Robert Owen and William Maclure, and included among its departments a School of Industry—the first vocational school in Indiana—with courses in drawing, painting, music, lithography, printing, and bookbinding. On its faculty was that extraordinary artist, Charles Alexander Le Sueur. He made sketches of the settlers, illustrated books, explored the Indian mounds, and collected data on the natural history specimens of this section of the country. David Dale Owen, a geologist by profession, painted a few portraits in New Harmony in the 1830's.

Another art form that arose in the same neighborhood and played a peculiarly interesting part in the early history of the State was the designing of panoramas. John Banward became inspired by the picturesque scenery of the Midwest and painted an immense canvas representing the course of the Mississippi River. The work was received with unbounded enthusiasm wherever it was shown, and it inspired other Indiana painters of the nineteenth century to make equally expansive pictures of beautiful scenes or historical episodes. The last notable example represented the Battle of Gettysburg and was exhibited in Indianapolis around 1886, housed in a building especially erected for its display.

The desire to record the customs and manners of the Indians was another force in bringing artists to the West. George Winter, an Englishman by birth, came to Indiana in 1837 specifically for this purpose and devoted the first part of his career to a serious study of the Indian in his natural environment. Though much of Winter's work tends to emphasize the ethnological rather than the artistic elements, his paintings admirably suggest the early character of the State and its inhabitants. He had no other profession than that of an artist, and in spite of the limited appreciation of art at the time, he was able to provide for himself and his family. He devoted much of his time to landscape painting along the Wabash River.

The most prominent figure in local art circles during the Civil War period was Jacob Cox. He came to Indianapolis from Cincinnati to establish a stove and tinware business, but his reputation as an artist soon eclipsed that of a tinner. He was self-taught, but he rapidly acquired a good technique and commendable style, which gained for him many portrait commissions and a steady sale for his landscapes and 'sketches of fancy,' as the Indianapolis *Journal* of 1857 stated. With the assistance of the scenic painter Henry Waugh, he tried his hand at panoramas but soon abandoned this form for the more congenial easel picture. Many of the younger artists who came to Indianapolis at that time learned to know Cox and became frequent visitors to his studio—William M. Chase was among these—and he was always ready to help them, even to the point of securing financial backing for their studies. Among his students were Joseph O. Eaton and Thomas W. Whittredge, who became prominent in the East a few years later. Other well-known artists of the period were Barton S. Hays, W. R. Freeman, Peter F. Reed, John Love and James R. Gookins. Love and Gookins organized the first art school in Indianapolis, which opened in 1877.

While the names of many Indiana painters are known, very little information is obtainable about the first craftsmen: the cabinetmakers, weavers, potters, and stonecarvers who played such important roles in the growing communities. In several of these crafts the artisans received slight personal recognition, and the omission of trade-marks or signatures makes it difficult today to discover their names. On the other hand, it is doubtful if Indiana produced anything outstanding in the field of the minor arts. Furniture design reflected the models brought in from the South and East, which in turn were based on European prototypes; carpenters and woodcarvers used the same books of plans as their Eastern colleagues, and pottery was designed for utility rather than beauty.

Doubtless the most significant of Indiana's early crafts was the hand-woven coverlet, both from the standpoint of decoration and utility. The wool came from local farms, where it was washed, spun, dyed, and—in the early days—woven; and although the women were limited to narrow single-weave coverlets with simple geometric patterns in two colors, the results were often rich and effective. The designs were based on early Colonial fabrics or on coverlets brought into the State by the settlers, while the actual weaving was done from homemade 'drafts' composed of lines, spaces, and numbers, which guided the weavers as they passed the wool through their looms. These 'drafts' were probably exchanged among the women in much the same way as recipes are today. With the appearance of the professional weavers and their elaborate looms, the home industry gradually ceased; the double-weave coverlet came into vogue, with more elaborate designs and finer texture. The wool was prepared on the farms, as formerly, and then sent to the weaver to be made up in accordance with the design selected by the family. Most of the professional weavers came from Scotland, England, or Germany; they had been trained in Europe and had brought their designs and patterns with them. John S. La-Tournette and his daughter Sarah were probably the best known of

Agriculture

tograph by J. C. Allen and Son

EASTERN INDIANA FARMSTEAD

'WHEN THE FROST IS ON THE PUNKIN AND THE FODDER'S IN THE SHOCK'

tograph by W A Sills

HEREFORD STEERS

FEEDING TIME

TIPPECANOE COUNTY CORNFIELD

SPRAYING PEACH TREES, KNOX COUNTY

TOBACCO WAREHOUSE, MADISON

MINT FIELD IN ST. JOSEPH COUNTY

DISTILLING MINT, NEAR ELKHART

ograph by courtesy of Elkhart Daily Truth

Photograph by courtesy of Purdue Unive

THE ANNUAL STATE TOMATO PICKING CONTEST BEGINS

FARMERS SPEND A DAY AT SCHOOL ON A PURDUE HOG FARM

Photograph by courtesy of Purdue Unive

FOUR-H CLUB MEMBERS LEARN TO JUDGE DAIRY CATTLE

HORSE SHOW AT A COUNTY FAIR

GRAIN ELEVATORS, VINCENNES

Photograph by courtesy of Farm Security Adminis

those in Indiana, because of the perfection and beauty of their work.

Sculpture has not developed into as significant an art in Indiana as the abundance of good stone would warrant. Probably the most interesting early work was done in connection with grave markers, many of which are still to be seen in southern Indiana. Delicate traceries and graceful designs give these stones an appearance of elegance and restraint that contrasts strikingly with the flamboyant cemetery monuments of more recent date. In the years following the Civil War this modest craft was eclipsed by more monumental carvings and sculptured figures, brought about by the expansion of business and the growing patriotic sentiment regarding local heroes. The most notable from the standpoint of the profusion of sculptured groups is the Soldiers and Sailors Monument in the heart of Indianapolis, executed under the direction of Rudolph Schwartz. When the development of the limestone industry in the State and the number of monuments that have been erected are taken into account, it is somewhat surprising to find that no local school of sculpture, in the true sense of the word, has developed. Several men and women of ability received their early training, as well as their first commissions here, but most of them went elsewhere when they reached their maturity as artists. Among these are Janet Scudder, Myra Richards, Warner Williams, Seth Velsey, and Robert Davidson.

There are several memorials and public monuments in Indiana that are important both as works of art and historical documents, and although they are the work of out-of-State sculptors, their significance to the cultural status of Indiana is obvious. The following may be ranked as the best: *The Young Lincoln* by Paul Manship, at Fort Wayne; *General Lew Wallace* by Andrew O'Connor, at Crawfordsville; *Schuyler Colfax* by Lorado Taft, *Benjamin Harrison* by Charles H. Niehaus, *Henry Lawton* by Andrew O'Connor, and the *Depew Memorial Fountain* by Sterling Calder, at Indianapolis; and the *Appeal to the Great Spirit* by Cyrus E. Dollin, at Muncie.

Painting, unlike sculpture, developed rapidly in all parts of the State between the Civil War period and the close of the nineteenth century. Many students were going to Europe to study and others were returning from the East well equipped with technical knowledge and fortified with sufficient enthusiasm to withstand the indifference shown toward their profession. Studios were fixed up in available buildings, exhibitions were held, and critical reviews of paintings began to appear in the newspapers. Picture raffles, based on the sale of shares or on memberships, were the most successful means of selling paintings and arousing the interest of the public.

During this period there occurred a decline in portrait painting and the rapid development of a landscape movement, which reached its height in the opening years of the present century. The change was most noticeable upon the return of artists from Munich and Paris between 1885 and 1890, with their sincere enthusiasm for this section of the country combined with an alert interest in the Impressionists' tenets. This singleness of purpose on their part brought about two important results: first, every section of the State was explored in search of sketching grounds, leading to a wide variety of subjects for easel pictures and ultimately making the people of the State conscious of the beautiful scenery around them; and second, a lyrical school of painting developed, characterized by hazy atmosphere, rolling hills, and winding streams. The most popular theme was the wooded landscape in autumn.

This local spirit was so strong that the painters made little effort to exhibit their paintings outside the State. Their work became conservative and provincial, pleasant in its mood, and reassuring in its optimistic point of view. Indiana art was not only consistently rural in its representation of outdoor themes, but no stress was laid on the fact that groups of painters were working in different communities. This movement was less a composite of small colonies of artists working in remote areas than a State-wide activity, kindred in point of view and on the whole harmonious. The Brown County artists' colony at Nashville reflects most vividly this characteristic type of Indiana landscape painting.

The names and works of Indiana painters are too numerous to include in a survey of this kind; more detailed information may be found in Mary Q. Burnett's comprehensive book, *Art and Artists of Indiana* (1921). The men who expressed most capably the character of the State in the first quarter of the present century and who are regarded as the founders of a true Indiana school of landscape painting are J. Otis Adams, William Forsyth, Otto Stark, Theodore C. Steele, and John E. Bundy. To them has been attached the familiar name, the Hoosier Group.

The passing of these artists and their contemporaries marks the beginning of modern Indiana painting. Although the transition has not been startling, certain new tendencies have appeared to modify the interpretation of the local scenes and expand the scope of subjects used by the painters. These tendencies are more or less in keeping with contemporary American art as a whole—more concentrated in feeling, more direct in expression, and bolder in the choice of theme—displaying a greater interest in activities around the farms and in smaller communities.

The stress on mural painting, motivated to a large extent by the active participation of the Federal Government in this field, has had something to do with this tendency, both in the emphasis on certain themes and the change in technique from broken, spotty colors to strong, clear patterns.

One of the first important mural projects, and probably the most ambitious, was the series of decorative panels and murals placed in the Indianapolis City Hospital during 1914 and 1915, in which 12 local artists participated, supervised by William Forsyth. The themes range from Biblical subjects to fairy-story illustrations. Under the Public Works of Art Project few murals, in the true sense of the word, were made because the program in Indiana was confined to relatively small decorative panels for public buildings; but the more recent competitions conducted by the Division of Painting and Sculpture of the Treasury Department has given the State several noteworthy examples, including those by Donald Mattison at Union City and Henrik Mayer at LaFayette. That Indiana murals are varied in their technique and points of view is clearly seen by comparing Robert Grafton's historical episodes at Culver Military Academy with Gilbert Wilson's expressionistic pronouncements at Terre Haute.

In addition to the work of residents, some important murals have been painted in the State by outside artists. Among them are the subjects dealing with the Northwest Territory by Ezra Winter, in the George Rogers Clark Memorial at Vincennes; episodes in local history by J. Scott Williams, in the Indiana State Library, Indianapolis; a chronological story of Indiana's industrial, political, and cultural history by Thomas Benton, originally designed for the Chicago World's Fair and now (1941) installed at Indiana University; and the court-house murals at Covington. Two of these were executed by Eugene Savage, a native of Covington now living in New York, and the remaining ones are the work of local artists, supervised by Savage.

Concurrent with the development of Indiana art there has been a steady growth of organizations and societies that conduct art programs, promote the work of native artists, and form public collections. The Art Association of Indianapolis was organized in 1883, and since 1906 has had as the center of its expanding program the John Herron Art Institute. The museum of the Institute includes a permanent collection of paintings ranging from the productions of Flemish and Italian artists of the early Renaissance period to the work of present-day Indiana artists, as well as a group of art objects representing important phases in the development of the plastic and decorative arts since the earliest civilizations. Two exhibits are held each year and the Institute also presents concerts, lectures, and marionette shows.

The Art School, housed in an adjacent building erected by an anonymous donor in 1928, offers courses in drawing and painting, sculpture, advertising art, and allied subjects. For three successive years (1937–9) students of this school won the coveted Prix de Rome, a two-year fellowship at the American Academy in Rome.

The Richmond Art Association, Fort Wayne Art School and Museum, Evansville Society of Fine Arts and History, and others have followed the lead of the Art Association of Indianapolis, carrying on their activities year after year and forming an effective network of art organizations over the State. An extensive collection of paintings is owned by Notre Dame University; the most recent and up-to-date gallery is that of the Ball State Teachers College at Muncie. To this collection Mr. and Mrs. W. H. Thompson of Indianapolis added in 1940 a notable group of Italian Renaissance paintings and art objects, including works by Titian, Raphael, Andrea del Sarto, Donatello, Lorenzo di Credi, and others. Four later artists—Rembrandt, O. P. Pannini, Renoir, and Degas—are also represented. These paintings are hung in a separate room of the Arts building on the college campus, and the gallery is fitted with a collection of Italian furniture of the fifteenth and sixteenth centuries.

State-wide exhibitions have been noteworthy among the activities of Indiana artists and three major shows are held each year. Important from the standpoint of its tradition and prestige is the annual exhibition at the John Herron Art Institute; the Indiana State Fair exhibit is significant in its scope of displays and the audience it reaches; and the Hoosier Salon in Chicago plays a unique role in placing the work of Indiana artists before out-of-State groups and extending the market for local pictures and sculptures. All of these exhibitions are made up of current work and serve to familiarize the people with the latest expressions of the local artists.

Music and the Theater

D URING the pioneer era Indiana was handicapped culturally
by isolation and prejudice. Early Midwestern centers—Cincinnati, Lexington, Louisville, and St. Louis—were linked to New
Orleans and the East by the Ohio and Mississippi Rivers. Detroit
welcomed travelers and wandering theatrical companies by way of
the Great Lakes. But in Indiana, settlement was slow and the first
important towns were not on the main routes of early travel. The
churches, the most powerful single influence in early Indiana, disap-
proved of such devil's devices as dancing, music, and play-acting; sectarian prejudice ruled even among the lettered, and was so strong that
even the Indianapolis *Journal* refused to advertise theatricals until
1851. It was not without reason that Indiana in the early nineteenth
century was said to have the crudest and most provincial population
in the United States.

The folk impulse was active, however. From the earliest period
music in Indiana has been a flowering of community experience, burst-
ing through Puritanical restrictions, eventually emerging in civic singing societies and concert groups, and reaching personal expression in
the work of a number of composers.

The frontier made its own genuine folk music. Song books were
unknown, but the first settlers to enter Indiana from the South brought
the traditional 'white spirituals' of Virginia and Carolina. A typical
example is the famous 'What a Meeting':

> Our fathers will be there, will be there,
> Our fathers will be there, will be there,
> Our fathers will be there, for a crown of life to wear,
> When we meet around God's white throne.
>
> *Chorus:*
> What a meeting, what a meeting that will be,
> What a meeting, what a meeting that will be,
> What a meeting that will be, that in Heaven we shall see,
> When we meet around God's white throne.

The stanza was repeated for each member of the family and sometimes sinners, friends, mourners, and others were included.

Methodists and Baptists, the largest sects, sang these songs for many years before song books came into use. Book songs, however, were never sung with the same hearty enjoyment and abandon as the old spirituals, into which people threw not only fervor but physical strength. They were sung in rural camp meetings in Indiana until comparatively recent years.

Many religious groups feared the violin as an instrument of Satan (there were no musical instruments in the early church), and almost all of them drew the line at dancing. They saw no evil, however, in simple games and the rhythmic verses that were chanted in accompaniment; before long the chanting became outright singing, sometimes—in more daring communities—helped out by a fiddler. Other songs were sung to rhythmic motions, hops, and skips, which only a sophist could have distinguished from the brimstone-tainted dance. Most popular of these were the famous 'Skip to My Lou,' and 'Weevily Wheat,' a version of the Virginia Reel. Such songs persisted even after the passing of the log cabin and the frontier. A generation still living recalls with affection the play-parties of the eighties and nineties, with their lusty singing, stamping feet, and the strains of 'Skip to My Lou.' But this rich material has not yet been extensively used by Indiana composers.

With the growth of town life and the influx, after 1848, of music-loving Germans, the difference between the musical taste of rural groups and that of the increasingly sophisticated city dwellers became pronounced. The backwoods and small towns still enjoyed their games and songs, but urban centers turned to the music of Europe. For many years the German element in the population was responsible for the musical education of Indianapolis. German singing societies, notably the Liederkranz, Saengerbund, and Maennerchor, were active. The Maennerchor, through the generosity of the Frenzel family, sponsored a concert series annually for many years and presented such artists as Gregory, Piatigorsky, Joseph Szigeti, and Vladimir Horowitz.

The long tradition of this organization, still a fine male chorus, is linked with the name of Alexander Ernestinoff, who probably contributed more to the development of Indiana music than any other one person. Coming to Indianapolis from Russia in 1882, Ernestinoff for 40 years gave all his energies to the singing societies, the first symphony orchestra, and other musical groups.

Since 1930 a State symphony orchestra, supported by the Indiana Symphony Society, has presented a series of concerts annually in Indianapolis. The orchestra was directed by Ferdinand Shaefer until he retired in November 1936; the present conductor (1941) is Fabien Sevitzky, formerly a member of the Philadelphia Orchestra. The concerts are presented at the Murat Temple, a large and handsome building built by the Mystic Shrine in 1909. The Symphony Society has enlisted State-wide support and concerts are now given in several other cities.

Another name closely linked with the musical development of Indiana is that of Franz Xavier Arens, a native of Rhenish Prussia, who conducted a notable series of May Music Festivals in Indianapolis from 1892 to 1896. He was president of the Metropolitan School of Music of Indianapolis and head of its vocal department until he moved to New York in 1897. There he established and directed the People's Symphony Society.

Other factors in the growth of Indiana music are the privately sponsored concert series, of which Ona B. Talbot's was outstanding; the work of the Indiana Federation of Music Clubs; and the excellent music instruction in the public schools and colleges. One musical center in the State, St. Meinrad's Abbey (*see Tour 11A*), is probably better known in Europe than in this country. The abbey has a magnificent Gregorian choir and in the cloister here the great traditions of the plain chant and other forms of medieval music are continued.

Paul Dresser, or Dreiser (1858–1906), a brother of Theodore Dreiser, was long one of the most popular song writers in the country. Among his compositions are, 'Just Tell Them That You Saw Me,' 'The Blue and the Gray,' and 'On the Banks of the Wabash, Far Away,' the Indiana State song that has won a permanent place in American folk music. Almost as well known is Cole Porter (b.1892), of Peru, who wrote the lyrics and music for *Anything Goes,* and the music for the film version of *As Thousands Cheer.* Among his most popular songs are 'Old Fashioned Garden,' and 'Night and Day.' Hoagland (Hoagy) Carmichael (b.1900), a native of Bloomington, is another popular composer, best known for 'Lazy Bones' and 'Star Dust.'

Drawn more from local folk material are the compositions of Charles Diven Campbell (1877–1919), who taught music at Indiana University for 13 years. He composed and directed the music for the State Centennial pageants presented at Indianapolis, Bloomington, and Corydon in 1916. His 'Hymn to Indiana' is still often heard in schools and club gatherings. Van Denman Thompson, who has been professor of organ and composition at DePauw University since 1911 and now (1941) heads the university's school of music, has made excellent use of indigenous material. His oratorio *The Evangel of the New World* (1934), with libretto by Edith Arnold Tilden, is based on old hymns and spirituals. The composition was presented by the DePauw Choir and was also sung in Baltimore by a chorus of nearly 1,000 voices. Dr. Thompson has written anthems, piano, and organ compositions. Among his best-known works are 'A Dance for Phyllis' and 'Daffodils,' for the piano, and 'Album Leaf,' 'To Patience,' and 'Woodland Sketches' for organ.

Brief accounts of the work of these and many other Indiana composers are given in the booklet *Indiana Composers, Native and Adopted*, compiled in 1936 by the Indiana Federation of Music Clubs and printed and distributed by the Extension Division of Indiana University. Among the State's eminent musicians (in addition to those listed above) are Adolph H. Schellschmidt, teacher, cellist, and composer; Elmer Andrew Steffen, composer and teacher, widely known as director of choirs and choruses; Frederic Krull, who set some 30 of Riley's poems to music and also wrote for piano and orchestra; Charles F. Hansen, blind since infancy, one of the outstanding organists of the Midwest and composer of numerous hymns; and Mildred Dilling, internationally known concert harpist.

The Music Project of the Work Projects Administration has greatly advanced interest in music in Indiana. During 1940 the project maintained a concert orchestra, a teaching unit, and white and Negro dance orchestras in Indianapolis; one or several groups in these categories and folk-song units were functioning in South Bend, Terre Haute, Evansville, Fort Wayne, Hammond, and five other cities. The Indianapolis concert orchestra gave 300 performances attended by more than 60,000 persons during the year; approximately 6,000 concerts, classes, and music appreciation sessions were held elsewhere in the State, drawing a total attendance of more than a million persons.

THE THEATER

For many years the theater was a stepchild in Indiana, opposed by the churches and throttled by the moralistic attitude of the period. Yet from the first it was welcomed and fostered by inveterate playlovers. When people were unable to pay professional actors they organized amateur companies, even with the breath of hell-fire hot upon their necks. If they had no theater, they played in a foundry or a stable; if their audience's taste was uneven, they performed *Othello,* or *Pocahontas,* and followed it with a bawdy skit and a wrestling match.

The French settlers did not develop a native theater during the early period, either at Vincennes or anywhere else in the Ohio Valley. By 1814, however, a theatrical association had made Vincennes a center of amateur theatricals, and New Harmony during the Owenite period likewise fostered an amateur company. The hostility of religious groups had relaxed somewhat by 1840, and LaFayette, Logansport, Brookville, and Indianapolis had all set up amateur theaters. Later in the century most of the larger towns had their 'op'ry houses,' where local groups provided entertainment and where road companies sometimes performed for one night only.

The best professional troupes in the Middle West neglected Indiana, for the most part, until the railroad supplanted the Ohio River as a means of transportation. But in 1820 Samuel Drake, returning from St. Louis to Louisville, played for a summer season in Vincennes on a tiny stage that was hardly large enough for even his small company. Vincennes was later visited occasionally by traveling stock companies on their way to and from Cincinnati, Lexington, and St. Louis.

The first theatrical performance in Indianapolis was given on December 8, 1823, in Carter's Tavern, near the present site of the *News* Building. The tavern owner, mindful of his reputation as the sole dramatic entrepreneur of the town, said that the 'orchestra' (one violin) would play only 'solemn' music. After this venture, however, there was no further theatrical activity until the winter of 1837–8, when William Lindsay's company arrived from Cincinnati. It played in an old wagon shop on Washington Street across from the courthouse—an unfloored, uncomfortable place, lit only by tallow candles and with hard two-inch planks for seats. The program consisted usually of a serious play, followed by songs, recitations, tableaux, and a farce. The most popular plays of the season were *Othello,* Home's *Douglass,* and Robert Dale Owen's *Pocahontas.* Two years later the company returned, this time to present its plays in the dining room of the old Browning Hotel. The outstanding event of the season was the performance of *Pocahontas* under the personal supervision of its famous author. This Indian romance, first published in New York in 1837, was said to have a 'Shakespearean' sweep and grandeur; but the qualities of rhetoric and melodrama that made it popular on the frontier doomed it to oblivion a few years later. It had its first and only New York performance at the Park Street Theater, February 8, 1838.

The theater struggled along, in spite of the hostility of newspapers and church groups. In 1843-4, John Powell brought an excellent company to Indianapolis and played on the second floor of an old wagon shop. The admission fee was 25¢ and the crowds were large; but one night a citizen named Richard Corbaley fell off the outdoor stairway by which the audience ascended and was killed—furnishing a solemn point to the warnings of the puritans. In the same year Mrs. Alexander Drake, the popular star of the Ohio Valley, appeared for her second season, giving fine performances in *Othello* and *Macbeth*.

The Indianapolis of the 1850's owed much to Austin H. Brown, owner of the *Sentinel*. Brown brought shows to Indianapolis on a profit-sharing basis, guaranteeing their publicity. His first ventures were distinctly popular in appeal: panoramas, gaudy spectacles, and concerts. In 1851 the Shire and Toledo Company gave a series of plays and concerts in the Masonic Temple, where during the day the historic Constitutional Convention was meeting.

During the first State Fair, in October 1852, Brown engaged all the halls in the city and brought in several companies of minstrels, variety players, and concert performers. Later he toured the State with these same companies. 'Yankee' Robinson, who came to Indianapolis with his stock company to play for the Fair crowds, finding all the halls taken, opened in a tent, moving to Washington Hall after the Fair was over. In 1854-5 the Athenaeum was opened by Robinson and became a very popular theater. A number of famous players appeared here, including the elder John Drew. The Athenaeum had a varied career and finally became a gymnasium.

The first building in Indianapolis devoted wholly to plays was the old Metropolitan Theater (later known successively as the Park, Strand, and Capitol), erected in 1857 by Valentine Butsch. Seating an audience of 1,500, it opened in September 1858, but its managers had a difficult time until the Civil War. So great was the need at that time for lively patriotic programs to keep up public morale that all opposition to the theater disappeared from press and pulpit and has never been revived. During this period several famous actors, including Edwin Forrest and James H. Hackett, played at the Metropolitan.

In 1868 Butsch completed the Academy of Music. Even larger than the Metropolitan, it cost nearly $150,000 and for seven years was the unchallenged center of Indianapolis dramatic activities. A rival theater, the Grand Opera House (now B. F. Keith's) was opened in 1875—luxuriously appointed and with a seating capacity of 1,600, it was built in 100 days at a cost of $50,000. The Academy burned in 1877 and the older Metropolitan, which had become merely a mildly naughty variety theater, was renovated and rechristened the Park. It opened in 1879 with Joseph Jefferson as the star attraction.

Despite newspaper opposition to additional theaters in Indianapolis, William H. English built the English Opera House the following year. Here America's greatest tragedians alternated with light comedy, concerts, lectures, and vaudeville. Lawrence Barrett opened the theater September 27, 1880, with *Hamlet;* early in 1881 Sarah Bernhardt appeared in *Frou Frou* and *Camille* and Jan Auschek in *Bleak House.* Outstanding among the scores of popular actors who have appeared at the English since that time are Edwin Booth, Henry Irving, John Drew, Minnie Maddern Fiske, Richard Mansfield, E. H. Sothern, Julia Marlowe, Maude Adams, Ethel Barrymore, Mrs. Patrick Campbell, and George Arliss. Closed temporarily in 1930, the theater is now (1941) once more housing an annual season of stage productions.

While nationally known actors were playing in Indianapolis, showboats were offering a different kind of theatrical entertainment along the Ohio. *Price's Sensation,* which left Point Pleasant, West Virginia, in 1883, was the first showboat to embark upon a long voyage, although the Chapman family's *Floating Theater* had tied up at Indiana river towns 50 years before. Evansville, Madison, and New Albany, because of their location on the Ohio, were important stops for these fascinating craft that floated downstream and were towed back to their starting point by mules or poled back by deck hands. Visits from the showboats were eagerly awaited and the day of their arrival ranked with election day for bustle and excitement. The boats became more and more ornate until they were in reality floating theaters. The famous *Golden Rod,* pushed by little steamboats, was built in 1904 and is still (1941) an exciting spectacle with its auditorium seating 1,200 and its equipment rivaling that of many land theaters. Its route includes the Ohio, Monongahela, Illinois, and Mississippi Rivers, and varies each season according to channel conditions.

Indiana has had many good stock companies, but the finest of them all, without doubt, was Stuart Walker's Portmanteau Theater, which played in Indianapolis during the summer seasons of 1917–23 and 1926–8. After serving as stage director under Belasco in New York, Walker set up as an independent producer in 1914 and originated the

Portmanteau Theater, a production unit with a folding stage that could be easily transported and set up indoors or out. In Indianapolis his repertory company presented plays of great variety and excellence, many of them written by Walker. After directing a similar company in Cincinnati, Walker went to Hollywood where he now (1941) directs a dramatic school for screen actors.

The earliest amateur group in Indianapolis, the Thespians, was organized in 1840. Its first play, the perennial *Douglass,* was performed in an old foundry at the corner of Market and Senate Streets, on a stage 15 by 20 feet. Finding the moral rectitude of *Pocahontas* a better instrument with which to break down church opposition, the Thespians frequently gave this play. For its first performance, in 1840, Jacob Cox, well-known artist, painted the scenery; young William Wallace, later a noted Indiana politician, played the heroine, since women did not at that time act in amateur theatricals; and the heroine's sister, Nomony, was played by William's brother, Lewis, who was later to win fame as general, diplomat, and author of *Ben-Hur.*

After the Thespians ceased to be active, theatricals languished in Indianapolis for 20 years. In 1864, however, a dramatic club was organized to play at a Sanitary Fair, held to sell needlework and all manner of handicraft to raise funds for dressings and food delicacies for wounded Union soldiers. In 1872 the Indianapolis Dramatic Society was formed. Including both men and women, this group was largely devoted to social affairs enlivened by decidedly amateurish skits, and was a forerunner of such clubs as the more accomplished and fashionable Players' Club of the present day. But it was not until the rise of the little-theater movement in the 1910–20 decade that the amateur theater exerted any serious influence in Indianapolis or elsewhere in the State.

In February 1915 the Little Theater Society of Indiana was organized in Indianapolis, with the aim of enabling the State to take part in the 'world-wide movement for reclaiming drama as the method of communal self-expression.' The first production was launched, under the presidency of George Ade, at the Herron Art Institute in October 1915. By 1925 a season of full-length plays was presented; in the following year a playhouse was constructed and the organization was rechristened the Civic Theater of Indianapolis. For ten years the group has maintained its noncommercial spirit while giving plays of professional caliber, including the work of Ibsen, Shaw, Pinero, Molnár, and Noel Coward. It has not, however, produced plays by native playwrights.

George Somnes, the able director, went to Hollywood in 1931 and was succeeded by Hale MacKeen and later by Frederick Burleigh. Richard Hoover is the present director (1941). There is now a Civic Theater in Fort Wayne also.

Two other recent dramatic ventures are the Indiana University Traveling Theater, which toured the State under the direction of Volney Hampton in the spring of 1935; and the Federal Theater Project, which Dr. Lee Norvelle directed from March 2, 1936, to July 15, 1937, when the project was closed. In addition to many popular stand-bys, the project presented four new works, including *The Hoosier Schoolmaster,* by Dr. Norvelle; *Do Unto Others,* by H. K. Burton; *One Night at Brenda's,* by Miles Tiernan; and *Bringin' Back the Drama,* written by Ralph Stuart for Charles Withers, popular impresario of 'Withers' Op'ry,' who appeared as guest star. The Theater Project, it is estimated, played to a total of 150,000 persons during its brief existence.

The works of Indiana dramatists do not conform to any one pattern. At least two hits have been made from novels by Hoosier writers— *The Copperhead,* adapted from *The Glory of His Country,* by Frederick Landis; and *Ben-Hur,* from the novel by Lew Wallace. Theodore Dreiser's *Plays of the Natural and Supernatural,* although less known than his novels, have power—especially his tragedy, *The Hand of the Potter.*

The three plays that most closely portray the Indiana scene and the Hoosier type are George Ade's *The County Chairman,* Booth Tarkington's dramatization of his novel *The Gentleman from Indiana,* and his *The Man from Home,* written in collaboration with Harry Leon Wilson. Tarkington's light-hearted pictures of comfortable middle-class life— as drawn in *Clarence* and *Seventeen*—have an interesting if not commanding place in the American theater; while Ade's lively musical satires, *The College Widow, Speaking to Father,* and *The Old Town,* have contributed almost as much to American humor as his *Fables in Slang.*

Literature

UNTIL the 1840's, the most vigorous writing in Indiana was being produced by men of science. Many scholars came from Europe and New England to study in the West; Indian tribes still living in the region, archeological remains left by prehistoric peoples, unclassified flora and fauna, and unexplored rivers and geological systems offered these scientists tempting inducements. In New Harmony (*see New Harmony*), for many years the principal center of research in the Middle West, were published some of the most notable books of the period. To this category belong Thomas Say's *American Conchology, or Description of the Shells of North America, Illustrated by Coloured Figures from Original Drawings Executed from Nature* (1830); the same author's *Descriptions of Some New Terrestrial and Fluviatile Shells of North America* (1840); David Dale Owen's numerous State and Federal geological reports and his *Catalogue of Mineralogical and Geological Specimens at New Harmony, Indiana;* and William Maclure's *An Essay on the Formation of Rocks* (1832).

In the field of imaginative literature, John Finley, a native of Virginia who lived in Wayne County for 40 years, wrote 'The Hoosier's Nest,' which was perhaps the first genuine poem of the frontier. The Indianapolis *Journal,* in 1833, published this poem, an account of a stranger's visit in the cabin of an Indiana settler. Within a year it was reprinted in almost every American newspaper and widely quoted in England. Terse and vivid, precise and realistic in its evocation of disagreeable detail, 'The Hoosier's Nest' has even today a fresh and living quality.

Other writers were slow to follow Finley's lead, however, and throughout the region both poetry and fiction remained stilted and imitative for 30 years or more. But when Midwestern realism did begin to mature, another Indiana writer was the trail blazer; and the publication in 1871 of *The Hoosier Schoolmaster* marked an important step in the development of American fiction.

Edward Eggleston, the author, was born in 1837 in the quiet little village of Vevay (*see Tour* 11) on the Ohio, the son of a cultured and successful lawyer. Many elements in his early life conspired to prepare him for his life work—the natural loveliness of southern Indiana; the large library in his father's home; the delicate health that forced him to make the most of his reading and of every experience. But it was not an academic existence that young Eggleston led. He was reared on a farm, with a real knowledge of rural life and its problems. At the age of 16 he visited his father's family in Virginia, a visit that sharpened his observation of the contrast between the new country and an older, more cultivated scene. Soon afterwards, he was sent West for his health, arriving in Kansas during the free-soil excitement. These experiences enlarged his critical knowledge of men and manners and quickened his democratic idealism into sturdy political conviction.

Torn between the desire to write and a sense that religion was his true vocation, young Eggleston in the next few years was first a Methodist circuit rider, then editor of a juvenile magazine in Chicago. In 1870, however, when he went to New York as a preacher, he was also irrevocably committed to literature. With a clearer perspective in relation to his native State, he soon wrote *The Hoosier Schoolmaster*, a vigorous portrait of the illiterate people of southern Indiana in the 1850's. It was first published, curiously enough, in France in *La Revue des Deux Mondes* under the title, 'Le Maître d'École de Flat Creek.'

This first success was followed by many others. Eggleston's later novels include *The End of the World* (1872), an account of the Millerite hysteria of 1842–3; *Roxy* (1878), a powerful study of religious conflict in a dreamy Swiss village on the Ohio; *The Circuit Rider* (1874), a vivid picture of the strenuous religiosity of the frontier; and *The Graysons* (1888), a fine novel, celebrated both for its artistic perfection and its accurate and beautiful record of folk dialect. Eggleston was profoundly interested in dialect, as well as in the social and domestic history of the American people. In 1896, after 16 years of research in the course of which he assembled a vast collection of Americana, he published *The Beginners of a Nation*, one of the most important pioneer works in American social history.

Unquestionably an important figure in American realism, Eggleston is especially noteworthy as the first Indiana writer to master and recreate thoroughly the experience of the frontier. Steeped in an intimate knowledge of the life of his own day and of the era that had just vanished, yet nourished and stimulated by books of travel, he was able

—as the writers of an earlier generation were not—to deal imaginatively with native material.

Before the Civil War a few literary journals were started in the State, but the flourishing periodicals of Cincinnati overshadowed them as outlets for most Hoosier literary output of this period. For many years the literary vigor of Cincinnati and Lexington was to draw off the cream of Indiana writing.

The most famous figure in the State's literature during the later nineteenth century was James Whitcomb Riley. Like Eggleston, Riley worked in the main current of the democratic tradition, but he was sunnier, gayer, more genial in temperament, far less conscious of the ethical implications of the faith by which he lived; and perhaps for this reason he was—more than any other American writer of the last 60 years—a poet for the people. In popularity only Longfellow, with whom he had much in common, surpassed him; and even Longfellow did not deal with folk themes in so thoroughgoing a fashion.

Born in Greenfield (*see Tour* 8) in 1849, Riley came to maturity in the kindly, expansive, rural period of Indiana life. He grew up casual and open-eyed in his little county-seat town—a bright, prankish boy with no particular liking for formal education. Trained for no trade or profession, he drifted tentatively but happily into a dozen occupations —observing the lives of farmers and townspeople with the artless attentiveness of a child. Apparently he began to write for the same reason that he played the guitar—because he was clever.

Riley's verses, good, bad, and indifferent, were published for years in the weekly newspapers of Indiana; and the common people he wrote about took him warmly and uncritically into their affections. His first book, *The Old Swimmin' Hole and 'Leven More Poems* (1883), was immensely popular, as were *Afterwhiles* (1888), *Rhymes of Childhood* (1891), *An Old Sweetheart of Mine* (1891), *Out to Old Aunt Mary's* (1904), and a dozen or more other volumes that appeared in steady succession for many years.

Riley is best known today as a children's poet, and his 'Little Orphant Annie,' 'The Raggedy Man,' and 'The Old Swimmin' Hole' are still universally read. Throughout his life he remained the spokesman of children and extremely simple adults—the rustic philosophers and rude farm moralists from whose point of view many of his best poems are written. Basically the dialect spoken by these rural types is probably a fairly accurate report—although not as scientific as Eggleston's —of the careless speech of uneducated farmers.

While Eggleston and Riley drew their characters and backgrounds from Indiana sources, there were other and equally famous members of the Indiana group who escaped into exotic themes and remote periods for their literary material. During the period between 1840 and 1870 a number of young men with literary leanings grew up and were educated in Indiana—young men to whom the life about them apparently gave no imaginative quickening. They were swept into the fields of historical romance, bookish poetry, or sheer fantasy.

The most widely read of these was Lew Wallace (1827–1905), who won fame as soldier, painter, and writer. *The Fair God* (1873), a novel of the Spanish conquest, was written as a result of his campaign in the Mexican War. *Ben-Hur* (1880) was an outgrowth of his concern to defend his faith in Christianity; and *The Prince of India* (1893) was written during his residence in Constantinople as minister to Turkey under Garfield. All three novels have panoramic brilliance, historic fidelity, and striking dramatic episodes. In sales *Ben-Hur* probably exceeds even *Uncle Tom's Cabin*. It has been translated into almost all the European and several Asiatic languages. Maurice Thompson (1844–1901), Wallace's neighbor in the quiet little city of Crawfordsville (*see Tour 8A*), capped a lifetime of poetry and scholarship with *Alice of Old Vincennes* (1900), a vivid historical romance of the George Rogers Clark expedition. Charles Major's *When Knighthood Was in Flower* (1898) and *The Bears of Blue River* (1900) are still popular with younger readers; and many people still remember George Barr McCutcheon's *Graustark* (1901) and *Brewster's Millions* (1903). More important than any of these men except Lew Wallace, however, was Meredith Nicholson, essayist and writer of romantic mystery, a form which he perfected in *The House of a Thousand Candles* (1905).

Nicholson was born in 1866, coming to manhood a little later than the older members of the Indiana group. Although he never attempted imaginative realism in his own fiction, he had an unusual sense of the richness of Indiana as theme and material for literature. In 1900 he published *The Hoosiers,* an authoritative study of Indiana background, history, and social psychology. A volume of essays, *Valley of Democracy,* which appeared 15 years later deals vividly with the Middle West.

During the years that Eggleston, Wallace, Riley, and Nicholson were building a reputation for Indiana as a literary center, several other writers, born or reared in Indiana but making their permanent homes elsewhere, were rising to prominence. For a few years in his troubled youth Ambrose Bierce lived in Elkhart. But the brilliant, mordant short stories with which he left so deep a mark upon literature reflect nothing of this period of his life. David Graham Phillips, a leading journalist of the muckraking movement and the author of more than 20 novels dealing with social problems, was born at Madison and attended the Indiana public schools and Indiana Asbury (now DePauw) University. His journalistic career, however, was in New York and London. His novels are concerned with national problems, and when their setting is Indiana they do not, as his fellow-Indianian, Elmer Davis, has pointed out, 'create an Indiana recognizable to anyone who has lived there.' Phillips' most important novel is *Susan Lenox: Her Fall and Rise* (1917), a study of the position of women in society, with industrial and political corruption as a minor theme.

Joaquin (christened Cincinnatus Heine) Miller was born at Liberty. But while he was a youth, his father moved with his family to Oregon and the poetry and drama that were to make Miller famous dealt with the Far West. William Vaughn Moody was born at Spencer and brought up at New Albany, but he attended Harvard, taught in the East and at the University of Chicago, and used little of the background of his youth in his writing. He is best known for his earliest play, *The Great Divide*, first produced in Chicago in 1907.

In the early twentieth century, literary activity began to have an important role in everyday Indiana life. Literary societies became as common as women's clubs today. Bankers, merchants, doctors, lawyers, teachers, and housewives competed successfully with professional writers in the production of novels, short stories, essays and poems. The Bobbs-Merrill publishing house was established in Indianapolis. Once for a charity performance at almost a moment's notice it was possible to assemble on the platform of an Indianapolis theater Riley, Nicholson, Wallace, and Booth Tarkington.

Three women writers—Gene Stratton Porter, Annie Fellows Johnston, and Margaret Weymouth Jackson—made the State one of the Nation's leading producers of light fiction. Over a long period of time the novels of Gene Stratton Porter, native Indianian writing chiefly of the Limberlost region of the lake country, surpassed in total sales those of any other writer of her day. In a steady stream of literary confections, the best known of which are *Freckles* (1904) and *The Girl of the Limberlost* (1909), Mrs. Porter presented a sentimental picture of life in an idealized Limberlost. Annie Fellows Johnston was a prolific writer of children's books, of which the Little Colonel series, with its romantic version of Southern plantation life, was the most popular.

Margaret Weymouth Jackson is well known today as an author of light novels and short stories.

Most successful among modern writers in reflecting Indiana life have been Frank McKinney ('Kin') Hubbard, with his penetrating, yet good-humored, sketches and essays, and George Ade, with his lively satires. Born at Bellefontaine, Ohio, in 1868, Hubbard early learned the journalist's trade in the office of the local newspaper, which his father owned. As a sketch artist, he was entirely self-taught. In 1891 he went to work for the Indianapolis *News* as a police reporter and artist. He later successively joined the staffs of the Cincinnati *Commercial Tribune* and the Mansfield (Ohio) *News,* but returned to the Indianapolis *News* in 1901 and remained there until his death in 1930.

While touring Indiana on a campaign train in 1904 he made several sketches of rural characters. Printed in the *News* with a few lines of comment, one of these caught the fancy of the editor, who urged Hubbard to do a series. Christened Abe Martin, Hubbard's rustic philosopher became one of the most beloved characters in American fiction. Collections of these sketches appeared at frequent intervals, beginning with the appearance in 1906 of *Abe Martin, Brown County, Indiana,* and concluding with the publication in 1929 of *Abe Martin's Town Pump.* Hubbard's humor was principally that of indirect allusion, thinly screened by dialect and drawing. Will Rogers, his famous contemporary, maintained: 'No man within our generation was within a mile of him.'

Born near Kentland in 1866, George Ade has spent his life in or near his native State and has devoted his truly extraordinary talents to interpreting it. After his graduation from Purdue in 1887, he worked for several years on newspapers in LaFayette and Chicago. On the staff of the Chicago *Daily News,* he inherited Eugene Field's celebrated column, *Sharps and Flats.* His greatest achievement has been his *Fables in Slang.* Modeled on the old serio-comic form, these were widely syndicated in the press, and first appeared in book form in 1902. In them, he has drawn largely on the Indiana countryside for his characters, portraying them with the sympathy and truth of actual acquaintance. He shares with Hubbard the honor of producing the most authentic portraits yet created of Hoosier life, and with Riley the ability to give a touch of native Hoosier philosophy to his humorous sallies. In his most characteristic work, he satirizes the conceit, pretenses, and follies of that very 'city feller' at whom Riley also poked fun. It happened to be Riley—but it could have been Ade—who attended a solemn art lecture at the John Herron Art Institute. After a long and tiresome definition of art Riley leaned over to a neighbor and grunted: 'Speakin' o' art—I know a fellow over 't Terry Haute 'at kin spit clean over a box car!' The remark was characteristic of both men, even more characteristic of the rural type each understood so well.

Following the success of *Fables in Slang,* Ade turned to the stage, where he achieved a remarkable triumph with *The County Chairman* (1903), *The College Widow* (1904), and other productions in the field of prose comedy and musical satire. Today (1941) he lives the life of a country gentleman at Brook, disputing—although by the will of neither—with Booth Tarkington the place of Grand Old Man of Indiana literature.

Among Indiana's contemporary novelists, the best known are Newton Booth Tarkington and Theodore Dreiser. Born in Indianapolis in 1869, the son of the Honorable John Stevenson Tarkington, Booth Tarkington was reared in the extremely comfortable and genial atmosphere of the upper middle class. His first novel, *The Gentleman from Indiana,* published in 1899, was based, as one of his contemporary novelists, James Branch Cabell, phrased it, on 'the quaint legend that virtue and honest worth must rise inevitably to be the target of both rice-throwing and of respectful consideration of the bank cashier.' When in 1939, at 70, he was hailed the dean of American writers, he had produced 36 novels and collections of short stories, 19 plays and a volume of reminiscences. He has twice won the Pulitzer Prize (in 1919 with *The Magnificent Ambersons,* in 1922 with *Alice Adams*), the only novelist to attain this distinction. He is one of the three fiction writers ever awarded the gold medal of the National Institute of Arts and Letters (the two others having been William Dean Howells and Edith Wharton). He is a member of the American Academy of Arts and Letters.

As a fluent and engaging storyteller, Tarkington has few rivals in American literature. His prose is silken and lucid. He unfailingly shows poetic insight and elfin liveliness of fancy. One fundamental reason for his popularity lies in his warm, friendly attitude toward the basic assumptions of the American middle class. Tarkington's values are those of the Indiana of his boyhood; the Indiana of the Riley era, when families like the Tarkingtons could sit upon their front porches and gaze upon a comfortable region of trim homes, kerosene lamps, plush furniture, and calico dresses.

In his early years Tarkington essayed pure romanticism, producing *Monsieur Beaucaire* (1900) and *Cherry* (1903). Both reveal his lucent style. Both are lightly shot through with satire on the side of the established order, and both are slight and conventional in plot.

When he turned to more realistic themes, Tarkington's attitude was often similar to that of the professional booster. His *In the Arena* (1905), a collection of short stories based upon a term served in the State legislature in his youth, comes close to approving the political *status quo* in its entirety. In the tales of youth, *Penrod* (1914), *Penrod and Sam* (1916), and *Seventeen* (1917), on which so large a part of his fame is based, Tarkington presents a satire on the awkwardness of youth in which its problems are presented as a farce to be enjoyed by those who have passed beyond them.

During the first decades of the twentieth century, Riley paid a weekly visit to the Tarkington home. Although Riley's poetry was frequently discussed, Tarkington's work was never mentioned—Riley did not approve of its portrayals of Indiana. But when *The Flirt*, with its story of the pitiful struggles of middle-class women for prestige, appeared in 1913, Riley made a special visit to offer congratulations.

In the work of Theodore Dreiser, more complex canvases of American life are presented. Born in Terre Haute in 1871, reared in Sullivan, Evansville and Warsaw, this son of a poor German Catholic family was exposed to all the moral sentimentalism and cultural poverty of the hinterland. Disillusionment was bitter and early. His wild young vitality had fed on dreams of success—grandiose dreams of power, luxury, and beautiful women—but he was soon aware of the blind pressure of an environment where success was increasingly difficult, and failure often the portion of the helpless individual. This recognition of almost universal frustration served to purify his own aspirations, lifting them above their crass materialistic level. An equally important influence was his early reading. Herbert Spencer and Thomas Huxley revealed to him a blind, deterministic universe, which he found more awe-inspiring, yet more stimulating to creative effort, than the orderly religious hierarchy of his childhood. Reading Balzac, he was filled with a desire to do for America of the twentieth century what Balzac had done for France of the mid-nineteenth.

Dreiser attended the Indiana public schools, Catholic parochial schools, and, for a brief period, Indiana University. Revisiting his childhood homes in middle life, he wrote *A Hoosier Holiday* (1916), a series of essays, catching in a mood of both nostalgia and critical appraisal, the mellowness of Victorian Indiana and the grimness of the modern industrial State. Its vignette of an Indiana boyhood is one of the most delightful portraits of the Middle West in all literature.

Dreiser's first novel, *Sister Carrie,* was published in 1900. Although it was suppressed for several years in the United States because of alleged 'immorality,' it immediately was hailed in England as a masterpiece of realism by H. G. Wells, Arnold Bennett, Hugh Walpole, and other literary leaders. Eleven years later, Dreiser published *Jennie Gerhardt.* Both were studies of daughters of the people forced into prostitution by economic necessity.

Jennie Gerhardt was followed by *The Financier* (1912) and *The Titan* (1914), the first two volumes of a proposed Trilogy of Desire, which never has been completed. Based on the career of the Chicago and Philadelphia traction magnate, Charles T. Yerkes, they present a massive, somber canvas of the conflicts of individual ambitions and desires among the ruling class. Mr. Dreiser's next novel, *The Genius* (1915), was a portrait of an artist driven by a world in which success is measured primarily by material standards to egomaniacal overestimation of his talent and personal tragedy.

The climax of Mr. Dreiser's career was reached with the publication in 1925 of *An American Tragedy,* a painstaking, detailed study of an average young American of working class origin. As the economic and social problems of the twentieth century became more complex, Mr. Dreiser's tone deepened. In the career of Clyde Griffiths, he traces the whole course of the American tradition of success, presenting Clyde's tragedy as the tragedy of his class, and, by implication, that of all America. Through Dreiser's grim realism, moreover, runs not only a strain of pity but a thin, persistent thread of mysticism; he is often, to quote Lawrence Gilman, 'a sentimental mystic who employs the mimetic gestures of the realist.'

With *An American Tragedy,* he emerged as the most important realistic fiction writer in the United States. He was the first novelist to mirror the changes that industrialism had wrought in America, portraying the era of capitalism as an inevitable outgrowth of events and forces, not as an arbitrary arrangement effected by a few individuals. He paved the way for Sherwood Anderson, John Dos Passos, John Steinbeck, and other American realists.

Some of the most important twentieth-century scholars in the fields of history and sociology were born and brought up in Indiana. In 1924 Robert S. Lynd, a sociologist, returned to his native Indiana to write *Middletown.* Collaborating with his wife, Helen M. Lynd, in this book and its successor, *Middletown in Transition* (1937), he made a candid and penetrating appraisal of Muncie as the 'representative American city.' Among political historians, Albert J. Beveridge and Claude Bowers are notable. Beveridge, for 12 years a member of the United States Senate and for a generation or more the most incisive political thinker in the Republican party, may be remembered longest for his unfinished *Life of Abraham Lincoln* (1928), although his *John Marshall* (1916), winner of the Pulitzer Prize in 1920, is likewise notable. Claude Bowers, editor, orator, and ambassador to Spain under President Franklin D. Roosevelt, has written party history that is also literature in *The Party Battles of the Jackson Period* (1922), *Jefferson and Hamilton* (1925), and *The Tragic Era* (1929). Most distinguished of all, however, is the work of Charles Austin Beard and his wife, Mary Ritter Beard. Their *Rise of American Civilization* (1927) is an outstanding contribution to our national self-knowledge. Other works by Dr. Beard include *An Economic Interpretation of the Constitution* (1913), *The Supreme Court and the Constitution* (1912), and, again in collaboration with Mrs. Beard, *America in Midpassage* (1939).

Among other contemporary novelists, dramatists, essayists and poets born or reared in Indiana are Elmer Davis, Don Herold, Will Cuppy, Kenyon Nicholson, Albert Edward Wiggam, Frederick Austin Ogg, Marjorie Hill Allee, Ernest Kidder Lindley, LeRoy MacLeod, Lloyd Douglas, Max Ehrmann, Marcus Dickey, George Jean Nathan, Louis Ludlow, Bertita Harding, Sister Mary Madaleva, and Lucy Fitch Perkins. Few of these have remained in their native State and fewer still have written of it. Some of the novels of Marjorie Hill Allee deal with the schoolteachers of ante-bellum Indiana. LeRoy MacLeod's *The Years of Peace* (1932) and *The Crowded Hill* (1934) have their setting in the Wabash Valley, and one of Louis Ludlow's best-known books is *In the Heart of Hoosierland* (1925).

Although 'the Indiana group' is a phrase heard often in reference to Hoosier authors, the State's writers have formed no school and followed no single literary trend. Eggleston and Wallace, Riley and Nicholson, Dreiser and Tarkington have little in common beyond the accidental fact of birth in the same State. And Indiana's contribution to the main stream of American literature might, from one point of view, have had greater significance if Hoosier authors had applied their talents more to the problem of interpreting their native State and less to the creation of sentimental fiction. As the twentieth century enters its fifth decade, virtually all of Indiana, from the tranquil life of the southern hills to the lusty industrialism of the Calumet, remains a virgin field for literary interpretation.

Architecture

EXCEPT for rude forts and stockades the earliest buildings in the territory that is now Indiana were those at the French trading post of Vincennes. Most of the inhabitants were trappers and fur traders who had come with their families by water from New Orleans or Quebec. Constantin François Volney, French writer and explorer, who visited there in 1796, said, 'The village contains about 50 houses, whose cheerful white relieves the eye, after the tedious dusk and green of the woods.'

A few of these early houses are still to be found in Vincennes. Most of them were one story high, with a central hall running through from front to rear, and with a wide veranda across the front and a similar one at the back, often overlooking a garden. They were usually built of hewed logs, with the intervening spaces filled with a mortar made of clay and straw. In many, the logs were placed upright instead of parallel to the ground. The walls were often whitewashed with lime made by burning mussel shells that were abundant along the banks of the river. The straight, sloping roofs, gabled at each end, and covered with thatch or hewed shingles, extended over the two long verandas. The larger structures, at the time of Volney's visit, included the blockhouse with its stockade, the little log church of St. Francis Xavier, and the two-story log storehouses of the fur traders, Francis Vigo, Laurient Bazidon, and Lasselle.

Perhaps the first house of consequence in Indiana Territory to be influenced by the Colonial style found along the Atlantic seaboard was the one built at Vincennes by Colonel Francis Vigo, soldier of fortune and fur trader. It was a two-story, white frame house with green shutters and was, at the time of its completion, the most impressive residence in the town. When, in 1801, young William Henry Harrison came to Vincennes, as the first governor of Indiana Territory, he was a guest in this house until he had arranged to build a home for himself.

Harrison's house, which he named Grouseland, is still standing, cared for by the Francis Vigo Chapter of the Daughters of the American Revolution. There is no record of the way in which the plans for this house were made. It was built of brick in the Georgian style characteristic of the country homes with which Harrison had been familiar in his native Virginia. At that time a knowledge of architecture was considered part of the education of a gentleman, and it is probable that Harrison consulted some of the books written by English and American architects for the use of master builders.

Grouseland took more than a year to build, since it was necessary to burn the brick, cut the timber, and even hammer out the nails by hand. When the house was completed, it was surrounded by lawns and gardens that have now been destroyed. It was, for a time, the political and social center of the vast Northwest Territory.

Work was begun in 1825 on the Cathedral of St. Francis Xavier at Vincennes. The plans apparently were adapted from those for the Cathedral at Bardstown, Kentucky, of which it is recorded that John Rogers of Baltimore was both architect and builder. Both of these buildings were constructed under the administration of Bishop Flaget of Bardstown. The Cathedral at Vincennes is built of brick. The interior columns that support the roof, cut from great trees from the surrounding forests, were coated with stucco. The design of the graceful spire, typical of the period, undoubtedly was influenced by the work of Sir Christopher Wren.

After the organization of Indiana as a territory in 1800, many new settlers came down the Ohio, through the Cumberland Gap, and across Tennessee and Kentucky. Most of their early cabins and houses were built of logs of the black walnut, yellow poplar, and other trees common in southern Indiana. Nearly every man was familiar with the use of the saw, ax, adz, and auger. Cabins, taverns, and general stores were built with hewed and squared timbers, lapped or dovetailed at the corner; they had roofs of split shingles and puncheon floors. So substantial was the construction that a number of these buildings are standing today in a good state of preservation. In the Lincoln village at Rockport some of the early log buildings have been reproduced.

About 40 miles down the river from Vincennes the village of Harmonie was established in 1815 by the patriarchal religious leader, George Rapp, and his group of 800 German peasants, as a place where they could develop an ideal communal society. They erected a number of substantial buildings that in their simple design were unlike any

others in Indiana. They probably were influenced by records and recollections of buildings in their fatherland.

Among the buildings still standing are a two-story community house
and a structure designed for storage and protection of grain and other
commodities. The first story of the latter building, sometimes called
the fort, is of stone, while the roof is of tile. It is evident from the
loopholes in the masonry walls that the building was planned for
possible use as a place of defense against hostile Indians or envious
neighbors.

In 1824, when the members of the community moved back to their
former home in Pennsylvania, the Rappite properties were purchased
by Robert Owen and the settlement became known as New Harmony.
The Rapp homestead, which had been partly burned, was rebuilt in a
different style by William Maclure, an associate of Owen. The wide
portico that was added followed in design the classic tendency of the
day, and its columns were turned by hand. This house and other
Rappite buildings are still standing.

In 1813 the Territorial government was moved to Corydon, where
the legislature and the Constitutional Convention of 1816 met in the
Harrison County Courthouse, designed and built by Dennis Pennington.
This square building of blue limestone, now preserved by the State,
shows the influence of books prepared for builders of that period by
capable architects. Without experience or training as an architect, Pennington constructed a building of simple design that is today a credita-
ble example of early American architecture.

In a number of towns that grew up along the National Road there
are interesting specimens of the architectural work of a century and
more ago. At Centerville, houses were built flush with the sidewalks
and close together; they had arched passageways leading to the yards
at the back in much the same manner as many of the homes of that
period in Philadelphia and other Eastern cities.

With the development of river traffic, several important towns grew
up along the Ohio. In Lawrenceburg, Vevay, Rising Sun, Madison,
Jeffersonville, and New Albany, excellent homes and public buildings
were constructed, nearly all of them following American adaptations
of the Georgian style. The Vance house, still preserved at Lawrenceburg, was completed about 1820 for Samuel Vance from plans that had
been brought from England. When this well-designed brick house was
built, it was thought by many to be the finest on the river. There are
also a number of fine homesteads still standing in Vevay, founded by

a group of Swiss settlers. Silver plates on the newel posts at the foot of the stairs in several of these houses record the fact that they were the work of 'George A. Kyle, architect and builder.' Among the homes worthy of note are the Schenck house, the Thiebaud house, and the Craig house, all built of brick in a free translation of the Georgian style.

In Madison, at one time the largest and most prosperous community in the State, are to be found a number of attractive homes built a century or more ago. The brick house built about 1818 for Judge Jeremiah Sullivan has a well-proportioned doorway, with fanlight, sidelights, and a wrought-iron balustrade. It has been photographed and sketched many times. Along the back wing of the house is a two-story open gallery, such as those that characterized many Southern homes of the period.

Many of the Madison houses were designed by Francis Costigan, an architect of unusual ability who received his training in Baltimore and Philadelphia. The house he built in 1844 for James F. D. Lanier, in the manner of the Greek Revival, is one of the finest examples of this style in the Middle West. One notable feature of this house, and of many others in Madison and neighboring towns, is the unusual excellence, in both design and craftsmanship, of the wrought- and cast-iron work used for exterior balconies and railings. At that time a great deal of beautiful iron work was made in Madison and shipped by boat on the river as far south as Louisiana. The Neal foundries, where much of the iron work was made, were among the largest in the United States.

Near the Lanier home is the Shrewsbury house (1846), another gracious residence designed by the same architect. It contains a freestanding spiral stairway that is considered remarkable by builders of today.

Among the early churches in Madison is the Second Presbyterian Church, designed in the Greek Revival manner by Edwin J. Peck. The exterior walls are of brick covered with stucco. The Doric columns, with the pediment and classic cornice, are combined in an effective composition. Other good churches built at about the same time are the well-proportioned Episcopal Church (1835), designed in the English Gothic manner, and St. Michael's Roman Catholic Church (1837–9), a stone building showing Italian influence. An unusual feature of the latter structure is the location of the spire-topped tower at the rear instead of the front.

The courthouse at Madison, designed by David Dubach and built in the 1850's of stone brought up the river from quarries at Marble Hill, is classic in style. This same style of architecture was used for most of the courthouses built in southern Indiana at that time. Many of them have been torn down to make way for larger structures, often less attractive than the ones they replaced. A beautiful example of the older type is the courthouse at Paoli (1849).

In South Bend and Fort Wayne, in the northern part of the State, notable buildings of the mid-nineteenth century are still standing. Most of the old buildings in South Bend, as in other parts of the State, have been demolished, but the former St. Joseph County Courthouse, built in 1854, has been preserved as a home for the Northern Indiana Historical Society. This structure, designed by VanOsdol and Olmsted in the days of the Classic Revival's popularity, is a fine example of the simplicity and dignity of this mode.

West of South Bend, in the little town of New Carlisle, is the Augustine homestead, built in 1834 by Henry Brown, carpenter and cabinet-maker. Squared logs and planks used in the construction are said to have been hauled by ox team from a sawmill many miles away. This house is a faithful reproduction of designs in the Greek Revival manner that were found in the handbooks of the time.

Several good examples of the Georgian and Greek Revival styles of residence architecture, built before the Civil War, are still standing in Fort Wayne. These include the Ewing homestead and the former homes of Hugh McCulloch and Judge Samuel Hanna. Also in Fort Wayne is an unusually fine example of ecclesiastical architecture—Trinity Church (1925) designed by Bertram Goodhue. The dignity of the tower, the outline of the graceful flèche, the harmony of mass and proportion, all combine to show the work of a great artist. In every detail this beautiful sandstone edifice is worthy of careful study.

During the last half of the nineteenth century, the tendency to follow prevailing modes led American—and Indiana—architects into strange vagaries. Improved woodworking machinery and an abundance of fine hardwoods, plus an urge for beauty in people willing to experiment but unschooled in architectural composition, resulted in the spread of the gingerbread style of the Victorian era. This vogue, particularly in domestic architecture, manifested itself in strange and wonderful towers, circular and bay windows, heavy overhanging cornices upheld by scrolled brackets, and porches with turned posts and jigsaw decorations. Examples of the Victorian and the so-called General Grant styles of the 1860's are still found in nearly every Indiana community.

The first public buildings in Indianapolis were little more pretentious than the log cabins of the pioneers, but it was not long until a small brick courthouse was built. It also served as a temporary statehouse, church, and public meeting place until the first statehouse, designed by Ithiel Town, was completed in the 1830's. Town, an architect of ability who had made plans for a number of important buildings in the East, designed this one in the popular style of the day. It followed in a general way the lines of a Greek temple, but was surmounted with a Roman dome.

This original statehouse was eventually replaced by a much larger building, completed in 1888 after nearly ten years' work. The architect, Edwin May, selected as the result of a competition, died within a short time after work was begun, and Adolph Scherer, who had worked with him on the preliminary plans, was chosen as his successor. The design is one of balanced symmetry, in the classic spirit of most State capitols. A feature of the interior is the grand hall, three stories in height, extending the full length of the building.

The elaborate Marion County Courthouse (1876) was built during the ostentatious period that followed the Civil War, when the classic manner was thought to be outmoded. The mansard roof and other features of the design suggest the architectural influence of the French style of the Third Empire. The interior arrangement is inconvenient in many ways, but the building is characteristic of a type popular when it was built.

One of the most important buildings in the Middle West, architecturally speaking, is the Central Library in Indianapolis, for which Paul Cret was the architect. It is described in *Masterpieces of Architecture in the United States* by E. W. Hoak and W. H. Church as follows: 'It almost seems as though the architects thought themselves into the Hellenic spirit, and so expressed themselves. The whole is not only Greek in form but penetratingly Greek in spirit, yet a thoroughly modern building and perfectly adapted to its function.' Mr. Cret also designed the distinguished main building of the John Herron Art School.

The State Library and Historical Building, completed in 1934, is marked by dignity of proportion and simplicity of design. The exterior is of Indiana limestone; richness is given to the interior by the use of St. Meinrad's limestone in variegated colors. The architects were Pierre and Wright.

Christ Church, also in Indianapolis, is surrounded by tall buildings, but the little stone church of English Gothic design is regarded by many as the most charming building in the city. The architect was William Tinsley, born and trained in Ireland, who came to Indiana about 1850. Another attractive Gothic edifice in Indianapolis is the Second Presbyterian Church for which Joseph Curzon was the architect.

The Scottish Rite Cathedral, designed by George F. Schreiber, is an imposing Gothic structure of Indiana limestone. The tower, rising 212 feet, houses a great carillon of 63 bells. Beauty of proportion and richness of detail are attained in the tower by the use of pilasters in receding stages, art glass windows in delicate designs, and by the spacings and forms of the crowning finial.

The desire of the people of Indiana to honor their soldiers and statesmen has been expressed in many forms. Memorial statues, monuments, and buildings are found throughout the State. The most notable of these memorials are the Soldiers and Sailors Monument and the World War Memorial, both in Indianapolis, and the George Rogers Clark Memorial at Vincennes.

The Soldiers and Sailors Monument was erected in 1887–1901. It was designed by Bruno Schmitz, a German architect who won a worldwide contest held by the commission in charge of the Memorial. The graceful outline of the tall, square, tapering shaft, built of ashlar limestone, is a well-known feature of the Indiana capital. On either side are terraced fountains above which are sculptured groups of heroic size, designed and executed by Rudolph Schwartz, and representing scenes of war and peace. Two hundred and fifty feet above the base stands a 38-foot statue of Victory, familiarly referred to by Hoosiers as 'Miss Indiana.'

At the north end of the World War Memorial Plaza, four city squares in length, rests a black granite cenotaph, flanked by fluted columns surmounted by gilded eagles with uplifted wings. It was erected in honor of the first Indiana soldier killed in the World War. In the center of the Plaza stands an obelisk of Berwick black granite 100 feet high and beautiful in proportion, which rests on a base of pink granite and is surrounded by fountain basins of pink Georgia marble. On the sides of the shaft are bronze bas-relief tablets designed by Henry Hering.

The Memorial Shrine itself is an imposing structure of Indiana limestone. The long approach of granite steps, the wide podium entirely surrounding the central tower, the colonnades of Ionic columns, surmounted by symbolic figures, the stepped, pyramidal top—all combine to form a monumental effect.

The George Rogers Clark Memorial at Vincennes is circular in form, nearly 90 feet in diameter and 82 feet high. The impressive peristyle supporting the entablature consists of 16 Doric columns, each 39 feet high and more than 6 feet in diameter. Hirons and Mellor were the architects.

The interior contains a bronze statue of Clark, heroic in size, by the sculptor Hermon A. MacNeil, and seven large murals by Ezra Winter, depicting important scenes in the history of the Northwest Territory. On the grounds surrounding the Memorial are two noteworthy statues: the one of Francis Vigo, carved in granite, facing the river, was executed by John Angell; the bronze figure of Father Gibault near the Cathedral is the work of Albin Polasek.

Buildings on the campuses of Indiana colleges and universities represent many periods and styles. Some were completed more than a century ago. Others are modern structures built chiefly in the 1930's with the aid of PWA grants or private funds.

Among the older buildings are Classic Hall (1853) at Hanover College, located on a site that commands a magnificent view of the Ohio River, and the first little college building at Notre Dame (1834), built when Father Sorin and six Brothers of the Congregation of Holy Cross came to the Mission at Saint Mary's Lake.

All of the new buildings on the campus at Indiana University are built of limestone obtained from the famous quarries a few miles away. Among them are the Union Building and the new Administration Building, both of which were designed by Granger and Bollenbacher. Other well-designed buildings, for which A. M. Strauss was the architect, are the new Medical Building (1936), the School of Business (1939), and the Physical Science Building, known as Swain Hall (1939). All are in the collegiate Gothic style. The impressive new auditorium (1939) was also designed by Mr. Strauss, with Eggers and Higgins as associates. Five well-planned residence halls, built at Indiana University in the late 1930's, were designed by Burns and James.

The extensive building program that has been carried on at Purdue University since 1933 includes a group of five residence halls for men and three halls for women. These were designed in the collegiate Gothic manner. The large new Music Hall (1940), in which more than 2,000 people may be seated, is in the Renaissance style, as are the laboratory and classroom buildings of the departments of chemical engineering, mechanical engineering, electrical engineering, physics, and others. All of these were designed by Walter Scholer.

A new building of modified classic design has been constructed at the Indiana State Teachers College, Terre Haute, to house the departments of fine arts and commerce, as well as an impressive Student Union Building of collegiate Gothic design. The architects for these buildings were Miller and Yeager.

Several new buildings of modified Gothic style, designed by George F. Schreiber, have been built in recent years on the campus of Ball State Teachers College at Muncie. These include the Arts Building, Frank Elliott Ball Residence Hall, and Lucina Hall.

The main building of the University of Notre Dame, at the end of a broad avenue nearly a mile in length, housed all of the activities of the college for many years. It is built of pale yellow brick made from clay found near the St. Joseph River. The great metal dome, overlaid with gold leaf, is surmounted by a statue of the Blessed Virgin. The architect for this building was W. J. Edbrooke. The university church, which is nearly 300 feet long, was built of the same brick as the main building, with trim of Joliet limestone. In the tower is a carillon which is one of the oldest in the United States.

Butler University at Indianapolis has as its main building Jordan Hall, which is actually three separate buildings combined into one by passages through the towers. In this structure the architects, Daggett and Hibben, have used a modern treatment of collegiate Gothic in soft-toned granite that has weathered to a beautiful gray. A number of buildings of early American design have been built within recent years at DePauw University. Other private schools and colleges have constructed some noteworthy buildings, including the new Chapel at Wabash and new dormitories at Hanover.

PART II
Principal Cities

↑↑↑

Cities of the Calumet

The Cities of the Calumet—Gary, Hammond, East Chicago, Whiting—with a population of 250,000, have in little more than two decades become one of the world's greatest industrial centers. Perhaps nowhere else in the Nation is there such concentration of diversified industry in an area of similar size (70 square miles).

Lying in the most northwesterly county of Indiana, the Calumet area follows the curve of Lake Michigan for 16 miles. Through the region flow two branches of a sluggish river that the French called Calumet. A profusion of reeds used by the Indians for pipestems grew along this river so that the name Calumet is thought to have originated from the French *chalumeau* (little reed). Through usage *calumet* came to mean 'pipe with a reed stem.'

The romance of the growth of this region has been publicized the world over, and this amazing exhibition of modern industry at work attracts thousands of visitors annually. No writer concerned with the urban development of America has been able to omit Gary from his consideration. Whether his interest has been sociological, economic, or industrial, Gary, and in fact the entire Calumet region, has lain squarely across his path.

In 1905 the total population of the Calumet region was 19,000. Gary did not exist, Whiting and East Chicago were little more than villages, and Hammond, oldest of the group, had a population of 12,000. Today (1941) the population numbers 250,000, of which 8 per cent are Negro and 20 per cent foreign-born. In 1905 more than half of this area was swamp, swale, and sand dunes, uninhabited and uninviting. Today it presents a massing of four modern cities with a multiplicity of industries, a maze of paved motorways, and a huge network of railroad tracks.

Industry dominates the entire region. There are 175 major and minor factories, including giant steel and rail mills, cement plants, one of the largest soap-manufacturing factories in the country, oil refineries, and enormous electric generating units. Manufactured products have an annual value of more than $600,000,000. About 73,000 persons are employed, and the yearly pay roll approximates $83,000,000. Three commercial harbors serve 15,000,000 tons of water-borne world-traffic annually.

This industrial panorama is striking by day and beautiful by night. Broken only by three small parks, the 16-mile crescent of the lake shore, from the Illinois Line on the west to the eastern edge of Gary, is a continuous array of manufacturing plants. In sections of Hammond and East Chicago, factories hug the water front and sprawl southward into these cities. Over the entire district are the smoke of the steel mill, the smell of the oil refinery, and the glow of the blast furnace. Always there is the clang of forge, the roar of wheels, and the thunder of dumping slag.

Column after column of stacks pour forth steamy white or heavy black smoke. Giant steel towers supporting high-tension cables stride over the region. Great gas reservoirs move imperceptibly up and down in huge steel frameworks. Cranes, oil distilleries, collieries, and giant factories stand silhouetted against the sky. Hundreds of oil tanks, silver gray or oyster gray, dot the area like mammoth mushrooms.

Barrack-like buildings of gray corrugated iron blend into the monochrome. Freight engines weave in and out with long strings of cars. Great banks of coal lie waiting for blazing furnaces. Bridges lift over the ship canal so that steamers and ore boats may pass. Everywhere in the composite of movement and noise thousands of workers hurry in and out. The only variations in the whole smoky, busy picture are occasional administrative, laboratory, or hospital buildings of brick, surrounded by small landscaped plots.

At night, myriads of lights outline shafts, tanks, and framework. Flames from open-hearth furnaces light the sky for miles. Black smoke gathers into clouds. It was of this picture that Carl Sandburg wrote in *Smoke and Steel:*

Ears and noses of fire, gibbering gorilla arms of fire, gold mud pies, gold bird wings, red jackets riding purple mules, scarlet autocrats tumbling from the humps of camels, assassinated czars straddling vermilion balloons;
I saw then the fires flash one by one: good-by: then smoke, smoke . . .

Realizing that it is without the background of age, the Calumet region exploits its industrial pre-eminence. Visitors are told of the complete topographical transformation necessary before either house or factory could be built. Building was an engineering feat that involved all the new methods in wet excavation, drainage, building caissons and floating foundations, and 'making land.'

Residents draw attention to the fact that this area was the birthplace of refrigeration for the transportation of dressed meat, of large-scale utilization of by-products, and of the use of electricity as driving power in a large steel mill. They point to the crude oil pipe line from the mid-continental oil fields which has its northern terminal here. They tell visitors that some of the longest bridges in the world, steel rails, gasoline, oil, antifreeze compound, and steel frames and tops for automobiles are manufactured here as well as cement for the highways upon which automobiles are driven. The show places are the massive industrial plants. Instead of a museum the stranger is shown a bridge spanning 67 railroad tracks or an insect farm where bedbugs, flies, and roaches are bred scientifically to test the efficiency of insect sprays.

In development this region is only as old as its oldest industry, but for those who look beneath the surface of the present there is the echo of things past. Marquette and Louis Joliet passed through here in 1673 and for an unrecorded period it was a Potawatomi hunting ground. Later, the flags of France, Great Britain, and the United States waved in succession over these dunes and swamplands.

The Cities of the Calumet are an industrial and geographical unit. Their city limits are contiguous. Physically they merge so completely that those who have lived here for 30 years often do not know where the city limits are. Many of the industries are related and in some cases interdependent. Highway, park, and city planning is done in co-operation with the Chicago Regional Planning Commission. However, socially and municipally, the cities are separate, each with its own residential districts, schools, civic buildings, and park systems. Each is an administrative entity and each has a distinctive social structure.

Gary

Railroad Stations: Union Depot, 3d Ave. and Broadway, for New York Central R.R. and Baltimore & Ohio R.R. (suburban stations, Clarke, and two points on Lake St.); W. 5th Ave. and Chase St. for Pennsylvania R.R. (suburban station, Broadway and 21st Ave.); 1045 Broadway for Michigan Central R.R.; 9th Ave. and Broadway for Wabash R.R.; Broadway and 40th Ave. for Nickel Plate R.R.; 330 Broadway for South Shore & South Bend R.R. (electric).
Bus Stations: Gary Union Bus Depot, 470 Broadway, for Indian Trails, Greyhound Lines, Bluebird Lines, Southern Limited, Shore Line Motor Coach; Gary Trailways Bus Depot, 477 Broadway, for Lincoln Trail System, Santa Fe Trails, Yankee Trailways, DeLuxe Motor Stages, Empire Trails.
Airports: None. Gary Travel Bureau, 470 Broadway, books passage over all air lines using Chicago Airport.
Taxis: 35¢ first mile or fraction thereof, 20¢ per mile thereafter.
Streetcars: Gary Railways Co. maintains city and interurban service. City service, cars every 6 min. on Broadway, transfers E. and W. at 5th Ave. and 11th Ave.; fare 5¢ within certain zones, 10¢ to city limits, tokens, three for 25¢. Gary to Hammond, 30-min. service, fare 20¢. Bus lines connect with streetcars by transfer for Miller, Crown Point, Hobart, East Chicago, Garyton.
Traffic Regulations: Usual traffic regulations; curb parking permitted. Time restrictions indicated by signs. Public parking lots, 5th Ave. and Massachusetts St., 7th Ave. and Massachusetts St., 8th Ave. and Washington St., 5th Ave. and Madison St. No one-way streets. Left-hand turns permitted except on Broadway.
Street Order and Numbering: City laid out on rectilinear system with unbroken uniformity. Hub of city, Broadway and 5th Ave.; streets running N. and S. parallel to Broadway, on W. side named after presidents of the United States in order of service; on E. side named after States of the Union in order of admission to Union. E. and W. thoroughfares termed avenues; numbered from one, going S. Numbering of streets starts from Broadway and First Ave.

Accommodations: 34 hotels.

Information Service: General information, Gary Commercial Club and Chamber of Commerce, Gary Hotel, Broadway and 6th Ave. Social information Y.M.C.A., 5th Ave. and Adams St. Road information, Chicago Motor Club, 916 W. 5th Ave.

Theaters and Motion Picture Houses: Civic Theater, 2323 W. 11th Ave., and Dunes Theater, Hemlock and Lake Sts. offer seasonal performances. In Memorial Auditorium, 29 E. 7th Ave., the Gary Concert Guild sponsors performances by nationally known artists and the Gary Municipal Choral Society presents cantatas and other musical programs. 10 motion picture houses.

Radio Station: WIND (560 kc.).

Swimming: Gary Municipal Bathing Beach, modern bathhouse, life guards, pavilion, parking areas, picnic grounds, etc., in Marquette Park on Lake Michigan.

Fishing: Streams and lakes near by well stocked with fish; license required.

Athletics: Baseball, football, Gleason Park, S. on Broadway to 35th Ave.

Tennis: Public courts, Gleason Park.

Golf: Municipal course, Gleason Park, 18 holes, greens fee 25¢.

Shooting: Municipal Gun Club, rifle range in Marquette Park.

Recreation such as bowling, indoor tennis, basketball, etc., at Y.M.C.A. and K. of C. club-hotel.

Annual Events: Gary Independent Basketball Tourney, automobile show, Jan.; Golden Gloves Boxing Tournament, Feb.; Indiana High School Basketball Tourney, sectional, Mar.; South Shore Music Festival, May; amateur golf tourney, June; Art Salon presentation, the *Messiah,* by Gary Municipal Chorus, Dec.

GARY (613 alt., 111,719 pop.), key city of the Calumet and site of the United States Steel Corporation's Midwest plant, is the youngest metropolis in the country having a population of more than 100,000. Twelve parks (one a scenic dune area on the lake front), a well-planned system of boulevards, a certain architectural distinction in its churches, libraries, and civic buildings, and its internationally known school system give an undeniable individuality to Gary.

The hub of the city is the intersection of Broadway and Fifth Avenue, the latter the continuation of US 12 and US 20 through Gary. In the downtown section Fifth Avenue is zoned for business; in the outlying district it is lined with modern homes and apartment buildings.

Another line of demarcation is the Wabash Railway tracks, paralleling Ninth Avenue. Since the beginning of the city, 'south of the tracks' has meant differentiation. In this section are congested foreign centers, shops, taverns, and drab homes. Here too live most of Gary's 18,000 Negroes, although segregation is largely self-imposed. This melting pot of race, creed, and color has its own residential distinctions, its parks and racial centers—the Union Español, Sokol Hall, Centro Español, and the like. It has schools and libraries, and many of the churches are patterned after those of other lands. Bizarre shops and markets, and signs and advertisements in many tongues give to this section almost an Old World atmosphere.

The plants of the steel corporation are separated from the rest of the city by the Grand Calumet River and the embankments of several railroad lines. The mills lie along the lake, the houses of the workers extending southward into the town. Between 20,000 and 30,000 persons pass in and out daily through the plant's four entrances, on foot, in special streetcars, in busses, and in automobiles.

Thousands of the city's foreign-born have been naturalized, and many are leaders in social and industrial life. In helping the foreign-born to adapt themselves to American ways, the International Institute and numerous settlement houses in the city have been of primary importance. More than half of the work of the Institute, which is affiliated with the National Institute of Immigrant Welfare, has to do with assisting persons who wish to be naturalized.

The large Negro population, for the most part, has adjusted itself to living in a northern industrial city. Notwithstanding the hardships imposed by the depression, especially upon those who were employed in heavy industries, the people have responded admirably to rehabilitation work. School facilities for Negroes are excellent, and many members of the race have succeeded in business and the professions. Negroes maintain a hotel, two theaters, two hospitals, a social center, a Y.M.C.A., and a weekly newspaper. An outstanding development of Gary Negroes' increasing sense of self-reliance is the organization of a co-operative.

The Gary school system, inaugurated by the late Dr. William Wirt, has won attention from educators everywhere. In the United States his system has been widely copied, and the schools of Gary are visited annually by many foreign and American educators and sociologists. The basic idea is to wean the child from the streets, and attach him to the school by making it the more attractive of the two. Summer school is optional, but has a surprisingly large attendance. The child's day is divided into periods of work, study, and play. Training includes shopwork, sewing, cooking, helping in the cafeterias, and school management. The playgrounds have unusual features such as lagoons, small zoos, and aviaries, which are open during the daylight hours. At night the buildings are used for night school sessions and weekly community programs, and for student dances and· other social events. (Permission to visit the schools may be obtained at the offices of principals.)

The community church school, which has been widely adopted throughout the United States, originated in the Gary schools. Each child whose parents express in writing the desire to have him enrolled attends a daily church school class for a required period. Classes are divided into Protestant, Jewish, and Catholic units, and the religious organizations of the city provide instruction.

In Gary the relation between capital and labor has on the whole developed along peaceful and, until lately, paternalistic lines. Elbert H. Gary contributed to every church, hospital, and civic or fraternal building erected in the city during his lifetime. Within the plants he provided better sanitary conditions, opportunities to buy stock on easy payments, and loans to buy houses. Under his leadership, the corporation set aside $8,000,000, to which Andrew Carnegie added $4,000,000, for pensioning employees who had reached retirement age (55 for women, 65 for men) and who had been in the corporation's service for 25 years.

The most noteworthy break in industrial peace was the Gary and East Chicago phase of the Nation-wide steel strike called in August 1919 under the leadership of the A. F. of L. Gary became front-page news. General Leonard Wood and 1,500 United States Regulars were called in. A peak of 350,000 strikers throughout the Nation was reached in October 1919, and Youngstown, Cleveland, Johnstown, and Wheeling were affected. Seeing no hope of victory, labor leaders ended the strike in January 1920; the strikers returned to work apparently without having won a single concession. But the strike had dramatized the evils of the 12- and 16-hour day, and by September 1922 the 8-hour day was in effect in Gary and in 97 per cent of the other plants of the steel corporation.

From that time until April 1937, the Gary mills functioned under an employee representation plan, which was a branch of the Industrial Relations Department of the corporation. However, on April 1, 1937, a contract was signed with the Committee for Industrial Organization, and the company unions were disbanded.

The early history of Gary is a story of industrial pioneering. 'It has been decided to construct and put in operation a new plant to be located on the south shore of Lake Michigan in Calumet Township, Lake County, Indiana, and a large acreage of land has been purchased for that purpose.' This conservatively worded statement of Judge Elbert H. Gary, for whom the city was later named, appeared in the annual report of the United States Steel Corporation for 1905.

Of all the tracts in the Calumet region the one selected by the steel corporation was the most desolate. Wholly uninhabited, it was an area of sloughs, sand dunes, and small streams, crossed by a meandering river and several trunk line railroads. However, almost overnight the new steel plant and a new city were in the making. The mill site was elevated an average of 15 feet by pumping material from Lake Michigan through huge suction pipes and spreading it over a wide irregular terrain; towering hills of sand were pulled down into the sloughs and valleys, a whole river was picked up and carried 100 yards and then set down again; a water tunnel extending 2 miles from the Jefferson Park powerhouse to the Lake Michigan shore line, and an additional mile into the lake, was constructed 95 feet underground. Three railroad right-of-ways were relocated. The region was a wilderness of chilling winds, and driving sand so deep that a quarter-mile walk was exhausting. The population during the first few years was mostly male—young huskies who went about 'encased in thick sweaters' and lumber jackets. In 1907 the town consisted of a long, narrow street of shacks 'engulfed in white sand from one building line to the other.'

The Gary Land Company took over this crude camp and erected the city of Gary. It was obvious that the city would expand as the steel plant grew, and the steel corporation purchased practically all the land contiguous to the plant—some 7,000 acres—and platted the town according to the best principles of municipal design and zoning. A water system capable of supplying a city of 200,000 was installed, miles of streets were paved, gas mains and sidewalks were laid, and electrical facilities were provided.

Grass would not grow in the sand, so trainloads of black soil were brought in. Trees and shrubs were planted and two thoroughfares, Broadway and Fifth Avenue, each 100 feet wide, were graded and paved. In order to avoid rows of identical houses, common to most industrial cities, architects were instructed to draw up diversified plans. Lots were offered by the company with the stipulation that a certain class of houses be erected within 18 months. The 500 houses under construction in 1907 were for sale only to employees of the steel company, at cost. Employees were permitted to rent, but were encouraged in every possible way to buy.

With the United States Steel Corporation as a magnet, other industries were soon attracted to the site. Important subsidiaries of Republic Steel (the Union Drawn Steel Plant), the Standard Steel Spring Company, and the Pittsburgh Screw and Bolt Corporation were building factories in Gary before long. Other industries today include the Bear Brand Hosiery Mills, and the Anderson Company, manufacturing windshield wipers and similar devices.

Architecturally, Gary's business section, despite its brief life, has had three distinct periods. The first was that of the tar-paper shack. From 1908 to 1921 these shacks were gradually replaced by more ambitious structures, many of stone or brick, and by 1921 the general picture was that of a small but thriving metropolis. In that year the city began a complete architectural renaissance. Though the oldest structures were hardly 20 years old, civic buildings, churches, banks, and hotels were razed and the buildings of today were substituted. There are as yet (1941) no skyscrapers in Gary, but many 10- and 12-story modern office structures accent the skyline.

POINTS OF INTEREST

(Points of interest in the Cities of the Calumet are numbered consecutively, beginning with Gary)

1. MARQUETTE PARK, Grand Blvd. between Hemlock and Montgomery Sts., bordering Lake Michigan at the eastern limits of Gary, is dedicated to the memory of Père Jacques Marquette, French Jesuit missionary and explorer, who passed through this region in 1673. Standing in a landscaped area is a heroic-sized bronze STATUE OF MARQUETTE, which depicts him advancing, holding aloft the Cross. The park, a 133-acre tract, has excellent bathing and other recreational facilities.

2. The PUBLIC LIBRARY (*open 9-9 weekdays, 2-6 Sun. and holidays*), 220 W. 5th Ave., contains a large collection of books of interest to steel workers, most of them for readers with less than high school education. There is also an excellent metallurgical reference library.

3. The CARNEGIE-ILLINOIS STEEL PLANT (*open 9-5 weekdays May-Oct.; conducted tours*), on the lake front N. of 3rd Ave., covers 1,400 acres. By day piercing the sky with tall chimneys, towering der-

ricks and massive buildings, it is outlined against the sky at night by fantastic flames and myriad lights. This plant has broken many records for quantity and economy in the production of steel. Nearly 12,000 persons, with an annual pay roll of $25,000,000, are employed in normal times. Twelve blast furnaces have a capacity of 300,000 tons a month, and 52 open hearths have a capacity of 13,000 tons daily. The electrically driven rail mill, largest in the country, has a yearly production of 900,000 tons of rail. The plant is served within its borders by 260 miles of railroads and 30 miles of improved roads. A coke plant, including 976 by-product coke ovens, using 613,000 tons of coal monthly, produces 440,000 tons of coke per month and about 225,000,000 cubic feet of gas per day. Other departments of this giant plant are the billet mill, plate mills, axle and wheel mills, 13 merchant mills, laboratories, a hospital, a restaurant, schools, welfare centers, and electrical department. In the last named, power is generated for all mill requirements, for subsidiary companies in Gary, the Buffington works, and the city of Gary. This plant is one of the most important in 'Big Steel.'

4. The AMERICAN SHEET AND TIN PLATE PLANT (*open 9–5 weekdays May-Oct.; conducted tours*), Buchanan St. and the lake shore, occupying 376 acres on the lake front, in 1938 was said to be the world's largest sheet and tin mill. The tin mill is equipped with a 42-inch hot strip mill that has an annual capacity of 500,000 gross tons. The cold reduction department has a five-stand tandem with an annual capacity of 350,000 gross tons. There are in each unit two 20-inch forged steel, motor-driven rolls; two 49-inch cast steel backing-up rolls; and two large cast housings to support the four rolls. These units, called stands, are placed in series of five, in tandem, the strip being reduced about 30 per cent as it passes through each unit. The hot mills produce about 184,000 gross tons of steel products in the lighter gauges. Combined production of the cold reduction units is about 500,000 gross tons annually. About 1,500,000 sheets of tin are produced daily, running in thickness down to about a fourth that of a sheet of bond paper.

The sheet mill has an 80-inch hot strip mill with an annual capacity of 750,000 gross tons, a cold reduction mill with an annual capacity of 500,000 gross tons, and other hot mills capable of producing about 175,000 gross tons annually. A 90-inch continuous hot strip mill placed in service in March 1936 has a rated capacity of 60,000 tons per month, but has on many occasions exceeded this output. This plant is a subsidiary of the U. S. Steel Corporation and employs 11,500 persons.

5. The UNIVERSAL ATLAS PORTLAND CEMENT PLANT (*open by arrangement*), end of Cline Ave. at the lake shore, is a subsidiary of the U. S. Steel Corporation, manufacturing more than 20,250,000 barrels of cement annually. About 600 persons are employed. Basic materials used are limestone screenings, granulated blast furnace slag,

and gypsum. The plant has a private harbor, the basin of which has an area of 56 acres enclosed by two piers, one 1,800 feet long and the other 1,950 feet long. On the shore is a 30-acre, 1,000,000-ton storage yard for limestone. An electrically operated bridge, 633 feet long, facilitates boat unloading, and an electrically operated belt conveyor carries limestone from the dock to the plant at the rate of six tons per minute. The mouth of the harbor is guarded by a government approved lighthouse.

POINTS OF INTEREST IN ENVIRONS

Indiana Dunes State Park, 15 *m*. (*see Tour 2*).

Hammond

Railroad Stations: 423 Sibley St. for Erie R.R., Chesapeake & Ohio Ry., and Monon R.R.; 475 Plummer St. for Michigan Central R.R.; 5310 Oakley Ave. for Nickel Plate R.R.; 4601 Hohman Ave. for Wabash Ry.; 4531 Hohman Ave. for South Shore & South Bend R.R. (electric).

Bus Stations: Union Bus Depot, 5036 Hohman Ave., for Northern Trails, Bluebird Lines, DeLuxe Lines, Empire Trailways, Santa Fe Trails, Yankee Trailways; Hammond Bus Depot, 5035 Hohman Ave., for All American Lines; Greyhound Bus Station, 4919 Hohman Ave., for Greyhound Lines, Southern Limited, Indian Trails, Bluebird Coach Lines, Gold Star Lines; Central Bus Station, 147 State St., for Shore Lines, Blue Motor Coach Lines; Schappi Line Depot (interurban), Hohman at Plummer Ave.

Airports: None. Lansing Field of Ford Airplane System 10 m. SW. of Hammond; municipal airport at Chicago, 20 m. NW.

Taxis: 25¢ first mile or fraction thereof, 15¢ for each additional mile.

Streetcars: Gary Street Railways operates cars between Hammond and Gary on a 30-min. schedule, fare 20¢; city fare 8¢. Free transfers from Gary Street Ry. to Shore Line bus lines for city service.

Street Order and Numbering: Numbering for E. and W. streets begins at Indiana-Illinois State Line, continuing the system of Chicago to the eastern limits, such as 150th, 160th, etc. There are a few named streets in business districts. N. and S. streets numbered from Columbia Ave., even numbers on W. side of streets, numbers 1000 to the block. Hence, the SW. corner of Columbia Ave. and 160th St. is 16,000 Columbia Ave., abbreviated through local usage to 6000 Columbia Ave.

Accommodations: 9 hotels.

Information Service: Hammond Chamber of Commerce, 423 Fayette St.; Chicago Motor Club, A.A.A. branch office, 5444 Hohman Ave.

Theaters and Motion Pictures Houses: Orak Shrine Auditorium, 45 Muenich Court, used for concerts, lectures, etc.; 7 motion picture houses.

Radio Stations: WHIP (1520 kc.); WJOB (1230 kc.).

Golf: Wicker Park, on Hammond's southern boundary (take Hohman Ave. to 165th St., R. from 165th St. on Wicker Ave. to park), 18 holes, 9 holes, greens fee Mon.-Fri. 25¢, Sat. and Sun. 50¢.

Swimming: Lake front, beach on Lake Michigan, no charge for use of bathhouse, 25¢ parking charge; swimming beach on Wolf Lake; modern swimming pool in Harrison Park.

HAMMOND (598.5 alt., 70,184 pop.) is in the extreme northwest corner of the Calumet region and merges with Chicago on Indianapolis Boulevard. The Grand Calumet River traverses the city from east to west, and Wolf Lake is partly within the corporate limits. The width of a street separates Hammond from Calumet City, Illinois, and it is only two blocks from the dividing line to the heart of Hammond's business district, at State Street and Hohman Avenue. When Calumet City was incorporated in 1893, nine years after Hammond was advanced to the rank of city, the effect was to place a part of what was considered Hammond proper in a city of another State. There are few landmarks in Hammond reminiscent of the past. A network of railway tracks in the downtown commercial district dominates the scene, cutting diagonally through the principal streets. Traffic in the shopping district often waits for a train to pass.

A slaughterhouse, built in 1869, was the beginning of industry in Hammond. Now (1941) there are 94 manufacturing establishments, with an annual output valued at more than $71,000,000. Hammond factories employ approximately 4,600 persons and have a total annual pay roll of $4,500,000. They produce such articles as corn syrup and allied products, railway supplies and equipment, hospital and surgical supplies, tile roofing, dairy products, cold-drawn steel, car wheels, forgings, candy, chains, steel fabrics, casting and tanks. Other industrial activities are printing and bookbinding. About 85 per cent of the population is native white; the foreign-born are mostly Germans and Poles.

Previously called Hohman for an early settler, then State Line, because of its geographical location on the Indiana-Illinois Line, Hammond was finally named in honor of George H. Hammond, a Detroit butcher, founder of the local slaughterhouse and originator of refrigeration of dressed beef for shipment. When the Davis brothers, of Detroit, invented a refrigerator box to ship fish in good condition from Lake Huron and Lake Superior to Detroit, it occurred to Hammond that dressed beef might be transported in the same way, with great economy as compared to the old method of shipping live cattle. He organized a company and in 1869 bought the site where the original slaughterhouse was erected. Hammond died in 1886 and an English syndicate purchased the packing plant from his widow for $6,000,000.

With the establishment of the packing plant, butchers, carpenters, and laborers came to the community. The coming of the Erie and Nickel Plate Railroads in 1882 and the Monon in 1883 helped to develop Hammond. As a result it was incorporated as a city in 1884, and by 1900 it was a lively city of 12,000. In 1901 the packing plant was destroyed by fire, and thousands of families moved away. However, in 1903 and 1904 other factories began to arrive and Hammond again expanded, new factories being built even during the panic of 1907. The industrial growth of the entire Calumet region has contributed to the increased importance of this city since 1910.

POINTS OF INTEREST

6. The CONKEY PRINTING PLANT (*open 8–5 weekdays; guides*), 601 Conkey Ave., is a large printing and bookbinding establishment with an annual output of more than 15,000,000 books, exclusive of pamphlets and catalogues. The plant covers 14 acres, employs 600 persons, and has a capacity of 40,000 bound volumes a day.

7. The LEVER BROTHERS PLANT (*open 8–5 weekdays; guides*), 1271 Indianapolis Blvd., is a 5-story soap manufacturing plant, employing 500 persons. This is a branch of Lever Bros., Port Sunlight, Cheshire, England.

8. The AMERICAN MAIZE PRODUCTS PLANT (*open 8–5 weekdays; guides*), 113th St. at Roby, is a large producer of salad oil, starch, corn syrup and sugars, and a variety of other by-products of corn. On a 100-acre site, 18 buildings cover approximately 50 acres. About 500,000 bushels of corn are used monthly and 11,000,000 gallons of water flow daily through the mains of this plant—enough to supply a city of 60,000 persons.

9. The PUBLIC LIBRARY (*open 9–9 weekdays, 2–5 Sun., except in July and Aug.*), Hohman St. and Michigan Ave., contains a general collection, and books of special interest to steel and petroleum workers and chemists.

East Chicago

Railroad Stations: Michigan Ave. and Guthrie Sts. for Pennsylvania R.R.; Regent and Watling Sts. for New York Central R.R. and Baltimore & Ohio R.R.; 819 Chicago Ave. for South Shore & South Bend R.R. (electric).
Docks: Port of Indiana Harbor; industries have wharves along canal; ocean passenger service between East Chicago and European ports from East Chicago Dock Terminal.
Bus Stations: Harbor Bus Depot, 3448 Guthrie St., for Greyhound Lines, DeLuxe Lines, Great Eastern Lines. All bus lines leaving Chicago for points east pass through either East Chicago or Hammond.
Airports: None. Region served by municipal airport in Chicago, about 20 m. distant.
Taxis: 25¢ first ⅓ mile, 5¢ each additional ⅓ mile.
Street Order and Numbering: E. and W. streets begin numbering at the western boundary of the city, where it adjoins Hammond, continuing thus to eastern boundary, adjacent to Gary. N. and S. streets take their numbering from the Chicago system.

Accommodations: 19 hotels; tourist homes and rooming houses.

Information Service: Chamber of Commerce, 4618 Magoun Ave.; Chicago Motor Club, 4815 Indianapolis Blvd.

Motion Picture Houses: 8.
Swimming: Public bathing beach on Lake Michigan; wading pools for children in city parks.
Golf: Wicker Park course (*see Hammond*), maintained by all cities of North Township, 9 and 18 holes, greens fees Mon.-Fri. 25¢, Sat. Sun. 50¢.

Parks: Todd Park, Indianapolis Blvd. and Columbus Drive; Washington Park, which houses the only zoo in the Calumet District.

EAST CHICAGO (610 alt., 54,637 pop.) is only 11 square miles in area, of which one square mile is 'made land.' Adjoining Gary on the east and Whiting and Hammond on the northwest and southwest, hemmed in on the north by Lake Michigan and on the south by swamps and dune lands, it is the most distant from farmland of all the Indiana cities. Nowhere else in the Calumet region is there such a dense concentration of industries, including steel works, blast furnaces, and coke ovens; rolling mills and petroleum refineries; chemical and packing house by-product establishments; railway car and equipment shops; lead, zinc, oxide aluminum, gypsum, silver and gold bullion works; steel fabricating and tin plate mills. These industries, which reach into the inland sections of the city, flank Lake Michigan, the Indiana Harbor Ship Canal, and the Grand Calumet River.

East Chicago is divided into two distinct business and residential centers. One, along the shore of Lake Michigan, is commonly referred to as Indiana Harbor; and the other, about two miles southwest, centering about the intersection of Chicago and Forsythe Avenues, is usually known as 'East Chicago proper.'

Indiana Harbor consists of an outer harbor and an inner channel (Indiana Harbor Canal) to the Grand Calumet River and Lake George, 4.7 miles long. Government figures show water-borne commerce approximating 5,000,000 tons annually. Ocean as well as lake vessels arrive and depart from the port, which has more than five miles of wharves and is served by trunk and belt line railroads, an electric railway, local and through bus lines, and motorized highway freight carriers. Principal imports are iron ore, coal, limestone, gypsum rock, wood pulp from Baltic ports, and palm oil from Africa. The bulk of this freight is for the Youngstown Sheet and Tube Company and the Inland Steel Company, both of which maintain extensive docks, and for the United States Gypsum Company. Leading exports are steel products, gasoline, kerosene, and fuel oils, heavy shipments being made by Shell, Sinclair, Cities Service, Standard Oil (Ind.), and Socony-Vacuum. The value of the petroleum commerce alone exceeds $40,000,000 each year.

East Chicago has extensive school, church, library, and park systems. With the exception of the Federal building, however, and a few business and school structures, both its residential and business sections are dingy in appearance. Industry rules, and the dirt, according to East Chicago citizens, is 'pay dirt.' About 25 per cent of the population is foreign-born—mostly Poles, Czechs, Yugoslavs, Hungarians, and Rumanians—and there has been little intermarriage with native stock. There are about 5,000 Negroes and nearly the same number of Mexicans.

Almost contemporary with the beginning of East Chicago was the advent of the Standard Oil Company in Whiting, where the Rockefeller interests built the world's largest complete oil refinery in 1889. This plant later was extended into East Chicago. During its first dozen years East Chicago grew slowly. Incorporated as a town in 1889, it had 1,255 inhabitants in 1890; by 1900 the population had reached only 3,411.

However, America's industrial growth had created a constantly expanding demand for steel. When in 1901 Block Brothers built a small steel mill here, the lonely, unsettled Indiana Harbor sand dunes to the north of East Chicago suddenly came to life. Since the company needed a harbor to obtain ore shipments by water, work was begun in 1903 on the Indiana Harbor and Ship Canal. By 1928 the first mill had expanded to 100 times its original size; today (1941) this concern, now the Inland Steel Company, employs more than 10,500 men.

After the first steel mill was built, related industries soon followed, chief among them the American Steel Foundries and the Standard Forgings Company. At this time, also, East Chicago still housed the employees of the Universal Atlas Portland Cement plant, erected just over the line in the still unborn city of Gary. In 1916 the Youngstown Sheet and Tube Company, employing 5,500 persons, started a factory in East Chicago. From a population of 19,000 in 1910, the city grew to almost 55,000 in 1930.

The development of the automobile industry during the last two decades accounts for much of the expansion in the steel business, and has also made East Chicago an important petroleum refining district. The five refineries in this area have a daily crude oil cracking capacity of 190,000 barrels and employ some 7,000 persons.

A strike in June 1937 in the Youngstown Sheet and Tube and Inland Steel plants disrupted the progress of collective bargaining in the area and resulted in an unusual settlement. 'Little Steel' contended that the Steel Workers' Organizing Committee was not a responsible union and refused to deal with it. When the tension approached the breaking point, Governor Townsend proposed that each party sign an agreement with the State, thus eliminating 'Little Steel's' objection to dealing with the union and assuring that the pact would be kept. The agreement was signed, and the State has not been called upon to make good any breach of contract.

POINTS OF INTEREST

10. The CUDAHY PACKING PLANT (*open 8–5 weekdays; guides*), Cline Ave. near South Shore Electric Line, includes refrigerator car repair shops and a wool pullery—an establishment for removing wool from slaughtered sheep. The most important unit is a soap factory where a nationally advertised cleanser is manufactured. High above the plant is a gigantic reproduction of the Dutch Girl, a guide post for travelers in this region.

11. The GENERAL AMERICAN TANK CAR PLANT (*open 8–5 weekdays; guides*), 4405 Euclid Ave., on a 90-acre site, was originally started to repair refrigerator cars. It now repairs all classes of car equipment, besides building, owning, and leasing tank cars to manufacturers, and building freight cars for railroads. In this plant a car for the transportation of helium gas was designed and constructed for the Bureau of Aeronautics, U. S. Department of the Navy.

12. The GRASSELLI CHEMICAL PLANT (*visited by permit from superintendent only; write several days in advance*), corner 151st St. and Kennedy Ave., a Du Pont subsidiary, has 250 of its 400 acres covered with buildings. Normally 1,000 persons are employed. The plant produces more than 300,000 tons of chemicals annually, including those used in the oil and steel industries; plant foods, fertilizers, and insecticides; and calcium arsenate used in fighting the boll weevil.

13. The WEBER INSULATION PLANT (*open 8–5 weekdays; guides*), 4821 Railroad Ave., produces insulation material for ovens, boilers, steam pipes, refrigerating cabinets, and buildings from the steel slag formed by the foam that boils up from iron ore in the process of making steel. The slag is porous and has the consistency of rock. It is melted and, by a special process, air is forced through the mass to form a fluffy, hairlike fiber that is further treated to increase its strength and resiliency. In this form the insulation is effective at temperatures as high as 2,000° F.

14. The HARBISON-WALKER REFRACTORIES PLANT (*open 8–5 weekdays; guides*), 4343 Kennedy Ave., was built to supply the Calumet mills with silica firebrick for building open-hearth furnaces and coke ovens. The discovery of ganister beds in the Devil's Lake district, near Baraboo, Wisconsin, and cheap lake transportation made East Chicago an ideal site for this industry. Beginning with 6 kilns in 1907, the plant had increased to 16 kilns in 1938. The company investigated the German tunnel-kiln process of firing silica brick, owned by the Heinrich Koppers Company, shipping hundreds of tons of its own ganister rock to Germany for testing. The experiment proved a success, and the Harbison-Walker Refractories acquired sole American rights to the German process in 1937. Both periodic and tunnel kilns are in use.

15. The EDWARDS VALVE PLANT (*open 8–5 weekdays; guides*), 1200 W. 145th St., produces high-pressure and high-temperature valves. Twenty years ago steam pressure of 250 pounds and temperatures of 400° F. to 500° F. were considered high; valves are produced now that will retain a working steam pressure of 1,800 pounds and temperatures up to 800° F.

16. The SINCLAIR REFINERY (*open 8–5 weekdays*), 3301 Indianapolis Blvd., was established here in 1917. Its present capacity exceeds 20,000 barrels daily. More than 1,000 men are employed.

17. The INLAND STEEL COMPANY PLANT (*open by arrangement*), 3210 Watling St., established in 1893, was the pioneer steel

company of the Calumet. Normally employing 12,000 persons, Inland has constantly added new equipment and anticipated new developments. During the recent depression a steady program of expansion and improvements was carried on. The company purchased coal properties in Kentucky, limestone quarries in Michigan, and in 1932 added a new continuous sheet and strip mill. The plant produces a variety of steel products, including sheets, tin plate, plates, bars, shapes, and piling.

18. The YOUNGSTOWN SHEET AND TUBE PLANT (*open by arrangement*), corner Riley Road and Dickey Road, employing 5,000 men, is an important unit of 'Little Steel.' Wrought iron, pipe, steel plate, billets, coke, and coke by-products are produced in large quantities.

19. WASHINGTON PARK, W. of Grand Blvd., covers about 20 acres landscaped with trees, shrubs, and flowers. Though the collection of animals is not extensive, the Zoo (*open 9–4 daily; free*), at the south end of the park, is noteworthy as the only one in the Calumet. The park also has a conservatory, and flower shows are held here in season.

Whiting

Railroad Stations: Front and 119th St. for New York Central R.R.; Ohio and 117th St. for Pennsylvania R.R.
Bus Stations: None. Greyhound Lines, Indian Trail Lines, DeLuxe Lines, and all lines from Chicago to the East pass through city by way of Indianapolis Blvd.; stops made at specified street crossings. Bus to Gary, fare 25¢.
Taxis: 35¢ to any point in city.
Street Order and Numbering: E. and W. street extensions of Chicago numbered streets, as 117th St. Numbering begins with 1200 at Atchison St., W. boundary of city. N. and S. streets are locally named, taking house numbers from streets immediately N. by dropping first numeral, as 119th St. = (1) 1901 Atchison St.

Accommodations: 1 hotel; rooming houses.

Information Service: Whiting-Robertsdale Chamber of Commerce, Illiana Hotel, 119th and Atchison Sts.; Memorial Community House, Clark St. and Community Court.

Theaters and Motion Picture Houses: Concert halls in Slovak Hall, Clark and 119th St., and Community House, Clark and Community Court. 2 motion picture houses.
Swimming: Lake Front Park, reached via 117th St.; tennis, baseball, and playground facilities also provided.
Fishing: Lake George and Wolf Lake.
Golf: Wicker Park course (*see Hammond*), maintained by all cities of North Township; 9 and 18 holes, greens fees Mon.-Fri. 25¢, Sat. and Sun. 50¢.

WHITING (589.7 alt., 10,307 pop.), for many years a predominantly German settlement clustered around a railway crossing (now the Calumet Terminal), has been called successively Whiting's Crossing, Whiting's Station, Whiting's, and finally, Whiting. It was a one-industry town until the Carbide and Carbon Chemicals Corporation became an across-the-street neighbor of Standard Oil in 1934.

Despite the fact that about 90 per cent of Whiting's population is foreign-born or of foreign-born parentage, the town is like any other industrial city in appearance. Its geographical compactness and the unity conferred by the presence of only one large industry have done much to foster civic spirit. However, there has always been in Whiting a definite cleavage between foreign and native groups. The former, mainly Slavic and Polish, have been slow to adopt American ways; 119th Street is the dividing line between the foreign-born and native inhabitants.

Whiting's residential streets are clean and well paved, and the city maintains a lake-front park of 22 acres, fully equipped with modern recreational facilities.

The Standard Oil Company plant at the eastern edge of Whiting is one of the most striking sights in this region, with switch engines, trains of tank cars, row upon row of glistening storage tanks, labyrinths of pipe of all sizes and, breaking the skyline, hundreds of stacks of varying heights. At night, vaguely outlined by lights, it becomes a thing of beauty.

As might be expected in a city largely made up of persons of music-loving nationalities, music is an integral part of community life. The Symphonic Boy's Band, under the direction (1941) of Father John L. Lach, pastor of the Church of the Immaculate Conception, in addition to giving public concerts in Whiting, makes an annual tour of the United States and foreign nations.

POINTS OF INTEREST

20. The MEMORIAL COMMUNITY HOUSE (*open for meetings and civic gatherings*), 1938 Clark St., is a memorial to those who served in the first World War. The building, a gift of the Standard Oil Company, is Southern Italian in design. It is headquarters for civic groups and 35 other organizations use it for meetings and social events.

21. The STANDARD OIL COMPANY (INDIANA) PLANT (*open by arrangement*), Standard Ave. and Front St., Whiting, began in 1889 with construction of a refinery on a few acres on Lake Michigan. Now (1941) occupying 750 acres, it covers portions of Whiting, East Chicago, and Hammond, but is principally in Whiting. The refinery produces a wide variety of petroleum products in large quantities: gasoline, kerosene, motor oils, lubricants ranging from heavy grease for locomotives to the lightest oil for wrist watches, a varied line of asphalt products, fuel for cigar lighters, and candles. When operating at capacity it employs about 4,000 persons. The coal used daily would supply the normal domestic requirements of a city of 500,000 people and

the water used in cooling the gasoline each day would suffice for a city of 1,250,000 inhabitants. To paraphrase the packing house story, everything except the *odor* of crude oil is used. From a by-product, coal tar, chemists obtain substances that provide the scents for synthetic rose water and artificial musk and jasmine perfumes.

Corydon

Railroad Stations: Corner Water and Walnut Sts. for Louisville, New Albany & Corydon R.R.
Bus Stations: Old Capital Inn, Chestnut St. (State 62), for Greyhound Lines; Rosenbarger's Restaurant, Chestnut St., for Corydon Bus Line.
Traffic Regulations: Speed limit 20 m.p.h.

Accommodations: 3 hotels.

Information Service: A.A.A., Old Capital Inn, Chestnut St.

Motion Picture Houses: 1.
Athletics: Recreation Island Park, flood lights for night games (baseball, softball, track).
Basketball: Corydon High School Gym.

Annual Events: County Fair, 3 days in Sept. at fairgrounds, including horse and cattle shows, agricultural exhibits, and horse racing.

CORYDON (715 alt., 1,865 pop.) is built on a hillside between Big and Little Indian Creeks in a valley of the Harrison County hill country. At one time it was the seat of Indiana government and the residence of much of the State's aristocracy; later, it was the scene of the only Indiana battle of the Civil War.

The community is the center of a dairy cattle country whose products are carried by truck lines into New Albany and Louisville. The region also possesses great rock resources; quarries of varying size and importance are scattered along the highways leading into town. Natural gas is available and many homes are heated by it.

From its wide, shaded, and precipitously steep residential streets in the north and northeast sections, clean, dignified homes, most of them white frame or mellow old brick, look down on the level little business district with an air of aloofness. Streets of the business and shopping district (Walnut to Poplar and Market to Maple Streets), narrow in contrast to those of the residential district, are lined with a curious mixture of old, one-story frame buildings and glossy new modern fronts. Horse teams stand at the curb side by side with trucks and automobiles. Meals served in smartly fronted little restaurants and lunch stands retain the unmistakable tang of country cooking. In the center of this heterogeneous business section stands the old State Capitol.

The town's major industries are wagon works and a glass factory, survivals of a more gracious era when the roar of gasoline motors and the glare of incandescent lamps were unknown. Their products, farm wagons and chimneys for coal-oil lamps, are sold throughout the Nation. There are several smaller industrial establishments, including chicken hatcheries, a lumber mill, and a cannery. All the industries are in the eastern and western outskirts of the town where the terrain slopes sharply downward.

General William Henry Harrison originally owned the site of Corydon and named the town. Harrison, later governor of the Northwest Territory and hero, before he became the Nation's chief executive, of the Battle of Tippecanoe (*see Tour* 18*b*), entered the land in 1804. He sold it to Harvey Heth, who laid out the town as the seat of government of the newly organized Harrison County in 1808.

General Harrison, while governor of the Territory, named the community Corydon for the young shepherd in his favorite song, the 'Pastoral Elegy,' one of a number of songs in the then popular songbook, *Missouri Harmony*. Miss Jenny Smith often sang it for him when he stayed overnight with her family on his many trips between the Territorial capital at Vincennes and the Government Land Office at Jeffersonville. The Edward Smith Home, where the General stayed, was on the present fairgrounds.

The courthouse, later the State Capitol, was built in 1811–12. On May 1, 1813, after the Northwest Territory had been divided, the seat of Indiana Territorial government was moved here from Vincennes and the structure was used as the capitol building. Here the 44 delegates to the Indiana Constitutional Convention assembled in June 1816, when Corydon was chosen as the new State's capital.

Until 1825, when Indianapolis became the capital, Corydon was the hub of the State's governmental and social activity. After the removal, it was just another county seat, distinguished only by the aristocratic background that still seems to lift it above the rusticity of other Indiana country towns.

Traditional stories about the Battle of Corydon preserve the town's one other outstanding historical event. On the night of July 8, 1863, General John Hunt Morgan and his Confederate raiders crossed the Ohio River from Brandenburg, Kentucky, to Mauckport, on commandeered steamboats. On the 9th he attacked Corydon, which resisted his advance with 400 Corydon Home Guards. Three of the defenders were killed and 2 wounded, while 8 of the invaders were slain and 33 wounded. The Home Guards surrendered as Morgan's men rode into town and were held prisoners in the public square during the few hours the famous raider remained. That night Morgan camped near Palmyra, north of Corydon.

A Confederate veteran, reminiscing years later at a reunion in Louisville, Kentucky, told of the 'enjoyable time' he had in Corydon during the raid. 'As we rode to the northwest corner of the square,' he recalled, 'we met two young ladies who we later learned were Emma

Jones and Mary Mitchell. Upon being dared, they mounted behind a couple of boys and we decorated their hair with bolts of ribbon that trailed out behind them as we rode.'

To save their flour mills from being burned, each of the town's millers was required to pay General Morgan $1,000. When Morgan counted one of the rolls of bills handed him and found it contained $1,200 he returned the $200 saying that $1,000 was his price. While the Confederates 'lived off the country' in the raid, their conduct was so considerate that they were leniently remembered by their victims.

In five days during which the main body of General Morgan's troops covered 200 miles of Indiana territory, sallies of his foraging and feinting parties added appreciably to the area touched upon. Morgan's constantly zigzagging course gave rise to many erroneous conclusions about his ultimate destination, and Union forces and Home Guards were rushed nervously from one point of imagined peril to another. The pursuing troops of General Hobson were always just a few hours behind him. In the last phase of the raid through Indiana, pursuer and pursued spent 21 hours a day in the saddle. General Hobson had crossed the Ohio into Indiana a day behind Morgan; he had cut this difference to five hours as the raiders left the State at West Harrison Monday evening, July 13 (see Tour 18a).

On his second day in Indiana, July 10, Morgan passed through Palmyra and Salem, and then eastward through Vienna to Lexington, where he camped for the night. At Salem the defending Home Guards fled without firing a shot. They were taken prisoners, but were released as Morgan moved on after burning the highway and railroad bridges, the water tank and depot. At Vienna, Morgan took over the telegraph station and, before destroying it, listened in on military dispatches being sent between Indianapolis and Louisville regarding his raid and plans for his capture. He heard orders to the militia to fell trees across the roads over which he was supposed to be advancing. After camping for the night at Lexington, he continued his zigzagging tactics.

On the morning of July 11, after severing the last telegraph line at Lexington connecting Louisville and southern Indiana with Indianapolis, he headed north along what is now State 3 through Scottsburg toward Vernon.

At Vernon he found the Home Guards and militia under arms and called upon the town to surrender. The Federal commander refused and asked time in which to evacuate noncombatants. Morgan granted the request and, screened by a detachment of skirmishers, moved his main force out and southeastward to Dupont. Darkness came on as the defenders of Vernon awaited the expected attack. Suddenly, in the salient along the ford at the southeastern edge of town, a great splashing was heard. The Home Guards occupying the sector took to their heels. In the scramble to get away, many of them fell from the 20-foot embankment at their rear. More men were hurt in this fall in the 'Battle of Finney's Ford,' than in any brush with Morgan's men. While the guardsmen were falling off the embankment, Morgan's raiders were miles away. The noise had been made by livestock that neighboring farmers were driving across the ford to safety in the town.

Morgan camped for the night in Dupont, leaving there early Sunday morning, July 12, for Versailles just five hours before General Hobson's forces arrived. The raiders surprised a Home Guard council of war at Versailles and broke it up without bloodshed. By mock troop movements leading Union forces at his front to believe he would strike Lawrenceburg next, Morgan proceeded to Sunman after the 1,200 militiamen stationed there had been dispatched to the 'threatened' city. He camped at Sunman overnight and, on July 13, marched eastward through New Alsace and Dover to West Harrison and into the State of Ohio.

POINTS OF INTEREST

The OLD STATE CAPITOL (*open* 10–4 *weekdays; adm.* 25¢), Market St. between Beaver and Walnut Sts., has become a shrine of Hoosier history. Lacking in architectural grace, the structure nevertheless suggests enduring strength. Cube-shaped with a hip roof surmounted by a bell tower, it is built of rough blue limestone quarried in the neighborhood. After the removal of the State capital to Indianapolis, the old statehouse was the Harrison County courthouse until 1898. The building has been restored inside and out, with exact reproductions of all the original furniture and other articles. Letters exchanged by State and National leaders of the period are included in the history exhibit. The old capitol building is maintained by the State, under the jurisdiction of the Department of Conservation.

CONSTITUTION ELM, High St. between Market and Water Sts., with limbs that measured 132 feet across, formed a shaded retreat for the delegates who framed the Constitution of Indiana during 20 hot days of June 1816. A sandstone pergola with open archways enshrines the dead trunk of the historic tree.

The OLD STATE TREASURY (*private*), NW. corner of Walnut and Mulberry Sts., has been the Brewster home since 1871. A one-story brick building, it was built as a residence in 1817 by Davis Floyd, implicated in the Aaron Burr conspiracy and later judge of the Circuit Court. The house was rented to the State as a treasury building during the time Corydon was the capital. The east room was the office of the State auditor; the west room the office of the State treasurer. The State's money was kept in strongboxes in the cellar under the west room. Between 1829 and 1850, the residence housed the Harrison County Seminary.

SITE OF THE GOVERNOR'S MANSION (*private*), Walnut St. between Mulberry and Maple Sts., is occupied by the Ben Yeager residence. The eastern side of the Yeager home is built on the original mansion's foundation and the north wall of the basement was the south wall of the mansion's cellar. Presidents James Monroe and Andrew Jackson visited here. Governor Jonathan Jennings was the first and only governor to occupy the mansion.

The MANSION OF COLONEL THOMAS LLOYD POSEY (*open 9–4 weekdays*), Oak St. at W. end of Cherry St., is an assembly hall for the Hoosier Elm Chapter of the D.A.R. and houses a comprehensive museum of pioneer relics. Included in the collection is a cannon ball fired into the town by General Morgan's raiders. Colonel Posey, son of Governor Posey, was a great church worker and well known for his philanthropies. Although a bachelor, he reared 14 orphans in his home. The two-story house, built in 1811, is of brick.

The HARRISON COUNTY FAIRGROUNDS, corner of Cook and Market Sts., are in a natural amphitheater formed by surrounding hills. On these 43 acres of level green meadows, the Harrison County Fair has been held annually since September 11–14, 1860. The home of Edward Smith, where General William Henry Harrison, later President of the United States, used to visit, formerly stood here.

The W. H. KELLER WAGON WORKS (*open 8–5 weekdays*), W. end Keller St., covers 10 acres and includes three railroad sidings, a powerhouse, sawmill, spoke and rim factories, lumber and dimension sheds, dry kilns, woodworking departments, and warehouses. The factory, founded in 1894, employs 125 men, with an annual output of 15,000 wagons.

The CO-OPERATIVE GLASS PLANT (*open 6 A.M.–10 P.M. weekdays*), at E. edge of town, manufacturing coal-oil lamp chimneys, is operated by employee-owners. The plant was started here in 1925 after fire had destroyed its predecessor at North Vernon, Indiana. 'Gatherers' prepare the molten glass for the 'blowers,' who, with a few deft twirls and an occasional puff, convert it into finished lamp chimneys. Special crimping machines are used on the tops.

The KINTNER HOTEL BUILDING, SW. corner of Market and Chestnut Sts., occupied by mercantile establishments, housed the hostelry that General John Hunt Morgan made his headquarters for several hours in his raid through Indiana. Reminiscences of Mrs. Sallie Kintner Jones, daughter of the former proprietor, are part of the traditional history of the raid. She met all the Confederate officers and liked best General Morgan's brother and General Duke, second in command of the invading cavalrymen. She recalled that, while the commander spent his time roughly questioning prisoners on the second floor of the hotel, his brother loitered in the yard 'talking to the girls.'

CEDAR GLADE (*private*), Market St. N. of Keller St., is the two-story brick McGrain homestead, where General Morgan's men, while scouring the countryside for fresh mounts, left in exchange the thoroughbred mare, Lady Morgan. Her descendants were the Edward Everett horses, well known in southern Indiana. Through the raiders' custom of leaving a tired horse for the one commandeered, many fine animals were introduced in the region they traversed. The architecture of the house shows the Georgian influence; a long front porch has been added.

POINTS OF INTEREST IN ENVIRONS

Wyandotte Cave, 9.9 *m.* (*see Tour 11A*).

Evansville

Railroad Stations: Union Station, Fulton Ave. and Ohio St., for Louisville & Nashville R.R., Chicago & Eastern Illinois R.R., and Cleveland, Cincinnati, Chicago & St. Louis R.R.; Illinois Central Station, Franklin St. and 6th Ave., for Illinois Central R.R.; Southern Station, Division St. and Elsis Ave., for Southern R.R.
Bus Stations: Greyhound Bus Terminal, Third and Sycamore Sts., for Greyhound, Southern Limited, and Wabash Valley Coach Co. bus lines; 15 SE. Fifth St. for Evansville Suburban and Newburgh bus lines; 214 Locust St. for Evansville and Ohio Valley bus lines.
Airport: Municipal Airport, 5 m. NE. on US 41, for Eastern Airlines; taxi, $1.
Taxis: 30¢ to any point in city, 20¢ per mile outside city.
City Busses: Fare 7¢, service at 15 min. intervals.
Traffic Regulations: Parking unlimited in all streets except those of business district. Parking lots with nominal charges on 4th St. between Main and Sycamore Sts., on 5th St. between Sycamore and Vine Sts., and at 419 Locust St.

Accommodations: 11 hotels; lodging houses. Tourist camps 1 m. S. and 5.5 m. N. on US 41.

Information Service: Chamber of Commerce, Third and Main Sts.; Evansville Automobile Club of Southeastern Indiana, 300 SE. Riverside Drive; Junior Chamber of Commerce, 209 NW. Fifth St.

Theaters and Motion Picture Houses: 13 motion picture houses; 2 concert halls, the Coliseum, Court St. between Market St. and First Ave., and Washington Avenue Temple, corner Washington Ave. and Sixth St.; amusement park, Mesker Park and Zoo, corner Mesker Park Drive and Bement Ave., free.
Radio Stations: WGBF (1280 kc.); WEOA (1400 kc.).
Swimming: East Side Pool, Division St. between Rotherwood and Weinbach Aves.; Garvin Park Pool, corner N. Main St. and Morgan Ave.; Julius Artes Pool, Keller St. between Fulton and Fifth Aves.; Howell Pool, corner S. Barker Ave. and Floyd St.; Booker T. Washington Pool (colored), 650 S. Governor St.; Beach Grove Beach, across river on Kentucky side, 10¢ round trip by boat.
Tennis: 25 public courts, all free.
Golf: Municipal Course, corner Mesker Park Drive and Bement Ave., 18 holes, greens fees 25–50¢.
Hunting and Fishing: Angling in Ohio River and tributary streams; rabbits, squirrels, and quail in season.
Baseball: Bosse Field, SE. corner Garvin Park on N. Main St., Evansville Bees (Three I League).
Football and Basketball: Bosse Field, Evansville College and city high schools.
Horse Racing: Dade Park, 2 m. SE. on Shawnee Drive, running horse racing.

Annual Events: New Year's Ball, Jan. 1; Aviation Show, July 26; Dade Park Races, Aug. 8 to Sept. 7; German Day, Aug. 20–22; *Volksfest,* Sept. 14; Fall Flower Show, Sept. 27; West Side Fall Festival, for three nights preceding Halloween; Auto Show, Nov. 12–15.

EVANSVILLE (383 alt., 97,062 pop.), seat of Vanderburgh County, is a link between the unhurried Old South and the bustling, industrial North. Still an important avenue for commerce, the romantic Ohio River recalls the great days of steamboat traffic, when Evansville was a prominent port of call. Located at the mouth of Pigeon Creek, halfway between the falls of the Ohio and the river's mouth, the town has one of the best harbors on inland waterways. For many years it was a vital link between Northern farmers and the markets of the South, and even now the impressive volume of its river freight and its busy water front give Evansville the characteristic atmosphere of a river town. The bordering horse country adds an air of easy leisure. In August the business and industry of Evansville continue almost automatically, while attention focuses on running horses at the Dade Park race course southeast of town.

The city, fifth largest in Indiana and largest on the Ohio River west of Louisville, covers 11 square miles of land—level except for a number of hills in the northwest section. From the lofty roadway of the Evansville-Henderson bridge in the southeast, or from the high hills of the fashionable Forest Hills section in the west, the great horseshoe bend of the city's water front can be seen in its entirety—Sunset Park with its splendid view across the two expanses of the turning river; the city wharf; railroad freight depots, yards, and shops; and the great Mead-Johnson river-rail-highway terminal, through which an average of 321,000 tons of freight is shipped annually. The romance of the old steamboat days, however, is recalled only by Sunday excursion boats and an occasional showboat making its way down the river from Pittsburgh.

The center of Evansville's business district is on Main Street for about 10 blocks back from the river. A second mercantile area is on West Franklin Street (the only through east-and-west street), across the Pigeon Creek Bridge. Streets in the city's comparatively small downtown section run northwest to southeast and southwest to northeast, parallel and at right angles to the northeast segment of the horseshoe curve of the river. This was the original Evansville. As the city grew, later streets were laid out north-south and east-west. Colonial mansions of early Evansville are along SE. Second Street.

The city's importance as a transportation center contributed to the rise of industry early in its history. Today Evansville's 225 factories employ 16,700 workers. Major products are auto bodies, steam and electric shovels and cranes, electric and gas refrigerators, tools, electric headlights, infant foods, glass bottles, grain products, clothing, textiles, beer, and cigars.

The population is almost entirely native-born. The German ancestry of many citizens, however, is apparent in the Germania Mannerchor, a male chorus, and in a miniature German village where the Volksfest, a German celebration, is held annually.

Evansville's location on the Ohio made it easy for wandering theatrical troupes to give occasional performances even in the early frontier period. In 1852 the first theater, Mozart Hall, was built and the show-boat period of the 1880's (*see Music and the Theater*) brought added theatrical importance to the town. In recent years, in addition to performances by road companies, theater-goers have enjoyed the productions of the Community Players, an amateur company that gives several plays annually. Concerts are given by the Evansville Philharmonic Orchestra. Among its outstanding natives the town is proud of Marilyn Miller, Joe Cook, and Louise Dresser, stage celebrities.

When in 1812 Colonel Hugh McGary built his cabin on a spot that became the foot of Main Street, he had no plan to found a town. In the days when he lived west of Princeton, it occurred to him that if he were to live at this U-bend of the river—some 30 miles to the south of his old home—it would be simpler for him to visit his wife's relatives in Henderson (then Red Banks), Kentucky. He started a ferry at this point, which became known as McGary's Ferry. In 1814 the growing village was made the seat of the new county of Warrick.

Almost immediately after its selection as county seat, the village lost the honor and seemed about to dwindle away when McGary enlisted the aid of General Robert Evans and James W. Jones. In 1818 he sold the section above Main Street to General Evans and the town was replatted. In the same year, to settle a three-cornered political controversy, Warrick County was divided into three counties. McGary's and Evans's town was named Evansville and made seat of the newly created Vanderburgh County. A brick courthouse was built.

The population, 200 in 1819, when the town was incorporated, grew with the migration westward by flatboat. Usually several flatboats traveled together with a frontiersman as guide and navigator. These 'western boatmen,' as the guides were called, were usually tall and thin, sinewy and capable of unbelievable endurance under hardship. Among their accomplishments was a precise accuracy with tobacco juice, many being exact at a range of 15 feet.

In Evansville and similar Ohio River towns, flatboat operators traded powder, lead, salt, and flints for pork, venison, hams, skins, fur, and other products of the region. They carried the new cargo to New Orleans where they sold it, together with the lumber of which their boats were made, making the return trip afoot or on horseback.

The coming of the steamboat opened a golden age for Evansville. The *Robert Fulton,* first steamboat to ply the Ohio River, appeared in 1809, but more than a decade passed before this form of transportation was accepted as practicable. Early steamboats were remarkable for their noise and slowness. Flatboaters often walked along the banks from Natchez to Evansville and made the trip in as short a time as did the steamboats. By 1822, however, the steamboats had cut the time for the trip to New Orleans to 7 days from the 30 required for flatboats, and made the upstream trip, New Orleans to Evansville, in 16 days instead of 90. As the river schedules improved, increasing quantities of goods were shipped by boat, and by 1854 the Ohio River was the 'grand avenue of prosperity for the thriving town of Evansville.'

But with all its natural advantages the city did not escape troubles. It suffered losses in the financial depression of 1824–9, and the coincident epidemic of milk sickness took its toll. (When Dr. William Trafton, an Evansville physician, discovered a cure for this malady during the epidemic, he won Nation-wide prominence.) Cold weather added to the city's troubles in the winter of 1831–2, when the river froze to a depth of 22 inches, crippling business by stopping river traffic. With spring came the first of Evansville's four disastrous floods, making an island of the village for a time. In the summer 391 persons died in an epidemic of cholera.

To crown misery with disillusionment, Colonel Hugh McGary, patriarch of the town, was charged in 1832 with horse stealing. When arrested for riding an animal said to have been stolen, he explained that he had traded with a relative for it. He was not prosecuted, but community whispering forced him to leave town.

Meanwhile, in 1828 several shops for blacksmiths, hatters, and cobblers were established, and as Evansville grew, sawmills were erected on Pigeon Creek to supply heavy timbers for shipbuilding and fuel for steamboats. In 1836 the Mammoth Internal Improvement Bill, which named Evansville as southern terminus of the Wabash & Erie Canal, brought new immigration. Real-estate prices collapsed in the financial depression of that year, however, and the period until 1844 was a lean one. Recovery began to be felt in 1844 and 1845. In 1848, when its population had grown to 4,000 and its area to 230 acres, Evansville was chartered as a city. The legislature authorized completion of the canal, construction of which had been halted by the depression; several flour mills and foundries, a furniture factory, two wharf boat plants, and new sawmills were established on the strength of anticipated canal trade.

But at almost the same time that the first canalboat from Petersburg arrived in April 1853, the first railroad train arrived from Princeton. The last boat came through the canal to Evansville in 1860. River traffic, which today is wholly confined to freight shipments, declined appreciably with the development of the railways.

Although the canal was a failure financially, its construction greatly helped the development of Evansville. Because of it, the population grew and manufacturing was stimulated; even before the Civil War the city had become a factory center as well as a shipping point for southwestern Indiana. After the war this industrial growth continued. With craftsmen from Europe attracted by foundries and woodworking factories, the population jumped to 50,756 by 1890, despite a second inundation by the river in 1884. In the early 1900's furniture factories, a number of stove foundries, and a buggy factory were established.

By 1920 Evansville had a population of 85,000, and growth since that time has been steady.

The river overflowed in 1913 and again in 1937, when on January 30 water reached a flood level of 53.74 feet and covered 46 per cent of Evansville's area. Although every relief agency was taxed to the limit and several rescue workers died from pneumonia, little evidence of this deluge, the worst in the city's history, could be seen three months later. With Government aid, a huge levee to prevent future floods has been built.

POINTS OF INTEREST

1. The MEAD-JOHNSON TERMINAL, corner St. Joseph and Ohio Sts., is a modern, completely equipped river-rail-highway terminal. Part of the great building juts out over the river permitting loading, unloading, and interchange of truck, train, and boat cargoes under cover. In the building is the office of the U. S. customs collector.

2. The MARINE HOSPITAL, 2700 W. Illinois St., was established in 1892 for the care of river-boat sailors. Its services are now available for merchant seamen, Coast Guardsmen, enrollees in the CCC and other Government employees. Fitted with 100 beds, this hospital is one of a chain operated by the United States Public Health Service and accommodates a daily average of 85 patients.   •

3. MESKER MUNICIPAL PARK, corner Mesker Park Drive and Bement Ave., includes 212 wooded acres and is the most popular of the city's recreational resorts. Among the park's attractions are the largest Zoo in Indiana, a SUNKEN GARDEN, an AMUSEMENT PARK (*all open; free*), and an 18-hole golf course. The summer home of the zoo monkeys is a ship modeled after the *Santa Maria*.

4. The GRESHAM MEMORIAL HOME (*open; apply Service Star Legion, 405 S. Kentucky Ave.*), NE. corner Wedeking Ave. and Herndon Drive, a remodeled two-and-a-half-story brick Georgian residence, was built and furnished by popular subscription for the late Mrs. Gresham Dodd, mother of Corporal James Bethel Gresham, one of the first three American soldiers killed in the World War, November 3, 1917. The home is the meeting place for Gresham Chapter, Service Star Legion War Mothers.

5. The SERVEL PLANT (*open* 8:30–9:30 A.M., 1:30–2:30 P.M. *weekdays*), Morton Ave. between Division and Franklin Sts., a refrigerator factory with 1,000,000 square feet of floor space, is the city's largest industry, employing 6,000 persons in times of peak production. The business evolved from the old Hercules Buggy Works of the early 1900's. In turn this plant manufactured one-cylinder gasoline motors, truck bodies, and even a few automobiles.

6. The WILLARD CARPENTER HOMESTEAD (*open* 9:30 A.M.– 12 P.M. *daily*), corner Third, Ingle and Carpenter Sts., is a fine example of Georgian architecture. Built in 1848 by Willard Carpenter, mer-

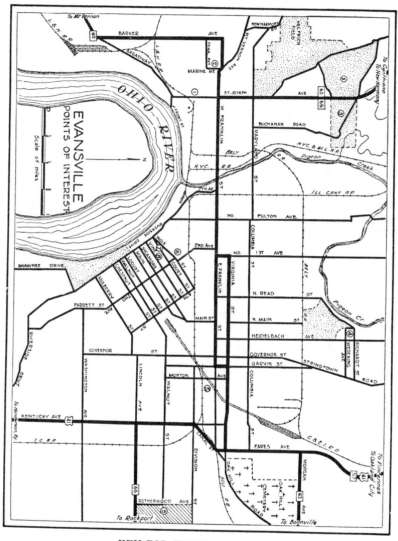

KEY FOR EVANSVILLE MAP

1. Mead-Johnson Terminal   2. Marine Hospital   3. Mesker Municipal Park   4.
Gresham Memorial Home   5. Servel Plant   6. Willard Carpenter Homestead   7.
Soldiers and Sailors Memorial Coliseum   8. Temple of Fine Arts and History
9. Evansville College

chant and civic leader, it is the home of the American Legion Post. In 1937, the Historic American Buildings Survey included this house among 28 Indiana architectural landmarks.

7. The SOLDIERS AND SAILORS MEMORIAL COLISEUM (*open* 8:30–5 *daily*), Court St. between First and Second Sts., Greek Doric in design, is a center of civic activity. In its front limestone gable is the flag-and-eagle emblem of the Grand Army of the Republic. The main auditorium has 3,000 seats, a completely equipped stage, and a fine pipe organ.

8. The TEMPLE OF FINE ARTS AND HISTORY (*open* 10–5 *weekdays; 2–5 holidays*), 216 W. Second St., 2 two-story brick houses joined by a one-story reception hall, contains an extensive collection of original paintings, as well as reproductions and historic relics. On display is a framed London *Daily Times* issue of July 22, 1815, the day following the Battle of Waterloo. No mention is made of the famous conflict, an illustration of the slowness of communication in that day.

9. EVANSVILLE COLLEGE (*open* 8:10–5 *weekdays*), corner Rotherwood and Lincoln Aves., is a Methodist institution, conferring bachelor degrees in Arts and Sciences. ADMINISTRATION HALL, built of irregularly cut buff and blue Indiana limestone, is an excellent example of Gothic architecture. The COLLEGE MUSEUM (*open school hours*) contains the Otto Laval collection of 5,000 Indian relics, including arrow points, drills, grinding stones, flint hoes and spades, tomahawk blades, pottery, clay and stone images, and a large collection of natural-history specimens.

POINTS OF INTEREST IN ENVIRONS

Lincoln City, 37.9 *m.;* Santa Claus, 45.3 *m.* (*see Tour* 11*A*). State Hospital, 4 *m.;* Angel Mounds, 6.4 *m.;* Government Dam No. 47, 9.8 *m.* (*see Tour* 11*B*). Dade Park Racetrack, 2.5 *m.* (*see Tour* 20*b*).

Fort Wayne

Railroad Stations: SW. corner Harrison and Baker Sts. for Pennsylvania R.R. and Grand Rapids & Indiana R.R.; Grand St. between Calhoun and Harrison Sts. for Wabash R.R.; 912 Cass St. for Lakeshore R.R., a branch of the New York Central System; Calhoun St. between Columbia and Superior Sts. for New York, Chicago & St. Louis R.R. (Nickel Plate).

Bus Stations: 223 W. Jefferson St. for Greyhound Lines, ABC Coach Lines, Central Coach Lines, Greenville-Dayton Transportation Co. Lines, Shortway Lines, Paulding Bus Lines, Kalamazoo Coach Lines, Warsaw Bus Lines, and North Manchester Line; 205 W. Washington Blvd. for Lincoln Trailways; 314 W. Main St. (Interurban Station) for Indiana Railroad System bus service to Indianapolis via Peru and Kokomo, and via Bluffton, Muncie and Anderson; also for Indiana Motor Coach Lines, Empire Trails, and All-American Bus Lines.

Airport: Smith-Baer Field, 5 m. N., on Ludwig Road, between State 3 and US 27 (municipal). TWA scheduled day and night passenger, mail, and express.

Streetcars and City Busses: Fare 7¢, four tokens 25¢, free transfers, weekly passes $1.

Taxis: 30¢ for 3 passengers within city limits.

Traffic Regulations: U turns prohibited at all stop lights. Left turns prohibited on Calhoun St. at Main, Berry, Wayne, Washington, and Jefferson Sts. Park with right side of car next to curb, no double parking.

Accommodations: 12 hotels, tourist lodges, auto camps; no seasonal rates.

Information Service: Fort Wayne Motor Club, 924 S. Clinton St., and Police Department booth, corner Calhoun and Main Sts., Courthouse Square.

Radio Stations: WOWO (1180 kc.); WGL (1450 kc.).

Theaters and Motion Picture Houses: Shrine Theater, W. Berry St. between Ewing St. and Fairfield Ave., occasional road shows; 15 motion picture houses.

Swimming: Municipal Bathing Beach, St. Joseph River below St. Joe Dam at N. end Anthony Blvd., lifeguards, electrically lighted, picnic and playgrounds, ample parking space; Lawton Park Pool, between Spy Run Ave. and Clinton St. on US 27, and West Swinney Park Pool, on US 24 W. of city, lifeguards.

Golf: Municipal course, S. Broadway at Rudisell Blvd., 18 holes, and Fairview course, S. end Calhoun St., 18 holes, greens fee 30–60¢.

Baseball: Pennsylvania Ball Park, 2400 S. Anthony Blvd. (semipro.); softball leagues at Public Parks.

Football: Concordia College, corner Washington Blvd. and Hanover St., and high school games at their respective fields.

Riding: Saddle and Bridle Club, Centlivre Park, N. Clinton St., US 27; Indian Village Club, Bluffton Road, State 1, across river from Foster Park.

Parks and Playgrounds: 25 city parks totaling 865 acres, 39 horseshoe courts, 67 tennis courts, 27 softball and hardball diamonds, 6 football fields, 2 archery courts, 3 bridle paths, 12 supervised playgrounds.

Amusement Park: Amusement Park in West Swinney Park, US 24, a continuation of W. Washington Blvd.

FORT WAYNE (765 alt., 118,410 pop.), seat of Allen County, second largest city in Indiana and historically one of the most significant, is an industrial and railroad center in the heart of a rich agricultural region. Its traditions recall the chief town of the Miami Indians once occupying this spot, and the era when General Washington envisaged an American outpost here and General 'Mad Anthony' Wayne made the dream a reality. Gateway to the northern Indiana lake region, Fort Wayne is a recreational rendezvous as well as a manufacturing and trading center. Within a radius of 50 miles are 300 lakes varying from quiet fishing resorts to those offering more elaborate entertainment.

In the heart of the city the St. Mary's and St. Joseph Rivers join to form the Maumee River. Dividing Fort Wayne into three parts, these waterways have a combined length within the city of 10 miles and are spanned by 21 bridges, 11 of which are stately and ornamental. From the junction of these rivers, four blocks from the business center, the flat land rises to a low range of hills partly encircling the northern environs. To the south lies a gently lifting plain.

Calhoun Street is the principal business street and the city's meridian. Century-old structures still sound and serviceable, grimy anachronisms amid modern stores and office buildings, stand in the narrow streets of the original part of town. Principal lanes for east-west traffic are Washington Boulevard and Jefferson Street; Clinton Street, the longest in Fort Wayne, is the main north-south traffic thoroughfare. The Italian Renaissance courthouse, in the square bounded by Calhoun, Main, Court, and Berry Streets, is the geographic center of the city. Towering over the entire business scene at 116 E. Berry Street, stands the 22-story Lincoln National Bank & Trust Company Building, the tallest in Indiana. A steel structure of modern design, it is faced with Indiana limestone, and has lead spandrels, terra-cotta top, and a cupola and observation tower.

Fort Wayne's location at the confluence of three rivers has led to its present importance. Seeing the advantage of the site for travel and defense, the Indians established Kekionga, or Miami Town, at this place; here early French traders and soldiers erected Fort Miami for the same reason. A prosperous fur-trading post for more than a century, Fort Wayne later developed as a commercial and industrial city. Owners of sawmills and gristmills found plenty of water power available, and industrial growth was stimulated by the building of the Wabash & Erie Canal, begun here in 1832. This canal, one of the longest ever constructed, connected the Ohio River and Lake Erie. By the time the railroad from Pittsburgh to Chicago was built, Fort Wayne had become such a center of trade and manufacture that its location on the main line of that road was inevitable.

Today (1941) the city's industry is thriving and highly diversified. The electrical industry leads in value and employment, with 10,000 persons working in peak times in the General Electric Company's plant. Since 1891, when the Wayne Knitting Mills opened to produce the first full-fashioned hosiery in the United States, the manufacture of this product has been one of Fort Wayne's chief industries. In 1885 Sylvanus F. Bowser began to manufacture self-measuring oil tanks for kerosene; since then the city has become a leading producer of filling-station equipment. At present (1941) three factories here manufacture 70 per cent of the Nation's output in this field. Other Fort Wayne products include railroad car wheels, boilers, tanks, washing machines, steel, medicines, motor trucks, automatic phonographs, display cases, meat-packing products, mining machinery, and tents and awnings. One of the largest brewing industries in the State is also located here.

Since 1890, Fort Wayne has been one of the most thoroughly unionized cities in the State and has had fairly stable labor conditions. Occasional strikes have affected single industries, notably the walkout at the Wayne Knitting Mills in 1935; and a few railroad strikes begun elsewhere have involved local workers. In general, however, the city has been free from serious labor disputes. In 1936 a convention was held in Fort Wayne at which the United Electrical and Radio Workers of America was organized.

In cultural and civic endeavor, as well as in industry and trade, Fort Wayne is a center for northeastern Indiana. Music and the theater are fostered by the Lutheran Choral Society, a Civic Symphony Society, a Civic Theater, and the Old Fort Players. Art instruction and current art exhibitions are provided by the Fort Wayne Art School and Museum. A coeducational college, a Bible training school, and three public and four parochial high schools are included in Fort Wayne's system of higher education. Fourscore churches serve all leading denominations.

For years before and after the coming of white men, the site of Fort Wayne was the headquarters of the Miami Indians. Known at different times as Kekionga, Kiskakon, Omee Town, Twightwee Village, Frenchtown, and Miami Town, the village was a center of trade, travel, and communication for the greater part of the area that later became known as the Northwest Territory. A 7-mile portage from this point to the Wabash River joined the waterways of the Great Lakes with those of the Wabash and the Mississippi.

When white men first came to the site is not known with certainty. Dr. Charles E. Slocum, historian, says Samuel de Champlain reached the head of the Maumee River as early as 1614, and that La Salle crossed the portage in 1669 or 1670. But even the date of the building of the first French fort, Fort Miami, is obscure; and the name of the builder is not known. According to Dr. Slocum, this fort, built on the east bank of the St. Mary's River, was begun between 1682 and 1686.

Jean Baptiste Bisset, Sieur de Vincennes, appears definitely to have 'rebuilt and strengthened the first French fort in 1697.'

In 1750 M. de Raimond, commandant of the fort, warned his government that English traders, by paying twice the French price for beaver skins and underselling the French on rifle balls, were capturing the business and ultimately would defeat the French. For his pains he was relieved of his command. True to his prediction, the fort was surrendered to the English at the close of the French and Indian wars in 1760.

In 1763 the English lost the fort temporarily to the followers of Pontiac, but soon recaptured it. They discontinued the garrison, however, and until the close of the American Revolution the site at the junction of the three rivers was a lawless trading settlement known as Miami Town. In commercial importance it was surpassed in the West only by Detroit and Vincennes, but in spite of the presence of English traders the Indians were powerful and defiant. Here many settlers captured in savage raids on settlements in Kentucky, Ohio, and southern Indiana were brought to die by torture; and the fame of Little Turtle as a soldier began in this vicinity with the massacre in 1780 of Colonel Auguste de la Balme and his troops (*see Tour 4 and History*).

At the close of the Revolution General Washington, writing to General Richard Henry Lee, said, 'I cannot forbear observing that the Miami village points to an important post for the Union.' In 1790, the second year of his presidency, Washington sent General Josiah Harmar to establish a post at Miami Town, but Harmar was outwitted and defeated by Little Turtle on October 19, only four days after his arrival. The next year General Arthur St. Clair led the second American army to defeat at Little Turtle's hands. But for the third expedition Washington selected as leader that master disciplinarian, Anthony Wayne, who drilled his army scientifically and finally defeated Little Turtle in 1794 (*see History*). After marching his army back up the Maumee, Wayne built the stockade (across the river from Miami Town) around which grew the American village of Fort Wayne.

For the next two decades the settlement was a crude military and commercial outpost—a stockade guarded by a handful of hard-drinking, often insubordinate soldiers, surrounded by squatters, traders, and hangers-on. The American Government was represented by the garrison, an Indian agent, and a factor who conducted the trading house.

From 1799 to 1809 the Indian agent was William Wells, white son-in-law of Chief Little Turtle. Kidnapped as a child in Kentucky, and adopted as a member of Little Turtle's family, Wells had become an Indian in everything but blood. He helped Little Turtle win his victories over Harmar and St. Clair, but after the St. Clair massacre he asked if he might return to his own people. Little Turtle granted his request, and from that time on Wells served the American Government, becoming chief of scouts for General Wayne in his campaign in

1794. Wells helped build the Fort Wayne stockade and with Little Turtle signed the Treaty of Greenville, opening to settlement half of Ohio and a strip of eastern Indiana. Soon after this he was appointed Indian agent.

Although Wells was a heroic figure in this pioneer period, he seems not to have been entirely trustworthy at times. Governor Harrison suspected him of bad faith when the Indians became menacing after the Treaty of 1803 (see History); but he managed to explain his actions satisfactorily and performed his duties faithfully for several years. In 1806 when Tecumseh and the Prophet began marshaling the Indians against American expansion, Wells warned Governor Harrison, and he and Little Turtle kept their Miamis aloof from the Shawnee confederacy. In 1809 he revealed to the governor Tecumseh's plan to 'destroy all the white people at Vincennes and all those that live on the Wabash and the Ohio as low down as the mouth of the Ohio and as high up as Cincinnati.' In spite of these valuable services to the Government, however, Wells was dismissed as Indian agent in 1809 for his failure to deliver $350 in annuities to the Eel River Indians; and soon afterward he seems to have had a part in agitation among the Indians against the Treaty of 1809.

To utilize Wells's recognized capabilities and keep him from thwarting Government plans, as he would if left unemployed, Governor Harrison in the spring of 1811 sent him to Prophet's Town (see Tour 17) to investigate Tecumseh. More and more Fort Wayne had become a meeting place for armed Indians passing between Prophet's Town and Malden, the British fort on the Canadian side of the Detroit River. Wells's report was enlightening and led to the Battle of Tippecanoe, in which Harrison crushed the incipient Indian rebellion.

On July 14, 1812, Little Turtle died at Wells's home in Fort Wayne and was buried with military honors. About a month later Wells himself was killed at Fort Dearborn, vainly fighting to prevent the massacre of the beleaguered garrison that Harrison had sent him to help evacuate. Both Little Turtle and Wells had been faithful to the treaty with General Wayne, signed 17 years before. Soon after Wells's death the Potawatomi besieged Fort Wayne. The restraining influence of their leaders no longer operating, the neighboring Miami also participated, and not until General Harrison arrived with an army was the siege lifted.

The last Indian fighting about Fort Wayne was the massacre of several of Major Joseph Jenkinson's men late in 1813. While flatboating garrison supplies, the victims were ambushed at a bend in the St. Mary's River in what later became the 500 block of West Superior Street. With the end of the war, however, in 1815, British agitation ceased among the Indians, who abandoned the warpath with no hope of further gains. The fort was evacuated April 19, 1819, and Benjamin F. Stickney, Indian agent and civil authority, took possession.

In 1819 Judge Samuel Hanna settled here and with his brother-in-law, James Barnett, built a log-cabin trading post and the town's first gristmill. Called the 'builder of the city,' Hanna was later the guiding genius of the Fort Wayne section of the Wabash & Erie Canal, the first railroad, and other progressive enterprises. In the year after Hanna's arrival came Francis Comparet and Alexis Coquillard, partners in the fur trade; they were followed in 1822 by Colonel Alexander Ewing and his four sons. Coquillard soon moved on to found South Bend, but two of Ewing's sons, G. W. and W. G. Ewing, amassed large fortunes in Fort Wayne from the fur trade.

At the government land sale October 22, 1823, John T. Barr of Baltimore, Maryland, and John McCorkle, of Piqua, Ohio, pooled resources and bought for $1.25 an acre the tract that became downtown Fort Wayne. In the same year William Rockhill, Joseph Holman, Jesse L. Williams, Hugh Hanna (Samuel Hanna's brother), and Allen Hamilton established homes and businesses here. Several years later Hugh Hanna and Holman pushed westward to found, respectively, Wabash and Peru, Indiana. On April 1, 1824, at a meeting held in the community's first tavern, built by Colonel Ewing, Allen County was organized and Fort Wayne named the seat of government. A brick store building at 236 East Columbia Street occupies the site of the old hostelry.

For several years the principal support of the village was the fur trade. Fort Wayne grew, however, and in 1829 it was incorporated as a town, with a population of 300. Three years later the Wabash & Erie Canal was begun, and the population, stimulated by the building and operation of the canal, reached 2,080 by 1840. When the canal was completed from Toledo, Ohio, to LaFayette, Indiana, in 1843, yards for building canal boats were added to Fort Wayne industries, which already included tanneries, distilleries, breweries, and water-power sawmills and gristmills.

By now the presence of the Indians had become a problem. Quarterly payments of annuities brought large numbers of them to Fort Wayne, where they were preyed upon by white scalawags who cheated and robbed them in trade and gambling and sold them villainous liquor at outrageous prices. The Indians would neither work nor hunt game in the forest; their habits became squalid and obscene, their manner of life miserable. Finally in 1846, except for a few families for whom special reservations were made, the Miami were removed to lands in Miami County, Kansas, and in 1867 to Miami, Oklahoma.

They were led westward by Chief Francis La Fontaine. In 1847, while returning to his home in Huntington, Chief La Fontaine died in LaFayette, believed to be the victim of a poison plot (*see Tour 5*). His predecessor as chief had been his father-in-law, Jean Baptiste Richardville, son of a French father and Indian mother. Undoubtedly interested in the funds which he, as chief, would receive from the sale of reservation lands, Richardville had persuaded his Indians to cede the last of their territory to the Government. His people felt he had betrayed them and he was forced to leave Fort Wayne for safety until feeling among the Indians subsided. Five years before the removal of the tribe, Richardville died, wealthy, in a large brick house the Government built for him on the St. Mary's River four miles south of the city. None of his vast holdings about Fort Wayne remains today in the hands of his descendants, the Miami Godfroys.

The decade before the Civil War saw the foundation of Fort Wayne's later industry and commerce. In 1853 the Brass Foundry and Machine Company was founded, one of the oldest factories in Indiana in point of continuous operation and once the world's largest manufacturer of railroad car wheels. The next year brought the first railroad into Fort Wayne, the Ohio & Indiana, built from Crestline, Ohio. The Fort Wayne & Chicago was constructed in 1856. Later these two lines were consolidated with the Pennsylvania & Ohio (Pittsburgh to Crestline) to become the Pittsburgh, Fort Wayne & Chicago Railway System, backbone of the great Pennsylvania Lines. The city's population jumped from 4,200 to 8,400 in the first decade of railroad building.

Between 1869 and 1871, four other railroads were built through the city; and by 1874, except for a small amount of traffic between Fort Wayne and some Ohio points, the Wabash & Erie Canal passed out of the transportation picture. The city shared in the industrial boom that followed the Civil War, the lumber business being outstanding until the hardwood forests of the region were exhausted. Branch industries included those manufacturing wagon beds and wheels, organs, and pianos. In 1871 the Horton Manufacturing Company, a pioneer in the washing-machine field, opened its factory here. From initial production of a crude hand-operated invention of Dr. Theodore Horton, the company later claimed the distinction of having been first to apply electrical power to operation of domestic washing machines.

Fort Wayne claims to be the birthplace of night baseball. On Saturday night, June 2, 1883, at the old League Park, which was then on the 'flats' at what is now the foot of Calhoun Street, a team of professionals from Quincy, Illinois, played a team made up of students of the Fort Wayne Methodist Episcopal College under the 'rays of electric light.' The game was witnessed by some 2,000 persons, who saw the professionals defeat the students by a score of 11 to 10. The arc-lighting system was installed by the Fort Wayne Jenney Electric Light Company, predecessor of the present General Electric Company. The park was lighted by 17 arc lights of the Jenney low-tension type, using half-inch carbons, which furnished illumination equal to 4,857 gas burners. In brilliancy the spectacle was a great success, but as a specimen of ball playing it was poor indeed.

From 1870 to 1930 the city's population grew at the rate of about 35 per cent every 10 years, but since 1930 the rate of increase has dropped to less than 3 per cent. Among notable natives of Fort Wayne are Dr. Alice Hamilton, renowned authority on occupational and industrial diseases and assistant professor of Industrial Medicine at Harvard; Carole Lombard, motion picture actress; and Dr. George Frederick Dick and his wife, Dr. Gladys Dick, who developed the Dick test for scarlet fever.

POINTS OF INTEREST

1. The McCULLOCH HOMESTEAD (*private*), 616 W. Superior St., was built in 1838 by Hugh McCulloch, banker and Secretary of the Treasury under Presidents Lincoln, Johnson, and Arthur. Formal Colonial in style, this fine old mansion retains much of its original beauty in spite of remodeling.

2. REMAINS OF THE OLD AQUEDUCT are on the west bank of St. Mary's River, 150 ft. N. of W. Main St. Bridge. The Nickel Plate R.R. Bridge crosses the river where the aqueduct once crossed carrying the waters of the Wabash & Erie Canal.

3. The SITE OF POST MIAMI is immediately north of the aqueduct on the east bank of St. Mary's River. The fort was burned by the Indians in the Chief Nicholas conspiracy of 1748. Repaired by the new commandant, Monsieur de Raimond, the same year, it was abandoned in 1750 for a new site on the east bank of the St. Joseph River.

4. The SITE OF THE CANAL-FEEDER JUNCTION, Rumsey Ave. and Wheeler St., is where the feeder canal joined the Wabash & Erie Canal. The feeder's northern terminus connected with the St. Joseph River six miles north of town, where the House of the Keeper of the Dam Gate still stands. As part of the Fourth of July celebration in 1834, the year the feeder canal was completed, the first canal boat in Indiana, laden with excursionists, was navigated up this intake canal.

5. SWINNEY PARK, W. end of Jefferson St., 90 acres of landscaped woodland cut through by the winding St. Mary's River, is Fort Wayne's third largest park. At the east entrance, Jefferson and Garden Sts., is the Fort Wayne-Allen County Museum (*open 9–4 daily*), housed in the old farm homestead of the park donor, the late Colonel Thomas W. Swinney. The two-and-a-half-story brick home was built in 1844. In the museum's collection are pioneer relics, archeological objects, historical documents and letters, rare books, and mementoes of the Indian wars. Most cherished is a camp bed used by General Wayne. Here also is the sword given Little Turtle by President Washington.

In the central area of the eastern part of the park is a Boulder Memorial to Johnny Appleseed, whose real name was John Chapman, a strange character who began preaching the gospel and planting orchards through the Midwest in 1801 (*see Folklore and Folkways*).

The portage of early river travel crossed the St. Mary's River in Swinney Park just north of State 24. West of the river is a Japanese Garden.

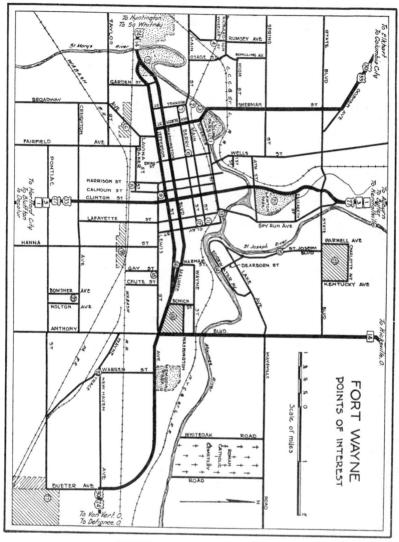

KEY FOR FORT WAYNE MAP

1. McCulloch Homestead   2. Remains of the Old Aqueduct   3. Site of Post Miami
4. Site of the Canal Feeder Junction   5. Swinney Park   6. General Electric Company Plant   7. Fort Wayne Art School and Museum   8. Lincoln National Life Insurance Building   9. Cathedral of the Immaculate Conception   10. Old Ewing Homestead   11. Old Fort Park   12. Site of the First American Fort   13. Site of East End of Portage   14. Site of Wyllys Massacre   15. Site of Fort Miami   16. Anthony Wayne Monument   17. International Harvester Company Motor Truck Plant   18. Samuel Hanna Memorial   19. Concordia College   20. Site of the Parade of Armies   21. Lawton Park   22. Fort Wayne State School

6. The GENERAL ELECTRIC COMPANY PLANT (*open; guides furnished*), along the Pennsylvania and Wabash R.R. tracks E. and W. of Broadway, is the largest industrial plant in Fort Wayne. Its 30 factory buildings have 1,506,182 square feet of floor space and are chiefly of concrete construction with brick and stone trim. There is a large administration building. A clubhouse with gymnasium, lockers and shower rooms, bowling alleys, billiard and pool tables, and motion-picture equipment is used exclusively by employees and their guests. Products include AC generators and synchronous motors, DC motors and generators, dynamometers and brakes, printing press devices, elevator and shovel sets, fractional horsepower motors, transformer specialties, refrigeration machinery, switchboards, and textolite products. At peak of production about 10,000 persons are employed. A part of the plant is at Winter and Lanternier Streets, where the refrigeration machinery is manufactured.

7. The FORT WAYNE ART SCHOOL AND MUSEUM (*open* 8:30–4:30 *Mon.-Fri.*, 9–3 *Sat.*, 2–5 *Sun.; Wed. lectures* 25¢), 1026 W. Berry St., a remodeled residence with auditorium added at rear, contains a reference library on art subjects, 2,000 reproductions, and a permanent collection of paintings and prints. Founded in 1888, the school has included in its staff notable Indiana painters such as J. Otis Adams, William Forsyth, and Homer Davisson. The organization maintains a day school, Saturday school, and night school, with an average enrollment of 100, and brings art exhibitions to the city. In a financial crisis early in its history, the school was saved by Miss Margaret V. Hamilton, daughter of a pioneer family of the city.

8. The LINCOLN NATIONAL LIFE INSURANCE BUILDING (*open* 8–4:30 *Mon.-Fri.*), 1301 S. Harrison St., is a U-shaped structure of three full stories, penthouse, and observation tower. Doric in design, the building is of steel and Indiana limestone finished in Vermont granite. The portico has four fluted columns extending to the second floor. In the forecourt is a STATUE OF LINCOLN AS A BOY, for which Paul Manship, noted sculptor, had neither model nor photograph. The statue is symbolic of youth and its attributes. The building contains an outstanding MUSEUM OF LINCOLN LORE and a very extensive library of Lincolniana.

9. The CATHEDRAL OF THE IMMACULATE CONCEPTION, a Roman Catholic church on Calhoun St. between Jefferson and Lewis Sts., mainly Gothic in design, has some of the most beautiful Bavarian stained-glass windows in the United States. The secret staining process used on the glass was lost with the passing of the German family that perfected it. The main altar is said to be one of the finest examples of wood carving in America.

10. The OLD EWING HOMESTEAD (*private*), corner Berry and Ewing Sts., a good example of architecture of its period, Georgian Colonial in feeling, was built in 1854 by Judge William G. Ewing, son of Colonel Alexander Ewing, one of the pioneer settlers.

11. OLD FORT PARK, NW. corner Main and Clay Sts., a small triangular plot with flower beds, shrubbery, and a Spanish War monument, marks the site of the second and last American fort at Fort Wayne, built by Major John Whistler in 1815. It was torn down in 1857.

12. The SITE OF THE FIRST AMERICAN FORT, NW. corner Clay and Berry Sts., is designated by a marker. The fort was built in 1794 by General Anthony Wayne following his successful expedition against Little Turtle, whose Indians he defeated twice in Ohio before marching his army up the Maumee to build the stockade at Miami Town.

13. The SITE OF EAST END OF PORTAGE is on St. Mary's River between LaFayette and Clay Sts. Here the *pirogues* and canoes of early river travelers were taken from the water, carried westward across the territory that became downtown Fort Wayne and Swinney Park, and launched again in Little Wabash River.

14. The SITE OF WYLLYS MASSACRE, on the north bank of Maumee River at Edgewater Ave. and Dearborn St., is designated by a marker. Here Major John Wyllys and 60 regulars were slaughtered by Indians. President Washington had sent Colonel John Hardin to make an establishment at Fort Wayne. On October 19, 1790, Colonel Hardin was ambushed and defeated by Little Turtle at the site of Heller's Corners, 11 miles northwest of Miami Town. Following this engagement Colonel Hardin, accompanied by Major Wyllys, attempted to encircle Miami Town on October 22, but his impetuous militia were destroyed by a stratagem of the crafty Indians and Wyllys and his men were left to face the Indians alone, resulting in the whites' slaughter.

15. The SITE OF FORT MIAMI is on the east bank of St. Joseph River at Delaware Ave. and St. Joseph Blvd. A marker designates the site. This, the second and last French fort built here, was surrendered to the English in 1760. In the Pontiac War of 1763 (*see History*) the English fort fell after its commandant, Ensign Robert Holmes, was lured from the stockade by his Indian sweetheart and slain. The Indians displayed Holmes's severed head before the garrison while a French Canadian in the fort urged submission. The British recaptured the fort soon afterward but did not garrison it again.

16. The ANTHONY WAYNE MONUMENT, NW. corner Hayden Park, Harmar St., and Maumee Ave., is a heroic-size equestrian statue of the general for whom the city is named. The statue, sculptured by Charles E. Mulligan of Chicago, was dedicated in 1918.

17. The INTERNATIONAL HARVESTER COMPANY MOTOR TRUCK PLANT (*open 9–12 Mon.-Fri.*) occupies 137 acres at the intersection of Pontiac St., extended, and the Bueter Road. Six factory buildings have 996,000 square feet of floor space. An 80-acre proving ground is maintained for the testing of motor trucks. Daily capacity is about 175 trucks. Normally, there are about 4,000 employees.

18. The SAMUEL HANNA MEMORIAL (*open*), SE. corner Lewis and Gay Sts., is a two-story, 18-room brick house reflecting the Georgian Colonial influence. It is the former home of Judge Samuel Hanna, 'the builder of Fort Wayne,' and was given to the school system of Fort Wayne by Eliza Hanna Hayden. It is now used as a children's museum of natural history and four rooms are devoted to the teaching of crippled children. In this vicinity Stephen Johnston, assistant Indian agent, was shot and killed August 28, 1812, when he left the fort to get aid for the beleaguered garrison in the Indian siege of the Fort Wayne stockade.

19. CONCORDIA COLLEGE, Washington and Anthony Blvds., is maintained by the German Lutheran synod as a coeducational high school and junior college to prepare students for the Lutheran ministry. The 1940 enrollment was about 500.

20. The SITE OF THE PARADE OF ARMIES is at the corner of Wayne Trace and New Haven Ave. A marker at the spot designates it as a point on the route into Fort Wayne traveled in 1790 by the ill-starred army of General Josiah Harmar; by General Harrison's army in 1812; and from the town in 1794 by the victorious army of General Wayne.

21. LAWTON PARK, Spy Run and Tennessee Aves., Fort Wayne's oldest park, was named for the city's most distinguished soldier, General Henry W. Lawton, veteran of the Civil War and captor in 1886 of the Apache chief, Gerónimo, after a chase of 1,400 miles. As a major general in the war with Spain, he led the charge up El Caney at Santiago, Cuba. He was killed by an enemy sharpshooter in the Aguinaldo rebellion in the Philippines December 19, 1899. The park is cut through by Spy Run Creek.

22. The FORT WAYNE STATE SCHOOL, 801 E. State Blvd., is a $2,000,000 State institution for feeble-minded women and children. Institutional buildings on the 54-acre reservation include residential cottages, factories, greenhouse, hospital, laundry, bakery, and heat, light, water, and cold-storage plants. Two farms provide employment for part of the inmates.

The school course includes kindergarten, primary and advanced academic work, domestic science, wood and metal work, physical education, sense training, vocal and instrumental music, sewing, basketry and weaving. Children and adults are kept busy in the institution's dressmaking, tailoring, shoe, and printing shops at tasks within range of their abilities.

POINTS OF INTEREST IN ENVIRONS

Site of Eel River Post and Village of Little Turtle, 18.5 *m.* (*see Tour* 4). Gronauer House and Canal Lock, 8.3 *m.;* Vermilyea Tavern, 11.5 *m.* (*see Tour* 5). Heller's Corners, 11.2 *m.* (*see Tour* 15).

Indianapolis

Railroad Stations: Union Station, S. Illinois St. and Jackson Place, for Big Four, Pennsylvania, Illinois Central, Baltimore & Ohio, and Monon; Suburban Station, 1100 E. 38th St., for Chicago Division Monon passengers; Union Ticket Office, 210 Guaranty Bldg.

Interurbans: Indiana Railroad, Inc., N. Illinois St. at Market.

Bus Stations: Traction Terminal, Illinois and Market Sts., for Greyhound, American Stage, Central Indiana Coach, Central Swallow Coach, Hoosier Transit, Indianapolis Railway, Indianapolis and Southeastern, Swallow Coach, Indianapolis-Martinsville, Indianapolis-Sheridan, Indianapolis and Vincennes, ABC Coach, Indiana Motor Bus, White Star, Indianapolis-Crawfordsville Transit, Del Ray, Indianapolis-Rockville-Clinton Line, Beech Grove, Indianapolis-Danville, and Scenic Bus Lines of Indiana; 226 N. Illinois St. for All American and Yankee Coach Lines.

Airport: Municipal, 6 m. SW. on High School Road, for Transcontinental and Western, American, and Eastern Airlines; ticket offices, TWA, 108 W. Washington St., Amer., 609 Merchants Bank Bldg.

Taxis: Rates 15¢ first 1.5 m., 10¢ each mile thereafter.

Streetcars, Trackless Trolleys: Fare 7¢, 4 tokens 25¢, transfer car to car 2¢, transfer to bus 4¢.

Motor Busses: Common terminus Monument Circle, fare 10¢, transfer bus to bus or bus to streetcar, free.

Traffic Regulations: No turn on red light; U-turns only at corners where not prohibited; drive to right of safety zones; stop with streetcars at non-zoned stops. Parking limit in downtown area indicated by signs. No double or all-night parking. Lights on 30 min. after sunset to 30 min. before sunrise. 20-mile speed limit in business district, 30 m. otherwise: enforced.

Accommodations: 73 hotels. Tourist camps along highways entering city.

Information Service: A.A.A., Hoosier Motor Club, 1840 N. Meridian St., phone WAbash 3311.

Street Order and Numbering: Washington St. dividing line for north-south numbers; Meridian St. dividing line for east-west numbers.

Theaters and Motion Picture Houses: 2 legitimate; 4 first-run movies, 1 vaudeville. Neighborhood movies in all sections of town.

Radio Stations: WFBM (1260 kc.); WIRE (1430 kc.); WIBC (1070 kc.).

Baseball: Indianapolis 'Indians' (American Association), Perry Stadium, W. 16th St.

Football: Butler University, Butler Stadium.

Basketball: Amateur, Butler University, and finals of State high school tournament, Butler University Fieldhouse, 46th and Sunset. Professional, Indiana National Guard Armory, 711 N. Pennsylvania. All games as scheduled.

Automobile Races: International 500-mile Sweepstakes at Speedway City, W. 16th St., on Memorial Day; gen. adm. $2.50 plus 25¢ tax; infield parking free; reserved seats $1 to $10; reserved parking $10 to $25; adm. qualif. trials, 50¢.

Horse Racing: Grand Circuit harness races, State Fairgrounds, E. 38th St. and Fairgrounds Ave., week starting Labor Day.

Riding: Indiana Saddle Horse Association, administrative offices, 646 Indianapolis Athletic Club, 350 N. Meridian St.

Archery: Range in N. end Riverside Park; no fees.

Tennis: 85 courts in larger parks, open daily, no fees.

Golf: Charles E. Coffin Course, W. 30th and Cold Springs Road, 18 holes, fee 50¢; Riverside Course, W. 30th and Riverside Pkwy., 18 holes, 50¢; South Grove, W. 18th St. and Riverside Pkwy., 18 holes, fee 50¢; Douglas (Negro), 25th and Martindale, 9 holes, fee 25¢; Pleasant Run, Arlington and 9th St., 18 holes, fee 50¢; Sarah Shank, Keystone and Troy, 9 holes, fee 25¢.

Parks: Brookside, 2200 Brookside Pkwy.; Christian, English Ave. and Denny St.; Douglas (Negro), 25th and Martindale; Ellenberger, Pleasant Run and Ritter; Garfield, Southern Ave. and Shelby St.; George Washington, Dearborn and 30th St.; Haverford, Arsenal and 46th St.; Little Eagle, Eagle Creek and Tomlinson; Holliday, Spring Mill Road and 64th St.; Northwestern (Negro), Fall Creek and Northwestern; Rhodius, Belmont and Reisner; Riley, Kentucky and Ray; Spades, Newman and Nowland; Thomas Taggart Riverside, between W. 16th and 38th along White River, 12 tennis courts, rowboats and canoes for rent, 1 football field, 10 horseshoe courts, 3 softball diamonds, 2 hockey fields, and archery range; University, Meridian and New York; Big Eagle, 4400 W. Michigan, 93 acres; Willard, Washington and State; Broad Ripple, 62nd and White River, amusement; Riverside, W. 30th and White River, amusement. Supervised playgrounds open June to September.

Swimming: Swimming and wading in Broad Ripple, Douglas, Ellenberger, Garfield, and Rhodius Parks, June to September, 10 A.M. to 2 P.M. free; 2 P.M. to 10 P.M. adm. 10¢; lockers 10¢; towels 5¢; suits 25¢. Willard Park, swimming 10 A.M. to 10 P.M. free. Lifeguards in attendance.

Beaches: White River at W. 26th St.; Big Eagle Creek at Rowena Ave.; Fall Creek at Millersville Road; White River Dam at Riverside (Negro); all beaches patrolled.

Annual Events: Golden Gloves Boxing, Armory, Jan. 30; Fine Arts Exhibit, John Herron Art Institute, Jan. 30; President's Birthday Ball, Jan. 30; Indiana High School Athletic Association Amateur Basketball Finals, Butler Fieldhouse, Mar.; Indianapolis Home Show, State Fairgrounds, Apr.; Opening Day Baseball, American Association, 'Indians,' Perry Stadium, Apr.; Easter Sunrise Service, Monument Circle, Easter Morning; outboard motor races, Westlake, May; 500-Mile Motor Race, May 30, Motor Speedway; Amateur Swimming Championship, sponsored by Park Board, July; Soap Box Derby, Williams Hill, US 31, July; Gladiolus Show, State Fairgrounds, Aug.; Indiana State Fair, State Fairgrounds, Aug.-Sept.; outboard motor races, Ravenswood, Labor Day.

INDIANAPOLIS (750 alt., 386,972 pop.) is the capital of Indiana and seat of Marion County. Embracing 54.13 square miles in the heart of a fertile, undulating agricultural area, it is the largest city in the United States not on navigable water. An important commercial and railroad center in the Middle West, Indianapolis has become a popular convention city the year round, although the outstanding event of the year is undoubtedly the Memorial Day auto race at the Motor Speedway.

The visitor's first impression is one of spacious friendliness—broad streets, an almost Southern leisureliness, and fewer tall buildings than are seen in most cities of comparable size. Washington Street (US 40), the chief east-west thoroughfare, is nine miles long and as wide as any village Main Street; Meridian Street, less important commercially but first in residential stateliness, expands northward into a broad avenue.

This quiet spaciousness of Indianapolis results both from the terrain and from deliberate planning. Built on level ground with plenty of room to expand, the city was patterned after Washington, D. C. Its streets intersect at right angles and four great avenues cut away diagonally from the business section. Central to this plan and most memorable to the visitor is Monument Circle, from the heart of which towers the Soldiers and Sailors Monument. Also in the center of the city, scattered among stores and office buildings, are the State Capitol, the State and city libraries, and the Scottish Rite Cathedral.

South of the theater and shopping section are the warehouses of the wholesale district, freight yards, and the smoke stacks of many of the city's factories. Beginning several blocks south of Washington, Meridian Street is a miniature New York Lower East Side, with a large proportion of foreign and Jewish shops and restaurants; still farther south are neighborhoods of trim houses, here and there a belt of slums, and Garfield Park with its sunken gardens. Westward along White River lie packing houses and factories, rising in the midst of drab streets of workers' homes; and Indiana Avenue, slanting northwest into the densely populated Negro section, is lined with little shops and stores. Northwest along White River is Riverside Park, a kind of inland Coney Island. Farther north are the Gothic halls of Butler University set in a park-like campus; a few miles westward on 16th Street is the Indianapolis Motor Speedway.

A mile and a half east of Monument Circle between Michigan and 10th Streets is an incorporated town within the city—Woodruff Place, which has never been annexed by Indianapolis, although it is wholly surrounded by it. A residential district, platted in 1872 and incorporated four years later as a suburb of Indianapolis, it covers 80 acres and has a population of about 1,200. Grass and flowers in the center of drives ornamented by fountains, urns, and Victorian statuary, together with tall trees, wide lawns, and gingerbread architectural details give this district an air of respectable old age. No business building of any kind is permitted.

North on such streets as Delaware and Pennsylvania are many fine old houses, set deep in shaded lawns and still inhabited by the descendants of their builders. Many newer residences of architectural distinction are on the curving, well-shaded lanes of Irvington, the extreme eastern section of the city, and in large sections in the north, where winding drives and wooded avenues provide desirable residential areas for the well-to-do. Probably the most beautiful of these drives is Fall Creek Parkway. Beginning at the Thomas Taggart Memorial Archway in Riverside Park it follows the meanderings of Fall Creek for nearly 12 miles past small parks and playgrounds. East of Keystone Avenue the drive is flanked by a bicycle path and a bridle path and, after passing Woollen's Gardens of Birds and Botany and the Boy Scout Reservation, ends near Fort Benjamin Harrison.

A source of community pride is the street railway system of Indianapolis, ranking, according to government officials throughout the United States and Canada, as one of the finest in the world.

The site of Indianapolis was selected for the State capital because of its central location, which also became a great commercial advantage. More than half of all the farming in Indiana is done within 75 miles of this city, now the third largest corn and livestock market in the United States as well as an important banking center and the home of several insurance companies. Also because of its location Indianapolis has become one of the leading railway centers of the country. The first Union Station was built here in 1853; in 1877 the first Belt Railroad in the country was completed here. This 14-mile double-track belt, surrounding much of the city, greatly facilitates freight transportation. Most large cities have since adopted the idea.

Although the location of Indianapolis was a great advantage commercially, it was less beneficial to the development of industry. In spite of excellent railway facilities, the absence of navigable water has been a real handicap; the great quantities of coal and iron required for the basic industries cannot be transported cheaply enough by rail to attract large-scale enterprises. Hence Indianapolis has remained the home of relatively smaller manufacturing plants, highly diversified in their products and scattered widely throughout the city.

As an agricultural market, Indianapolis has attracted the meat-packing and milling industries, and large quantities of canned goods are produced. Industries using wood are also important—with a number of plants devoted to the manufacture of paper and furniture. Serums and pharmaceutical products are made, notably by Eli Lilly and Company, one of the largest biological laboratories in the country. Many plants manufacture textiles and clothing of all sorts; one of the largest plants in this field is the Real Silk Hosiery Mills, with an annual capacity of 1,750,000 dozen pairs of socks and stockings. Finally a number of factories manufacture machine-shop products, aircraft engines, and automobiles, bodies, and accessories.

This pattern of decentralized industry has affected the social character of the city. Partly because workers are scattered in so many small factories, Indianapolis was until the winter of 1936-7 nearly 95 per cent an 'open shop' town. This percentage, however, has decreased, since several thousand steel (machine shop), textile, and automobile workers have joined CIO unions. The same factors have kept Indianapolis from acquiring the tempo and aspect of a metropolitan center. Among large cities it is remarkable in the number of its churches (340, embracing all important denominations, with a heavy Protestant majority), which constitute the chief social and community tie of a large section of the population. It is also known as a city of homes. Forty per cent of the families own their homes, and there are 228 houses for every 1,000 persons. But undoubtedly the most important effect of the city's lack of large-scale industry is its racial composition. More than most cities of its size, its population is predominantly native-born white.

The outstanding racial minority is the Negro group. Although there are naturally many cultural levels and ways of life among Indianapolis Negroes, their Southern origin is still apparent—in their soft, slow speech, in the Saturday night 'revivals' held on street corners in warm weather, and in the popular 'chitlin' parties. Chitlins are a highly esteemed delicacy prepared from the entrails of the hog, usually served with high seasoning, cornbread, and slaw. Other indications of Southern origin are to be found in the closeness of even the most highly educated Negro groups to the folk roots and traditions, the folk humor and vocabulary of the masses of the race.

Thus in respect to racial composition and religious interests, Indianapolis differs from the typical small town in Indiana less in quality than in mere size. It offers little of the brilliant or the bizarre; hence, only with the deeper understanding of long intimacy comes the knowledge that the Indiana capital is an intriguing cross section of American life—that 'typical American life' which Booth Tarkington so well described.

The earliest settlers near what is now Indianapolis were George Pogue and John McCormick and their families, who came in February 1820. They built their cabins in the woods, more than a mile apart—Pogue's on high ground near where today East Michigan Street crosses Pogue's Run; McCormick's on the east bank of White River, just north of what is now Washington Street. Indian settlements were near by, and at night the lights of 'fire fishing' parties could be seen on the streams. Other settlers soon came, and by summer a dozen or more cabins had sprung up along the east bank of the river. Fur traders and travelers dubbed the spot the Fall Creek settlement.

Meanwhile, in January 1820, the legislature at Corydon chose 10 commissioners and instructed them to select a site for a new capital, as near as possible to the center of the State. On June 7, 1820, the commissioners decided on the Fall Creek site.

The new city was laid out in a mile square by E. P. Fordham, a surveyor. Attracted by the prospect of settling in the future seat of State government, many settlers soon arrived; and after legislative approval of the site in 1821, the city was named Indianapolis (*Indiana* plus *polis,* Gr. city). Alexander Ralston, who had helped to lay out the city of Washington, D. C., was then appointed to complete the task of surveying. In 1821 Marion County was organized, with Indianapolis as the county seat. Stores, taverns, and homes were built; more new settlers kept arriving; and in 1822 the first newspaper, the *Gazette,* made its appearance.

In 1824 the courthouse was built, a brick structure that served later as the State Capitol. At this time the capital was only a village of 600 people; but after January 1825, when the first legislature met, the town boomed because of its political importance. Roads were constructed, a brickyard was opened, and a ferry was established across the White River. In 1830 the building of the National Road through Indianapolis gave further impetus to its growth, and in 1836 it was incorporated as a town. An engineer was appointed, and sewerage and street improvements were begun.

The panic of 1837 delayed progress but in 1839 the State completed the construction of the Central Canal from Broad Ripple to Indianapolis. Water power was then available; factories were built; and gristmills, paper mills, woolen mills, and sawmills sprang up. In a few years the volume of water diminished to such an extent that the canal was useless, and water transportation was replaced by the railroad. The first steam train puffed into the city on the Madison Railroad in February 1847, hailed with wild excitement and feted by parades and banquets.

In the same year Indianapolis was incorporated as a city and its citizens first voted for tax-supported schools. From 1840 to 1847 Henry Ward Beecher, famous writer, preacher, and brother of Harriet Beecher Stowe, author of *Uncle Tom's Cabin*, lived in Indianapolis. While here he was pastor of the Second Presbyterian Church, then on Monument Circle, and edited the *Indiana Farmer and Gardener*.

By the outbreak of the Civil War, Indianapolis had emerged from the pioneer stage. Sidewalk and street improvements and gas street lights had been installed; fire and police departments were operating. By 1860 more than 100 manufacturing concerns were here, and the yearly pay roll for factory workers was nearly $250,000, a large figure for that era in the Middle West. During the 1850's many Germans had arrived, bringing the *rathskeller, Saengerbund,* and Lutheran Church. Musical and literary organizations were thriving, and the Masonic Temple and newly erected Metropolitan Theater were available for lectures and plays.

When war was declared, Indianapolis, under the inspiration of Governor Oliver P. Morton, immediately put its full quota into the field. During the war the city became State recruiting headquarters. There was a large ammunition factory; and Camp Morton, which was first used as an instruction camp and later as a Confederate prison camp, was occupied by six regiments of Union soldiers.

The period from 1865 to 1873 was one of rapid growth and expansion, during which the first streetcars were introduced and thousands of homes were built every year. This boom, the result of war inflation, collapsed in 1873. Recovery was slow, but in 1890 Indianapolis entered another expansion period. Natural gas was introduced, providing cheap fuel for manufacturing and causing an influx of new industries. In 1860 the annual value of manufactured products was less than $2,000,-000; in 1900 it was $60,000,000. The annual industrial pay roll, less than $250,000 in 1860, was more than $10,000,000 in 1900; and the city's total population had grown to 170,000. Meanwhile, increased traffic brought a need for economical short-distance transportation, and the interurban railway system was developed. By 1902 electric lines connected Indianapolis with all the principal towns of the State, and the city was known as the Nation's largest interurban center.

At about this time the automobile industry became important, and Indianapolis began to manufacture automobiles and accessories on a quantity production basis. As a matter of record, Indianapolis probably gave America its first gasoline automobile. Although Elwood Haynes of Kokomo built and operated the first mechanically successful clutch-driven car with electrical ignition in 1894, an automobile with an internal combustion gasoline engine was built in Indianapolis in 1891 by Charles H. Black. His 'horseless buggy,' however, used a kerosene torch for ignition; and it was this impracticable device, one that would blow out on a windy day, that prevented Black from being recognized as the inventor and builder of the first successful automobile.

Before the World War automobile factories hummed in Indianapolis. Many innovations and improvements in motorcar manufacturing originated here, notably four-wheel brakes and the six-cylinder motor. An important by-product of the city's automobile industry was the building of the Motor Speedway. The first 500-mile auto race, held in 1911, was won by an Indianapolis-made car, the *Marmon,* and subsequent races saw local automobiles making speed history.

In the 1920's the city's pre-eminence in the automobile industry declined. The growth of vast corporations succeeded in driving many independent manufacturers out of business, and those that survived had to operate more economically. Indianapolis was handicapped by its remoteness from sources of steel and coal, and by the fact that the long haul on the railroad is far more costly than by water. Thunderously surviving to remind the world of past supremacy, however, the annual 500-mile race is still the high point, nationally, of the automobile year.

Indianapolis has been the home of important figures in several fields: Benjamin Harrison, President of the United States; Vice Presidents Thomas R. Marshall, Charles W. Fairbanks, Thomas A. Hendricks, and Schuyler Colfax; the painters Otto Stark, T. C. Steele, and William Forsyth; Albert J. Beveridge, statesman and author; Kin Hubbard, humorist; Paxton Hibben, journalist and diplomat; and the poet James Whitcomb Riley. Among famous living sons who spend some of their time in the city are the novelist, Booth Tarkington; Meredith Nicholson, novelist and minister to Nicaragua; and the painters Wayman Adams, Marie Goth, Carl Graf, and Clifton Wheeler.

The Civic Theater was first organized in 1915 and for more than 25 years has produced both serious drama and light comedy. The Indianapolis Symphony Orchestra, sponsored by the Indiana State Symphony Society, is developing into a distinguished musical organization. Also important is the Mannerchor, founded in 1854 by a group of Germans, which for many years has provided excellent concerts.

POINTS OF INTEREST

1. INDIANA CENTRAL COLLEGE (*open 9–4 weekdays, Sept. to June*), 4001 Otterbein Ave., University Heights, is a coeducational institution, opened in 1905 and supported by the United Brethren Church. Composed of a College of Liberal Arts, Teachers College, Academy Conservatory of Music, School of Oratory, School of Com-

merce, Bible Institute, and School of Art, it has a faculty of 50 and an average enrollment of 500 students.

2. The STOCKYARDS (*open 8–5 weekdays*), 1500 Kentucky Ave., occupy 200 acres of ground with a capacity of 50,000 head of livestock daily. These yards, opened in 1877, are today (1941) the largest east of Chicago.

3. The UNION STATION, S. Illinois St. and Jackson Place, is of red stone and brick, Romanesque in style. It was erected in 1888 to replace the original station built in 1853, which was the first Union Station in the United States. It is used by all passenger trains, a total of 116 entering and leaving daily.

4. FLANNER HOUSE (*open 8–5 Mon.-Fri.; 8–12 Sat.*), 802 N. West St., a Negro social service and training center, occupies four frame buildings, containing a number of departments and divisions adapted to social service work. A playground adjoins the building.

5. The INDIANA UNIVERSITY MEDICAL CENTER (*open 8–5 weekdays, apply at Administration Building*), 1040–1232 W. Michigan St., occupies 93 acres and consists of three hospitals, a nurses' school and home, medical school, dental school, and a convalescent park. It is controlled by the State.

The ADMINISTRATIVE AND CLINICAL BUILDING (*open 8–5 weekdays*), rear of Robert W. Long Hospital, is the nerve center of the Indiana University medical group. In this six-story brick, stone, and tile building of modern perpendicular design are administrative offices, admitting rooms, case histories of patients treated at all hospitals of the group, and all files and records. All patients are received here, except in extreme emergencies.

This building also houses the out-patient clinic, equipped with modern devices for combating disease. Radium and X-ray equipment used in the fight against cancer, a galvanic generator used to combat arthritis, ultraviolet lamps, diathermy heat current machines, and spark-proof switches to prevent explosion of ether are part of the equipment of this department. Living quarters for resident members of the medical staff are also provided. The building was completed in 1938.

The ROBERT W. LONG HOSPITAL (*open 7–8 P.M. Tues., Thurs.; 2–3:30 P.M. Fri., Sun.*) is a modern, general hospital for patients from rural districts and small towns without hospital facilities. It is named for the original donor, Robert W. Long, an Indianapolis physician.

The JAMES WHITCOMB RILEY HOSPITAL FOR CHILDREN (*open 2–4 Sun.*), largest unit of the Indiana Medical Center, is a charitable institution for treatment of physically handicapped children. The interior is decorated to appeal to youngsters. Illustrations of Riley's poems are found in the art-glass windows and wall decorations. Student nurses wear bright-colored uniforms; an occupational therapy workshop is maintained; the Cheer Guild, with 6,500 members, supplies books and toys, and gives parties for the children. New hydrotherapeutic pools are used in the treatment of infantile paralysis and other diseases.

The WILLIAM H. COLEMAN HOSPITAL (*open* 7–8 P.M. *Tues., Thurs.;* 2:30–3:30 P.M. *Fri., Sun.*), established in 1927 through a donation by Mr. and Mrs. William H. Coleman, is conducted exclusively for women patients.

The SCHOOL OF MEDICINE BUILDING (*open* 8–5 *Mon.-Fri.*) represents a union of several former medical schools of Indiana, the first of which was opened in 1869. Several mergers were made between that time and 1907, when the present school came into existence as part of the Indiana University Medical Center. The school occupies a four-story, Georgian-type, brick and stone-trim building. The first year of medicine is given at Indiana University at Bloomington and the remaining three years here. The faculty consists of 90 members; the average enrollment is 460. The SCHOOL OF DENTISTRY BUILDING (*open* 8–5 *Mon.-Fri.*), the ninth dental school to be established in America, was founded in 1879 as a private school and acquired by the State in 1925. The TRAINING SCHOOL FOR NURSES (*open* 8–5 *Mon.-Fri.*) was opened in 1914 in the Robert W. Long Hospital. Student nurses receive their training in all three hospitals in the Medical Center and in the City Hospital.

6. The STATE CAPITOL (*open* 8:30–5 *Mon.-Fri.;* 8:30–12 *Sat.*), between Washington and Ohio Sts. and Capitol and Senate Aves., is an impressive Indiana limestone structure of Neo-Roman design, erected in 1878–88.

A huge copper-covered dome surmounts a drum form of stone, with columns and carved stone ornaments. The east and south façades are adorned with Roman porticoes in the colonnade, with entablature and supporting sculptured stone figures representing the early days of the State. Flat pilasters of Roman order are engaged with the masonry walls of the building, and the caps of the windows are carved in classic forms of pediment, elliptical and keystone arch.

In addition to housing most of the State's governmental offices, the capital contains a large collection of battle flags used by Indiana regiments in the various wars, and a gallery of oil portraits of all the State's governors. In the basement is a STATE MUSEUM (*open*) containing more than 9,000 specimens, classified into nine groups: geology, history, archeology, conchology, forestry, ornithology, herpetology, zoology, and ichthyology. The C. T. Tarleton collection, loaned to the Museum, consists of swords of many types used by different nations, and steel beheading knives with wooden handles, used by savages.

7. The SCOTTISH RITE CATHEDRAL (*open* 3 P.M. *Sat. only for conducted tour*), NW. corner of Meridian and North Sts., is an imposing structure of Tudor Gothic design, built of Indiana limestone in 1929. Above the entrance on Meridian Street rises a square tower 212 feet high, with finials of the cross on top. In this tower is a great carillon, with 63 bells, the smallest 6 inches in diameter and weighing 12 pounds, the largest 7 feet in diameter and weighing 11,200 pounds. The lounge, lobby, and other rooms of the interior are elaborately decorated. The Elizabethan period banquet hall below the street level

seats 3,500 persons. The grand salon and ballroom of the same period has a balcony supported by free-standing square columns. Ritual work is given in the auditorium, which seats 1,200. The 5,000-pipe organ is played from a console on the upper balcony; an echo organ of 500 pipes is concealed above.

The auditorium, Tudor Gothic in style, has dark oak hammer beams. Eight sets of stained-glass windows represent symbols of the Rite. The stage, with complete modern electrical equipment, has a proscenium opening 38 feet wide and 28 feet high.

8. The STATE LIBRARY AND HISTORICAL BUILDING (*open 8-5 Mon.-Fri.; 8-4 Sat.*), 140 N. Senate Ave., is a four-story, air-conditioned structure, erected in 1934. The beauty of this building lies in its simple ornamentation. The entire outer wall is of Indiana limestone, with an ornamental cresting carved in scroll design. The outside walls of the fourth story and the space between the windows of the first and second floors are carved in low-relief panels of the Greek style. The approach to the central entrance is over a broad plaza of stone with large Grecian urns on either side of a classic lintel doorway.

The interior walls of the lobby, lower halls, exhibit hall, and foyer are built of variegated Monte Cassino sandstone from St. Meinrad, Indiana. To the right and left of the stairway are aisles leading to the first floor hallway, elevators, extension-division rooms, traveling library, and the newspaper and archives sections. A broad marble stair leads to the foyer of the second floor. This floor has high vaulted and paneled ceilings, large foliate burnished bronze chandeliers, walls of variegated St. Meinrad sandstone, five windows of 4,000 pieces of antique glass, and four large murals by J. Scott Williams, New York artist.

The State Library contains by far the greatest amount of material on Indiana to be found in any library, and includes a large collection of books in Braille. In addition to the State Library, the building houses the offices of the Indiana Pioneers, the Indiana Historical Society, the Delavan Smith Memorial Library, the Indiana Historical Bureau, and the department of conservation.

9. The U. S. COURTHOUSE AND POST OFFICE occupies the square between Ohio and New York Sts. and Meridian and Pennsylvania Sts. This structure is of Classic Ionic design, with exterior masonry of Indiana limestone. The central façade, on Ohio Street, is a long colonnade of Ionic order engaged with the wall masonry to the fourth floor entablature. Imposing porticoes of Ionic columns adorn the public hall entrances of the east and west wings, on Ohio, Meridian, and Pennsylvania Streets. This building houses the post office, Federal courts, and U. S. bureaus.

10. GARFIELD PARK, Raymond St. and Southern Ave., founded 1875, the city's oldest public park and named for President James A. Garfield (1831-81), contains 129 acres of wooded, rolling land. An impressive feature is the sunken garden and illuminated fountain with its scintillating rays of various colors from hidden lights. Beyond the esplanade is the lagoon with an elaborate illuminated fountain said to

be the first of its kind to be placed in any public park. A bronze statue of General Henry W. Lawton, killed in the Spanish-American War, originally placed in the courthouse grounds, was moved here in 1915. The sculptors were Daniel C. French and Andrew O'Connor. A granite shaft, erected originally in Greenlawn Cemetery as a tribute to Confederate prisoners who died in the Indianapolis prison camp, was moved here in 1929. The city's largest bathing pools for adults and children, the city's largest open-air theater, and baseball, softball, football, and tennis facilities are available. There is a large brick shelter house and community building with an assembly hall seating 500.

11. THOMAS TAGGART RIVERSIDE PARK, between 16th and 38th Sts. along the banks of White River, 930 acres in size, is the largest of the city's parks. At the Burdsal Parkway entrance is a limestone colonnade, a memorial to Thomas Taggart, senator and former mayor of Indianapolis, for whom the park was named. The southern end of the park was a Union camp (Camp Robinson) during the Civil War. There are two municipally operated bathing beaches, one at 26th Street for whites and one at 16th Street for Negroes.

EMERICHSVILLE BRIDGE, of notable design, spans the river at 16th Street. At 30th Street and White River is the NAVAL RESERVE ARMORY, a four-story modern structure of brick, steel, and concrete. Within the park is LAKE SULLIVAN, a 14-acre artificial lake named for Reginald Sullivan, former mayor of Indianapolis, who was again elected mayor in 1938. Hundreds of mallard ducks make their home in this lake.

At the north end of the park is the STATE FISH HATCHERY. It covers 22 acres and has 34 breeding ponds.

12. The INDIANAPOLIS CITY HOSPITAL (*open* 2–3 P.M. *Tues. and Fri.*), 960 Locke St., consists of 10 buildings of brick, stone trimmed, occupying a 10-acre tract of landscaped ground. The City Hospital is affiliated with the Indiana University School of Medicine as a clinical hospital but is operated and controlled by the Indianapolis Board of Health and Charities. The average annual number of patients is 14,600.

It has one of the finest interiors of any hospital in the Nation, owing to the murals donated by the St. Margaret's Hospital Guild. They were painted by Carl Graf, Simon Baus, William Forsyth, Walter Isnogle, J. Otis Adams, Otto Stark, Clifton Wheeler, Wayman Adams, William E. Scott, Francis Brown, and Emma B. King. These artists enthusiastically rendered their services for a nominal 'sum, producing a work that otherwise would have cost many thousands of dollars.

13. The BENJAMIN HARRISON HOME (*open* 10–4 *daily; adm.* 25¢), 1230 N. Delaware St., is marked by a boulder on the front lawn bearing an inscription to the 23rd President of the United States. The house is a two-story English Regency-style brick structure with bay windows, trimmed with stone. The home was taken over by the Arthur Jordan Foundation in 1937 and is kept as a memorial unit of the Arthur Jordan Conservatory of Music.

The home was built by General Harrison in 1872, 18 years after his arrival in Indianapolis to enter the practice of law; he occupied it continuously until his death in 1901, except when he was U. S. senator (1881-7) and President (1889-93). After he was defeated for re-election by Grover Cleveland in 1892 he resumed his law practice at Indianapolis. He was counsel for the Venezuelan Government before an arbitration tribunal in 1899 in a controversy with British Guiana. Much of the furniture in the house is from the Harrison family, and all is of the period of General Harrison's occupancy.

14. The COLUMBIA CONSERVE PLANT (*open* 7:30–5:30 *Mon.-Fri.*), 1735 Churchman Ave., is engaged in the canning of soups and fancy food specialties. The company was founded in 1903 by the Hapgood family as a private enterprise and in 1917 was turned over to the employees as an experiment in industrial democracy. The management, control, and ownership of the organization is vested in the workers.

15. CHRIST EPISCOPAL CHURCH, NE. segment of Monument Circle, in the business center of the city, is an ivy-covered stone structure of English Gothic style. Erected in 1857, it was for many years considered the finest church in Indiana. The spire, added in 1869, is surmounted by a finial containing the Greek letters χ ϱ (C.R.), meaning Christ. The interior is impressive in its beauty and simplicity. Flying arches of age-darkened wood sweep beneath the vaulted roof. Pews and chancel are styled after those of early English cathedrals. This structure was selected by the Indiana Advisory Committee for the Historic American Building Survey as the best type of early Indiana church architecture.

16. The KINGAN PLANT (*open* 9–3 *Mon.-Fri.*, 9–12 *Sat.; guide*), Blackford and Georgia Sts., is one of the city's largest industries and one of the Nation's largest meat-packing plants. It has a daily capacity of 10,000 hogs, 1,500 cattle, 1,000 calves, and 1,000 sheep. About 2,200 persons are employed here.

17. The JOHN HERRON ART INSTITUTE (*open* 9–5 *weekdays, 1–8 Sun., 1–6 holidays; Mon. Tues. Thurs. Fri., adm. 25¢, Wed. Sat. Sun., free*), 110 E. 16th St., was opened in 1891 for the preservation and exhibition of works of art. In front of the main building, which is modified Renaissance in design and two stories high, is a full-size plaster model of Verrocchio's noble equestrian statue of Bartolommeo Colleoni. A library, exhibition space, and collections of glass and prints occupy the main floor. On the second floor is a notable permanent exhibition of paintings and other art forms. Two art exhibits are held each year: one in January for artists who live in the United States and who participate by invitation; another in March for Indiana artists only. Concerts, lectures, and marionette shows are also given. To the north of the main building is the ART SCHOOL, operated by the Institute (*see Arts and Crafts*). The present buildings were erected in 1905 with funds bequeathed by John Herron.

18. BUTLER UNIVERSITY (*open* 8–5 *daily*), Sunset Ave. and W. 46th St., is situated on a landscaped campus of 246 acres of rolling land. Originally known as Northwestern Christian University, Butler

was founded in 1855 on a site at College Avenue and 13th Street, donated for its use by Ovid Butler. In 1875 it was moved to Irvington, where it remained until 1928, when it was removed to its present location, formerly Fairview Park.

Amidst the trees of the heavily wooded portion of the campus is JORDAN HALL, a large edifice of American Gothic design built of Indiana limestone and Salisbury granite from North Carolina. Here are the administrative offices, library, laboratories, recreation rooms, chapel, lecture rooms, and a zoological museum.

Butler University includes the Colleges of Liberal Arts and Sciences, Religion, Education, the Division of Graduate Instruction, and the Division of Evening Courses and Summer Session. The subjects taught cover the entire field of higher education. The Arthur Jordan Conservatory of Music and the John Herron Art Institute are affiliated with this university.

The STADIUM, seating 36,000, and the FIELDHOUSE, seating 16,000, are on the northeast part of the campus. Butler is a coeducational institution, with an average enrollment of 3,500 students including extension and evening classes.

19. The STATE SOLDIERS AND SAILORS MONUMENT (*open 8–5 daily; adm., 10¢; 15¢ extra for elevator service*), center of the Monument Circle, was completed in 1902. From the center of a plaza 342 feet in diameter, the monument rises to a height of 284 feet. It is said to be the first monument ever erected to the private soldier. A powerful battery of floodlights is trained on the shaft at night. Topping the monument and visible from almost any part of downtown Indianapolis is a 38-foot statue of *Victory*. Just below the statue is a glass-enclosed observation platform offering a complete view of the city.

At the base of the shaft and filling opposite sides of the pedestal are sculptured groups depicting War and Peace. On the north and south sides, standing guard at the entrance doors, are figures representing four branches of service during the Civil War: the scout, the cavalry, the sailor, and the infantry. To complete the decoration, bronze statues of General George Rogers Clark and Governors William Henry Harrison, James Whitcomb, and Oliver P. Morton commemorate four periods in the history and development of Indiana. Cascades, on the east and west sides of the monument, are covered during the summer months by a flow of water. The sculpturing in stone is the work of Rudolph Schwartz, and the bronze figures are by George T. Brewster. Bruno Schmitz was the architect.

20. CROWN HILL CEMETERY (*open 8–4 daily*), 3402 Boulevard Place, covering 540 acres, is the largest cemetery in the city and the burial place of many whose names are famous in Indiana history. Interred here are Benjamin Harrison, 23rd President of the United States, Charles W. Fairbanks and Thomas R. Marshall, Vice Presidents; Thomas T. Taggart and Albert J. Beveridge, U. S. senators; Oliver P. Morton, famous Civil War governor of Indiana; Kin Hubbard, author and humorist; and James Whitcomb Riley, poet.

21. The LOCKEFIELD GARDEN APARTMENTS (*open 2–8 week-days; 2–6 Sun.*), Indiana Ave. and Locke St., were completed in 1937 by the Public Works Administration as a slum clearance project to provide better housing for Negroes. There are 24 block type, fireproof plain brick buildings on a 22-acre tract in the heart of the Negro district. The apartments and group houses—three and two stories high, respectively—provide living quarters for 748 families.

22. The CARMELITE MONASTERY (*lobby open 7–5 daily*), 2402 Cold Spring Road, 'Fortress of Prayer,' is in charge of the Sisters of Our Lady of Mount Carmel, a Roman Catholic order. Resembling medieval European monasteries, it is a rough, brownstone structure, with parapets, deep small-paned windows, and walled courts; the castle-like entrance has huge, studded oak doors and hand-wrought hardware. The cloister section was closed forever to the public by Bishop Joseph Chartrand in 1932 when the monastery was dedicated. The number of nuns is limited to 21.

23. The WORLD WAR MEMORIAL PLAZA, occupying five city blocks between Meridian and Pennsylvania Sts. and New York and St. Clair Sts., was erected in honor of Indiana's participants in the World War, and as a memorial to those of Indiana who died in the service.

UNIVERSITY PARK, New York and Vermont Sts., the only downtown park, occupies the square south of Memorial Hall. This square was originally set aside by the State in 1827 as the prospective site of a university, which never materialized. In the center of the park is the DEPEW MEMORIAL FOUNTAIN, the work of A. Sterling Calder; and at the southwest corner is a bronze STATUE OF ABRAHAM LINCOLN by the New York sculptor, Henry Hering. A STATUE OF BENJAMIN HARRISON stands at the south entrance of the park, and occupying a central position is a STATUE OF SCHUYLER COLFAX, unveiled in 1887. This, the oldest statue in the city, is the work of Lorado Taft.

MEMORIAL HALL (*open 10–5 daily; guides*), north of University Park, is a magnificent structure faced with Indiana limestone, with granite steps and walks. The base, 230 feet wide and 400 feet long, consists of a ground-level floor, the basement providing space for a museum and auditorium. Forty feet above the street level is a podium entirely surrounding the tower. On this level is the cornerstone laid by General John J. Pershing, July 4, 1927. Between the tower windows on the four sides are six huge columns, surmounted by heroic stone figures representing *Courage, Memory, Peace, Victory, Liberty,* and *Patriotism.* Approaches are made by two grand stairways that form entrances from the north and south sides. On a granite base in the center of the south stairway stands the largest sculptural bronze casting ever made in America—Henry Hering's *Pro Patria.*

The VESTIBULE, Michigan St. side, is entered through huge bronze doors, over which are shields of the United States Army and Navy. Floors are white marble, walls are travertine and Brescia marble. Side wall lighting fixtures are in cup form set in vertical alignment. This vestibule opens into the Grand Foyer Hall, on both sides of which are neoclassic Ionic columns of verd antique marble.

The ALTAR ROOM, occupying the top floor of Memorial Hall, is entered from the Grand Foyer by two white marble stairways marked by Roman arched entrances. Framed on the stair walls and corridors are the names of the Indiana men and women who entered the service in the World War. The shrine, 115 feet from floor to apex, with impressive white and blue lighting, forms an appropriate setting for the large American flag that hangs from the vaulted space. Over all shines the crystal 'Star of Destiny,' symbolizing guidance of the future welfare of the Nation. The altar to the flag is composed of 17 kinds of marble. The top of the altar is a remarkable piece of craftsmanship, executed in colored enamels and resembling a blanket of precious stones. It embraces the American Golden Eagle, Shield of the United States, Wreath of Memory, Palms of Victory, and a broad golden ribbon on which is inscribed, in letters of blood red, the Pledge of Allegiance to the Flag.

Around the four walls is a 17-foot marble wainscot and 16 large columns of St. Alban marble in dark red hues. Between the corner pilasters and columns are groups of flags of the allied nations. On the east and west sides are niches framing portraits of the officers in command of the Allied Army. An allegorical, molded frieze above the wainscot depicts America joining the Allies and portrays the great struggle of mankind for ultimate peace.

The auditorium, seating 600, can be entered from the Grand Foyer Hall. It is octagonal in form with a domed ceiling finished in polychrome shades.

OBELISK SQUARE occupies the entire square to the north of Memorial Hall and is paved with macadam and bordered with grass plots and trees. The Obelisk, of black Berwick granite, rises from the center of the square to a height of 100 feet, representing the aspirations of the Nation. On the four sides of its base are bas-reliefs representing the four fundamentals on which the hopes of the Nation are founded— Law, Science, Religion, and Education. Around the base is a varicolored electric-lighted water fountain.

The CENOTAPH, Indiana's tribute to her World War dead, occupies the square to the north of Obelisk Square, and is a black granite structure resting on a floor of red and dark-green granite, in a sunken garden. In the floor of the north side is a bronze plaque placed there in memory of James Bethel Gresham, of Evansville, Indiana, Corporal, Co. F 16th Inf., 1st Division, A.E.F. Killed at Bethelmont, France, November 3, 1917, Gresham was one of the first three members of the American forces to lose their lives in action. At the four corners are majestic columns of black granite, surmounted by four golden Roman eagles. Around the Cenotaph is the Mall, a broad expanse of lawn with terraces and walks that are lined with trees and shrubbery.

The AMERICAN LEGION BUILDING, NW. corner of Cenotaph square, is a four-story Greek style structure of Indiana limestone. Erected in 1925, it is the national headquarters of the American Legion.

24. The INDIANA WOMEN'S PRISON (*open 1–3 Wed.; groups by appointment*), 401 N. Randolph St., is the country's first penal institution built for women and managed exclusively by women. It was established by an act of the State legislature in 1869 and opened in 1873. The Women's Board of Control, whose members are appointed by the governor, was created by the legislature in 1877. The average number of inmates (1941) is 150.

25. The INDIANAPOLIS PUBLIC LIBRARY BUILDING (*open 9–9 weekdays, 2–6 Sun.*), 40 E. St. Clair St., houses the administrative offices and central branch of the city's public library system. The building, which faces the War Memorial Plaza, was dedicated October 7, 1917. Constructed of Indiana limestone at a cost of $510,000, it is a thoroughly modern building, perfectly adapted to its functions, and at the same time an outstanding example of Greek Doric design. Suzanne La Follette, discussing the classical vogue in public buildings in *Art in America*, wrote: 'Some of the results have been impressive, and some have been even beautiful—Paul Philippe Cret's Public Library in Indianapolis, for example, which is the best Greek building in the United States . . .'

26. The VETERANS' HOSPITAL, Division of Veterans Administration Facility (*open 2–4, 7–9 daily*), 2401 Cold Spring Road, admits veterans of all wars. On a 30-acre tract of landscaped ground, the building, erected in 1931, is a functional type of brick, stone trimmed. The bed capacity is 172.

27. The CHILDREN'S MUSEUM (*open 1–5 Mon.-Fri., 9–5 Sat., 2:30–5 Sun.*), 1150 N. Meridian St., maintained by the Children's Museum Board of Trustees, contains approximately 30,000 objects of interest to children, displayed in the 24 rooms of the three-story brick house that was the John Carey homestead. Children take active part in the museum's management by means of a Junior Board of Directors.

28. The JAMES WHITCOMB RILEY HOME (*open 10–12, 2–4 daily; adm. 25¢, children accompanied by adults free*), 528 Lockerbie St., is a two-and-a-half-story Victorian-type house of brick trimmed with stone. The home is furnished just as it was when Riley occupied it, with furniture largely of the Civil War period. In addition to its furnishings the house contains many personal relics of the poet.

29. The INDIANAPOLIS MOTOR SPEEDWAY (*open 8–5 weekdays*), 2400 W. 16th St., scene of the world famous 500-mile Memorial Day race, is a noted proving ground and outdoor laboratory, where much of the safety and durability of automobiles and tires have been developed. Engineers claim that 70 per cent of the improvements in modern cars and tires are an outgrowth of races held here.

The 2.5-mile brick and asphalt oval track has two long straightaways of 3,300 feet each and two short ones of 660 feet each, connected by four wide, sweeping curves each of which is 1,320 feet. The track is 50 feet wide on the stretches and much wider on the turns, which have a gradient of 16° at the approach and 40° where the turn is sharpest. There are safety walls on the outside and wide safety aprons on the inside of all curves. Around the western and southern sides of the track are grandstands, paddocks, and bleachers seating 125,000. The infield, a large part of which is a golf course, has parking space for 25,000 automobiles. Inside the track are garages, pits, judges' stand, score boards, press pagoda, an emergency hospital, and refreshment stands.

Here on each Memorial Day from 125,000 to 175,000 persons, from shoeshine boys to overlords of the financial world, watch 33 crack drivers pilot America's fastest racing cars 500 miles. Before the race, each car and driver must pass rigid inspections and the cars must qualify (1941 rules) by running 10 miles at an average speed of not less than 115 miles per hour. From those qualifying the 33 fastest are allowed to start. The race itself is replete with thrills, sometimes with spills, and acts of heroism. The record for the race is an average speed of 117.2 miles per hour (1938) and the fastest lap recorded is 130.492 miles an hour.

30. The KIRSHBAUM COMMUNITY CENTER (*open* 9 A.M.–10 P.M. *Mon.-Thurs.*, 9–5 *Fri.*, 6–10 P.M. *Sat.*), 2314 N. Meridian St., a Jewish organization established by Raphael Kirshbaum in memory of his wife, is nonsectarian in membership. A swimming pool, gymnasium, and library provide recreation and educational facilities. The organization has for several years conducted open forums, bringing distinguished lecturers to the city from all over the world.

31. The INDIANA STATE SCHOOL FOR THE DEAF (*open* 8–4 *Mon.-Fri.*), 42nd St. between College and Keystone Aves., for pupils between the ages of 7 and 18, was founded in 1843 and is now situated on a 100-acre tract of land. Of the 11 buildings, 9 are brick and of Georgian design. The administration building has a Greek portico with Ionic columns.

32. The STATE FAIRGROUNDS (*open*), 38th St. between Winthrop Ave. and Fall Creek Pkwy., is the scene of the State Fair held annually since 1852 during the first week in September. The principal features of the grounds are a grandstand and race track; barns for the exhibition of horses, cattle, sheep, swine, and poultry; and a coliseum seating 12,000. Purdue and Indiana Universities, and the State departments of agriculture and conservation, have special buildings to house exhibits. A hotel, on the eastern side of the fairgrounds, is open throughout the year.

POINTS OF INTEREST IN ENVIRONS

Woollen's Gardens, 11.8 *m.*; Fort Benjamin Harrison, 12.5 *m.*; Sunnyside Sanatorium, 14.5 *m.*; Indiana Reformatory, 28.3 *m.* (*see Tour 7a*). Eli Lilly Biological Laboratories, 19.9 *m.* (*see Tour 8a*). Indiana School for the Blind, 9.2 *m.* (*see Tour 16a*).

Muncie

MUNCIE (949 alt., 49,720 pop.), seat of Delaware County, is situated on White River, in the east central sector of Indiana. Although the major portion lies south of a U-bend in the river, Muncie extends beyond it to the north and west, over an unevenly cross-shaped area of 9 square miles. The shopping and business districts have kept as their center the courthouse at Main and High Streets, and cover 15 blocks. Many new store fronts give the streets an up-to-date appearance. Normally, the city, which houses about 13,000 industrial workers and is the center of a rich farming district, enjoys comparative prosperity.

Early Muncie grew rapidly around its railroad station and little group of factories, a nucleus in what is now the southern part of town. The city is crossed from east to west by the railroad tracks, and, more haphazardly, by the river north of them, which winds past the cemetery, through the residential district, over the business center and golf course, through the largest park, and out of town. The airport, college, and hospital, as well as all the transverse highways, also lie north of the tracks. On the south side are the greater concentration of factories, a smaller park, and the homes of the workers.

Education

ON THE CAMPUS OF INDIANA UNIVERSITY, BLOOMINGTON

JOHN HERRON ART INSTITUTE, INDIANAPOLIS

JORDAN HALL,
BUTLER UNIVERSITY,
INDIANAPOLIS

CONVENT AND ACADEMY OF THE IMMACULATE CONCEPTION, FERDINAND

CAMPUS, UNIVERSITY OF NOTRE DAME, SOUTH BEND

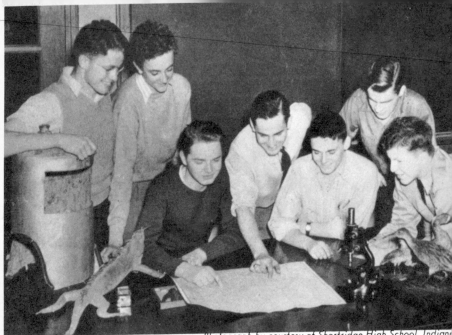

SCIENCE STUDENTS PLAN A FIELD TRIP

PURDUE TRAINS CHEMISTS FOR INDUSTRIAL RESEARCH

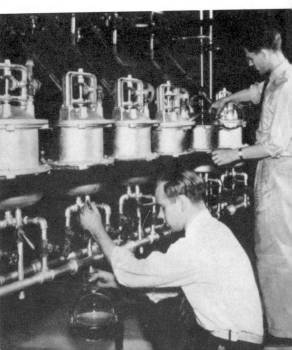

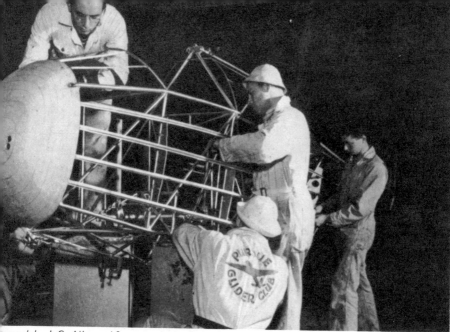

ENGINEERING STUDENTS BUILD A GLIDER AT PURDUE UNIVERSITY, LaFAYETTE

ZOOLOGY LABORATORY AT DePAUW UNIVERSITY, GREENCASTLE

STUDENT UNION BUILDING AT INDIANA STATE TEACHERS COLLEGE, TERRE HAUTE

A YOUTHFUL HOOSIER POLITICIAN—
CAMPUS ELECTION DAY AT INDIANA STATE TEACHERS COLLEGE

'THE CAISSONS GO ROLLING ALONG'—CULVER MILITARY ACADEMY, CULVER

PURDUE MEETS INDIANA IN THE ROSS-ADE STADIUM, LaFAYETTE

BACKSTAGE AT A HIGH SCHOOL DRAMATIC PRODUCTION

MURAL BY GILBERT WILSON, IN WOODROW WILSON HIGH SCHOOL TERRE HAUTE

Nine city bridges span White River, and a paved road parallels it, forming links between eight public parks and their network of drives that wind through 300 acres of grassed stretches. Muncie has 136 miles of paved streets, lined with shade trees in the residential districts.

Before the turn of the century, builders of pretentious houses, garnished with ornate gingerbread ornamentation, developed the east side into a fashionable district. It was later supplanted as the choice residential sector, however, by Normal City, in the northwest, following the founding of Eastern Indiana Normal University in 1899 and the acquisition of 10 acres for the campus. Adjacent to the town are the developments of Old Town Hill and Inlow Springs, situated along the west bank of the river, with their elaborate residences set in old oak groves.

Beginning in 1924, two sociologists, Robert S. and Helen Merrell Lynd, undertook a candid and complete appraisal of Muncie, which attracted Nation-wide attention when their findings were published in *Middletown* (1929). This book made the city a center of study and discussion, but at the same time it made Muncie citizens, who resented some of the investigators' conclusions, uncomfortable and self-conscious. Ten years after their first visit the authors returned to record the changes of the depression years in Muncie; and in 1937 *Middletown in Transition* was published.

The Lynds might have chosen Kokomo, Anderson, Marion, Peoria, Walla Walla, or any other of a hundred average American towns for their study; they chose Muncie not because it was exceptional in any way, but because it was thoroughly typical and had certain characteristics that made it more suitable for their purposes than any other small city.

Though it has grown rapidly in the last 50 years, Muncie still retains the stamp of 'country town' days, and its population is predominantly native-white. It possesses a highly industrialized pattern, with modern high-speed machine production, and it is not dominated by any single large industry. To balance its industrial activity there is a well-developed appreciation of art.

Muncie's past may be divided into three periods: settlement and a long period of agricultural simplicity; the decade of upheaval and transformation following the discovery of gas in the 1880's; and a later period of 40 years or more as an industrial city.

In 1818, when the Indians of the region were expropriated by the Treaty of St. Mary's, white families began to pour in from the East and South. A 672-acre tract had been given to Rebecca Hackley, half-breed daughter of William Wells, the white son-in-law of Little Turtle. This tract was bought by Goldsmith C. Gilbert, and, after passing through several hands, was platted in 1827. It was called 'Munsey-town' for the Munsee Indians, whose settlement it marked, and in 1845 was given its present name. By then, homes were rising rapidly, and in 1847 Muncie was incorporated as a town. In 1865 it reached the status of a city.

In 1876, a crew boring for coal at Eaton, 11 miles north of Muncie, struck a foul-smelling gas 600 feet down. The fumes and hissing from the two-inch bore caused reports that the drillers had struck Satan's caves, and the hole was condemned and plugged. Muncie was at the time a quiet town of about 6,000 inhabitants, retaining many of the traits of a pioneer settlement and the pioneer simplicity of living.

Ten years later, when large gas fields were being developed in the East, the plugged hole at Eaton was remembered, and a well was sunk. Gas was struck, with a roar heard for miles, and a wild high flame which could be seen in Muncie. It was a gala occasion. By spring a well was sunk in Muncie itself; excitement rose; drillers tried to anchor the seemingly limitless flow; boomers were arriving on special trains, real-estate prices doubled; there were wild predictions of endless supplies of natural gas and of endless expansion.

New industries flocked in—glass works, iron mills, pulp and rubber factories—lured by the offer of free fuel and free factory sites. Housing failed to keep pace with the influx of families. The only uninhabited section within city limits was Avondale, platted but undeveloped. In their rush to house themselves, newcomers bought up the lots and built shanties, adding a grotesque supplement of board, paper, and sheet-iron to an otherwise presentable town. Avondale became known as 'Shed-town,' a name that persisted for years, until the ramshackle dwellings were replaced by modern cottages. It is still (1941) the residential section of the factory workers, of whom about 91 per cent are native whites, 6.6 per cent Negroes, and about 2 per cent foreign-born whites.

The consensus was that the gas was inexhaustible, and it was spent recklessly. Great flambeaux burned night and day, in the streets and at the wells. When the pipe-lines were laid, nonindustrial consumers were charged by the fixture—$12 a year—and no one bothered to turn out a light. It was cheaper to let the gas burn than to strike another match.

By the summer of 1890 the town had grown to a manufacturing city, with a busy population of 12,000. Forty factories had been built; and Muncie continued its growth until the gas gave out, suddenly. By 1900 natural gas for manufacturing purposes was past. Plants moved away; but in this town of 20,000 the groundwork had been laid, and a population was here to stay. In this country town that had had big industry plastered over its surface, there was a foundation for today's city.

Most important of the industries which had come to Muncie in a search for cheap fuel was a glass products plant owned by the five Ball brothers of Buffalo, New York. After moving their homes and the central offices of the Ball Brothers Company to Muncie, this family entered into the city's economic and social life in many ways. They invested heavily in the Warner Gear Company and the Kuhner Brothers Packing Company, Muncie's two other large industries, as well as in other factories and large downtown stores. They revived the old Eastern Indiana Normal University, which had opened during the gas boom, and after it became Ball State Teachers College they aided its growth and prestige by donating funds for most of the buildings on its campus. They built a hospital and contributed to the building funds for the Y.M.C.A., Y.W.C.A., and other institutions.

At the same time they developed the Ball Brothers Company into a nationally known producer of fruit jars and other glass products, and built for themselves personal fortunes which are among the most extensive in Indiana. Today (1941), only two of the five brothers are living, but Muncie is still largely dominated by its wealthiest and most influential family; and Muncie is perhaps unique among mid-western cities in the extent to which its industry remains under local ownership and control.

POINTS OF INTEREST

The DELCO REMY CORPORATION PLANT (*open 8-5 week-days*), corner 5th and Elliott Sts., employs about 600 men and produces electrical automobile accessories for General Motors.

The MUNCIE PRODUCTS COMPANY PLANT (*open 8-5 week-days*), 1200 W. 8th St., employs about 1,500 men and manufactures automobile parts, chiefly for General Motors.

BALL MEMORIAL HOSPITAL (*open 2-4 daily*), 2400 University Ave., was opened August 8, 1929. Grounds, equipment, and Tudor-Gothic building were donated by the Ball Brothers Foundation. There are 142 beds, and an average of about 60 nurses train here, receiving additional instruction at Ball State Teachers College.

BALL STATE TEACHERS COLLEGE lies between Riverside Drive and University Ave. and McKinley and Tillotson Aves. Entrance to the campus is a semicircular drive between McKinley Avenue and Riverside Drive. The college buildings, four of them of Tudor-Gothic type, face a central quadrangle, wooded and landscaped.

The college opened in 1899 as the Eastern Indiana Normal University, but was short-lived. After closing and re-opening several times, each time under a different name, it was acquired by the Ball family in 1918 and presented to Indiana as Ball State Teachers College.

Entering the campus from McKinley Ave. and driving west, the visitor encounters first the LIBRARY (R), with 54,000 volumes; in the library is an auditorium seating 1,500 persons. The roof of the SCIENCE BUILDING (L) is equipped for the study of elementary astronomy and meteorology. The ADMINISTRATION BUILDING (L), oldest in the group, houses offices and the college bookstore. LUCINA HALL (L) accommodates 100 women residents; FOREST HALL (L), southeast of Lucina Hall, is also a women's residence. Past the curve of the drive is BALL GYMNASIUM. The ARTS BUILDING (R) contains an art collection and a museum of relics and curios. In a separate room of this building is a notable collection of Italian Renaissance paintings and art objects, presented in 1940 by Mr. and Mrs. W. H. Thompson of Indianapolis (*see Arts and Crafts*). The top floor houses the music department, with recital halls and practice studios.

At the northwest corner of the campus, at Tillotson Ave. and River-side Drive, is the ARBORETUM, a 14-acre tract, heavily wooded, used as a biological reserve and laboratory. At University Ave., the southern boundary of the campus, is the ATHLETIC FIELD. On the south side of University Ave. east of the Ball Memorial Hospital, between Celia and Tally Aves., is the BURRIS TRAINING SCHOOL for nurses. At University and Tally Aves. is the recently erected FRANK ELLIOTT BALL RESIDENCE HALL, a dormitory accommodating 100 men. The 1939 enrollment of the college was 2,710.

The DELAWARE COUNTY FAIRGROUNDS, Wheeling Ave. between Highland and Centennial Aves., cover 41 acres. There is a half-mile racetrack and a grandstand with seating capacity for about 5,000 persons.

The SITE OF AN INDIAN VILLAGE, N. of Minnetrista Blvd. between Crane and Walnut Sts., is marked with a boulder bearing a bronze tablet, erected June 14, 1914, by the Paul Revere Chapter of the D.A.R. Near by is an Indian burying ground, undisturbed. On this site the Munsee clan of the Delaware raised their crops, and here in March 1806 they burned at the stake John A. Christian, an Indian martyr of the Christian faith.

The 'APPEAL TO THE GREAT SPIRIT' STATUE stands on the N. bank of White River, at Walnut St. and Granville Road. A mounted Indian, head back and arms outstretched in supplication, this figure was erected and presented to the city as a memorial to Edmund Ball by his widow. It is a copy of Cyrus Dallin's noted work of the same name, in front of the Boston Museum of Fine Arts.

McCULLOUGH PARK, a well-landscaped tract between Broadway and Elm Sts., has a large shelter house, tables and furnaces for picnickers, tennis courts, playground equipment, and a baseball diamond. It is the largest park in town, and contains a life-sized statue of George F. McCullough, the donor, who promoted the suburb of Whiteley.

The INDIANA STEEL AND WIRE MILL (*open 8–5 weekdays*), corner Ball Road and Jackson St., is owned and operated by the Kitselman Brothers. Started in 1901 to manufacture wire for telephone lines, it has conducted laboratory experiments resulting in new standards for transmission wire and the development of a seven-wire steel cable strand for guy wires.

The WARNER GEAR PLANT (*open 8–5 weekdays*), Seymour St. from Hackley to Blaine Sts., occupies 72 acres and employs 3,000 men. Manufacturing automobile and truck transmissions, rear axles, motor heads, gears, and clutches, this plant is responsible for 'free wheeling,' 'overdrive,' and other innovations.

The OWENS-ILLINOIS GLASS COMPANY PLANT (*open 1–5 Thurs.*), Macedonia Ave. S. of 8th St., formerly the Hemingray Glass Company, produces both blown and pressed glass, but chiefly insulators and glass building blocks. It has been in operation for 47 years, expanding with the growth of the telephone industry. After the present firm took over in 1933, bottle manufacturing was shifted to another unit.

Most striking feature of all the new buildings of the plant is the extensive use of glass blocks in construction. Because of this there is little need for artificial lighting except at night. Raw materials are stored in the 'batch house' and hauled later in electric trucks to batteries of furnaces, where they are melted and fused for molding. From 425 to 750 persons are employed.

The BALL BROTHERS PLANT (*open 8–5 weekdays*), Macedonia at 9th St., covers 10 acres, with 37 factory buildings and 21 warehouses. The company manufactures glass jars and fittings for home canning, glass bottles for beverage uses, zinc battery shells, strawboard boxes, rubber rings for fruit jars, aluminum pressure cookers, and jelly glasses on a large scale.

The industry originally centered in Buffalo, New York, but during the gas boom of 1886 the five Ball Brothers, who developed the concern to its present scale, were tempted into establishing a branch factory in Muncie. As an inducement the city (in the heart of a farming region and near the necessary raw materials for glass manufacture) offered free fuel, 70 acres of land, and $5,000 cash. So profitable did this location become that the Muncie plant is now the main plant of the company, with large branches in other States. It employs about 3,500 persons.

HEEKIN PARK, between 8th and 12th and Madison and Penn Sts., is a recreation center with tennis courts, children's wading pool, and several cabins for rent.

POINTS OF INTEREST IN ENVIRONS

Chesterfield Spiritualist Camp, 13.9 *m.;* Mounds State Park, 15.7 *m.* (*see Tour 6*). Monument to Wilbur Wright, 14 *m.* (*see Tour 7a*). Highest point in Indiana, 30.8 *m.* (*see Tour 13*).

New Albany

Railroad Stations: Cavell and E. Market Sts. for Chicago, Indianapolis & Louisville R.R.; end of Vincennes St. between Market and Stone Sts. for Baltimore & Ohio R.R.
Bus Stations: 234 Vincennes St. for Greyhound Lines and Meadors and Allen Line; 310 Bank St. for Corydon bus.
Streetcars: Fare 5¢; to Louisville, Ky. 10¢; New Albany-Jeffersonville bus 10¢.
Taxis: 15¢ first 1.5 m., 10¢ each additional mile.
Toll Bridge: K. & I. Bridge, south end of Vincennes St., into Louisville, Ky., 25¢ for car and driver, 5¢ for each additional passenger, round-trip 50¢ with no passenger limit.

Accommodations: 3 hotels.

Motion Picture Houses: 3.
Radio Station: WGRC (1400 kc.).
Golf: Valley View Golf Course, directly north of Falling Run Park on Mosier Ave., 18 holes, greens fee 35¢.
Tennis: Falling Run Park, Mosier Ave.; Bicknell Park, Silver St.

Annual Events: Decoration Day Exercises at National Soldiers' Cemetery, May 30; Strawberry Festival, first week in June.

NEW ALBANY (459 alt., 25,414 pop.), seat of Floyd County, and populated almost exclusively by people of Anglo-Saxon stock, extends for two miles along the northern bank of the Ohio River, directly opposite Louisville, Kentucky. On the north and west a range of hills known as the Knobs rise 200 feet above the river level.

The town follows no set plan, but resembles a huge spider web, with sections angling off in every direction. The streets are wide, and in general well paved. Most of the business buildings are huddled together on Market Street, between First and Pearl Streets, as they were in the old days when the market house was the social and business center of the town. The site of the old market, in the middle of Market Street, is still the hub of activity.

New Albany's historic background is linked with that of the Ohio River, and much of its charm springs from its river-town past. It has always been dependent upon the river for its industry and shipping; at one time the Ohio was its only means of contact with the East and South. Today (1941) New Albany factories are served by three railroads and several bus and truck lines; but the proximity of the river— with steamboat lines from Pittsburgh to New Orleans—is still important and makes possible the large plywood and veneer mills along its banks.

Thus New Albany retains some of the flavor of a once great waterfront community. Mansions built in the 1850's and 1860's dot the old part of the city, lining East Main Street between Third and Fourteenth Streets. Most of those between Third and Fifth have been neglected, but east from Fifth Street they look much as they did when owners of steamboat lines and builders of river boats lived in them. Some of these fine old residences are surrounded by flower gardens, and the Southern influence is striking. A few have been converted into tenement houses, but although the interiors are badly marred, they still present a brave front to the world. Except for these 11 blocks, however, and the outlying hill sections where large modern homes are found, cottages—some old and drab, others new and comfortable— predominate.

Although it was the largest city in Indiana when Indianapolis was swampland and forest, New Albany failed to keep its position of prominence. Yet despite the collapse of two major industries, shipbuilding and glass manufacture, the city has managed to recover after each setback. Today, in addition to veneer, New Albany factories produce stoves, stokers, and boilers; suits, overcoats, and shirts; fertilizer, leather products, and automobile bodies. Although these industries are not large, they are sufficient to provide employment for almost half the gainfully employed townspeople. Slightly more than half of those engaged in clerical work are employed in Louisville, but most of the professional people and those engaged in trade have offices and shops in New Albany.

The original tract of the town comprised 86½ acres lying between the Grant Line road and the foot of the Knobs. In 1808 Colonel John Paul of Madison entered this land, because he believed the falls would provide water power for manufacturing establishments and because it was adjacent to Clark's Grant and Clarksville. Then in 1813 Joel, Nathaniel, and Abner Scribner, three enterprising brothers from New York, bought Colonel Paul's holdings for $8,000 and platted New Albany, naming it for the capital of their native State.

Meanwhile in 1806 an event of more than local significance had occurred on what was later to be New Albany soil. Near the mouth of Silver Creek, which lies between the modern city of New Albany and Clarksville, Major Davis Floyd built and assembled a small fleet and recruited men for a highly questionable expedition down the Ohio and Mississippi Rivers (*see Tour* 12). The purpose of this expedition (engineered and commanded by Aaron Burr) was undoubtedly to invade Mexico, then a possession of Spain.

Floyd, a member of the first General Assembly of Indiana Territory and the major of the Clark County militia, first met Aaron Burr in 1805 in Jeffersonville, at the home of Judge Thomas T. Davis. He became interested in the former Vice President's project for a canal through Jeffersonville around the Falls of the Ohio; and in the midst

of the somewhat devious proceedings of the Indiana Canal Company
he had ample opportunity to acquaint himself with Burr's more far-
reaching ambitions. Mexico was a glittering prize, but Spain was at
that time friendly to the United States. It is doubtful, therefore, if
the prospect of money and glory would have lured Floyd into the conspiracy without substantial reassurance. This was forthcoming in the
summer of 1806, when Burr came West again and showed Floyd and
William Prince, of Vincennes, another prospective associate, a letter
purporting to come from the Secretary of War and apparently sanc-
tioning the invasion.

Continued peace with Spain, however, made it dangerous to advocate such an invasion openly. Floyd did his recruiting more subtly,
hiring young unmarried men as colonists for a land grant on the Washita, at $12.50 per month and a bonus of 150 acres of land after a
year's service. But apparently the recruits had an inkling of the real
purpose of the voyage, for several of them later recorded that—when
the flotilla assembled—there were no farming utensils and no women
and children among the armed 'colonists.'

Two boats departed from Silver Creek in the second week of December 1806, after a skirmish with the local militia that detained the
rest of the fleet. After uniting with contingents led by Burr and Blennerhassett, the combined flotilla consisted of only nine boats manned
by some 60 men. Before they reached the mouth of the Ohio, Floyd
had told his men that, reinforced by other troops that would join
them, they were going to take Baton Rouge and Mexico. By that time,
however, he undoubtedly knew that an agreement had already been
reached with the Spaniards and that no war was possible for a long
time.

Just what Floyd's purpose actually was at this point is shrouded in
mystery. Unaware that Burr was entertaining the wild hope of founding an independent empire west of the Alleghenies, he probably believed that they were acting for the United States Government on a
dangerous secret mission. Burr, on the other hand, was now desperate,
and (dissuaded by arbitrary arrests of colleagues in New Orleans, and
the failure of various contingents of his followers to show up) took
a position on the west side of the Mississippi, a few miles above
Natchez.

A little later, deserting his fellow officers, he surrendered to the
Territorial courts, and warrants were issued for the arrest of the others.
Burr was questioned but soon acquitted after stating that his sole destination had been the Washita. He fled, and after his flight, the conspiracy frittered away to an ignominious conclusion. His followers were
arrested—among them Davis Floyd, who was tried in Indiana, convicted of treason, fined $20, and sentenced to three hours' imprison-
ment. Territorial politics were upset over this trial, since many people
considered Floyd a conscious traitor to the United States while others
felt that he had been an honorable (although misguided) servant of

the Republic. In any event, 10 years later he was elected to the Constitutional Convention that met in Corydon.

From the founding of New Albany in 1813 to the passing of the era of river traffic, the city grew and prospered. For the greater part of this period it was the largest town in the State, and much activity centered here. Ferries operating between Indiana and Kentucky and steamboats running from Pittsburgh to New Orleans made it a Midwestern gateway to the South.

In 1838 New Albany was chartered as a city. From four to seven shipyards were in operation between 1830 and 1860, and the excellence of the boats turned out brought more orders than the builders could fill. The famous *Robert E. Lee* was built in 1866 for Captain John W. Cannon, by Hill & Company, of New Albany. Over the racing course of the lower Mississippi between New Orleans and Natchez, the *Robert E. Lee* set a record of 17 hours and 10 minutes for the 256 miles, and also won a historic race against the *Natchez* from New Orleans to St. Louis.

The largest and most ornate craft on western waters was the *Eclipse*. Built in 1851–2 in New Albany at a cost of nearly $400,000, she made her maiden trip to New Orleans in March 1852. In addition to her great size and elaborate equipment, the *Eclipse* was the fastest long-distance boat on the Mississippi. Her records for short distances have been surpassed, but for long distances her time is still unbeaten. In 1853, in a race against the *A. L. Shotwell*, another New Albany-built boat, the *Eclipse* ran from Canal Street, New Orleans, to the Portland Wharf, Louisville, in 4 days, 9 hours and 20 minutes. The *A. L. Shotwell* came in one hour later.

These and many other boats added to the fame of the New Albany shipbuilders, and the taverns of the town were filled with Southern steamboat captains and their families, who were in New Albany to superintend the construction of their boats. In this period, too, many Southerners brought their families here for summer vacations. The Hale Tavern, or High Street House; the Black Horse, later known as the Hole in the Wall; and Marsh's Goose Horn Tavern were among many hostelries where a constant succession of brilliant social affairs took place.

Among these taverns the Black Horse, at Main and 4th Streets, had a particularly varied and colorful career. In 1827 Darius Genung, New Albany's first blacksmith, erected the large brick and sandstone building and conducted it as a tavern. During the Civil War an opening into the basement was made in the wall on the 4th Street side, and the barroom there became known as the Hole in the Wall. Abandoned as a tavern with the decline of the steamboat era, the Black Horse fell into ill repute. Tradition has it that it became the rendezvous of thieves and desperadoes, and that a gang of counterfeiters once operated in the dingy basement. In old photographs of the structure a door is visible, opening into space on the third floor on the 4th Street side. From this opening, according to the story, 'They' once hanged a man by the neck, although how he had offended these un-known but vigorous denizens of the building remains unclear. Its virile past forgotten, however, the old Black Horse was condemned and razed in April 1936.

During the Civil War, since the greater part of the commerce of southern Indiana had been with the South, businessmen in this part of the State—including New Albany—lost thousands of dollars. But after the war had depleted the wealth of the town and the railroads had ended steamboat transportation to a large extent, New Albany came back to prosperity with the growth of the glass industry, developed by John Ford and W. A. DePauw. The transformation from a center of wealth and social life to a manufacturing community took away much of the color and glitter of the city, but led to the employment of about 3,500 men. The glass works were moved to northern Indiana during the gas boom of the 1880's.

The next major industrial activity was the fabrication of plywood. Large amounts of hardwood timber near by, climatic conditions favorable for aging the veneer, and low transportation costs have made New Albany one of the largest veneer centers in the Nation. It slumped badly during the last few years, however, and is now (1941) attempting to recover its former position.

The flood of 1937, which broke all previous records for high water in the Ohio Valley, was a severe blow to New Albany. On January 27 the river reached a height of 57.1 feet, nearly 10 feet higher than ever before. More than half of the town's 6,617 homes were flooded; many were washed away. Public utilities were cut off, water stood 4 to 10 feet deep in the business section, and the town was placed under martial law to prevent looting. By February 7 the river had returned to its banks, leaving property damage estimated at $5,000,000. Work of rehabilitation got under way immediately, and now (1941) there are few signs of the disaster.

POINTS OF INTEREST

1. At SILVER CREEK BRIDGE, on State 62 at the eastern city limits near the mouth of Silver Creek, Major Davis Floyd, Aaron Burr's agent at Jeffersonville, assembled a small fleet and recruited men for his ill-fated expedition down the Ohio and Mississippi Rivers.

2. The NATIONAL SOLDIERS' CEMETERY, 1943 Ekin Ave., established in 1862, contains graves of Civil, Spanish-American, and World War veterans. A drive running through the cemetery is lined with rows of white granite gravestones. Memorial Day ceremonies are held here annually.

3. KENTUCKY AND INDIANA BRIDGE (*toll for car and driver, 25¢; each additional passenger, 5¢*), New Albany entrance at E. Main and Vincennes Sts., connects New Albany with Louisville, Kentucky. This bridge, lacking one foot of being a mile in length, is crossed by the Dixie Highway, the Midland Trail, and the Jackson Highway!

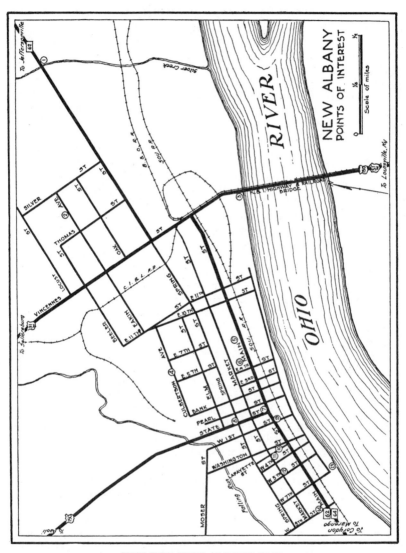

KEY FOR NEW ALBANY MAP

1. Silver Creek Bridge 2. National Soldiers' Cemetery 3. Kentucky and Indiana Bridge 4. Home of Byron Forceythe Willson 5. Sloan House 6. Site of the Old Hole in the Wall Tavern 7. Scribner House 8. County Jail 9. Site of Hale's Tavern 10. Scribner Park 11. Site of the Anderson Female Seminary 12. Home of William Vaughn Moody 13. Site of Hill Shipyards 14. Western Border of Clark's Grant

4. The HOME OF BYRON FORCEYTHE WILLSON (*private*), 520 Culbertson Ave., is a white, low cottage formed from two small houses joined by a long corridor. Willson, born in Genesee Falls, New York, moved here in 1853, and shortly after became an editorial writer on the Louisville (Kentucky) *Journal,* under the editorship of the poet, George D. Prentice. In this house Willson wrote his best verse, including 'In State' and 'The Old Sergeant.' The latter poem, written for distribution by the *Journal* carrier boys as a Christmas souvenir, attracted the attention of President Lincoln, who asked Oliver Wendell Holmes if he knew who wrote it. Holmes wrote to Prentice, who informed him that it was the work of Willson. It was widely circulated and led the New England writers to recognize the New Albany poet; but his slender output consisted of only one volume of verse, *The Old Sergeant and Other Poems,* published in 1866.

5. The SLOAN HOUSE (*private*), 600 E. Main St., was built about 1853 by Dr. John Sloan, to resemble a river steamboat. It is a large, square, two-and-a-half-story brick building, high above the street, topped by a glass tower resembling a pilot's cabin. The house later was the home of Rear Admiral George A. Bicknell, U.S.N. (1848–1925), who added other ship's features, one being a set of mirrors to reflect a visitor's face before he was admitted.

6. The SITE OF THE OLD HOLE IN THE WALL TAVERN is on the NE. corner of E. Main and E. 4th Sts. This tavern was for many years a rendezvous of robbers, murderers, counterfeiters, and other desperadoes.

7. The SCRIBNER HOUSE (*open 9–5 daily; adm. 10¢*), E. Main St., third house E. of State St., is the oldest frame residence in town, built in 1814 by Joel Scribner. The original furnishings are still in the house, now owned by the Piankeshaw Chapter of the D.A.R.

8. The COUNTY JAIL, NE. corner State and Spring Sts., is an old structure of brick and stone. Here occurred the lynching that put an end to one of the worst outlaw gangs that ever operated in Indiana—the Reno gang. They terrorized southern Indiana from 1864 to 1868; in the latter year three of the Reno brothers and a man named Anderson were captured in Floyd County and placed in the New Albany jail, from which they were taken and hanged by a mob of infuriated citizens.

9. The SITE OF HALE'S TAVERN is on the SE. corner W. Main and W. 1st Sts. This was the finest of the early New Albany taverns. It occupied half a block, with an 80-foot front and two large ells extending back toward the river. Here were entertained Daniel Webster, Henry Clay, Zachary Taylor, Andrew Jackson, Aaron Burr, William Henry Harrison, Martin Van Buren, Benjamin Harrison, and many other famous persons.

10. SCRIBNER PARK, between LaFayette and Washington, Main and Market Sts., was donated for a park site by the Scribner brothers when they platted the town in 1813.

11. The SITE OF THE ANDERSON FEMALE SEMINARY is on the SW. corner LaFayette and Market Sts. Established in 1841 by Colonel John B. Anderson and his wife, this select and nationally popular school was soon divided into the Anderson Female Seminary and the Anderson Collegiate Institute for Boys. The Confederate general, John Hunt Morgan, was a student at the latter institution.

Colonel Anderson became affiliated with the old New Albany & Salem Railway (now the Monon) and was later a division superintendent with the Pennsylvania Railroad. Andrew Carnegie was a telegraph operator for the company and Anderson gave him the freedom of his library, pointing out to young Carnegie the benefits that would accrue if education could be placed before everyone in this way. Profoundly impressed, Carnegie later made this dream a reality, giving much of his large fortune to a foundation for the establishment of libraries over the entire country.

12. The HOME OF WILLIAM VAUGHN MOODY (*private*), 411 W. Market St., is a large old two-story house with open galleries on the east side, both upstairs and down. Here William Vaughn Moody (1869–1910), poet, dramatist, and artist, lived until he was 17 years old.

13. The SITE OF HILL SHIPYARDS is on Water St. between W. 4th and W. 8th Sts. This was one of the largest and most famous of the old New Albany shipyards and furnished steamboats for the Ohio and Mississippi River transportation.

14. WESTERN BORDER OF CLARK'S GRANT, N. side of W. Main St. at its junction with W. 8th St., the western boundary of the land grant made to George Rogers Clark by the State of Virginia, is indicated by a large boulder bearing a bronze plate.

POINTS OF INTEREST IN ENVIRONS

First State Prison, 6.2 *m.;* Clarksville and Silver Creek, 8.7 *m.;* Charlestown, 19 *m.;* Rose Island, 21.8 *m.;* Tunnel Mill, 22 *m.* (*see Tour 11A*).

New Harmony

Railway Stations: Church St. (Ind. 66) at eastern city limits for Illinois Central R.R.
Bus Stations: Tavern Hotel, Church St., for Egyptian Bus Line.
Bridge and Ferry: W. end of Church St. (Ind. 66) for Wabash River ferry to Illinois.

Accommodations: 1 hotel; tourist accommodations.

Information Service: New Harmony Commercial Club.

Theaters and Motion Picture Houses: 1 motion picture house. Murphy Auditorium, concert hall.
Swimming: In Wabash River. No formal facilities.
Fishing: In Wabash River.

Annual Events: Golden Rain Tree Festival, June. New Year's Eve Ball.

NEW HARMONY (365 alt., 1,390 pop.), at one time a center of social experiment and scientific research that bore fruit of great importance to nineteenth-century progress, is a quiet little town on the lower Wabash River. In an atmosphere of serenity and solid dignity, well-built, attractive houses line streets shaded by majestic trees; and here and there, inconspicuous but significant, stand the old brick and stone structures so massively reared by the Rappites. New Harmony has thousands of 'gate' trees, which flower in June, shedding their blossoms in a golden rain. These hardy, round-topped trees (*Koelreuteria paniculata*), native to China and Korea where they are called the 'Tree of the Golden Rain,' were introduced by William Maclure a century ago and planted near the gate of the Owen-Maclure home; hence the local name 'gate' tree. They have spread freely over southern Indiana and their long sprays of yellow blossoms are a striking feature of New Harmony in early summer.

For nearly a century New Harmony has existed chiefly as a trading center for a rich agricultural community. There are no industries, and many citizens are retired farmers or professional people, although some work in the factories and commercial houses of Evansville. In more than a century the population has increased very little.

In spite of its placid present, New Harmony belongs to the world-aristocracy of villages that have made history. Students of cultural evolution and social reform remember it as the scene of two notable efforts to build a perfect communal society. The forests were cleared, the soil was cultivated, and the first sturdy buildings were erected by the Rappites, an ascetic religious group that came from Germany to Pennsylvania in 1805 and in 1815 founded the village of Harmonie on the Wabash. Then in 1824 the Rappites sold their village to Robert Owen, Scotch philanthropist, industrialist, and social reformer, who attempted here in New Harmony, as he called it, to found a new social order, a communal mode of living that was expected to eradicate the evils of exploitation, poverty, and competition. His great dream was destined to failure; but even in failure it exerted a lasting influence on the life and thought of this country and Europe.

The national influence of New Harmony seems on the whole to have lain in the direction of social and cultural improvement. The seed-idea—social perfection—disintegrated with the failure of the experiment itself, but this disintegration brought forth several vital ideas in more limited fields. The Owen colony and those whom it directly inspired were leaders in the struggle for the liberation of women, the abolition of slavery, and progressive education. Even in the field of scientific investigation their contribution was notable.

The New Harmony colony had international implications as well. Robert Owen was the first nineteenth-century critic of capitalism. The success of his particular type of experiment depended upon a perfection of human nature that, if it had existed, would no doubt have made all such experiments unnecessary. His failure, with many others during the next 20 years, became an important object lesson to Karl Marx and Friedrich Engels, and to other students of economics and sociology who hoped to reconstruct society scientifically.

For the making of the actual physical town—the buildings, old homes, and churches—the Rappites were responsible. They toiled for 10 years in Harmonie to build a perfect co-operative community. The leader of this group was George Rapp, a native of Württemburg, Germany, who preached to hundreds of devoted followers the principles of celibacy, primitive Christian communism, and strict obedience to the spiritual head of the flock. Petty persecutions awakened in these people a desire to find more religious freedom, and in 1805 Rapp, with his adopted son Frederick and a few followers, purchased 5,000 acres of Government land in western Pennsylvania. Here they were soon joined by the rest of the band and a 'community of equality' was established, based on implicit obedience to communal law, mutual protection and support, and common ownership of property. Although husbands, wives, and children entered the band, it was not long before Rapp's principle of sexual abstinence was enforced, former married couples becoming 'brothers and sisters in Christ.' Not satisfied in Pennsylvania, in 1814 they purchased 30,000 acres of unimproved Government land on the Wabash in Posey County, Indiana, and in the summer of 1815 the entire colony came to the new home.

Here these sturdy Germans faced a gigantic task. Dense forests covered the land and swamps stood where now lie choice farms. Within three years, however, they had cleared land, drained swamps, and built houses that were the wonder and envy of the backwoodsmen of adjacent regions. It was a deeply religious community, in which Father Rapp guarded his flock like a true shepherd. For 10 years they labored to create a town much of which remains to bear testimony to the skill of its builders. According to William Blaney, who visited the colony in 1823, they had extensive vineyards and numerous flocks and herds, and manufactured their own clothes. Significantly enough, however, he added: 'During the whole time I was at Harmonie I never saw one of them laugh.'

The Rappites appear to have taken their driving power from religious passion; and the patriarchal leader was invested with his immense authority solely because he was considered to have received divine inspiration. This great authority enabled him to discipline his followers rigidly; to enforce laws of labor that allowed for practically no leisure; and to require from the people lives of monastic self-denial. Unrest eventually came upon the colony, however, and in 1825, after selling their holdings to Robert Owen, the Rappites returned to Pennsylvania. Some authorities believe that Rapp was influenced to sell by the fact that with the passing of primitive conditions and the need for ceaseless toil, his followers had too much time to think (and thus to become discontented), and that for this reason Rapp wished again to set them to the task of building a communal city.

Be that as it may, in 1824 Father Rapp sent to England an English settler, Richard Flower, to offer the Harmonie estate for sale. Since at this time Robert Owen had a wide reputation in England and on the Continent as a great philanthropist and experimenter, Flower naturally sought him out as a prospect. The vast Harmonie domain seemed to Owen an ideal site for the venture he was contemplating, and the bargain was closed in the spring of 1825, the whole tract with all its improvements and much valuable equipment going for less than $150,000.

The New Harmony experiment is only one episode in the long life of Robert Owen, a life rich in practical achievement as well as visionary effort. 'Every social movement,' wrote Friedrich Engels, 'every real advance in England on behalf of the workers, links itself on to the name of Robert Owen.'

Owen was born in Wales in 1771, of humble parentage, and grew to manhood in the early days of the industrial revolution. His childhood and youth were spent in grinding toil as apprentice and draper; but by thrift, self-denial, and enterprise he was able to climb the legendary ladder of success as cotton-mill superintendent, partner, and owner. In spite of this self-made success, however, he was clear-sighted enough to realize that his lot was inevitably an exceptional one. For throughout his youth he saw thousands of English craftsmen forced to work 18 hours a day in order to exist; he saw women and children dying of starvation and overwork. At the same time he observed the rise of the industrial class of England, and the increasing concentration of wealth and power in the hands of this group. In revolt against these conditions he analyzed the difficulty as a matter of faulty distribution, and ruthless competition instead of co-operative effort.

When still in his twenties Owen became the son-in-law and business partner of David Dale, of Glasgow, who owned a great manufacturing establishment in New Lanark, Scotland. In 1800 he took over control of the New Lanark mills and began his career as a practical philanthropist. Although David Dale was not a cruel employer by the standards of the time, Owen found among the workers extreme poverty, malnutrition, long hours of toil, child labor, miserable hovels, drunkenness, and crime. In a few years he succeeded in giving the workers good wages, shorter hours, neat homes, and progressive schools. Despite these reforms, he operated the business profitably and his success in making humanitarianism 'pay' won for him an international reputation. From all parts of Europe statesmen, princes, and philanthropists came to study his methods.

But Owen's partners began, nevertheless, to complain that he was sacrificing possible profits, and eventually he was forced to sell out. Convinced that an appeal to capitalist 'good will' was ineffectual, he turned more and more to public agitation for legislative reform and many progressive measures were due to his incessant activities before 1824. Opposition from the industrialists, however, and failure of the workers to support him in an election campaign, convinced him that only a radical change in the structure of society could remove the evils of the competitive system.

The basic tenet of Owen's creed was that 'circumstances form character.' He expected to establish at New Harmony a perfect society in which equal opportunity, full co-operative effort, and advanced educational facilities would combine to develop perfect human beings and to alleviate social ills. He elaborated these ideas, not only in his numerous American lectures, but in his book, *The New Moral World,* which explained how he hoped to change society 'from an ignorant, selfish system to an enlightened social system which shall gradually unite all interests into one, and remove all causes for contest among individuals . . .'

To establish the 'superior circumstances' of his new moral world, Owen, by published invitation, threw open the door to all who were in sympathy with his views. The comfortable Rappite homes and buildings were soon filled with a strangely assorted crew, representing almost every State in the Union and many countries of Europe. By Christmas 1825, a heterogeneous population of nearly 1,000 persons had come to New Harmony. Owen himself, no doubt aware that a bad start had been made, returned to England in 1825 to solicit the aid of trained specialists.

The most important of the figures whom Owen gathered about him in the effort to make the experiment a success was William Maclure, a wealthy scientist and a man of broad and varied experience, who invested a considerable sum of money in the colony. His reason for doing so, however, was not altogether identical with Owen's. Owen envisaged a complete transfiguration of the social order; Maclure, who was interested solely in education, wanted to make New Harmony a laboratory test of the Pestalozzian system.

Maclure's enthusiasm for Pestalozzi was the culmination of a long life of effort as scholar and educator. Born in Ayr, Scotland, in 1763, he came to America in 1796 to make a geological survey of the United States. His Herculean work on this subject was first published in 1809, earning for him the title of 'Father of American Geology.' He was a leader in the founding of the Philadelphia Academy of Natural Sciences in 1812, and for 23 years was president of that body. In 1805 he first visited Pestalozzi's school at Yverdon in Switzerland and was soon convinced of the importance of the revolutionary new methods. The basic concept of the Swiss teacher was that education must pursue the course laid down by nature, a natural outgrowth of the doctrines of Rousseau and the French Revolution. The child's right to happiness was considered as important as the adult's right to liberty; knowledge was to be given in accordance with desire. These principles Maclure wished to put into practice in America.

To carry out his plans he invited to New Harmony a distinguished group of educators, trained Pestalozzians, including William D'Arusmont, Mme Marie Fretageot, and Joseph Neef. He had a keelboat built at Pittsburgh to carry most of the company down the Ohio and up the Wabash; and after a difficult voyage this famous 'Boatload of Knowledge' arrived at New Harmony January 26, 1826. Joseph Neef had settled in New Harmony a short time before, as had also the distinguished painter and scientist, Charles Alexander Le Sueur, and Frances Wright, brilliant writer, lecturer, and reformer, and niece of Jeremy Bentham, English philosopher.

The Boatload of Knowledge contained not only a dozen or so distinguished teachers, but also several men of science, including Thomas Say, conchologist and naturalist, and Dr. Gerard Troost, Dutch geologist. But perhaps the most important passenger of all—at least from the point of view of citizens of Indiana—was Owen's oldest son, Robert Dale Owen, then 24. He later made Indiana his permanent home, and in his long and useful life many of the ideals of his father and of Maclure were given effective expression.

The Boatload of Knowledge landed and for a time all went well in the colony. Maclure's schools were genuinely progressive, with infant classes, manual training, equal opportunities for girls, and insistence on interest rather than punishment. In the community there was a constant round of lectures and concerts, balls and entertainments; this was part of the theory of education for responsibility. There was also an attempt to divide the work fairly, although it was on such practical economic questions that the experiment seems finally to have been wrecked.

Before long dissension set in. Only a small part of the residents accepted, or even understood, the views of the founders or engaged in any honest efforts to carry them out. It seems certain that a large part of the community had come merely seeking an easy way of living. Factories built by the Rappites were soon in disorder, fences had holes in them, and everything was common property to pigs and cattle. Inexperienced farmers produced meager harvests, and thievery was not unknown. Painful suspicions, disappointment, and quarrels led to various splits in the ranks. Small colonies of dissenters sprang up within earshot of the main village.

At last even Owen's sons, in an editorial in the New Harmony *Gazette* early in 1827, were forced to admit that the experiment had failed. The egotism, rivalry, laziness, and greed of the members were too much for Owen's easy-going government. But although Owen's sons were willing to admit defeat, their father refused. In May 1827, he left for England, and in his farewell speech expressed, in spite of an awareness of the difficulties that had been endured, an unquenchable optimism concerning the outcome of the experiment. With his departure, however, the entire structure fell to pieces, forced into chaos by the undisciplined individualism of people who had never been prepared to live in Utopia. In the midst of the squabbles Robert Dale Owen and William Owen, who had recently arrived, managed to salvage some of their father's share of the property. For the rest of his life he received only about $1,500 annually.

Although the New Harmony experiment was from a practical point of view a failure, it was the parent of many similar experiments. Some of these, notably Frances Wright's antislavery colony in Nashoba, Tennessee, were in existence between 1825 and 1828. In spite of her interest in her own colony, Frances Wright was intimately associated with the Owen experiment throughout its existence. Beautiful, wealthy, and rebellious against injustice and oppression (which she felt poignantly as a woman in spite of her privileged social position), she had seen in Owen's community an opportunity for human emancipation regardless of sex, color, or poverty. During the years of the experiment she lectured about the emancipation of women and founded in New Harmony what was probably the first women's literary club in the United States. After the break-up of the colony she became a radical lecturer of note, arousing large audiences in New York, Philadelphia, and Baltimore on the subjects of socialism, women's rights, and slavery. When in 1829 the New Harmony *Gazette* was moved to New York as the *Free Enquirer,* she became one of the editors with Robert Dale Owen.

New Harmony itself continued to be an intellectual and cultural capital after the colony failed. Owen's two younger sons, Richard and David Dale Owen, arrived in November 1827, long after the most casual observers had been able to predict the colony's downfall. Several eminent scientists and scholars, including Gerard Troost, Thomas Say, and Charles A. Le Sueur, remained in the community for some time, continuing their studies and research. Le Sueur explored many of the prehistoric mounds of southern Indiana, wrote voluminously on the fishes and mollusks of the West, and made his living by painting and sketching. The Thespian Society was organized in 1828 and continued as a drama club for 50 years; one of its first plays was Robert Dale Owen's *Pocahontas*. For many years Le Sueur painted the scenery for the group's productions.

One of New Harmony's chief contributions to Midwestern culture came through William Maclure. Maclure went to Mexico in 1828, sick and disappointed, leaving Thomas Say in charge of his affairs; but his interest in the colony did not die. Nine years later, by correspondence, he rejuvenated the Workingmen's Institute, which he had founded during the early days of the colony, and donated large sums for its continuation. In 1838 the institute was incorporated un ˙ r the laws of Indiana. Maclure sent the organization an order on a L · ıdon bookseller for books to the value of $1,000, and conveyed to it as permanent quarters a wing of the old Rappite church. But before he could return to New Harmony to execute a trust for his anticipated 'model library and institute,' Maclure died in Mexico in March 1840.

In his will he provided for the inauguration of a system of libraries for workingmen's clubs; and in spite of long opposition from his heirs, the estate was converted into funds in 1855 and the distribution began. In Indiana, 144 groups styling themselves 'Workingmen's Institutes' or 'Mechanics' Asssociations' received, according to the will, $500 each; 16 groups in Illinois were also aided, making in all 160 libraries created by the distribution of $80,000. Most of these libraries were pitifully short-lived, but it seems certain that they aided greatly in stimulating public interest in the township libraries that eventually absorbed them. Maclure was also a pioneer in establishing traveling libraries.

Until shortly before the Civil War New Harmony was one of the scientific centers of America. For a year or so it was the headquarters of Prince Maximilian von Neuweid and his corps of explorers; Audubon, the ornithologist, and Sir Charles Lyell, eminent Scotch geologist, visited here; and for 17 years the town was the headquarters of the United States Geological Survey. David Dale Owen had studied in Europe after the colony broke up, and in 1837 was commissioned to make a preliminary geological survey of Indiana. In 1839 he was appointed United States geologist, a post he held for seven years. In a short time (with New Harmony as his base) he conducted a geological survey of the Northwest. The old Rappite granary-fortress was turned into a museum, in which were stored not only the specimens collected by Owen's surveyors, but the collections made by Say in the surrounding States, and by William Maclure in Spain, Portugal, Italy, France, Mexico, and the West Indies.

When in 1856 the headquarters of the Geological Survey were removed to the new Smithsonian Institution in Washington, a part of this immense collection was taken there, another to the Indiana State University at Bloomington, and a third to the American Museum of Natural History in New York. Among the eminent scholars aiding Dr. Owen in his work were Charles Whittlesy, F. B. Meek, the paleontologist, and Leo Lesquereux, noted fossil botanist. One of Owen's most valuable assistants was his younger brother, Richard, who later became State geologist of Indiana, and from 1864 to 1879 professor of natural science in Indiana University.

But the member of the Owen family to whom Indiana owes most was Robert Dale Owen. After his marriage in 1832 he returned to New Harmony from the East and in 1836 entered politics as a member of the legislature. From 1842 to 1846 Owen was in Congress, where he originated and introduced the bill providing for the application of the long-neglected Smithson bequest to the founding of the Smithsonian Institution. As a member of the State Convention in 1851 he was largely responsible for the clauses in the new constitution providing for free tax-supported schools; his speeches on this subject and on equal rights for women reveal a vision and statesmanship unequaled by any other delegate. Defeated in the convention on the question of women's rights, he was successful in the 1852 legislature in improving the divorce laws and in giving separate property and income rights to married women. Perhaps his most notable achievement, however, was his contribution to the emancipation of the slaves. After advocating for 30 years a peaceful and legal emancipation, he became at the outbreak of the Civil War a flaming champion of forcible emancipation. His letter to President Lincoln, written in 1862, had in the words of Secretary Chase 'more influence upon him [Lincoln] than any other document which reached him on the subject—I think I might say than all others put together.' The democratic ideals of New Harmony still had power to affect history. Owen died in 1877 in New York, and in 1937 his bones were removed to New Harmony for final interment.

With the exception of the Owens, most of those who made the village illustrious were gone before the Civil War. The famous scientists who clustered about the United States geological station naturally left after its removal to Washington in 1856. But the later history of the village has not been commonplace. Its influence upon the development of the library system has already been noted. Another great contribution was the origination of the women's club movement. In 1835 Robert Owen's daughter married Robert Henry Fauntleroy and settled down in one of the sturdy old Rappite houses in New Harmony. Here their daughter Constance, in 1859, founded the Minerva Club, the first organized women's club in the United States. The earlier literary club founded by Frances Wright, much less formal in structure, was the inspiration of the later organization.

Meanwhile Maclure's Workingmen's Institute grew into the community's proudest civic center. It got off to a bad start after Maclure's death, since the old Rappite church soon tumbled into ruins, and the London bookseller who was to have sent so many books turned out to be bankrupt. Maclure, however, had breathed real life into the organization, and corporation members and townsfolk enriched the institute by liberal donations. In 1874 the later followers of George

Rapp, then known as the Economy Society, bought the dilapidated old church, tore it down, and built a school building which they presented to New Harmony. In one wing the institute and its library were housed.

The chief benefactor of the library was Dr. Edward Murphy, who had come to New Harmony a barefoot, penniless boy. Befriended by citizens, he became a successful physician, accumulated a considerable fortune, and devoted the major part of it to benefiting the town that had been kind to him. In 1893 he induced the Library Society to sell its old quarters and helped it to erect the brick building it now occupies, housing not only the library but a large auditorium, museum, and an art gallery. He made contributions of books, specimens for the museum, and costly paintings for the gallery. At the time of his death in 1900, the sum of his financial gifts amounted to $155,000. At present (1941) the library contains about 28,000 volumes; a lecture course is given by the Institute every year; and the estimated wealth of the society is $200,000.

The 1938 session of the Indiana legislature created the New Harmony Memorial Commission for the purpose of acquiring and restoring the many historic landmarks of the town. To date (1941) the labyrinth, focal point of Rappite mysticism, has been replanted and a stone house in its center is under construction. This labyrinth and house signified that after tortuous ways comes rest. The Tavern has been acquired and its restoration is anticipated early in 1941. It is expected that the remaining buildings will be purchased in the near future and preserved for posterity. Soon after the formation of the Commission the Indiana Federation of Women's Clubs, owner of the Fauntleroy home, presented it, complete with furnishings, to the Commission.

Today New Harmony looks back to a past the true significance of which is all too often not understood. But in its civic consciousness, its cultural level, and the beauty and interest of its landmarks, the little town expresses its living pride in a great tradition.

POINTS OF INTEREST

1. The OLD RAPPITE FORT (*private*), Granary St. between Main and West Sts., built as a defense against possibly envious neighbors, served as a granary and storehouse for much of the Rappite wealth. The Rappites quarried the stone and made the bricks themselves; the three-story building is 70 feet long, 40 feet wide, and has walls 4 feet thick at the base.

2. COMMUNITY HOUSE NUMBER TWO (*private*), Main St. between Church and Granary Sts., is one of four community houses, two of which have been razed. This two-story brick structure with dormer windows and a mansard roof, built between 1816 and 1822 and substantially as the Rappites left it, is typical of all the Rappite buildings. It is insulated in the peculiar manner called 'Dutch biscuit.' The 'biscuits' are slabs of wood between 3 and 5 feet long, wrapped with

straw cemented with mud or clay; they were placed between the outer and inner walls for insulation, providing warmth in winter and coolness in summer. Community House Number Two was once used as a residence hall for men. On the first floor is a large room that served as a meeting place; the upper rooms, furnished with antiques, were originally bedrooms and are now used as meeting places for organizations. The 'Christian door,' closing a stairway from the third floor to the attic, has cross pieces connecting the panels to form a true cross. The stairway is open underneath, and on the back of one of the stairs is written in chalk, undoubtedly by a departing Rappite, these words: 'In the 24 day of May we have departed. Lord with thy great help and goodness protect us.' The words are now covered with glass. On the third floor is the old printing plant, including a Washington hand press, where for more than 66 years the New Harmony *Register* was printed.

3. The TAVERN, once known as COMMUNITY HOUSE NUMBER THREE, S. side of Church St. between Main and Brewery Sts., built in 1823, is three stories high with two huge chimneys and a flat roof. It still (1941) provides lodging but no food.

4. The SCHNEE HOUSE (*private*), Tavern St. between Main and Brewery Sts., was built in 1815 and named for a family that lived there for many years. It has never been painted, but the yellow poplar and walnut of which it is built remain sound.

5. The OLD FAUNTLEROY HOME (*open 9-12, 1-5 weekdays; 2-5 Sun.; adm. 25¢*), West St. between Church and Granary Sts., was built in 1815 of hand-hewn walnut, oak and hickory, with pegged and mortised joints. After 1840 it was for years in the possession of the Fauntleroy family, and is now (1941) owned and maintained as a shrine by the New Harmony Memorial Commission. In this house, in 1859, Constance Owen Fauntleroy, the granddaughter of Robert Owen, founded the Minerva Club, the first women's club in the United States organized with constitution and by-laws. The Old Fauntleroy Home, still in good condition, is a spacious, well-arranged two-story house, considerably enlarged from the original five-room Rappite cottage. It was occupied by Thomas Say, Robert Dale Owen, David Dale Owen, and other well-known New Harmony figures, and contains many of the possessions of its former occupants.

6. The RAPP-MACLURE HOME (*open 9-5 daily June-Sept.; adm. 25¢*), NW. corner Main and Church Sts., was erected in 1814 for Father Rapp, and was remodeled by Maclure as his home during his stay in the colony. The dignified mansion was later owned by Mrs. Thomas Say and by David Dale Owen. It contains antique furniture and other relics. Around the house are 'golden rain trees.'

In the yard of the Rapp-Maclure Home is GABRIEL'S ROCK, two limestone slabs, originally one stone, about 10 feet by 5, and 5 inches thick. On one is an unintelligible figure, or series of lines; on the other appears the impression of two large, bare human feet. According to popular tradition, these footprints were made by the Angel Gabriel, who alighted there to bring Father Rapp a message from Heaven. The

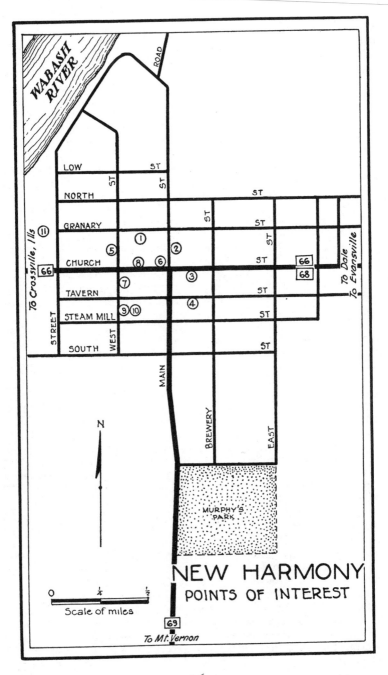

WABASH RIVER

ROAD

LOW ST

ST ST

NORTH ST

GRANARY ST

ST ST

① ②

⑤

To Crossville, Ills. ⑪

CHURCH ⑧ ⑥ ST ST

66 66

68

③

To Dale
To Evansville

⑦

TAVERN ST

④

STEAM MILL ⑨⑩ ST

STREET WEST

SOUTH ST

MAIN

N

BREWERY

EAST

MURPHY'S
PARK

NEW HARMONY
POINTS OF INTEREST

0   ¼   ½
Scale of miles

69
To Mt. Vernon

truth of the matter seems to be that Frederick, Rapp's adopted son, bought the rock near St. Louis; but in spite of the debates of archeologists it is not known whether the footprints are prehistoric or cleverly sculptured.

7. The ROSE DOOR is the west entrance to the high school, SE. corner Church and West Sts. This fanlit door was designed for the Rappite church by Frederick Rapp. Its graceful hand-hewn columns of limestone support a perfectly proportioned lintel. Above the lintel and beneath a hood is carved the date, 1822, and in a raised oval a rose and the words 'Micah 4, V8.' These refer to the passage in the Lutheran Bible used by the Rappites: 'Unto thee shall come the golden rose, the first dominion.' The Rappites believed that the world would end during their lifetime, and this verse meant much to them.

8. The OWEN HOME (*private*), Church St. between Main and West Sts., was built in 1859 by David Dale Owen for use as a laboratory. Prior to this date Owen had his laboratory in the old Fort. When he died in 1860, the building was made into a residence; it still contains many relics of the Owen family, including paintings supposedly done by pupils of Michelangelo, given to Richard Owen by Maclure.

9. The WORKINGMEN'S INSTITUTE, LIBRARY AND MUSEUM (*open 8–5 Mon.-Fri.; 8–8 Sat.; 3–5, 6–8 Sun.*), SE. corner Tavern and West Sts., is the only remaining visible evidence of all the benevolent schemes of William Maclure in behalf of the men who, in his words, 'earn their living by the sweat of their brows.' With his liberal donations, the citizens of New Harmony in April 1838 organized the Workingmen's Institute and Library. Numerous other donations to the library have been made from time to time, the most important being those of Dr. Edward Murphy, who built the library building and an auditorium, endowed a lecture course, and in 1894 endowed the library itself.

The upper floors house a MUSEUM AND ART GALLERY (*open*), also a part of Maclure's plan to 'provide free education to the masses.' In the museum are many geological specimens assembled by scientists of the Owen regime, personal relics of the Owen colony, and relics of three wars.

10. MURPHY AUDITORIUM (*open for lectures and entertainments*), next to Workingmen's Institute, Library and Museum, is a square, two-story brick building, given to New Harmony by Dr. Edward Murphy, where a lecture course endowed by Dr. Murphy is still held annually. On this site was the old Rappite No. 11 building, a school and printing office.

KEY FOR NEW HARMONY MAP

1. Rappite Fort 2. Community House Number Two 3. Tavern 4. Schnee House 5. Old Fauntleroy Home 6. Rapp-Maclure Home 7. Rose Door 8. David Dale Owen Laboratory 9. Workingmen's Institute, Library and Museum 10. Murphy Auditorium 11. Rappite Cemetery

11. The RAPPITE CEMETERY, W. end of Granary St., is a plot of three acres where about 230 Rappites are buried. They were laid in what was then an orchard, side by side, with no mounds or stones as markers. After burial each grave was sodded over at once, the only record being a plan that indicated the site of each grave and the name of the person buried there. In 1874 descendants of the original Rappite colony returned to New Harmony and bought their old church, razed it and from the bricks built a wall one foot thick and five feet high around the cemetery. Within the enclosure are also some Indian mounds.

POINTS OF INTEREST IN ENVIRONS

Mt. Vernon, 15 *m.;* Hovey's Lake, 23.8 *m.* (*see Tour* 11A).

South Bend

Railroad Stations: Union Depot, 326 W. South St. for New York Central R.R. and Grand Trunk Western R.R.; Pennsylvania Depot, 791 S. Main St. for Pennsylvania R.R.; 301 N. Michigan St. for Chicago, South Shore and South Bend R.R. (electric).

Bus Stations: Union Bus Station, 133 S. LaFayette St., for A.B.C. Lines, Indian Trail Lines, Enders Greyhound Lines, Indiana Motor Bus Co., and Greyhound Lines; Central Bus Station, 230-32 W. Jefferson St., for De Luxe Motor Stages, National Trailways, Martz Bus Lines, Safeway Bus Lines, People's Rapid Transit Co.; Great Eastern Depot, 119-21 W. Jefferson St., for Great Eastern Bus Lines; Main St. side of Courthouse square for Northern Indiana Railway, Elkhart Bus Line, Niles Bus Line.

Airports: Bendix Field, 3 m. W. of courthouse on US 20. Flat taxi rate, 50¢ per person. Used by American Air Lines, scheduled East-West service.

City Busses: Fare 10¢, 3 tokens 25¢. Free transfer between busses.

Taxis: 25¢ first mile, 5¢ each additional ⅓ mile.

Accommodations: 8 hotels. During football season reservations should be made in advance. Y.M.C.A. and Y.W.C.A. open to public.

Information Service: South Bend Association of Commerce, 107 N. Main St.; South Bend Branch, Chicago Motor Club, 209 N. Main St.

Motion Picture Houses: 13.

Radio Station: WSBT (960 kc.).

Swimming: Public Natatorium, 1044 W. Washington St. (adults 25¢, children under 15, 15¢).

Golf: Erskine Park, Miami St. and State 20, 18 holes, greens fee 50¢; Studebaker Park, 7 blocks west from intersection of State 31 and Calvery St., 9 holes, greens fee 25¢.

Tennis Courts: Leeper Park, N. LaFayette St. and St. Joseph River; Potawatomi Park, end of Greenlawn Ave.; Howard Park, E. Jefferson Blvd. and St. Joseph River (all free).

Annual Events: Fencing Tournament, Notre Dame University, Jan. 12; Golden Gloves Tournament and University of Notre Dame indoor track meet, Feb. 21-8; annual exhibit Midland Academy of Art, Mar.; State Conservation week, Apr. 1-7; Polish holiday observance, May 3; Air show, Bendix Airport, Aug. 5; Automobile Show, Granada Theater, Nov. 11.

SOUTH BEND (657.8 alt., 101,268 pop.), seat of St. Joseph County, lies in northern Indiana in the valley of the St. Joseph River, at the crest of the watershed dividing the St. Lawrence basin from the basin of the Mississippi. It covers 19.92 square miles on both sides of the St. Joseph River at its southernmost bend. From this location comes the name, South Bend.

Situated in a rich farming, dairying, and fruit-raising area, South

Bend also is the center of an important mint-growing and mint-distilling section. Its industrial importance, coupled with the presence of Notre Dame University, gives it a thriving, energetic, cosmopolitan atmosphere unusual in the Midlands. It has been shaped for more than 90 years by the creative influence of two great industries that settled here—the Studebaker plant and the Oliver Farm Equipment Company.

Downtown South Bend is a bustling business center, locally called 'Michiana' because it is the trade and financial heart of southern Michigan and northern Indiana. The center of activity is Michigan Avenue and Washington Street. Most of the streets are usually crowded, and noisy. Most of the office buildings are from five to eight stories high, with the exception of the Building and Loan Tower, which is twelve. On week ends during the collegiate football season the town is crowded with visitors who come to see Notre Dame teams in action. Crowds often number 60,000 and tax hotels and rooming facilities to capacity.

The skyline of the western and southern sections of the city is broken by the stacks of many factories, an impressive industrial scene. Here more than 25,000 persons are employed with an annual pay roll of about $40,000,000. South Bend has long been the scene of great industrial and commercial activity and is widely known for the production of aircraft and aviation devices, sewing machines, fishing tackle, automobiles, farm machinery, and farm implements. All the larger industries are unionized, either in the A. F. of L. or the C.I.O.

Surrounding the more than 150 factories are the homes of thousands of foreign-born employees: Poles, Hungarians, Belgians, and many other nationalities. Most of these houses are kept in good condition, with a small lawn in front and often a carefully tended vegetable garden in the rear. South Bend has no slum district, and of the 25,000 dwellings in the city about 70 per cent are owned by their occupants.

More than 15,000 Poles live here, chiefly in the western and southwestern sections of the city. They maintain their own churches, parochial schools, mercantile establishments, and one newspaper, printed in Polish. Preserving many of the traditions and customs of their homeland, they partake, on Christmas Eve, of the *oplatek,* a thin wafer with the outline of the Manger impressed upon it; and observe the ancient *dyngus* rite, in which men switch the women's legs with twigs or sprinkle the women with water on Easter Monday. Food for the Easter feasts is blessed by the priests. The outstanding Polish celebration is an annual field day in the summer, including gymnastics, music, and speeches.

Other racial groups also contribute to the cosmopolitan character of South Bend. Four thousand Negroes live here, with their own welfare agency and community house at Dunbar Center, 732 Western Ave. But perhaps the most colorful group are the Hungarians. About 10,000 have settled just southwest of the center of the city where they support Indiana's only Hungarian newspaper, *Varosi Elet,* two Roman Catholic churches, and one Presbyterian. Their social life centers in two church halls and in the Verhovay Home. For their Harvest Dance they gather in native costume to dance the *czardas,* adopted by their ancestors from the dances of the wandering gypsies of their homeland.

The north and east sections of the city are given over to residences ranging from comfortable cottages and bungalows to mansions set in spacious, landscaped lawns. In the northern portion of the town along Michigan Avenue (US 31) are many stately old houses, particularly in Navarre Place. Curved residential streets, tree-lined and quiet, lead to the river. Along its northern bank is North Shore Drive, with many of the city's finest old houses. Just where the drive leads off from the highway is the spot where Pierre Navarre built his first log cabin in 1820. Near by on the drive is the crown of a hill that affords an excellent view of the city and river, as well as the morainal hills to the south.

Civic leaders are conserving the city's natural beauty spots: Rum Village Park is a tract covered with virgin timber on the southern edge of the city, named for Chief Rum of the Potawatomi Indians, who once maintained a village here; retaining walls, both picturesque and utilitarian, line the St. Joseph River between South Bend and Mishawaka; and a beautiful boulevard parallels the river connecting the two sister cities. (Although separate municipalities, South Bend and Mishawaka are virtually one. There is no physical line of demarcation.)

South Bend claims to be the first city in the United States to enforce a law requiring all commercial food handlers to take a Wassermann test; public health work in general receives much attention. Scattered over the city are 120 established churches. There are 19 public elementary schools, 2 schools for the mentally and physically handicapped, 10 junior and 3 senior high schools, 14 parochial elementary schools, and 2 parochial high schools. At the northern city limits, and visible from practically every vantage point, is the great golden dome of the Administration Building of the University of Notre Dame.

Near this point, on December 5, 1679, René Robert Cavelier, Sieur de la Salle, man of letters and explorer, made a portage between the St. Joseph and Kankakee Rivers and continued on his way to the Illinois, the Mississippi, and the unexplored western waters. On a second trip in May 1681, La Salle met with the chiefs of the Miami and Illinois confederations under a tree known as the Council Oak, which still stands (1941) in Highland Cemetery. At this meeting he brought about a treaty of peace between these nations that banded them together against their common enemy, the savage Iroquois from the east. This alliance of the Miami and Illinois with the French against the eastern tribes that were backed by the English had far-reaching consequences in the development of the fur trade and the history of this region.

The first white man to make a permanent home in what is now

St. Joseph County was Pierre Freischütz Navarre, an educated French-man who arrived in 1820 as an agent of the American Fur Company and established the first trading post in this section. He married a Potawatomi whom tradition represents as having been exceptionally intelligent. When the Potawatomi were removed to the West in 1838, Navarre went with them but returned and died in 1864 at the home of one of his daughters in South Bend. Both Navarre Place and Navarre Street perpetuate his name.

Alexis Coquillard, the founder of South Bend, first named the site Big St. Joseph Station to distinguish it from a trading post operated by relatives on the Little St. Joseph River near the present site of Fort Wayne. Settlers, however, soon dubbed the post 'The Bend,' or 'South Bend.' In 1823, Coquillard, a man of energy and force, per-suaded his father-in-law, Francis Comparet, to become his partner and invest a sum said to have approximated $75,000 to the purchase of the agency of John Jacob Astor's American Fur Company for the region of the Upper Lakes.

Four years later Colonel Lathrop M. Taylor opened a trading post for Samuel Hanna & Company and became a friendly business rival of Coquillard. In 1827 Colonel Taylor renamed the settlement St. Jo-seph's and in 1829 the name was changed to Southold. Finally and officially, in 1830, the Post Office department named it South Bend.

Working together, Coquillard and Taylor laid the foundation of South Bend's industrial future. Ferries, dams, and mills resulted from their efforts. They encouraged settlers with gifts of money and land and, in 1831, after laying out the town site, brought about the selection of South Bend as the county seat.

Henceforth the town's growth was steady. But it was slow until 1852, when Henry and Clement Studebaker came to South Bend. With $68 and two forges they opened a blacksmith and wagon shop, fore-runner of the extensive Studebaker Corporation of today. Building farm wagons, fine carriages, prairie schooners for western emigrants, and, later, automobiles, they served a world-wide market and laid the basis for South Bend's future prosperity.

Further industrial impetus was given to the town by the rise and growth of the Oliver Chilled Plow Works. In 1855 James Oliver came to South Bend and in the following year joined with T. M. Bissel, who had been in the plow-manufacturing business in Ohio, and George Milburn in the manufacture of plows under the name of Oliver, Bissel & Company. Later a stock company was formed under the name of the South Bend Iron Works. It subsequently passed into the control of James Oliver and eventually became the Oliver Chilled Plow Works. In 1864 Oliver discovered a process for chilling and hardening steel so that the curved moldboards of plows could be made of steel instead of the softer iron, formerly used. This plow would remain sharp for a long time, and the moldboard would not become encrusted with sticky earth. Today the Oliver Plow is known the world over. Together with the Studebaker wagon, it played no small part in the agricultural development of the Nation.

POINTS OF INTEREST

1. ST. JOSEPH COUNTY'S ORIGINAL COURTHOUSE (*open 8–5 weekdays*), 112 S. LaFayette Blvd., an excellent example of Colonial type public building, was erected in 1855. It is now a museum in which the Northern Indiana Historical Society maintains a collection of Indian relics, early northern Indiana historical documents, and bones of prehistoric animals found in the region. A cannon used in the Revolutionary War stands in the vestibule. On the grounds is a 75-foot masonry monument, with bronze tablets, by Rudolph Schwartz, erected in honor of the soldiers and sailors of St. Joseph County who have served in the Nation's wars.

2. The BENDIX AVIATION CORPORATION PLANT (*open 8–5 weekdays; guide*), city limits, between Michigan Central R.R. and US 20, is almost a city within itself. Factory buildings, paved streets, electric transportation, small parks, boulevards, and homes of workers occupy many acres of former Kankakee marsh wasteland. This corporation manufactures four-wheel brakes, carburetors, automatic clutch controls, finger-tip gearshift apparatus, and many other parts of modern motor cars; marine and general industrial appliances; and practically all devices used in airplanes. It is one of the largest plants in the world for the manufacture of airplane parts.

The Bendix-Westinghouse Airbrake Company, a subsidiary, manufactures air brakes and air-control appliances for motor vehicles; while the Lubrication Corporation, owned jointly by the Bendix Corporation and the Standard Oil Company (Indiana), produces automotive and industrial lubrication equipment. About 7,000 persons are normally employed.

3. The OLIVER FARM EQUIPMENT PLANT (*open 8–5 weekdays*), 533 Chapin St., is one of the largest plants in the world making farm machinery and tools. It covers 99 acres, normally employs 2,000 persons, and exports its products to 50 countries. Founded in 1856 by James Oliver and known the world over as the home of the Oliver plow, the firm has grown in industrial importance since 1929 as a result of mergers.

4. The STUDEBAKER CORPORATION PLANT (*open 8–5 weekdays; guide*), S. LaFayette and Bronson Sts., covering 125 acres, was the first of South Bend's industrial plants to attain national prominence. In 1852 Clement and Henry Studebaker arrived in South Bend from Ashland, Ohio, and established a wagon-making and blacksmith shop. In 1899 the firm began the manufacture of bodies for electric automobiles. Electric runabouts and trucks were manufactured from 1902 to 1912, when electric motive power was abandoned. The peak of business in automobile manufacturing was reached in 1923, when 145,167 motorcars were produced. Financial reorganizations have taken

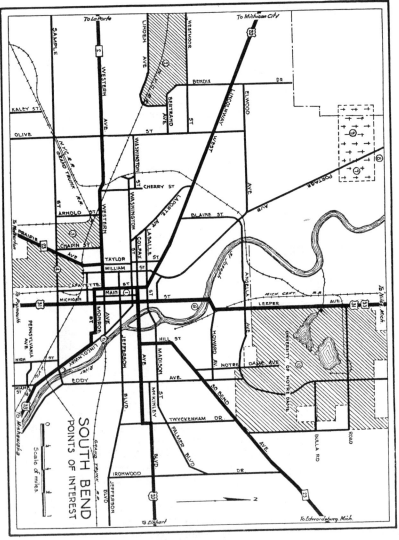

KEY FOR SOUTH BEND MAP

1. St. Joseph County's Original Courthouse 2. Bendix Aviation Corporation Plant
3. Oliver Farm Equipment Plant 4. Studebaker Corporation Plant 5. First Shot
Marker 6. Leeper Park 7. La Salle's First Portage 8. La Salle Monument 9.
Highland Cemetery 10. University of Notre Dame Du Lac

place since that time, but large-scale manufacture continues. Early in 1911 the firm was incorporated under the name of the Studebaker Corporation with assets of $22,000,000.

The MUSEUM (*open*), in the Administration Building, contains a covered wagon made by John Studebaker, father of the founders, in 1830; early buggies and other vehicles; a carriage used by LaFayette when he visited the United States in 1824-5; the carriage used by President Lincoln on the night of his assassination; carriages made by the firm for President Benjamin Harrison and President Ulysses S. Grant; a large collection of vehicles of many periods, and all models of Studebaker automobiles.

5. FIRST SHOT MARKER, 615 Lincolnway E., honors Sergeant Alex Arch, a native of South Bend, who was in command of Battery C, 6th Field Artillery, U. S. Army, when that battery fired the first shot discharged by American forces in France, at 6:05 A.M. on October 23, 1917.

6. LEEPER PARK (*open 8-5 daily*), Michigan St. and St. Joseph River, where Pierre Navarre's original log cabin stands, is the homestead of this district's first white settler, who arrived in 1820. His heirs presented his cabin to the Northern Indiana Historical Society. Most of the original logs are intact, but a new fireplace has been added.

7. LA SALLE'S FIRST PORTAGE between the St. Joseph and Kankakee Rivers is designated by the St. Joseph-Kankakee marker in Riverview Cemetery, across the river from Pinhook Park. At this point, in 1679, La Salle, first recorded white man to cross this region, set out for the Kankakee on an ancient Indian trail between the two rivers.

8. The LA SALLE MONUMENT, E. side of Portage Ave. just beyond the northern boundary of Riverview Cemetery, is a granite shaft about 6 feet high, 18 inches thick and 4 feet wide, erected to the memory of La Salle by the South Bend Park Board.

9. In HIGHLAND CEMETERY, Portage Ave. near N. city limits, is the COUNCIL OAK under which La Salle held council with the Miami and Illinois Indians in May 1681. Near this tree, said by botanists to be about 700 years old, was the portage trail in the heart of the Miami village, which was an important Indian gathering point and the capital of the Miami nation. La Salle's western enterprise had been seriously threatened by the Iroquois' destruction of Illinois villages farther down the Illinois River in 1680. He knew that singly the western tribes could not withstand the powerful Iroquois, and planned to unite them against this common enemy. Accordingly, he assembled a group of Illinois chiefs and a few representatives of eastern tribes that had been scattered by King Philip's War in New England four years before and were then guests of the Miamis. A confederation against Iroquois aggression was formed, and under its protection La Salle finished his exploration of the Mississippi and claimed all the territory drained by it, naming it Louisiana in honor of his sovereign.

The GRAVE OF KNUTE ROCKNE, 400 feet north of Council Oak, is marked by a simple stone. Rockne, nationally known football coach of Notre Dame University, was killed in an airplane accident March 31, 1931.

10. UNIVERSITY OF NOTRE DAME DU LAC, Notre Dame Ave., NE. city limits, N. of Angela Blvd., E. of US 31, is one of the leading Roman Catholic universities of the United States. Its 1,700-acre campus, said to be the largest in the world, is landscaped and beautifully shaded. Students, annually numbering more than 4,000, all live on the campus.

The university consists of five colleges: Arts and Letters, Science, Engineering, Law, and Commerce. In addition, there are summer sessions and a graduate school. Emphasis is placed on business administration, law and science. Notable graduates include: Father Nieuwland, creator of synthetic rubber, Lewisite gas and other chemical compounds; Professor J. A. Reyniers, who developed the germ-free guinea pig; Knute Rockne, of football fame; Edward N. Hurley, former Secretary of Commerce; Angus McDonald, president of the Southern Pacific Railroad; Frank C. Walker, former co-ordinator of the National Emergency Council; Edward J. Kelley, mayor of Chicago; Frank E. Hering, founder of Mother's Day and the *Eagle Magazine;* Charles Butterworth, actor; Francis Wallace, novelist; and Paul Mallon, journalist.

It was at Notre Dame that Knute Rockne introduced his spectacular and successful system of football, developing the famous 'Four Horsemen' and 'Seven Mules' of 1924, and many other All-American stars. Rockne's system has been widely adopted and many men coached by him now hold important coaching positions throughout the Nation.

The university was a pioneer in offering graduate work in Boy Guidance. This division, sponsored by the Knights of Columbus, was made a part of the general graduate program in social work in 1935. Its purpose is to prepare young men for positions in the field of community recreation, scouting, boys' clubs, and in industrial welfare and settlement work.

On November 26, 1842, Father Edward Sorin, coming overland from Vincennes with seven Brothers of the Congregation of the Holy Cross, reached the site of Notre Dame. About 600 acres, 10 of them cleared, and then known as St. Marie des Lacs, had been given to Father Sorin by Bishop Hailandière of the diocese of Vincennes on condition that he establish a college there within two years. A log house was already standing and Father Sorin and his colleagues at once set about raising funds. A small log building that still stands on the shores of St. Mary's Lake was erected. The first student was Alexis Coquillard, founder of South Bend.

Funds were gradually obtained and in the fall of 1843 an architect arrived from Vincennes and work was started on new and larger buildings. During the first quarter century the pinch of poverty was never absent, but with the completion of the Lake Shore Railroad in 1851 a few more students began to arrive and this condition was gradually alleviated. In April 1879 the university was destroyed by fire, but

Father Sorin immediately set to work to rebuild and since that time the growth of the institution has been unimpeded.

CAMPUS TOUR

(Buildings, unless otherwise stated, are open 9–5 weekdays; apply Administration Building for guide.)

Entering the campus from Notre Dame Avenue, the drive passes through a group of buildings arranged in a rectangular plan with the long dimension east and west. Beyond is the U-shaped arrangement of the older buildings showing French influence in its symmetry. The Administration Building is at the end of the vista with the Church of Our Lady of the Sacred Heart to the west, and Washington Hall and the university auditorium to the east. Erected in 1879, the Administration Building shows the Neo-Gothic influence of that period. Its most notable feature is an immense golden dome crowned with a figure of the Virgin, by Giovanni Meli. In the background are several halls, not open to the public, that are used by the community of priests and brothers.

To the left of the campus entrance, the shafts of Cedar Grove cemetery are seen, with the east end of the golf course between the cemetery and the roadway. To the right, across an open field, the west wall of Rockne Stadium is visible. Dedicated October 4, 1930, as a memorial to Knute Rockne, this concrete stadium, seating 57,000 persons, occupies the site of old Cartier Field.

The College of Law Building, at the right of the entrance, is a Gothic-type building of light-colored brick, trimmed with stone. Just west of it is the College of Engineering Building, functional in design, the gift of John F. Cushing, '06, of Chicago. It houses the famous high-tension laboratory where a gigantic 'atom smasher,' nearly twice as large as any existing electrostatic generator, is being built. This 8,000,000-volt instrument, which is to be in operation during 1941, will be in addition to the 1,800,000-volt 'electron gun' now in use. When completed this generator will drive streams of electrons down a long evacuated porcelain tube to bombard atoms and cause them to disintegrate. It will also generate tremendously powerful and penetrating X-rays. Operators will be compelled to observe the progress of experiments through a five-foot wall through which runs a large sewer pipe filled with water with its ends closed by heavy glass.

Just north are the College of Commerce Building, Chemistry Hall, where Father Nieuwland discovered processes for making synthetic rubber and Lewisite gas, and the College of Architecture Building. The Hall of Science, beyond the College of Architecture, is where Professor Reyniers developed his germ-free guinea pig.

The Administration Building is the main structure on the campus. In the long, high-ceilinged hall are murals by Luigi Gregori who came from Rome in 1874 to become Director of the Art Department of the University. The murals depict incidents in the life of Columbus. The interior of the dome is decorated by allegorical paintings, also by Gregori.

The CHURCH OF OUR LADY OF THE SACRED HEART, immediately west of the Administration Building, is an impressive structure that follows the French plan of an ambulatory and chevet chapels. All the paintings are the work of Gregori. The 42 painted glass windows were made by Carmelite nuns at Le Mans, France. The main altar, a double one, came from the atelier of Froc-Robert in Paris, and stood originally in the Church of St. Étienne in Beauvais, France. Carvings depict subjects from the 21st chapter of the Apocalypse. Under the altar are the bones of Saints Stephen, Vincent, and Sebastian. The sanctuary lamp of gold and silver, decorated with semiprecious stones, is noteworthy. In the rear of the main altar is one of the university's greatest treasures, a baroque altar carved by Giovanni Lorenzo Bernini (1598–1680), architect of the colonnade of St. Peter's in Rome. The RELIQUARY CHAPEL (open) is the third apsidal chapel to the right. Its altar contains relics of the Twelve Apostles and of many saints. Above the altar is a copy by Gregori of Raphael's *Disputa* in the Vatican. The Stations of the Cross, also by Gregori, are very fine.

CORBY HALL (open by arrangement), in the rear of the Church, is a residence hall before which is a monument to Father Corby, chaplain of the Irish Brigade in the Civil War. It is a copy of the monument erected to him on the battlefield at Gettysburg and shows him giving general absolution to the soldiers on the second day of the battle. A short distance behind Corby Hall is the GROTTO OF OUR LADY OF LOURDES, a reproduction of the original in the French Pyrenees. In a niche high up on the rock wall is the figure of Our Lady of Lourdes. Near by is a small statue of the recently canonized St. Bernadette. An outdoor WAY OF THE CROSS starts in the rear of the Grotto. It consists of tall wooden crosses with a cupola over each, much like the roadside shrines of Bavaria. The Way extends around St. Joseph Lake and ends at the Hill of Calvary.

The FIRST BRICK MISSION HOUSE (not open) built on the campus is about 1,000 paces to the left of the Grotto. It is the headquarters of the mission priests of the Congregation of the Holy Cross. A log chapel, near the Mission House, is a reproduction on the site of the first log chapel erected here by Father Badin, first priest to be ordained in the United States. His remains rest under a stone slab in the middle of the chapel floor.

The LIBRARY, just east of the Log Chapel, is a four-story gray limestone building, which houses the university's collections of art and literature. Most famous among the books are the 3,000-volume Dante collection, assembled and endowed by Father Zahm, and rare books and documents bearing on early American history.

The art collection is on the second floor. In the five galleries are original canvases by such masters as Van Dyck, Tintoretto, Guido Reni, Veronese, Correggio, and others, some 15 fine Russian and Italian primitives, and some excellent moderns. Paintings by Roos, Albini,

Murillo, Poussin, Ribera, Bartolommeo, and many others are in the Wightman Memorial collection, the gift of Charles A. Wightman of Evanston, Illinois, in memory of his wife. Many of the canvases once were owned by the Capuchin monks of Benevento, by the Sciarri-Colonna family, and by Cardinal Fesch, uncle of Napoleon I.

Also on the second floor is a collection of furniture and art objects once owned by the Borgias and the Medici, which was given to the university by Mrs. Frederick H. Wickett of Chicago, in memory of her husband. An outstanding Mortlake tapestry is included. On the same floor is the Vincent Bendix Foundation Tapestry Exhibit, a loan collection of 16 tapestries, including several Gobelins. This exhibit exemplifies the work of tapestry makers from the fourteenth to the eighteenth centuries.

About 7,500 meals are served daily in the DINING HALL (*cafeteria open* 7–8), which is in the residence hall area west of the entrance. This building, opened in 1927, contains several small dining rooms, a cafeteria, and two large halls, paneled in oak with tables arranged in the manner of a medieval refectory and a high table at the end of each hall for the use of faculty members. Residence halls, HOWARD, BADIN, MORRISSEY, LYONS, ALUMNI, and DILLON are grouped around the Dining Hall. Other buildings include the GYMNASIUM, MUSIC BUILDING, INFIRMARIES, FRESHMAN RESIDENCE HALL, and the BIOLOGY BUILDING. The latter houses 6,000 volumes on botany, said to be the largest collection west of Harvard.

POINTS OF INTEREST IN ENVIRONS

Bendix Municipal Airport, 3.7 *m.;* Studebaker Proving Grounds, 13.6 *m.* (*see Tour* 1). St. Mary's Academy, 2.2 *m.* (*see Tour* 16a).

Terre Haute

Railroad Stations: Union Station, 9th and Spruce Sts., for Pennsylvania R.R., Chicago and Eastern Illinois R.R., and Chicago, Milwaukee, St. Paul and Pacific R.R. (the latter with passenger service south of Terre Haute only); Big Four Station, 7th and Tippecanoe Sts., for Cleveland, Cincinnati, Chicago and St. Louis R.R.
Bus Stations: Union Bus Terminal, 6th and Cherry Sts., for Greyhound Lines, Wabash Valley Coach Company, Ricauda Stage Line, National Motor Transit Company, Western Motor Lines, Southern Limited, Inc., Swallow Coach Line and Rankin Coach Lines; Indiana R.R., 637 Cherry St.
Airport: Paul Cox Field (municipal), 7th St. and Davis Ave.; no scheduled service.
Taxis: Minimum 25¢ for 2 m. in city limits, 1 to 4 passengers.
City Bus Lines: Fare 5¢.
Traffic Regulations: U turns on Wabash Ave. prohibited. No double parking.

Accommodations: 18 hotels; many tourist camps.

Information Service: Terre Haute Auto Club, Terre Haute House, 7th St. and Wabash Ave.

Theaters and Motion Picture Houses: 1 theater, the Hippodrome, 8th and Ohio Sts., occasional road shows; 12 motion picture houses.
Radio Station: WBOW (1230 kc.).
Swimming: Municipal Swimming Pool (25¢ adm.), Fairbanks Park, First and Park Sts.; Y.W.C.A. Pool (25¢ adm.), Y.W.C.A. Building, 131 N. 7th St.; Y.M.C.A. Pool (25¢ adm.), Y.M.C.A. Building, 200 S. 6th St.; Teachers College Pool, Student Union Building, 7th and Mulberry Sts.
Golf: Stadium Course, 9 holes, municipal, 35th St. and Wabash Ave., greens fee 25¢; Rea Park, 18 holes, municipal, 7th St. and Davis Ave., greens fee 50¢.
Baseball: Memorial Stadium, Midwest Semipro Tournament yearly, May 30 to Sept. 2.
Football: Rose Polytechnic Institute, 4.3 m. E. on US 40; Indiana State Teachers College; high school teams at City Schools Athletic Field, 13th and Locust Sts.
Basketball: Two colleges and city high schools in own gymnasium.
Riding: Saddle Club, clubhouse and stables 7 m. W. on US 40.

Annual Events: Indiana State Teachers College Foundation Day, Jan. 6; Rose Show, biannually, Apr. 20–30, at Rose Polytechnic Institute; Boy Scout Circus, May 4; Boat Races on Wabash River, May 30; 4-H Club Stock Exhibit at Memorial Stadium, Aug. 30 (approximate); Wabash Valley Golf Tournament, Sept. 15; Foundation Day at St. Mary-of-the-Woods College, Oct. 22; Annual Shoot of Terre Haute Gun Club, Nov. 11.

TERRE HAUTE (495 alt., 62,693 pop.) is the commercial and banking center of a wide Midwestern trade area, situated in a district of farms and coal mines. Seat of Vigo County and industrial, commercial, and cultural hub of the fertile Wabash Valley, this alert city covers a 10-square-mile plateau on the east bank of the Wabash River. The principal places of business lie along the main thoroughfare, Wabash Avenue. The population of Terre Haute is predominantly native white.

Numerous suburban developments lie north, south and east of the city. In sharp contrast is Taylorville, near the west end of the Wabash River bridge, now partly eliminated by Paul Dresser Memorial Park. There, on the river bank in shacks built of tin and river debris, the very poor and the outcast live in poverty and squalor.

Three institutions of higher learning—Indiana State Teachers College, near-by Rose Polytechnic Institute, and St. Mary-of-the-Woods (*see Tour* 8)—offer scholastic opportunities usually to be found only in much larger cities. There is wide support for two little-theater groups, the Terre Haute Symphony Orchestra, art exhibits and frequent platform appearances of distinguished speakers.

Terre Haute was the home of Eugene V. Debs, labor leader; Claude Bowers, historian and diplomat; Janet Scudder, sculptor; Theodore Dreiser, novelist; Paul Dresser, song writer; Daniel Voorhees, political debater; Lyman Abbott, minister, author, and magazine editor; Colonel Richard W. Thompson, Secretary of the Navy under President Hayes; Rose Melville, original 'Sis Hopkins' of the plays *Zeb* and *Sis Hopkins;* Gilbert Wilson, mural painter; Anthony ('Skeets') Gallagher, stage and screen comedian; and Max Ehrmann, poet.

More than 200 industrial establishments manufacture such diverse products as brick and tile, glass bottles, heating boilers, steel plates and angle iron, paint and varnish, commercial solvents, liquor, canned goods, beer, and corrugated paper and pasteboard shipping containers.

The principal industry since 1875, however, has been coal mining, and three-score mining companies have business offices in the city. During a period almost as long as the history of the coal industry, Terre Haute has been regarded as a strong 'union town' and Terre Haute workers have been leaders in labor progress. Great influence was exerted by Eugene V. Debs, who for half a century preached from his home here the economic brotherhood of man; and by the farmer organizations that began with the formation of the first Indiana Grange in 1869 in Honey Creek Township.

The site of Terre Haute was known to white men—Jesuit missionaries and French traders—early in the eighteenth century. Called *terre haute* (high land) by the French, it once was the home of a band of Wea Indians. Here, according to tradition, the Illinois Indians fought a savage battle with the invading Iroquois, in which the invaders suffered the worst defeat in all their forays into the Midlands.

From about 1720 until the end of French occupation in 1763, the site of Terre Haute was a point on the dividing line between the French colonial provinces of Canada and Louisiana. Americans first settled in the vicinity in 1811, when General William Henry Harrison built Fort Harrison on the Wabash River three miles north of where the city was later built. A small settlement grew up about the fort, but in 1816 a group of southern Indiana and Kentucky businessmen formed the

Terre Haute Town Company, bought a tract from the United States Land Office at Vincennes for $30,376.28 and platted Terre Haute. Their surveyor, in recommending the site, said: 'If a town is started on this location, it will some day become a flourishing city.'

In the year following the founding only two cabins were built. In 1818, however, the company, by promising to erect public buildings, had Terre Haute designated as the seat of government of newly organized Vigo County. With prestige thus gained, the river assured the success of the town. Over the river came settlers hoping to earn fortunes in the West, and over it their produce was sent to market. Before the coming of the steamboat, farm products went down the Wabash and Ohio Rivers to New Orleans by flatboat. The first Wabash River steamboat, the *Florence,* docked in the spring of 1822 at the old flatboat yards south of the foot of Oak Street. Steamboats often could go no farther north because of low water and numerous sandbars; this gave the town a strategic location as a terminal for river shipping.

The first industrial activity was processing resources of the Wabash Valley. Salted and smoked pork, raw and tanned hides, hominy and whisky were among the first products of Terre Haute factories. In 1832 the thriving village, grown in population to 600, was incorporated as a town.

In 1838, completion of the National Road (now US 40) from Washington, D. C., to Terre Haute, brought stagecoaches and wagon trains with more settlers. The Wabash & Erie Canal reached Terre Haute in 1849, giving the city its most direct and lowest-cost outlet to the Atlantic seaboard. Along the canal within the town new factories and warehouses were established, among them a flour mill, foundry, planing mill, brewery, ice house, candle factory, tannery, and blast furnace. Railroad service to Indianapolis was inaugurated in 1852 by Chauncey Rose and other public-spirited citizens, and to Evansville in 1858. The town was organized as a city in 1853, and the Civil War found Terre Haute a thriving industrial community that was rapidly becoming a railroad center.

Coal in this region was first mentioned in 1816 in a letter from David Thomas, a New Yorker, to Eastern friends. Thomas observed that outcroppings of coal at many points along the river and its tributaries in the vicinity of Terre Haute indicated an important industrial future for the settlement. Development of the coal fields did not start, however, until about 1875. In 1838 Jacob Thomas tried unsuccessfully to ship coal from Terre Haute by flatboat. Before he completed loading, the river receded to a low level that left the boat stranded. When the river rose again, the loaded boat sank. As there was little demand for coal at that time because firewood was plentiful and cheap, the venture was not attempted again. With the railroad building boom in the last quarter of the nineteenth century, however, large-scale coal production became possible. When the coal mines in the vicinity were developed, new factories sprang up also, attracted by low fuel costs.

After peak production for war demands totaled more than 30,000,000 tons (4.59 per cent strip, 95.41 per cent shaft) in Indiana in 1918, coal production declined to a low figure of little more than 12,500,000 tons for the State in 1932. Thereafter production increased gradually, with strip mining steadily gaining in importance. In Vigo County, always one of the leaders in coal production, trends followed the figures for the State. Decline in coal production is attributed partly to diversion of demand to other fuels when the Indiana supply was shut off by the strike of 1922, and partly to substitution of coal of higher thermal values from other fields.

Before the American Federation of Labor was organized, coal miners were members of the Knights of Labor. When, in 1890, the United Mine Workers of America was formed, District 11 headquarters made the city, already the home of the Indiana Coal Operators' Association, arbiter of coal-mining relations in Indiana.

Some of Terre Haute's strikes have attracted Nation-wide attention. One was the 9-months coal strike of 1922, out of which came coal-mining relations that were peaceful for many years. Another was the general strike of July 1935, the third in the Nation's history and the first east of the Rockies. It was called in support of nearly 600 Columbian Enameling and Stamping Company workers who had walked out March 23, 1935, for a 10 per cent wage increase and a union shop. On July 18 the company imported 58 professional strikebreakers. Officials disregarded warnings from the 48 American Federation of Labor unions that unless the strikebreakers were removed a general sympathetic strike would be declared, whereupon on July 22 nearly 26,000 workers and many merchants quit work in a strike described by the New York *Times* as 'virtually 100 per cent effective.'

The governor ordered 2,000 National Guardsmen into the city. Martial law was declared, picketing was forbidden, and on July 23 troops tear-gassed 1,800 pickets. In spite of State-wide liberal protest, martial law was not lifted until February 1936, although the general strike was called off July 24, 1935. The dispute was placed in the hands of Federal mediators and later the demands of the strikers were sustained by the National Labor Relations Board. A number of employees were discharged for participating in the strike and the National Labor Relations Board ordered the company to rehire them. The company appealed to the United States Supreme Court, which held that the finding of the National Labor Relations Board that the company refused to negotiate with a union was without support, and ordered the decision of the Board to be set aside.

POINTS OF INTEREST

1. The SITE OF THE OLD CANAL TURNING BASIN, 9½ St. and Wabash Ave. Here canalboats of the old Wabash & Erie Canal used to dock and turn.

2. The PHOENIX or PROX OIL WELL, 201 N. 9th St., is of international geological interest, having for 39 years produced oil from a

stratum that experts agreed should not contain oil. Recent discoveries do not confirm that opinion. Three drillings made in 1937 near Middletown on Prairie Creek, 11 miles southwest of Terre Haute, flow more than 50 barrels a day each. It is now believed oil is to be found in numerous dome-shaped formations, small in area and subjected to considerable water pressure that forces the oil to the top of the dome or through sealed faults such as that on which the Phoenix or Prox well is located. It is believed that production of oil may partially compensate for decreased demand for coal. The Phoenix or Prox well was plugged in 1928 by order of the State fire marshal. Once it produced 1,000 barrels a month and it was averaging 100 barrels a month when plugged.

3. The HOME OF EUGENE V. DEBS (*private*), 451 N. 8th St., is a two-story frame house, unpretentious and quite in keeping with the character of the noted Socialist and labor leader. Called a great constructive thinker by his followers, a destructive agitator by his foes, he was beloved personally by all who knew him—even his most bitter political opponents. Many of the things he fought for have been embodied in present-day social legislation.

Born in Terre Haute in 1855, Debs received a public school education and in 1871 started work as a locomotive fireman. A brief excursion into local politics brought him the post of city clerk in his home town, but he soon devoted himself to the labor movement as secretary-treasurer of the Brotherhood of Locomotive Firemen and editor of the magazine of the order. In 1893, dissatisfied by what he termed the conservatism and weakness of the craft of Brotherhoods, he organized the first industrial union, the American Railway Union, and in 1894 attracted national attention as a leader of the great Pullman strike. Jailed for six months in 1895 for violation of a Federal injunction issued during that strike, he decided workers ought to form a political party of their own and in 1898 founded the Social Democratic party, liberal rather than socialist in character. On March 6, 1900, at a 'unity convention' held in Indianapolis by Debs and his Social Democrats and a large faction split from the Socialist Labor party, the Socialist party of the United States was launched. Debs ran for President on the Socialist ticket in 1900 and received about 88,000 votes.

From that time to his death Debs was the Socialist leader and spokesman, running for President in 1904, 1908, 1912, and 1920. In 1918 he was arrested in Cleveland, charged with violation of the Espionage Act because of an anti-war speech made in Canton, Ohio, convicted, and sentenced to ten years in a Federal prison. From prison he conducted his most successful campaign in 1920, polling nearly 1,000,000 votes. President Harding released him December 23, 1921. He died October 20, 1926, mourned as America's greatest and best-beloved labor leader.

4. The EMELINE FAIRBANKS LIBRARY (*open 9-9 weekdays, 2-6 Sun., 9-6 holidays*), 7th and Eagle Sts., a memorial gift by Crawford Fairbanks, Terre Haute financier, honoring his mother, houses more than 103,000 volumes. The main library contains many exhibits

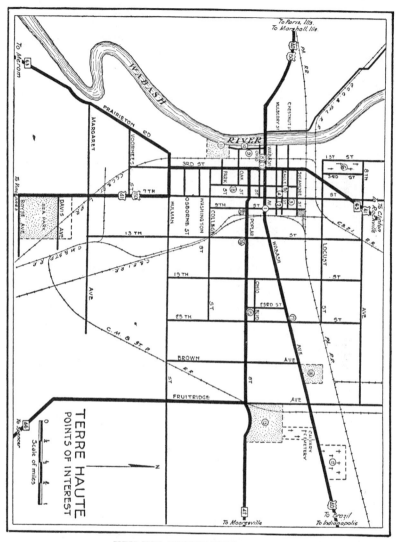

KEY FOR TERRE HAUTE MAP

1. Site of the Old Canal Turning Basin 2. Phoenix or Prox Oil Well 3. Home of Eugene V. Debs 4. Emeline Fairbanks Library 5. Indiana State Teachers College 6. Woodlawn Cemetery 7. Vigo County Courthouse 8. Memorial Hall 9. Dresser (Dreiser) Home 10. Dresser Drive 11. Wabash Valley Boat Club 12. Highland Lawn Cemetery 13. Deming Park 14. Memorial Stadium 15. Woodrow Wilson Junior High School 16. Preston Home 17. Chauncey Rose School 18. Temple Israel

of special interest because the Terre Haute artists who created them achieved distinction and fame in later years. Examples are the first work of Janet Scudder, sculptor, and Amalia Kussner Coudert, noted miniature painter.

5. INDIANA STATE TEACHERS COLLEGE, 6th and 7th Sts., Mulberry to Chestnut Sts., covering approximately six city blocks, is one of the older institutions in the United States for preparation of teachers. Created as the Indiana State Normal School by act of the Indiana General Assembly December 20, 1865, the school opened on January 6, 1870. The City of Terre Haute gave the land on which the buildings stand and $50,000 cash; it also pays half the upkeep of the buildings and grounds. All other expenses are borne by the State. The college buildings represent an investment of $6,000,000. The Administration Building is of early English tower-and-battlement design. Gilbert Wilson's murals enrich the Laboratory School. The college is coeducational, with 3,000 students enrolled in courses leading to degrees of A.B. and B.S. More than a fourth of all teachers and administrators in the public schools of Indiana received at least part of their training at this school, and more than 600 graduates are professors and administrators in American colleges and universities.

Newest additions to the Indiana State Teachers College campus are the FINE ARTS AND COMMERCE BUILDING and the STUDENT UNION BUILDING AND AUDITORIUM. Both were built with State and Federal Public Works Administration funds, and cost respectively $360,000 and $427,000. The Fine Arts and Commerce Building, housing the departments of art, music, and commerce, contains a music hall, art studios, an art gallery, and modern commercial equipment such as bookkeeping and calculating machines. The eight Hoosier Art Salon prize paintings, which the Kappa Kappa Kappa sorority placed on permanent exhibit here, form the nucleus of the art collection. The Student Union Building and Auditorium contains a theater seating approximately 2,000 persons, a swimming pool, meeting and recreation rooms, cafeteria, and limited hotel facilities. The cafeteria and swimming pool are open to the public.

6. In WOODLAWN CEMETERY, N. 3rd St. between Locust St. and 8th Ave., is a monument to 11 Confederate soldiers who died here as prisoners in the Civil War.

7. The VIGO COUNTY COURTHOUSE, 3rd St. and Wabash Ave., has a tower in which hangs the Vigo Bell, bought with $500 bequeathed for the purpose by Colonel Francis Vigo (1740–1836), financial backer of General George Rogers Clark's conquest of the Northwest Territory (see Vincennes). Vigo died in poverty, but his will provided for the money for the bell, if and when the Government allowed his claims for financing supplies for General Clark to the amount of $8,616. The claim was allowed and paid in 1875, 40 years after Vigo's death. By this time interest had increased the amount of the claim to $49,898.60, which was paid to Vigo's estate. The lumber for the courthouse was sawed by Chauncey Rose.

8. MEMORIAL HALL (*open* 9–4:30 *daily*), Ohio St. between 2d and 3d Sts., of Greek Doric design, is used as a meeting place for Civil and Spanish War veterans and their auxiliaries, and also as a museum of war relics. When a child, Amalia Kussner Coudert, miniature painter born in Terre Haute March 26, 1873, lived upstairs in this building, which then was the old State Bank Building.

9. The DRESSER (DREISER) HOME (*private*), 115 Walnut St., is a small brick house where the Dreiser family lived in poverty. Paul Dresser (1858–1906) wrote Indiana's State song, the beloved 'On the Banks of the Wabash,' and other songs. Theodore Dreiser (1871–   ) became a noted American novelist (*see Literature*). When Theodore was three years old the family moved away from Terre Haute. Paul was sent to St. Meinrad Academy at St. Meinrad, Indiana, at 15, to be educated for the priesthood. He tired of life at the academy, ran away, changed his name to Dresser and joined a medicine show at Indianapolis. In 1892 he joined a music publishing firm in New York and in the following decade became the country's most popular song writer and a music publisher. The publishing firm failed just before he died January 20, 1906, leaving him broken in health and finances. Dresser, rather than Dreiser, the family name, is the name Terre Haute knows and honors.

10. DRESSER DRIVE, a scenic boulevard, was built in honor of Paul Dresser. It follows the east bank of the Wabash River south from Wabash Ave. to Fairbanks Park, the Municipal Swimming Pool and the Wabash Valley Boat Club.

11. The WABASH VALLEY BOAT CLUB (*private*), river bank at foot of Park St., has a clubhouse, landing barge, and specially constructed harbor. The club has a large membership of owners of speedboats, large cabin craft and canoes. Several river regattas are conducted each year.

12. HIGHLAND LAWN CEMETERY, on US 40 a short distance outside the eastern city limits, is the city's principal burying ground. Among its graves are those of Senator Daniel Wolsey Voorhees (1827–97) and Colonel Richard W. Thompson, Secretary of the Navy under President Hayes.

Voorhees, the 'tall sycamore of the Wabash,' was one of the most effective orators of his day, and his speeches in the United States Senate rank almost with those of Calhoun and Clay. His defense of John Brown, John E. Cook and others, for the burning of Harpers Ferry just before the Civil War, brought him national fame. So powerful were his pleadings in a damage case in a District of Columbia court that the presiding judge set aside the verdict of the jurors as excessive, declaring the jury to have been 'unduly influenced' by the senator's powerful appeal.

13. DEMING PARK, Fruitridge Ave. and Ohio St., named in honor of Terre Haute's pioneer banker, is the city's largest and most beautiful park. In its 155 acres of wooded and hilly terrain are a small zoo,

fish breeding pond, facilities for group outings, a bridle path, and several hiking trails.

14. MEMORIAL STADIUM, 30th St. and Wabash Ave., dedicated to World War soldiers and sailors of Vigo County, is the city's recreational center. It is constructed of concrete, with a seating capacity of 20,000. At the entrance is a memorial arch of Greco-Roman design.

15. WOODROW WILSON JUNIOR HIGH SCHOOL, 25th and Poplar Sts., is Collegiate Gothic in design. The famous Wilson Murals on the north and south walls of the main entrance hall are gifts to the school by Gilbert Wilson, of Terre Haute, an outstanding painter of murals in the modern style (*see Arts and Crafts*).

16. The PRESTON HOME (*open on application*), SE. corner 13th and Poplar Sts., built of stone in Georgian Colonial style at a cost of $20,000 in 1830, is one of the city's few remaining old landmarks. When it was built the area about it was prairie and a bit of its old detachment is preserved by many shade trees in the spacious yard. Some of the mansion's furnishings were purchased in Baltimore in 1835.

17. CHAUNCEY ROSE SCHOOL, first called the Rose Orphans Home, Wabash Ave. at 25th St., was established October 27, 1874, by Chauncey Rose (1794–1877), the city's famous benefactor. Born in Wethersfield, Connecticut, Rose first crossed Indiana in the fall of 1817, a year after Terre Haute was laid out. He financed promotion of interest in education in 1847 and contributed much to the city's progress. The architectural style of the Chauncey Rose School is said to be similar to that of Sandringham Palace in England. His other benefactions include the Rose Ladies Aid Society, Sisters of Providence Hospital at 13th Street and 6th Ave., the Rose Dispensary, and Rose Polytechnic Institute.

18. TEMPLE ISRAEL, 540 S. 6th St., is used by both branches of the Jewish faith, the Reformed congregation and the Orthodox. This house of worship and the orthodox Temple B'Nai Abraham, 300 South 5th St., are managed by one board. Members of both congregations attend services at either temple. The union of the two groups has been operating since 1935 with great success.

POINTS OF INTEREST IN ENVIRONS

Dresser Memorial Park, 1.2 *m.;* Rose Polytechnic Institute, 3.9 *m.;* Bobolink Strip Mine, 7.9 *m.* (*see Tour 8b*). St. Mary-of-the-Woods, 6.6 *m.* (*see Tour 12*).

Vincennes

Railroad Stations: Union Station, Washington and Wabash Aves., for Baltimore & Ohio R.R., Chicago & Eastern Ill. Ry., Pennsylvania R.R., and Big Four Route.
Bus Stations: Terminal, 429 Main St., for Capitol Greyhound, Bluebird, Southern Limited, Inc., Indianapolis-Vincennes, and Wabash Valley Lines.
Taxis: 25¢ for 1 to 3 passengers anywhere in city, 50¢ up to 6 passengers; 25¢ for stops in excess of 1; hourly rate $1.50.
Ferry: At St. Francisville, 9 m. S., short cut to southeastern Illinois; 25¢ for passenger automobiles.
City Busses: 10 min. service to all parts of city; fare 5¢.
Traffic Regulations: Main highways routed on through streets. Watch for limitations on Main St. traffic lights, and for numerous stop streets in all parts of the city. Parking space and periods clearly marked.
Street Numbering: N. and S. from Main St., E. and W. from Park St.

Accommodations: 4 hotels.

Information Service: Chamber of Commerce, City Hall, 4th and Main Sts.

Motion Picture Houses: 5, two of which have occasional local or road productions.
Radio Station: WAOV (1450 kc.).
Recreation: A total of 200 acres of parks and playgrounds, including 13 public tennis courts, all free; Rainbow Beach (municipal swimming pool), in Gregg Park (*adm.*, 25¢); Buena Vista Golf Course (*private*), 1.5 m. E. of city on US 50.

VINCENNES (431 alt., 18,228 pop.), capital of the Old Northwest and the oldest town in Indiana, has preserved many visual reminders of its historic past. Once the seat of government for an area of United States territory greater than that of the original thirteen States, Vincennes today has an air of mellow maturity in keeping with the traditions that center here.

The city is a combination, rare in the Middle West, of the past and present. It stretches for more than two miles along the east bank of the Wabash River, flanked on the north and east by a rim of mound-shaped hills sloping down to its outskirts and on the south by the level Cathlinette prairies that extend some 10 miles southward along the river. Surrounded by rich farm lands and orchards, and within 15 miles of one of Indiana's richest coal fields, Vincennes is a brisk trading and shipping center with a limited industrial section. On every hand, however, are timeworn buildings and sites that are landmarks in the history of the Midwest and the Nation. Many of these shrines are near the Wabash River, immediately north and south of Main Street. A semicircle with a radius of half a mile, having the Indiana end of the Lincoln Memorial Bridge as its center, would encompass the 'old town,' pioneer Vincennes, in which are the stately George Rogers Clark Memorial, the Old Cathedral of St. Francis Xavier, and other points of historic interest. Farther north are the William Henry Harrison Mansion and the old Territorial Legislative Hall.

Tumble-down shanties of fishermen and musselers that a few years ago lined the river front have been razed to make way for the attractively landscaped area bordering the new Memorial Drive. Running at right angles to the river is Main Street, for the most part a succession of adjoining two- and three-story brick business buildings, with a scattering of structures six and seven stories high. Hemming in the downtown section as far as the southern city limits and extending about a half mile north and east is a well-shaded residential section, its two-story brick and frame houses reminiscent of the architecture of the 1870's and 1880's. Farther north is the newer section of the city, once known as 'Goosetown,' with frame cottages occupied by the city's workers. Burnett Heights, an exclusive residential section in the eastern part of town, overlooks Gregg Park.

At a ford on the site of the Lincoln Memorial Bridge, a buffalo trail from the hills and salt licks of southern Indiana once crossed the Wabash River to grazing grounds farther west. Upstream a short distance, there was, during the eighteenth century, an Indian village known as Chip-pe-coke, and to the south and east of the city are four mounds that bear witness to a still more ancient culture.

Authorities differ about the exact date of the first settlement at this point. Some contend that a French fur trading post was established here as early as 1683; some fix the date at 1702. It is quite generally agreed, however, that settlers arrived before 1727, and certainly a fort was built about 1732 (see History) under command of François Morgane de Vincennes. Referred to for some time by a variety of names, such as Au Poste, Poste Ouabache (Wabash), and Post St. Francis Xavier, the settlement received its present name shortly after 1736 in honor of Vincennes, who in that year was captured and burned at the stake by Chickasaw Indians.

Three flags have flown over Vincennes: French, British, and American. It was an important French trading post until 1763, when by the Treaty of Paris it was ceded to Great Britain; with the capture of Fort Sackville by George Rogers Clark in 1779 it came under the American flag.

After the close of the French and Indian War, in 1763, settlers began to penetrate the territory that is now western Pennsylvania and Kentucky and soon after the outbreak of the Revolution the British began to give the Indians firearms and incite them to raids on the frontier settlements. In 1777 Vincennes became one of the principal posts from which the British operated, and for this reason it was the major objective of George Rogers Clark, who saw clearly the importance of the frontier posts. Even if defeated in the East, he reasoned, the British might be able to hold the western country. Accordingly, he organized the settlements of Kentucky as a base of operations and late in 1777 laid his plans before Governor Patrick Henry. Having been commissioned a lieutenant colonel and authorized to draw 1,200 pounds from Virginia's treasury and to enlist 17 companies of 50 men each, Clark, in January 1778, set out to recruit his force. By the following May he had assembled about 150 men on Corn Island, then lying in the Ohio River between the present cities of Jeffersonville and Louisville. From this point he launched his expedition against the British.

He decided to strike first at Kaskaskia. Reaching there on the night of July 4, he took the town and Fort Gage by surprise attack without firing a shot. Father Gibault, resident priest, learned that Clark's government guaranteed political and religious freedom and cast his powerful influence on the American side.

On July 14, after taking Cahokia (on the Mississippi opposite St. Louis), Clark dispatched Father Gibault and Dr. Jean-Baptiste Lafont to Vincennes. Lieutenant-Governor Edward Abbott, British commandant at Vincennes, had left the fort with his garrison the preceding January, leaving it in charge of the Creole villagers. Influenced by Gibault, these Creoles, who had little love for England, quickly swore allegiance to America, and Captain Leonard Helm was sent to hold the fort and begin peace conferences with the Indians. When the news of Clark's successes reached General Hamilton, the British commander at Detroit, he immediately set out with about 600 men for Vincennes. On December 17, 1778, Captain Helm, deserted by his Creoles, surrendered the fort. Clark learned of these developments through a wealthy Italian fur trader, Francis Vigo, and decided to attack Vincennes immediately, with Vigo's financial support. Additional money and men also were furnished by the Kaskaskian Creoles.

On February 5, 1779, with about 70 of his old company and 60 Creoles, Clark started a 240-mile march across flooded prairies to Fort Sackville. Food was almost impossible to obtain and much of the march had to be made through icy water. After enduring almost incredible hardships they reached Warrior's Island on February 23. Vincennes and the fort were about two miles away, and while the men put their arms in order Clark sent a message to the inhabitants of Vincennes telling them of his intention of attacking that night. With the coming of darkness Clark's forces entered the town, which immediately surrendered, and the inhabitants produced a supply of dry powder that had been hidden from Hamilton. The fort was surrounded and was the target of harassing rifle fire throughout the night. With the coming of dawn the riflemen rained so deadly a hail of fire on the fort that it was impossible for its defenders to show themselves at a porthole to use their cannon. When Hamilton's French volunteers from Detroit saw that their Vincennes brethren had joined Clark, they 'hung their heads' and refused to fight against them. Left with only 30 able-bodied defenders and 600 miles from help, Hamilton decided to accept 'honorable terms if they could be procured.'

Clark demanded unconditional surrender, which Hamilton refused. However, a conference was arranged and Hamilton capitulated. The formal surrender took place at 10 o'clock on the morning of February 25.

The capture of Fort Sackville has been called everything from a 'miracle of war' to a 'mere skirmish.' Whatever its military character, it was of decisive importance to the Colonial cause in the West. Following Clark's victory, Virginia claimed all the lands northwest of the Ohio and the county of Illinois was organized. John Todd, Jr., was made county lieutenant but soon returned to Virginia on business. Left with little or no organized government, Vincennes degenerated into a state of anarchy. Indians were debauched and robbed, with the usual reprisals. Murder was common. Efforts of orderly inhabitants to drive away lawless traders and thieves served only to increase the chaos. Finally Virginia, finding herself unable to govern this vast area, ceded it to the United States in 1784. The formation of the Northwest Territory followed in 1787, with the capital at Marietta, Ohio, and General Arthur St. Clair as first governor.

The principal actors in Clark's triumph were never properly rewarded. Virginia refused the claims of Francis Vigo, whose timely information prompted Clark's march on Fort Sackville and whose money outfitted it, and when the Federal Government finally paid them, it was to the second generation of Vigo's heirs. Father Gibault in his declining years asked Governor St. Clair for $1,500 and two acres of land but was refused. The aged priest then withdrew across the Mississippi to Spanish territory, where he died in obscurity and poverty, supposedly at the little town of New Madrid in what is now southeastern Missouri. His burial place is unknown. When the Northwest Territory was ceded to the Union, Virginia gave Clark and his men a strip of about 150,000 acres of land on the north bank of the Ohio River, in what are now Clark, Scott, and Floyd Counties. Just across the river from Louisville he founded the little town of Clarksville. But Clark was a warrior and not a real-estate operator and the town failed to prosper. In his old age, beset by ill health and poverty, he gave himself over to rage and excessive drinking. He died on February 13, 1818, and his remains now rest in Cave Hill Cemetery, Louisville, Kentucky.

When Indiana Territory was created in 1800, Vincennes became the seat of government and William Henry Harrison was appointed governor. He was succeeded by John Gibson and the Territorial capital was moved from Vincennes to Corydon in 1813.

Vincennes was for many years populated almost entirely by Creole descendants of the early French settlers and soldiers. Up to 1845 the only vehicles seen on the streets of the town were French *calèches,* two-wheeled carts made entirely of wood and drawn by a horse or mule. As late as 1855 the French controlled elections in Knox County. The Indian strain in these early citizens was easily discernible in the high cheek bones and straight black hair of many Creoles. The common attire of the men consisted of buckskin coat, knee breeches, and leggings. During the winter they added moccasins and a *capote*, a long, hooded overcoat made of fur. Neither men nor women wore shoes in the summer. The most common garment worn by the women was the *habit*, reaching to the knees; under it was usually worn a gaudily colored petticoat that hung down to the ankles. Both sexes were fond of bright colors around the throat and waist, and costumes were often decorated with bright beads in the Indian fashion.

The Creoles were a musical, fun-loving people, caring little for either formal government or tilling the soil. All they wanted was a living, which was easy to get in those days—hence they became known as a race of pleasure-loving idlers. Life in a frontier outpost could not have been one of complete ease, but these people always seemed to take the line of least resistance and in spite of inevitable hardships they remained gay and easygoing. Certainly they were driven by no compelling urge to accumulate lands or goods.

In the early days Vincennes was also the home of the majority of the Negroes in Indiana. Early French families often imported slaves, and, although the Ordinance of 1787 forbade slavery, many clung to their chattels on alleged constitutional grounds. Indentured Negroes were brought into the Territory by later settlers and slavery was common, in a modified form at least, even after the adoption of the State constitution in 1816. A local census of 1830 revealed 32 Negro slaves in Vincennes, and not until 1843 were the last vestiges of the practice eradicated.

On November 5, 1834, the Most Reverend Simon William Gabriel Bruté de Rémur, first Bishop of the Diocese of Vincennes, arrived to find the St. Francis Xavier church, dedicated in 1826, still unfinished. Bishop Bruté caused the church to be completed, and founded an ecclesiastical seminary, an academy for girls, and two free schools—open to children of all creeds, one for girls and one for boys—before he died June 26, 1839. He has been called the founder of free education in Indiana.

In 1837 a combination town hall and market house, a two-story frame structure, was completed on the same lot on which the present City Hall was erected in 1887. The population of Vincennes around 1837 was predominately French and the old Market House was a busy place. Around it each weekday morning could be seen many of the Creole *calèches*, French farmers from the Cathlinette section, who had brought their produce to town, and Creole womenfolk, carrying their market baskets. A passageway ran the length of the Market House flanked on either side by stalls filled with the various things brought in by the Creole farmers. An ordinance prohibited anyone from selling or bartering before the market was officially opened by 'the marketmaster blowing his horn.' The busiest place in town, however, was Water (now First) Street. Here were most of the stores, saloons, poolrooms, gristmills, and 'porkhouses' (slaughter houses).

In the 1830's Vincennes was a picturesque county seat town, predominately French and Roman Catholic. Below Main Street, most of the houses were built of logs. The river front was usually lined with steamboats, barges, and smaller craft. The amount of commerce on the Wabash is indicated by the record that 54 steamboats called at Vincennes between March 1 and April 16, 1831, and that, during the same period, from 450 to 500 flatboats stopped at its docks or passed by. The cargoes consisted for the most part of pork, beef, lard, horses, oats, corn, meal, and wheat. The value of produce shipped annually by boat from Vincennes was estimated at $740,000.

Prior to 1844, when the township voting system was established, voters from all over Knox County came to Vincennes to cast their ballots. Election day was a full holiday for the townspeople and neighboring farmers, a day filled with hilarity and rough-and-tumble fun. No place in town held more excitement and interest than the old 'French Corner,' at Third and Main Streets, the favorite gathering place.

As Vincennes grew in the following decades, the influence of its Creole founders declined. The character of the town was changed partly by marriages between the French and the American settlers in and near Vincennes, and partly by the presence of German families, most of them Roman Catholics and many of them Alsatians, who had been arriving in Vincennes in noticeable numbers since 1840. In answer to their pleas Bishop Hailandière had not only allotted to them a special time for services at his Cathedral of St. Francis Xavier but had provided them with a German priest who conducted services in German, the only language most of them understood. They continued to attend church in this manner until the completion of their own church of St. John the Baptist, July 1852. Marriages between the French and Germans were frequent.

By 1853, when the first free public schools were inaugurated in Vincennes, the town was divided, so to speak, into three parts. 'Frenchtown,' which covered all the town below Main Street and from the Wabash to 8th Street, was still populated almost entirely by descendants of the town's Creole founders, who with their farmer cousins in the Cathlinette Prairies were still carrying on to a noticeable extent the customs of their forefathers. In the 'Dutch Flats,' below Main Street and extending from 8th Street southward to the town limits, stood the homes of the Germans, mostly members of the parish of St. John the Baptist. The remainder of the town, north of Main Street, was typically American and predominately Protestant.

The completion of the Cincinnati-St. Louis Division of the Ohio & Mississippi (now B & O) Railroad through Vincennes in 1857, and the location in Vincennes of the Ohio & Mississippi shops brought into the town a number of Irish. They located in what was then the north end of town, between the river and the shops, which stood just across the railroad tracks from the present Union Depot—at the time 'out of town.' In 1859 the first gas light company in Vincennes was incorporated. The estimated population in 1860 was 3,960.

When the Indianapolis & Vincennes Railroad (now the I & V Division of the Pennsylvania) was completed in 1867, and the Bicknell coal fields were opened up in 1875, Vincennes' potentialities as an industrial city were recognized and widely advertised. None were more active or astute in the promotion and management of the budding business and industrial advance than the German citizens. Thrifty and far-sighted, a good number of them moneyed people when they located in Vincennes, the Germans soon adapted themselves to American ways and speech. They continued, however, to hold their church services in German, to teach German in their parochial schools, and in some cases to use the German language at home. By 1870 Vincennes' population was 5,438, and ten years later it was 7,680.

Those were the 'good old days,' old-timers recall, when everybody had a job, when new dwellings and business houses were being built and the town was spreading, when smoke from the stove works, the foundries, the railroad shops, flour mills, paper mill, plow works, sawmill, spoke factory, ice houses, slaughter house, and the Hack and Simon Brewery darkened the skies.

By 1900, the old-time French customs, never backed by an organized effort to perpetuate them, were no longer in evidence. Old Frenchtown was no longer French. The quaint old songs and observances no longer held any interest for a generation growing up in an environment that had for 50 years been conforming to the American pattern. After more than a century of intermarriage, the characteristic black-haired, black-eyed Creole type was rare. A few of the early log houses, covered with weatherboarding, were still standing, but they were rotting away.

The Germans, however, had taken steps to preserve the culture of their homeland by organizing on July 8, 1888, the *Harmonie Verein,* a society composed exclusively of Germans or German-speaking people. It drew its membership from all three of Vincennes' German churches— St. John's (Catholic), the Lutheran, and the Evangelical. By the turn of the century, Vincennes, founded by the French, had only one cultural influence not essentially American—the German one.

During the first two decades of the twentieth century, the city experienced its period of greatest growth, and the last vestiges of Old Vincennes were swept away. The Dutch Flats and other special sections lost their separate entities, and Frenchtown received its final *coup de grâce* in 1903, when a window glass factory was established at its southern edge. Skilled Belgian workers, at first employed almost exclusively in the factory, lived in and near the French section. They still live there and the factory is today (1941) one of the city's principal plants.

Since the first World War the population of Vincennes has remained fairly stationary, but its diverse elements have been merged. Only the city's name, the Old Cathedral of St. Francis Xavier, and several near-by spots of historic interest are left as reminders that Vincennes was once French.

Vincennes is today (1941) in many ways as progressively new as it is historically old. The seat of Knox County, agriculturally one of the richest in the State, it is the home of 40 plants manufacturing window glass, shoes, paper products, canned foods, steel bridges, and flour.

POINTS OF INTEREST

1. The LINCOLN MEMORIAL BRIDGE, Vigo St. and Wabash River, a concrete structure of seven spandrel arches built in 1931 by Indiana, Illinois, and the Federal Government, is an impressive link of the Lincoln National Memorial Highway from Hodgenville, Kentucky, to Springfield, Illinois. In 1938 a suitable memorial, commemorating the passage of the Lincoln family across the Wabash here in their migration from Indiana to Illinois in 1830, was completed just off the Illinois end of the bridge. In the stone wall at the foot of the stairway on the south side of the Indiana approach, an integral part of the landscaped 18-acre George Rogers Clark Memorial Plaza, are three massive granite tablets with inscriptions summarizing the history of Vincennes and the Old Northwest.

2. The GEORGE ROGERS CLARK MEMORIAL BUILDING (*open 8–5 daily*), W. end of Barnett St., stands in the center of the Clark Memorial Grounds. It was erected on the site of Fort Sackville in 1931–3 by the Federal Government at a cost of $1,500,000 and dedicated by President Franklin D. Roosevelt, June 14, 1936. The memorial grounds were purchased jointly by the State of Indiana, Knox County, and the city of Vincennes, at an additional cost of $900,000.

The Memorial Building proper is a round room encircled by a colonnade of 16 massive Greek Doric columns. It rests at the top of a series of three circular stepped granite terraces surrounded by a wide pebbled terrace at the top of an octagonal wall. At the bottom of this wall is a broad base formed into a square by a curb wall. Thirty-three steps lead from terrace to terrace up to the Memorial Room, which contains a bronze statue of Clark, by Hermon MacNeil.

Pilasters divide the circular wall of the Memorial Room into eight sections—the entrance and seven historical murals by Ezra Winter depicting episodes in Clark's conquest and the opening of the West. Cut in stone above the murals are words from Clark's letter to Governor Patrick Henry: 'Great things have been effected by a few men well conducted—our cause is just—our country will be grateful.' A carving above the entrance door shows Clark before Governor Patrick Henry, receiving his commission as lieutenant colonel, January 2, 1778. Also depicted are George Mason, Thomas Jefferson, George Wythe, Benjamin Harrison, and an unnamed clerk. The wainscot and seat around the wall below the murals are of French marble; the circular black marble step in front of the seat is from Italy, in honor of Italian-born Vigo.

3. Between the river wall and the Memorial is a granite STATUE OF FRANCIS VIGO, by John Angell; it shows Vigo seated.

4. The OLD FRENCH CEMETERY, extreme W. end of Church St. on Old Cathedral grounds, is a shady area of less than an acre holding

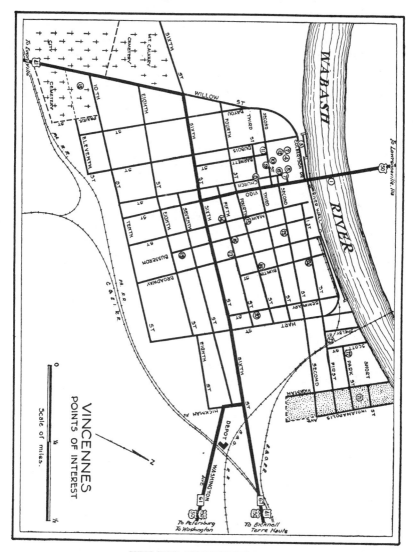

KEY FOR VINCENNES MAP

1. Lincoln Memorial Bridge 2. George Rogers Clark Memorial Building 3. Statue of Francis Vigo 4. Old French Cemetery 5. St. Francis Xavier (Old) Cathedral 6. Old Cathedral Library 7. Statue of Father Pierre Gibault 8. Site of the Home of Madame Godare 9. Chapel 10. Old College of Vincennes 11. Home of Alice of Old Vincennes 12. Marker 13. Old City Cemetery 14. Bonner-Allen Mansion 15. Old Post Museum of History 16. Vincennes University 17. Masonic Temple 18. Niblac Residence 19. Knox County Courthouse 20. St. Rose Academy 21. Old Territorial Legislative Hall 22. William Henry Harrison Mansion 23. Old Treaty Tree 24. Site of the First Newspaper Plant 25. Old Ellis Mansion

unmarked graves of Indians, missionaries, and early French and American settlers. Near the center, surrounded by many of Clark's soldiers, including Captain Joseph Bowman, and men killed at the Battle of Tippecanoe (*see Tour* 18*b*), is the unmarked grave of Father John B. Rivet, first public schoolteacher in the Northwest Territory, who died from overwork and privation in 1804. The first interment was in 1741, the last in 1846.

5. ST. FRANCIS XAVIER (OLD) CATHEDRAL (Roman Catholic) (*open* 9–5 *daily, adm.* 15¢), 2nd and Church Sts., begun 1825, dedicated 1826, gradually enlarged and completed in 1841, is a venerable gray brick structure of Romanesque design standing on or near the site of the historic log chapel erected about the time Vincennes was founded. The See of the Diocese of Vincennes from its establishment in 1834 until 1898, when the Vincennes district was incorporated into the Diocese of Indianapolis, the aged church has lost little of its sturdiness and charm and each year increases in sentimental appeal as it continues to serve the needs of the oldest parish in Indiana.

Above the clock in the belfry of the high stone steeple is the little 'Liberty Bell of the Old Northwest.' According to tradition, this bell (since recast) was brought from France during the 1740's and placed in the original log chapel. It is said to have called the inhabitants of Vincennes to the log church when, on July 20, 1778, Father Gibault administered to them the oath of allegiance to the United States, and it rang out the tidings of liberty at the capture of Fort Sackville.

Above the stone steps extending across the façade are three entrances. Above them in niches stand statues of St. Patrick, St. Francis Xavier, and St. Joan of Arc—that of St. Joan was the first erected to her in the United States after her canonization in 1919.

Graceful beauty and perfection of detail characterize the arched ceiling supported by eight circular columns. The art-glass windows and transoms are notable. Overlooking the wooden pews is a delicately carved canopied pulpit, the handiwork of early Alsatian craftsmen.

In the crypt under the sanctuary lie the remains of four of the five bishops of the old Diocese of Vincennes, as well as those of St. Aufidia, 12-year-old Roman martyr whose remains were brought here by the first of the four bishops, the Most Reverend Simon William Gabriel Bruté de Rémur.

6. The OLD CATHEDRAL LIBRARY (*open* 9–5 *daily, adm.* 15¢), Church St. next to the church, is a small one-story brick structure housing the oldest library collection in Indiana. Carrying out the wishes of Bishop Bruté, the Most Reverend Celestine de la Hailandière, Vincennes' second bishop, completed the building in 1843. In it he placed the parish records dating from June 25, 1749, Father Gibault's missal, and an extensive library brought from France by the learned Bishop Bruté to form the nucleus of the present collection. This includes more than 10,000 items—rare manuscripts, beautiful and historic art specimens, as well as about 5,000 books and periodicals, many printed before 1700 and nearly all before 1800.

Outstanding items include a thirteenth-century book of sermons printed and illuminated by hand on parchment and valued by collectors at $40,000; Bibles and other books bearing fifteenth-century dates; an original manuscript of Claude La Salle, French monk, dated 1705; dictionaries and geographies printed from 1636 to 1665, containing maps and other information so valuable that copies have been made and placed in the Library of Congress; accounts of the voyages of Fathers Hennepin and Charlevoix; early missionary records dated 1660, 1702, and 1707; an original letter written by St. Vincent de Paul; the original copy of the Ordinance of 1787; a Bible used (as her notes and markings show) from 1819 to 1835 by Elizabeth Ann Bayley Seton, foundress of the Sisters of Charity in America; a fine miniature of the illustrious Bishop Rohan of Strasbourg; and a highly prized *Ecce Homo* on ivory by Guido Reni of Bologna (1575–1634), presented to Bishop Bruté by the King of Naples.

7. A bronze STATUE OF FATHER PIERRE GIBAULT, across Church St. from Old Cathedral and facing N., is the work of Albin Polasek.

8. On the SE. corner 3rd and Church Sts. is a marker on the SITE OF THE HOME OF MADAME GODARE, 'Betsy Ross of the Northwest Territory.' Before Clark's arrival, she was authorized by a group of patriots to fashion a flag with which they hoped soon to replace the British colors over Fort Sackville. Charge for the cloth she used— 3¾ ells of green serge and 5 ells of St. Marion's red—was made in Clark's financial account rendered to the State of Virginia. The story is told that Madame Godare's flag was the one raised triumphantly over the fort by the legendary 'Alice of Old Vincennes.'

9. The small red brick CHAPEL, E. side of 2nd St. between Church and Barnett Sts., was used by the students of near-by St. Clare's Convent, a Catholic school for girls founded in 1824 by Sisters of Charity from Nazareth, Kentucky. This school was the predecessor of St. Rose Academy, whose students attended chapel here as late as 1911.

10. A small one-story brick building with a porch across the front, W. side of 2nd St. between Church and Barnett Sts., is said to be one of the buildings of the OLD COLLEGE OF VINCENNES, an institution for the education of young men for the Catholic priesthood founded in 1837 by Bishop Bruté. With the purchase by the bishop of the old 'Seminary Building' at the 'north end of town' in 1839, the college was moved there and given a new name—St. Gabriel's College. It passed into oblivion a few years later.

11. A marker, SE. corner 2nd and Barnett Sts., designates the supposed SITE OF THE HOME OF ALICE OF OLD VINCENNES, heroine of Maurice Thompson's historical novel of the same name. Alice Roussillon, it is said, was the adopted daughter of Gaspard Roussillon, Vincennes' leading citizen when the French surrendered the post to the British in December 1778. Rather than see the French colors taken by General Hamilton, Alice jerked the flag from its staff and hid it. When Clark heard of her exploit he gave her the honor of

raising the flag—emblematic of American supremacy after Hamilton's surrender. Another spot, also marked, extreme W. end (S. side) of DuBois St., is said to have been pointed out by Thompson as the probable site of Alice's home.

12. A MARKER, on Memorial Grounds, midway between corner 2nd and Barnett Sts., and Memorial Building, designates the spot where the housewives of Vincennes fed Clark's soldiers while Clark and Hamilton were conferring, February 24, 1779.

13. The OLD CITY CEMETERY, 10th St. between Prairie and Willow Sts., contains the graves of Francis Vigo and of General Washington Johnson (1776–1833), founder of the first Masonic Lodge in Indiana, first man admitted to the bar west of Ohio, and a prominent opponent of slavery in the Indiana Territory. A large tombstone just off the main drive marks the burial place of five unknown soldiers, members of Clark's force at the capture of Fort Sackville. (Arrows along the main drive indicate all these graves.)

14. The BONNER-ALLEN MANSION (*open 9–6 daily*), 505 Main St., was built in 1842 by David Bonner, a Virginian, and sold in 1845 to Colonel Cyrus M. Allen, Vincennes attorney and friend of Abraham Lincoln. It is a massively built brick structure with an interesting portico and panelled doorways. A bronze plate on a second floor door marks a room where Lincoln once slept. The building is (1941) occupied by a mortuary.

15. The OLD POST MUSEUM OF HISTORY (*open 9–4 weekdays*), 2nd Floor of City Hall, NW. corner 4th and Main Sts., was founded in 1932. Exhibits include loaned collections of pioneer relics, Indian weapons and artifacts, and some early deeds and records.

16. VINCENNES UNIVERSITY (*open*), NW. corner 5th and Busseron Sts., founded December 6, 1806, with William Henry Harrison on its original Board of Trustees, was the second oldest institution of its kind in the old Northwest Territory. After the establishment of the State University at Bloomington in 1820, Vincennes University struggled to maintain itself and occupied several sites until the present three-story brick structure was completed in 1878. It is (1941) a coeducational junior college with about 150 students. Sigma Pi fraternity was founded here in 1897.

17. The two-story yellow brick and stone MASONIC TEMPLE, SE. corner 5th St. and Broadway, houses Vincennes Lodge No. 1, A.F. & A.M., the oldest Masonic Lodge in Indiana and the oldest established lodge of continuous existence in the Old Northwest. It was organized March 13, 1809.

18. The NIBLACK RESIDENCE (*private*), SW. corner 4th and Buntin Sts., former home of Judge William Niblack, once chief justice of the Indiana Supreme Court, is a spacious two-story gray brick structure standing on the site of Knox County's first brick courthouse, erected in 1813. Congress in 1809 provided for the separation of the Illinois and Indiana Territories and named Vincennes as the dividing

line. When the survey was made in 1821, the old courthouse was chosen as the exact point from which a line projected directly north became the boundary between the two States north of the Wabash River boundary.

19. The KNOX COUNTY COURTHOUSE, on an elevation in the middle of the square bounded by 7th, Broadway, 8th, and Busseron Sts., is a commanding five-story building of light-colored Bedford limestone with a luminous clock in its tower. Modified Romanesque in design, its exterior has bas-relief tablets and carvings of historical subjects. The structure, erected 1873-4, is a memorial to Knox County's soldiers and pioneers.

20. ST. ROSE ACADEMY, NW. corner 5th and Seminary Sts., is a three-story yellow brick Catholic high school for girls, an institution that has been under the supervision of the Sisters of Providence ever since it was founded in the old St. Clare's Convent buildings in 1843. It stands almost on the exact SITE OF THE ORIGINAL BUILDING OF VINCENNES UNIVERSITY, erected 1807-19. This was a brick structure in the center of a spacious campus that included all of the four city blocks that surround the present street intersection. Used occasionally for meetings of the Territorial legislature, converted into a hospital for men wounded at the Battle of Tippecanoe (*see Tour* 17), the building was the home of Vincennes University until 1824 when the property was acquired by the Knox County Seminary, an educational venture that failed to prosper. After being put to a variety of uses, it was taken over in 1875 by the St. Rose Academy and was finally razed in 1884 to make way for the city streets. The present St. Rose building was erected immediately afterward. St. Rose's enrollment is usually about 100 students.

21. The OLD TERRITORIAL LEGISLATIVE HALL (*open* 9-6 *daily, adm.* 15¢), in Harrison Park, W. side of Park St., midway between Hickman St. and Indianapolis Ave., built on 'Market' (now Main) St. as a residence about 1800 by Antoine Marschall, Vincennes Frenchman, was soon converted into Indiana's first capitol by William Henry Harrison. All the original Indiana Territory and part of the Louisiana Purchase were once governed from it. After the removal of the Territorial capital to Corydon in 1813, the old capitol again became a residence. In 1858 the structure was moved to N. Third Street. It was rescued in a dilapidated condition in 1919, moved to its present site, and reconditioned and refurnished in conformity with its original state. There is one room on each floor of this two-story frame building. The lower floor with its whitewashed walls and large fireplace contains the governor's desk, equipped with candles and quill pens and surrounded by well-worn hickory chairs; here also is the original desk of General Gibson, Territorial secretary. A narrow outside stairway leads to the upper story, the legislative hall where the first general assembly of the Indiana Territory met July 29, 1805, and where for several years the weighty problems of the time were discussed by early Hoosier law-

makers. Here are their hard benches overhung by crude candle lanterns and the original walnut table used by the governor and judges, upon which were signed the first code of laws for Indiana Territory as well as for the District of Louisiana.

22. The WILLIAM HENRY HARRISON MANSION (*open 8–5 weekdays, 9–5:45 Sun.; adm. 25¢*), NW. corner Park and Scott Sts., was erected in 1803–4 at a cost approximating $20,000. Previous to its completion, Governor Harrison lived in the home of Francis Vigo. Only about 100 yards from the Wabash River and built in the style of an old Virginia plantation mansion, this palatial structure served not only as a home for Harrison, his family and servants, but also as military headquarters and a fortress against Indian attacks. Once surrounded by an extensive grove of walnut trees, it was the hub of activity on Harrison's 300-acre estate, called Grouseland, which fronted the Wabash between present Hart and Hickman Streets. Here was concluded the important Treaty of Grouseland.

The main house, containing 26 rooms, is 60 by 75 feet, two stories high with basement and attic. Practically all the material used in its construction, with the exception of the doors, stairways, and windows, was fashioned by hand of local resources—limestone foundation blocks quarried near Fort Knox (*see Tour* 16), 200,000 bricks made from clay on a near-by farm, and massive wooden joists and studdings, twice as thick as those used today, fastened together with hand-forged nails and thousands of wooden pegs. There are 13 fireplaces, with richly carved mantels. On the left of the first-floor hallway is Harrison's old council chamber and on the right the living room. Furnished throughout in the style of its period, the house contains relics of Harrison's occupancy, such as his desk, chairs, tables, and other household articles, and part of Colonel Francis Vigo's furniture, and his last will and testament.

23. A bronze tablet on the OLD TREATY TREE, NW. corner 1st and Shelby Sts. (behind a filling station), states that this tree is the only survivor of a magnificent grove of walnuts in which Governor Harrison held a momentous council with Tecumseh, August 12–16, 1810.

24. A marker in a vacant lot, NE. corner 1st and Buntin Sts., designates the SITE OF THE FIRST NEWSPAPER PLANT in Indiana, where the *Indiana Gazette* was printed July 4, 1804. Two years later the plant was destroyed by fire; when the publication reappeared it was called the *Western Sun*. Here, in 1830, Abraham Lincoln first saw the process of printing. Later named the *Sun*, this newspaper continues (1941) as the *Sun-Commercial*.

25. The OLD ELLIS MANSION (*private*), 111 N. Second St., erected in 1830 by Judge Abner T. Ellis, is a two-story structure with a gable roof, built entirely of stone quarried by hand near Vincennes. The interior woodwork, including mantels and high wainscoting, is of hand-carved cherry and black walnut. Judge Ellis was a pioneer in efforts

to establish steamboat navigation on the Wabash River, as well as a promoter and first president of the Ohio & Mississippi R.R., now part of the Baltimore & Ohio. He was an intimate friend of Abraham Lincoln and often entertained him here.

POINTS OF INTEREST IN ENVIRONS

Sugar Loaf Mound, 1 *m.* (*see Tour* 10). Site of Fort Knox, 4.7 *m.;* Deshee Farms, 9.2 *m.;* Clark's Ferry, 11 *m.* (*see Tour* 20*b*).

PART III
Tours

Tour 1

(Toledo, Ohio)—Elkhart—South Bend—Gary—(Chicago, Ill.); US 20. Ohio Line to Illinois Line, 155 *m.*

Concrete roadbed, two- to four-lane, throughout.
New York Central R.R. roughly parallels route west of Elkhart; Chicago, South Shore & South Bend R.R. (electric) west of South Bend; and Michigan Central R.R. from Furnessville to Illinois Line.
Accommodations of all kinds at short intervals.

In its eastern section US 20 crosses a gently rolling agricultural country dotted with spring-fed lakes of varied size. Pickerel, bass, pike, and other fish are plentiful and fishing is good. In the middle portion of the route are the flat muck lands of St. Joseph County, the first part of Indiana to be explored by white men. The dune country lies along Lake Michigan, and west of it the highway leads into the Cities of the Calumet—Gary, East Chicago, Whiting, and Hammond.

US 20 crosses the INDIANA LINE, 0 *m.*, 71 miles west of Toledo, Ohio (*see Ohio Guide*).

At 3.7 *m.* is the junction with a graveled road.

Right on this road to a junction with State 120, a blacktop road, 8.2 *m.;* R. here to CLEAR LAKE, 10.3 *m.* (*cottages, hotels, water sports, and other recreational facilities*). In winter cottages, inns, and refreshment stands are boarded up and there are about 30 permanent residents, but with the first warm days of summer Clear Lake blossoms into a vacation colony of more than 1,500 population.

At 5.7 *m.* is the junction with State 1, an oil mat road.

Left on State 1 to HAMILTON LAKE, 6 *m.* (*hotel and cabins; bathing, boating, dancing, good fishing*). On its southern shore is the century-old town of HAMILTON (392 pop.), incorporated in 1914, but founded in 1836 as Enterprise. The site was selected because of water power, and a WATER-DRIVEN MILL is still in operation.

ANGOLA, 10.1 *m.* (1,055 alt., 3,141 pop.), clean and quiet, is the seat of Steuben County, a college town and a vacation center. Within easy walking distance are a number of lake resorts in the midst of wooded hills.

At the northwestern edge of Angola are the three brick buildings and wooded campus of TRI-STATE COLLEGE, which offers courses in engineering, commerce, and music. The college does not require high-school graduation for entrance, awards bachelor's degrees at the end of a two-year course, and depends primarily upon student fees for income. The average enrollment is about 1,400.

287

Angola is at the junction with US 27 (*see Tour* 13).

Steuben County's frontier stories are almost as well known as its lakes. Early tales of the prowess of Abraham Walters, Jr., son of a pioneer family living near Fremont, grew to epic proportions through the years. Stories of 'Old Goldin,' an enormous buck that roamed Steuben County, were also legion. This deer was occasionally seen, but was so elusive that it was impossible to get a good shot at him. One evening when young Walters was hunting near Lake Withington, he glimpsed a huge pair of antlers through the tall reeds only a short distance away. Slowly the antlers lifted, and Old Goldin rose to his feet. Walters's hastily-aimed shot struck the deer's horn close to his head and knocked him down. Knife in hand, Walters ran forward, seized the deer's horns, and attempted to cut his throat. All night the two struggled, in and out of the water, from shore to shore, first one and then the other on the offensive. When the sun rose, Old Goldin lay dead.

At 11.6 *m.* is the junction with a blacktop road.

Right on this road to a junction with another blacktop road, 2.8 *m.;* L. here to CROOKED LAKE, 3.1 *m.* (*cabins and boats*), six miles long and one and a half miles wide. Fishing, particularly for bass and bluegill, is good.

SILVER LAKE (*cabins*), 13.6 *m.*, is a fishing resort (L). The mile-long OTTER LAKE (*good accommodations and fishing*), 19.2 *m.* (L), is noted for large-mouthed bass.

LaGRANGE, 32.3 *m.* (913 alt., 1,814 pop.), is a dairying center with wide, tree-lined streets. Seat of LaGrange County since 1844, the town was named by its French founders in 1836 for the Marquis de LaFayette's country residence near Paris. The site was purchased from the Government in 1835 and platted in the following year; the town was incorporated in 1855.

LaGrange is at the junction with State 9 (*see Tour* 14).

West of LaGrange the route passes through a level and prosperous farming country that a century ago was swampland—a region of fever and ague, and the haunt of stock-destroying wolves. An epidemic of ague swept away the settlers in 1838 and this country lay desolate for several years. It was later cleared, drained, and became excellent farm land.

At 41.7 *m.* is the junction with State 5, a blacktop road.

Right on this road is SHIPSHEWANA, 1.2 *m.* (903 alt., 286 pop.), a busy little trading center for Amish farmers of the neighborhood (*see Tour* 15). The closed buggies of members of this religious sect may be seen in the town and along the near-by roads.

Left from Shipshewana on a blacktop road to a junction with a graveled road 2.2 *m.;* R. here to SHIPSHEWANA LAKE (*cottages and boats*), 2.5 *m.*, a crescent-shaped, 176-acre lake, excellent for bass, bluegill, and perch fishing. Near a camp maintained by the United Brethren Church is a 12-foot stone marker, a MEMORIAL TO CHIEF SHIPSHEWANA. The Potawatomi leader, who is buried beneath the monument, was taken away from his beloved lake in 1838 and sent to Kansas under military escort, but three years later was permitted to return to its shores to die.

At 48.2 *m.* on US 20 is the junction with State 13, a paved road.

Right on this road is MIDDLEBURY, 1 *m.* (852 alt., 722 pop.), a farming village with a WATER-POWER MILL. Old-style burrs, operated by an undershot wheel, are still used for grinding feed. At the northern end of the village are the KRIDER NURSERIES, one of the largest in the Midwest, with 12 gardens modeled after typical gardens of different nations. The *Lilideum*, an Aztec sacred lily, has been developed here in five colors.

The range of hills (R) between the junction with State 13 and Elkhart is of glacial origin. From atop several of them the little town of White Pigeon, Michigan, 12 miles north, can be seen on clear days.

ELKHART, 63.1 *m.* (753 alt., 33,434 pop.), a city of diversified manufacturing, lies at the confluence of the St. Joseph and Elkhart Rivers. These rivers, with Christiana Creek, divide Elkhart into several sections, and it is almost impossible to go far in any direction without crossing at least one of the city's ten bridges. At the confluence of the Elkhart and St. Joseph Rivers is a small island in whose shape the imaginative Indian saw an elk's heart and so named the island. This name was recorded by Isaac McCoy, a Baptist missionary, in 1822, and was gradually adopted by the white settlers. The site was long popular with the Indians and lay at the junction of several of their trails.

Dr. Havilah Beardsley, who had bought a section of an Indian reservation from Pierre Moran (Pierish), a Potawatomi chief, platted the town of Elkhart in 1832. Settlement started immediately, and by 1835 there was a village of 50-odd dwellings and 200 to 300 inhabitants. Through the influence of Dr. Beardsley the Michigan Southern Railway Company built its shops here in 1850, and from that time on, Elkhart's growth was inseparably linked with the development of the railroad and the evolution of the New York Central system. After 1850 Elkhart grew rapidly and 27 years later was incorporated as a city. The water power attracted industries and after the construction of a hydraulic system in 1867–8, several small factories sprang up. In 1875, Charles G. Conn, who had been making cornet mouthpieces in his home, rented a one-room building and started the manufacture of plain brass cornets. From this beginning sprang the largest band-instrument factory in the world. Nine years later Dr. Franklin Miles established the Dr. Miles Medical Company, manufacturing proprietary medicines. These and other manufactories have given to Elkhart its essentially industrial character.

Elkhart is predominantly a city of small homes grouped around industrial plants, a practical and sober arrangement that has been relieved to some extent by nine public parks and four recently developed residential sections—St. Joseph Manor, East Jefferson Boulevard, Greenleaf Boulevard, and Riverside Drive. The shopping district extends three-quarters of a mile along Main Street, and includes a few modern office buildings on 2nd Street, just off Main. The foreign-born population, most of them Italian railroad workers, live in the southwestern part, between the 'Hump,' or railroad shop district, and the center of Elkhart.

Elkhart's distinction as a manufacturing city arises from the quality and variety of its products. Twenty-seven types of industry are represented by its 74 factories, which employed 5,550 persons in 1937, according to the U. S. Census of Manufactures for that year. Ten musical instrument factories produce 70 per cent of the wind and percussion instruments made in the United States.

The C. G. Conn Band Instrument Company Plant (*open* 9–5 *weekdays; guides*), 1000 E. Beardsley Ave., employs more than 900 craftsmen and produces 5,000 musical instruments a month. When Captain Charles Gerard Conn returned to Elkhart after the Civil War, he conducted a small grocery and bakery and was the cornetist in the local band. Shortly thereafter he suffered a badly bruised upper lip in a fight with a neighborhood bully, and to retain his job as cornetist, he contrived a soft rubber mouthpiece that enabled him to play. Conn was soon besieged with requests for these mouthpieces and started to fill orders as a sideline, using a lathe devised from an old sewing machine. The business increased and in 1875 he organized the Conn & Dupont Company, and started the manufacture of brass cornets. This was the first wind instrument factory in the United States. The company now manufactures all types of wind and percussion instruments and is said to maintain the only band instrument research laboratory in the world.

The Miles Laboratories (*open* 9–5 *weekdays*), 117 Franklin St., is the outgrowth of a small medicine business formed to market the popular prescriptions of Dr. Miles, who had been a practicing physician and was active in the management of the company in its early years. For more than half a century the company has enjoyed a steady growth. The three-story main building is a modern structure of brick, granite, steel, and concrete. The company employs about 550 skilled workers and a large office and sales force.

The Ambrose Bierce House, 518 W. Franklin St., has been reconstructed as a modern two-story frame residence. In the original house, Ambrose Bierce, noted journalist and author of short stories, spent his boyhood and part of his young manhood, and hated Elkhart with as much fervor as he hated other things in later life. The man whose pen was to earn for him the name of 'Bitter Bierce' worked as a youth as an off-bearer of brick in Steeple's brickyard and later as a waiter in Faber's restaurant, both in Elkhart. Bierce's birthday is not known, but he was old enough in 1861 to enlist in the Union army. When he returned to Elkhart on furlough with a slight scalp wound, he was admonished by a friend to be more careful, but he replied characteristically, 'The damn Rebels can't shoot.' His experience when General Buell's forces rushed to the aid of the Union army at Shiloh is lucidly described in 'What I Saw of Shiloh,' one of his best pieces on the war. When he was mustered out he accepted a post in the Treasury Department and was stationed in Alabama. He then joined General Hazen's surveying expedition into Indian Territory. In 1867 he was in San Francisco, and with the exception of brief visits to England, where he married Mary Ellen Day, daughter of a wealthy Englishman, his life and his writing centered in the West. Bierce suddenly disappeared into Mexico in 1913 and no trace of him was ever found.

In Elkhart is the junction with US 33 (*see Tour* 15).

West of Elkhart there are several good views (L) of the wide St. Joseph River, flowing slowly beyond the trees which line US 20.

SOUTH BEND, 78 *m.* (733 alt., 101,268 pop.) (*see South Bend*).

In South Bend is the junction with US 31 (*see Tour* 16).

Left from South Bend on paved State 23 to a junction with State 123 (Mayflower Road), a paved highway, 5 *m.* Near by is a little pond, all that is left of FATHER HENNEPIN PONDS, a chain of small lakes that once were the source of the Kankakee River. In these ponds, at the eastern end of the great Kankakee Marsh, the canoes of the early French explorers, traders, and missionaries were launched after being carried over the Portage (*see South Bend*) from the St. Joseph River. The ponds were named for Father Louis Hennepin, Jesuit priest who accompanied La Salle in his explorations of the region. The boggy prairie land is now (1941) being drained and transformed into farms.

That part of the St. Joseph Valley that lies in St. Joseph County and in southern Michigan was the locale of many of the writings of Simon Pokagon, last chief of the Potawatomi in Indiana (*see Tour* 13), who was born in 1830 in a village not far from the Old Sauk Trail about six miles northwest of South Bend. His work shows an unusual personality and a rare feeling for nature combined with an appreciation of Indian history, poetry, and romance. The semi-autobiographical *O-gi-maw-kwe Mit-i-gwa-ki* (Queen of the Woods) is a beautifully written forest romance.

The BENDIX MUNICIPAL AIRPORT (*visitors welcome*), 81.7 *m.*, is a 500-acre landing field (R) with five hangars, an administration building, and a café. Owned by the Bendix Corporation, of South Bend, the port is strategically located between Detroit and Chicago. It is rated by the Department of Commerce as one of the most efficiently operated in the State. Five private air schools use the port and it also is used as an army base.

TERRA COUPEE, 87 *m.* (747 alt., 25 pop.), in the heart of an extensive prairie of the same name, was founded in 1837. In its early days the village was a prosperous and important trading post on the principal stage line between Detroit and Chicago. The importance of Terra Coupee declined after the building of the Lake Shore Railroad through New Carlisle, and it is now merely a trading point for the farmers of the immediate vicinity. Wheat and corn are the principal crops of the area.

NEW CARLISLE, 91.6 *m.* (778 alt., 747 pop.), situated on a plateau that overlooks the Terra Coupee prairie, is the only town between South Bend and La Porte. It is a prosperous-appearing trading community for the surrounding rich farm lands. The town was founded in 1835 by Richard R. Carlisle, a traveler and adventurer, who purchased the land from the half-breed heirs of the French trapper, Laza-rus Bourissau.

Among the early settlers of the locality were two shrewd, hard-working young men named Wash and Elias Baldwin. During the gold rush of '49, both boys sold out and left for California. Elias was a bold trader and gambler who took unheard-of chances and made them pay unheard-of profits. He became known the country over as the famous 'Lucky' Baldwin.

Left from the eastern edge of New Carlisle, on Timothy Road (improved), 2.6 m. to the junction with State 2, a concrete road; L. here to the STUDE-BAKER PROVING GROUNDS, 3.6 m. (*visitors must obtain permits at Studebaker plant in South Bend*). The 800-acre outdoor testing laboratories (R) include fast tracks with curves to test the responsiveness of cars at high speed, rough tracks to determine durability, and many similar facilities for measuring per-formance. On the grounds are machine shops and garages for checking motors and for repairs and adjustments.

ROLLING PRAIRIE, 98.5 *m.* (815 alt., 450 pop.), is a village built on a site selected by Ezekial Provolt in 1831, and platted in 1853. A large oak that shaded the cabin that Provolt built in 1834 still shades the frame house he erected in 1845.

At 108.5 *m.* is the junction with US 35 (*see Tour* 17), which unites with US 20 for one mile.

The junction, 109.5 *m.*, with the Michigan City business route of US 20 (straight ahead) is a cloverleaf crossing, where a four-lane con-crete highway sweeps above US 20 on an overpass.

West of the cloverleaf crossing, US 20, which by-passes Michigan City, is a broad, busy highway with gradual curves, the main traffic artery between Chicago and lake resorts in Michigan. At 114.6 *m.* is the eastern end of a mile-and-a-half stretch of lighted highway. Se-lected by the safety division of the State Highway Department be-cause of heavy traffic conditions, accident frequency, and fog, this stretch serves as a demonstration place for highway lighting. Spaced at 24-foot intervals, sodium vapor lights of 10,000 lumen intensity make it possible for a driver to see a pedestrian or a vehicle at a dis-tance of 2,000 feet.

At 116.3 *m.* is Pines Cut-Off (R), a hard-surfaced road two-tenths of a mile long connecting US 20 with US 12 (*see Tour* 2).

US 20 curves along the southern edge of the crescent-shaped In-diana sand dunes area (*see Tour* 2), which extends from Michigan City to Gary. Southward (L) the land is gently rolling, with fields of corn, hay, and grain.

FURNESSVILLE, 119.8 *m.* (642 alt., 150 pop.), grew up around the OLD FURNESS HOUSE. The two-and-a-half-story red brick dwell-ing, built in 1856 by Edwin L. Furness, is on an elevated site (R). Glass-enclosed porches have been added to the original structure. Fur-ness, a New Englander, acquired a large tract of land in the vicinity and engaged in farming and lumbering. He was the first postmaster of the village. The house is now (1941) occupied by the third and fourth generations of the Furness family.

PORTER, 123.7 *m.* (641 alt., 1,190 pop.), lies on both sides of the highway, extending from south of US 20 to Lake Michigan, nearly three miles north. Many of Porter's residents are employed in the town's brickyards, on the railroad, or in the steel mills of Gary.

Set back from the highway (L) under wide-spreading, century-old oaks is the CARLSON PLANETARIUM (*open Thurs., adm.* 25¢), 124.5 *m.*, a 16-sided structure of rustic design in which the solar system is depicted. There are five observation and lecture platforms, a reception parlor, a number of exhibition rooms, and a collection of newspaper clippings of astronomical and archeological interest. The planetarium is owned and operated by Edward Carlson.

Between 136.5 *m.* and 138.8 *m.* US 20 and US 12 (*see Tour* 2) are identical. At their western junction US 20 forks L. on 5th Avenue, Gary, and for 10.7 miles follows a route through GARY (*see Gary*) and HAMMOND (*see Hammond*) a few blocks to the south of US 12 (*see Tour* 2). The two routes are reunited at 149.5 *m.*, in EAST CHICAGO (*see East Chicago*), and follow Indianapolis Boulevard through WHITING (*see Whiting*) to the ILLINOIS LINE, 155 *m.*, at the eastern limits of Chicago (*see Illinois Guide*).

↑↑

Tour 2

(New Buffalo, Mich.)—Michigan City—Gary—Hammond—(Chicago, Ill.); US 12.
Michigan Line to Illinois Line, 45.5 *m.*

Concrete roadbed, two- to four-lane, throughout.
Route paralleled by Michigan Central R.R. between Michigan Line and Illinois Line; by Pennsylvania R.R., Baltimore & Ohio R.R., New York Central R.R., and Chicago, Indiana & Southern R.R. between Gary and Illinois Line; and by Chicago, South Shore & South Bend R.R. (electric) between Michigan City and East Chicago.
Accommodations of all kinds at short intervals.

This route, called the Dunes Highway, swings around the southern tip of Lake Michigan, never more than two miles from the lake. Its eastern section traverses the beautiful dunes region, one of Indiana's most popular recreational areas, and the western section runs through the highly industrialized Cities of the Calumet—Gary, East Chicago, Whiting, and Hammond.

US 12 crosses the INDIANA LINE, 0 *m.*, four miles southwest of New Buffalo, Michigan, and skirts the lake shore residential and resort developments of MICHIANA SHORES and LONG BEACH.

At 4.5 *m.* is the junction with Liberty Trail, a blacktop road that forms the eastern boundary of Michigan City.

Left on Liberty Trail is POTAWATOMI PARK, 0.5 *m.* (615 alt., 29 pop.), a fashionable residential village, without business establishments, set in a beautifully wooded section that was once the site of a Potawatomi Indian village. Father Marquette visited this region. In 1675 he is said to have preached to the Indians at MARQUETTE SPRING (R), alongside the two-mile circuitous park driveway, though this is doubtful as he was in ill health at the time. Here in 1831 Blackhawk, the Sauk chief, is said to have tried unsuccessfully to enlist Potawatomi aid in a projected Indian revolt.

Visible from Marquette Spring are the INTERNATIONAL FRIENDSHIP GARDENS, which, when completed, will include flowers of all Nations. The project, inaugurated in 1934, has received flowers and plants for resetting from 300 well-known persons, including King Boris III of Bulgaria, Neville Chamberlain, King Gustav V of Sweden, Adolf Hitler, Benito Mussolini, and Ignace Jan Paderewski. Created and supervised by J. E., J. V., and C. L. Stauffer, the gardens are being developed as a public museum of flora.

TRAIL CREEK, which runs through Potawatomi Park, figured briefly in an incident that occurred in the fur trade days. In 1780 a small party of French-Canadians, Indians, and one American left Cohokia under the leadership of a half-breed, Jean Baptiste Hamelin, intending to pillage Fort St. Joseph of its rich store of furs. The expedition was timed to arrive at the fort, near the present site of Niles, Michigan, when the Indian garrison would be away on a hunt. Hamelin and his men sacked and burned the post, and escaped with 50 bales of valuable furs. When the commandant learned what had happened he sent the Indians in pursuit and both parties crossed Trail Creek, probably near Marquette Spring. The report of Major Arent DePeyster, British commandant at Detroit, states that the fugitives were overtaken at Petite Fort, near the present site of Tremont, Indiana, on December 5, 1780. Four were killed, two wounded, seven taken prisoners, and three escaped into the wilderness. The furs were recovered and Major DePeyster treated the captives as prisoners of war.

MICHIGAN CITY, 6 *m.* (621 alt., 26,476 pop.), on Lake Michigan at the mouth of Trail Creek, was founded in 1832 as the northern terminus of the old Michigan Road. The city is best known as a summer playground, although in the early 1840's it was a greater lake port than Chicago, and is still an industrial city of consequence. Its bathing beach, boating facilities, dunes, and lake front make it a popular resort; the population increases by 5,000 to 7,000 each summer.

A three-day Dunes Water Sports Carnival, held early in August, is ruled over by Miss Indiana, who is selected in competition as the most beautiful girl in the State. Festivities are opened by a street parade, with 35 to 50 bands and drum corps and more than 100 gaily festooned floats. Contests include yacht, outboard-motor, scooter, bicycle, and foot races. There are daily band concerts and fireworks displays. A Venetian Water Parade of beautifully decorated yachts and boats is held on the second night, and a visit by the governor and another grand parade feature the final day.

WASHINGTON PARK (*dancing, tennis, baseball*), at the northern end of Franklin Street fronting Lake Michigan, is the city's recreational center. Its public bathing beach covers a wide expanse of the 'singing sands,' which respond to high winds or footsteps with an ·eerie rustle. Within the park is a Zoo (*free*) in which 50 monkeys stage a continuous trapeze performance. A large collection of rare fowl and birds of prey is also housed here. Near the zoo is a 200-foot brown sandstone OBSERVATION TOWER (*free*), commanding a magnificent view of the lake and the duneland region. At the entrance to the park is the WASHINGTON MEMORIAL BRIDGE over Trail Creek, named *Rivière du Chemin* (river of the trail) by the French because of the old Indian path along its bank.

At the western end of the park is the MICHIGAN CITY HARBOR, around which the city's first dwellings were built, and the U. S. COAST GUARD STATION. In the harbor are stationed the warships U.S.S. *Sacramento* and U.S.S. *Wabash,* the only Navy vessels in Indiana waters. The Michigan City lumber business attained its peak in 1884, when 160,000,000 feet of lumber were received and distributed. Eight lumber yards stood along the harbor, and it was not unusual for 15 lake boats to be unloading at the same time.

On the lake front in 1837 Daniel Webster made the Fourth of July speech in which he briefly discussed the National debt. Wined and dined to repletion by the people of Michigan City, he mounted the platform none too steadily, it is said. Holding to a chair, he began, 'The national debt—' He paused to marshal his thoughts, began again, 'The national debt—' Then, putting a hand in his trouser pocket, he demanded, 'How much is the damned thing?'

Behind the harbor is the OLD MICHIGAN CITY LIGHTHOUSE, built in 1856, now the residence of the keeper of the NEW LIGHTHOUSE at the end of the long eastern pier. The fixed white light of the new lighthouse is visible for 13 miles.

The harbor is still the nucleus of Michigan City's industrial life. Between 300 and 400 tons of fish, worth about $150,000, are taken from the lake each year by eight Michigan City fishing companies. There are 10 trucking firms with lake shipping connections that give employment to 400 persons. Products of the city's other industries include bicycles, metal furniture, clothing, gloves, hats, and cough drops.

Robert Wadsworth Grafton, who painted portraits of President Coolidge and President Hoover, is a Michigan City resident. Murals by Grafton are in the study room of the ISAAC C. ELSTON SENIOR HIGH SCHOOL, Michigan City; the First National Bank and Anthony Hotel at Fort Wayne; the gallery of the Richmond Art Association (*see Tour 8a*); the LaFayette Art Museum (*see Tour 18b*); and the lobby of the Rumely Hotel, La Porte.

Along the highway (R) at the western edge of Michigan City is the INDIANA STATE PRISON (*visiting restricted; apply at office*), for male convicts 30 years of age and over. About 2,400 men are confined here, including life prisoners and prisoners awaiting electrocution. Great gray walls, with constantly patrolled catwalks, surround the 23-acre prison area. The prison is largely self-supporting, operating its own heat, light and power, cold storage and ice plants, its own canning and coffee-roasting factories, and clothing, tobacco, and print shops. Of the 80 acres outside the walls, 12 are used for parks, lawns, and homes of prison officials, the remainder for gardens and vineyards.

A major prison break occurred at the institution on September 26, 1933, when 10 convicts serving long terms escaped. They made their way to Lima, Ohio, where they entered the county jail, killed the sheriff, and liberated John Dillinger, subsequently classified as Public Enemy No. 1. Dillinger was later recaptured in Tucson, Arizona, and brought to the Lake County jail in Crown Point, Indiana, from which he escaped with the aid of a wooden gun (*see Tour* 5). He was finally killed by Federal agents in Chicago.

At 9.7 *m.* is the Pines Cut-Off (L), a hard-surfaced road, 2 miles long, connecting US 12 with US 20.

BEVERLY SHORES, 11.6 *m.* (578 alt., 300 to 1,000 pop., depending on season), is a fashionable residential village on Lake Michigan. Many of its houses, which range from rustic log cabins to large country mansions, are from the Century of Progress Exposition in Chicago (1934–5). Several are from the Colonial Village. They are furnished in the styles of their respective periods and closely resemble the originals. After the Fair these buildings were dismantled and shipped by boat to this point, where they were reassembled.

Between US 12 and the lake is Broadway, the main thoroughfare of the village. Right on this street, in the rear of the Beverly Shores Hotel (L), are the BOTANICAL GARDENS (*free*), used exclusively for experimentation with ornamental plants under dune and bog conditions. White lizard tail, the only representative of tropical flora in this latitude, and gleaming white bog callas from the far North grow within a few yards of each other; hardy cacti, delicate orchids, trailing arbutus, and wild iris are among the many species exhibited. The gardens, which have more than 75 varieties of plants, were planned for the promoters of Beverly Shores by Mrs. Louis Van Hees Young, Chicago art collector and designer.

Along Broadway in the following order are buildings from the Century of Progress Colonial Village:

VIRGINIA TAVERN (R), a restaurant, said to be a reproduction of the tavern in Georgetown which was patronized by George Washington. It is a two-story, white frame structure with a wide curved veranda supported by tall wooden pillars. In the roof are 22 dormer windows.

WAKEFIELD HOUSE (*private*), a reproduction (R) of Washington's supposed birthplace in Virginia, is Georgian Colonial in style, with five dormer windows. HOUSE OF SEVEN GABLES (*private*) is an approximate duplicate (R) of the Salem, Massachusetts, house that was the scene of Nathaniel Hawthorne's novel. WAYSIDE INN (*private*) is a reproduction (R) of the Sudbury, Massachusetts, tavern that inspired Henry Wadsworth Longfellow to write *Tales of a Wayside Inn.*

Just east of the Wayside Inn is the gabled VILLAGE SMITHY (*pri-

vate garage), built to resemble the blacksmith shop formerly in Cambridge, Massachusetts, the scene of Longfellow's poem, 'The Village Blacksmith.' GOVERNOR'S MANSION (*private*), a two-story brick structure (L) painted white, duplicates on a smaller scale the home of John Winthrop (1588–1649), first governor of the Massachusetts Bay Colony. BENJAMIN FRANKLIN HOUSE (*private*), a two-story frame house (R), is a counterpart of Franklin's home in Boston. PAUL REVERE HOUSE (*private*) is an exact reproduction (R) of Paul Revere's house in Boston. It has an overhanging second story with ornamental drops, and small window casements with diamond-shaped glass panes. Large beams support the rafters on the second floor. The OLD NORTH CHURCH (L) is a reproduction of the church from whose belfry Paul Revere received the signal for his historic ride. This building is used regularly for religious services. It is brick veneered, has a wide veranda with six two-story pillars, and windows with small panes. MOUNT VERNON (*private*) is an approximate reproduction (L) of George Washington's home.

At 16 *m.*, is the junction with State 49, a paved road.

Right on State 49 to the INDIANA DUNES STATE PARK, 0.9 *m.* (*adm.* 10¢; *hotel, tourist camp, cottages, picnicking and camping facilities*), an area of three-and-a-half square miles on the southern tip of Lake Michigan in the dunes region. A high ridge of sand along the shore has been anchored and held together by growths of vegetation; yet here and there the wind has torn away the vegetation and cut great gaps into the rampart of sand. Behind the ridge are dunes of all sizes and shapes, verdant valleys, and low, flat marshlands. Blanketing much of the country are many varieties of flowers, shrubs, plants, and trees.

Near the lake front the park road widens into a paved parking space, accommodating more than 800 cars. Fronting the lake at the end of the parking space is the DUNES ARCADE PAVILION, a Moorish-style limestone structure housing the grill and bathhouse. Access to the flat roof and promenade is by stairways at each end of the long building. West of the pavilion is the DUNES ARCADE HOTEL, faced with stucco, painted green, and faintly Chinese in appearance. The cottages lining the beach vary in size; the GOVERNOR'S HOUSE is the most impressive. This summer house of the State's chief executive is located on a bluff near Mount Tom, the highest of the dunes, and is a semirustic structure built of drop siding. Similar in appearance is the PRAIRIE CLUBHOUSE, the dunes home of a group of Chicago scientists and nature lovers. The GROUP CAMP, on the site of a Potawatomi Indian village, is composed of eight tepee-shaped bunkhouses, built of upright slabs of wood covered with bark. There are, in addition, a large mess hall and kitchen, a director's cabin, and a bathhouse. The sandhills, marshes, and forests of the park are traversed by nine marked foot trails that converge at the terminus of the Tremont Road.

The formation of dunes is a curious process. Sand swept upon the shore by the waters of Lake Michigan is carried inland by the prevailing north and northwest winds. Then a struggle begins between the invading and shifting sand and the hardy vegetation that may spring up and threaten to block its way. Grasses, vines, shrubs, and small cottonwood trees sink long surface and lateral roots and provide a nucleus around which small cones of sand are formed. In time the cone is increased in size by the wind-driven sand, and slowly a dune is formed. Mount Tom, the loftiest of the dunes, is 190 feet high and covers an area of more than 100 acres.

There are 'dead' or stationary dunes and 'live' or traveling ones. The 'dead' dune is covered with small trees, grasses, shrubs, and perhaps flowers; the 'live' dune is bare, the picture of desolation. The 'life' of a dune depends upon its vegetation. Unless the sand composing the dunes is anchored by vegetation, the dunes shift—small forests are buried and, years later, uncovered as the dunes advance.

A dune sometimes becomes an amphitheater of sand and is then called a 'blowout.' Sparse vegetation is cut away by high winds, and whirling sands retreat until a bowl-shaped excavation is formed. The leeward side of the dune, now a fan-shaped heap of sand, may then become a traveling dune. Some traveling dunes are called 'complex,' when portions of them travel in different directions. The principal course of the dunes as a whole is south or southeast.

Soil conditions and abundant moisture make it possible for a large number of rare and beautiful flowers and plants to grow in this otherwise desert-like area. Plant growth is almost tropical in its luxuriance. Shrubs and plants ordinarily found far to the north and south of this region grow side by side.

The trailing arbutus is the first to bloom, sometimes appearing at the edge of a snowdrift. Hepatica blooms amidst dead leaves. Acres of marsh-marigold, patches of yellow and white dogtooth violets, anemones, cranesbill, wintergreen, and partridge berry spring up. The first of the orchids, the yellow lady's slipper, begin to bloom early in June; a month later the large white or snowy lady's slipper, a beautiful wild orchid, appears in swamps. Also blooming in early June are many varieties of roses, including the Captain Robinson, which grows only in the Indiana dunes; the yellow meadow or Canada Lily; and the bright green Turk's cap, the most beautiful of the dune lilies. The flat-leaf cactus, asters of many kinds, water-blooming plants, and goldenrod are not uncommon. Among the flowering shrubs and trees found here are the spicebush, service berry, wild cherries, crab apples, and tulip trees. In the shallow waters of the creeks are hibiscus, and the white blooms of the sand cherries dot the beach. In all, more than 300 varieties of plants, shrubs, and flowers grow in this natural botanical garden.

During migratory seasons a great variety of land and shore birds visit the dunes. Climatic conditions are favorable, and edible fruits and berries provide ample food. The golden eagle, horned owl, and blue heron are indigenous, as well as the common varieties of game birds. Grosbeak, crossbills, and pine finches come in the winter searching for food.

At 18.4 *m.* on the main route is the junction with a graveled road.

Left on this road and R. at the first turn to the HOME OF JOSEPH BAILLY, 2 *m.* Built in 1822, this house (L) and the three neighboring log cabins are all that is left of BAILLYTOWN, a projected municipality that Bailly's death in 1835 left without a promoter. Except for new weatherboarding on the house and new roofs on the cabins, the structures are just as Bailly built them. The house is of logs, with hand-wrought hardware and floors of walnut and oak.

Bailly, in his early years, was a fur trader on Mackinac Island, where, having married the daughter of a native chief, he was in special favor with the Indians. In 1812 he was imprisoned by the Government as a British spy. On his release after the war he divorced his first wife, married a French-Ottawa woman, and in 1822 established his new trading post here, blazing the trail for the settlement of northwestern Indiana. In addition to the cabins he built for his helpers, he erected a log warehouse and a chapel, conducting in the latter religious services for his family and neighboring Indians.

Near the Bailly home is the MARRIAGE TREE, an oak and an elm planted so close together that the trunks, limbs, and roots of the two trees have become interwoven into what appears to be one tree bearing both elm and oak leaves. In accordance with the pioneer custom, Bailly's daughter and her husband planted these trees on their wedding day (1840), believing that if the trees thrived, their marriage would endure.

At 22.8 *m.* on US 12 is the junction with a paved road.

Right on this road is OGDEN DUNES, 0.7 *m.* (578 alt., 144 pop.), a residential suburb of Gary and other cities of the Calumet. The village covers 432 acres of dune country along Lake Michigan. Boating, bathing, fishing, golfing, and skiing are popular.

It was here, before the village was founded, that the nationally publicized 'Diana of the Dunes,' female hermit, lived in an abandoned fisherman's hut made of driftwood. She was discovered in 1916 when fishermen observed the nude young woman taking a daily plunge in Lake Michigan, but she refused to see newspaper reporters and avoided would-be visitors. The thwarted periodicals dubbed her 'Diana of the Dunes' and carried many stories of her mysterious behavior. According to various reports she was the beautiful daughter of a Chicago physician; she made wine from the wild berries of the dune hillsides, selling it for the little money required for her limited needs; she lived alone to study nature, and knew and loved every plant and animal of the region, every mood and color of the lake and dunes. It was hinted that there had been a disappointment in love. Continued publicity brought her many offers of marriage and in 1922 she married a Texan. While preparing to leave for her new home, she suddenly became ill and died.

Between 28 *m.* and 30.3 *m.* US 20 (*see Tour 1*) and US 12 unite. At the western junction, within the limits of Gary, US 20 forks L.; US 12 continues ahead on 4th Avenue.

GARY, 31 *m.* (613 alt., 111,719 pop.) (*see Gary*).

EAST CHICAGO, 40 *m.* (610 alt., 54,637 pop.) (*see East Chicago*).

Between East Chicago and the Illinois Line US 12 and US 20 (*see Tour 1*) unite.

WHITING, 43 *m.* (595 alt., 10,307 pop.) (*see Whiting*).

HAMMOND, 44.5 *m.* (598 alt., 70,184 pop.) (*see Hammond*), is at the junction with US 41 (*see Tour 20*), which unites with US 12–20 on Indianapolis Boulevard to the Illinois Line, 45.5 *m.*, at the eastern limits of Chicago (*see Illinois Guide*).

ⵜⵜ

Tour 3

(Bryan, Ohio)—Waterloo—Nappanee—Gary—(Calumet City, Ill.); US 6.

Ohio Line to Illinois Line, 154.6 *m.*

Two-lane concrete roadbed to Gary; four-lane to Munster; two- and four-lane in Hammond.

Route paralleled by New York Central R.R. between Ohio Line and Wawaka; by Baltimore & Ohio R.R. between Nappanee and Gary; and by Michigan Central R.R. and Chicago, Indianapolis and Louisville R.R. between Gary and the Illinois Line.

Accommodations of all kinds at frequent intervals.

This route, a section of the direct route between New York City and Chicago, follows a beeline through Indiana, avoids cities and rail crossings, and permits speedy movement of transcontinental traffic. The highway passes through a number of small rural communities that are curious combinations of industrial towns and crossroad hamlets. Agriculturally, the region is noteworthy for its truck gardening and contains one of the two principal mint-growing sections of the United States (the other is in Washington). Dairying and poultry and sheep raising are also important. At the western end of the route is the Calumet steel district.

US 6 crosses the OHIO LINE, 0 *m.*, 16 miles west of Bryan, Ohio (*see Ohio Guide*).

BUTLER, 3.6 *m.* (838 alt., 1,794 pop.), is a small industrial town and rural trading center. Its cramped and crowded business district contrasts sharply with its residential area, which contains wide, tree-shaded streets and dignified old homes with spacious lawns. The towns-people are railroaders, retired farmers, and factory workers employed in small industries that produce leather jackets and helmets, house slippers, windmills, tanks, pumps, and condensed milk.

WATERLOO, 11.6 *m.* (900 alt., 1,257 pop.), at the intersection of two widely traveled highways, caters to tourists and consequently is a strange admixture of new gasoline stations, modern lunchrooms, and old-fashioned brick buildings. Although it is not an industrial town, Waterloo has a small broom factory, a bentwood factory, and a sawmill.

In Waterloo is the junction with US 27 (*see Tour* 13).

KENDALLVILLE, 24.9 *m.* (975 alt., 5,431 pop.), in the northeast corner of Noble County, is the shipping center of the onion-growing area. Noble County leads the State in onion production. David Bundle first settled on the site of Kendallville in 1833 and, noticing that many travelers passed his log hut, turned it into a tavern. This tavern prospered and was sold to Mrs. Francis Dingman, who improved it with a frame facing. Around it grew a tiny wilderness community that developed slowly until 1857, when the building of the New York Central Railroad through the county hastened its growth. The frame house, still enclosing the original studding and beams of the old BUNDLE TAVERN, stands at 118 Gold Street.

The bulk of the town's industry is concentrated in two factories: the McCRAY REFRIGERATOR PLANT, one of the largest of its kind in the United States, and the FLINT & WALLING MANUFACTURING PLANT. The latter was founded in 1865 as a small machine shop and expanded gradually until today (1941) it is a large producer of windmills, electric and hand pumps, and pump accessories.

In the MULHOLLAND MUSEUM (*open*), 315 N. State St., are Indian relics, stoves of the early pioneers, early firearms, glassware, tables, and chairs. The owners, Mr. and Mrs. Ora Mulholland, spent 17 years assembling the exhibits, which fill four rooms.

Right from Kendallville on State 3, a paved road, is the old WALTERHOUSE FARMHOUSE, 1 *m.*, an Underground Railroad station before the Civil War.

BRIMFIELD, 31 *m.* (960 alt., 175 pop.), laid out in 1861 by William Bliss, has never developed beyond the status of a trading village located on a railroad. Life is still as uneventful as it was in 1861, when Reason Dye and Manhood Jones joined Bliss and the settlement had a population of about 30.

West of Brimfield there are no towns on the highway for a distance of 32 miles. This stretch passes through the Indiana lake region and, although there are few lakes in the immediate vicinity of the highway, dozens of small resorts lie to the north and south of the route. The highway traverses the muck-farm area, where the black, wet mucky soil produces great quantities of onions, mint, and truck produce. This raising of garden vegetables on a large scale is referred to as 'knee farming' and, while it requires a great deal of work, is highly profitable.

Off the highway (R) is WAWAKA, 37.4 *m.* (952 alt., 400 pop.), named from an Indian word meaning Big Heron. The village owes its existence to the New York Central Railroad and was laid out in 1857, when the railroad was built. It is a shipping point for muck farmers and an outlet for many tons of onions yearly.

At 43.4 *m.* is the junction with US 33 (*see Tour* 15).

At 51.9 *m.* is a junction with State 13, a blacktop road.

Left on State 13 to SYRACUSE, 1.6 *m.* (840 alt., 1,346 pop.), a summer resort town on Lakes Syracuse, Wawasee, and Papakeechee. LAKE WAWASEE (pronounced Wawa-see' and named for an Indian chief otherwise known as 'Old Flat Belly'), has 21 miles of shore line and is the largest lake in Indiana. There are hotel accommodations and facilities for golf, tennis, and horseback riding. The WAWASEE FISH HATCHERY, in the southeastern corner of the lake, is one of the oldest of the State's fish hatcheries. Its ponds are fed by the artificial PAPAKEECHEE LAKE, a privately owned lake whose use is restricted to owners of adjacent lots. LAKE SYRACUSE is a small body of water adjoining Lake Wawasee on the north. This chain of three lakes has a combined area of 7,000 acres and a shore line of 40 miles.

NAPPANEE, 65.5 *m.* (880 alt., 3,028 pop.), lies in the midst of the prosperous mint and onion country. It is a compactly built town, platted in 1874 and developed along the Baltimore & Ohio Railroad. Furniture manufacturing is a principal industry. The business district, old fashioned but clean and neat, stretches one block north and south of the public square. The wide streets are paved and the old, one-story buildings are in good repair. Many Amish farmers (*see Tour* 15) live in and about Nappanee and their covered buggies are common sights around the public square.

BREMEN, 73.9 *m.* (820 alt., 2,179 pop.), is a country town in the mint-growing belt, whose chief claim to fame is that its fire department won the State championship in hose and engine maneuvers in 1882 and 1887. There is a MUNICIPAL PARK (*playgrounds, shelterhouse, tennis courts*) with an electrically lighted softball diamond for night games. Many of the farmers about Bremen are of Dutch descent, and there are several large settlements of Amish, who are almost without exception prosperous farmers.

At 74.9 *m.* is the junction with Bremen Road, an improved county highway.

Left here to the junction with North Lake Road, 1.6 *m.;* R. to LAKE OF THE WOODS (*cottages and boats for rent; fishing*), 3.6 *m.* Surrounded by a forest of virgin hardwood, this lake, two miles long and one mile wide, is one of the most beautiful lakes in Indiana.

At 82.8 *m.* is the junction with US 31 (*see Tour 16a*).

WALKERTON, 92.6 *m.* (724 alt., 1,178 pop.), is a shipping point in the heart of one of the Nation's two largest peppermint-growing areas (*see Agriculture*). There are few empty buildings in this busy town, and the weathered brick fronts in the shopping district are painted and clean. St. Joseph County alone—in which Walkerton is located—has more than 10,000 acres planted in mint, and the whole region, including land lying across the Michigan Line, produces 90 per cent of all the oil of peppermint used in the United States. Spearmint is also grown. About 100,000 pounds of mint oil are shipped from Walkerton annually.

The peaty mucklands surrounding the town are planted early in the spring. Late in July or in early August, the harvesting of the green, knee-high mint begins and often lasts until October. Mint is cut and raked like hay, and hauled by team or tractor to huge vats in the distilleries that dot the countryside. An average yield is 20 or 30 pounds of oil to the acre. The mint farmers of this region have formed the Northern Indiana and Southern Michigan Peppermint Growers Association, a co-operative marketing organization, to find markets for their product; the chief market is in New York, where the oil is used to flavor chewing gum.

Mint growing began in this country more than a century ago in New York, where the plant was introduced from Europe. Until 1926, Indiana peppermint was free from pests, but in that year the flea-beetle, which attacks both the roots and the foliage of the plants, made its first appearance in St. Joseph County. The mintlooper also feeds on the growing plants. Both pests are combated by chemical treatment.

Onions are also grown extensively around Walkerton, as the muck is particularly well suited to this crop. A mucklands crop fair is held each November and prizes are awarded for individual exhibits and greatest yields. Westward from St. Joseph County, many of the truck farmers, especially in Lake County, are Polish, Hungarian, and Lithuanian; they seem to take naturally to 'knee farming.'

At 100.6 *m.* is the junction with US 35 (*see Tour 17*), with which US 6 unites westward for 5 miles.

At 109.4 *m.* is the junction with an improved county road.

Left on this road is UNION MILLS, 1.9 *m.* (747 alt., 400 pop.). About the edges of the town is a cluster of 11 INDIAN MOUNDS. Human skeletons, clay pipes, copper hatchets, and other Indian artifacts that have been excavated here are on exhibit at the La Porte County Museum (*see Tour 17a*) and the Three Oaks (Michigan) Museum.

At 124.6 *m.* is the junction with State 49, a paved road.

Left on State 49 to WAHOB LAKE (*cottages for rent*), 1.6 *m.,* third largest of the Porter County lakes, and noted for its good fishing. A GOLF COURSE (*9 holes; greens fee 35¢*) lies along the south side of the lake.

At 126.2 *m.* on the main route is the junction with a blacktop road.

Left on this road to a junction with a graveled road, 2 *m.;* L. here to LONG LAKE (*hotel, cottages, boats, good fishing*), 2.8 *m.,* so named because of its long, cigar-like shape.

At 128.1 *m.* on US 6 is the junction with a graveled road.

Left on this road to the junction with a second graveled road, 1 *m.;* L. on this road, 1.2 *m.,* to a junction with a third graveled road; R. here to BUTTERNUT SPRING (*artificial lake, game preserve, tennis courts; adm. 25¢*), 1.7 *m.,* an old Indian watering place frequented by several tribes because of the medicinal value of its water. The spring is so named because the waters originally sprang from the ground near a large butternut tree. This recreational area is privately owned and the lake is stocked with game fish, wild mallard ducks, and Chinese swans. The densely wooded game preserve, the rustic bridges, and the formal gardens make this spot attractive. An Indian burial ground, marked by a tree bent by Indians into the shape of a camel's hump, is in the rear of the gardens.

The McCOOL AIRPORT, 132.8 *m.,* an emergency landing field (R) under the supervision of the Bureau of Air Commerce, United States Department of Commerce, furnishes information for government and commercial airlines using this route. More than 50 ships pass the McCool port daily. Six times each hour the station broadcasts data on visibility, dew point, ceiling, wind velocity, and temperature. The field is illuminated for night landing.

Left from McCool Airport on a graveled road (following signs), to the SHRINE OF THE SEVEN DOLORS, 2.6 *m.,* built in 1932 by the Franciscans of Oldenburg (*see Tour 9a*), and dedicated 'to suffering Divinity to console suffering humanity.' A broad, tree-lined lane leads across a lagoon to the Seven Stations, depicting in bronze and stone the seven periods of sorrow in the life of the Virgin Mary. The stations encircle a life-size statue of St. Francis of Assisi showing his love for the crucified Saviour. Surrounding this central unit stand the Stations of the Cross. Hundreds visit the shrine daily, many bringing their lunches and spending the day in the adjoining grove.

At 137 *m.* is HOBART (600 alt., 7,166 pop.), whose citizens take great pride in the fact that the local high school band has won the Class B national band championships for several years. The town, platted in 1849, was named for a brother of George Earle, founder of the community. Earle, an English gentleman and painter, built a low rambling house, imported plants and shrubs from an old English garden, and assembled a private art collection, later donated to the town. The GEORGE EARLE HOUSE still stands on Main Street, two blocks west of the traffic light.

The CRESSMOOR GOLF CLUB (*public; greens fee* 50¢) is at the corner of US 6 and Wisconsin Street. Left on Wisconsin Street to LAKE GEORGE (*swimming, boating, fishing*), formed in 1846 when a dam was built across Deep River to provide power for the town's first mill. The lake is now crossed by several bridges carrying city traffic over the winding, two-mile body of water.

NEW CHICAGO, 138.8 *m.* (597 alt., 466 pop.), stands on the site that was once the council grounds of the Potawatomi Indians in Indiana. It was in this village that the United States Electric Carriage Company built their first electric buggy in 1898, seven years after the electric car was invented. The company ran this advertisement in a local paper: 'Costs less to keep than a horse. Doesn't get sick. Doesn't eat when it doesn't work.'

GARY, 142.1 *m.* (613 alt., 111,719 pop.) (*see Gary*).

In Gary are junctions with US 20 (*see Tour* 1) and US 12 (*see Tour* 2).

HIGHLAND, 147.5 *m.* (600 alt., 2,723 pop.), is principally a Dutch settlement in the midst of a truck-gardening community. The business district lies along the old highway about 500 feet north (R) of present US 6. To the southwest are sand hills that were once beaches of Lake Michigan, although they are now approximately seven miles from the lake. There is seldom activity upon the main thoroughfare; life moves at a leisurely pace. The town hall is a stucco adaptation of Dutch design. Many of the inhabitants work in the industrial plants of the Calumet cities.

Near the western edge of Highland is the junction with US 41 (*see Tour* 20), which coincides with US 6 to MUNSTER, 151.4 *m.* (615 alt., 1,751 pop.). Occupying an area between a sand ridge and the swamplands, Munster seems merely a continuation of the suburban homes that line the highway, here called Ridge Road, and there is no business section except at the western junction of US 41 and US 6. The route is bordered with almost solid lanes of open-air markets, gasoline stations, and lunch stands. Munster's inhabitants work in factories or on truck farms, or operate tree and shrub nurseries. Their homes are built along either side of the highway, with lawns running to the edge of the road. Much garden produce is shipped from Munster to the Chicago markets.

US 6 crosses the Little Calumet River at 153.1 *m.* into HAMMOND (598 alt., 70,184 pop.) (*see Hammond*).

At 154.6 *m.* US 6 crosses the ILLINOIS LINE into Calumet City, Illinois (*see Illinois Guide*).

Tour 4

(Van Wert, Ohio)—Fort Wayne—Warsaw—Valparaiso—(Chicago Heights, Ill.); US 30.
Ohio Line to Illinois Line, 156 *m.*

Roadbed hard-surfaced throughout.
The Pennsylvania R.R. parallels the route.
Accommodations of all kinds at frequent intervals.

US 30 is one of the most heavily traveled routes across northern Indiana; it is also, for 20 miles, a part of the transcontinental Lincoln Highway. The road carries a steady stream of traffic across one of the State's rich agricultural regions, passing for most of its course over level and almost treeless plains. Near by is historic Indian country, including the home of Little Turtle, Miami chief who was one of the greatest of all Indian leaders. Outstanding among the many lake, resort, and recreational areas are Lake Tippecanoe, deepest in Indiana, and Lake Winona, a religious center where Billy Sunday once lived and which is now the setting for a number of camps for the youth of the Middle West. Near the Illinois Line is the Kankakee River, its valley a great swamp and a haven for wild life of all kinds.

US 30 crosses the INDIANA LINE, 0 *m.*, 15 miles northwest of Van Wert, Ohio.

BESANCON, 8.2 *m.* (775 alt., 30 pop.), is clustered around a beautiful white stone church, visible for miles. The little Roman Catholic settlement exists today almost as it did a century ago when the land was cleared by French immigrants. Rich in legends of the early settlers, Besancon is a reminder of the efforts made by the French people to develop Allen County. In the old, well-kept cemetery adjoining the church are gravestones inscribed with epitaphs in French patois.

At 14 *m.* is NEW HAVEN (759 alt., 1,872 pop.) (*see Tour 5a*). At 15.1 *m.* is a junction with US 24 (*see Tour 5*) and the two highways coincide into Fort Wayne.

FORT WAYNE, 20.1 *m.* (829 alt., 118,410 pop.) (*see Fort Wayne*).
In Fort Wayne is the western junction with US 24 (*see Tour 5*), and junctions with US 27 (*see Tour 13*) and US 33 (*see Tour 15*), which unites northwestward with US 30 for 4.3 miles.

At 30.1 *m.* is the junction with a graveled road.

Right on this road to LAKE EVERETT, 2 *m.*, a 90-acre natural lake, popular as a fishing and recreational resort. Several tamarack swamps in the vicinity are typical of the surrounding farming land before it was reclaimed by drainage.

305

At 34.9 *m.* on US 30 is the junction with a graveled road.

Right on this road to the junction with a second graveled road, 1.3 *m.;* R. to the junction with a third graveled road, 3.2 *m.;* L. to the SITE OF EEL RIVER POST OF LITTLE TURTLE, 3.7 *m.* Little Turtle (1751–1812), Chief of the Miami Confederacy and a great Indian leader, spent most of his life in this region. On two occasions he was responsible for the failure of American troops to establish a military outpost at what is now Fort Wayne. He defeated General Harmar's army at Post Miami (*see Fort Wayne*) and at Heller's Corners (*see Tour* 15) in 1790. Leading a force composed of ten or more Indian tribes, Little Turtle decisively defeated troops under the command of General Arthur St. Clair at Fort Recovery, Ohio, in 1791. From this plateau, bounded on three sides by the Eel River and swamps and on the fourth by a rampart, the remains of which are still discernible, Little Turtle conducted a flourishing trading post and ruled the Miami Confederacy.

1. Right from the site of the post, 0.5 *m.,* to a monument marking the SITE OF THE LABALME MASSACRE, Little Turtle's first major military success. Here on November 5, 1780, Little Turtle ambushed and destroyed a force of 100 cavalrymen commanded by Colonel Auguste de LaBalme, a French soldier of fortune who had launched a private military venture to restore to France the territory she had lost to Britain in the French and Indian War. The British rewarded Little Turtle and influenced him to lead hostile expeditions into Kentucky, thus hoping to prevent American colonists from settling in Indiana. These raids continued long after the close of the American Revolution.

2. Left from the site of the post, 2 *m.,* to the SITE OF LITTLE TURTLE VILLAGE, home of Little Turtle. The chief's family included the 'white Indian boy,' William Wells, who was taken captive by Little Turtle on one of his Kentucky raids and reared as an adopted son. Wells became Little Turtle's lieutenant and married the chief's sister Anahquah. After her death he married Wahmangopath (Sweet Breeze), Little Turtle's daughter. According to some historians, Wells was so shocked by the massacre of St. Clair's army that he decided, with Little Turtle's permission, to return to his own people. The story handed down in the Wells family is different. After learning that General 'Mad Anthony' Wayne was to lead an expedition against the Indians, Little Turtle and Wells decided that peace was desirable and that Wells might implement its coming. That Wells, as a captain in Wayne's army, and Little Turtle did work for an end to hostilities until just before the Battle of Fallen Timbers (*see History*) is evidenced by Wayne's offer of peace as he marched to the scene of the conflict. Little Turtle unsuccessfully urged the Indians to accept the offer.

After Wayne's victory Wells returned to the Indians, living with his wife and children near the Fort Wayne stockade and frequently visiting Little Turtle, who devoted the last years of his life to the economic and social welfare of his people. Respected by both whites and Indians, Little Turtle died at Wells's home in 1812. Wells met a heroic death several weeks later in the Fort Dearborn (Chicago) massacre (*see Fort Wayne*).

At 37.5 *m.* on US 30 is the junction with a graveled road.

Left on this road to PAIGE'S CROSSING, 0.6 *m.,* where a punitive expedition, sent by General William Henry Harrison against the Miami in retaliation for attacks on Fort Wayne and Fort Harrison, decisively defeated the Indians on September 12, 1812. According to tradition the slaughter of the Indians was so great that the Eel River ran red with blood.

COLUMBIA CITY, 40.1 *m.* (839 alt., 4,219 pop.), is a prosperous industrial and agricultural town that has considerable transient trade because of its location at the intersection of US 30 and State 9 (*see Tour* 14). The stores that line the town square, on which the red brick courthouse stands, are for the most part modern and attractive in appearance. An overall factory, a meat-packing plant, and a woolen mill are the principal industries. Thomas Riley Marshall (1854–1925), Vice President for two terms under Woodrow Wilson, and governor of Indiana from 1909 to 1913, practiced law in Columbia City from 1875 to 1909. While presiding during a Senatorial debate, he made his famous remark, 'What this country really needs is a good five-cent cigar.' Major General Merritt W. Ireland, surgeon general of the U. S. Army from 1918 to 1931, was born in Columbia City.

Lloyd Cassel Douglas, author of *The Magnificent Obsession, The Green Light,* and other novels (*see Tour* 5), was born in Columbia City in 1877. His parents took him to Kentucky at the age of five and returned to Columbia City when Douglas was 16. He spent seven years at Wittenberg College and Seminary in Ohio, later becoming a Lutheran minister.

At 60.3 *m.* (eastern city limits of Warsaw) is the junction with a concrete road.

Left on this road to WINONA LAKE, 0.5 *m.* (833 alt., 743 pop.), a popular vacation retreat set in the shady hills that surround the lake on three sides. The town is the largest Chautauqua headquarters in the Middle West and is also the scene of numerous religious activities, including a summer normal school, song directors' school, mission school, and school of theology. About the lake are many children's camps, sponsored by churches and other organizations. The BILLY SUNDAY TABERNACLE, a one-story frame building seating 7,500, was built by the famous evangelist. The influence of Billy Sunday (1863–1935) is still felt in the community and observance of the Sabbath as a day of worship is strictly enforced. Stores are closed, entertainment is forbidden, and the smoking of a cigarette on the street or the causing of any noise or disturbance is punishable by arrest. There are no bars or taverns and no intoxicating drink is sold in the town. The BILLY SUNDAY HOUSE, an unpretentious frame bungalow, is the former home of the evangelist and is now occupied during the summer by his widow.

The INDIANA UNIVERSITY BIOLOGICAL STATION, on the grounds of the Winona Assembly, is a field laboratory for work in biology. Three buildings house the laboratories and classrooms.

On the western side of the lake and south of the city limits of Warsaw is the WARSAW COUNTRY CLUB (*open to public; greens fee* 50¢). The nine-hole golf course extends along the lake, its well-kept greens high above the water.

WARSAW, 62.3 *m.* (824 alt., 6,378 pop.), the seat of Kosciusko County and center of a diversified farming area, is in the heart of Indiana's lake region. Like Winona Lake, it is primarily a resort town with seasonal residents. Two plants manufacturing surgical supplies are among the largest in the Nation, and there are also cut-glass and vacuum-cleaner factories.

Kosciusko County was named for Thaddeus Kosciusko (1746–1817), Polish national hero and aide to Washington in the American Revolution. Warsaw was named for the capital of Poland. The northern part of town, now the finest residential district, was formerly a swamp that served as a rendezvous for horse thieves and counterfeiters.

1. Right from Warsaw on State 15, a concrete highway, to LEESBURG, 6.5 *m.* (935 alt., 389 pop.); R. from Leesburg on a blacktop road to TIPPE-

CANOE LAKE (L), 11.5 *m.*, source of the Tippecanoe River. Secluded in its beautiful valley from noisy highways, the lake is popular with vacationists, sportsmen, and nature lovers.

2. Left from Warsaw on State 25, a concrete highway, is PALESTINE, 6.8 *m.* (850 alt., 100 pop.), a farming and stock-raising center. On Trimball Creek in the middle of the village is LONE EAGLE MILL, a water-powered flour mill still operating after more than 100 years of service. Here the men of the neighborhood gather to exchange stories and to pass the time.

The TIPPECANOE RIVER, 67.6 *m.*, an important waterway in the early history of Indiana, flows southwestward through productive farm lands. To the Indians, whose villages lined its banks, it was known as Kethippecamunk.

At 67.7 *m.* is the junction with a graveled road.

Right on this road to an enormous BURR OAK TREE, 1.5 *m.*, said to be the largest tree in Indiana. Estimated to be more than 500 years old, the 150-foot tree stands in the center of a 35-acre tract of virgin timber and can be seen for miles, towering above its neighbors of the forest. The trunk, 35 feet in circumference at its base, rises unbrokenly for more than 70 feet. At one time arrangements were made to sell the tree and it was marked for 12-foot logs, but before the sale was consummated a clause was discovered in the will of David Phillips, who acquired the land from the Government in 1834, that protected the tree from anything but a natural death.

ATWOOD, 70.4 *m.* (823 alt., 250 pop.), settled by the Pennsylvania Dutch in the 1850's, and ETNA GREEN, 73.6 *m.* (813 alt., 423 pop.), are small trading and shipping points.

In BOURBON, 78.8 *m.* (840 alt., 1,145 pop.), an active farm trading village, is a MONUMENT TO THE OLD TOWN PUMP. In the heart of the town, this colored rock monument, topped with a stone likeness of the old pump, replaces with a fountain the original supply of drinking water.

PLYMOUTH, 89.5 *m.* (795 alt., 5,713 pop.), is a thriving county seat and a shipping center for the surrounding countryside. Founded in 1834, Plymouth has been swept by several destructive fires and by epidemics of malarial fever caused by adjacent swamp lands; reclamation permitted the town's steady growth. At the northern edge of Plymouth, on US 31, is CENTENNIAL PARK (*camping facilities*).

Plymouth is at the junction with US 31 (*see Tour* 16).

Left from Plymouth on State 17, a blacktop highway, to the junction with a graveled road, 7.8 *m.*; L. here to the junction with another graveled road, 10.5 *m.*; L. to the CHIEF MENOMINEE MONUMENT, 10.9 *m.*, an impressive granite monument supporting a life-size statue of Menominee, chief of the Potawatomi (*see Indians*). The statue stands between Pretty Lake and Twin Lakes on the site of the Indian village and Roman Catholic Mission.

Chief of the last Indian village held after the 1832 treaties, Menominee refused to acknowledge the purchase or to evacuate his tribe. In 1838, surrounded by squatters ready to move in, the Potawatomi made a final stand against Colonel Abel C. Pepper and soldiers secretly sent by Governor David H. Wallace. Trapped in the council house during a conference with Colonel Pepper, the Indians fought bravely but uselessly. The 859 men, women, and children were permitted a last visit to the graves of their dead and then started on their long and tragic journey to Kansas. Malaria was common that hot summer;

at every camp the dispossessed Indians stopped for new burials. They were led through Chippewanung, Logansport, Tippecanoe, and Williamsport. On September 13, they crossed into Illinois near Danville, where Father Petit, their village priest, rejoined them and accompanied them to their reservation on the Osage River.

In DONALDSON, 96.6 *m.* (789 alt., 128 pop.), is the junction with a blacktop road.

Left on this road to the RETREAT OF ST. AMALIA (*visitors welcome*), 1.6 *m.*, Mother House of the Ancilla Domini (Handmaidens of the Lord), a Roman Catholic institution. The five-story French-Gothic building stands on a beautifully landscaped tract of 160 acres. Copper towers and a cross, 140 feet above the ground, surmount the building, which houses 800 girls in 400 rooms, and contains a library, auditorium, recreation hall, oratories, and a chapel.

St. Amalia is primarily a training school for girls who intend to enter a religious order. A high school and junior college are maintained, and training is offered in nursing, teaching, and in the administration of hospitals and homes for children and the aged. First vows are made after a novitiate of two years; perpetual vows after a training period of three years. The sisters are then assigned to various institutions for which they have received special training.

In GROVERTOWN, 99.9 *m.* (720 alt., 75 pop.), is the junction with blacktop State 23.

Right on State 23 to 200-acre KOONTZ LAKE (*hotel, cottages; fishing, boating, bathing*), 3.5 *m.* The lake is shallow in comparison with most northern Indiana lakes.

HAMLET, 103.7 *m.* (702 alt., 519 pop.), was platted in 1863 by John Hamlet. It owes its existence to its location at the crossing of the Pennsylvania and New York Central Railroads, and is a shipping point for the surrounding country. The town has good tourist accommodations and an 18-hole golf course (*open to public; greens fee 35¢*).

At 105.3 *m.* is the junction with US 35 (*see Tour 17*).

US 30 crosses the KANKAKEE RIVER, 110 *m.*, which, like the Tippecanoe, flows through almost level country. The Indians called the river A-ki-ki (wolf) because a band of Mohicans of that name once lived along its banks. Formerly a vast swamp (*see Natural Setting*), the Kankakee region once furnished more than 30,000 pelts yearly to the fur trade. In the early 1900's the river was dredged, its channel straightened, and about 600,000 acres of marshland were drained and cleared for farming. Because the experiment was only partly successful, some of this land is being restored to its original state, and the Kankakee State Game Preserve (*see Tour 17*) has been established.

The river was used by early white explorers as a connecting link between the Great Lakes and the Mississippi. La Salle, with 32 *voyageurs* in eight large *pirogues*, passed this point on his first recorded trip through Indiana, early in December 1679, after a portage at South Bend from the St. Joseph River to the Kankakee.

WANATAH, 121 *m.* (752 alt., 750 pop.), is a farming village named for Wa-na-tah (keep knee deep in mud), an Indian chief who is said to have been noted for his laziness.

At 122.2 *m.* is the junction with a graveled road.

Right on this road to the PINNEY-PURDUE EXPERIMENTAL FARM, 0.7 *m.*, a 480-acre tract of rich farming land donated to Purdue University in 1909 by W. E. Pinney and his daughter, Mrs. F. R. Clark, for experimental work in animal husbandry, crop control, and scientific farming methods. There is a beautiful plantation-type house and many barns, silos, and poultry sheds.

DOLSON, just off the highway (L) at 127.2 *m.*, was formerly the loading station for the dairy train running daily from Wanatah to Chicago, and marks the center of a rich dairying country. The area around the old loading station is a part of the VALPARAISO MORAINE, an accumulation of earth and stone deposited here by the last glacier. This is the highest ridge in northern Indiana.

VALPARAISO, 130.8 *m.* (805 alt., 8,736 pop.), seat of Porter County, has contributed liberally to the industrial and social progress of northern Indiana and to the educational development of the Nation. For the greater part of its century of slow but steady growth, the town's claim to fame has been VALPARAISO UNIVERSITY, a group of time-worn buildings in the southeast part of town, overlooking 16 miles of Kankakee marshlands. Len Small, former governor of Illinois; George W. Norris, progressive Republican senator from Nebraska; Flem D. Sampson, former governor of Kentucky; and Lowell Thomas, radio commentator, attended Valparaiso University.

Founded in 1859 as a Methodist school and called the Valparaiso Male and Female College, the institution suffered financially during the Civil War and was forced to close its doors in 1870. It was reopened soon afterward by Henry Baker Brown, then a 26-year-old professor in an Ohio normal school. Endorsed by the Methodist Church and Porter County, it was conducted as a nonsectarian, self-supporting, and self-governing coeducational college. Under Brown's excellent management it became nationally known as the 'poor man's Harvard,' and in 1914–15 boasted a student body of 6,000, second only in size to that of the older Eastern university. The death of Brown in 1915 and the entrance of the United States into the World War seriously hindered the school's program, progress, and enrollment. The university was purchased by the Lutheran Church in 1925, but is open to students of all faiths. The 1939–40 enrollment was 513.

The INDIANA STEEL COMPANY PLANT (*visitors welcome*), in the northwestern part of town, produces 80 per cent of all the magnets made in the United States. Among the town's other industrial products are electrical insulation, paints and varnishes, ball and roller bearings, and bronze die castings.

A marker in the yard of the public library, one block east and one block north of the courthouse, commemorates the site as a point on the OLD SAUK TRAIL, over which the Sauk Indians traveled yearly from Illinois and Wisconsin to Detroit to collect annuities from the British for services in the War of 1812.

A ROUGH BARK MAGNOLIA TREE, one of the few in the northern part of the State, grows in the yard of the B. J. Barrington home,

355 Garfield Avenue. It is believed that the tree was transplanted here by an early settler from the South. It is 75 feet high and its trunk is four and a half feet in diameter, a size rarely attained by the tree in sections of the country where it is common.

Right from Valparaiso on State 49, a hard-surfaced highway, to FLINT LAKE, 4 m., buried (L) among wooded cliffs and grass-covered hills. BLACK-HAWK BEACH (bathing, boating, fishing), almost hidden in a beautiful park overlooking the eastern shore of the lake, attracts many tourists and vacationists. The highway winds around the lake to HILLCREST PARK AND GOLF COURSE (open to public; greens fee 40¢), high above Flint Lake and the smaller Long and Loomis Lakes that flow into it.

A 14-mile stretch of double-lane super-highway begins at 138.5 m. A broad parkway between the lanes is landscaped with shrubs and evergreen trees.

At 145.9 m. is the junction with State 55, a concrete road.

Right on State 55 is MERRILLVILLE, 1 m. (645 alt., 150 pop.), once the point at which 16 Indian trails converged upon the old Sauk Trail. The SOLO-MON ZUVER HOUSE, directly across the street from the Methodist Church, is probably the oldest house in Lake County. The SITE OF THE CALIFORNIA EXCHANGE INN, widely known as a stopping place during the gold rush of 1849, is within the village. The inn burned in 1913.

At 15.3 m. is the junction with US 41 (see Tour 20).

DYER, 155.8 m. (635 alt., 976 pop.), a dairying center, is the last town in Indiana on this route. The STATE LINE HOUSE, built in 1838, a two-story yellow tavern in the center of town, is still conducted as a hostelry.

US 30 crosses the ILLINOIS LINE, 156 m., seven miles east of Chicago Heights, Illinois (see Illinois Guide).

✓✓✓

Tour 5

(Defiance, Ohio)—Fort Wayne—Huntington—Peru—Logansport—Kentland—(Sheldon, Ill.); US 24.
Ohio Line to Illinois Line, 159.4 m.

Two-lane concrete roadbed throughout.
Route is paralleled by the Wabash R.R. between Fort Wayne and Peru; by the Pennsylvania R.R. between Peru and the Illinois Line.
Accommodations at short intervals; hotels chiefly in cities.

Across eastern Indiana, US 24 follows the course of the Wabash and Erie Canal, an ambitious and ill-advised project that bankrupted the

State. The highway and the bed of the canal parallel in turn the Maumee, the Little Wabash, and the Wabash Rivers, which together formed an important link in the early French waterway from the Great Lakes to the Gulf of Mexico.

This region is rich in Indian tradition, for it was the home of the major branch of the Miami nation. At the forks of the Wabash and the Little Wabash many treaties between the United States and the Miami nation were negotiated, and here still stands the home of La Fontaine, a Miami chief. Along the bank of the Mississinewa River is the battlefield where the Miamis made their last organized fight against the whites. Near by are the graves of Francis Godfroy, their leader in this fight, and Frances Slocum, a white girl who became the wife of a Miami chieftain and an Indian in spirit and appearance.

At the mouth of the Mississinewa are the wintering quarters for several large circuses, where giraffe, elephants, and zebra graze along the roadside in early spring and fall. The western part of the route falls off into level prairie lands of rich, black soil, passing through one of the finest farming sections of the Middle West.

Section a.   OHIO LINE to PERU, 79.1 m.   US 24

From the State Line to Huntington, US 24 passes through a pleasantly rolling country rich in vegetation, with occasional glimpses of the tree-bordered Maumee River. Westward the road dips and rises through the hilly terrain near the Wabash River, which is the most heavily wooded section of northern Indiana.

US 24 crosses the OHIO LINE, 0 m., 27 miles west of Defiance, Ohio.

The SITE OF SAYLOR'S LOCK, 0.5 m., Indiana's easternmost lock of the Wabash and Erie Canal, is now occupied by a gasoline station. Directly across the road is the SAYLOR HOUSE, built in 1837 by Ulrich Saylor. It was originally a two-story frame structure at the front and one and a half stories high at the rear, but its appearance has been altered by new shingle siding and a modern veranda.

The GRONAUER HOUSE and LOCK SITE, 11.8 m., is a landmark dating back to canal days. The house (R) is directly across the highway from the lock site, and is a red brick building with an ell extension on one side. Behind the house, built in 1860 by George Gronauer, is a large barn built ten years earlier and formerly used as winter quarters for mules that towed the canal barges.

NEW HAVEN, 14 m. (759 alt., 1,872 pop.), a small farming center that owes its origin to the canal, has been kept alive by the Wabash Railroad. A placid and dignified residential town with a number of fine homes, it has become practically a suburb of Fort Wayne. Early New England settlers named it for the Connecticut city.

Between 15.1 m. and Fort Wayne, US 24 and US 30 (see Tour 4) are united.

FORT WAYNE, 20.1 *m*. (829 alt., 118,410 pop.) (*see Fort Wayne*).

In Fort Wayne are junctions with US 27 (*see Tour 13*) and US 33 (*see Tour 15*), and the western junction with US 30 (*see Tour 4*).

A large brick residence, 31.6 *m*., was once the popular VERMILYEA TAVERN (R). This nondescript old house was the most patronized amusement place along the canal for the hard-working, hard-drinking, canal laborers. It also drew a large transient trade and many celebrities spent the night here at a time when transcontinental travel was slow and laborious. The bed of the canal is still visible about 1,000 feet from the house.

The SITE OF RACCOON VILLAGE, at the junction with the Allen-Whitley County Line road, 32.7 *m*., is the last of the Indian reservations of Allen and Whitley Counties.

ROANOKE, 36.7 *m*. (757 alt., 808 pop.), an unpretentious country town, was known locally as the 'Athens of Indiana' when its seminary was considered the last word in culture by Hoosiers. Founded by Frederick S. Reefy in 1861, the ROANOKE CLASSICAL SEMINARY played an important role at a time when high schools and normal schools were unknown in this part of the country. Reefy successfully conducted the school for several years, with an enrollment of about 250. The institution grew in reputation throughout the State and eventually was sold to the United Brethren Conference for use as a preparatory school for Otterbein University in Westerville, Ohio. Later it came into the hands of D. N. Howe, who moved it to North Manchester, where it became Manchester College.

In the southeastern part of the town is a simple little house that was once the HOME OF KILSOQUAH, beloved granddaughter of Little Turtle, the famous Miami chief. Kilsoquah was born in May 1810 at the forks of the Wabash near Huntington. She lived in the forests along the Wabash River near Roanoke where her father, Little Turtle's son, owned 320 acres of land. She was twice married; once to a French-Indian named John Owl, who died within a year, and the second time to Anthony Revarre, also a French-Indian. Four children were born to the couple. Although Kilsoquah lived near English-speaking people most of her life, she never learned the language and her son Anthony acted as interpreter. She died in September 1915 at the age of 105 years and was at that time the only full-blooded Indian inhabitant of the county. She is buried in the Odd Fellows Cemetery in Roanoke.

HUNTINGTON, 46 *m*. (736 alt., 13,903 pop.), is the home of John R. Kissinger, who in 1900, while a United States army private in Cuba, submitted to the yellow fever tests of Dr. Walter Reed. During the experiments Kissinger developed a virulent case of yellow fever from which he never fully recovered. Today he walks with crutches. Dr. Reed said of him, 'In my opinion, there has never been a higher exhibition of moral courage in the annals of the Army of the United States, than that exhibited by John R. Kissinger.' So impaired was Kissinger's health that he has been pensioned by the Government.

Huntington was originally called Wepecheange (place of flints), but was given its present name in 1831 in honor of Samuel Huntington, a member of the first Continental Congress. This relatively small community has the hustle and atmosphere of a much larger city, and the imposing HUNTINGTON COUNTY COURTHOUSE is more suggestive of a State capitol than a Hoosier county seat. It is a four-story granite building and its four entrances converge at a circular opening under the dome. The building is a combination of Greek and Roman styles and each of the four entrances is surmounted by a Greek pediment containing a clock.

The JEFFERSON STREET BRIDGE, one block south of the courthouse, strikes a bizarre note in the otherwise conventional-looking city. One side of this bridge, which spans the Little Wabash River, holds an entire city block of stores and business houses, suspended over the river and facing the traffic of the bridge's four highways. It is said to be the only bridge of this kind in the United States.

Overlooking the Little Wabash River and one block west of the courthouse, is the $1,000,000, six-story brick LA FONTAINE HOTEL, named for a chief of the Miami Indians (see below). It was built in 1923 and endowed with a trust fund to help defray maintenance expenses.

HUNTINGTON COLLEGE, on a wooded campus at the northeastern edge of the city, was founded in 1897 by the Church of the United Brethren in Christ, after fire had destroyed the denomination's school at Hartsville (see Tour 9). Its approximately 200 students may take courses in theology, music, and commerce, as well as regular liberal arts work.

SUNDAY VISITOR PUBLISHING HOUSE, NE. corner Warren St. and East Park Drive, a Roman Catholic enterprise founded in 1912 by the Right Reverend J. F. Noll, bishop of the diocese of Fort Wayne. Here are published the Sunday Visitor (weekly circulation 400,000), one of the most widely circulated Roman Catholic papers in the world, and the magazines Family Monthly, Acolyte, and Missionary Catechist.

In the HOME OF MRS. HOWARD OWENS (open), 828 Poplar St., is the huge ARMCHAIR used by Chief La Fontaine. As the chief weighed 368 pounds, the chair was especially constructed of heavy walnut, reinforced with metal and bolts at each joint. It is about three and a half feet wide between the arms. Mrs. Owens is the granddaughter of La Fontaine.

Huntington is at a junction with State 9 (see Tour 14).

Right on State 5 (paved) is the beautiful mission-type MONASTERY OF ST. FELIX (open), 1 m., home of a group of Capuchin monks and a novitiate school with a one-year term. Capuchins take their name from the cowl attached to their habit, and they wear a beard. Most austere of the several orders of St. Francis, they are mendicants, and the poorest order of the Roman Catholic Church. Their food is coarse and plain, their existence without material comforts. The special work of the order is home and foreign missions, assisting the secular clergy in parish work, and the training of boys for the priesthood. All classes are taught in Latin. At present (1941) the monastery houses about 32 persons, including priests, brothers, and novices.

At 1.5 *m.* on State 5 is MT. CALVARY CEMETERY (R), where Chief La Fontaine is buried. La Fontaine, son of a French trader and a Miami squaw, became chief of his tribe in 1828, when he was 18 years of age. His tribe of 300 Miami were forced to leave the State in 1846, and were removed to Kansas. Overcome by a longing for his old home, La Fontaine started back to Huntington in 1847 for a visit, unaware that the broken-spirited Miami, believing their chief was deserting them, had secretly given him a slow poison. He fell ill on his way to Indiana and died upon reaching LaFayette, in 1847. LA FONTAINE'S GRAVE is marked by a granite shaft.

At 47 *m.* on US 24 is the junction with a graveled road.

Left on this road, across the bed of the old Wabash and Erie Canal, is the LAMBDIN P. MILLIGAN HOUSE, 0.1 *m.,* once the home of one of the most active figures in the Knights of the Golden Circle, an organization of men who, weary of the Civil War, were engaged in subversive activity. Milligan, a Huntington attorney, was arrested with Dr. William A. Bowles of French Lick, Horace Heffren of Salem (*see Tour* 11), and Stephen Horsey of Shoals (*see Tour* 10) in the closing years of the war. Milligan was a popular figure in the Huntington community, and to prevent interference, the military authorities who arrested him backed a train at night all the way from Indianapolis to the track beside his house, seized him, and took him to the military prison in Indianapolis. In the trial before a military court in 1864, Heffren turned State's evidence and was released after accusing Bowles, Milligan, and Horsey of plotting to kidnap Governor Oliver P. Morton and hold him as hostage during an insurrection planned for August 16, 1864. All three men were convicted of treason and sentenced to be hanged. By the intervention of friends they were taken out of the State before the sentence could be carried out. After a series of legal stalemates the case was carried to the United States Supreme Court and the decision was reversed, the higher court ruling that a military court had no jurisdiction except in cases where martial law prevailed. The decision stated that an emergency does not create any additional power to cope with that emergency. This is considered one of the most important decisions in the history of the Supreme Court.

Milligan's rambling house sits almost on the banks of the Little Wabash River. The thin limestone slabs of the original structure are retained in what is now the kitchen; the front of the house is weatherboarded with wide poplar boards still in good condition. Milligan, a wealthy horse lover, kept a stable of fine racing horses. The outline of his training track is still well defined at the rear of the estate.

At 47.3 *m.,* in MOUNT HOPE CEMETERY (R), is the GRAVE OF LAMBDIN P. MILLIGAN (1812–99).

The VICTORY NOLL MISSIONARY SCHOOL, 47.5 *m.,* a Spanish-Byzantine building atop a beautifully landscaped hill overlooking the river, was founded in 1925 by Bishop Noll of the Roman Catholic Diocese of Fort Wayne. The school educates young Catholic women to serve as missionaries to Catholic children of outlying churchless sections of the country.

At the confluence of the Wabash and the Little Wabash Rivers, 48.1 *m.,* known during pioneer days as the FORKS OF THE RIVERS, many treaties between the government and the Indians were negotiated. The last great treaty of the Miamis, in which they relinquished all their land holdings in Indiana and promised to move beyond the Mississippi, was signed here in 1840.

This place was a key point on the continental route from the mouth of the St. Lawrence to the mouth of the Mississippi, for the Wabash-Maumee portage extended from near the Forks to a point in Fort Wayne where the junction of the St. Mary's and the St. Joseph Rivers formed the Maumee. Today five routes, closely paralleling one another, illustrate the development of travel and transportation: the Wabash River, the old Wabash and Erie Canal, the old Indian trail (now a paved highway), the Wabash Railroad (steam), and the Indiana Railroad (electric).

Directly north of the highway where it passes the Forks is the field (R), where Little Turtle, famed Miami chief (*see Tour* 4), conducted what was probably the first agricultural school in America sometime between 1795 and 1800. He brought a Quaker farmer from Philadelphia to teach the young braves scientific farming, but after doing all the manual labor for one season while the unenthusiastic braves fished and hunted, the farmer gave up the experiment in disgust.

During the War of 1812, immediately after the siege of Fort Wayne, General Harrison burned the Miami village at the Forks and destroyed the crops in the fields, as a disciplinary measure to thwart any further uprisings among the Indians. The village was afterwards rebuilt and continued until 1840. The small spot of ground between the Forks and the Miami Inn (L) has never passed from Indian ownership.

The LA FONTAINE HOMESTEAD (*private*), built over a century ago by Chief La Fontaine and used as his residence, still stands (R) less than 100 yards from the Forks. The front of the house with its recessed doorway faces the highway and the wide poplar weatherboarding is still well preserved, although the house itself has commenced to sag. Here La Fontaine distributed to his tribe the government money, in coins which were brought to the house in barrels. Each Indian would bring what money he had retained from the previous payment, throw the old money on the floor, and receive its equivalent in new and shiny coins.

At 50.4 *m.*, about 50 ft. R. of the highway bridge over Silver Creek, is the STONE AQUEDUCT that carried the Wabash and Erie Canal over the stream. The creek was so named because a marauding Indian, attempting to escape with $500 worth of silver stolen at the Forks, dropped the money into the stream for safekeeping.

At 52.3 *m.* is the junction with State 105.

Left on State 105 is ANDREWS, 1 *m.* (716 alt., 954 pop.), birthplace of Ellwood Patterson Cubberley, nationally known educator. Dr. Cubberley was graduated from Indiana University in 1891 when Dr. David Starr Jordan was its president. He taught at Vincennes University, later became president of that school, and then joined Dr. Jordan in the development of Leland Stanford University.

In 1938 Dr. Cubberley presented Stanford with a three-story, $500,000 building to house a school of education. The funds came from 'pin money' that he and his wife had saved over a period of 20 years: royalties on books, receipts from lectures and consultation services, dividends and interest. He made many profitable investments, studying stock trends and statistics, as he said, 'just like preparing for an examination.'

In the Cities

SOLDIERS AND SAILORS MONUMENT, INDIANAPOLIS

ARCHITECTURAL DETAIL, TRINITY ENGLISH LUTHERAN CHURCH, FORT WAYNE

PUBLIC LIBRARY, INDIANAPOLIS

WORLD WAR MEMORIAL, INDIANAPOLIS

AIRVIEW, EVANSVILLE (Ohio River in the foreground)

LOW-COST PREFABRICATED DWELLING BUILT BY FORT WAYNE HOUSING AUTHORITY

LOCKEFIELD GARDENS, INDIANAPOLIS—U. S. HOUSING AUTHORITY PROJECT

COURTHOUSE SQUARE, BEDFORD

DOWNTOWN TERRE HAUTE

MICHIGAN STREET, SOUTH BEND

HAMMOND CELEBRATES
Basketball Fans Welcome a State Championship High School Team

THE DRESSER (DREISER) HOUSE, TERRE HAUTE
This cottage was the family home of Theodore Dreiser, novelist, and his brother
Paul Dresser, composer of the State song—'On the Banks of the Wabash'

GENERAL LEW WALLACE'S STUDY, CRAWFORDSVILLE

LAGRO (pronounced La-grow'), 59.3 *m.* (704 alt., 542 pop.), named for an Indian chief, Les Gros, is now a little community of retired farmers. The bed of the Wabash and Erie Canal runs alongside the main street where garages, chain grocery stores, and lunch stands line the edge of the 100-year-old ditch by means of which the area was settled and developed. The interurban station marks the SITE OF THE TOLL LOCK. Through the length of the town there are several locks in a good state of preservation.

The KELLER HOUSE (R), overlooking the Wabash Valley at the intersection of Davis St. and US 24, was a tavern popular with the Irish laborers on the canal. The substantial two-story brick structure, built about 1840 by Ephraim Keller, was considered the finest hotel between LaFayette and Toledo.

Left from Lagro on a graveled road is the SALAMONIE RIVER STATE FOREST (*shelter house, picnic area*), 3.4 *m.*, a 300-acre preserve; the natural beauty of its timber and of the Salamonie River is enhanced by an artificial lake.

At 63.2 *m.* is the junction with State 13, which unites with US 24 to Wabash.

Right on State 13 is NORTH MANCHESTER, 13 *m.* (774 alt., 3,170 pop.), in the valley of the beautiful Eel River. This sedate town with its tree-lined streets and vine-covered houses has a large population of Dunkers, members of a religious sect founded in Germany in 1708. The Dunkers came to Pennsylvania in 1719 and later spread over the Middle West. Dunkers strongly stress nonconformity with the world and strive for simplicity in dress and habits and a close following of Scriptural teachings. The name Dunker comes from the German 'tunker' meaning 'to dip,' for they believe in triple immersion as the only true baptism. Dunkers refuse to take oaths, to give military service, or to own any kind of a musical instrument.

North Manchester is the birthplace of Thomas R. Marshall (*see Tour* 4), former governor of Indiana and Vice President of the United States under Woodrow Wilson. A bronze plaque on the Oppenheim Building on Main Street marks the SITE OF THE MARSHALL HOME.

MANCHESTER COLLEGE, which has an enrollment of 1,264 (1939-40) and is conducted by the Church of the Brethren, is at the northeast edge of town. Founded in Roanoke, Indiana, in 1860, the school was taken over by the Dunkers and moved to North Manchester in 1884. The athletic field, east of the college, occupies the SITE OF A POTAWATOMI VILLAGE, in which a street 30 feet wide (still visible) ran between the rows of tepees to the Eel River. Adjacent to the athletic field on the north is the CHIEF PIERISH HOUSE, a remodeled log cabin formerly the home of a Potawatomi leader. Although it is definitely known that Pierish ruled a large Potawatomi village at this place and is himself buried beneath the floor of this house, he remains a nearly legendary figure. The only tangible evidence of his existence is his signature on the Treaty of 1826, between the Government and the Potawatomi, by which the Indians ceded a portion of land between the Wabash and the Eel Rivers.

ZION LUTHERAN CHURCH, Main St., was founded in 1846 and is one of the town's oldest churches. The pastor of this church from 1903 to 1905 was Lloyd Cassel Douglas (*see Tour* 4), author of *The Magnificent Obsession* and *The Green Light*. Grace Van Studdiford (1875-1927), light opera singer of note, also lived in North Manchester.

At the west end of 7th Street is the ESTELLE PEABODY MEMORIAL HOME for aged persons. Intending it as a memorial to his wife, James P. Peabody founded the home in 1930, but died before it was finished. His son, Thomas Peabody, built two units instead of one, in honor of each of his parents. Both the north and south units are large Georgian-style buildings of brick with white trim, and are identical in size and detail. In 1936, Thomas Peabody added a chapel of the same style and equipped it with a pipe organ and an amplifying system. He has also added a Gothic singing tower at the base of which his parents are buried. The entire memorial has been turned over to the Presbyterian Church of Indiana. This home for the aged is open to all persons of any denomination who can pay a fee of $1,500 for admission. Married couples are not separated, but are permitted to establish themselves as though in their own homes. Living conditions and quarters would do credit to a fashionable hotel or resort.

WABASH, 65.6 *m.* (744 alt., 9,653 pop.), built on the side of a hill overlooking the Wabash River, was a gathering place for the Indians, who named it Oubache (water over white stones). Wide, tree-shaded streets lined with comfortable middle-class homes make up the residential area. Wabash is the seat of Wabash County and above its courthouse square towers a soot-stained courthouse. At the foot of the hill, along the river and below the courthouse, is the shopping district.

A boulder with a bronze plaque, one block south and three blocks east of the courthouse, marks the SITE OF THE SIGNING OF THE TREATY OF PARADISE SPRINGS. This treaty, signed in October 1826, opened the surrounding territory to settlement by white men.

Nine years later the Wabash and Erie Canal was dug through this section, and with the canal came a new element into the melting pot of the frontier. Much of the labor was done by Irish immigrants, who brought with them all the rivalries and traditions of the old country. The 'Irish War,' a protracted series of fights between the men of Cork, called 'Corkonians,' and men from the north of Ireland, called 'Fardowns,' made a lively chapter in the story of the canal.

There were about 300 laborers on each side, and their differences finally culminated in plans for a pitched battle to be fought near the site of the present city of Wabash. On July 12, 1835, the 145th anniversary of the Battle of the Boyne, the opposing forces were drawn up. A few shots had been fired when the timely arrival of a large body of militia averted what promised to be something worse than a Donnybrook Fair.

By September 1853 the 460-mile canal extended from Ohio, through Wabash, to Evansville—only to be overtaken by the railroads. The canal was completed the very week that the Union Station in Indianapolis was opened. The iron rails had already begun to write the final chapter in the story of tow-path and barge.

Wabash was one of the first cities in the country to use electricity for public lighting. In a corridor of the courthouse is a glass display case containing one of the four large CARBON LAMPS that were first used on March 31, 1880, to light the dome of the building. On this occasion a large dynamo was set up in the courthouse yard and persons from far and near gathered to witness the spectacle.

On the northeast corner of the courthouse square is the LINCOLN OF

THE PEOPLE STATUE, a 35-ton bronze statue of Abraham Lincoln, by Charles Keck of New York. In the city park is the LINCOLN MEMORIAL CABIN, a restored cabin of unknown origin, that in construction and arrangement resembles cabins occupied by Lincoln. It was erected in the park in 1909 by the Old Settler's Association of Wabash County.

PERU, 79.1 *m.* (658 alt., 12,432 pop.), the 'Circus City of the World,' is near the confluence of the Mississinewa and Wabash Rivers. The surrounding territory is rich in memories of the Indians who once used these streams as highways. Peru is the seat of Miami County and is essentially a one-street town. Main Street, which runs east and west along the Wabash River, comprises about four-fifths of the shopping district. Peru's 'uptown' section is a cluster of new granite buildings and many more that are nondescript left-overs from the middle of the last century. The BEARSS HOTEL, Broadway and 3rd Sts., once known as the Western House, has served uninterruptedly as the town's leading hostelry since 1837. It is a plain three-story brick building that has been remodeled and given an outside finish of stucco.

In the residential section are many beautiful houses along exceptionally wide paved streets. The massive BEN WALLACE HOUSE, 6th St. and Broadway, is a Georgian-style structure, painted canary yellow and trimmed in white. The house and grounds occupy nearly half of a city block. Ben Wallace laid the foundation for the city's fame as the winter quarters for a majority of the leading circuses in the United States. Buying a defunct traveling show in 1883 that consisted of a band wagon, a one-eyed lion, a camel, two monkeys, a few dogs, a spotted horse, and an elephant named Diamond, Wallace and a partner, James Anderson, started their show. The elephant they trained in a railroad roundhouse. They staged their first exhibition in Peru, and started what later became the Hagenbeck-Wallace Circus.

In the public library, Main and Huntington Sts., is the city's HISTORICAL MUSEUM (*open weekdays* 9–5, *free*), containing a comprehensive collection of Indian and pioneer relics; there is a large supplementary museum on the fourth floor of the courthouse.

Peru is at the junction with US 31 (*see Tour* 16).

Left from the courthouse, the Frances Slocum Trail, an old Indian road (partly macadamized and partly graveled) leads across the Wabash River bridge and southeast, first along the Wabash and then along the Mississinewa.

At 2.7 *m.* is the junction with a graveled road (R).

Right on this road 0.5 *m.*, is the SITE OF THE OSAGE VILLAGE (R), now a farm but once a flourishing Miami village named for Chief Osage. On the grassy hillside that forms a small natural amphitheater back of the barnyard was held the last important council of the chiefs. Here on May 15, 1812, Tecumseh built the fire for the last Great Council of the Mississinewa, his final attempt to organize the Indians of the Middle West into a confederation and to enlist them with the British against the United States. But the disaster of Tippecanoe, resulting from the counsel of the Prophet, Tecumseh's brother, was still fresh in the minds of the visiting warriors. After a session in which the wrathful eloquence of Tecumseh was directed against the white settlers, the chieftains of the Wyandot, Delaware, Potawatomi, and Miami nations arose and stated firmly that they were done with strife and bloodshed, and intended to live in peace with the whites. Tecumseh, realizing that his influence had waned and his power was ended, left for Canada where he joined the British in the War of 1812.

The AMERICAN CIRCUS CORPORATION, 3 m., provides winter quarters of some of America's foremost circuses. Scores of large red sheds (L) house animals and equipment. The land on both sides of the Slocum Trail for about half a mile is owned by the Circus Corporation and is used as a pasture for the circus animals.

At 3.9 m. is the junction with a graveled road.

Left on this road 0.9 m., in the GODFROY CEMETERY, are the graves of Francis Godfroy, last of the Miami war chiefs, and other members of the famous Indian family that took the name of a French nobleman who married the daughter of one of their chiefs. Godfroy was selected as chief on the exact spot where he is now buried. He led the Miami in their last battle on the Mississinewa, when General Harrison destroyed the Miami villages as a precaution against Indian assistance to the British in the War of 1812. Retiring from war, Godfroy devoted his time to the trading post on the Wabash that had been started by his father. He became very rich, living in feudal splendor. The SITE OF GODFROY'S MOUNT PLEASANT HOME AND TRADING POST is across the road from the present cemetery. Godfroy, wise, generous, and a fearless leader, was a man of extraordinary strength and physique, weighing nearly 400 pounds. He died in 1840, beloved by both Indians and whites.

At 4.7 m. on the Slocum Trail is the palatial HOME OF COLE PORTER (*private*), internationally known song writer, author of 'Old-Fashioned Garden,' 'Night and Day,' and many other songs. Porter now (1941) lives in New York, and this house is occupied by his mother. It is a huge, three-story, red brick structure, Georgian in design, set in the middle of a large estate surrounded by a high iron fence.

The OLD-FASHIONED GARDEN, 5.1 m., was the inspiration for Porter's song.

The CLIFFS OF THE SEVEN DOUBLE PILLARS, 5.5 m., were cut in high relief by erosion of the rock ledge overhanging a bend of the river. It is claimed by Indians living in the surrounding area that the first white man's trading post in Indiana was located on this high bank, but no one remembers his name or the date of his arrival. At this point the Mississinewa is very flat and shallow, flowing over a shale bed. The Indians fished with bow and arrow in the clear, sparkling stream.

At 7.4 m. is the farming village of PEORIA (673 alt., 100 pop.), founded early in the settlement of the country by a group of pioneers bound for Peoria, Illinois. The beauty and fertility of the Mississinewa Valley satisfied them so completely that they named their community for their original objective.

The entrance to the FRANCES SLOCUM STATE FOREST is at 7.6 m. This 981-acre tract is being developed by the State Department of Conservation.

From Peoria the trail winds around the Mississinewa to a junction with a graveled road at 8.5 m.

Left on this road, 0.5 m., to the HOME AND BURIAL PLACE OF FRANCES SLOCUM, the 'White Rose of the Miamis,' who was stolen from her Quaker home in Pennsylvania in 1773, at the age of four. The Slocum family had always been immune from attack by Indians, who respected the peaceful ways of the Quakers. However, one of the Slocum boys had fought against the Indians without the knowledge or consent of his father, and feeling that they had cause to retaliate, a band of Delaware descended upon the Slocum home, killed a neighbor boy who was playing in the yard, because he had on a soldier's coat, and carried off the auburn-haired Frances. Some three weeks later the father and grandfather were killed as they worked in a field. Mrs. Slocum never gave up hope that Frances was alive and kept up a lifelong hunt for her kidnapped daughter. The brothers and sister later carried on the search, offering large rewards for her discovery. Their last efforts, in 1826, proved futile and convinced them that Frances was dead.

Nine years later, George Ewing, an Indian trader from Logansport, arrived at the Deaf Man's Village on the banks of the Mississinewa. He was hospitably received in the cabin of Ma-con-a-qua, the widow of She-po-ca-nah, the Deaf Man, who had been an old acquaintance of Ewing. After supper the conversation in the Miami language gradually waned as the other members of the household dropped out and retired, leaving only Ewing and Ma-con-a-qua, who was visibly agitated. When Ewing arose to retire, she objected, saying that she was old and weak and, fearing that she would die, must unburden herself of a secret.

She told him that she was a white woman who had been carried away as a small child by three Delaware Indians. She did not remember when, and she had forgotten her mother tongue and her Christian name. She said that the Indians had treated her kindly and that she had been adopted by a chief named Tuck Horse and his wife and raised to womanhood. She had married a young Delaware who treated her badly, and had left him and returned to her Indian parents. They had then moved to Indiana where she had lived for a time in the village of Little Turtle. After the defeat of the Indians by Wayne the family went to Ohio to visit some of their former home sites. It was here that she met a young Miami chief, She-po-ca-nah. He was badly wounded and she nursed him back to health, returning to his tribe with him as his wife. They lived at Fort Wayne until it became too densely populated with white men to suit She-po-ca-nah, and then moved to the Osage village where he became chief and successor to Osage, the founder of the village. When age and increasing deafness overcame him he resigned as chief and moved to the banks of the Mississinewa and built the little settlement of his own family. She forbade Ewing to tell her story because, with her Indian belief in the power of the white man, she feared that her relatives would force her to return to them. He assured her that she would be safe, and immediately set about to locate her brothers.

Not knowing where to inquire, he wrote his strange story to the postmaster at Lancaster, Pennsylvania, who considered the tale too vivid and threw the letter aside. It was found two years later by his successor. Frances' brothers and sister were finally located and in 1837—all then over 60 years of age—they started on their last search. The meeting was embarrassing. Ma-con-a-qua received them with typical Indian indifference and calm. They identified her by her hair and a maimed finger and told her the circumstances of her kidnapping and the history of her family. She was interested, but stolid. As neither could understand the other's language, the conversation was carried on through an interpreter. Eventually the constraint wore off and she visited them at the Bearss Hotel in Peru. She was glad enough to see them but would not consider even visiting Pennsylvania with them, fearing, since she was very old, that she might not live to return to the land along the Mississinewa so that she might be buried with her husband and sons. She finished her life here, respected and beloved, and died March 9, 1847.

In JALAPA, 21.3 *m.* (736 alt., 100 pop.), the Slocum Trail turns east (L) and crosses the Mississinewa River.

On the MISSISSINEWA BATTLEFIELD (L), 21.8 *m.*, the Miami made their last fighting stand as a nation on December 18, 1812. When it became evident that the Miami were being incited to hostilities against the white settlers, General Harrison sent Colonel Campbell to attack and destroy their villages on the Mississinewa. Campbell was cautioned that no harm should come to any of the relatives of Little Turtle or any of the Godfroys, as these two families had always been friendly to the United States.

After destroying villages and stores of provisions, the army moved up the Mississinewa to the camp site near Jalapa, planning to continue along the river to its junction with the Wabash, destroying settlements on the way. Before daylight the following morning the camp was attacked by more than 300 Miami braves who had gathered during the night, and the Battle of the Mississinewa was fought in the cold and snow of early dawn. Colonel Campbell estimated that about 30 Indians were killed, and that his force lost 8 men, with 48 wounded. The officers thought it best to return to Ohio immediately, as they feared another attack. Thus the heroic resistance of the Miami protected their homes, but the campaign struck terror into the hearts of the Indians and prevented them from taking any further active part in the War of 1812. The Indian attack was so ably directed that Campbell thought that the great Tecumseh was in command, but it later developed that the commanding chief was Francis Godfroy.

At 23.7 m. is the junction with paved State 15, now the route, called the Slocum Trail between this point and Marion.

Right on State 15 to the junction with State 9 (see Tour 14) at MARION, 28.9 m. (852 alt., 26,767 pop.) (see Tour 14).

Section b.   PERU to ILLINOIS LINE, 80.3 m.

West of the rolling Wabash River country, the landscape along the route is level to the point of monotony, relieved only by heavily wooded skylines and well-kept, productive farms. The rich black soil makes for an abundance of vegetation, and wild flowers and vines are profuse during the spring and summer. Fields thick with black-eyed Susans, buttercups, and cowslips give color to the flat landscape, and wild roses and honeysuckle climb the fences along the highway.

West from PERU, 0 m., US 24 and US 31 (see Tour 16) coincide for two miles.

At 11.4 m. is the junction with the Adamsboro Road. Opposite, in the Wabash River, is Cedar Island (L), part of the Logansport Country Club.

Right on this road is ADAMSBORO, 2 m. (658 alt., 60 pop.). From Adamsboro the Eel River road leads, 1.9 m., to the SITE OF 'OLD TOWN,' called Kenapocomaqua in the days when it was a rendezvous for Indian bands that made constant war on the whites. So menacing was this concentration of hostile Indians that President Washington sent General Wilkinson with 525 mounted men to destroy the village. Wilkinson captured the town on August 7, 1791, razed it, and laid waste to 430 acres of growing corn (see History).

LOGANSPORT, 16.2 m. (617 alt., 20,177 pop.), at the confluence of the Wabash and the Eel Rivers, was in the early days a trading post of the Indians and white settlers. Today it is an attractive and progressive small Midwestern city. Because all entrances into the municipality are made across one of the several waterways, Logansport is called the 'City of Bridges.'

At 3rd and Ottawa Sts. is the SITE OF CAMP LOGAN, occupied in 1861 by the 46th Indiana Infantry Regiment, commanded by Colonel G. M. Fitch of Logansport. LOG PIONEER INN, Cicott St. and Cliff Drive, was built in 1828 by Alexander Chamberlain, the first permanent settler and tavern keeper; it is now weatherboarded. At the NE. corner of 17th and Market Sts. is the former HOME OF FREDERICK LANDIS (1872–1934), Hoosier lecturer, writer, newspaperman, and congressman, and brother of Kenesaw Mountain Landis, 'czar' of baseball.

On BIDDLE'S ISLAND, 3rd and Gate Sts., is the beautiful BIDDLE MANSION (private), purchased from General John Tipton by Judge

Horace Biddle (1811–1900), jurist, writer, illustrator, and painter. The central section of the house is one and a half stories, with dormer windows and a Georgian portico, flanked by one-story wings. In the yard, at the foot of one of the great elm trees that shade the house, is the GRAVE OF NO'KAMENA, a Miami chieftain. Judge Biddle permitted the Indian to be buried on this spot because it was the chief's early home site.

Logansport is at the junction with US 35 (*see Tour* 17), which unites westward with US 24 for 1.9 miles.

1. Right (southwest) from Logansport on State 25 is (R) the LOGANSPORT STATE HOSPITAL (Longcliff), 2.5 *m.*, one of five State-supported institutions for persons suffering with mental disease. The capacity of the hospital is 690 men and 650 women.

2. Left (southwest) from Logansport on State 25 to ROCKFIELD, 14 *m.* (650 alt., 300 pop.), a thriving rural community noted as a center of co-operatives. Following the organization of telephone and grain elevator co-operatives, the Farmer's Co-operative Breeding Association was formed in 1915 and the first act of the group was the purchase of 'Long Chief,' a grand champion Poland China boar. This boar sired 'Evolution,' which later sold for $25,000, a record price. A litter of seven sired by 'Evolution' sold for $9,500 at the age of four months. These prices focused attention of breeders throughout the Nation upon Rockfield, and also gave great local impetus to co-operatives. Since this success, co-operative grocery, drygoods, hardware, and farm implement stores have been organized; all are operating successfully and paying steady dividends.

DELPHI, 20 *m.* (555 alt., 2,213 pop.), seat of Carroll County, was an important port of call in the days of the old Wabash and Erie Canal. The town presents a conspicuously neat and orderly appearance with its small, square brick business buildings and comfortable residences.

On the north side of Main Street, about 130 feet east of the corporation line, is a marker designating the SITE OF THE CABIN OF SAMUEL MILROY (1780–1845), a member of the State Constitutional Convention of 1816, and a leader in the organization of the county. It was Milroy who suggested the name of Delphi to the county commissioners and sold the first lots in 1828.

Across Deer Creek, at the southern edge of town, is RILEY DAM, named for James Whitcomb Riley (*see Tour 8a*), who spent many hours fishing near the spot. The dam, constructed with funds obtained by public subscription, was completed in July 1930. It was here that Riley got his inspiration for the poem, 'On the Banks o' Deer Creek.' RILEY PARK (*public bathhouses*) is a 20-acre recreation area extending from the pool to a high bluff to the south.

AMERICUS, 27 *m.* (550 alt., 85 pop.), is a tiny survival of a great dream. When it was laid out in 1832 by William Digby, founder of LaFayette, it was the western terminus of the Wabash and Erie Canal, and gave promise of being the county's principal town. Diversion of the canal by way of LaFayette led to virtual abandonment of the town-building project, and the community has remained an unimportant trading center for farmers.

LaFAYETTE, 37 *m.* (540 alt., 28,798 pop.) (*see Tour 18b*), is at the junction with US 52 (*see Tour 18*).

LAKE CICOTT (pronounced Si-cot), 25 *m.* (575 alt., 75 pop.), is a country village on the edge of the only lake in Cass County. From the bed of the lake, which covers 100 acres and is 65 feet deep, about 2,000 carloads of sand are taken annually.

In BURNETTSVILLE, 28.6 *m.* (711 alt., 436 pop.), the FIRST NORMAL SCHOOL IN INDIANA and the fifth such school in the United

States was opened in 1852 by Isaac Mahurin. It closed in 1863 when the Union Army claimed most of its students. The old brick building, now used for storage, is at West Street and US 24.

MONTICELLO, 38.2 *m.* (678 alt., 3,153 pop.), seat of White County, is principally a resort town (*fishing, boating, and swimming; good accommodations*) on the Tippecanoe River between Shafer Lake and Freeman Lake. These lakes, formed by power dams built across the Tippecanoe River by the Indiana Hydroelectric Power Company, are among the most popular summer resorts in Indiana.

1. Right on Main St. to a fork in the road, 2.1 *m.*, R. from this fork to NORWAY DAM, 2.5 *m.*, built in 1923, which generates electric power for the surrounding country. The 1,200-foot dam backs up the waters of the Tippecanoe for 10 miles, forming the 1,400-acre SHAFER LAKE, and furnishes hydroelectric power for more than 100 communities with a combined population of 110,000. Left from the fork of the road is IDEAL BEACH, 5.1 *m.* (*cottages, hotel, restaurants, dancing pavilion*), recreational center of Shafer Lake and a favorite spot for campers and fishermen. This resort has a large sanitary beach where the water changes every 30 minutes.

2. Left from Monticello on State 39 to a junction with a graveled road, 7 *m.;* R. here to the 2,800-acre FREEMAN LAKE, 8.4 m. (*cabins, restaurant; black and silver bass fishing*). OAKDALE DAM, a third of a mile long, backs up the river to form the lake, and to develop hydroelectric power. It was completed in 1925.

WOLCOTT, 54.6 *m.* (714 alt., 736 pop.), is the self-styled 'Biggest Little City in the World.'

In REMINGTON, 60.7 *m.* (731 alt., 869 pop.), are the PEONY FARMS (*open*), two blocks (L) from the southern end of Main Street, founded in 1900 by Walter L. Gumm.

Right (north) from Remington on State 53 is ST. JOSEPH COLLEGE, 10 *m.*, a Roman Catholic high school and junior college for men, founded in 1891. About 300 students are enrolled (1939–40). Across the highway is a mission-type three-story, brick structure that once housed ST. JOSEPH'S INDIAN NORMAL SCHOOL, closed in 1896. In 1887 Miss Catherine Drexel, of a wealthy Philadelphia family, gave money for the purchase of a 420-acre tract and for the erection of the building.

At 11 *m.* is the MONNETT SCHOOL FOR GIRLS, an elementary school founded in 1903 and maintained by the Methodist Episcopal Church of Rensselaer. The school accommodates 40 pupils.

RENSSELAER, 12 *m.* (664 alt., 3,214 pop.), seat of Jasper County, is a residential town and a trading center for a prosperous farming area. At the entrance to MEMORIAL PARK, on the opposite side of the Iroquois River from the business district, is a bronze STATUE OF GENERAL ROBERT HOUSTON MILROY, veteran of the Mexican and Civil Wars. When Fort Sumter was fired on, Milroy recruited a company of Indiana volunteers and was made its captain. At Winchester, Virginia, men under Milroy's command held back Robert E. Lee's troops for three days when the Confederate general began operations to invade Pennsylvania. After the war Milroy became a trustee of the Wabash and Erie Canal and later superintendent of Indian affairs at Olympia, Washington.

In the Presbyterian churchyard, Cullen and Cornelia Sts., is the GRAVE OF JAMES VAN RENSSELAER, a Utica, New York, merchant who founded the town in 1837 and operated the community gristmill.

At 36 *m.* the route crosses the Kankakee River, over which La Salle and other early explorers and missionaries made their way westward from the portage at South Bend, through the Illinois country and on down the Mississippi (*see South Bend*). Much of the valley of the Kankakee, once a great marsh, has been drained and now is farmed, but wild game still finds refuge in this area (*see Tour* 4).

CROWN POINT, 52 *m.* (701 alt., 4,643 pop.), is the seat of Lake County, which includes the industrial cities of the Calumet—East Chicago, Hammond, Whiting, and Gary. It is prosperous and independent, refusing to be absorbed by the larger industrial centers. Many of Crown Point's citizens are retired farmers or business people and their houses and landscaped gardens make the town attractive. Most of the large hickory trees that shade the streets were here prior to the founding of the town by Solon Robinson, who came from Connecticut in 1834. A marker in the courthouse yard points out the SITE OF THE SOLON ROBINSON CABIN. Robinson, earliest resident of Crown Point and Lake County's first justice of the peace, built the original courthouse where the present one now stands. The community was first known as Robinson's Prairie, but when Robinson earned the sobriquet 'King of the Squatters' by saving his neighbor's lands from scheming speculators, it was renamed Crown Point—'crown' for the 'king' and 'point' for the elevation on which his cabin and courthouse stood. As a prolific contributor of articles to New York newspapers, Robinson attracted many Easterners to his new town. He left Crown Point in 1849 to become agricultural editor of the New York *Tribune*, then under the editorship of Horace Greeley. While on the *Tribune's* staff he also operated an experimental farm at East Yonkers, New York, where he demonstrated his agricultural theories.

The LAKE COUNTY JAIL, one block south of the courthouse, is almost hidden behind the home of the county sheriff. From this jail John Dillinger, once Public Enemy No. 1, escaped to resume a campaign of terror that claimed the lives of several law enforcement officers before his death in Chicago, July 22, 1934, at the hands of Federal agents. Dillinger escaped by using a wooden gun he had whittled in his cell. With this spurious weapon, he forced the turnkey to release him and a Negro prisoner, and fled in a commandeered automobile.

LAKE COUNTY FAIRGROUNDS, south end of Court Street (*open; camping and picnicking grounds; zoo*), is a beautiful natural park with spring-fed FANCHER LAKE in its center and with wooded hills forming a natural amphitheater. The grounds include a dirt race track. Modern brick buildings house the exhibits of the annual Lake County Fair, one of the most successful of Indiana's fall fairs.

At 56 *m.* is the junction with US 30 (*see Tour* 4).

In KENTLAND, 76.3 *m.* (680 alt., 1,608 pop.), the county seat of Newton County, is an unusually large WHOLE MILK CHEESE FACTORY, one block south of the business district. The BIRTHPLACE OF GEORGE ADE, opposite the courthouse, on E. Graham St., is now (1941) used as a doctor's office. After graduation from Purdue University, Ade (b.1866), Hoosier author, humorist, and playwright, began newspaper work in LaFayette. He turned then to the Chicago *Record* where his column, 'Stories of the Streets and Town,' furnished the background that served him in his later literary works. He is probably best known for his *Fables in Slang*, excellent examples of his style of satirical humor. Some of his plays are *The County Chairman, The College Widow,* and *The Fair Co-ed*. Ade lives on a country estate in the Iroquois River Valley near Brook (*see Tour 20a*).

Kentland is at the junction with US 41 (*see Tour* 20).

At EFFNER, 80.3 *m.* (676 alt., 20 pop.), US 24 crosses the Illinois Line, two miles east of Sheldon, Illinois (*see Illinois Guide*).

Tour 6

(Greenville, Ohio)—Muncie—Anderson—Crawfordsville; State 32. Ohio Line to Crawfordsville, 122.6 m.

Concrete roadbed interspersed with short sections of brick between Ohio Line and Farmland; asphalt between Farmland and Muncie; concrete between Muncie and Noblesville; oil mat to Crawfordsville.
Cleveland, Cincinnati, Chicago & St. Louis R.R. parallels the route between the Ohio Line and Anderson; Central Indiana R.R. between Anderson and Lebanon.
Accommodations of all kinds at short intervals.

State 32 traverses a rich, flat farming region with soil composed of glacial drift—a closely intermingled mixture of clay, sand, and gravel. The farmsteads along the eastern part of the route are large and well kept. The highway passes the Chesterfield Spiritualist Camp, one of the largest in the Nation, and Mounds State Park, once an important center for the Mound Builders in the Mississippi Valley. The only large industrial centers are Muncie and Anderson, in the former natural-gas belt. In its western section the route crosses a countryside that becomes gradually rougher and more wooded.

State 32, a continuation of Ohio 71, crosses the Ohio Line at UNION CITY, 0 m. (1,111 alt., 3,535 pop.), 12 miles northwest of Greenville, Ohio. Union City straddles the State Line, with three-quarters of its population on the Indiana side. It has several industries, among them furniture, carriage, and trunk manufacturing plants, and is a shipping point for produce and livestock brought in from surrounding farms.

The ISAAC PUSEY GRAY HOUSE (*visitors welcome*), 305 N. Union St. on the Indiana side, is a two-story, 12-room red brick house, erected in 1870 and occupied by the builder until 1890. Gray (1828-95) was governor of Indiana from 1885 to 1889.

At 4.7 m. is the junction with a blacktop road, formerly the QUAKER TRACE. Opened in 1817 by a group of 25 or 30 early settlers, the trace extended from Richmond to Fort Wayne and was the first road through Randolph County. Its name is derived from the fact that it was used extensively by the Quakers who settled here and later became active in helping slaves to escape.

WINCHESTER, 10.2 m. (1,087 alt., 5,303 pop.) (*see Tour 13*), is at the junction with US 27 (*see Tour 13*).

The JAMES A. MOORMAN ORPHANS HOME (*open*), 12.4 m., was established in 1888 from a trust fund created by the will of James A. Moorman. A lane passes under a stone gateway (R) flanked by red barberry and evergreens to the large square red brick house of 40 rooms. The landscaped grounds consist of 160 acres. This is a privately supported institution where Randolph County orphans live without charge to the county.

At 18.4 *m.* is the junction with State 1.

Left on State 1 to the junction with a blacktop road, 4 *m.;* L. on the blacktop road is UNIONPORT, 5.6 *m.* (1,054 alt., 85 pop.), a cluster of unpainted houses and barns. On a slight elevation (R), is the former HOME OF ELIZABETH MARINE (*visitors welcome*), mother of James Whitcomb Riley. It was here that Reuben Riley came to court the girl who later became the mother of Indiana's best-loved poet. The house is a two-story, tin-roofed, unpainted structure. The lower floor formerly housed a general store, and the second story was used as living quarters. It is now a residence.

FARMLAND, 19.1 *m.* (1,040 alt., 914 pop.), and PARKER CITY, 24.6 *m.* (850 alt., 786 pop.), are trading towns, the latter a 'Saturday night' town. Deserted during most of the week, its streets and stores are filled with shoppers, farmers, and residents on Saturday afternoons and nights.

At 29.6 *m.* is the DELAWARE COUNTY INFIRMARY (R), a well-kept institution set in 193 acres of farm land. This modern infirmary is an evolution from the neglected 'poor farm' of other days. Although nearly all Indiana counties still provide infirmaries, the trend since the passage of the Federal and State Social Security Acts in 1936 has been to maintain the indigent aged in their own homes through the payment of old-age assistance benefits.

Wide-spreading farms on either side of the highway produce great quantities of wheat, oats, and corn. Grains in Delaware County are harvested by old-fashioned, high-wheeled steam engines, rarely seen in other parts of Indiana. During the threshing season these machines, with grain separators attached, chug complacently along the roads, indifferent to the demands of swifter traffic.

MUNCIE, 34.6 *m.* (947 alt., 49,720 pop.) (*see Muncie*).

Muncie is at the junction with US 35 (*see Tour 17b*).

Between Muncie and Anderson the highway is the improved OLD GOVERNMENT ROAD along White River, built in 1821 to facilitate transportation of the Delaware Indians to reservations west of the Mississippi.

DALEVILLE, 45.2 *m.* (916 alt., 100 pop.), a trading point for farmers, was laid out in 1838 with the expectation that a canal would be built through its site and a feeder dam constructed. The canal failed, but a railroad built in 1852 revived the sleepy town for a time.

In CHESTERFIELD, 48.5 *m.* (900 alt., 581 pop.), is the CHESTERFIELD SPIRITUALIST CAMP (*adm.* 10¢; *free camping and parking space; hotel rates $5 single, $9 double rooms, weekly; cottages, $8 to $10 per week*), second largest enterprise of this sort in the United States. The camp was founded in 1890 by Dr. J. Westerfield of Anderson and a group of his followers. Each year from July 15 to September 1 thousands of persons from all parts of the Nation come here to attend spiritualist meetings and to hear the doctrine of Spiritualism expounded.

The camp buildings include two modern hotels, one of 180 rooms and the other of 74 rooms; an auditorium with a seating capacity of 3,000 persons; a cafeteria; and 75 summer cottages. Ten of the 34 acres of grounds are reserved for free camping and parking for those who come to attend the meetings.

At 50.3 *m.* is MOUNDS STATE PARK (*adm.* 10¢; *hiking trails, riding horses, picnicking facilities*), given to the Indiana Department of Conservation in 1930 by the people of Madison County. The park (R) covers 251 acres of rolling woodlands extending from the highway to a bluff above the White River.

In the park area, once an important center for that little known and vanished race, the Mound Builders (*see Archeology*), is the largest single earthwork in Indiana. It is 9 feet high, 1,200 feet in circumference, 384 feet in diameter, and excellently preserved. Surrounding it are evidences of 10 other mounds, some of which have been almost obliterated. A rare 'fiddle back' mound was nearly destroyed when the area was used as an amusement park and a merry-go-round spun giddily upon the ancient earthworks. A highway was cut through another mound.

At the peak of their culture the vanished Mound Builders engaged in agriculture, hunting, and pearl fishing, mined copper and flint, and manufactured pottery. Their copper mines are believed to have been located in Michigan, on the shores of the Great Lakes. The metal was transported considerable distances and hammered into warriors' breastplates, royal headdresses, and ceremonial objects. Art designs included the swastika, the doubleheaded eagle, and conventional designs of snake heads. This ancient people used flint for weapons and for household and agricultural tools.

At 51.2 *m.* is the junction with the graveled Range Line Road.

Right on this road to a junction with a concrete road, 1.1 *m.;* L. here to the MORAVIAN MISSION MONUMENT (L), 1.7 *m.* The mission was three-fourths of a mile south of the monument, across a field, on the north bank of White River. It was here that a Moravian missionary from Pennsylvania, John P. Kluge, with his wife and a little band of Indian converts, established a mission in the summer of 1801. For five years they labored, enduring more than the ordinary privations of pioneer life. By their simple faith and humble, helpful ways they entered into Indian life more deeply perhaps than any of the other missionaries. With true Moravian zeal Kluge and his wife gradually brought about conversion of many Delaware Indians, including the chief, Ta-ta-pach-sit. When Ta-ta-pach-sit was burned at the stake at the insistence of the Prophet (*see Tour 17b*) and several other converts were killed, the missionaries realized that their work was likely to bring only death or ruin to their followers; upon the advice of their superiors, they withdrew in the fall of 1806.

ANDERSON, 54 *m.* (885 alt., 41,572 pop.), lying among low glacial hills on the south bank of White River, is the seat of Madison County and occupies the site of an old Delaware Indian village. It takes its name from Chief Kikthawenund, whose English name was Captain Anderson. Its situation above great pockets of natural gas gave the city its chance for industrial development.

Many obsolete structures, relics of the gas boom, still stand on Main Street. Upper floors are used for small offices and most of the street floors have been converted into storerooms. The courthouse square is lined with small shops, restaurants, and clothing stores. Meridian Street, south of the square, is modern and progressive in appearance.

In 1937, according to the U. S. Census of Manufactures, 13,883 wage earners were employed in 62 factories, producing automobile ignition systems, storage batteries, headlamps, wire fencing, corrugated shipping containers, pottery, glassmaking machinery, stoves, tile, and many other articles.

The original site of Anderson was held by William Conner before the establishment of Madison County. He sold it to John Berry, who platted the town in 1823 and four years later conveyed a part of it to the county as an inducement to make it the seat of government.

During the first 10 years of its existence the growth of Andersontown, as it was then called, was slow; in 1837 the population was about 200. In that year, however, a system of internal improvements was begun throughout the State. The Indiana Central Canal, a branch of the Wabash and Erie Canal, was to extend from Logansport to Indianapolis, passing near Andersontown. Settlers flocked to the young community. When Andersontown was incorporated in 1838 it had 350 inhabitants. Then came news of the abandonment of work on the canal. The population soon began to decline and the town surrendered its incorporation, remaining a village until 1853, a year after the establishment of an Indianapolis and Bellefontaine Railroad station at Anderson, as the settlement was renamed. In 1868 a company was formed to build the canal as a private project, stock was sold, and contracts let. The canal was opened on July 4, 1874, but as soon as it was filled with water the banks collapsed in several places. It was repaired and again filled, and again the banks caved in. After an expenditure of some $80,000 on repairs, the property was sold to satisfy judgments.

Anderson had been incorporated as a city in 1865. A municipally-owned water plant was installed in 1886, and the discovery of gas the same year ushered in a boom (*see Labor and Industry*). Within two years, 37 factories sprang up, lured by the apparently inexhaustible supply of fuel. In a decade the boom was over, and the city returned to a less spectacular expansion.

The automotive industry has been the chief factor in the later growth of the city. By 1916 Anderson had 24,000 inhabitants; in 1920, after General Motors acquired the Remy Electric Company here, the population was 29,797. On December 31, 1936, members of the United Auto Workers of America called a sitdown strike in the Guide Lamp unit, and operations ceased in all General Motors plants in Anderson. During the ensuing tension Governor Townsend declared martial law, sent in the National Guard, and suspended the right of public assembly. Work was resumed on the basis of a Nation-wide agreement that granted the workers the right to bargain collectively.

Within a week after settlement of the strike the Anderson plants were running at capacity and employing 11,500 persons.

The GUIDE LAMP CORPORATION PLANT (*open 9–5 weekdays; guides*), 25th St. and Arrow Ave., manufactures automobile headlights, pilot lights, fender lights, marker and dome lights. The corporation employs about 3,000 persons in its Anderson offices and factory.

The DELCO-REMY CORPORATION PLANT (*open 9–5 weekdays; guide*), 25th St. and Columbus Ave., consists of five plants covering six city blocks. Delco-Remy, a subsidiary of General Motors, manufactures all types of distributors, generators, starting motors, and other electrical equipment for General Motors cars, and for many others. This factory was established in 1895, when Frank L. and B. Perry Remy developed an ignition system for marine and stationary engines and then turned their attention to automotive ignition. The company grew rapidly and in 1919 was sold to General Motors, who continued its expansion. About 10,000 persons are employed.

The SITE OF CHIEF ANDERSON'S CABIN, 9th and Fletcher Sts., on the grounds of the Pennsylvania Railroad Station, is marked by a large boulder. Kikthawenund (Captain Anderson) was the best known and most influential of the Delaware chiefs. He was not unfriendly toward the whites, and his daughter, Oneahye, or Dancing Feather, was married to a white settler. When Tecumseh visited Kikthawenund to enlist the support of his tribe in a last stand against the white advance, the old Delaware opposed the ill-fated venture.

ATHLETIC PARK (*open daily; free*), 8th St. and White River, includes the fairgrounds and has stables for 150 horses. The grandstand seats 4,500 persons, and the half-mile track is lighted to permit night racing. In the infield of the racetrack are a football field and two baseball diamonds. Within the park, at the East 8th Street entrance, is the municipal swimming pool.

ANDERSON COLLEGE AND THEOLOGICAL SEMINARY (*open Mon.-Fri., Sept.-June*), 5th St. and Union Ave., occupies a large four-story concrete building formerly housing employees of a publishing house of the Church of God, the denomination controlling the college. The school was established in 1917 as the Anderson Bible Training School and became a coeducational college of liberal arts in 1929. The (1939–40) enrollment was 355 students from 35 states and four foreign countries.

The GOSPEL TRUMPET COMPANY PLANT (*open 9–5 weekdays*), 5th St. and Union Ave., said to be the largest religious publishing plant in the United States, is sponsored by the nonsectarian Church of God. Anderson is the national headquarters of this religious organization.

Anderson is at the junction with State 9 (*see Tour 14*).

EDGEWOOD, 58 m. (880 alt., 229 pop.), is a restricted residential suburb inhabited mainly by executives of manufacturing plants in Anderson.

NOBLESVILLE, 73.3 m. (801 alt., 5,575 pop.), seat of Hamilton County, was founded in 1823 by William Conner, Indian trader and the county's first settler. Hamilton County is widely known as a breeding center of pure-bred Percheron and Belgian draft horses.

West of the courthouse, across White River and one-eighth mile north is FOREST PARK AND TOURIST CAMP (R), a forested camp of 149 acres (*community buildings, dance and concert hall, log cabins, tennis and horseshoe courts, baseball diamond, and children's playground*).

1. Right from Noblesville on State 13 is CLARE, 5 *m*. (800 alt., 90 pop.), a summer resort town on the east bank of the White River. At the southern edge of the community is the CONCRETE DAM of a generating plant owned by the Northern Indiana Power Company.

At 7.5 *m*. is STRAWTOWN (780 alt., 75 pop.), named for Chief Straw of the Delaware, whose village was on this site. A monument of boulders and concrete has been erected in his memory at the north edge of town.

Left from Strawtown on a concrete road is CICERO, 11.7 *m*. (837 alt., 943 pop.), named for a Delaware chief of that name. The town is largely inhabited by Seventh-Day Adventists, who maintain an academy one mile north.

2. Left from Noblesville on State 13 is the WILLIAM CONNER HOMESTEAD (R), 4.7 *m*. In 1818, Conner opened a trading post here in one part of his double log cabin. Both he and his brother John, founder of Connersville (*see Tour 18a*), had been captured by Indians when young and were reared as members of the tribe. Both had Indian wives. William Conner became a prominent citizen of Indiana and State senator from Hamilton County. When in January 1820 a commission of ten men was appointed by Governor Jennings to select a site for the new State capital (*see History*), the commission met at Conner's trading post and spent some time looking over this section before finally deciding on the present site of Indianapolis.

The two-story, red brick house (*obtain visiting permit from Eli Lilly, Indianapolis*), built in 1823, stands at the end of a long driveway lined with Lombardy poplars and occupies the site of the trading post. In 1935 Mr. Lilly purchased the estate and furnished the house approximately as it was in the days when Conner occupied it. On the halltree near the door hang a coonskin cap, a quilted bonnet, and an old plaid shawl.

WESTFIELD, 79.7 *m*. (901 alt., 709 pop.) (*see Tour 16a*), is at the junction with US 31 (*see Tour 16*). JOLIETVILLE, 85.3 *m*. (920 alt., 100 pop.), is a country village set in a level farming area where there are many gravel deposits.

At 88.3 *m*. is the junction with State 29 (*see Tour 17A*).

LEBANON, 98.5 *m*. (900 alt., 6,529 pop.) (*see Tour 18b*), is at the junction with US 52 (*see Tour 18*).

Between SHANNONDALE, 111.4 *m*. (850 alt., 50 pop.), and CRAWFORDSVILLE, 122.6 *m*. (800 alt., 11,089 pop.) (*see Tour 8A*), the countryside gradually becomes rougher and more forested. At Crawfordsville is the junction with State 34 (*see Tour 8A*).

Tour 7

(Greenville, Ohio)—Pendleton—Indianapolis—Danville—Rockville—
(Newman, Ill.); US 36.
Ohio Line to Illinois Line, 157 *m*.

Narrow highway with short intermittent stretches of oil mat between Ohio
Line and junction with State 67; three- and four-lane concrete roadbed to
Indianapolis; two-lane concrete remainder of route.
Cleveland, Cincinnati, Chicago & St. Louis R.R. roughly parallels the route be-
tween Ohio Line and Mooreland, and between Pendleton and Danville.
Accommodations of all kinds at short intervals.

US 36, cutting through the heart of central Indiana, crosses a glacial
plain that is part of the rich Indiana corn belt. The highway, which
misses most of the industrial cities, runs for mile after mile past prosperous farms and through small towns that are agricultural trading
centers. East of Indianapolis the land is predominantly flat, while to
the westward it is gently rolling with a few low hills; but throughout
the tour the general impression is of quiet, level country cut by placid
streams.

Section a. OHIO LINE to INDIANAPOLIS, 82 m.

The eastern half of the route crosses a countryside given over to
general purpose farming. There are no large towns between the Ohio
Line and Indianapolis. Near Pendleton rise the high brick walls of one
of the State's two penal institutions for male felons, and northeast of
Indianapolis is Fort Benjamin Harrison, a United States Army post.

US 36 crosses the OHIO LINE, 0 *m*., 13 miles west of Greenville,
Ohio.

LYNN, 7 *m*. (1,162 alt., 1,014 pop.), laid out in 1847, prospered
after the Indianapolis to Bellefontaine railroad was completed in 1852.
It is now a quiet trading center for farmers.

In Lynn is the junction with US 27 (*see Tour* 13).

MOORELAND, 27 *m*. (1,000 alt., 496 pop.), a rural town with a
grain elevator and a bank as its main enterprises, was named for Philip
Moore, one of its first settlers. A row of soft maple trees lines the highway for a quarter of a mile at the northern entrance to the town.

MOUNT SUMMIT, 34 *m*. (1,088 alt., 265 pop.), so named because
it occupies one of the higher elevations in Henry County, is surrounded
by hilly farm lands.

Left from Mount Summit on paved State 3, 3.3 *m.*, to the MONUMENT TO WILBUR WRIGHT (R), a propeller mounted on a stone base. Wilbur Wright, son of a Methodist minister, was born on a farm near New Castle, April 16, 1867. The family left Henry County for Dayton, Ohio, before Orville was born, and their former residence east of New Castle has since burned. Wilbur, with his brother Orville, was the first to fly in a heavier-than-air gasoline-engine-powered machine. Their first airplane was flown at Kitty Hawk, North Carolina, December 7, 1903.

NEW CASTLE, 5.6 *m.* (1,058 alt., 16,620 pop.), is a busy industrial city and the seat of Henry County. More than 300 products are manufactured by the city's 24 industrial enterprises (1937). The largest factories are those of the Chrysler Corporation, the Perfect Circle Company, and the Ingersoll Steel and Disc Company.

In the HENRY COUNTY HISTORICAL BUILDING (*open daily* 9–12, 1–4), 614 S. 14th St., are many pioneer relics, some of them dating back to the founding of the city in 1822.

At 51.9 *m.* is the junction with State 9 (*see Tour* 14), which unites with US 36 for two miles.

At 52.2 *m.* is the junction with State 38.

Right on paved State 38 is PENDLETON, 0.6 *m.* (850 alt., 1,681 pop.), a lively town with shady streets and attractive well-kept homes. FALLS PARK (*picnicking facilities; swimming pool*) is on Fall Creek within the city. Seventy-five feet north of the park pool is a MONUMENT marking the spot where three white men were hanged for the murder of a party of nine Indians in 1824. At that time Pendleton was the county seat, and many Indians stalked silently into the settlement to see a new kind of justice done. Although an uprising was feared, the Indians withdrew immediately after the execution, leaving as quietly as they had come. This was said to be the first time white men were hanged for the murder of Indians.

The INDIANA REFORMATORY (*limited visiting; obtain permission from warden*), 53.7 *m.*, is a State penal institution (R) for male convicts between the ages of 16 and 30, accommodating approximately 1,400 men. The State has invested about $4,000,000 in the 1,554 acres of land and in equipment and buildings, which include a library with 14,000 volumes, trade schools, cell houses, and officers' living quarters. Inmates attend classes in the School of Letters and are taught a useful trade, producing for the State sheet metal, job printing, brooms, cement products, uniforms, underclothing, mattresses, woven furniture, and foundry products.

FORTVILLE, 60 *m.* (863 alt., 1,463 pop.), was laid out in 1849 by Cephas Fort. In 1852 when the old Bee Line Railroad reached the town, Fortville merged with Walpole, a small settlement to the north, located at a point called Phoebe's Fort. The Grasselli Chemical Company has a branch plant here.

At 68.2 *m.* is the junction with the graveled Springer Road.

Right on this road is the MARION COUNTY TUBERCULOSIS SANATORIUM (*visitors welcome*), 0.7 *m.*, on a 75-acre tract (R) of rolling land. There are 12 buildings, and a staff of 4 physicians, 1 dentist, and 31 nurses. The average number of patients is 250, including men, women, and children. James Whitcomb Riley named the hospital 'Sunnyside.'

The SALVATION ARMY FRESH AIR CAMP (*visitors welcome; guide*), 1.7 *m.*, is a summer camp (L) for undernourished children and mothers. Each week

100 persons selected by Indianapolis welfare agencies are taken to the camp to enjoy fresh air, sunshine, and nourishing food. Expenses are borne by the Salvation Army.

The INLAND MUSHROOM COMPANY PLANT (*visitors welcome*), 69.9 *m.* (L), produces an average of 50,000 pounds of mushrooms yearly. The crop is marketed in Indianapolis, Chicago, and New York.

At 70.5 *m.* is the junction with the paved Post Road.

Right on the Post Road is FORT BENJAMIN HARRISON (*open to public*), 1 *m.*, a United States Army Post established in 1903. On the 2,030-acre reservation are located the Schoen Field airport, a hospital, the administration building, machine shops, fire-engine house, polo field, bakery, storehouse, guardhouse, a theater, CCC barracks, and a clubhouse and library. At present (1941), about 4,000 men, including 2,800 trainees, are stationed at Fort Harrison, which has a capacity of nearly 8,000. In addition, thousands of recruits under the Selective Service program are received here each month. In the Induction Station and Reception Center the selectees are given a physical examination and general classification test, interviewed to determine occupation, education, hobbies, and desires in respect to assignment, and provided with equipment and basic training. They are then transferred to various parts of the United States according to their occupational classification and the needs of the service.

At 72.7 *m.* on US 36 is the junction with Shadeland Avenue, a graveled road.

Right on Shadeland Avenue to WOOLLEN'S GARDENS (*open to public; no fishing permitted*), 2.5 *m.*, 45 acres (L) of hilly, densely wooded land along the banks of Fall Creek. There are two bird observatories, 15 bird houses, and a station where birds are banded for tracing migration and mating habits. Presented to the city of Indianapolis in 1909 by William Watson Woollen, an attorney, the gardens are used by schools and nature-study clubs.

INDIANAPOLIS, 82 *m.* (750 alt., 386,972 pop.) (*see Indianapolis*).

In Indianapolis are junctions with US 31 (*see Tour* 16), US 40 (*see Tour* 8), US 52 (*see Tour* 18), State 29 (*see Tour* 17A), State 37 (*see Tour* 19), and State 34 (*see Tour* 8A).

Section b. INDIANAPOLIS to ILLINOIS LINE, 75 m.

West of Indianapolis US 36 crosses a prosperous farming country, passes through Danville, seat of an 'abducted' college; and continues to the coal mining region in the hill land of Vermillion County on the State's western border.

DANVILLE, 20 *m.* (922 alt., 2,093 pop.), seat of Hendricks County, is a farming center and home of Central Normal College. Most of the town's business establishments, housed in old but well-preserved brick buildings, are grouped around the courthouse square. Danville is sometimes known as 'Gable Town' because many of its private and public buildings have gabled roofs. There are no industries, and the majority of the inhabitants are engaged in business enterprises, or in furnishing room and board to students of the college.

The first building within the present city limits of Danville was built in 1824. It was the cabin of Daniel Clark, early justice of the peace, for whom the town was named.

In the spring of 1878 Central Normal College at Ladoga, 22 miles northwest, was experiencing difficulty in finding lodgings for its growing student body. The townspeople hesitated, in the financial panic of that year, to erect new buildings. Danville wanted a college. Quick to recognize an opportunity, its citizens subscribed $10,000, bought the buildings of the old Danville Academy from the Methodist Church, and turned them over to Professor W. E. Harper of Central Normal College. Loath to lose its institution of higher learning, Ladoga promised free tuition and free lodging to the students for the duration of the emergency. Plans were laid to secure an injunction against the removal. But at four o'clock on the morning of May 10, 1878, a delegation of Hendricks County citizens, under the leadership of Moses Keeney, hitched up their carriages, buggies, spring wagons, and drays, and headed for Ladoga. When the half-mile-long cavalcade arrived there, the vehicles were backed up to the college building; desks, bookcases, and the library were loaded in and well on their way to Danville before citizens of Ladoga realized that the abduction had occurred. Professor Harper and Miss Dora Leuellen, members of the faculty, rode with Keeney behind his finest team of horses. Most of the male students traveled with the equipment, but 65 young coeds, their fares paid by Danville citizens, arrived by train to be met at the station with a brass band.

The old DANVILLE ACADEMY BUILDING, erected in 1829, still stands as the east wing of Recitation Hall on the CENTRAL NORMAL COLLEGE campus. The college enrolls approximately 650 students. Just east of the shaded campus and its five brick buildings is DANVILLE PARK (*ball park, tennis courts*), a 20-acre recreational spot.

Between BAINBRIDGE, 35 *m.* (933 alt., 414 pop.), and BELLMORE, 51 *m.* (670 alt., 320 pop.), the highway dips into the wooded valley of Raccoon Creek.

Bellmore is at the junction with paved State 59.

Left on State 59 is MANSFIELD, 5.5 *m.* (660 alt., 100 pop.), a quiet Hoosier village of old farmhouses. The little settlement has always been a mill town, and its OLD GRISTMILL is still powered by the waters of Big Raccoon Creek. Two hundred yards downstream from the mill, a 250-foot COVERED BRIDGE spans the creek.

The most exciting event in the history of the village occurred during the Civil War, although it had no connection with that epochal struggle. Husband and wife trouble it was—and aggravated by the village saloon. Disturbed to the point of rebellion by the conduct of their several husbands, the women organized, raided the village saloon, rolled barrels of whisky into the street, and emptied them. When another saloon was opened on the creek bank, the embattled women of Mansfield hired a farmer to hitch his ox team to the structure and drag it into the creek.

The INDIANA STATE SANATORIUM (*visiting hours* 11-1, 4-7 *daily*), 54 *m.* (R), for tubercular patients, has cured most of the 5,000 cases it has treated since its opening in 1911. Preference is given to patients with low incomes; there is also a low-cost out-patient department. A new (1937) hospital wing, built partly with WPA funds, gives the institution a capacity of 300 beds.

ROCKVILLE, 58 *m.* (677 alt., 2,208 pop.), is the county seat of Parke County. The large limestone courthouse in the center of the business district is the hub of the town and county activities. The population is chiefly retired farmers and professional people. The

A small, one-story building one block east of the square is the former LAW OFFICE OF JOSEPH A. WRIGHT, tenth governor of Indiana. Wright began his law practice here at the age of 20. He was elected governor in 1849, was re-elected in 1852, had a leading part in the second constitutional convention (1850–51), and is remembered as 'the farmer's friend.' Though Wright was not a farmer himself, it was through his influence that the act of 1851 'for the encouragement of agriculture' was passed. This measure provided for the organization of the board of agriculture, empowered to conduct the annual State Fair, and encouraged the organization of local agricultural societies.

In Rockville is the junction with US 41 (*see Tour* 20).

At 61.5 *m.* is the junction with a graveled road.

Right on this road is COLOMA, 0.8 *m.* (450 alt., 50 pop.); a Quaker village. Prior to the Civil War an Underground Railroad station was maintained just south of the village. The present FRIENDS MEETING HOUSE, a white frame structure, replaces an old log building that had a wooden partition to separate men and women at the services. Changed, too, is the old custom of silent worship that began and continued without a sound, and was considered ended when the leader arose after an hour or so, and shook hands with the man next to him.

At 64.5 *m.* is the junction with the LaFayette Road, a graveled road that was one of the main thoroughfares through western Indiana in pioneer times.

Left on this road to a large two-story red brick house (*private*), 0.6 *m.*, built on the SITE OF THE HOME OF CHRISTMAS DAZNEY (R). The land and the house were given the Indian chief by the Government for friendly services as interpreter and peacemaker. His marriage in 1819 to Mary Ann Isaacs was the first Christian marriage ceremony performed in Parke County. The Dazneys used the house only when they had visitors, living most of the time in a wigwam in the back yard.

ARMIESBURG, 1.1 *m.* (450 alt., 30 pop.), is a rural hamlet of a half-dozen houses on the north bank of Big Raccoon Creek. In the days of the Wabash & Erie Canal, Armiesburg—platted to be the county seat—was a town of considerable importance. At that time all flatboats on Big Raccoon, Little Raccoon, and Leatherwood Creeks came to Armiesburg to enter the canal. It is said that the army of General William Henry Harrison encamped in the small pasture just south of the village on the night of October 30, 1811, en route to the Battle of Tippecanoe (*see Tour* 18).

Right from Armiesburg on a dirt road is the junction with Big Raccoon Creek and the Wabash River, 2.1 *m.*, one terminus of the TEN O'CLOCK BOUNDARY LINE, established by the treaty of Fort Wayne in 1809 between Governor Harrison and the Miami and Delaware Indians. This boundary line extended southeasterly to a point near Vallonia in Jackson County (*see History*). According to tradition, it was called the Ten O'Clock Line because the Indians, knowing that the boundary, as negotiated, should run parallel to a shadow cast by the sun at 10 o'clock on September 30, 1809, and distrustful of the white man's surveying instruments, requested that it be so determined and designated.

MONTEZUMA, 65 *m.* (495 alt., 1,366 pop.), a rambling town on the east bank of the Wabash River, was in its heyday a commercial rival of LaFayette and Terre Haute. Its importance grew with the completion of the Wabash & Erie Canal in 1848 and ended with the coming of the railroads and the subsequent abandonment of the canal. There are several small brick and tile factories and a canning plant that employs some 200 persons in season.

Originally the site of an Indian village with wigwams stretching away to the southeast for two miles, Montezuma was named by the early white settlers for the last Aztec emperor of Mexico. The first of the settlers was Samuel Hill, who came West in 1821 at the age of 71, and built Montezuma's first house, a pretentious two-story log structure around which the town grew.

On Water Street, just north of the bridge over the old canal bed, is a two-story frame house (*private*), built in 1848 and known in canal days as the BRADY BOARDING HOUSE. The boarding house was operated by an Irish couple, John and Ann Brady. It is said that Mrs. Brady charged 25¢ for a night's lodging, but never turned a penniless traveler from the door, saying, 'He might be back sometime and pay me.'

US 36 crosses the ILLINOIS LINE, 75 *m.*, 24 miles east of Newman, Illinois (*see Illinois Guide*).

Tour 8

(Lewisburg, Ohio)—Richmond—Indianapolis—Terre Haute—(Marshall, Illinois); US 40.
Ohio Line to Illinois Line, 148.7 *m.*

Concrete roadbed throughout; two to four lanes.
Route paralleled by Pennsylvania R.R. and Transcontinental & Western Airlines.
Accommodations of all kinds at frequent intervals.

US 40 cuts across central Indiana, traversing the farming area between the southern hill country and the flat lands of the northern part of the State. In this fertile, gently undulating plain nearly every crop raised anywhere in Indiana is successfully cultivated, with the exception of tobacco and mint.

The highway is the Old National Road authorized by an act of

Congress in 1806 to stimulate settlement of the public lands in the West. The section first surveyed, from Cumberland, Maryland, to the Ohio River at Wheeling, West Virginia, was graveled by 1818. By 1835 the road had been completed to Columbus, Ohio. When in 1839 the Government turned the road over to the States, Indiana leased its part to a private company, which paved it with planks and collected toll until the planks were worn out. The road then became a public thoroughfare, and was graveled. One of the greatest wagon roads in the country, it passed through Indianapolis, becoming that city's main street and first improved thoroughfare. Today blinking beacon lights along its course mark the route of a later transportation system—a transcontinental airway.

Section a.   OHIO LINE to INDIANAPOLIS, 72 m.

The route runs through attractive Richmond, home of a large settlement of the Society of Friends, and Centerville, which resembles the towns of New England with its old-fashioned houses built close to the streets. It passes the birthplace of James Whitcomb Riley, the Hoosier poet; the 'old swimmin' hole' he made famous; the boyhood home of Charles A. Beard, well-known historian; and the biological laboratories of the Eli Lilly Company.

US 40 crosses the OHIO LINE, 0 m., 15 miles west of Lewisburg, Ohio. At 0.6 m. is the junction with US 35, which coincides with US 40 to Richmond.

RICHMOND, 4.1 m. (954 alt., 35,147 pop.), seat of Wayne County, is an industrial city of 60 factories, large and small. The value of their annual collective output is estimated at nearly $30,000,000. Richmond was founded in 1805 by soldiers who had been with George Rogers Clark at the capture of Fort Sackville (*see Vincennes*). Settlers were attracted by the fertility of the soil, and the village grew rapidly. In 1816, the year Indiana became a State, Richmond was platted as a town. A community of Quakers soon sprang up, and a large population of Friends still exists. They gave the town Earlham College and, by stoutly and publicly challenging Henry Clay to free his slaves, contributed locally to the political turbulence preceding the Civil War.

On October 1, 1842, Clay addressed a gathering of 20,000 Whigs here. (The site, corner of 7th and A Sts., is commemorated by a marker.) At the close of his speech, a petition that he free his slaves, signed by 2,000 Richmond Quakers, was handed him by Hiram Mendenhall, a leader in the sect. Clay answered the petition by declaring that while he looked on the institution of slavery as an evil, it was 'nothing in comparison with the far greater evil which would inevitably flow from a sudden and indiscriminate emancipation.' He said he owned about 50 slaves, worth about $15,000, and asked his hecklers if they would be willing, should he be induced to free them, to raise $15,000 for their benefit. As a parting shot at the bearer of the petition, Clay advised him to return to his home and attend to his own business. The incident, widely publicized in the hotly contested presidential election of 1844, may have contributed to Clay's defeat by Polk.

The HILL FLORAL PRODUCTS COMPANY PLANT (open), Easthaven Ave. and Peacock Road, is one of the largest greenhouses in the United States. Among its products are roses, chrysanthemums, and grafted rose plants. Under 1,250,000 square feet of glass the company has 525,000 rose and 45,000 gardenia plants. Two great electric turbines and one steam pump distribute water through a system capable of supplying a city. E. Gurney Hill (1847–1935), noted for his introduction of new roses into America, founded the business. During his long experiments he rejected as many as 16,000 rose plants from all parts of the world, often working years to develop a new shade or a more shapely bud. The Richmond Rose, a beautiful hybrid produced in 1905, opened the way to international horticultural prominence for Hill. More than 50 prizes, acknowledgments of his success, are on display in the company's offices.

In GLENN MILLER PARK, at the eastern edge of the city, are a MEMORIAL FOUNTAIN, built by the city in honor of E. Gurney Hill, and the MUNICIPAL GARDENS, with blue spruce trees planted by Hill. In the park also is RICHMOND'S PIONEER SCHOOLHOUSE, built in 1812.

The OLD HICKSITE FRIENDS' MEETING HOUSE (open), N. A St. between 11th and 12th Sts., contains a museum of historic relics. Among them is the UNDERGROUND RAILROAD STATION DOOR through which Eliza Harris of Uncle Tom's Cabin crawled into the garret of the Levi Coffin home in Fountain City (see Tour 13).

The movement to establish municipal art galleries in Indiana originated in 1898 with the organization of the Art Association of Richmond. Daniel G. Reid gave $500 a year to the project from 1903 to 1912. The GALLERY OF THE RICHMOND ART ASSOCIATION (open), third floor Morton High School, N. 9th and A Sts., was the first gallery to be placed in an Indiana high school. From this small beginning sprang the Richmond art movement (see Arts and Crafts). John E. Bundy (1853–1933) and William T. Eyden (1859–1919) were the best-known painters associated with this group, which includes William T. Eyden, Jr., George H. Baker, Maude Kaufman Eggemeyer, Marston Hodgin, and Carolyn Bradley. A fine color sense and sincere feeling for nature characterize the landscapes of Bundy and the elder Eyden— particularly their pictures of the now-vanishing beech trees of the Whitewater Valley. The permanent exhibit includes work by William Forsyth, Robert Grafton, William Chase, R. B. Gruelle, and John Bundy. The gallery is entered through an archway from a side wall. In a niche in the east wall of the hall is the TORTOISE FOUNTAIN, sculptured by Janet Scudder. The central figure is an undraped urchin standing above an eight-foot pool.

EARLHAM COLLEGE (L), at the western edge of the city, was founded in 1847 as the Friends' Boarding School and chartered by the State under its present name in 1859. The institution was the outgrowth of a movement begun in 1832 by the Society of Friends to establish a school that would oppose war and all forms of oppression. In 1853 Earlham began the first natural-history collection in Indiana, from which has developed its present MUSEUM. The school also had the first students' chemical laboratory in the State; today (1941) it has five well-equipped scientific laboratories. During the period 1933–9 the college developed rapidly, and enrollment rose to 477 in 1939. In the astronomical observatory, the first established in Indiana (1861), is the FORT SUMTER TRANSIT, in use at the time of the fort's surrender.

Among Earlham's distinguished alumni are Joseph G. Cannon, for ten years Speaker of the House of Representatives; William Penn Nixon, for many years managing editor of the *Chicago Inter-Ocean;* Achilles Unthank, civil engineer who supervised the construction of many public works in Asia and South America; and Dr. Walter Jessup, president of the Carnegie Foundation for the Advancement of Teaching.

Richmond is at the junction with US 27 (*see Tour* 13) and US 35 (*see Tour* 17).

Along the highway west of Richmond many old homes of white or blue-gray brick, some ivy-covered, stand as pleasant reminders of the past. GRAY GABLES (*private*), 10 *m.*, is a large gray brick structure (R) with a two-story porch. Built in 1822 as a tavern, the house is now (1941) a private home for the feeble-minded.

CENTERVILLE, 10.6 *m.* (969 alt., 1,162 pop.), is a town of fine old residences. Above the entrance to the OLD BRICK JAIL, now the Masonic Hall, northwest corner of 1st and Main Sts., two holes bear witness to the reluctance of Centervillians to hand over the seat of Wayne County to Richmond. On August 14, 1873, the county seat was transferred to Richmond and the Centerville citizens barricaded themselves in the old jail; they refused, until shots were fired into the structure, to turn the county records over to the city they never have forgiven.

The OLIVER P. MORTON HOUSE (*private*), at the western edge of town (L), is a two-story brick structure resting on a foundation of limestone plates. A marker states that the homestead was built in 1848; county records, however, indicate that it was built in 1842. The interior is finished in yellow poplar.

Morton began the practice of law in Centerville in 1846. Elected circuit judge in 1854, he resigned to study law in Cincinnati. He was one of the founders of the Republican party and in 1856 was the Republican nominee for governor of Indiana. In 1860 he was elected lieutenant governor on a ticket with Henry S. Lane. When Lane resigned to become United States senator, two days after he was sworn in, Morton succeeded him as governor and piloted Indiana through the difficult years of the Civil War. Morton was elected to the United States Senate in 1867 and re-elected in 1873, serving until his death in 1877.

The GEORGE W. JULIAN HOUSE (*open* 8:30–4 *weekdays*), 323 E. Main St., is a two-story gray brick structure now occupied by an antique shop. Built in the Georgian style in 1846, the house was later enlarged and remodeled; the changes—Italian Renaissance and Greek Revival—reflect the styles of the periods in which they were made. Julian was in Congress from 1849 to 1851. Keenly interested in homestead legislation, he was vice-presidential nominee for the Free Soil party in 1852. Again in Congress from 1861 to 1871, he presented in 1868 the first resolution for a woman-suffrage amendment. He was surveyor general of New Mexico (1885-9), and exposed Spanish land grant frauds in that Territory. He died in Irvington, Indiana, July 8, 1899.

The JOHN NIXON COLLECTION (*open upon application*), northeast corner of Main and 4th Sts., is housed in the owner's residence and includes more than 150 canvases by Indiana artists. There are also 46 books and pamphlets printed in Indiana before 1850, many Indiana newspapers printed prior to 1850, 500 almanacs from 1767 to 1880, an extensive collection of Overbeck pottery, and a large number of selected first editions.

The ivy-covered, red brick MISSES CONKLIN RESIDENCE (*private*), 18.3 *m.*, is just east of the bridge over the Whitewater River at Cambridge City. Built in 1839, the house has an unusually attractive doorway. The stairway and much of the furniture in the house were made by George Whitman, a well-known early Indiana craftsman.

CAMBRIDGE CITY, 19.8 *m.* (940 alt., 2,207 pop.), a prosperous town on the west fork of the Whitewater River, was founded in 1836 as a depot on the old Whitewater Canal (*see Tour 18b*). Even Indianapolis merchants received their goods at this place for a time, and large quantities of wheat were milled here. The VINTON HOUSE (L), a three-story red brick tavern on Main St., built at the side of the canal in 1847, still serves as the town's hotel. A high stone curbing keeps passers-by from falling from the sidewalk into the old canal bed. The OVERBECK POTTERY SHOP, Church and S. Pearl Sts., operated by three sisters, has handmade decorative ware and art pottery.

In the settlement of MOUNT AUBURN, 20.5 *m.* (1,000 alt., 145 pop.), is the three-story brick HUDDLESTON INN (*private*), a well-known hostelry of early days (L). The building is now used as a residence by descendants of the original owners.

DUBLIN, 21 *m.* (1,030 alt., 751 pop.), is a peaceful rural town with several interesting old houses. The largest of the remaining early buildings is THE MAPLES, a tavern, at the intersection of US 40 and Middletown St. Built of handmade brick in 1825, it was for many years one of the most popular inns on this section of the old National Road. The owner now operates a grocery store in connection with the tavern.

In the heyday of the tavern-studded Old National Road, 12 stage-coach lines operated over the highway. Only the finest Virginia horses were used on the better lines and the notes of the stagecoach bugle were as certain an index of the time of day as are passing transcontinental limited trains today. The arrival of a coach was an event, and coachmen were persons of consequence. To see the coach wheel up, stop while the driver absorbed a pint of ale and regaled onlookers with the latest news from the East as the horses were changed, and then break away at a 15-mile-an-hour clip, was a splendid sight.

Amanda Way called together the first woman's suffrage group in Indiana at her home in Dublin in 1851. The next year the Women's Rights Society was formed and soon afterward filed a petition with the Indiana General Assembly. The petition was referred to the Committee on Rights and Privileges, which reported that legislation on the subject 'is inexpedient at this time.' Then the Civil War came. Slaves were freed and given the right to vote, but woman suffrage remained 'inexpedient' until ratification of the Nineteenth Constitutional Amendment in 1919.

DUNREITH, 33.5 m. (1,000 alt., 187 pop.), is a village of frame houses clustered around the Pennsylvania Railroad station and a grain elevator.

Right from Dunreith on paved State 3 is SPICELAND, 2.2 m. (1,025 alt., 645 pop.), settled in 1828 by a group of Quakers from North Carolina. SPICELAND ACADEMY, on a site, L. on W. Main St., now occupied by grade and high school buildings erected in 1919, opened in 1834 and was for 80 years one of the most important secondary schools in the region. Among its alumni is Charles Austin Beard, noted historian. Of the academy, Dr. Beard wrote on the occasion of the village's centennial: 'Mrs. Hannah Davis reigned for a while after the death of her noble husband, Clarkson Davis. She seemed both omniscient and indefatigable. She traveled widely in Europe and brought back great news of strange lands. She loved good books. She organized lecture courses and gave us an opportunity to hear distinguished speakers. In her spirit and tradition Thomas Newlin carried on. He taught me the rudiments of American history and the elements of physics with equal proficiency, in my youthful eyes. John Parker taught us the Latin tongue and displayed so great a love of it that he could scarcely wait for us to learn the conjugation, so eager was he for us to read Cicero and Virgil.

'The academy had two debating societies and I was a member of one, the name of which I have forgotten. In the room set aside for us we had our library of choice books, and there on Friday nights we assembled to solve the burning problems of the hour. Work and meditation were broken by play according to the season. Baseball, football, skating, sleighing and sledding were my favorites.'

Beard was graduated from the Knightstown High School in 1891, and then joined his father and his brother, Clarence, in publishing the Knightstown Sun. In 1893 he entered DePauw University and was graduated in 1898. A brilliant educator and political scientist, Beard is best known for his many books in the field of American history. With his wife, Mary Ritter Beard, he is co-author of The Rise of American Civilization, and other works.

KNIGHTSTOWN, 38.3 m. (978 alt., 2,323 pop.), an attractive community in a patch of wooded hills, was named for John Knight, government engineer in the construction of the National Road through the village. In early days it was a common occurrence for bears from the vicinity of Blue River to wallow in mudholes of the highway here.

The late William Herschell's poem, 'Ain't God Good to Indiana?' was inspired by the pastoral scenery along the Blue River just east of the town. According to Herschell (see Tour 9), he picked up the phrase from an old man who, while sitting on a log in the sun and fishing in

Blue River, took in the surrounding countryside with a wide sweep of his arms and said: 'Ain't God good to Indianny?'

Tradition has it that Marshal Ney, famous French general under Napoleon, once visited Count Lehmanowsky, a captain in Napoleon's army, in Knightstown. Lehmanowsky left France after Waterloo and eventually settled in Knightstown. While French history holds that Ney died before a firing squad, Miss Christine A. Reising, of Louisville, Kentucky, a great-granddaughter of Lehmanowsky, has publicized in a letter to *Time* the tradition of Ney's survival and visit. Lehmanowsky's story, handed down through succeeding generations of the family, was that the firing squad, commanded by a friend, fired over Ney's head; that Ney fell as though slain and was helped to escape; and that the French government buried an empty coffin thinking it contained the body of the former marshal. Ney escaped to America, settled in North Carolina, and worked as a French teacher and dancing master under the name of Peter Stuart Ney. It is a family tradition, too, that Lehmanowsky's autobiography, said to have revealed much regarding Napoleon and French state secrets, disappeared shortly after it was submitted to the printers.

Left from Knightstown on paved State 140 is the INDIANA SOLDIERS' AND SAILORS' CHILDREN'S HOME (*visitors welcome*), 2 *m.* Ordinarily about 1,000 orphans of the State's soldiers and sailors are reared here. Schooling is offered through a four-year high school course with vocational training.

CLEVELAND, 44.2 *m.* (972 alt., 40 pop.), is headquarters of the Eastern Indiana Holiness Association, an organization of Holiness, Pilgrim Holiness, and Methodist Protestant churches and Friends' Societies of the region. Two conventions are held here each year, in June and in September.

GREENFIELD, 51 *m.* (866 alt., 4,821 pop.), seat of Hancock County, is, like many other towns along this route, a busy tomato-canning center in the late summer and early fall. The city is the birthplace of James Whitcomb Riley, Hoosier poet.

JAMES WHITCOMB RILEY MEMORIAL PARK, at the eastern edge of town, preserves the OLD SWIMMIN' HOLE of Riley's poem. Near the Old Swimmin' Hole is a new and modern pool. A STATUE OF RILEY, purchased with funds contributed by the school children of Indiana, stands in front of the courthouse (L).

The RILEY HOMESTEAD (*open 9–5 daily;* 10¢ *and* 25¢), acquired in 1936 by the city from the Riley heirs and repaired and renovated by the Riley Old Home Society, has been converted into a museum. The ten-room frame house, built in 1850, is in the style of the period, with woodwork of walnut, carved doors, wide floor boards, large fireplace and built-in cupboards and clothes presses. The fireplace in the parlor has been rebuilt with old brick, the iron grillwork around the front porch repaired, and the floors, woodwork, and walls restored to their original condition. Much of the furniture was donated by members of the Riley family. Victorian bric-a-brac is prominent and Currier and Ives prints hang on the walls. The large collection of Riley memorabilia includes manuscripts, his pen-and-ink set, pictures, and letters.

Riley (*see Literature*) was born in a log cabin (the kitchen of the present house) October 7, 1849, the son of Elizabeth (Marine) and Reuben A. Riley. His father, a successful lawyer, was disappointed in his hope that his son would take up law. Riley attended school until he was 21, but was an uninterested pupil. Objecting to work in the garden at home, he accepted a job with a shoemaker. Later he went to Rushville to sell Bibles, the beginning of his wanderings over the State as an itinerant salesman, house painter, sign painter, and medicine show performer. As early as 1870 he contributed verse to the Greenfield *Commercial* under the name of Edyrn. Later he used the name of James Whit. In 1874 he joined the Greenfield *News* as associate editor and began his literary career in earnest. Three years later he was working for the Anderson *Democrat*. In this period of employment, with the sanction of the editor of the Kokomo *Dispatch*, he perpetrated the 'Leonainie' hoax, presenting this poem as an unpublished work of Edgar Allan Poe (*see Newspapers and Radio*). The poem attracted considerable attention, but the hoax was denounced widely. Riley, then 28, returned to Greenfield, which he continued to make his headquarters until he joined the staff of the Indianapolis *Journal*.

A Greenfield politician and his method of campaigning are said to have caused the Democratic party to choose the rooster for its emblem in 1840. Joseph Chapman, owner of a tavern that served as local headquarters of the Democratic party, was an optimistic stump speaker. He claimed every county in the State for the Democrats at the begin- of oratory 'crowing.' In the presidential campaign of 1840 between Martin Van Buren, Democrat, and William Henry Harrison, the Whig contender, things were going badly for the Democrats. An Indianapolis newspaper publisher sent to the Greenfield ballyhooer, a candidate at ning of every political campaign. The opposing Whigs called his style that time for the State legislature, a message to 'Crow, Chapman, crow!' Indiana Whigs seized upon the phrase as a target for ridicule. Unperturbed, the Democrats used it as a battle cry and adopted the rooster as a party emblem.

At 52.1 *m.* are the ELI LILLY COMPANY BIOLOGICAL LABORATORIES (L) (*open 9-4; guide service*), where thousands of small animals are kept for experiments in the development of the company's 2,500 pharmaceutical products.

PHILADELPHIA, 55.1 *m.* (860 alt., 200 pop.), was an important stopping place for early travelers on the old National Road.

Left from Philadelphia on a graveled road, 0.8 *m.*, to the ANNIE GRAY HOUSE (*private*). Annie Gray was the 'Little Orphant Annie' of James Whitcomb Riley's poem. In this little white cottage (R), the second house after the crossroads, the woman who worked in the Riley home and inspired the poem spent the last years of her life.

Between Philadelphia and Indianapolis the countryside for the most part is level and dotted with large, modern farmhouses and attractive tourist camps.

INDIANAPOLIS, 72 *m.* (750 alt., 386,972 pop.) (*see Indianapolis*). Indianapolis is at the junction with US 31 (*see Tour* 16), US 36 (*see Tour* 7), US 52 (*see Tour* 18), State 29 (*see Tour* 17*A*), State 37 (*see Tour* 19), and State 34 (*see Tour* 8*A*).

Section b.   INDIANAPOLIS to ILLINOIS LINE, 76.7 m.

Between INDIANAPOLIS, 0 *m.*, and the Illinois Line, US 40 traverses a gently rolling farming country. In its western section, between Brazil and Terre Haute, the highway crosses a part of Indiana's clay fields, and passes over coal deposits that, lying along the State's western border, reach two-thirds of the way from the Ohio River to Lake Michigan.

BEN DAVIS, 7 *m.* (810 alt., 800 pop.), is a small suburban community, and BRIDGEPORT, 8.8 *m.* (775 alt., 500 pop.), a dairy-farming center. At the western edge of Bridgeport is the C. M. Hobbs and Sons Nursery (R). On its 400 acres the company grows trees and shrubs that find markets in many parts of the Nation.

Right from Bridgeport on the Dandy Trail Road (graveled) is the Bridgeport Nutrition Camp (*open to public*), 0.7 *m.*, maintained by the Marion County Tuberculosis Association for undernourished children. The 80-acre camp is supported by public contributions and by the sale of Christmas seals.

PLAINFIELD, 13.7 *m.* (747 alt., 1,811 pop.), self-styled 'Village of Friendly Folk,' is the headquarters of the Society of Friends in western Indiana and eastern Illinois. The red brick Western Yearly Meeting House (L), in the center of town, is the assembly place for the annual August meeting of Quakers of the district.

Near Van Buren Elm, on the meeting-house grounds, the dapper and dignified Martin Van Buren was dumped into a mudhole, June 13, 1842. Van Buren, defeated for re-election to the Presidency in 1840, was making a swing around the circle—New York to St. Louis by stage; thence to New Orleans and to New York by boat—surveying the political situation preparatory to entering the 1844 campaign. While President, Van Buren had vetoed a bill providing for improvement of the National Road, and tradition has it that residents of Plainfield decided to give him an object lesson in the need for good roads. At any rate, the stagecoach overturned near this elm, and Van Buren was bespattered. The story that the incident was the result of a plot is supported by a granddaughter and a niece of Mason Wright, driver of the stage, who is said to have received a silk hat for his trouble; and by the fact that a crowd was on hand to witness the 'accident.' The local chapter of the D.A.R. has placed a wooden marker on the tree.

The Indiana Boys' School (*open 8-4:30 Mon.-Fri.; 9-2:30 Sun., except holidays*) (L), at the western edge of Plainfield, was established in 1867 for the reform and education of juvenile offenders. Near the administration building is a life-size STATUE OF WHITTIER'S BAREFOOT BOY, carved by Gabriel Gariby, a 15-year-old inmate, from a single block of Bedford limestone. A MONUMENT near the entrance to the Administration Building marks the site of the building where the song, 'I'l' Take You Home Again, Kathleen,' was first played in 1875. The composer, Thomas Paine Westendorf, an official of the Boys' School, was inspired by loneliness for his wife, who was visiting her parents in New York. Northwest of the administration building is the MUSEUM, containing a fine collection of relics, pioneer tools, mounted birds, old documents, a picture of Abraham Lincoln on his deathbed, and a duplicate of the first McCormick grain reaper. Students in the woodworking department made the exhibit cabinets.

At 17.9 *m.* is the CADLE LOG TABERNACLE (L), a large log structure, with sawdust floor, log pulpit, and plain board seats. The tabernacle seats 4,000 persons and the choir platform seats 600. An electrically operated pipe organ can be heard for miles.

In BELLEVILLE, 18.6 *m.* (775 alt., 120 pop.), known as a tourists' village, most of the inhabitants operate camps, filling stations, restaurants, or stores.

West from STILESVILLE, 28.3 *m.* (875 alt., 273 pop.), US 40 passes through Putnam County, 25 miles of varied topography—rugged hills, gently rolling farm land, and stretches of level prairie.

At 37.9 *m.* is the junction with State 43.

Right on State 43 (paved) is GREENCASTLE, 5 *m.* (683 alt., 4,872 pop.), the home of DePauw UNIVERSITY, whose main entrance is on Locust Street in the center of town. The institution was founded in 1837 by the Methodist Episcopal Church as Indiana Asbury University. The original name was changed to DePauw in 1884, several years after Washington C. DePauw, New Albany glass manufacturer, had saved the institution from closing with a substantial gift of money. Supported today by a $6,000,000 endowment, the university is nonsectarian, and enrolls approximately 1,400 young men and women. Several hundred men students are aided yearly by a scholarship fund of $2,250,000 donated by the late Edward Rector, Chicago manufacturer. The university includes a College of Liberal Arts and a School of Music.

Among noted alumni are Willis Van Devanter, U. S. Supreme Court Justice; Albert J. Beveridge, U. S. senator; Charles Austin Beard, historian; and William Wirt, superintendent of the Gary schools and father of the Gary System (*see Gary*).

The AMERICAN ZINC PRODUCTS COMPANY PLANT (*open 9–4 weekdays*), at the east end of Washington St., is one of three factories in the United States in which sheet zinc is rolled.

PUTNAMVILLE, 39.9 *m.* (683 alt., 145 pop.), looks much as it did in the days when it was a popular stagecoach station. It is said that Abraham Lincoln once dined in a Putnamville tavern.

At 40.9 *m.* (L) is the INDIANA STATE FARM (*apply at office of superintendent*), opened in 1915 for the confinement of men convicted of misdemeanors and sentenced for short terms. The average population is about 800. On the 2,397-acre farm are shops and factories in which

Industry

SECTION OF HOT BLAST STOVE AND FURNACES IN A GARY STEEL MILL

Photograph by courtesy of Carnegie-Illinois Steel Corpor

POURING MOLTEN STEEL FROM OPEN HEARTH FURNACE IN A GARY MILL

CONTROL EQUIPMENT FOR COLD ROLLING STEEL, GARY

AUTOMOBILE BODY FINISHING ON ASSEMBLY LINE, SOUTH BEND

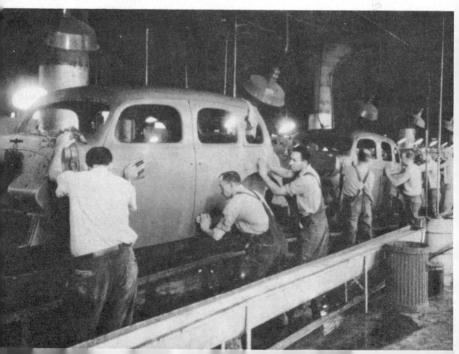

88-TON LIMESTONE COLUMNS QUARRIED AT BEDFORD

ELECTRIC CHANNELING MACHINES IN A LIMESTONE QUARRY NEAR BEDFORD

GANG SAW CUTTING OIL STONES

STONE CARVERS AT WORK IN A BEDFORD MILL

STRIP-MINING COAL NEAR TERRE HAUTE

MOTOR-DRIVEN LOADER IN DEEP COAL MINE

GREAT LAKES ORE BOAT UNLOADING AT INDIANA HARBOR

LAND-RAIL-WATER TERMINAL, EVANSVILLE

MACHINE USED IN BLOWING FRUIT JARS, MUNCIE

Photograph by courtesy of Ball Brot

prisoners produce brick and tile, crushed limestone, willow baskets, rustic furniture, rock wool, and canned goods.

Directly across the highway from the penal farm is an INDIANA STATE POLICE POST, one of nine along Indiana highways. Of modern design, it is built of bricks in several colors.

MANHATTAN, 43.2 m. (819 alt., 100 pop.), was founded in 1829, and is now a stopping point for the many interstate trucks which rumble down US 40.

Left from Manhattan on the Bowling Green Road (improved) is HOOSIER HIGHLANDS (*cabins, boating and fishing facilities*), 6 m., a popular summer resort. Before the coming of the white man, this wild, broken section on Eel River was a common hunting ground for Indian tribes in the region. Tradition has it that Indians panned gold from streams of the Highlands.

US 40, now a winding road, runs past heavy woods (R) and through rocky hills covered in late summer and early fall with a blanket of goldenrod.

TEN O'CLOCK LINE, 47.2 m., was the boundary of white settlement established by the Indian Treaty of 1809 (*see History*).

SHADY LANE, 48.9 m., is a 400-yard stretch, bordered on each side by sycamore trees, their overhanging branches making a bower through which motor traffic roars unceasingly. This is one of the few scenic reminders of the once rural lane that was the wagon trail of the pioneers of the West. The McKINLEY TAVERN (L), 50.5 m., built in 1834 and one of the oldest brick buildings in this vicinity, is today a refreshment stand.

HARMONY, 51.8 m. (669 alt., 2,100 pop.), once a booming coal-mining town, is now almost wholly a residential village.

BRAZIL, 54.5 m. (650 alt., 8,126 pop.), seat of Clay County, is an important mining center, known for its brick and tile and Brazil block coal. A bituminous coal field adjoins the town on the west. The nine clay plants manufacture glazed building brick, conduits, sewer pipe, roofing, floor and decorative tile, building blocks, and other products. US 40 is the town's main street and the elongated business district makes the town seem larger than it is. Brazil was named by William Stewart who, when asked to suggest a name, had just finished reading a magazine article on Brazil, South America.

One of the first electric interurban lines in the United States ran between Brazil and Harmony. Built in 1893, it was 4.4 miles in length. The CLAY COUNTY HISTORICAL MUSEUM (*open 9–5 daily*), third floor of the courthouse, in the eastern part of town, has a large collection of early relics, including the first railroad spike driven on the interurban line.

Left from Brazil on paved State 59 are FOREST PARK (*open-air auditorium, stadium, swimming pool*) and MEMORIAL LOG CABIN (*open Sundays and holidays June-Oct.*), at the southern city limits. The cabin, built in 1853 by Philip Fernsel when he came to Clay County from Ohio, was moved to the park from its original site as a typical early Clay County home. The furniture is rustic, and there is an exhibit of pioneer relics. The cabin was restored by the Clay County Historical Society.

At 3 *m.* are some of the STRIP COAL MINES of Clay County. Great power shovels strip the soil that covers the coal, sometimes to a depth of 35 or 40 feet, and dump it into large piles known as spoil banks. As mining continues, more and more of the level Clay County farms are converted into a wasteland of dumps and water-filled pits. After the surface cover is removed, the big shovels load the coal into trucks that carry it to tipples to be screened, graded, and loaded into other trucks for shipment.

SEELYVILLE, 62.4 *m.* (583 alt., 807 pop.), a ramshackle village of coal miners' cottages, was once a prosperous little mining center.

Left from Seelyville on a graveled road to the unusually large BOBOLINK STRIP MINE (*apply at office*), 2 *m.* It is equipped with a power shovel that towers 108 feet at the top of the boom, has a 30-cubic-yard capacity, and can remove 90,000 pounds of soil at one scoop. This electrically powered juggernaut works silently, smoothly, almost gracefully, as it bites off a carload of soil, swings it away, dumps it, and returns for more. Trailer trucks, carrying 25 to 30 tons, are part of the mine's equipment.

ROSE POLYTECHNIC INSTITUTE, 64.4 *m.*, is an endowed engineering college for men, founded in 1874 by Chauncey Rose. The campus (R) covers 123 acres. The main building is a red brick structure housing laboratories, classrooms, library, gymnasium, shops, and offices. Enrollment is limited to 261 students.

TERRE HAUTE, 68.3 *m.* (495 alt., 62,693 pop.) (*see Terre Haute*).

Terre Haute is at the junction with US 41 (*see Tour* 20) and State 46 (*see Tour* 9).

At the western end of the bridge carrying US 40 over the Wabash River is DRESSER MEMORIAL PARK, which stretches along both sides of the highway, with an underpass connecting the two parts. The park is dedicated to the memory of Paul Dresser (1858–1906) (*see Terre Haute*), composer of the Indiana State song, 'On the Banks of the Wabash Far Away,' and a popular song writer and publisher in the 1890's. He was a brother of Theodore Dreiser, the novelist.

WEST TERRE HAUTE, 71.7 *m.* (490 alt., 3,729 pop.), once a prosperous coal-mining town, is now largely a residential suburb of Terre Haute.

At 76.7 *m.* US 40 crosses the ILLINOIS LINE, nine miles east of Marshall, Illinois (*see Illinois Guide*).

Tour 8A

Indianapolis—Crawfordsville—Covington—(Danville, Illinois); State 34.
Indianapolis to Illinois Line, 83.4 *m.*

Hard-surfaced road throughout.
The Cleveland, Cincinnati, Chicago & St. Louis R.R. parallels the route.
Accommodations at frequent intervals; hotels chiefly in cities.

State 34, a direct route between Indianapolis and Danville, Illinois, passes through agricultural and dairy country. For the first 40 miles, the land is level and rich; numerous groves break the monotony of the prosperous pastoral landscape. In the western half of the route (nearly to the Illinois Line) the countryside is rolling, more heavily wooded, most beautiful in the summer when iris grows in profusion along the roadside. The level fields of the extreme western section are planted to corn and wheat, and stock raising is carried on extensively.

INDIANAPOLIS, 0 *m.* (750 alt., 386,972 pop.) (*see Indianapolis*).

Indianapolis is at the junction with US 31 (*see Tour 16*), US 36 (*see Tour 7*), US 40 (*see Tour 8*), US 52 (*see Tour 18*), State 29 (*see Tour 17A*), and State 37 (*see Tour 19*).

SPEEDWAY CITY, 5.7 *m.* (816 alt., 2,325 pop.), is the home of the INDIANAPOLIS MOTOR SPEEDWAY (*see Indianapolis*), scene of the annual 500-mile International Sweepstakes automobile race. The town was laid out in 1912 by Carl Fisher, James T. Allison, and Frank H. Wheeler, with the stipulation that no land ever be sold or rented to one of Negro blood, and that no Negro own or operate a business within the city. Many streets are named for makes of cars, such as Cord, Auburn, and Ford.

Most of the local workers, as well as many Indianapolis citizens, are employed by Speedway City factories. Plants include those of the Prest-O-Lite Storage Battery Company, American Art Clay Company, Esterline-Angus Company, Electric Steel Castings Company, and Allison Engineering Company. The latter plant is an important unit in the manufacture of airplane motors for the United States Army.

The SPEEDWAY GOLF COURSE (*public; 75¢ weekdays, $1 Sun., holidays*) is one of Marion County's longest 18-hole courses.

At 8.7 *m.* is a junction with the Girls' School Road (graveled).

Left on this road is the INDIANA GIRLS' SCHOOL (R), 0.1 *m.*, a school of correction for girls between 10 and 18. The institution consists of 10 cottages, a hospital, a school, and numerous auxiliary buildings, on a 250-acre tract.

It was established in 1889 as a part of the Indiana Reformatory Institution for Women and ·Girls; in 1907 it was separated from the prison and moved to its present site. The girls are provided with entertainment, recreational facilities, physical training, and a well-stocked library. The average number of inmates is 285.

At 0.3 m. is the junction with a graveled road; L. on this road, 0.7 m., to CAMP DELLWOOD (L), conducted by the Indianapolis Girl Scouts, and occupying a 140-acre woodland tract along the banks of Big Eagle Creek. A vine-covered LOG CABIN, built in 1821, stands near the road. Camp sessions are held in June, July, and August. On the grounds is a concrete swimming pool.

CLERMONT, 10.7 m. (748 alt., 465 pop.), platted as Mechanics-burg in 1849, was renamed six years later because there was another Mechanicsburg in Indiana. State 34 is the main street of this attractive village of rambling buildings and shady· yards. Many of the residents are employed in Indianapolis. The post office was once a popular tavern, but alterations and additions have so changed the appearance of the old log building that its identity is almost lost.

In BROWNSBURG, 15.3 m. (896 alt., 1,136 pop.), is the junction with S. Green Street, a blacktop road.

Left on S. Green Street to the junction with a graveled road, 0.6 m.; R. on this graveled road to the junction with another graveled road, 1.9 m.; L. here is the KELSCH DUDE RANCH, 2.9 m. (open; cabins, saddle horses, shooting range, fishing, swimming pool), on a large, prairie-like area (L), broken with woodland-bordered fishing streams.

LIZTON, 24 m. (1,000 alt., 200 pop.), was founded in 1851 in the middle of a wet and swampy forest area and its inhabitants earned the reputation of being web-footed. Artificial drainage has since converted this swampy land into fertile and productive farms. Lizton figures in James Whitcomb Riley's poem, 'A Lizton Humorist,' in which the small-town conversation around the grocery store stove is recorded.

At 28.7 m. is the PUMPING STATION (R) of the Illinois Pipe Line Company, one of a number of stations that pump crude oil from Oklahoma, Texas, and Illinois to refineries at Whiting, Indiana, and Lima, Ohio.

The route traverses a corn, hog and cattle raising region, where fine herds of milk cows browse in pastures along the highway. JAMESTOWN, 29.4 m. (830 alt., 583 pop.), now a quiet village, was once a busy stage stop and later a center of boisterous activity while the Peoria Division of the New York Central Railroad was being built. NEW ROSS, 34.8 m. (830 alt., 355 pop.), is a trading point for near-by farmers.

CRAWFORDSVILLE, 46.7 m. (750 alt., 11,089 pop.), former home of three men of letters—General Lew Wallace, Maurice Thompson, and Meredith Nicholson—and the seat of Wabash College, is known as the 'Hoosier Athens.' The town was laid out in 1823 by Major Ambrose Whitlock, who named it in honor of Colonel William Crawford of Virginia, a famous Indian fighter. The early development of Crawfordsville was helped by the establishment of a Government land office.

At one time it was the only town between Terre Haute and Fort Wayne.

In sharp contrast with the residential section's shady streets, stately houses, and grassy lawns is the business district, with its two- and three-story brick buildings, dingy and old. The courthouse, in the center of the city square, is a time-scarred brick and stone structure. Crawfordsville is a busy manufacturing and trading city, surrounded by a productive agricultural area.

The LEW WALLACE STUDY (*open* 9–5, *except Sun.*), Pike St. and Wallace Ave., occupies a central position on a beautifully landscaped tract of three and a half acres enclosed by a brick wall. The entrance gate is designed after that of a French abbey. The study, a square, tower-like structure of red brick in Byzantine design, was planned and its construction supervised by General Wallace, whose statue, in bronze, stands on the grounds. The portico has Doric columns and the frieze above the door is sculptured to represent literary characters created by Wallace. Within the study are many war relics, letters, and objects of art.

Lew Wallace was born in Brookville (*see Tour 18a*) in 1827 and moved to Crawfordsville in 1853. At the outbreak of the Civil War he assisted in organizing the 11th Indiana Regiment and was later made a major general for his gallantry at Fort Donelson. While stationed at Baltimore in 1864 Wallace helped save Washington, D. C., from capture by engaging the Confederate General Jubal Early until Grant could bring up reinforcements. Wallace was a member of the court that tried the conspirators for the assassination of Lincoln. From 1878 to 1881 he was territorial governor of New Mexico, and from 1881 to 1885 United States minister to Turkey.

Wallace is best known, however, as a writer (*see Literature*). His book *Ben Hur* had an enormous sale for many years and was translated into many languages. His other books include *The Fair God, Prince of India, The Wooing of Walkatoon,* and an autobiography. He died in Crawfordsville in 1905.

The former MEREDITH NICHOLSON HOUSE (*private*), 205 S. Walnut St., is a modest story-and-a-half frame cottage. Nicholson, United States minister to Paraguay and a well-known novelist, was born in Crawfordsville and lived there until he joined the staff of an Indianapolis newspaper at the age of 19 (*see Literature*). He is the author of *The House of a Thousand Candles, The Hoosiers, The Port of Missing Men, The Valley of Democracy,* and many essays.

The HENRY S. LANE PLACE (*open* 10–5, *except Sun.; adm.* 25¢; *children under* 12 *free*), Pike and Water Sts., is the headquarters of the Montgomery County Historical Society. Housing a large collection of antique furniture, the two-story, 14-room brick house is of Georgian Colonial style. The grounds are beautifully landscaped.

Henry Smith Lane moved to Crawfordsville in 1833 from Kentucky, where he was born in 1811. He was admitted to the bar and became an authority on criminal law. In 1840 and 1842 he was elected to Congress. In 1846 he organized a company for the Mexican War and was made lieutenant colonel on the battlefield. After the war he returned to Crawfordsville and became a prominent figure in the People's party, later the Republican party, of which he was the first national chairman.

In 1860 Lane was the Republican candidate for governor of Indiana, with Oliver P. Morton as candidate for lieutenant-governor. Both were elected; Lane, however, resigned to fill a vacancy in the United States Senate. He was a delegate to the Republican National Convention where his efforts were directed toward nominating Lincoln for the Presidency.

Maurice Thompson (1844–1901), poet, scholar, and author of the vivid historical romance, *Alice of Old Vincennes,* spent most of his life in Crawfordsville. The site of his home, long since demolished, is on the southwest corner of E. Pike and Pine Sts.

Bounded by Wabash Ave., Crawford and Grant Sts., and the Big Four Railroad is WABASH COLLEGE, a nonsectarian college of liberal arts for men. Forest Hall, built in 1833 and the first building owned by the college, still stands among the red brick, stone-trimmed buildings on the 40-acre campus. Goodrich Hall of Physical Sciences was named for its alumnus-donor, former Governor James P. Goodrich. Among other alumni are former United States Vice President Thomas R. Marshall (*see Tour* 4) and General Lew Wallace. The Yandes Library contains 82,000 volumes, and other buildings include a chapel, classroom structures, and the president's house, built in 1836 and once occupied by Caleb Mills, father of the public school system of Indiana (*see Education*). Enrollment of the college in 1938–9 was 446. Each spring seniors attend a study camp held at Turkey Run State Park.

In Crawfordsville is a junction with State 32 (*see Tour* 6).

Left from Crawfordsville on paved State 47 to the junction with State 234, 10 *m.;* R. on State 234 to THE SHADES, 14.9 *m.* (*adm.,* 10¢), the largest private park in the State. Marked trails lead through much of the 2,000-acre preserve and along Sugar Creek, which flows beneath high, tree-crested rock cliffs. Accommodations include a hotel, 14 cottages, and a dance hall.

Near WAYNETOWN, 56.7 *m.* (735 alt., 644 pop.), and HILLS-BORO, 61.7 *m.* (760 alt., 516 pop.), the soil of the rough countryside is not good for farming, but furnishes excellent clay for manufacture. Tile factories and brick kilns are the principal industrial plants.

STERLING, 67.3 *m.* (605 alt., 350 pop.), is at the junction with US 41 (*see Tour* 20).

VEEDERSBURG, 67.9 *m.* (622 alt., 1,781 pop.), grew rapidly in its early days because of excellent railroad facilities. The chief industry—the manufacture of bricks—accounts for the many brick streets and the few frame dwellings.

On S. Mill Street, at the edge of town, is the plant of the VEEDERSBURG PAVER COMPANY (*visitors welcome,* 9–5 *weekdays*), one of the oldest brick kilns in this part of Indiana. It has 30 ovens for the manufacture of building tile and building and paving brick. This plant, now closed, furnished the brick for paving the Indianapolis Motor Speedway (*see Indianapolis*). When operating it employed about 100 men. The VEEDERSBURG BRICK COMPANY (*open 9–5 weekdays*), which employs about 70 persons, has 12 kilns.

COVINGTON, 75.6 *m.* (506 alt., 2,096 pop.), the seat of Fountain County, was laid out in 1826 on the east bank of the Wabash River. A new, three-story limestone courthouse rises from the square, flanked by shabby, time-worn buildings. On the courthouse walls are murals by Eugene F. Savage and eight other Indiana artists, depicting the history of the State and county.

During canal days Covington, suspecting that Attica was holding back the water supply, marched there under the leadership of Edward A. Hannegan and threw open the floodgates. This was followed by a free-for-all of such intensity that the towns were bitter enemies for years.

At the corner of Fifth and Jefferson Streets is the former HOME OF EDWARD A. HANNEGAN (1807–59), United States senator and minister to Prussia. Hannegan was a fiery, attractive, extravagantly impulsive man. Born in Ohio, he was admitted to the bar in Fountain County at the age of 20. His rise was rapid: circuit rider in 1829, prosecuting attorney in 1830, representative from 1832 to 1840, and U. S. senator in 1842. Daniel Webster said of him, 'Had Hannegan entered Congress before I did, I fear I never should have been known for my eloquence.' But Governor Willard used to say, 'Start Hannegan downstream at high tide, and he can gather more driftwood than any man I know, but he isn't worth a curse to row upstream.'

A leader in the Northwest Boundary dispute, Hannegan raised the 'Fifty-Four Forty or Fight' slogan in his Indiana campaign. When President Polk agreed to a compromise, Hannegan delivered a scathing attack in the Senate. Polk resented him bitterly until Hannegan, against his convictions, cast the deciding vote in a party caucus in favor of declaring war on Mexico, and was forgiven.

Polk appointed Hannegan minister to Prussia in 1849. With his high color and firm build, his charm and liveliness, he dazzled the court. The Queen was infatuated, it is said. Frederick Wilhelm IV jealously seized on a point of court etiquette, and demanded Hannegan's recall when he publicly kissed the' Queen's hand. Hannegan returned to Covington early in 1851.

Defeated in the State elections, he entered the race for the presidential nomination. Pierce was unknown, and Hannegan, the only man on the Democratic ticket who could match Daniel Webster, had the pledged support of nine States. He was drinking heavily during the canvass; and since his nomination seemed certain, he went home to rest. When Captain Duncan, his wife's brother, told him he was drinking too much, a quarrel flared up; Duncan followed Hannegan upstairs, called him a coward and slapped his face. Hannegan reached for a dagger and drove it into Duncan's throat. The captain died the next day. Although he made a deathbed statement absolving Hannegan, the damage was done. Hannegan was not nominated for the Presidency.

Shocked and desperate, he moved to St. Louis to practice law. His prestige gone, his wife dead, he continued drinking and became addicted to morphine; but he was still eloquent and charming, and in 1859 friends persuaded him to start over, to speak for Douglas. His was to be the principal address at a great meeting; well-primed, feeling fine, he sat and listened to a ruinously long introduction, which praised him, going over his long career. As the speech continued, the alcohol wore off; the drugs numbed him, and when he finally spoke, he was a hopeless failure. Next morning he was found dead of an overdose of morphine.

Daniel Voorhees, 'the Tall Sycamore of the Wabash,' was a close friend of Hannegan and occupied this house for some time after Hannegan left. Voorhees became prosecutor after Lew Wallace resigned from the office, but was so sharply criticized by the local press for refusing to take action against his friend Hannegan that he moved to Terre Haute, where he became United States senator from Indiana.

The FORMER RESIDENCE OF LEW WALLACE (*private*), in which he wrote *The Fair God,* is at Eighth and Crockett Streets. Wallace was prosecuting attorney of Fountain County until 1853, when he resigned and moved to Crawfordsville to escape the unpleasant duty of prosecuting his friend Hannegan on a murder charge.

At 78 *m.* is the junction with State 63, a blacktop road.

Left on State 63 to the KENFLEUR HORSE FARMS (*open*), 8.8 *m.*, owned by H. C. Horneman. On this 160-acre farm are bred registered Belgian draft horses. At 9.9 *m.* are the HORNEMAN GUERNSEY FARMS (R) (*open*), where pure-bred Guernsey cattle produce a special grade of milk for infants and invalids. The farm has taken many prizes for its cattle and for the Duroc hogs which it also raises.

State 34 crosses the ILLINOIS LINE, 83.4 *m.*, 6 miles east of Danville, Illinois (*see Illinois Guide*).

↗↗

Tour 9

Junction with US 52—Greensburg—Columbus—Bloomington—Terre Haute; 164 *m.* State 46.

Roadbed hard-surfaced throughout.
Route paralleled by Cleveland, Cincinnati, Chicago & St. Louis R.R. between

Batesville and Columbus, and between Riley and Terre Haute. Accommodations at short intervals.

State 46, in its devious route across Indiana, twists over hills and sweeps down valleys through some of the most beautiful country in the State. Brown County, famed for its scenery, and Nashville, its rustic little county seat, are on this route, as are also Brown County and McCormick's Creek State Parks. The route leads through Bloomington, site of the State University, crosses the northern tip of the oölitic limestone belt, and passes many strip coal mines before reaching the Wabash at Terre Haute.

State 46 branches left from US 52 (*see Tour* 18), 0 *m.*, at a point 3 miles west of West Harrison (*see Tour* 18a). On the northern border of PENNTOWN, 17 *m.* (1,010 alt., unincorporated), is a junction with State 1 (*see Tour* 18a).

BATESVILLE, 24.3 *m.* (1,000 alt., 3,065 pop.), a neat, compact, furniture-manufacturing center, is peopled almost exclusively by thrifty Germans, whose comfortable mode of living is little disturbed by economic depressions. Master craftsmen, they are employed in the six large furniture factories of the town and are seldom without work. Batesville homes are scrupulously clean and neat, and at the western edge of town are many attractive houses set in large lawns.

NEW POINT, 30.2 *m.* (986 alt., 328 pop.), a small trading center, enjoyed a prosperous quarrying business before the centralization of Indiana's stone industry near Bloomington and Bedford.

At 36.2 *m.* is a junction with State 29 (*see Tour* 17A), with which State 46 is united westward for four miles.

GREENSBURG, 40.2 *m.* (1,000 alt., 6,065 pop.), seat of Decatur County, is renowned for its COURTHOUSE TOWER TREE, a nine-foot maple that grows out of the sloping concrete block roof of the county's house of justice. There have been stories that the tree is secretly cultivated, but this is emphatically denied. It is explained that the tree is of a species which thrives in rocky soil, and that the tower is filled with crumbled bricks and mortar, capable of nourishing the tree through the longest drought.

Greensburg is principally a city of retired farmers, and has little industry. Natural gas is plentiful near by and is used extensively for heating and cooking. Many of the farms near the city have their own gas wells. At the eastern end of Main Street are the 180-acre grounds of the INDIANA ODD FELLOWS HOME (*open*), an institution provided by the State Grand Lodge for its needy, aged, and infirm, and for orphans of deceased members. Buildings include dormitories, farm buildings, and a hospital.

In Greensburg is the western junction with State 29 (*see Tour* 17A).

In HARTSVILLE, 53.4 *m.* (668 alt., 318 pop.), a park marks the SITE OF HARTSVILLE COLLEGE, a coeducational school founded by the United Brethren denomination in 1850. The college building was destroyed by fire in 1898, and the school moved to Huntington, where it continues as Huntington College (*see Tour* 5).

COLUMBUS, 66.3 *m.* (637 alt., 11,738 pop.) (*see Tour 16b*), is at the junction with US 31 (*see Tour 16*).

GNAW BONE, 80.3 *m.* (600 alt., 8 pop.), was named in the early days of the settlement when one of the inhabitants, asking the whereabouts of another, was told, 'I seed him a-settin' on a log above the sawmill a-gnawing on a bone.' Several years ago the State Highway Commission changed the town's name to West Point, but the citizens continued to call it Gnaw Bone and this is once again its official name.

The settlements in this region are poor and sparse and the land sterile and hilly, yet agriculture is the principal occupation, and corn grows on the narrow strips of bottom land. Farther west fruit-growing is increasing, and some tobacco is grown in the lowlands. The inhabitants take pride in their beautiful but undeveloped country, and depend upon farming and the tourist trade for a livelihood. Log cabins are still numerous, and nearly every house is heated by wood-burning stoves or fireplaces, and lighted by coal oil lamps. Slopes in this area are too steep for cultivation, and the region is a jumbled and heavily foliaged wilderness of hills and valleys.

In GROUCH CEMETERY, 81.2 *m.*, is a POPLAR TREE MONUMENT (R) to John Allcorn, who was crushed to death by a poplar tree he had felled. There were no sawmills in the vicinity and consequently no lumber available for a rough box. A neighbor sawed off seven feet of the trunk of the tree that had killed Allcorn, and hollowed it out for a coffin. Some time later a poplar shoot appeared at the head of the burial mound and became the tree that is John Allcorn's memorial.

At 83.7 *m.* is a blacktop road (L), and across a covered wooden bridge on this road is the entrance to the BROWN COUNTY STATE PARK AND GAME PRESERVE (*adm.* 10¢; *nature-guide service; park map free*). The 3,822-acre park and the adjoining 11,390-acre game preserve constitute the largest publicly owned land unit in Indiana.

Virtually isolated for years because of inadequate highways, this hill country is now easily accessible to thousands of motorists who visit it annually. In the park and game preserve are ten miles of well-marked scenic driveways.

Near the entrance is the stone and timber ABE MARTIN LODGE (*cabins, meals, swimming pool, saddle horses*), named for a pen character of Kin Hubbard (1868–1930), Indianapolis cartoonist, whose Brown County characters won him Nation-wide fame.

WEEDPATCH HILL (1,167 alt.), highest of the southern Indiana hills, commands an unobstructed view of 15 to 20 miles. On its crest are the BROWN COUNTY AIRPORT, highest airport in the State, and a FIRETOWER. The LAFE BUD TRAIL (*time:* 1 *hour*), leading to Weedpatch Hill, is one of the most beautiful foot trails in the park. The SQUIRE MARSH SWALLOW TRAIL (*time:* 2½ *hours*) leads along one of the highest ridges from which, on clear days, smoke from Columbus, 20 miles away, can be seen.

At the GAME FARM are permanent display pens of deer, bears, coyotes, badgers, opossums, owls, hawks, weasels, ferrets, foxes, and other animals and birds. Two ARTIFICIAL LAKES supply thousands of blue-gills to other lakes in Indiana.

A 1,500-acre ARCHERY HUNTING AREA (*hunting in season; bow and arrow only*), the first of its kind in Indiana and the second in the Middle West, has been well stocked with small game, chiefly rabbits and quail.

At 85.8 *m.* is the junction with the Greasy Creek Road (improved).

Right on this road is STINSON'S CABIN (*visitors welcome*), 0.9 *m.*, an old log structure (R) that has been the subject of many paintings.

On BEAR WALLOW HILL, 3.9 *m.*, is the spruce-bordered HOME OF MARCUS DICKEY (L), for many years secretary to James Whitcomb Riley. In the front yard is a BEAR WALLOW, a natural basin long ago hollowed out by wallowing bears. It is now dry, and a sign reads, 'Bears Not Wallowing Today.' Across the road from the house is an OBSERVATION TOWER (*free; parking space provided*), from which landmarks of eight counties are visible. Thunderclouds over the Ohio River can often be seen with binoculars.

NASHVILLE, 86.1 *m.* (700 alt., 493 pop.), county seat and largest town of Brown County, lies between the ranges of hills that stretch from Columbus to Bloomington. Because the town is in the heart of the loveliest scenery in Indiana, it is a mecca for painters, photographers, and tourists who mingle on the streets with the permanent residents. The latter are not unmindful of their opportunities, and living costs for tourists are higher here than in many Indiana cities. Men, women, and children stand along the highway selling baskets of wild flowers, bittersweet, sassafras root, berries and nuts, and pails of maple syrup.

In the center of the village is the two-story COURTHOUSE (1874) of scarred and faded red brick, heated with wood-burning stoves. On the courthouse lawn is the LIARS' BENCH, rendezvous of the accomplished dawdlers who gather here to prevaricate in pleasant and friendly rivalry. Famous over the county, the bench is armless at one end and has a seating capacity of six. Here disciples of Munchausen gather, bask in the sun, and exchange magnificent tales. When a bigger and better story is told by some person standing, the man seated at the armless end is pushed off to make room for the expert. Behind the courthouse is the LOG JAIL (*adm.* 10¢), built in 1837, with walls five feet thick. It houses a fine collection of Indian relics.

The ART GALLERY (*adm.* 10¢), a half block west of the courthouse, is owned and operated by Brown County artists, many of whom occupy log cabin studios in Nashville and its environs. Pottery of Brown County clay, made by local artists, is displayed one block south of the courthouse on State 46.

In BROWN COUNTY MUSEUM (*adm.* 10¢), one block north of the courthouse on State 135, Indian relics, pioneer tools and utensils, spinning wheels, and looms are on display.

At 91.6 *m.* is a junction with a crushed rock road.

Right on this road, 2.5 *m.*, to YELLOW WOOD LAKE AND PICNIC AREA (*adm. free; fishing, picnic area, shelter house*), a 20,000-acre recreational area (L) developed by the Resettlement Administration. An earth dam backs up the waters of Jackson Creek to form a 147-acre lake between wooded slopes. Roads within the area are marked and the JACKSON CREEK ROAD leads over fords and through a rugged valley to State 45 (7 *m.*). Adjoining the area on the west is the purchase unit of the HOOSIER NATIONAL FOREST, extending from Bloomington to the Ohio River. The 545,000 acres in the unit are to be the nucleus of a permanent national forest (*see Tour* 19).

BELMONT, 94.4 *m.* (650 alt., 25 pop.), is a crossroads trading hamlet.

Left from Belmont on a graveled road is (R) the HOUSE OF THE SINGING WINDS (*adm.* 25¢), 1.3 *m.*, named for the pleasant sound of the wind blowing through the evergreen trees near the house. It was built in 1907 by Theodore Steele, first artist to realize the possibilities of Brown County for landscape paintings.

At 100.9 *m.* is a junction with the KNIGHT RIDGE ROAD, built in 1834 between Brownstown and Bloomington.

Left on this crushed rock road to the ASTRONOMICAL OBSERVATORY (L), 0.9 *m.*, owned and operated by Indiana University. The observatory was completed in 1936 to house a telescope with a 24-inch reflector, developed after 25 years of research by Professor W. A. Cogshall, head of the department of astronomy.

BLOOMINGTON, 104.4 *m.* (752 alt., 20,870 pop.), is the seat of the State University, the home of a large furniture factory, and a center of oölitic limestone quarrying. The town was settled in 1815 and its name suggested when a group of pioneers, picnicking on a near-by hillside, were impressed by the blooming flowers and foliage below them. The principal factor in Bloomington's steady growth during the last half century has been the development of the stone industry. In the vicinity are 17 stone quarries and mills valued at more than $50,000,000. Indiana University, founded in 1820, has also played an important part in the city's development.

On the PUBLIC SQUARE in the 'center of town' stands the MONROE COUNTY COURTHOUSE (1908), a Neo-Roman limestone structure with a metal fish weather vane on the clock tower. Surrounding the square are two- and three-story business buildings of brick or stone, and an eight-story hotel. The presence of the State University accounts for the gaily dressed groups of young men and women seen on the streets. The first-floor lobby of the courthouse and the sidewalks of the west side of the square are meeting places for farm folk who come to Bloomington in large numbers, particularly on Saturdays. Here occasionally may be found a legless pencil salesman, a Townsendite selling old-age pension magazines, or an itinerant peddler demonstrating kitchen knives, glass cutters, or china cement. The twang of Hoosier dialect is heard in curbstone conversations. It is in Monroe County that the language of the common folk begins to shade off into the southern Indiana hill country speech. 'Swimmy-headed' means dizzy, cream gets 'blinky' during a thunderstorm, and 'hep git shet of' means to help get rid of. Until 1936 local grocery and fruit stores stretched awnings over outdoor counters and conducted many sales on the walks. A city ordinance has since restricted this pleasant custom to an occasional sidewalk display of sweet potatoes, sorghum, or watermelons.

That part of the business section sloping down to the railroad tracks one block west of the square is known locally as 'the levee.' Taverns, low-price grocery stores, and second-hand furniture salesrooms merge into the industrial district of wholesale houses, flour mills, creameries, and small factories. SHOWERS BROTHERS FURNITURE FACTORY (*visitors welcome; guides*), 601 N. Morton St., employs 1,500 persons at an annual pay roll of $1,000,000; its 11 plants have a yearly output of 22,000 pieces valued at approximately $7,500,000. It is the city's largest industry.

INDIANA UNIVERSITY, five blocks east of the public square, was established as a State seminary in 1820, and opened four years later with one professor and ten male students in a single brick building on a hill south of Bloomington. One member of the first group of students was Joseph A. Wright, later governor of Indiana (1850–54) and United States minister to Prussia. The University has borne its present title since 1838, and has received appropriations from the State legislature since 1867, in which year the school became coeducational. In 1883, after a series of disastrous fires, the University was moved to its present site. Its period of greatest growth was under the administration of William Lowe Bryan, an alumnus, president from 1902 to 1937. Instruction is offered in arts and sciences, education, graduate studies, law, business, and music. The medical center is in Indianapolis (*see Indianapolis*). Enrollment at Bloomington is 8,000 (1939–40); more than that number of additional students are enrolled in extension classes and correspondence courses. Extension teaching centers are maintained in East Chicago, South Bend, Fort Wayne, and Indianapolis. Among alumni and former students of the University are Wendell Willkie, Republican presidential candidate in 1940 (*see Tour* 14); Theodore Dreiser, novelist, who wrote of the University in his *Dawn;* Don Herold, humorist; 'Hoagy' Carmichael, composer of 'Star Dust' and other popular songs; and Paul V. McNutt, former dean of the law school, governor of the State, and now (1941) administrator of the Federal Security Agency.

More graduates have entered teaching than any other profession, and 75 alumni have become college presidents. The school of business (1939–40) had the largest enrollment of the professional schools.

The main entrance to the 173-acre campus is at E. Kirkwood (Fifth St.) and Indiana Avenues. At the right is the ADMINISTRATION BUILDING, a modern limestone structure, where descriptive literature and free campus guide service may be obtained at the Registrar's Office, first floor. At the left is the LIBRARY, of collegiate Gothic design, containing 312,526 volumes. Seven levels of glass-floored stacks house the main collection. East of the library is the STUDENT BUILDING, built in 1906 with funds contributed partly by John D. Rockefeller, which houses the women's gymnasium and swimming pool. The university chimes are in the tower.

MAXWELL HALL contains the classrooms and library (33,000 volumes) of the School of Law, founded in 1838. South of this building in a wooded section of the campus is the WELLHOUSE, built around stone doorways removed from the Old College Building (1854). Old College is still standing on the present grounds of the Bloomington High School. North of Maxwell Hall is the MEMORIAL UNION BUILDING, of English-Gothic design with an eight-story tower, containing ALUMNI HALL, used for convocations and dances, and lounges, student meeting rooms, alumni headquarters, guest rooms, and a cafeteria. The BOOKSTORE in the east wing has a beamed ceiling and leaded casement windows. Behind the building meanders the 'Jordan River,' a small stream named for David Starr Jordan, University president from 1884 to 1891.

OWEN HALL and WYLIE HALL, which housed the original classrooms, are of red brick, but many of the later buildings are of limestone. Six new structures, completed in 1940, include dormitories, an auditorium seating 6,000, and a School of Business building. A MUSEUM, on the top floor of the Business Administration Building, contains many relics of domestic life a century ago, and the first automobile built in Bloomington in 1895. On the top floor of BIOLOGY HALL is a large collection of fishes, reptiles, and other zoological specimens. Under construction near by is the PHYSICAL SCIENCES BUILDING, which will house an 87-ton cyclotron, or 'atom-smasher,' the second largest machine of this type in the country. Near the School of Music Building—where the university's broadcasting studios are located—is the UNIVERSITY SCHOOL, a laboratory for practice teachers, who observe and conduct classes from kindergarten through high school.

The MEMORIAL STADIUM, seating 22,000, the MEN'S GYMNASIUM and adjoining FIELDHOUSE, and the men's dormitories are on or near Tenth Street (State 45). From this street there is a pleasant prospect across the playing fields to the towers and spires of the University proper. South of the fields the tall chimney of the POWER HOUSE rises near the UNIVERITY PRESS, an old-fashioned red brick building where undergraduates publish the *Indiana Daily Student*, campus newspaper founded in 1867. In a stone-fenced cemetery near by, myrtle-covered graves date back to 1830.

Flanking the University campus on three sides is a student rooming-house district. In the northwest corner of the city, on and near West Eleventh Street, is a part of town known locally as 'Pigeon Hill,' an area of poorly constructed homes and underprivileged families. A Negro district, with a grade school for Negro children, is located south of Pigeon Hill.

Some fine old houses of an earlier day survive, particularly in the vicinity of tree-shaded College Avenue, once the principal thoroughfare from the public square to the old University campus. The JOSHUA

OWEN HOWE HOUSE, 421 S. College Ave., built in 1834 by Howe, a merchant, is now occupied by the local American Legion post. In this house Dr. James Maxwell and his wife, daughter of the original owner, entertained the trustees and faculty of Indiana University and their wives twice a year. The ANDREW WYLIE HOUSE (*open*), 307 E. Second St., was built in 1835 by the University's first president; its broad halls, beautiful doors and hand-carved woodwork give it unusual distinction. Built of brick and half concealed by trees and shrubbery, the residence is known as 'The Treasure House.' Its spacious rooms are filled with rare jewelry, cloth of gold, linens, and other articles that its present tenant, Mrs. A. S. Hershey, has collected from many parts of the world.

The Hugh Hinkle House, 703 E. Cottage Grove Ave., contains a COLLECTION OF RELICS (*adm. free, by appointment*). Included in the more than 2,000 articles are a 150-year-old ox yoke, old Bloomington newspapers, a cannon ball used at the battle of Bunker Hill, and many Indian artifacts.

Bloomington is at the junction with State 37 (*see Tour* 19).

Left from Bloomington on State 45 is the SITE OF HARMONY, 7.5 *m.*, founded in 1826 as the Blue Springs Community, an experiment in communism. All property was held in common as it was in Robert Owen's New Harmony settlement (*see New Harmony*). Lasting one year, the experiment was wrecked by dissension when the industrious argued that the lazy fared as well as they.

ARLINGTON, 106.7 *m.* (740 alt., 125 pop.), is a small quarrying settlement suburban to Bloomington. At the HOADLEY QUARRY (*visitors welcome*), dimension blocks, weighing between 10 and 12 tons, are cut into building blocks in the adjoining mill.

ELLETTSVILLE, 112.2 *m.* (685 alt., 863 pop.), a stone-quarrying town, is the source of the stone used in the Scottish Rite Cathedral in Indianapolis. Some of the quarries operating here specialize in fine stonework, carving, and ornamentation, particularly in the Gothic style. The town was named for Edward Elletts, who kept a tavern here long before the settlement was platted in 1837.

McCORMICK'S CREEK STATE PARK (*adm.* 10¢; *hiking trails, swimming, bridle paths, picnic and camping areas, free nature-guide service*), 124 *m.*, was the first of Indiana's State parks, acquired by the State in 1916. The mile-long, 100-foot canyon of McCormick's Creek winds through the park; the valleys, plateaus, and wooded slopes of this area still retain their natural charm. WHITE RIVER, bordering the park on the north, is noted for its black bass, pike, and other game fish. Other attractions are the beech woods, a pine forest, an observation tower, and an abandoned quarry that furnished the stone for the foundation of the State Capitol in Indianapolis. A PIONEER LOG CABIN, built by Abel Carpenter at Adel, Owen County, in 1810, has been restored near the barrack-like group camps. A MUSEUM (*free*) houses examples of handicraft, and mounted exhibits of wild life native to the park and region, as well as a few live animals.

SPENCER, 123.1 *m.* (577 alt., 2,375 pop.), seat of Owen County, was named for a Captain Spencer, of Kentucky, killed in the Battle of Tippecanoe. Farming, coal mining, and quarrying are the principal industries around Spencer. A large printing establishment employs many of the town's residents. The business buildings are low and rambling and the atmosphere is that of a quiet county-seat town.

Spencer was the home town of two American poets. At Franklin and Short Streets is the HOUSE OF WILLIAM HERSCHELL (1873–1939), whose most famous poem is 'Long Boy,' popular World War song. The BIRTHPLACE OF WILLIAM VAUGHN MOODY stood on the site now occupied by a white house adjacent to the post office on Washington Street. Moody (1869–1910), dramatist, poet and educator, was best known for his play, *The Great Divide*.

Just south of the library on Washington Street is a house built around, and using as one of its rooms, the old LOG COURTHOUSE, erected in 1820 on a $51.35 contract. Before this courthouse was built, Spencer's first trial was held under the trees of the public square. At this trial, Thomas Adams, first resident lawyer, ended an argument with the opposing counsel by knocking him down with a law book.

Spencer is at the junction with State 67 (*see Tour 19A*).

BOWLING GREEN, 138.3 *m.* (600 alt., 219 pop.), is a country village of large, weather-beaten, frame structures that served as hotels and general stores in days when Bowling Green was the seat of Clay County. The town was founded in 1825 on a high bluff overlooking Eel River. Several efforts were made to jam bills through the Indiana General Assembly relocating the county seat, and on two occasions elections were held on this issue. Bowling Green staved off these attempts, but Brazil (*see Tour 8b*), 25 miles northwest, finally succeeded in becoming the permanent seat in 1877.

The old brick COUNTY JAIL (*private*) stands near the PUBLIC SQUARE. Every fall pioneers from all over the county gather in the square for an Old Settlers' Reunion.

The highway crosses EEL RIVER at the western edge of town, over a new concrete and steel bridge. This Eel River, which joins the east fork of White River near Worthington, is to be distinguished from the Eel River of northeastern Indiana, which joins the Wabash at Logansport. The Eel River here is that of the Delaware Indians, called by them Shakamak, meaning snakefish or eel. It still abounds with eels.

RILEY, 154 *m.* (562 alt., 287 pop.), a small coal-mining town, was known as Lockport in the days of the Wabash and Erie Canal.

Left from Riley on State 159 (oil mat) to the junction with a graveled county road, 1 *m.* Left here to RAY PARK (*adm. free; shelter house, dance hall*), 2 *m.*, a private recreational area. A short stretch of the WABASH AND ERIE CANAL is preserved in the park. The canal is used as a fish hatchery by the Izaak Walton League.

At 9.3 *m.*, where State 159 makes a sharp right turn, is a junction with a graveled county road. Straight ahead on this road to the old WABASH AND ERIE CANAL RESERVOIR, 10.8 m. The bowl-shaped area, dry now, is 6,000 acres in extent and served, when it was flooded, as a feeder for the old canal. From a grove in the center of the reservoir, the old earthwork walls can be seen above the corn growing in the basin.

TERRE HAUTE, 164 m. (495 alt., 62,693 pop.) (*see Terre Haute*). Terre Haute is at the junction with US 40 (*see Tour* 8), US 41 (*see Tour* 20), and US 150 (*see Tour* 12).

ⵏⵏ

Tour 10

(Cincinnati, Ohio)—Seymour—Shoals—Vincennes—(Lawrenceville, Illinois); US 50.
Ohio Line to Illinois Line, 171.3 m.

Hard-surfaced road throughout.
The Baltimore & Ohio R.R. roughly parallels the entire route.
Accommodations of all kinds at frequent intervals.

Wide, sweeping curves, varied at intervals by several miles of straightaway, mark the route between the Ohio Line and Shoals. Most of the country is hilly, and the eastern section is especially rugged, with abundant brush and wild flowers. In spring violets grow thickly along the roads and large patches of bluebells occasionally spangle the hillsides. In late summer trumpet vines festoon the fences. Autumn brings goldenrods and purple gentians and spreads multicolored panoramas of bright foliage on the hills of Lawrence and Martin Counties. The western section—rolling to level, and extensively cultivated—presents a uniformly pleasant pastoral scene.

The route passes through one of the Nation's largest distilling centers and the great quarries of the Indiana limestone belt. Some of the region was traversed by General John Hunt Morgan in his raid of 1863, and Vincennes, on the western border, is rich in historic interest.

US 50 crosses the Indiana Line 21 miles west of Cincinnati, Ohio, at the INDIANA-OHIO STATE MARKER, 0 m., a weather-stone column erected in 1838.

GREENDALE, 3.5 m. (490 alt., 1,548 pop.), is a bustling town filled with the odor of fermenting whisky mash. Although separately incorporated, Greendale is generally considered a part of Lawrenceburg (*see below*).

The distilling of whisky has long been associated with this area, largely because of the supply of clear, cold well water. In 1809 the local manufacture of distilled liquors was begun on the site now occupied by the Old Quaker Plant. From a crude apparatus with an output of two barrels a week, the industry grew steadily until the prohibition era. With the repeal of the Eighteenth Amendment, equipment that had lain idle for 15 years was purchased and the plants enlarged and rehabilitated until they are now among the largest and most modern in the United States.

A trip through either of the two large distilleries requires about four hours. Visitors are shown the various processes of distillation from the time the raw grain is received until liquor is bottled and packed for shipment. A force of 35 Federal agents is maintained here to gauge whisky as it is removed from the warehouses, where more than 2,000,000 barrels of liquor are being aged.

At the intersection of US 50 and Brown St. is a small sign (R) inviting visitors to drive two blocks (R) to the OLD QUAKER PLANT (*visiting permits at office, Brown and Railroad Sts.; 8–4 daily; 8–12 Sat.; guide*). This distillery, originally W. P. Squibbs and Company, was built in 1868, and began operations with a capacity of five barrels a day. The property was bought in 1933 by the Schenley Corporation, rebuilt, and named the Old Quaker Company. A new building was added in 1936 for the distillation of other Schenley whiskies. The original plant has a capacity of about 700 barrels per day and the new plant of about 500 barrels. Approximately 1,200 persons are employed.

The JAMES WALSH & COMPANY DISTILLERY (*visiting permits at office; guide furnished*), four blocks west of the Old Quaker Plant and north of US 50, is the oldest distillery in Lawrenceburg by name but the youngest in operation. The O'Shaughnessy brothers built the present plant in 1934, and adopted the name of the old Rossville distiller, James Walsh. The smallest of the Lawrenceburg distilleries, this plant has a yearly output of 20,000 barrels, much of which is bottled under special labels for customers who market the product under their own names. It has a storage capacity of 40,000 barrels and about 75 persons are employed.

The JOS. E. SEAGRAM PLANT (*visiting permits at office; 8–4 daily; 8–12 Sat.; guide*), three blocks west of the James Walsh & Company Distillery, started in Greendale with the alcohol plant of the Commercial Solvents Company. The Seagrams, Canadian distillers since 1857, purchased this plant in 1933. Subsequent expansion has made their plant the largest in Lawrenceburg; it includes 54 buildings and covers 25 acres. Between 10,000 and 16,000 bushels of grain are used daily. The plant has a daily capacity of 30,000 cases of liquor and storage space for more than 600,000 barrels. During the peak season the Seagram Company employs between 1,200 and 2,000 workers.

LAWRENCEBURG, 4.8 m. (480 alt., 4,413 pop.), a prosperous town with the mellowness of age, was founded in 1801 by Captain

Samuel C. Vance. During the steamboat era it was a favorite port of call on the Ohio River. Boisterous, slave-driving captains, mates, and deckhands caroused in GAMBLERS' ROW, a vice district notorious from Pittsburgh to New Orleans. The district once occupied the river front at the foot of Walnut Street, where the 72-foot levee now extends. Secure for 24 years behind this levee, Lawrenceburg was temporarily turned into a ghost city when on January 21, 1937, the Ohio River swept over the embankment and engulfed the town. The crest of the flood at Lawrenceburg reached 82.6 feet and about 6,000 persons were made homeless.

INDIANA'S FIRST SKYSCRAPER, a block from the river at Walnut and High Sts., is a three-story brick structure built in 1819. This building was an awe-inspiring sight to the pioneer folk. Still well preserved, it is now used as a hotel.

The BEECHER PRESBYTERIAN CHURCH, west side of Short St., between Center and William Sts., is a plain red brick building on the site of the church where Henry Ward Beecher held his first pastorate in 1837. The famous pulpit orator and lecturer served here for two and a half years.

The VANCE-TOUSEY HOUSE (*visitors welcome; weekdays 8–5*), 504 High St., is a two-story brick structure built in 1818 by Captain Samuel Vance. It is now (1941) the office of the Lawrenceburg Roller Mills. Until the Lanier Mansion was erected at Madison (*see Tour 11*), the Vance-Tousey House was considered the finest residence on the Ohio between Cincinnati and Louisville.

AURORA, 8.7 *m.* (499 alt., 4,828 pop.), where stately old houses overlook the Ohio River, was founded in 1819 and named for the goddess of the dawn by Judge Jesse Holman, one of the first judges of the Indiana Supreme Court. Aurora's east and west streets run along the hillsides, so that houses on one side are approached from the sidewalks by high and precipitous flights of steps; houses on the opposite side are built with the second story on the sidewalk level and the first floor below the street. Aurora's industries consist of two furniture factories, a coffin factory, and a paper-box factory.

Like other Ohio River towns, Aurora suffered heavily from the 1937 flood. The water reached a height of 80.9 feet, three-quarters of the city was inundated, and more than 3,000 persons were driven from their homes.

This unassuming little river town was the birthplace of Edwin C. Hill and Elmer Davis, well-known writers and radio commentators.

For several miles up and down the Ohio, the river banks are peopled with families who live in shacks or houseboats. They raise a small patch of tobacco for their own use, and subsist mainly on catfish and greens, accepting the periodical high waters with philosophic calm. They move up the hills into deserted barns until the water recedes, and then return to their shanties to resume their usual occupation of gazing dispassionately at the river.

Aurora is at the junction with State 56 (*see Tour 11*).

In DILLSBORO, 18.4 *m.* (650 alt., 558 pop.), is the DILLSBORO SANATORIUM, a 100-room hotel in which arthritis, rheumatism, and nervous disorders are treated with medicinal waters.

At 23 *m.* is the junction with State 1, a paved highway.

Right on State 1 to the junction with State 350 in MILAN, 5 *m.* (950 alt., 1,000 pop.); R. on State 350 to MOORES HILL, 7.3 *m.* (917 alt., 359 pop.), a quiet village on the highest point in Dearborn County. Here in 1854 a Methodist college was founded, forerunner of the present Evansville College (*see Evansville*). In 1915 the old college building burned and Evansville succeeded in having the college removed and renamed in 1919. The only remaining college building here is the three-story CARNEGIE HALL, now used as a consolidated school.

The main entrance to the VERSAILLES RECREATIONAL DEMONSTRATION AREA (*visitors welcome*), 29 *m.* (R), leads to a 6,000-acre, Federally owned tract of hilly woodland in the valley of Laughery Creek. The area was developed by the National Park Service in co-operation with the Ripley County Park Board. Organized camping facilities are available for short-term, low-cost rental by accredited groups of this region. Three large lodges and kitchens may be rented by camping, hiking, educational, or character-building agencies. A camp with nine cabins, each containing eight cots, occupies the grounds of a former country estate.

Within the area is GORDON'S LEAP, a huge cliff more than 100 feet high. In the early days of the county Dr. William Anderson, graduate of the University of Dublin, settled in Versailles, planning to start a medical college. Two of his most promising students, Gordon and Glass, went to the cemetery near the cliff one night, following the death of a prominent citizen, to exhume his body and use it for dissection. They were detected and a group of indignant villagers pursued the young ghouls. Glass made his way through the foliage and escaped but the pursuers forced Gordon to the edge of the cliff. To the surprise of his would-be captors, Gordon leaped over the precipice. Escaping with a broken leg, he dragged himself across the creek to a cabin where he obtained a horse and fled the county. He later enlisted in the Union Army at Indianapolis, became a major, and after the war was nominated for attorney general of Indiana. Glass went to Missouri and became a prominent physician. Also in the park is a LOG CABIN, a one-room shack reputedly built in 1837. It was the only dwelling in the vicinity at that time and is presumed to be the place where Gordon obtained the horse on which he escaped.

VERSAILLES (pronounced Ver-sales'), 30 *m.* (990 alt., 582 pop.), a farm center founded in 1818, is no larger now than it was in 1880. An outstanding annual event is the Pumpkin Show and Farmers' Fair, held on the second Saturday in October, which attracts between 10,000 and 12,000 persons.

In strange contrast to the nineteenth-century appearance of many of Versailles's buildings, is the TYSON TEMPLE, one block north (R) of US 50. The use of contemporary materials in this structure has resulted in a bizarre church building, completed in 1937. An open-work, cast-aluminum spire soars 100 feet from the ground, rising above the building of concrete, steel, glazed brick, and glass tile. All angles have been rounded, even to the roof covering the auditorium. The ceiling simulates a concave blue sky, with the North Star and constellations of gold and silver leaf. The church is air-conditioned and indirectly lighted. It was built from proceeds of a trust fund given to the town by James H. Tyson, former resident, and co-founder of a Chicago chain drugstore organization.

On the grounds of the Ripley County Courthouse, built in 1852, a MORGAN RAID MARKER recounts the fact that General John Morgan (*see Corydon*) passed through on July 12, 1863. Morgan's men looted the general store at Rexville and came to Versailles, where they were met in the square by the local militia and citizens. The raiders seized the guns belonging to the militia and broke them against the corner of the courthouse. The office of the county treasurer was looted and $5,000 taken; the bulk of the county's money had previously been buried. Morgan had come to Indiana expecting enough help from the Knights of the Golden Circle to capture Indianapolis. The Knights failed him, however, and his men were scattered, captured, or lost during the hurried drive through Indiana and Ohio. A CIVIL WAR MUSEUM (*adm.* 10¢), S. Tyson St., contains pioneer relics and saddle bags, bullets, side arms; and remnants of clothing forgotten or discarded by Morgan's raiders.

A huge stump (L), one block east and two blocks·north of the courthouse, is all that remains of the HANGING TREE, scene of a multiple lynching. In 1897 Versailles was harassed by repeated burglaries, apparently perpetrated by an organized band. The torturing of an old couple spurred citizens to hire a private detective. He gained the confidence of the suspects and was admitted into the gang. When a robbery was planned and the detective informed the officials, five of the gang were captured and lodged in jail at Versailles. A mob of 400 overpowered the jailer and removed the bandits to the tree where they were hanged. The coroner said they 'came to their death at the hands of unknown parties.'

Versailles is at the junction with State 29 (*see Tour 17A*), which unites briefly with US 50.

The water tower and roofs of the MUSCATATUCK COLONY, 47.2 *m.*, a 2,071-acre farm and institution for the care and custody of feeble-minded men, are visible (R). This State-supported colony was opened in 1920. Inmates are employed in various duties or, if harmless, released on furloughs to their families.

NORTH VERNON, 51.1 *m.* (750 alt., 3,112 pop.), a railroad and trading center, was platted in 1854, an offspring of the older town of Vernon. By reason of its transportation facilities North Vernon has become the largest town in Jennings County.

Left from North Vernon on paved State 7 is MUSCATATUCK STATE PARK, 1.1 *m.* (*adm. free; ovens, picnic tables, shelter house*), a 205-acre tract of hilly land overlooking the Vernon fork of the Muscatatuck River, known for its plentiful supply of game fish. At MUSCATATUCK INN (*meals and lodging*), near the entrance, a series of marked trails, arranged in loops, start and end. The park has wide stretches of woods, a circling canyon, fresh-water springs, and cliffs.

VERNON, 2 *m.* (650 alt., 413 pop.), seat of Jennings County, is an old-fashioned town of white houses and red brick county buildings. One of the provisions of the grant of land in 1815 was that Vernon should forever be the county seat.

Vernon was the only town in Indiana that Morgan's raiders could not take. News of Morgan's coming had preceded him and every available man from Jennings County awaited the invader and his 2,200 men at the south edge of Vernon on July 11, 1863. The strength of the little force of 400 was overestimated by Morgan and he sent a flag of truce and demanded a surrender. Colonel Williams, in charge of the Home Guards, replied that he was able to hold the place and would not consider capitulation. Morgan deployed skirmishers along the roads, apparently preparing for battle, and under cover of these demonstrations withdrew the main body of his force. The Confederate raiders then sent a second messenger to Colonel Williams demanding his surrender. Williams detained the messenger until the arrival of General Love with reinforcements, raising the number of defenders to 1,000 men. General Love at once sent the answer, a summons to Morgan to surrender. He asked Morgan for two hours in which to remove the women and children, and although greatly outnumbered and illy equipped, made preparations for battle. After a feeble skirmish and a few desultory shots, the enemy withdrew.

SEMON MILL (*adm. free*), two blocks north of the courthouse, was erected in 1837 and was originally a station and tavern on the old Madison Railroad. The mill is powered by a single-cylinder engine made in 1833 and formerly used in an Ohio River steamboat; the connecting rod is of wood. The engine has supplied power for the mill for more than 80 years.

At 63.4 *m.* is the junction with US 31 (*see Tour* 16), which coincides with US 50 to SEYMOUR, 66.3 *m.* (614 alt., 8,620 pop.), a progressive factory town at the junction of three railroads. Seymour's industries include printing, wood products, stoves, pottery, and woolen goods.

The H. VANCE SWOPE MEMORIAL ART GALLERY (*open weekdays* 8–5), adjoining the library at Walnut and Second Sts., was erected in 1928 with funds bequeathed by H. Vance Swope (1879–1926), a native of Jackson County. Swope became a prominent New York artist.

BROWNSTOWN, 76.6 *m.* (561 alt., 1,860 pop.), founded in 1816, is the seat of Jackson County and a typical Hoosier farm town with a beautiful public square shaded by large maple trees. The building of the Ohio & Mississippi Railroad (now the Baltimore & Ohio) in 1857 fostered the growth of Ewing, just a short distance west. Jealous of the rival town, Ewing refused to give up its post office even when it was annexed to Brownstown; consequently, Brownstown maintains that it is the only town in Indiana with two main post offices.

1. Left from Brownstown on State 250, a blacktop highway, is the entrance (L) to the JACKSON COUNTY STATE FOREST (*adm. free; ovens, shelter houses, tables*), 2 *m.* These 4,000 acres of forested hills and valleys are comparable in beauty with any in Indiana, and are easily accessible on a network

of forest roads. KNOB LAKE, an artificial lake of 10 acres, is well stocked with fish.

2. Left from Brownstown on paved State 135 is VALLONIA, 3.5 m. (550 alt., 486 pop.). At the northwest corner of the schoolhouse lawn is a stone marker on the SITE OF OLD FORT VALLONIA, a pioneer fort built in 1805. Vallonia, platted in 1810, was the first seat of Jackson County.

BEDFORD, 102.1 m. (703 alt., 12,514 pop.), Lawrence County seat, is the center of the Indiana limestone industry, to which the city owes its development. Three stone companies in the vicinity in normal times employ approximately 5,000 men. Bedford is a neat city with fine stone residences and tree-lined streets.

From 16th Street (US 50) at D Street, a dirt driveway leads (R) downhill through a wood for 200 yards; a footpath here leads L. 150 feet to FOOTE'S VAULT, the mausoleum of Dr. Winthrop Foote and his brother, Ziba. A large limestone boulder, approximately 10 feet square and 4 feet high, was hollowed out and made into a tomb. In this was sealed the body of Ziba, who was drowned in 1840; in 1856 Dr. Foote was interred beside him. Dr. Foote is reported to have been one of the first residents to realize the possibilities of Bedford limestone as a building material. He persuaded a stonecutter from Louisville to come to Bedford and start his trade here—the beginning of one of Indiana's foremost industries.

Lending itself easily to carving and delicate tracery, and possessing both beauty and durability, the limestone quarried and fabricated near Bedford has long been a favorite among architects. It has been used in the construction of many of America's best-known buildings, including those of the Federal Triangle in Washington, D. C., the Empire State Building in New York City, the Chicago Museum of Fine Arts, the World War Memorial in Indianapolis, and the Mellon Institute in Pittsburgh.

The MILLS AND QUARRIES OF THE INDIANA LIMESTONE CORPORATION (*open Mon.-Fri.; guides furnished for parties by previous arrangement; permits at office, 4th & I Sts.*) are typical of the companies operating in and about Bedford. Cuts of stone are extracted from the solid floor or ledge of the quarry. These blocks, with an average dimension of 4 feet in thickness, 10 feet in width, and ranging from 50 to 120 feet in length, are turned and laid on the new floor of the quarry by electrically powered steel derricks. Drilled and broken up into mill blocks, the stone is hoisted from the quarry, placed on railroad cars, and transported to the mill for fabrication. Planers work it to the desired shape by anchoring it on moving steel beds, which pass back and forth between stocks or heads that hold currying tools. The smooth block is then cut to required dimensions by hammers operated by electricity or air.

Right from Bedford on State 58 (oil mat) to the junction with State 158, 4 m.; R. on State 158 (oil mat) to the MOSES FELL ANNEX FARM (*visitors welcome;* 6:30–5:30 *Mon.-Sat.,* 6:30–4 *Sun.; guide furnished*), 5 m. This farm (L), given to Purdue University in 1914 by Moses Fell for experimental purposes in horticulture, livestock raising, bee and poultry keeping, has greatly benefited Indiana farmers with information on scientific farming. Livestock and poultry, and specimens of scientific breeding and crossbreeding are on exhibit.

Between Bedford and 105.8 *m.*, south of the bridge across the WHITE RIVER, US 50 and State 37 (*see Tour* 19) are united.

In BRYANTSVILLE, 111.8 *m.* (675 alt., 20 pop.), is the junction with a graveled road.

Left on this road to the junction with another graveled road, 1.5 *m.*; R. on this road to the GRAVE OF DAVID ELKINS, 1.6 *m.*, about 50 yards (R) on a wooded knoll, and marked by a limestone shaft. Elkins claimed that he was the Methodist preacher who came to the Pigeon Creek settlement in Spencer County some months after the death of Nancy Hanks Lincoln and preached a belated funeral sermon over Lincoln's mother and other members of the community who had died of the 'milk-sick' plague. He came to Lawrence County in the early 1840's, settling on a farm near Bryantsville, and preached in that vicinity until he died.

Between Bryantsville and Shoals the highway winds around hillsides and through cuts of shale outcroppings that rise 25 feet on either side. The country is covered with a heavy growth of walnut, maple, oak, and other hardwood trees.

In MARTIN COUNTY STATE FOREST (*adm. free*), 122.1 *m.*, thousands of pine trees have been planted by CCC enrollees. There is a 100-foot FIRE TOWER and a network of firetruck trails extends throughout the 2,000-acre area. These one-way roads are not designed for public traffic, but a motor road extends from US 50 to a developed PICNIC AREA (*shelter house, ovens, water*).

SHOALS, 126.3 *m.* (490 alt., 1,031 pop.), the seventh town to be the seat of Martin County, lies on both sides of the White River. In an area of caves and cliffs around which have been woven tales of Indian treasures, the town is surrounded by high hills and woodlands. This region was frequented by moonshiners and bootleggers during the prohibition era, and in Civil War days by Knights of the Golden Circle, of which Stephen Horsey, grandson of a Martin County pioneer, was a leader. Founded in 1816, Shoals was so named because of its situation at a ford across a shallow place, or shoals, in the river. Lumbering, farming, fishing, and making buttons from mussel shells are the occupations of the townsfolk.

Shoals is at the junction with US 150 (*see Tour* 12), which unites westward with US 50 for 44.5 miles.

Left from Shoals on 'old State 50,' a blacktop road, 1 *m.* to the CLIFFS OF BEAVER CREEK AND SPOUT SPRING (R). The cliffs, also known as the White River Bluffs, extend about one mile north of this point along Beaver Creek and White River, and about 600 feet west along the highway. They are between 60 and 100 feet high, and the loftiest point, about 400 feet north of the highway, is a honeycombed rock of beautifully blended colors, with a large cavern in its north side. The cliff and cavern are reached by the county road that branches R. Spout Springs, about 500 feet west of the junction with this road, is situated under an overhanging sandstone cliff (R).

At 127 *m.* is JUG ROCK PARK (*adm.* 10¢; *picnic area, ovens, tables*), containing a natural rock formation that from a distance resembles a huge jug. The rock, 60 feet high and 15 feet in diameter, is formed of variegated rock strata in which hikers and picnickers have carved names, initials, and dates. Also in the park is PINNACLE ROCK, a high cliff overgrown with moss, ferns, and lichens, which rises 150 feet above White River.

At 127.6 *m.* is a junction with blacktop State 450.

Right on State 450 is DOVER HILL, 3.5 *m.* (610 alt., 285 pop.), a village strung out for half a mile along a high ridge above the White River. This village was the county seat between 1848 and 1857.

At 5 *m.* is the junction with a graveled road.

Right on this road to the junction with a country lane, 5.5 *m.;* R. on this lane to a winding road at the edge of the White River, 6.3 *m.*, the beginning of McBRIDES BLUFFS, a range of precipitous, rocky cliffs about 175 feet high. Numerous small caves, bear holes, and springs are among the rocks. According to legend, McBrides Bluffs were the headquarters of the Choctaw Indians for about 100 years, and somewhere among the bluffs is a closed cave in which they lived during severe weather. Absalom Fields, an early settler, is said to have been seized one autumn evening by a band of Indians who blindfolded him and took him to their place of concealment, removed the blindfold, and showed him their treasure. According to Fields's story there was a fabulous amount of silver molded into crude bricks. The Indians then replaced the blindfold and returned Fields to his home. He spent the remainder of his life—the legend relates—in a futile effort to find the cache. The Indians left this section shortly after the incident, but in 1866 an old Indian sent his son-in-law back to the bluffs to find the silver. This man dug into the cliffs repeatedly but the secret hoard was never found. The land had been cleared and the trees that the old Indian had cited as landmarks were gone. Twice, bars of silver similar to those described by Absalom Fields have been found above ground in this vicinity, but the treasure cave defies all searchers.

At 7 *m.* on State 450 is TRINITY SPRINGS (590 alt., 120 pop.), once a popular resort that boasted two large hotels and much activity because of the medicinal properties of two wells at the north end of the village. One hotel burned, the other has closed, and the resort is now (1941) almost deserted.

LOOGOOTEE (pronounced La-goat′ee), 134.3 *m.* (546 alt., 2,325 pop.), a town of well-kept residences, is peopled mainly by retired farmers. Its name is a corruption of the combination of Lowe, for the engineer of the first train through town and Gootee, the owner of the land upon which the town was built.

Natural gas was struck in this vicinity in 1899, and four glass factories were established. Loogootee enjoyed a period of prosperity until the prohibition era, when its two bottle factories and a fruit-jar plant were closed; the window-glass plant was destroyed by fire. A partial recovery has been accomplished by inducing work-shirt, veneer, and tile factories to begin operation in the town.

Right from Loogootee on paved State 45 to BURNS CITY, 11 *m.* (710 alt., 160 pop.), a sleepy, century-old village typical of the several small settlements in the rugged upland country of northern Martin County. Once the site of flourishing tanneries, gristmills, and barrel factories, these villages have declined owing to eroded farm lands and the loss of population to urban centers. Here, now, are one-room schoolhouses, hillside coal mines, dirt roads, and the descendants of restless, independent men who pushed into the forests from Kentucky and Ohio when Indiana was young.

At 16 *m.* is the entrance to the WHITE RIVER LAND UTILIZATION PROJECT (*free; shelter houses, picnic areas*), a 32,000-acre Federal development to provide recreational facilities and to convert unproductive farm land to pasture and forest. A 1,900-foot earth dam impounds an 800-acre lake, stocked with fish. Other developments include the building of 5,000 check dams as a part of the erosion control project, construction of 1,000 upland game shelters, and clearing of 15 miles of linking trails. Controlled cutting of timber will eventually reimburse the government for part of the cost of the area. The land for this project was sold voluntarily by the farmer-owners, although in Greene County, which adjoins the area on the north, protest meetings were held in country schoolhouses when it was believed that the government planned to buy eroded land there and retire it from production.

At 142 *m.* on US 50 is the junction with a graveled road.

Right on this road is the village of MONTGOMERY, 0.2 *m.* (537 alt., 510 pop.), built around St. Peter's Church, which was founded in 1818 at Black Oaks, a small settlement near by. The church, on the crest of a hill (R), is a red brick structure of Gothic design. Montgomery was at one time seriously considered as the site for a great Catholic university. Here in 1841, Father Edward Sorin, rector of St. Peter's and later founder of the University of Notre Dame (*see South Bend*), planned to build the university. The Bishop of Vincennes, to show his appreciation of Father Sorin's earnestness, offered to deed him in perpetuity the properties of St. Mary-of-the-Lake, as the site of Notre Dame was then known, on the sole condition that he open a college for young men there within two years.

An AMISH SETTLEMENT, which lies mainly R., begins at 5 *m.* and covers an area of 64 square miles. There are no towns or villages, for the Amish are all farmers. A very thrifty and industrious people, they live according to the strictest interpretation of the Bible, stressing humility and simplicity in their customs and dress (*see Tour 15*).

At 11 *m.* is the junction with another graveled road; R. on this road to its junction with State 58, 14 *m.* Left on State 58 is ODON, 14.7 *m.* (545 alt., 958 pop.), a farm town with pleasant, tree-shaded streets. A stone marker stands on the CAMP SITE OF GEORGE ROGERS CLARK and his soldiers, near a spring that supplies water for the city hall. Here Clark's men stopped for water and to hunt buffalo. An annual event at Odon is the Old Settlers' Reunion, held on August 22, 23, 24, and said to be the largest picnic of its kind in the State.

GRAHAM FARMS (*adm. free*), 146 *m.*, cover approximately 5,000 acres of fertile land between the two branches of the White River, and have more than 800 head of registered cattle, 500 hogs and 2,500 chickens. They are operated scientifically on an extremely large scale; corn is planted in rows a mile and a half long, and a ton and a half of cheese is made every day. There is a privately owned grain elevator with a capacity of 150,000 bushels. The Graham Farms Fair, held annually in late August, is of State-wide interest.

WASHINGTON, 149.1 *m.* (443 alt., 9,312 pop.), Daviess County seat, is an attractive trading and industrial center, with large Baltimore & Ohio Railroad shops. The first settlement on the site of Washington was made in 1805, when Fort Flora was erected during the Indian uprising. Nothing remains of this old fort that stood on the present corner of Second and Main Streets.

The old VAN TREES MANSION (*private*), northeast corner of Main and Sixth Sts., was built in 1843 by Colonel John Van Trees, a successful merchant, on the site where his father, Emmanuel Van Trees, one of the founders of Washington, built his cabin in 1817. This house reflects the Greek Revival style of a century ago, with fluted Doric columns hand-carved from solid tree trunks. Originally this was an imposing, two-story, ten-room structure, but the upper story was destroyed by fire in 1906 and never replaced. Henry Clay was a guest here at one time, and Van Trees gave a stately and sumptuous ball for Governor Oliver P. Morton. Van Trees was county clerk for 37 years and administered the oath to a young Illinois attorney named Abraham Lincoln, who appeared in court in the interest of a client.

In MAYSVILLE, 153 *m.* (450 alt., 150 pop.), US 50 crosses the Big Four Railroad, which is built on the towpath of the old Wabash and Erie Canal.

At 156.4 *m.* is the junction with a graveled road.

1. Right on this road 1 *m.* is the STANDARD MINE (*visitors welcome; State laws prohibit taking visitors into mine*), operated co-operatively by 160 men, all of whom are stockholders of the Standard Coal Company. Completed in 1928 and one of the most modern deep mines in the State, it is electrically lighted and the coal is loosened by compressed air instead of blasting. The coal seams are between 4 and 6 feet thick and approximately 160 feet deep. The mine produces about 2,000 tons of bituminous coal daily.

2. Left on this gravel road to the junction with State 61, 4.2 *m.;* L. on State 61 through MONROE CITY (480 alt., 518 pop.), to graveled Walnut Grove Road, 8.8 *m.* Left here, 10.9 *m.*, to WALNUT GROVE CEMETERY (R), final resting place of James D. 'Blue Jeans' Williams, 17th governor of Indiana. 'Blue Jeans' was born in Ohio, January 16, 1808, and grew to manhood under unfavorable circumstances. Schools were infrequent and education was obtained with difficulty. When he was 20 years old his father died, leaving a large family in his care. Williams entered public life as a justice of the peace in 1839, holding the office until elected to the legislature in 1843, in which he served until 1874. Following his election to Congress in 1874, he was nominated and elected governor in 1876, defeating Benjamin Harrison. Harrison gave him the name of 'Blue Jeans' because of his addiction to this apparel. One of Williams's favorite expressions was that he 'just grew up between two corn rows.'

WHEATLAND, 157.3 *m.* (483 alt., 713 pop.), and FRITCHTON, 163.2 *m.* (530 alt., 50 pop.), are trade centers for a rich apple and peach orchard district.

VINCENNES, 170.8 *m.* (442 alt., 18,228 pop.) (*see Vincennes*).

In Vincennes are junctions with US 41 (*see Tour 20*) and State 67 (*see Tour 19A*), and the western junction with US 150 (*see Tour 12*).

Left from Vincennes on State 61 (St. Clair St.) to the junction with a paved road, 0.9 *m.;* R. on this road, 1 *m.*, is SUGAR LOAF MOUND (*adm. free*), a truncated cone (L) 140 feet high. The mound has an east-west diameter of 216 feet and a north-south diameter of 180 feet at the base. The level area at the summit is 16 by 25 feet. The mound was used for burials by a prehistoric race. In 1873 John Collett, an archeologist, sank a shaft straight downward from the center of the summit, revealing three burial layers, consisting of a mixture of ashes, charcoal and bones, at varying depths. Below the third layer is a stratum of red altar clay that forms the interior bottom of the mound. According to one theory, the presence of charcoal mixed with bones indicates that the mound builders attempted to cremate their dead. Many archeologists disagree and say that the bodies of deceased tribesmen were buried in charcoal because it is a durable substance and an excellent preservative. Sugar Loaf has been an object of curiosity for 200 years, but the shaft sunk by Collett is the only systematic investigation ever made of its interior.

US 50 crosses the Wabash River into Illinois over the LINCOLN MEMORIAL BRIDGE, 171.3 *m.*, nine miles east of Lawrenceville, Illinois (*see Illinois Guide*).

ʯʯʯ

Tour 11

Aurora—Madison—Scottsburg—Salem—Paoli—French Lick—Jasper —Princeton—(Mt. Carmel, Illinois); State 56, 156, 61, 64. Aurora to Illinois Line, 217.9 *m.*

Paved roadbed throughout.
Route paralleled by Monon R.R. between Paoli and French Lick; by Southern R.R. between French Lick and Illinois Line.
Accommodations at short intervals.

The eastern portion of this tour follows the Ohio River, winding through towns that retain hints of the faded glories of steamboat days in their stately old homes and outmoded business districts. The broad Ohio, nearly always visible from the highway, dominates the scene, and its valley is Indiana's largest tobacco-growing district. Turning away from the river, the route traverses a region of yellow clay soil, bleak and sparsely inhabited in some sections, but always rugged and hilly. The landscape becomes more heavily wooded as the route progresses westward from the cone-shaped knobs between Scottsburg and Salem. Then the highway descends into the beautiful Lost River Valley and passes through French Lick, one of America's foremost health and pleasure resorts. Near the Illinois Line, in the valley of the Wabash River, is a level stretch of fertile farm land.

State 56 branches south from US 50 (*see Tour* 10) in AURORA, 0 *m.* (499 alt., 4,828 pop.) (*see Tour* 10). Leaving the banks of the Ohio but still following its general course, the route crosses rolling woodlands.

On the north bank (R) of Laughery Creek, 2.3 *m.*, is a granite MONUMENT TO COLONEL LOCHRY AND HIS MEN, who were massacred here by Indians in 1781. Archibald Lochry and 107 men were marching to join George Rogers Clark at the Falls of the Ohio (Louisville), to plan an expedition against Detroit. On the forenoon of August 24,

1781, as Lochry's men were preparing to make camp at the Laughery Creek site, they were attacked by a large force of Indians. Thirty-six of the whites were killed, 64 were captured, and 2 escaped. Following the battle, Lochry was tomahawked and scalped, as were also the wounded who were unable to walk. The prisoners were handed over to the British, who took them to Detroit. Several escaped and some were later exchanged.

At 2.9 m. is a junction with a graveled road.

Right on this road, along the banks of Laughery Creek, to HARTFORD, 6.1 m. (530 alt., 39 pop.). Once a stopping point on the old Madison-Aurora stagecoach road, Hartford is now a cluster of time-worn houses and store buildings huddled together beside the road. Small fields of bottom land and century-old, square-built brick houses flank the road, which parallels the creek in its meandering course through the narrow valley. Life here is leisurely and uninfluenced by progress in the outside world. The soft-spoken natives are of stock that generations ago came to terms with their environment—green hills stepping down to the winding stream.

RISING SUN, 8.4 m. (520 alt., 1,545 pop.), seat of Ohio County, is an old river town, platted in 1814. For many years it was the scene of considerable steamboat building and an important shipping point. The name was suggested by the grandeur of the sunrise over the Kentucky hills above the town of Rabbit Hash, across the river. On Front Street, which runs along the river, are several warehouses that date from the heyday of the river traffic. The town's jumbled little business district contrasts sharply with its dignified residential section of broad streets and shaded walks.

Outstanding among the many old structures is the two-story gray brick SEMINARY BUILDING, 4th and Walnut Sts., erected in 1827 and for some time a Presbyterian seat of higher education. The building is now (1941) a private residence. The OHIO COUNTY COURTHOUSE, Main, Broad, and Mulberry Sts., is a two-story structure built in 1845. Large round pillars support a pediment in front and open stairways lead to the courtroom on the second floor. This building is the seat of government for Indiana's smallest county—both in size and population. The population of the area has been dwindling steadily since the turn of the century, and according to the 1940 census, numbered only 3,782.

At 11 m. is the junction with State 156, now the route, which follows the river—south, east, and then southwest.

PATRIOT, 21.2 m. (525 alt., 257 pop.), an active settlement during the era of river transportation, has for many years been merely a quiet community of retired farmers and river men. Patriot's serenity was abruptly shattered in 1937 when flood waters swept through the village and all but destroyed it.

There are several hamlets and ferry landings along the river road southwest of Patriot. White-painted arms of river signals and lanterns stand beside the highway on the banks of the curving Ohio. At filling stations and on village porches are old men who can recall the long-gone steamboat days when the valley was black with the smoke of proud stern-wheelers. Now past the faded river towns rolls the Ohio, silent and empty save for an occasional excursion boat, or a chuffing tug pushing a row of barges.

VEVAY (pronounced Vee′vee), 39.2 m. (495 alt., 1,209 pop.), seat of Switzerland County, was founded in 1801 by a group of Swiss immigrants, who started vineyards and made wine of excellent quality. The settlement became widely known in early years and played host to many prominent citizens, among them Henry Clay, who prized the quality of the Swiss wine and once had a dozen bottles sent to his home in Lexington, Kentucky. Intending to regale some distinguished visitors with his choice wine, he found that all 12 bottles were filled with whisky, substituted by his son James, who had also found the product of Vevay's vineyards much to his liking.

Wine-making in time gave way to agriculture, for a bushel of potatoes would buy as much as a gallon of wine and was far easier to produce. During the period of river transportation Vevay had several furniture factories and woolen mills, but the development of railroads in other sections of the State (there are still no railroads in Switzerland or Ohio Counties) gradually discouraged industrial activity. Today, the SWISS INN, Main and Ferry Sts., which has been operated uninterruptedly as a hostelry since 1823, plays host to Vevay's visitors.

In a wide, tree-shaded lawn, surrounded by a spiked iron fence, stands the SWITZERLAND COUNTY COURTHOUSE, a two-story brick structure topped by a dome and four clock faces of wood. Four columns support the front pediment, and tall, square-paned windows open on a balcony enclosed by a wrought-iron railing. Large wood-burning stoves stand in cleared spaces among the box-like pews of the courtroom on the second floor. The judge's chambers and each of the county officials' rooms, all clean and orderly, are heated by stoves. A narrow stairway leads to the dome which, through its louver boards, affords an excellent view of Vevay and the Kentucky shore. The courthouse was completed during the Civil War.

One-half block west of the courthouse on Main Street stands the two-story brick BIRTHPLACE OF EDWARD EGGLESTON (see Literature). In The Hoosier Schoolmaster, which has been printed in eight languages, Eggleston used the experiences of his brother, George, who was only 16 years old when he taught school at the Ryker's Ridge District School in Jefferson County. The setting and some of the incidents were drawn from the northern part of Decatur County, where Eggleston had spent a year clerking in a village store.

In the historical room of the CARNEGIE LIBRARY, one block east of the courthouse on Ferry St., is a MUZIO CLEMENTI PIANO, brought from England to this country in 1817. Made in the style of the clavichord with five and a half octaves, it was recognized as a fine instrument, a great improvement over the pianos of that period. Clementi (1752–1832), the Italian composer and pianist who created it, is known as the father of modern piano-building technique. The piano belonged to Mary Wright, daughter of an aristocratic but impoverished English family that came to this country in 1817 and settled on a land grant near Vevay. Deserted by her English fiancé, she lived bewildered and heart-broken in this wild, rough country. An accomplished musician, she found outlet for her grief and loneliness in weekly concerts which she gave for the pioneer folk of the community. On each occasion she descended the ladder from the second floor of her father's rough log cabin attired in court dress and jewels, and with a gracious bow seated herself at the piano and played her entire repertoire. Then without a word she would retire to her second-story room, and the guests would quietly depart. These concerts con-,'nued for 40 years without the piano ever being tuned, or the introduction of a new composition. The court dress grew faded and the jewels tarnished, but the same dignified procedure endured year after year. The only time Mary Wright ever left the house was to wander alone in the moonlight. She was found dead in her room in 1874, at the age of 82.

Among the historic homes of Vevay is the FERRY HOUSE, on the river bank opposite the ferry landing, which has always been owned and occupied by the owners of the ferry. Its concrete-covered stone walls, three feet thick, have withstood every flood of the river since its construction more than a century ago.

The Switzerland County Poorhouse, in the northwestern part of town, occupies the AMIE MOREROD HOUSE, a two-story brick structure built by General John Dumont more than 100 years ago. A winding path, bordered by Lombardy poplars, leads to the building.

The old brick DUMONT HOUSE (*private*), facing the river at the western edge of town, is set in a lawn shaded by fir trees. In the wine cellar beneath the house is a huge 500-gallon cask typical of those used by the first wine-makers here. Julia C. Dumont, beloved teacher of Edward Eggleston, taught many of her pupils here.

In Vevay is the junction with State 56, again the route, which follows the river westward through high, wooded hills, used by the Indians as lookout stations before the coming of the white man. At several places there are commanding views of the river (L).

The HENRY HOUSE, 41.3 *m.*, a small brick residence (L), is set in the midst of an old-fashioned garden at the Riverair Recreational Camp. In the attic is a chest of European workmanship, more than 400 years old, that contains several very old quilts, one of which is made of more than 8,000 pieces. The old gabled, frame building behind the house was the INK FACTORY of John Henry, who conducted a thriving business during the 1850's and 1860's, manufacturing ink by a process known only to himself. His secret was finally stolen by a crafty visitor who started a factory in Louisville and forced Henry out of business. The ink vats, machinery, and an old book-binder remain as Henry left them.

In LAMB, 47.5 *m.* (501 alt., 18 pop.), a ferry (*car* 50¢, *pedestrians* 10¢) runs to Carrollton, Kentucky; it operates day and night, but maintains no regular schedule, and passengers may have to call across the river. Carrollton's steeple and red brick warehouses are visible across the Ohio.

From the top of high, wooded CEDAR CLIFFS, 55.9 *m.*, that parallel the highway and the river westward for a mile or more, there is a 12-mile view of the river. The only productive land along this route is a strip about 300 yards wide between the highway and the river bank, utilized to the last foot for the growing of tobacco and corn.

MADISON, 59.8 *m.* (650 alt., 6,923 pop.), seat of Jefferson County, occupies a peninsula between Crooked Creek on the west and north, and the Ohio River on the south. North and east are ranges of high hills; westward is densely wooded Clifty Falls State Park.

Madison is bisected by Main Street, on which are most of the business establishments and some of the better residences. Many fine houses stand along the river front on 1st and 2nd Streets, the fashionable neighborhood of an earlier day. Built between 1830 and 1860, these dignified structures reflect the Southern style of pre-Civil War days. Most of the buildings in the business district—the city hall, the courthouse, the National Bank, and many others—have a mid-nineteenth-century atmosphere. Along the river bank at the western edge of town are shipyards that flourished in 1830 and are still sometimes used to repair large river boats. Here were built a Union gunboat during the Civil War, and, in the eighties and nineties, many of the Ohio River's famous packets. Madison's small industrial plants employ about 400 workers.

The first settlers arrived in 1805. In 1809 the entire peninsular tract was purchased at a public land sale at Jeffersonville by Colonel John Paul, a Revolutionary War soldier, who platted the town, named it for President James Madison, and gave lavishly of his means for public use. Advantageously situated in the river transport days as the nearest port for interior Indiana, Madison grew swiftly. Its population in 1850 exceeded 5,000, making it the largest city in Indiana, a position it held for five years. It was outstripped, however, when new direct routes to Eastern markets were established from Louisville and Cincinnati.

Tobacco is all-important to the farmers of Jefferson County, where limestone soil produces leaf second to none in the Burley district for color and texture. The first day of the sale in December is a ceremonial occasion, when the auctioneers with their musical lingo, completely unintelligible to the layman, start down the rows of baskets in Madison's five large warehouses. When tobacco 'starts moving' it means money for growers and increased business for Madison merchants and bankers. Tobacco is unloaded in the basements, removed from sticks and re-graded if necessary, then placed in baskets with the grower's name on each basket and brought to the sales floor above. Buyers from the large manufacturing companies go from one warehouse to another as the auctions are held. TOBACCO WAREHOUSES include the Farmers, 2nd and West Sts.; the Independent, a one-story brick building at the foot of West St.; the Maddox, a sheet-iron warehouse covering a block at Central and West Sts.; and the two-story brick Planters Warehouse, Central and Front Sts.

THE PAUL HOUSE (*private*), 1st and Jefferson Sts., oldest brick building in Madison, is a two-story structure with dormers, a bracketed cornice, and a hip roof. It was built by Colonel John Paul in 1809. Surrounded by its original stone-fronted terrace, a precaution against high water, it is still used as a residence.

MADISON HOTEL, NW. corner 2nd and Mulberry Sts., is a hipped-roof, stone building with marble floors and mantels, and spiral iron stairways. Designed and built in 1849 by Francis Costigan, it has been operated as a hostelry since that time.

The SCHOFIELD MANSION, SE. corner 2nd and Poplar Sts., a red-brick structure of Southern Colonial style, was built in 1817 by Major Alexander Chalmers Lanier, father of James F. D. Lanier. The Grand Masonic Lodge of Indiana was organized here on January 12 and 13, 1818.

SULLIVAN HOUSE, NW. corner 2nd and Poplar Sts., now an antique shop, is a two-story brick house, painted white. It was built in 1818 by Judge Jeremiah Sullivan, a Virginian, who proposed the name 'Indianapolis' for the State capital. Of architectural interest is the entrance, with its graceful iron railing and its doorway of Palladian influence, set off by delicate moldings, fluted pilasters Corinthian-capped, side panels of glass, and a fanlight above. The yard is enclosed by a high stone wall with a formal entrance of wrought iron.

The SHREWSBURY HOUSE (*open*), SW. corner 1st and Poplar Sts., was designed by Francis Costigan and built in 1846 for Captain Charles Lewis Shrewsbury, who came from Virginia and accumulated a fortune operating a fleet of Ohio River boats. His home, known from Pittsburgh to New Orleans, was the scene of many brilliant social gatherings. The house is of red brick trimmed with wrought iron. The interior has marble fireplaces and a spiral staircase.

The JAMES F. D. LANIER HOME (*open 9:30–5 daily; adm. 25¢*), 1st St. between Elm and Vine Sts., was designed and built by Francis Costigan in 1844. Much of its ornamental work was produced by the architect himself, who was trained as a carpenter's apprentice in Baltimore, and studied architectural design before migrating West. He followed classical precedents, but was original in his refinements of cornice, column, scroll, and cupola.

An elaborate structure of great dignity and luxury of detail, the Lanier mansion was in its day considered unsurpassed in architectural beauty. Its 50-foot portico, which includes four 30-foot pillars, commands a panoramic view of the Ohio River and the Kentucky hills, with beautifully landscaped grounds and gardens in the foreground. Both the Lanier mansion and the Shrewsbury house are distinguished by three-story spiral stairs that rise unsupported except for their own thrust. Costigan's signature, engraved on silver plates, is set in the newel posts.

James F. D. Lanier, great-grandson of George Washington's maternal aunt, was a wealthy pioneer banker. He advanced approximately $1,000,000 as an unsecured loan when Indiana, without money or credit, needed money to equip soldiers for the Civil War. The Lanier Home was given to the State by his descendants. Most of the original furnishings remain.

The MADISON LIBRARY, corner of Main and Elm Sts., a three-story stone-trimmed brick building with Gothic gables and dormers, is an outgrowth of the first public library in the old Northwest Territory. In 1811 a group of Easterners met in an inn at Madison under the leadership of Alexander Meek, an attorney, to form the Madison Society Library. Twenty-four subscribers paid $5 each for borrowing privileges in that first year. The library soon outgrew its quarters in the inn and was moved to a store building. After the Civil War it became a county enterprise. Among its present volumes are many worn, rare books from the original library.

Madison is connected by bridge (50¢ *toll for automobile and* 4 *passengers*) with Milton, Kentucky, and is at the junction with State 29 (*see Tour 17A*).

> Right from Madison on State 7 is SPRINGDALE CEMETERY, 1.1 *m.*, where the parents of the late George Grey Barnard, noted sculptor, are buried. Near their graves is a marble reproduction of one of his most famous works, 'Let There Be Light.'
>
> Near the top of an exceptionally long, steep hill, SHELVING ROCK, 1.8 *m.*, a small waterfall (R), leaps from a wide rock shelf into a cement catch basin some 40 feet below.
>
> NORTH MADISON, 2.9 *m.* (877 alt., 316 pop.), is a quiet village on an eminence above the older town. Founded in 1847 and once a prosperous meat-packing center, this village has declined rapidly since 1900. MADISON STATE HOSPITAL (also known as Cragmont) consists of 1,200 acres and 30 modern buildings, and accommodates 1,600 patients. This institution for the insane is the most modern and beautifully situated of the State's benevolent institutions. At the south edge of the grounds, traversed by a three-mile concrete drive, there is an excellent view of the housetops of Madison and the winding Ohio.

JEFFERSON COUNTY POOR FARM, 61.3 *m.*, is a large, whitewashed, two-story brick structure (L) built around the four sides of a hollow square or patio. This is the poor farm that inspired Will Carleton to write the poem, 'Over the Hill to the Poorhouse,' while he was a resident of Madison. Beginning near the farm, the DEVIL'S BACKBONE, a serrated ridge, runs parallel to the highway for a mile. The ridge, about 200 feet high and a quarter of a mile in width, is so named because it resembles the vertebrae of a huge crouching monster.

A stone gatekeeper's lodge, 62.1 *m.*, marks the entrance to CLIFTY FALLS STATE PARK (*adm.* 10¢; *shelter houses, picnicking areas*), a 617-acre preserve of wild and rugged beauty. Along the roads within the park are high rocky bluffs, rock-strewn canyons, and deep ravines into which the sun shines only at noon.

CLIFTY FALLS, the principal attraction, at the north end of the park, is reached by a series of stairs down the side of the gorge into Clifty

Canyon. Here Clifty Creek flows over wide ledges of rock and drops in a silvery shower into a huge stone basin 90 feet below. For nearly two and a half miles, the deep-cut canyon winds southward, bordered by foot trails and occasionally spanned by a rustic bridge. An abandoned railroad tunnel leads into a hill beside one of the hiking trails. CLIFTY INN, a three-story, red brick building of Colonial style, stands on the brow of a bluff that rises 400 feet above the Ohio River. The view from the veranda is the finest in the park.

At 65.4 m. is the junction with a paved road.

Left on this road is HANOVER, 0.4 m. (820 alt., 406 pop.), founded more than a century ago and widely known as the seat of HANOVER COLLEGE. The oldest private institution of higher education in Indiana, the college was founded in 1827 by the Presbyterian denomination as a manual labor academy. After many vicissitudes, including temporary removal to Madison (in 1844 the students moved the library back to Hanover in wagons), the college achieved its present status as a four-year college of liberal arts, and in 1880 became coeducational. The 2co-acre campus is on a high bluff. The windows of the Thomas A. Hendricks Library—named for a Vice President of the United States (1885–9) who was graduated from Hanover College in 1841—afford a wide, sweeping panorama of the Ohio River Valley. The white pillars of the red brick CLASSIC HALL, built in 1853, face the front campus and the river. Other buildings include an observatory, science building, gymnasium, faculty residences, and dormitories. DONNER RESIDENCE HALL, a three-story red brick dormitory housing 116 girls, was completed in 1939; it is the gift of William H. Donner, a former student. A small frame building, erected in 1883, is the FIRST COLLEGE Y.M.C.A. BUILDING in the country. The oldest building in Indiana used continuously for college functions is the small brick HANOVER PRESBYTERIAN CHURCH, Gothic in design, used for religious services and commencements since 1832.

Three-fourths of Hanover's approximately 375 students are residents of Indiana. A high point of student life is the annual boat trip each spring; students and faculty spend the day steaming up the broad Ohio in a four-decked stern-wheeler, complete with calliope and dance floor.

At 68.9 m. is the junction with State 62 (see Tour 11A).

In SCOTTSBURG, 83 m. (596 alt., 2,189 pop.), is a bronze STATUE of WILLIAM HAYDEN ENGLISH (L), a native of Scott County and once a candidate for Vice President of the United States. It stands in the yard of the weather-beaten old courthouse in the center of town. English represented Indiana in Congress, served as Secretary of the State Constitutional Convention of 1850, and was the author of a history of the Northwest Territory.

Scottsburg is at the junction with US 31 (see Tour 16).

The KNOBS, 90.9 m., huge, wooded, cone-shaped hills, stretch away southward into the distance. These ancient hills were cut by stream erosion (see Natural Setting.)

At 102.2 m. is the junction with a graveled road.

Right on this road, 0.2 m., is the old HICKSITE MEETING HOUSE (L), built in 1816 by Quaker settlers from North Carolina. The structure became the property of the followers of Elias Hicks after a controversy over the divinity of Christ had split the Society of Friends in 1828. It was remodeled in 1870 but has long been almost entirely unused. Descendants of the early members are buried in the adjacent cemetery.

The BLUE RIVER FRIENDS MEETING HOUSE, 1.4 *m.*, stands on the site of the original structure built by the Orthodox Friends, who opposed the Hicksites. Services are still (1941) held here each Sunday. Before the Civil War, this Quaker community was active in the operation of the Underground Railroad (*see Tour* 13), and was one of the places visited by General John Hunt Morgan, the Confederate raider (*see Corydon*). Until 1888 the township school-house near by was occupied by the BLUE RIVER FRIENDS ACADEMY.

SALEM, 103.5 *m.* (623 alt., 3,194 pop.), seat of Washington County, has long been under Quaker influence. It was named by the wife of William Lindley, first surveyor of the county, for her native Salem, North Carolina, because German members of the community had difficulty pronouncing the suggested name of Mount Vernon. Founded in 1814, Salem grew slowly. This was partly owing to an epidemic of cholera in 1833, which nearly depopulated the town and caused many of the survivors to move away. Salem never fully recovered from this setback.

In the same year Washington County was the victim of an unusual raid. Coming from the north, countless thousands of squirrels invaded the county, filling the trees, covering fences, and devastating cornfields. Killing or capturing them did not seem to lessen their numbers, until one morning they disappeared as abruptly as they had come.

From the courthouse square, with its stone courthouse, shade-blanketed streets descend to the outskirts with varying degrees of steepness. One block east of the courthouse is College Avenue, a cheery, flower-clustered thoroughfare less than a city block in length. The BIRTHPLACE OF JOHN HAY, 106 College Ave., is a one-story yellow brick house. Hay, statesman, diplomat, poet, and historian, was born on October 8, 1838, the son of Dr. Charles Hay and Helen Leonard Hay, and spent the first three years of his life in Salem. A brilliant lawyer, he began his career as secretary to Abraham Lincoln and held the post of Secretary of State under President McKinley and President Theodore Roosevelt. His most noteworthy achievements were promotion of the Open Door policy in China at the time of the Boxer Rebellion in 1900; his handling of the Alaskan boundary question; and his promotion of friendly relations between the United States and Great Britain when he served as British Ambassador under McKinley.

In collaboration with John G. Nicolay, another of Lincoln's secretaries, Hay wrote an authoritative biography of Lincoln. He was also the author of a novel, *The Breadwinners,* and a book of verse, *Pike County Ballads.* His 'Jim Bludsoe' and 'Little Britches' have become almost folk poetry. Hay was said always to have considered himself a 'man without a state,' showing a pronounced distaste for Indiana, to which he constantly referred as 'this barbarous west.' He died in 1905 at his home in New Hampshire.

Just off the highway (R), beyond the southern extremity of South Main Street, is a MORGAN RAID MARKER. Here, 150 poorly armed Home Guards attempted to resist Morgan's entry into Salem, on July 10, 1863. On the public square was a small swivel cannon, about

18 inches long, used to celebrate holidays. This was loaded for the Confederate onslaught, and the gunner waited to discharge the cannon with a hot coal. So unnerved did he become when the Confederate cavalry charged that he dropped the coal, which fell down into his boot top. At that point the cavalry charge became of secondary interest. The cannon was never fired.

Morgan entered Salem at about nine o'clock in the morning and left at two o'clock in the afternoon. The banks had sent all their money out of town and the telegrapher had escaped with the instruments, but the depot, the water tank, and all the bridges were burned and the stores were looted for clothing and provisions. Colonel Basil Duke, one of Morgan's staff officers, writing of the raid said: 'They did not pillage with any sort of method or reason; it seemed to be a mania, senseless and purposeless. One man carried for two days a bird cage containing three canaries. Another rode with a huge chafing dish on the pommel of his saddle. Although the weather was intensely warm, another slung seven pairs of skates around his neck. I saw very few articles of real value taken; they pillaged like boys robbing an orchard.' A number of the raiders carried bolts of calico with them, which they unrolled and gave to the women and girls as they rode out of Salem. A strong force of Federal cavalry was threatening Morgan at this time, and it was here that he abandoned his intention of proceeding north to Indianapolis.

In 1864, in a trial before a military court in Indianapolis, several of the State's leading citizens were proved to be leaders in the Knights of the Golden Circle, called the Order of American Knights in Indiana. One of the surprises of the trial was the release of Horace Heffren, a Salem attorney, who was Deputy Grand Commander of the order. Heffren turned State's evidence and appeared as a witness for the Government, revealing that Dr. William A. Bowles, of French Lick, was the military leader of the order; that plans had been made to kidnap Governor Oliver P. Morton, who was to be held as a hostage; and that an insurrection had been planned for August 16, 1864. Several leaders were convicted of treason and sentenced to death, but were later freed by the United States Supreme Court (*see Tours 5 and 9*).

Among the interesting figures of early-day Salem was Christopher Harrison, an Easterner who came to Indiana because of an unhappy love affair with Elizabeth Patterson. Harrison, born in Maryland in 1775, was a graduate of St. John's College and a promising young artist. He was poor, however, and found it necessary to seek employment. Entering the counting rooms of William Patterson, wealthy merchant, he met Patterson's beautiful daughter, Betsy, a Baltimore belle. He was employed as Betsy's tutor and was accepted as an equal in the Patterson home, but when he and Betsy became engaged, her father protested so vigorously that the engagement was broken.

Harrison considered it a point of honor not to press his suit further and came West. He built a cabin in Jefferson County, near the present site of Hanover College, on a promontory overlooking the Ohio River.

Here he lived as a solitary hunter, devoting his spare time to his books and pictures. He was probably the first painter in Indiana, and some of his watercolors are still preserved.

While Harrison was here Jerome Bonaparte, brother of Napoleon, married Elizabeth Patterson in Baltimore and took her to England. In spite of the Pope's intervention the Emperor had the marriage annulled and compelled Jerome to desert his wife and infant son. Elizabeth Patterson Bonaparte returned to Baltimore and reared the child, Charles Joseph Bonaparte, who was destined to hold two cabinet posts in the Theodore Roosevelt administration—Secretary of the Navy and Attorney General.

In 1815 Harrison moved to Washington County and opened a general store. Living in a small brick house, long since destroyed, he pursued his painting and gardening. A gentle and kindly man, he loved children and was never happier than when they were clustered about him. He soon moved to a small farm outside of Salem, so that he could have more solitude. It is said that more than once before starting to town, he selected a load of watermelons and carved each melon with the name of one of his little friends. These he passed out as he drove through the streets of Salem.

Notwithstanding his reticence, Harrison was recognized as one of the leading citizens of southern Indiana, and in 1816 was elected lieutenant governor. In 1820 he was named, with James M. Jones and Samuel P. Booker, to survey and lay out the city of Indianapolis. Soon after the completion of this project he returned to Maryland, where he died in 1863.

Left from Salem on paved State 135 to the junction with the Salem-Fredericksburg road, 1.1 *m.;* R. on this road, 6 *m.*, through hilly countryside to the village of BECK'S MILLS (850 alt., 23 pop.) and BECK'S MILL AND MUSEUM OF ANTIQUES (*adm.* 10¢; *picnic grounds, meals*). The mill, in constant operation since 1808, is owned and run by the fifth generation of the Beck family. The stone burrs were brought from Louisville by ox teams. The village, founded at the same time, was the first permanent settlement in Washington County. In 1809 a log fort was built opposite the mill and by 1833 the place had become a tiny pioneer industrial center. The mill, sole surviving industry, contains a museum on the second floor; among the exhibits are two canopied beds more than a century old, wool-carding machines, flax brakes, candle lanterns, Indian relics, and old paintings.

CLICK'S CAVE (*adm.* 50¢), 6.4 *m.*, is three-quarters of a mile in length, winds around under the hill on which the village stands, and ends at Beck's Mill. Here originate the springs that provide water power for the mill. Throughout the length of the cave are stalactites and stalagmites, as well as blind fish and salamanders.

LIVONIA, 114.4 *m.* (795 alt., 192 pop.), is a crossroads village containing several houses, log cabins covered with boards.

North from Livonia on a graveled road is SALTILLO, 8.3 *m.* (800 alt., 125 pop.), a hamlet that links Washington County, by legend, with the much-questioned history of Marshal Ney, famous general of Napoleon's armies. Here lived Dr. E. M. C. Neyman, who asserted that he was the son of Marshal Ney (*see Tour 8a*). A grave marker in the cemetery near Saltillo reads: 'Dr. E.

M. C. Neyman, a native of France, son of Marshall Ney, Feb. 29, 1808—Jan. 4, 1909.'

Neyman is said to have been a remarkable old man of striking appearance, with a heavy white beard, waist-long. He was married three times and practiced medicine until he was 96 years old. On the occasion of his one-hundredth birthday, a celebration was held in Saltillo. In his talk that day he said: 'I was born in Paris on February 29, 1808. My father was Grand Marshal Ney and my mother was Madame Ney, whose maiden name was Mlle. Aglos Angine. I was the third of four children and was between seven and eight years old when Waterloo crashed over our house. Of course, I remember it. And then came the days of sorrow. It was along in 1821 when I again saw my father. That was in Baltimore. I had been sent across the ocean by my mother and was met by my father, who was then a country school teacher living under the name of Peter Stuart Ney. He picked out for me a medical career and put me in a school in Philadelphia, where I studied at the Jefferson Medical College under Dr. James Rush. I never lived with my father in this country, but I saw him a half-dozen or more times. The last time was in the 40's at a tavern kept by Thomas Allison, at Statesville, North Carolina. He was then teaching in Rowan County, North Carolina, where he died Nov. 15, 1846, insisting that he was the great French Marshal.'

Marshal Ney is said to have visited this section of Indiana soon after coming to America. He and his companion, Count Lehmanowsky, are reported to have killed a panther in a small cave near Saltillo. The ex-grand marshal later expressed a wish to be buried in this cave. Dr. Neyman, accordingly, bought the cave in 1876 and went to North Carolina for his father's remains, but because he could furnish no documentary proof that he was the son of the deceased man, the officials refused to allow the body to be moved.

In PAOLI, 124.9 *m.* (638 alt., 2,218 pop.) (*see Tour* 12), are junctions with State 37 (*see Tour* 19) and US 150 (*see Tour* 12), with which State 56 unites westward for nine miles. At 133.9 *m.* State 56 swings southward, dipping down a long curve.

WEST BADEN, 135.2 *m.* (486 alt., 949 pop.), in the valley of Lost River and backed by steep wooded slopes, is one of the hilliest towns in Indiana. Its streets climb up hillsides and curve down into valleys, the houses of its precipitous residential section screened by dense foliage.

Just off the highway (R), in the center of town, is WEST BADEN COLLEGE (*guide service*), a Jesuit school for men, affiliated with Loyola University, Chicago. The massive circular structure of yellow brick is the shell of what was once the West Baden Springs Hotel. Built here because of the presence of seven medicinal, saline-sulphur springs, the hotel became one of the most fashionable resorts in America—a gambling casino in which almost unlimited stakes were wagered. On the arched stone entrance is the inscription: 'West Baden Springs—Carlsbad of America.' The entire interior was furnished lavishly and the hotel enjoyed an international reputation. While a guest at the hotel Paul Dresser (*see Terre Haute*) is said to have composed 'On the Banks of the Wabash.'

This 700-room building, in which was once heard the whir of roulette wheels and the tinkle of champagne glasses, now houses 100 theological students, some 20 priests, and 10 brothers. Under the hotel's glass and steel dome, which is 200 feet in diameter and mounted on rollers to allow for expansion and contraction, is a beautiful marble lobby. The sunken gardens, intricately designed and planted with rare flowers and shrubs from Europe and the Orient, are now weed-grown and overrun by rabbits. The terraces and walks are cracked and broken, and weeds have sprouted from the crevices. The rich marble, tile and wrought-iron Roman-type baths have been wrecked and hauled away. The rattle of chips has been replaced by the resonant tones of 170 Swiss bells and 36 cathedral chimes.

Long before the coming of the white man, wild animals were attracted to this region to lick the minerals that the springs deposited upon near-by rocks. Hostile Indian tribes are said to have declared this a neutral area where all might hunt and partake of the medicinal waters.

Dr. John R. Lane, an itinerant medicine peddler, built the first resort on the site in 1851 and named it West Baden for the famous spa in Baden-Baden, Germany. The hotel was sold in 1875 to a group of Paoli and Salem residents for $23,000, and shortly before it was destroyed by fire in 1901, $1,000,000 was offered for the entire property. The present building, erected in 1902, was closed following the financial crash of 1929. In 1934 it was given to the Jesuit order for the establishment of a college.

WEST BADEN PARK, 100 yards from the highway (L), contains two SALINE-SULPHUR SPRINGS (no fee for water) made by piping the water here from the springs on the college grounds.

FRENCH LICK, 136.6 m. (484 alt., 2,042 pop.), built on the sides of steep hills, was founded in 1811. An animal lick within the borders of the settlement and the fact that a trading post had been operated here by the French in the early eighteenth century prompted the founders to adopt the present name. The community exists because of the French Lick Springs Hotel, which in turn owes its popularity to its medicinal springs and the promotional genius of Thomas Taggart.

The FRENCH LICK SPRINGS HOTEL, in the middle of town, is the largest hotel in Indiana and one of the most luxurious resorts in the United States. The seven-story structure has 1,000 rooms and 25 acres of floor space; the grounds comprise 4,000 acres of well-kept lawns, woodlands, and farms where much of the produce served in the hotel is raised. There is a model dairy farm with a registered herd that is electrically milked. The hotel operates its own electric light and water plants, and has a laundry adequate for a town of 20,000 persons.

Just north of the hotel and near the formal gardens are three ARTESIAN SPRINGS: Pluto, Proserpine, and Bowles. Pluto, covered by an elaborate springhouse of marble and tile, contains the highest concentration of minerals of the three. It runs 96.4 gallons per minute with a constant temperature of 55° Fahrenheit.

In 1840 Dr. William A. Bowles, realizing the commercial possibilities of the springs, built the first French Lick Springs Hotel, an ungainly frame structure that quickly gained widespread popularity. Guests came and went in creaking farm wagons, the homeward-bound vehicles laden with jugs of the medicinal waters. The doctor conceived the idea of marketing the spring water by boiling and bottling a concentrated solution. This was the origin of Pluto Water.

Near the close of the Civil War, Dr. Bowles came into national prominence when he was convicted of treason, with Lambdin P. Milligan and other leaders of the Knights of the Golden Circle (*see Tour 5a*). After his death in 1873, the hotel passed into other hands and was finally purchased in 1891 by a corporation headed by Thomas Taggart (1856–1929), the second owner to become a nationally known political figure.

For many years Thomas Taggart controlled the Democratic party in the State. Personable, genial, and considered one of the most astute politicians in the history of Indiana, he held many public offices, including the mayoralty of Indianapolis and a United States senatorship. While a Democratic national committeeman he helped shape the careers of United States Senator John Kern, Vice President Thomas R. Marshall, and Samuel Ralston, governor of Indiana and United States senator. At the elder Taggart's death, the French Lick Springs Hotel was taken over by his son, Thomas Taggart, Jr. It continues to be a gathering place for State and National Democratic leaders and a famous pleasure resort.

At 138.9 *m.* is the junction with a graveled road.

Right on this road to the junction with another graveled road, 0.4 *m.;* L. on this road, 2.4 *m.*, to the junction with a country lane; R. here to OUTLAW CAVE (L) 2.5 *m.* In 1886 Sam Bunch was brought to this cave by four members of the Archer family, a clan feared and mistrusted in the neighborhood. They seated their victim on a rock just inside the entrance to the cave, and tried to torture him into revealing the whereabouts of his farm hand, Marley, who they asserted had slain one of their family. Angered because Bunch refused to talk, the Archers fired 17 bullets into his body. Six feet to the left of the rock on which Bunch suffered torture and death is a flat rock on which his body lay while his slayers planned its disposal. Several days passed while they plotted destruction of the evidence. Meanwhile they moved the corpse about, in and out of the cave. After an unsuccessful attempt to burn it, they dragged the body down the dark, narrow passageway that branches (R) from the death chamber. About 50 feet down this corridor, the STONE FACE protrudes from the left wall, bearing across its nose an imprint such as is made by pince-nez glasses. Old-timers of the region say it is the image of the murdered man and that he always wore such glasses. The Archers were arrested soon afterward and placed in the jail at Shoals. Before they could be tried, a mob seized three of them on March 10, 1886, and lynched them in the courthouse yard. The fourth brother, held in another jail, was tried, convicted, and hanged.

At 143.4 *m.* on the main route is the junction with a dirt road.

Right on this road is VOWELL CAVE, 0.3 *m.* (*explorers should wear old clothing*), 100 feet R. on a wooded hillside. The mouth is just large enough to admit a person into the cave proper. Once inside, exploration is easy. The north passage, 664 feet long, contains Maiden's Spring, the Tower of Babel, and Roberta's Bell Rock, a limestone formation that gives out a clear ringing sound when tapped. In the south passage, 225 feet long, are the Tailor's Goose, Mollie's Rocking Chair, the Grand Canyon, the Devil's Flue, and Carrie's Iron, a flatiron-shaped stone 15 feet long and 4 feet wide.

At 152.2 *m*. a BUFFALO TRAIL MARKER (L) states that the approximate route of the present highway was first worn by herds of buffalo. Later an early settlers' trail, this route was often traveled by General William Henry Harrison, Colonel Francis Vigo, and General John Gibson. Across the highway from the marker and atop a knoll is the GRAVE OF JAMES HARRISON, soldier of the American Revolution and one of the earliest settlers of the region. During the war he was carrying important papers when surprised by a force of British soldiers. Harrison mounted his horse and fled, but as he jumped the animal over a fence, a British bullet cut off the queue of his wig. Reminded of the Biblical story of Absalom, Harrison vowed, as he raced for his life, that if he ever had a son he would be named Absalom. There have been many Absaloms in the local Harrison family since that time.

HAYSVILLE, 154.6 *m*. (505 alt., 175 pop.), is a neat group of white, frame houses on a low hilltop. Rising above the housetops is the steeple of ST. PAUL'S LUTHERAN CHURCH (German Evangelical), a Gothic type structure built in 1906, in which all services are conducted in German.

JASPER, 162.2 *m*. (467 alt., 5,041 pop.), seat of Dubois County, has been populated largely by German Catholics since 1838, 20 years after the founding of the town. One of the largest desk manufacturing centers in the Nation, Jasper has kept its factories running throughout the depression and enjoyed relative prosperity. A large percentage of the inhabitants own their homes.

Before the United States entered the World War, German was the chief language spoken here, but since the war it has been displaced by a colloquial speech—a combination of English and German and locally coined words—known as 'Jasper Dutch.' This broad, flat dialect is so general that it is soon acquired by newcomers. Strangers, however, will find it difficult to understand.

ST. JOSEPH'S CHURCH (Roman Catholic), on State 56 (R), is dedicated to Father Joseph Kundeck, the first resident pastor. The cornerstone of this massive stone structure was laid in 1868. The building was completed by members of the congregation, each doing his share in the work over a period of several years. The tile roof is supported by four huge trees, the largest that could be found in southern Indiana, which serve as 90-foot columns. Trees were used for rafters and braces in the roof structure; the walls are 6 feet thick. In the 206-foot steeple are chimes weighing 12 tons, which can be heard for miles. Art-glass windows, Italian marble altars, three mosaic frescoes, imported from Innsbruck, Austria, and Romanesque vaultings and columns make the interior impressive. This church is considered a fine example of the German ecclesiastic style.

The CROSS OF DELIVERANCE, in the church yard, was erected by George Bauman and three others as the fulfilment of a vow that they had made while crossing from Germany in 1847. Caught in a great storm that threatened to destroy the ship, they prayed for deliverance and swore that they would erect a fitting token of thanks if they were spared. Bauman, a sculptor, cut the inscription.

During prohibition, residents of Jasper refused to accept the situation passively, and this locality became noted for the excellence of its moonshine whisky. 'Jasper corn' soon achieved State-wide popularity.

At the southeastern city limits, on State 164 and the Patoka River, is ENLOW'S MILL (*open*), built in 1866 to replace the one where the Lincoln family often came to have their grain ground (*see Tour 11A*). The Lincolns lived about halfway between Enlow's Mill and the Hoffman Mill on Anderson Creek, and it is said they divided their trade between the two places. Here Abraham Lincoln's father once brought a desk he had made and traded it for meal. The desk was used at the mill for almost a century before becoming the property of Louis P. Joseph, who placed it in the employees' clubroom at the JASPER DESK FACTORY (*visitors welcome*), Sixth and Anderson Sts.

Left from Jasper on State 45 is HUNTINGBURG, 7.5 *m.* (467 alt., 3,816 pop.), a busy, smoke-filled German industrial town founded a century ago. Some of the finest clay mines in the Nation are in and around Huntingburg. At the UHL POTTERY WORKS (*visitors welcome*), one block R. of the highway, clay is turned, glazed and burned into the plant's 500 products, including 60-gallon jars weighing 400 pounds.

The HUNTINGBURG WAGON WORKS (*visitors welcome*), is the largest of the 17 establishments of its kind remaining in the United States. Here wagons and buggies are built of native timber, to be used on the western plains and in the mountains of southwestern United States and Mexico.

The PETER MORGAN GREENHOUSES (*visitors welcome*), E. Sixth St., one of the largest in southern Indiana, took prizes for seven consecutive years at the National Flower Show with its American Beauty rose.

At 179.8 *m.* is a junction with State 61, over which the route continues, turning south (L) at right angles.

This section of the route is part of the Lincoln National Memorial Highway, over which the Lincoln-Hanks-Hall clan passed in February 1830 on their way from Spencer County to their new home in Illinois. John Hanks had settled in Macon County, Illinois, and sent back reports of the rich prairie lands ready for the plow. Thomas and Sarah Lincoln spent the winter preparing for the journey. They sold their livestock and Thomas bought two yoke of oxen and a wagon. Three families—13 persons in all—made their way to Vincennes, where they stopped for a short time to view the largest town in Indiana. Early in March they reached their new home, selected for them by John Hanks. It was eight miles southwest of Decatur, on a bluff overlooking the Sangamon River.

WINSLOW, 184.1 *m.* (433 alt., 1,382 pop.), is a coal-mining town with a straggling little business district of old frame and brick buildings hooded by canopies out to the curb. At the northern edge of town is the COOPER MANUFACTURING COMPANY PLANT (*visitors welcome*), in which are made many of the triple-edged, grooved wooden rulers used by school children.

Left from Winslow on a dirt road to the entrance to the PIKE COUNTY STATE FOREST (*fishing, picnicking*), 1 *m.*, a 2,426-acre preserve on both sides of the Patoka River. There is a FIRETOWER in the forest, which is composed largely of reclaimed areas formerly used in strip mining.

At 185.1 *m.* is the northern junction with State 64, with which State 61 unites for 2.3 miles. From this point to ARTHUR, 187.4 *m.* (430 alt., 300 pop.), a mining settlement, side roads leading off the highway are made of waste coal, and 'spoil banks' thrown up in strip mining operations are occasionally visible.

At Arthur, State 64, now the route, turns west (R), while State 61 continues south.

OAKLAND CITY, 193.3 *m.* (640 alt., 3,068 pop.), a hilly town of narrow, shaded streets, is the home of OAKLAND CITY COLLEGE. The campus—a grove of native oaks in the northwestern part of town—contains the four main buildings; near by are a gymnasium-auditorium and a former factory remodeled to house laboratories and the library. The school, a Baptist institution, was opened in 1891. About 260 students are enrolled. Kitchens are provided in the dormitories for women students who wish to reduce expenses by boarding themselves.

FRANCISCO, 198.9 *m.* (430 alt., 611 pop.), according to legend, was named for a Spanish laborer on the Wabash and Erie Canal, which at one time brought much activity to this settlement.

PRINCETON, 206.4 *m.* (483 alt., 7,786 pop.), founded in 1814 and named for Captain William Prince, later a representative in Congress, is a residential county-seat town with a packing plant and several other small industries. One block west of the public square is the SITE OF THE EVANS MILL, a wool-carding mill that drew many pioneers to early Princeton. In 1827 Abraham Lincoln brought wool to the Evans Mill, and stayed overnight at the owner's home on West Broadway.

ROBERT STOCKWELL'S STORE stood at the southwest corner of State 64 and Hart Street. Years after his visit to Princeton, Lincoln was visited at the White House by Stockwell. When the latter introduced himself, Lincoln said, 'Oh, yes, I remember the name as the one I saw on a sign in Princeton, on the occasion of my visit there. It was the first gilt-lettered sign I had ever seen and it attracted my attention.'

Princeton is at the junction with US 41 (*see Tour* 20).

State 64 crosses the ILLINOIS LINE, 217.9 *m.*, over a bridge across the Wabash River, and enters Mt. Carmel, Illinois (*see Illinois Guide*).

Tour 11A

Junction with State 56—Jeffersonville—New Albany—Corydon—St. Croix—Dale—Boonville—Evansville—Mount Vernon—(Carmi, Illinois); State 62.

Junction with State 56 to Illinois Line, 191.6 *m.*

Concrete and high type bituminous roadbed to Mt. Vernon; oil stone and oil mat to Illinois Line.
Baltimore & Ohio R.R. parallels the route between Charlestown and New Albany; Southern R.R. between Dale and Evansville; Louisville and Nashville R.R. between Evansville and the Illinois Line.
Accommodations at short intervals; hotels chiefly in cities.

State 62 passes through a region of rugged beauty, heavy with oak, hickory, and poplar trees. It winds among hills ablaze in autumn with vivid colors, delicately mottled in spring with blooming redbud, dogwood, wild cherry, and wild plum. During the summer months Queen Anne's lace, elderberry bloom, and milkweed fringe the roadsides; September and October bring goldenrod.

Much of Indiana's early history was made in this region, for to the east are Jeffersonville and New Albany, once important shipbuilding centers; and Corydon, the first State capital. Westward, the route winds through hill country that still retains the flavor of days when life was hard and often precarious. Removed from large population centers, the people are quiet, self-contained folk among whose forebears Abraham Lincoln lived for 14 years. State 62 passes within a few miles of the farm on which young Abe went about his chores with a book under one arm, and where on a bleak autumn day his mother, the beloved Nancy Hanks Lincoln, died of the 'milk sick.' Along the route are St. Meinrad, the abbey town; Santa Claus, its post office famous for Christmas mail; and Evansville, metropolis of southwestern Indiana. In the uplands there is diversified farming, including tobacco and cane growing; in the lowlands, large-scale coal mining.

State 62 curves southward from the junction with State 56, 0 *m.* (*see Tour* 11).

CHARLESTOWN, 23.1 *m.* (590 alt., 939 pop.), the seat of Clark County from 1811 until 1878, was laid out north of Springville in 1808. As the latter declined, Charlestown grew in size and importance. It did not, however, alter greatly in population or appearance. In July 1940, Charlestown prepared for the biggest boom in its history when the Federal Government awarded a contract to E. I. du Pont de Nemours and Company for construction of a $25,000,000 smokeless powder plant on a 5,000-acre tract at the edge of the little town. Preliminary estimates that 5,000 persons eventually would be employed at the plant sent real-estate prices sky-rocketing.

In the next few months the original expenditure was more than tripled until, on May 1, 1941, when the first powder was produced, the estimated cost of the powder plant was $86,000,000. In addition, The Goodyear Tire and Rubber Company has constructed, under Government contract, a $20,000,000 bag-loading plant adjacent to the powder project.

In the CHARLESTOWN CEMETERY (R), at the northern edge of town, is the GRAVE OF JONATHAN JENNINGS (1784–1834), first governor of Indiana. The grave is just within the main entrance in a grassy plot at the center of the driveway. A log cabin (L), the FIRST METHODIST CHURCH IN INDIANA, was built in 1807 by the Robertson Methodist Society and called the Bethel Meeting House. The building was purchased in 1902 by the Indiana Conference of the Methodist Church, and restored. It is covered by an open shelter with a fireproof roof.

On Water Street opposite the Christian Church is the SITE OF THE GREEN TREE TAVERN, built in 1812 by Captain James Bigger, and named for an immense tree on which the tavern sign was hung. One of the famous early hostelries of this section, it was frequented by Jonathan Jennings, whose favorite mount, it is said, was always tethered to the tree. When the convivial Jennings was ready to go home, his friends would place him in the saddle and the horse would set out at a careful pace that would not dislodge his rider. The tavern was patronized by politicians of the times and was often the scene of spirited arguments. Here a brilliant inaugural ball was given for Jennings when he became governor in August 1816. The SITE OF JENNINGS' HOME, opposite the present Methodist Church, is indicated by a stone marker.

1. Left from the center of Charlestown on a graveled road is TUNNEL MILL AND DAM, 3 *m.*, built in 1820 by John Wade along Fourteen Mile Creek where it makes a hairpin turn around a ridge. Through the ridge Wade later dug a 300-foot tunnel high enough to accommodate a man on horseback. A new mill driven by a great overshot wheel was built at the lower end of the tunnel. This mill was considered one of the wonders of the section at the time of its completion and was operated until 1854. It burned in 1927, but the tunnel and the wheel remain, in a fair state of preservation. The site is now a Boy Scout camp.

2. Left from the southeastern edge of Charlestown, at the Baltimore and Ohio R.R. underpass, on a graveled road, 1.5 *m.;* L. here on a dirt road to ROSE ISLAND, 2.8 *m.*, a pear-shaped ridge about 280 feet high, bounded on the east by the Ohio River and on the west by Fourteen Mile Creek. Abrupt escarpments of rock, too steep to climb, rise from both streams, and these natural walls are joined by strong artificial embankments of earth and stones. Archeologists agree that this 'Stone Fort' was erected by Mound Builders of the Fort Ancient variant of the Upper Mississippi culture (*see Archeology*). A persistent though unreliable tradition, however, maintains that it was built by twelfth-century Welshmen.

In 1167, it is said, at the death of Owen Gwyneth, Prince of Wales, contention arose among his 17 sons about who should succeed him. One son, Madoc, decided to seek his fortune elsewhere, and sailed westward with a company of Welshmen. Several early writers believed that Madoc's colony eventually penetrated to this point on the Ohio and used the natural fortress for protection against the Indians. In 1582 Hakluyt's *Divers Voyages Touching the Discovery of America* mentioned the Welsh; and there is a curious reference in Captain John Smith's papers to 'white Indians' who spoke almost pure Welsh. George Rogers Clark reported that Chief Tobacco's son told him of a great battle at the Falls of the Ohio between the Indians and a 'strange race.'

Although archeologists give no credence to this tradition, several odd discoveries have been reported. George Catlin, an explorer, claimed that the Mandans, a Northwest Indian tribe, spoke a dialect in which occasional Welsh words were found, and that they used round basket boats that were exact duplicates of the Welsh coracle. There is also a legend, taken seriously by certain local historians, of Welsh armor found on the banks of the Ohio River near Jeffersonville in 1799. The armor is described as being of brass, bearing a Welsh coat-of-arms, the 'Mermaid and the Harp,' with a Latin inscription meaning 'Virtuous deeds merit their just reward.' The tale still persists that early hunters discovered a tombstone bearing the date 1186.

JEFFERSONVILLE, 35.9 *m.* (458 alt., 11,493 pop.), seat of Clark County and one of Indiana's oldest towns, was laid out and named in 1802 by William Henry Harrison according to a plan suggested by Thomas Jefferson. Of all the towns along the Ohio River's 980-mile course, Jeffersonville was probably damaged the most by the 1937 flood. Ninety-five per cent of its area was inundated; a tremendous property loss was sustained; and several years will be required to erase the physical effects of the high water.

The city prospered before the closing of the American Car and Foundry works and the Howard shipyards in 1931, but has never attained its promised stature, because of the overshadowing influence of Louisville, Kentucky, across the river, where many Jeffersonville residents are employed.

At Fort and Front Streets is the SITE OF FORT STEUBEN, where a settlement was made in 1786.

The SITE OF THE HOWARD SHIPYARDS, Front St. between Fulton and Watts Sts., is now overgrown by weeds. Once these shipyards were Jeffersonville's most important industry. With the exception of several years when its founder, James Howard, conducted the enterprise in Louisville, the Jeffersonville yards were in constant operation and in the hands of the Howard family from 1834 until 1931. Here were built many of the Mississippi River packets of the early days and some of the first large boats to steam up the Yukon River in Alaska.

The U. S. ARMY QUARTERMASTER DEPOT, 10th St. and Meigs Ave., is one of the largest in the Nation, employing about 600 persons. Here clothing and supplies are manufactured for that part of the Army and the CCC operating in Indiana, Kentucky, Ohio, West Virginia, Tennessee, Alabama, Mississippi, and Louisiana. During the Civil War it was the base from which all troops and supplies were shipped to points south of Louisville. One company of regular troops is situated at the depot for the repair and maintenance of motor vehicles, but all other work is done by civilians.

In WARDER PARK, Court Ave. and Spring St., is a MONUMENT TO LAFAYETTE, who visited Jeffersonville on May 11, 1825.

The remodeled buildings of the FIRST STATE PRISON IN INDIANA, Clark St. and Clark Blvd., are now used by the Colgate-Palmolive-Peet Company. The prison was established in 1821. The State, which built the prison with publicly subscribed funds, leased it to private individuals who contracted to care for criminals on a per capita basis. Captain Seymour Westover, the first lessee, was killed with David Crockett in the battle of the Alamo (1836).

West of Jeffersonville on Riverside Drive from the Municipal Bridge is CLARKSVILLE, 2.5 *m*. (805 alt., 2,386 pop.), founded in 1784 by George Rogers Clark on a tract of 150,000 acres in Clark, Scott, and Floyd Counties. Presented to Clark and his men by the State of Virginia in recognition of their military services, this land was selected by Clark on the north bank of the river, just above the Falls of the Ohio. It was divided into lots of 500 acres each and a town site of 1,000 acres was set aside by the State of Virginia and named Clarksville. This land overlooked Corn Island, on which Clark established his first military post and drilled his men in preparation for the expedition against Kaskaskia in 1778 (*see Vincennes*). He fortified the island and divided it among the families of his soldiers for the production of crops.

At the end of his campaign, Clark returned with his men and, upon the receipt of the land grant, settled here and founded the towns of Louisville, Clarksville, and Jeffersonville. He appears, however, to have been a soldier rather than a developer of communities. Living in his cabin overlooking the river and the city of Louisville, he made no effort to improve the settlement. It fell into decay and was deserted by all except himself. Clark died, impoverished, in 1818.

At the west edge of Clarksville, on the east bank of Silver Creek where it flows into the Ohio River, is the SITE OF THE CLAY-MARSHALL DUEL. Both Henry Clay and Humphrey Marshall were members of the Kentucky legislature, but opposites in looks, dress, and political beliefs. Clay wore homespun while Marshall, a Federalist, was the best-dressed man in the legislature. He was a person of violent prejudices and despised both Jefferson and Clay.

In December 1808, a debate between Clay and Marshall degenerated into a personal quarrel, and Clay challenged his opponent to a duel. For legal reasons they wished to fight outside of Kentucky and selected this site for its convenience. Each of the combatants fired a shot and each received a flesh wound. The seconds decided that 'honor was satisfied' and prevented further hostilities.

Two years before this duel, a part of the conspiracy headed by Aaron Burr, Vice President of the United States from 1801 to 1805, was hatched and frustrated near this spot. Burr had come West after killing Alexander Hamilton in a duel, an affair that ruined him politically in the East, and won many friends by plunging wholeheartedly into the civic life of Jeffersonville. He proposed and urged the building of a canal through Jeffersonville around the Falls of the Ohio and, although the project was unsuccessful, won for himself the reputation of a public-spirited citizen and leader. There is reason to believe that the canal had been conceived, not for the public good, but as a step toward greater power and wealth for Burr and his associates.

Burr had dreams of building an empire and annexing Mexico, and intended ultimately to utilize the disloyal sentiment then prevailing on the frontier because of heavy Federal taxes. Without moving too rapidly in the direction of actual rebellion, however, he first involved adventurous and enterprising frontiersmen in a plot to seize Mexico 'for the United States.' Recruiting an expedition of about 50 armed men, he proceeded down the Ohio River to Marietta, Ohio, where he was joined by Harman Blennerhassett.

Major Davis Floyd, a highly respected member of the Indiana General Assembly at that time, was Burr's agent in Jeffersonville. It is generally conceded that Floyd understood that Burr was acting with the approval of the United States Government; in fact the whole enterprise was represented in Indiana as a trading and colonizing voyage, with possibly a remote military objective (*see New Albany*). Floyd collected a number of recruits, and boats were built and launched on Silver Creek. Two of the boats succeeded in getting away and joining the expedition, but the remainder of the Jeffersonville fleet was captured by Captain William Prather of the militia, before it could embark.

Burr was arrested at Natchez and the expedition was broken up. Floyd was also arrested and indicted for treason, but because he had apparently been unaware that the expedition was disloyal, he was treated very leniently. Upon conviction he was fined only $20 and sentenced to three hours' imprisonment in Jeffersonville.

Jeffersonville is at the junction with US 31 (*see Tour* 16).

In NEW ALBANY, 42.1 *m.* (459 alt., 25,414 pop.) (*see New Albany*), is a junction with US 150 (*see Tour* 12).

The route swerves away from the river and takes an upgrade course. To the right are knobs decked with foliage from base to summit; on the left is a deep, densely wooded valley broken now and then by ridges that obscure the view of the river beyond. Much of the highway between New Albany and Corydon is built on a ledge that curves around hillsides. To the right of the highway are sheer rock walls; on the left, the edge of the road drops abruptly into canyon-like valleys 200 to 500 feet below.

LANESVILLE, 53.2 *m.* (750 alt., 267 pop.), a small trading center in a good farming section, was settled in 1792 and platted in 1817. It was named for General Lane, a Government surveyor who was one of its early and most prominent citizens. For many years Lanesville was an important stage stop between Corydon and New Albany.

CORYDON, 62.2 *m.* (715 alt., 1,865 pop.) (*see Corydon*).

WHITE CLOUD, 69.4 *m.* (760 alt., 59 pop.), nestles in the Blue River Valley between two ranges of lofty hills. Its name was suggested by a mist that often hangs lazily over the town. Tourist trade is the principal source of income, and there are many tourist cabins and summer homes.

WYANDOTTE CAVE (*adm.* $1.50 *long trip,* $1 *shorter trips; guide furnished; hotel accommodations May* 1-*Nov.* 1; *tourist cabins*), 72.1 *m.*, is one of the largest on the North American continent. It is a dry cave, easy of entrance and free of danger, with 5 floor levels and 23 miles of explored passages. The entrance is a natural opening on the hillside, a short distance from the hotel. A 400-foot passage, called Washington Avenue, leads into many spectacular caverns, among which are Bandit's Hall, Valley of the Shades, Coral Galleries, the Canopy, Lucifer's Gorge, the Natural Bridge, Hill of Humility, and the expansive Senate Chamber with its great Pillar of the Constitution. Monumental Mountain, 135 feet in height, is said to be the highest underground mountain in the world.

The walls and ceilings of many passages are mottled and striped with different-colored strata of limestone divided by bands of ebony-like flint. The Indians are known to have used the cave and some scientists believe there are evidences of prehistoric habitation.

At 73.3 *m.* is a junction (L) with a stone road.

Left on this road across the deep channel of the Big Blue River to the HARRISON COUNTY STATE FOREST, 2.1 *m.*, more than 7,000 acres of wooded hills and valleys along the Ohio River. From the FIRE TOWER, at the entrance, improved roads lead to a PICNIC AREA (*ovens, shelter house*) overlooking the river. Foot trails wind along the stone bluffs and stone steps lead down a steep cliff to the water's edge.

The rebuilding of LEAVENWORTH, 77.7 *m.* (785 alt., 394 pop.), gutted by the flood waters of the Ohio, was completed and the transplanted town dedicated on December 15, 1938. The site of the old town, founded in 1818, is (L) upon a curving bank of the Ohio. The town was the seat of Crawford County from 1843 to 1893 and, until the decline of river transportation, one of the principal shipping points along the Ohio.

Here, in 1824, a woodyard was established by David Lyon to furnish fuel for boats. In 1830 Lyon converted his enterprise into a boatbuilding industry, which operated for more than a century without shutting down for a single working day. It is still operated (1941), although on a much smaller scale, by Lyon's grandson.

In 1863 a group of Morgan's raiders under Captain Hines passed through Leavenworth, hotly pursued by Union forces that were attempting to retrieve a number of horses that the Confederates had stolen from the settlers of this region. Barely gaining the river, Hines's cavalrymen swam their horses to a small island that lay about a mile upstream from Leavenworth, and there they found themselves trapped. The river was too deep to ford to the Kentucky shore. Many tried it and a few succeeded. The rest drowned. The Union forces were joined by the Home Guards and a withering fire was poured into the marooned Confederates. Women and children gathered on the shore to watch the battle with breathless interest; the wives carried ammunition to the men, who kept up a continuous fire. Hemmed in on one side by nature and on the other by the enemy, the Confederates, about 80 in number, were finally forced to surrender.

The former site of Leavenworth was backed by high, wooded hills and bluffs that enclosed it on three sides like an amphitheater. Into this bend poured the full force of the 1937 flood. Almost without exception the buildings were swept away, smashed, or overturned. When the water receded it was evident that an attempt at salvage would prove useless, and that to rebuild the town on the same site would be a gamble against future floods, so it was decided to move the town up on the hills behind the old site. The highway has been relocated and passes by the new red brick church and clean white residences of the transplanted town in which, after the flood, rows of khaki tents with stovepipes sticking out of them housed the families whose houses were bobbing in the waters below. When the flood receded some persons moved back into the wrecked town under the bluff, but it remains a desolate settlement that owed its life—and death—to the river.

At 78.2 *m.* is the junction with State 66, a blacktop road.

Right on State 66 to MARENGO, 12 *m.* (574 alt., 812 pop.), a resort village and quarrying center in an area of caves and coldwater springs. The town is on a hill down which steep streets descend.

MARENGO CAVE (*adm.* $1, *children* 50¢; *guide service; free camping grounds*) was discovered by two children in 1883. The temperature within the cave remains at 54° at all times. Trips through the cave are over a long and a short route; the greatest distance covered is two miles, and the time required for the trip is slightly less than two hours. The cave is free from fallen rock, and its greatest depth is 286 feet. The stalactites and stalagmites are of pure calcium carbonate, and transmit a pearly glow when illuminated. Along the seams in the roof are 'curtain stalactites,' thin continuous formations that look like stone curtains. Many are so thin that they permit the passage of light. Among the chambers are Odd Fellows Hall, with its pulpit rock; Music Hall, with a bandstand and frescoed ceiling; and Flanders Fields, with low battlement-like partitions. The many unusual formations include Bunker Hill Monument, Niagara Falls, Devil's Washboard, and Mount Vesuvius with its 'frozen lava' shooting to the ceiling. The chimes are formations of different sizes and shapes that give off various musical tones when struck.

SULPHUR, 85.9 *m.* (800 alt., 27 pop.), named for the near-by sulphur springs, is a hamlet of several houses and two general stores. It is at the junction with State 37 (*see Tour* 19), which unites westward with State 62 for 6.9 miles.

Left from Sulphur on State 66, a blacktop highway that winds downhill through a rugged, heavily forested section, is WHITE SULPHUR SPRING, 1.5 *m.* (*cabins and rooms in private homes; hunting and fishing*), one of the largest of its kind in Indiana. In the 1860's several men who were drilling here for oil struck the powerful vein of sulphur water that created this artesian well. The medicinal properties of the water were advertised and a hotel built to accommodate 250 guests. A private light plant was installed, bathhouses built, and all manner of amusement facilities provided. The hotel did a flourishing business for many years, and the sulphur water was bottled and sold widely. The hotel burned down in 1910 and was never rebuilt. White Sulphur Spring is, however, a popular resort in the summer. Two near-by streams, West Fork Creek and Little Blue River, contain bass and pike.

ST. CROIX (pronounced Croy), 92.8 *m.* (800 alt., 50 pop.), a village perched on the top of a large hill, is at the junction with State 37 (*see Tour* 11B).

Upon rounding a curve into ST. MEINRAD, 107.7 *m.* (715 alt., 439 pop.), there is a sudden, unexpected view of the spired sandstone buildings of the abbey soaring above the village. The townspeople are German Catholics and the schools are taught by Sisters of St. Benedict. Many of the villagers are employed as lay-workers by the abbey.

A graveled road (L) leads to the Benedictine ST. MEINRAD ABBEY (Roman Catholic), set in rocky hills. The main group of buildings, quadrangular in form, includes the abbey church, monastery, major and minor seminaries, and library of 35,000 volumes. All buildings were constructed by the Abbey Fathers.

The ABBEY CHURCH, a massive structure of stone quarried from the grounds, is of pure Romanesque design, 200 feet long and 72 feet wide. In the tower is a chime of six bells. The windows were imported and the high altar, unusual in design and exquisite in detail, was made in Europe of Italian marble and firegilt bronze. A compound organ of 57 registers and 3,115 pipes voiced for Gregorian chant, occupies two lofts in the chancel. Beneath the chancel is a chapel with four grottos built of Ohio cave stone.

The church has 13 altars, including those in the Baptismal Chapel (R) and in the Chapel of Our Lady of Einsiedeln (L). The two large stained-glass windows above the main altar represent Pope Gregory, whose compositions are a part of the Roman Catholic ritual, and King David, whose psalms the Church chants. Eight other stained-glass windows illustrate the beatitudes by depicting scenes from the lives of Benedictine saints. In the chancel is the bishop's throne, of native woods carved by a monk who spent three years at the task.

The SEMINARY, founded in 1857, was largely rebuilt after a disastrous fire in 1887. The institution trains young men for the priesthood; the faculty numbers 27 and about 360 students are enrolled. The school is organized into a major seminary, which includes the theological department and two years of college, and a minor seminary comprising a junior college and a high school.

The abbey is almost self-sufficient. Industrial and agricultural activities are carried on by members of the order. In the valley to the south are the farm buildings, including a modern dairy barn sheltering a herd of 50 cows, a horse barn, a poultry house for 1,000 hens, an abattoir, and a milk house. The abbey also has its own carpenter shop, coal mine, and rock quarry. In addition to job printing and bookbinding for religious institutions, the printing department publishes several monthly magazines in English and German.

St. Meinrad, a descendant of the house of Hohenzollern, lived in solitude in the ninth century on the wild slopes of a mountain in Switzerland. He was murdered by robbers, but the hermitage was continued by his followers. Here, Everhard, one of the latter, erected a monastery and became the first abbot. A new monastery was built in 948. The present monastery and abbey of Maria Einsiedeln—Our Lady of the Hermits—was built on the original site of the hermitage in the early nineteenth century. In 1852 the Abbot of Einsiedeln yielded to the pleas of the vicar general of Vincennes and delegated two Fathers to seek a site for a Benedictine abbey in the New World. With their followers, the Fathers settled at St. Meinrad on March 21, 1854, the feast day of St. Benedict. Frame buildings were constructed and from this humble beginning grew the present abbey.

At 108.2 m. is the junction with a graveled road.

Left on this road, uphill through heavily wooded country, to MONTE CASSINO CHAPEL, 0.5 m., a small square building of sandstone quarried from the hill on which it stands. Here, in 1857, Father Isidore Hobi nailed to an oak tree a lithograph of the Immaculate Conception. It became a popular shrine for the Catholic families of this early backwoods community, and in 1866 Father Martin and the students of St. Meinrad built a little shelter of rough boards over the picture. The cornerstone for the present chapel was laid in 1868. At its completion a procession more than a half-mile long marched from the monastery to the chapel carrying the beautiful statue of the Madonna and Child, which still stands on the simple wooden altar within the chapel.

The walls are decorated with pictures of the Virgin. Pilgrimage services and processions are held here each May and October.

At 111.3 *m.* on the main route is the junction with State 162.

Right on State 162 to FERDINAND, 3.6 *m.* (500 alt., 990 pop.), a German Catholic community retaining the language and customs of the Fatherland. English, of course, is understood and spoken, as is also a strange admixture of the two languages. Rathskeller signs bear such names as Kunkler, Schnellenberger, and Hoppenjans. Many of the citizens carve and wear wooden shoes, or fashion wooden beer mugs and holders for pretzels.

The CONVENT OF THE IMMACULATE CONCEPTION is the mother home of about 300 nuns. There are about 70 girl students in the academy at present (1941). The church, one of the outstanding examples of ecclesiastical architecture in Indiana, is Romanesque in design. It is built of face brick with terracotta ornamentation; a dome topped by a gold cross rises 137 feet above the base of the structure, and two campanile towers above the entrance contain the four convent bells. The entire second story of the building is encircled by a spacious promenade; at each corner small pavilions of unusual design serve as roofs over the turret stairways to the colonnade below. The interior is decorated with white marble and plaster. The pews, confessionals, and the hand-carved sanctuary screening are of dark oak. The windows in the nave depict saints of the Benedictine order, those in the sanctuary show angels, and two rose windows in the balcony portray Christ the King and St. Benedict and his first disciples.

The industries of Ferdinand include an IRON FOUNDRY (*visitors welcome*), manufacturing steam engines, threshing machines, and saw-milling machinery, and a FURNITURE FACTORY that specializes in bedroom suites. Here, too, is the southern terminus of the one-locomotive FERDINAND RAILROAD, Indiana's shortest steam line, running to Huntingburg (*see Tour 11*), eight miles northwest. Two trips a day are made.

DALE, 117.7 *m.* (342 alt., 763 pop.), named for Robert Dale Owen (*see New Harmony*), has a canning factory, a cheese factory, and a sawmill. Near the sawmill is the HOME OF O. V. BROWN (*open by appointment*), which contains an extensive collection of pioneer relics, including old records, maps, pictures, furniture and utensils, and geological specimens.

GENTRYVILLE, 123.3 *m.* (414 alt., 258 pop.), was named for James Gentry, one of its first merchants, for whom young Abraham Lincoln frequently clerked. While in Gentry's employ Lincoln accompanied a flatboat of produce to New Orleans (*see Tour 11B*). In the village are the remains of an old WATER POWER MILL, owned by Eli Grigsby, one of the Grigsby family into which Abraham Lincoln's sister married.

Left from Gentryville on State 162 (oil mat), 1.8 *m.*, to LINCOLN CITY, (420 alt., 250 pop.), laid out in 1872 on ground that was once part of the farm of Thomas Lincoln, father of Abraham. Present-day Lincoln City is an unpretentious hamlet of frame dwellings, three stores, a hotel, a church, and a grade school. Most of the buildings are set on hillsides.

Adjoining Lincoln City on the south is LINCOLN STATE PARK (*adm. 10¢; picnic, camping, and recreation areas*), a 1,166-acre preserve. Within the park is the NANCY HANKS LINCOLN MEMORIAL, the grave of the Great Emancipator's mother. The SITE OF THE LINCOLN CABIN is marked by a low rectangular wall in which the Lincoln fireplace, made of the original stones, is set in its proper position. In the cemetery of the PIGEON CREEK BAPTIST CHURCH, built on the foundation of the original church in which the Lincoln family worshipped, is the grave of Sarah Lincoln Grigsby, Lincoln's sister. Thomas Lincoln helped to build the church and fashioned the rough benches that served as pews.

It was in this neighborhood that the Lincoln family settled in 1816, shortly after Indiana achieved statehood, when Abraham was seven years old and his sister nine. The Lincolns lived here during their 14-year stay in Indiana. Thomas Lincoln, a kindly but improvident man, entered a 160-acre tract, but was never known to have more than about 18 acres under cultivation. Most of his time was spent in hunting and doing odd jobs for more prosperous neighbors. Living conditions were primitive and the rough cabins dirty and vermin-infested. The entire family slept in the same room on a dirt floor covered with leaves. Bathing was not to be considered except during the summer, and clothing was probably not washed from fall until spring. Diet consisted almost exclusively of game, which was plentiful, and a little corn or roughly ground wheat. Cooking principally meant frying in grease.

In the autumn of 1818 the settlers were beset by a fever called 'milk sick' because it attacked cattle and particularly milch cows, as readily as men and women. No cure was known and the victims usually died quickly. Betsy and Thomas Sparrow, Nancy Hanks's foster parents, who had joined the Lincolns here soon after their migration from Kentucky, died of this plague about 18 months after their arrival. Soon after their death, Nancy was taken ill and died a week later in October 1818. Thomas made a rough coffin by whipsawing planks from a log and the body of Nancy Hanks Lincoln was hauled on a sled to a grave beside those of her foster parents, about a quarter of a mile from the cabin. Sometime after her death, an itinerant Baptist preacher, David Elkins (see Tour 10), coming from Kentucky, stopped at the Pigeon Creek settlement and preached a funeral sermon over the graves of those who had died of this plague during 1818. Nancy Hanks Lincoln's grave was unmarked during the lives of her husband and her son.

About a year after his wife's death, Thomas Lincoln went back to Kentucky and married Sarah Bush Johnson, a widow with three children, whom he had unsuccessfully courted before marrying Nancy Hanks. They returned to Pigeon Creek and Sarah immediately set about righting the slovenly household by a vigorous program of repairing and washing. An excellent mother and a patient and understanding woman, she appreciated Abraham's thirst for knowledge and aided him in his pursuit of an education. It was during this period that he learned to read and write. Schooling was sporadic and fragmentary and during his entire life, it is estimated, Abraham attended school for less than a year. However, his ability to concentrate was unusual and he invariably stood out among his fellow pupils. Although rather inept at figures, he found reading and writing easy. He was a voluble talker and liked nothing better than to entertain a gathering with speeches, jokes, and stories. He was eager to make everyone like him and was always careful not to offend. It is said that upon catching a group of boys stealing melons from his patch, he sat upon the fence and told them stories and helped to eat the melons.

Sarah Lincoln had brought with her a copy of the Bible, Aesop's Fables, Sinbad the Sailor, Pilgrim's Progress, and Robinson Crusoe. These young Abraham devoured eagerly and sought for more. From David Turnham, a young farmer near Grandview, he borrowed the Revised Laws of Indiana, which he read and re-read with great care. From Josiah Crawford, who lived near Pigeon Creek, he borrowed Weem's Life of Washington and Life of Franklin. The copy of Washington he left in the rain and the book was ruined. Crawford gave him the book and he 'pulled fodder' for several days to pay for it.

It appears that Lincoln was not the industrious rail-splitter of tradition. Although of prodigious physical strength, he disliked manual labor and never did more than was absolutely necessary. He afterward said that his father had 'taught him to work but could never teach him to love it.' He spent every spare moment with a book and even carried one with him into the fields, where he read through rest periods. Thomas Lincoln often treated him roughly, exasperated at this attitude, and hid or threw away the books with which 'Abe was foolin' away his time.'

One autumn, while Abraham was cutting corn for a Mr. Carter at a wage of 10¢ a day, his employer and Thomas Lincoln bargained to transfer one field of the Lincoln farm. Carter wrote the deed and brought it to the elder Lincoln for his signature. Abraham, knowing that his father could neither read nor write, asked to see the deed. He examined it and told his father, 'If you sign this, you've sold the farm.' Thomas Lincoln eyed Carter and said, 'Somebody's lied and 'taint Abe.' This bald statement caused the customary fist-fight which followed all affronts and disagreements. After this Thomas Lincoln never complained about Abraham's pursuit of knowledge.

The route continues to the junction with State 245, an oil mat road, 6.9 *m.*; R. on State 245 to SANTA CLAUS, 7.4 *m.* (425 alt., 54 pop.), a tiny, quiet community with two general stores on its one street. The village was platted in 1846, and the suggested name of Sante Fe for the post office was ruled out because there was another Sante Fe in Indiana. Santa Claus was jocularly suggested as an alternative, since it was the Christmas season, and the name stuck.

Santa Claus becomes a beehive of activity with the approach of Christmas. From all over the world parcels pour in to be re-mailed in order to bear the Santa Claus postmark. In 1937 more than 600,000 pieces of mail passed through the little post office. Santa Claus's outstanding citizen was 'Jim' Martin, postmaster for 38 years until his death in 1935, and Santa Claus to the Nation's children.

SANTA CLAUS PARK, on the highest hill of the village, has at its center a towering, smiling granite STATUE OF SANTA CLAUS, standing on a brightly silvered five-pointed star. The park and the statue, dedicated to the 'children of the world,' were sponsored by Carl A. Barrett, of Chicago, as a memorial to his family. In the park there is also a BELL, rung in celebration at Wilkes-Barre, Pennsylvania, when the Declaration of Independence was signed; an INDIAN TOTEM POLE, donated by the Hudson's Bay Company; and a WISHING WELL, locally built and donated, at which children can whisper their secret Yuletide desires.

A CRATER HOLE is being excavated in the park by the National Geographic Society and a RUSTIC CASTLE is under construction (1941). The cabins of the HOOSIER MEMORIAL VILLAGE will be outfitted with pioneer furnishings, including the toys and dolls of previous generations. Plans for the project include a nine-acre lake for swimming, boating, fishing, and skating. The roadway from the entrance to the center of the park is to be bordered by fir trees and will be called Christmas Tree Lane.

In the ENCHANTED FOREST (*free; guide service*), a woods that might have sprung from a Walt Disney fantasy, is a miniature village of brick and stone castles built of materials ingeniously arranged to resemble candy and ice cream. Each gaudily decorated room is stocked with shiny new toys of all sorts from the daintiest of dolls to the most deadly looking air rifles. Within the Enchanted Forest is conducted a SANTA CLAUS COLLEGE (*visitors welcome*), a unique institution moved here by its operator, Charles W. Howard, from Albion, New York. Howard hopes to supplant the usual bored and unconvincing department-store Santas with efficient, cheerful child psychologists. The untrained Santa Claus with a meager knowledge of his role will be replaced by craftsmen who know toys and how to make them and who can give a practical demonstration for the children. After practical store work successful graduates receive degrees of BSC (Bachelor of Santa Clausing).

BOONVILLE, 140 *m.* (408 alt., 4,526 pop.), Warrick County seat, is a coal-mining and farming center platted in 1818 and named for Jesse Boon, whose son, Ratliff, was instrumental in its selection as county seat. The town site was chosen because several wagon trails crossed here. Development was slow until 1880 when the construction of a railroad through the county gave impetus to tobacco growing, flour milling, and brick and tile manufacturing.

The RATLIFF BOON HOUSE, 116 N. First St., is a one-story weather-boarded, cabin-type structure, well preserved. Ratliff Boon came to Indiana from Kentucky and immediately engaged in politics. He was elected county treasurer when Warrick County was organized in 1813. The first State representative from Warrick County in 1816, he served for two terms and was then elected State senator. Before his term expired, he became lieutenant governor of Indiana in 1819, and served until 1825; he succeeded Governor Jennings as acting governor on September 12, 1822, and served until William Hendricks was inaugurated December 5, 1822. Between 1825 and 1839, with the exception of one term, Boon was a representative in Congress. He helped to organize the Jacksonian Democratic party in Indiana, later moving to Missouri, where he died in 1844.

Right from Boonville on Fourth St. to SCALES LAKE STATE FOREST (*free; picnic area*), 2.3 *m.*, a 477-acre tract in a reforested strip-mine region. There is a 68-acre artificial lake.

EVANSVILLE, 159.4 *m.* (383 alt., 97,062 pop.) (*see Evansville*). Evansville is at the junction with State 66 (*see Tour 11B*) and US 41 (*see Tour 20*).

MT. VERNON, 182.8 *m.* (340 alt., 5,638 pop.), seat of Posey County, was founded by Andrew McFadden, an Irish trader, in 1805. It was known as McFadden's Landing until 1816 when the present name was adopted. The southernmost city in Indiana, Mt. Vernon is primarily a trading center for the surrounding agricultural area. Fine houses in the heavily shaded residential districts reflect the architectural influence of the South. Oil was discovered near Mt. Vernon in the fall of 1938 and the quiet community hopefully awaits a boom.

The SOLDIERS AND SAILORS MONUMENT, Main St. entrance to the courthouse, is a tribute to the war heroes of Posey County. The monument was made by Rudolph Schwartz, sculptor for the Indianapolis Soldiers and Sailors Monument, to which it is similar in design. The courthouse, serving as a background for the monument, is a three-story red brick structure with stone trimming and a 'gingerbread' cupola.

In the old LEONARD CEMETERY, next to the High School building, Sixth and Canal Sts., is the GRAVE OF JUDGE J. E. PITCHER, a former Rockport attorney and friend of Abraham Lincoln (*see Tour 11B*). Pitcher, a Yale graduate and a man of unusual intellectual attainments, came to Indiana in his youth and became one of the State's leading figures. He served brilliantly in the Civil War, was wounded at Cedar Mountain, and retired at the end of the war with the commission of brigadier general.

At the foot of Main Street, three blocks south of the courthouse, SHERBURNE PARK (*children's playground; pavilion, benches*) affords an exceptionally fine view of the Ohio River.

1. Right from Mt. Vernon on State 69 (oil mat) is BELLEFONTAINE CEME-
TERY, 1 *m.*, in which are buried Alvin P. Hovey, Union Army officer and
governor of Indiana (1888–92), and General William Harrow, who rode the
Eighth Judicial Circuit (Illinois) with Lincoln. He stumped Indiana during
Lincoln's campaign for the presidency, and was his close friend for many years.

2. Left from Mt. Vernon on State 69 to 800-acre HOVEY'S LAKE (*fishing,
picnicking area*), 8.8 *m.*, one of the State's largest lakes south of Indianapolis.
Oaks, cottonwoods, maples, wild pecans, red birch, and a great number of
huge bald cypresses surround the lake. Holly, mistletoe, and networks of hanging moss aid in the creation of a semitropical atmosphere. In the spring and
fall, herons, cormorants, and wild ducks flock to this lake in great numbers.
Hovey's lake is in Point Township, southernmost part of Indiana, between the
Wabash and Ohio Rivers above their confluence. In the flood of January 1937,
every one of the township's 175 farms was inundated.

The Wabash River, 191.6 *m.*, at this point the Illinois Line, is crossed
at the MACKEY FERRY (*no regular schedule; ferryman answers a hail
from either side of the river;* 50¢ *for motor vehicle one way; round
trip* 75¢), 11 miles southeast of Carmi, Illinois (*see Illinois Guide*).

Tour 11B

St. Croix—Tell City—Troy—Rockport—Evansville—New Harmony—
(Carmi, Illinois); State 37, 66.
St. Croix to Illinois Line, 102.2 *m.*

Paved roadbed throughout.
Accommodations at intervals; hotels chiefly in cities.

Cutting almost straight south through the extremely rough but
pleasant hills of Perry County, this tour turns west and skirts the
Ohio River for several miles. It passes the point at which the Lincoln
family crossed the Ohio to begin their 14-year stay in Indiana, and the
Anderson River, at the mouth of which young Abraham conducted a
ferry. At Rockport, a few miles further west, is the famous Lincoln
Pioneer Village, a faithfully reconstructed collection of log buildings
like those in which Lincoln lived and worked. Beyond the Lincoln
country and Evansville, the route swings northwest to New Harmony
on the Wabash. Here are relics of the Rappite colony and of the 'Community of Equality,' where Robert Owen and a group of his followers
attempted to establish a new social system early in the nineteenth
century.

In ST. CROIX, 0 *m.* (800 alt., 50 pop.) (*see Tour 11A*), State 37
continues south from a junction with State 62 (*see Tour 11A*).

South of St. Croix the highway passes through the western edge of the 'knobs' country, rough and hilly and broken by deep stream valleys. This is one of the most heavily forested areas in Indiana and its hills are pleasant and restful. Because of its topography and the rocky nature of its soil, however, Perry County is less productive than most of Indiana and the inhabitants practice general farming with little success.

TELL CITY, 24.6 m. (483 alt., 5,395 pop.), settled in 1857 by a colony of Swiss, was optimistically laid out to accommodate 90,000 persons. Main Street is 80 feet wide and more than 2 miles long. The founders named the settlement in honor of the legendary hero, William Tell; present-day manufacturers and merchants use as their trademark an apple pierced by an arrow. Bordered with weather-beaten frame buildings, the streets run steeply uphill from the river, which is the west boundary of the town. The liberty-loving Swiss named streets for LaFayette, Steuben, Washington, Jefferson, and DeKalb; their respect for science and the arts is shown in streets named for Watt and Fulton, Humboldt and Pestalozzi, Schiller, Rubens, and Mòzart. Tell City is still largely populated by people of Swiss descent, although they have long since dropped the customs and mannerisms of the motherland. Since this area has access to much good lumber, and since woodworking is a traditional Swiss craft, the city's chief industry is furniture making. There are also a large distillery and a brick factory.

Left from Tell City on paved State 66 is CANNELTON, 3 m. (471 alt., 2,240 pop.), seat of Perry County. The town has the appearance of extreme age, mainly because of the many unimproved streets and the great number of old buildings constructed of sandstone quarried near the site in early days. Eastern capitalists founded the community in 1837 to exploit cannel coal deposits. During the era of steamboat transportation Cannelton was among the most important of Ohio River ports, but declined with the exhaustion of the coal deposits and the cessation of river traffic. Today its industries include the manufacture of cotton sheeting, toys and juvenile furniture, pottery, sewer pipe, and other clay products.

LaFayette Springs, 7 m., bubbles from a shallow cave (L) in the side of a huge cliff. Here LaFayette camped during his fourth visit to the United States, when the steamer *Mechanic,* on which he was traveling from New Orleans to Louisville, struck a rock and sank about 200 yards from the spring. No one drowned, but the Marquis's carriage, baggage, and about $8,000 in gold were lost.

In 1816, Thomas and Nancy Lincoln and their children, Abraham and Sarah, landed here on their way from Kentucky to Pigeon Creek to establish a new home. Borrowing a wagon—or more likely a heavy wooden sled—and a team of oxen from Francis Posey, whose farm was along the Anderson River, Thomas loaded his family and household goods and started through the thick undergrowth. The 16-mile trip required more than two days, for there was no road, and Thomas·Lincoln was forced to make his own path to the spot in the brush that he had chosen for a home. The Lincolns arrived early in December and hastily built a lean-to shelter. On the open side of this temporary home a fire, which served both for heating and cooking, was kept burning. It was too late to plant a crop and the family existed almost exclusively on wild game, which was plentiful, and water melted from snow. Their first winter in Indiana was one of innumerable hardships, a discouraging beginning of the 14 years they were to spend in the State (*see Tour 11A*).

State 66, a paved road and now the main route, roughly parallels the Ohio River westward between Tell City and Rockport, a distance of 21 miles.

TROY, 28.5 *m.* (505 alt., 599 pop.), sheltered by the protecting hill that furnished sandstone for its early houses, was one of the first settlements downstream from the Falls of the Ohio. Its founders were several Virginia families who, with their Negro slaves, made an important shipping point of the little town, and had it designated as the seat of newly formed Perry County, a distinction it retained until 1818.

At 29.4 *m.* ANDERSON RIVER is crossed near its mouth. Here Abraham Lincoln, in 1825, worked for James Taylor, a farmer near Maxville. He sometimes ran a ferry boat across the river for Taylor, and to increase his small income built himself a scow to take travelers to passing steamers in midstream.

For this industrious trait Lincoln was haled into the Kentucky court of Justice of the Peace Samuel Pate, on the complaint of a Kentucky ferryman that Abraham was conducting a ferry without a license. Lincoln explained that he merely took passengers to midstream to board passing boats, and therefore believed no license was necessary. Dill, the plaintiff, pointed out that the Kentucky boundary ran to the low water mark on the Indiana side, but Pate ruled that Lincoln was not guilty. He decided that taking passengers to midstream was not 'setting them over,' and that technically Lincoln had not violated the statute. Lincoln is said to have been so fascinated by this decision that from then on he attended sessions of this court at every opportunity.

GRANDVIEW, 40.3 *m.* (475 alt., 607 pop.), known to the Indians as Weesoe Wasapinuk (yellow tree and bank of big water), is another river town that has seen better days. It is situated atop a bluff that commands a view of the river for some five miles in either direction.

ROCKPORT, 45.8 *m.* (380 alt., 2,421 pop.), seat of Spencer County, is built on high bluffs overlooking the Ohio. Tradition has it that before 1807, when Daniel Grass became the first settler and landowner in Rockport and Spencer County, James Langford and his family made their home for one winter in a cave below the bluffs. 'Uncle Jimmy' Langford, it is said, was a leather-lunged exhorter and revivalist, and one of the earliest preachers in the neighborhood. Near the cave is a pit in which river pirates are supposed to have hidden the loot they stole from passing flatboats.

The Lincoln family settled 16 miles north of Rockport in 1816 and remained there for the entire 14 years of their stay. During this time Abraham Lincoln made many friends, among them John Pitcher, the first attorney of Rockport, who afterwards became the district prosecuting attorney. Pitcher had an exceptional library for that time, in which Lincoln read avidly of law, history, and fiction.

The Lincoln cabin was only a mile and a half from Gentryville (*see Tour 11A*) and Lincoln spent much of his time with the Gentrys. In 1828, James Gentry hired him to go with his son, Allen, on a flatboat loaded with produce to New Orleans. Lincoln 'worked the foremost oar' and received $8 per month as salary. The boys sold the cargo in New Orleans and returned upstream in a large passenger steamboat. Back in Pigeon Creek Lincoln resumed the old routine, but appears to have been dissatisfied with his limited surroundings. He read and wrote more than ever, and constantly attended court at both Rockport and Boonville.

The well-preserved two-story red brick SARGENT HOUSE, Second and Main Sts., was a tavern and inn where Lincoln stayed when he returned to Rockport in 1844 as a campaign speaker for Henry Clay. He spoke at the courthouse and was introduced by his old friend, John Pitcher.

The LINCOLN PIONEER VILLAGE (*adm.* 10¢) in the City Park, is the show place of Rockport. A memorial to Abraham Lincoln and the years he spent in Spencer County, the village represents in one group the crude homes and other buildings used by the people who played an important part in this formative period of his life. The buildings are all detailed and faithful reproductions, constructed by the Works Progress Administration under the direction of George Honig, sculptor, who has made a life study of Lincoln history. The village is surrounded by a stockade of poles, after the fashion of a pioneer settlement.

The ADMINISTRATION BUILDING AND MUSEUM ROOM is a double, one-story log house with a wide passageway between the rooms. On one side is the custodian's office, on the other a small museum of pioneer tools, clothing, weapons, old books and papers, and other interesting articles.

The JOHN PITCHER LAW OFFICE is a small one-room log cabin; the porch floor is of roughhewn planks. This building is located next to the AZEL DORSEY HOUSE, a two-story reconstructed log dwelling about 85 years old. Dorsey, who taught school near Pigeon Creek, was a fluent speaker from whom Lincoln received his liking for oratory. Beside this house is the DANIEL GRASS HOUSE, a two-story, four-room log building that was considered a mansion in the wilderness community of Rockport. It is really a double house with a corridor separating the two lower rooms, and a large fireplace on each side. Daniel Grass was one of the first settlers and by far the largest landholder and the wealthiest man in Spencer County. The interior, furnished by descendants of the Grass family, contains many of the original picture prints and pieces of furniture that belonged to the Daniel Grass family. Lincoln was a friend of the Grass children and once visited them for several weeks.

The AUNT LEPHA MCKAY HOUSE, erected as a memorial to the pioneer woman who once owned the land on which the village stands, is a simple one-room log cabin. Aunt Lepha was the first woman in this region to be interested in the education of the Negro, and in this cabin taught many of the Negro children of the vicinity. The GENTRY MANSION, so-called because it was a mansion compared with most of the rough shacks of that time, is a reconstructed two-story log house with a porch. The interior, furnished in the original manner, is maintained by descendants of the Gentry family. The FORMER HOME OF REUBEN

GRIGSBY, cousin to Aaron Grigsby, is a one-room cabin. Aaron married Lincoln's only sister, Sarah. She died in childbirth and Lincoln for a long time thereafter nursed a grudge against the Grigsby family, believing that her death was caused by negligence and lack of proper medical aid.

The PIGEON CREEK BAPTIST CHURCH is a large two-story cabin with two enormous fireplaces. The benches are roughhewn planks put together with wooden pegs. The Lincoln family worshipped here and much of the carpentry was done by Thomas and Abraham. The PIONEER SCHOOLHOUSE is a large one-room log house in which Abraham received a part of his limited formal education. Poorly lighted, it has a dirt floor and plank benches. BROWN'S INN is composed of two large rooms, both with dirt floors. It has a long dining table and a common sleeping room, usual in backwoods hostelries. During Lincoln's boyhood it was the only inn in the locality.

The LINCOLN CABIN is a reproduction of the last home of the Lincolns during their stay in Indiana. A one-story log house with an attic reached by a wooden peg ladder fastened to the wall, it has two rooms and a large fireplace, and was built by Thomas Lincoln after his second marriage brought two step-children that necessitated larger quarters. The MARKET AND BARTER HOUSE is a large single-room cabin to which the pioneers brought their produce to sell to outside buyers or to trade on a goods-for-goods basis. It was built by the settlers and held as common property for the disposal of stock and produce. The GRANDVIEW BLOCKHOUSE was originally located at Grandview as an Indian lookout and community fort in time of attack. It is a small square structure with an overhanging second story.

The FIRST HOME OF MR. AND MRS. JOSIAH CRAWFORD is a one-room cabin. Crawford was a young farmer who lived in the Pigeon Creek neighborhood and for whom Lincoln and his father worked at odd jobs (*see Tour 11A*). The JONES STORE is little more than a shack with a lean-to plank shed at the rear. Here Lincoln clerked for his friend Jones, while he told stories and made friends with the people of Gentryville. An avid reader of every newspaper that fell into his grasp, he became a self-appointed news commentator for the entire village. Very few of the settlers were able to read or write and to all of Jones's customers Lincoln gave a running account of the happenings in the outside world, while he weighed and sacked their purchases.

A covered wagon, oxcarts, sweep and windlass wells, mill-burrs, shaving horse, ash hoppers, soap kettles, hitch racks, grind stones, wooden moldboard plow, and similar articles are exhibited on the village grounds. Across the village is LAKE ALDA (*picnic tables, ovens, wading pool; boats for rent*), an artificial body of water bordered by pleasant outing grounds under century-old trees.

The ROCKPORT FERRY (*service every 15 min.; fare 10¢ per person each way, 50¢ for cars and trucks*) connects with US 60 at Maceo, Kentucky.

From this point the route leaves the river and crosses Spencer

County, through farm land that is productive and generally level to rolling in contour. The route strikes the Ohio again at 64 *m.*

GOVERNMENT DAM NO. 47 (*cottages for rent; fishing*), 66.2 *m.*, completed in 1928 at a cost of $5,000,000, extends for 2,050 feet across the Ohio River. It is one of several along the river that regulates the depth at low-water stage; the locks, which are on the Indiana side, have a nine-foot lift.

NEWBURGH, 66.6 *m.* (425 alt., 1,374 pop.), is a typical small river town of the last century. Its inhabitants now depend upon Evansville's industries for employment. Notable among the old structures of the town is the century-old WIES HOUSE (*visitors welcome*), Jennings and Market Sts. The bricks for this house were brought to Newburgh by flatboat and the timbers are not hewn out but merely cut to correct length and put together with wooden pins. The joists are the trunks of small trees hewn on one side in order to lay a floor.

From Newburgh the route continues due west through Evansville, while the river makes a deep loop to the south and continues in a series of loops until it meets the Wabash River at the southwest tip of Indiana.

At 69.7 *m.* is the junction with paved Stacer Road.

Left on Stacer Road, 0.1 *m.*, to the ANGEL MOUNDS, the largest group of prehistoric mounds in Indiana. Left here on Pollock Avenue is (L) BEEHIVE MOUND, 0.5 *m.* Seven other mounds are visible (R) at this point. The mounds are the property of the Indiana Historical Society, and excavations in this vicinity during the summer of 1939 uncovered a primitive Indian village believed to have had between 4,000 and 5,000 inhabitants.

The EVANSVILLE STATE HOSPITAL ('Woodmere'), 72 *m.*, is an institution (R) for the care and treatment of the mentally afflicted. The large, modern brick buildings are connected by a network of drives through the landscaped grounds. There are about 1,200 patients and all who are able to work are kept moderately occupied. The institution operates its own bakery, laundry, greenhouses, dairy, sewage disposal plant, and slaughterhouse; 503 acres of the 879-acre tract are devoted to gardens and farms.

At EVANSVILLE, 76 *m.* (383 alt., 97,062 pop.) (*see Evansville*), where the route again meets the Ohio River, are the junctions with US 41 (*see Tour* 20) and State 62 (*see Tour* 11*A*).

West of Evansville, State 66 leaves the Ohio River to take a north-westerly course through gently rolling pasture land and productive farms.

NEW HARMONY, 101.7 *m.* (475 alt., 1,390 pop.) (*see New Harmony*).

State 66 crosses the ILLINOIS LINE, 102.2 *m.*, on a bridge (*toll 50¢ per car each way*) spanning the Wabash River, 14 miles northeast of Carmi, Illinois (*see Illinois Guide*).

Historic Buildings

THE CAPITOL, INDIANAPOLIS

INDIANA'S FIRST STATE HOUSE, CORYDON
This building was erected in 1811-12 for use as Harrison County Courthouse

LEVI COFFIN HOUSE, FOUNTAIN CITY
(Grand Central Station of the Underground Railroad)

TERRITORIAL CAPITOL, VINCENNES
Erected about 1800 as a private residence, this
was the seat of Territorial government until 1813

THE LANIER HOUSE AT MADISON

STAIRWAY IN SHREWSBURY
HOUSE, MADISON
Designed by Francis Costigan

INTERIOR OF LANIER
HOUSE, MADISON

RAPPITE ROSE DOOR, NOW PART OF HIGH SCHOOL BUILDING, NEW HARMONY

RAPPITE FORT, NEW HARMONY (c. 1815)

RAPPITE COMMUNITY HOUSE NO. 2, NEW HARMONY

BOYHOOD HOME OF JAMES WHITCOMB RILEY, GREENFIELD

BIRTHPLACE OF EDWARD EGGLESTON VEVAY

Tour 12

(Louisville, Ky.)—New Albany—Paoli—Shoals—Vincennes—Terre
Haute—(Paris, Illinois); US 150.
Kentucky Line to Illinois Line, 180.7 *m.*

Concrete and high bituminous roadbed throughout.
Southern R.R. parallels the route from Paoli to Prospect; Baltimore and Ohio
R.R. from Shoals to Vincennes; Chicago and Eastern Illinois R.R. from Vincennes
to Terre Haute.
Accommodations at short intervals.

US 150, the principal route from Louisville to central Illinois, winds
northwest through the most rugged of Indiana's hill country. The highway is rich in historical association, for it was over this road that
many of the State's early settlers traveled north from the Ohio River
in search of homesteads, and it later became an important stagecoach
route. Paralleling parts of it are the Buffalo Trace, a well-defined path
once used by countless herds of bison; an Indian trail; and the Vincennes trace, cut through the forest early in the nineteenth century.

The highway passes through a section of the State that still retains
much of its original beauty and wildness. For many miles it is never
out of the hills, and in the southern portion there are few towns of any
size. Farther north and west are Vincennes, the State's oldest town, and
the vast coal fields that underlie every inch of the surrounding territory.

US 150 crosses the Ohio River by way of the Kentucky and Indiana
Bridge (*toll 25¢ for car and driver, 5¢ for each additional passenger*)
from downtown Louisville, Kentucky, to NEW ALBANY, 0 *m.* (459
alt., 25,414 pop.) (*see New Albany*).

In New Albany is the junction with State 62 (*see Tour 11A*).

FLOYDS KNOBS, 3.3 *m.* (846 alt., 182 pop.), in the center of a
strawberry-growing area, is set in a valley almost surrounded by towering hills called 'knobs.' The growth of the town dates from 1815, when
James B. Moore, of New York State, built a gristmill where the present
concrete bridge crosses Little Indian Creek. One of the settlement's
earliest industries was the making of beaver top hats. A sawmill, a
general store, and five quarter-sections of land were later acquired by
Moore, and the village, now strung along each side of the highway,
with no back streets or alleys, was named Mooresville. The present
name was adopted in 1843, in honor of Colonel Davis Floyd, of Jeffersonville. In spite of its proximity to New Albany and Jeffersonville,
Floyds Knobs has maintained its separate identity as a busy and enterprising town.

Since 1887—when strawberries were first cultivated in southern Indiana—the knobs and river bluffs of Floyd County have been noted for fruit growing. At present (1941) more than 500 acres are planted in strawberries; the crop yields an annual net income of about $200,000. The growers, for the most part, are of Swiss, Alsatian, German, and Irish descent.

In the early days the Old State Road, connecting Jeffersonville and Vincennes, ran over the top of the knobs or Silver Hills, as the Indians called them. According to Indian legend, the Silver Hills were formed when the Great Spirit dug up the ground searching for silver to put in the sky as stars. The Indians used the knobs as lookout points. From their summit Kentucky hills, 25 miles distant, can be seen on clear days. The townspeople of New Albany gathered on the knobs in July 1863 to defend their city against Morgan, the Confederate raider (*see Corydon*).

Years ago, according to the Louisville *Times*, Gilbert Vestison, the 'Hermit of the Knobs,' lived on a wild and lonely spot at the summit of a hill. As a youth—handsome, intelligent, ambitious, and poor—Vestison had lived in France and had fallen in love with a girl named Madeline (whose last name he would never reveal). For a short time they lived in their own personal paradise, completely happy. Then Madeline's wealthy parents parted the lovers. Gilbert was broken in heart and mind and became a wanderer. He finally came to the knobs, built a rude shack, and lived here for 30 years, nursing his grief and shunning the company of his neighbors.

Vestison became known throughout the neighborhood for his eccentricities. He said that he was 6,000 years old and that he expected to live another 1,000 years, after which he would be reunited with his Madeline in a second period of youth that would be unending. He was ordinarily gentle, kind, and apparently sane, but if a neighbor requested him to sing the 'Marseillaise,' his eyes would glow madly and the battle song of France would roll from his lips in an impassioned torrent.

His cabin finally collapsed and he spent the last years of his life in a hole dug in the side of a hill. One morning two passing hunters found Gilbert dead in his cave, a smile on his lips. Near by were the remains of a log cabin and a huge pile of old shoes he had collected. Clutched in his hand was the photograph of a beautiful girl. Gilbert had lived his remaining thousand years.

The St. Francis Proseminary, 5.8 *m.*, a Franciscan training school for the priesthood, was established in 1896 on 400 acres of forest and farm land given by Mary Anderson (de Navarro), an actress. The main hall is a rectangular, three-story brick building with dormer windows. Beside it is the new faculty home, of similar design, and the brick and stone Romanesque chapel, connected with the hall by a covered arch.

A large part of the seminary's land is under cultivation, and a dairy farm has been developed. A 10-acre artificial lake supplies water and furnishes facilities for recreation. The seminary offers high school and some junior college training and has a faculty of ten priests and one lay brother.

GALENA, 8.4 *m.* (840 alt., 162 pop.), was platted in 1836 in the vain hope that the Paoli Turnpike, then being surveyed, would make it a great city. It was first called Germantown, because of the large number of Germans in the community. Galena has two cooper shops and a factory making bellows for blacksmiths' furnaces. The GALENA MILL (R), built in 1857, was once a steam-powered flour mill; it is now the Odd Fellows Hall. Because of the many streams and salt springs in the vicinity, the site was a popular Indian camping and hunting ground and there are several Indian burial grounds in the neighborhood.

GREENVILLE, 11.7 *m.* (795 alt., 285 pop.), is the second oldest town in Floyd County and the intersecting point for a number of farm-to-market roads. It was first settled in 1807 and platted in 1816. Early in its history Greenville grew rapidly and at one time had a population of nearly 600. Situated in a region of fine white-oak timber, the town became a manufacturing center for barrels, wine kegs and, for a time, wooden clocks.

Greenville was an important stagecoach station on the Old State Road between Jeffersonville and Vincennes. This portion of the famous old road was later supplanted by the Paoli Turnpike, now US 150. Stages began running over the road—eastbound one day, westbound the next—in the 1820's and continued, despite the railroads, to run between New Albany and Paoli until the 1880's. Farming and dairying are now (1941) the principal occupations, and most of the homes are simple frame dwellings of mid-nineteenth-century construction.

In PALMYRA, 18.5 *m.* (800 alt., 274 pop.), a farming village founded in 1810, General John Hunt Morgan, the Confederate raider, stopped to rest and water his horses during his march through Indiana (*see Corydon*).

FREDERICKSBURG, 23.2 *m.* (715 alt., 205 pop.), first settled in 1805, is one of the many villages where toll stations were formerly operated on the New Albany-Vincennes plank road. Stations usually were placed at five-mile intervals and tolls were collected on the number of wheels on the vehicle and the number of horses pulling it. Persons going to church, funerals, musters, or elections were exempt from paying toll.

It is said that the part of the route between Fredericksburg and Hardinsburg was once a buffalo trail, made long before the coming of the white man by vast herds journeying between the prairies of Illinois and the salt licks in this vicinity.

The LICK CREEK FRIENDS CHURCH, 37 *m.*, built in 1815, was one of the first Quaker churches in this part of the country. A majority of the early settlers of this region were Quakers and many of them are buried in the adjacent cemetery. This is also the site of the Lick Creek Friends College, the first attempt to establish an institution of higher learning in Orange County. Today, on the site of the short-lived college, stands the Lick Creek grade school.

PAOLI, 40.9 *m*. (638 alt., 2,218 pop.), seat of Orange County, is sometimes called the 'crossroads of southern Indiana,' because of its proximity to intersecting latitude and longitude lines. There are a few light industries in Paoli—a canning factory, a chair factory, and a wooden-handle factory. The people are friendly and the town is neat and attractive. Its shaded streets are lined with brightly painted houses and well-tended lawns.

Most of the buildings of the shopping area are of the past century, but have been kept in a good state of repair. The business district forms a square about the two-story, gray brick ORANGE COUNTY COURTHOUSE, built in 1850, and an excellent example of the Greek Revival style. A portico, which has six fluted Doric columns that extend to the second-floor roof, fronts the building. Iron grillwork balustrades flank the portico, and over the first-floor entrance is an iron balcony with steps leading to the second floor. The building is surmounted by a large cupola containing a four-faced town clock.

Two blocks south of the courthouse square on a hill overlooking Paoli is the WILLIAM BOWLES HOUSE. Dr. Bowles was a leader in the Knights of the Golden Circle (*see Tour 5a*) and builder of the first French Lick Springs Hotel (*see Tour 11*). This large, two-story frame residence was built in 1825 before Bowles moved to French Lick.

In Paoli are junctions with State 37 (*see Tour 19*) and State 56 (*see Tour 11*), which unites westward with US 150 for 8.9 miles.

At 48.8 *m*. is the junction with a graveled road.

> Right on this road is ORANGEVILLE, 4.8 *m*. (628 alt., 50 pop.), where the elusive LOST RIVER, a stream of alternating underground and surface channels, rises from beneath a large, natural stone archway into a deep pool. East of here the river bed is dry, for the water flows in subterranean channels; but westward from this point to its junction with the White River nine miles south of Shoals, Lost River is a surface stream.

PROSPECT, 49.7 *m*. (600 alt., 210 pop.), is a rural village that forms a natural entrance into the bowl-like valley surrounding French Lick and West Baden.

In Prospect is the western junction with State 56 (*see Tour 11*).

In SHOALS, 63 *m*. (490 alt., 1,031 pop.) (*see Tour 10*), is the junction with US 50 (*see Tour 10*), with which US 150 unites westward for 44.5 miles to VINCENNES, 107.5 *m*. (442 alt., 18,228 pop.) (*see Vincennes*).

In Vincennes is a junction with US 41 (*see Tour 20*) with which US 150 unites northward for 56.1 miles to TERRE HAUTE, 163.6 *m*. (541 alt., 62,693 pop.) (*see Terre Haute*).

Terre Haute is at the junction with State 46 (*see Tour 9*), the northern junction with US 41, and the junction with US 40 (*see Tour 8b*) with which US 150 unites westward for 3.4 miles.

At WEST TERRE HAUTE, 167 *m*. (490 alt., 3,729 pop.) (*see Tour 8b*), is the western junction with US 40. Here US 150 turns right to 102-acre IZAAK WALTON LAKE (*open, nominal charge; fishing, swimming*), 167.9 *m.*, a recreational resort.

At 169.7 *m.* is the junction with a brick road.

Left on this road to ST. MARY-OF-THE-WOODS COLLEGE, 0.5 *m.*, a Roman Catholic girls' school with an enrollment (1939) of 929, founded in 1840. On the campus are gardens, tennis courts, lakes, golf links, and nine large buildings. The Anne Thérèse Guérin Hall is a handsome four-story Italian Renaissance building of buff brick ornamented with Bedford limestone, used as a freshman residence hall and for administration offices. Foley Hall is an imposing Italian Renaissance type structure with a frontage of 175 feet. Just east of it is the Church of the Immaculate Conception. The school operates its own bakery, farm, dairy, coal mine, and other service enterprises.

NEW GOSHEN, 176 *m.* (602 alt., 500 pop.), is a village populated chiefly by miners and retired farmers. Its major business establishments are several grocery and general stores.

A small mining town hard hit by dwindling coal markets is SHIRKIEVILLE, 178.6 *m.* (611 alt., 75 pop.). Founded only about 20 years ago and named for the owner of a near-by mine, Shirkieville is a settlement of Italians, many of whom have retained in part their European customs and traditions.

US 150 crosses the ILLINOIS LINE, 180.7 *m.*, eight miles east of Paris, Illinois (*see Illinois Guide*).

↑↑↑

Tour 13

(Coldwater, Michigan)—Angola—Fort Wayne—Richmond—Liberty—
(Oxford, Ohio); US 27.
Michigan Line to Ohio Line, 167.3 *m.*

Paved roadbed throughout.
The New York Central R.R. roughly parallels the route between Angola and Fort Wayne; the Pennsylvania R.R., between Fort Wayne and Richmond; and the Baltimore & Ohio R.R., between Liberty and West College Corner.
Accommodations at short intervals; hotels chiefly in cities.

In its northern section US 27 crosses a region of lakes and hills that were formed in the 'battle of the glaciers,' fought in prehistoric times when giant ice fields collided here. Between Fort Wayne and Decatur the route parallels the Wayne Trace, along which marched armies led by Generals Josiah Harmar (1790), Arthur St. Clair (1791), 'Mad' Anthony Wayne (1794), and William Henry Harrison (1812). Midway on the tour is Geneva, the village in which Gene Stratton Porter wrote *Freckles* and other stories about the Limberlost.

In pre-Civil War years the route now followed by US 27 was a main highway for runaway slaves bound for Canada and freedom. Many of the towns along the tour were 'depots' on the Underground Railroad, and one, Fountain City, at the junction of three lines of escape, was the 'grand central station.'

US 27 crosses the INDIANA LINE, 0 *m.*, 13 miles south of Coldwater, Michigan.

LAKE GEORGE, a popular resort, is intersected by the Indiana-Michigan Line. It is a part of one of three chains of lakes in this region, which can be explored through connecting streams by canoe; all of the lakes can be reached by good roads.

POKAGON STATE PARK (*adm.* 10¢), 3.6 *m.*, is a 937-acre recreational resort with deep forests and 2 miles of frontage on LAKE JAMES, third largest lake in Indiana. The park was named for Simon Pokagon (pronounced Po-kay'-gon), last chief of the Potawatomi Indians in this region. The area, as described years ago by Chief Pokagon at an old settlers' meeting in Angola, once teemed with elk, moose, beaver, and buffalo.

Chief Simon Pokagon attended Notre Dame University and Oberlin College and was considered the best educated man of his race (*see Tour 1*). In 1888 he succeeded in collecting $150,000 that the Government had promised to pay his tribe 55 years before. In 1833 Chief Leopold Pokagon, Simon's father, had surrendered the southern half of Steuben County and an additional 1,000,000 acres, including the land where Chicago now stands, and part of the purchase price was not paid. Simon Pokagon arranged for equal distribution of the $150,000 among the Potawatomi.

POTAWATOMI INN, a substantial two-story structure of 45 rooms, stands on an eminence in the park. Through a natural arch, formed by encroaching belts of timber on each side of the inlet, is a view of the broadest part of Lake James and the opposite shore, with its sky line of low forested hills rising behind the tiny cottages of Paltytown.

On a shaded elevation that slopes down to a sandy beach is a CAMPING GROUND (25¢ *per day*). At WELDON'S LANDING, on the west side of the lake, is a motor-boat livery (*rowboats available at park piers, 25¢ per hr.*).

ANGOLA, 8.7 *m.* (1,055 alt., 3,141 pop.) (*see Tour 1*), is at the junction with US 20 (*see Tour 1*).

PLEASANT LAKE, 13.1 *m.* (976 alt., 541 pop.), named for the near-by lake, is a small farming community. The lake was called Nipcondish (pleasant waters) by the Indians.

WATERLOO, 23.2 *m.* (900 alt., 1,257 pop.), is at the junction with US 6 (*see Tour 3*).

AUBURN, 28.6 *m.* (863 alt., 5,415 pop.), is the oldest, yet liveliest, town in the county. The business district about the DeKalb County courthouse square has attractive buildings and trim modern fronts.

Wide streets lead to pleasant, tree-shaded residential districts. The surrounding country is a fertile plain, and successful farmers have made a busy trading center of Auburn.

The WARNER AUTOMOTIVE PARTS PLANT, of the Borg-Warner Corporation, occupies the buildings of the Auburn Automobile Company on S. Jackson Street. Cylinder heads, axle shafts, ring gears and pinions, transmission gears, and clutch plates for all types of automobiles are manufactured here. The Auburn Automobile Company has ceased to operate in Auburn but still maintains the administration building of this plant as a distributing point for Auburn, Cord, and Duesenberg parts.

In GARRETT, 33.7 m. (893 alt., 4,285 pop.), the stores and business houses, many of which are new, two-story brick buildings, face a public square in the approved Hoosier fashion. This town was once a division point of the Baltimore & Ohio Railroad, with extensive shops and a roundhouse, but today only running repairs on steam heat, air hose, lubricators, and the like, are made here. It is now a farming center with an artificial bait factory and a few other small industries.

At 48 m. is (R) SAINT PAUL'S CEMETERY (German Lutheran), one of the oldest in Allen County; the inscriptions on the moss-covered headstones are in German.

At 50.1 m. is the junction with graveled Coldwater Road.

Right on this road to the FORT WAYNE SPEEDWAY AND EXPOSITION PARK (*open*), 0.5 m. There are three race tracks—one each for horse races, midget auto races, and regular auto races—and a grandstand seating 7,000 persons.

FORT WAYNE, 52.7 m. (779 alt., 118,410 pop.) (*see Fort Wayne*).
Fort Wayne is at the junction with US 24 (*see Tour* 5), US 30 (*see Tour* 4), and US 33 (*see Tour* 15), which unites southward with US 27 for 21 miles.

Paralleling the route between Fort Wayne and Decatur is the WAYNE TRACE. Along this famous old military road, General Anthony Wayne led his men after defeating the Indians under Little Turtle at the Battle of Fallen Timbers in Ohio in 1794, and after he had selected the site for a new stockade at what is now Fort Wayne. Although called the Wayne Trace, the route—about a mile and a half east of US 27—was the same one by which General Josiah Harmar's expedition against the Miami at Kekionga approached and left the site of Fort Wayne in 1790. Over this same road General Arthur St. Clair started for Kekionga in 1791. However, he was waylaid by Little Turtle at Fort Recovery, Ohio, and his army destroyed. General William Henry Harrison brought his army along this path to raise the siege of Fort Wayne in 1812.

In the ghost town of MIDDLETOWN, 64.2 m., is the RUCH TAVERN (L), a two-story rambling frame house, surrounded by a beautiful grove of maple trees. It was built in 1851 when the village was platted, a year after the road that is now US 27 had been laid with plank between Fort Wayne and Willshire, Ohio, and a line of stagecoaches put into operation. Soon railroads superseded the stage-coach lines, and the town declined.

MONMOUTH, 71 m. (788 alt., 60 pop.), is the center of a sugar-beet-growing section. South of the village the highway crosses Mc-KNIGHT's RUN. Legend has it that ever since a white man camping here for the night was murdered by a marauding Indian, his ghost has haunted the creek's banks after dark. More than one old resident avows that he was tapped on the shoulder by the restless spirit while walking along McKnight's Run.

DECATUR, 73.9 m. (800 alt., 5,861 pop.), was named for the American naval hero, Stephen Decatur. The city is the former home of Gene Stratton Porter (1868–1924), who was married and lived here for three years before moving to Geneva. A monument to her memory, erected by the school children of Adams County, stands in the courthouse yard.

Across the street from the courthouse is THE AUCTIONEERING SCHOOL of Colonel Fred Reppert, operated in July and December of each year, with 10 instructors and an average of 50 students. After one week of instruction the students are given practical experience, 'crying' public sales in the streets of Decatur. The auctions enable townspeople to dispose of odds and ends without paying a commission for the sale.

The auction method of sale is still popular in the Middle and Far West, particularly for disposing of pedigreed stock. The students of this school learn the history of all pure breeds of domestic animals, their characteristics and potentialities. They also are taught good English, oratory, physical culture, and 'pep,' as well as the importance of the psychological moment.

Decatur's industries include a small motor plant of the General Electric Company, a soy-bean mill and elevator, a cheese factory, a beet-sugar refinery, and a stone monument works.

Adjoining Decatur on the south are the DECATUR HOME-STEADS, a workmen's garden community, completed in 1935 under the supervision of the Resettlement Administration. Located here because of the diversity of industry and the shortage of houses, the project is designed to provide better housing conditions for part-time employees. On a landscaped 80-acre plot stand 48 one- and two-story houses of Dutch or Cape Cod Colonial design, each surrounded by a garden or fruit trees. The houses are purchased by long-term monthly payments.

In Decatur is the southern junction with US 33 (see Tour 15).

Right from Decatur on US 224 to the NUTTMAN-HANNA PARK, 1.5 m., a 40-acre preserve of virgin forest. The OIL PUMPING STATION (R), 4.5 m., of the Indiana Pipe Line Company, is one of the power units in the pipe line which carries 96,000 barrels of oil daily from Texas and Oklahoma to the Atlantic seaboard.

At 13.3 m. is the junction with State 1; L. on State 1 to the junction with

State 116, 18.2 *m.;* R. on State 116 to the DEAM OAK MEMORIAL (R), 2.5 *m.*
This tree, a rare hybrid that is not sterile, is a cross between a white and a
chinquapin oak; it is named in honor of a Bluffton botanist. The oak provides
viable acorns, which, with seedlings, have been distributed to many botanical
gardens over the United States.

Straight ahead on State 1 to BLUFFTON (829 alt., 5,417 pop.), 19.2 *m.,*
the century-old seat of Wells County, perched on the bluffs of the south
bank of the Wabash River. Streets are wide and paved with brick in the
shopping district but a majority of the residential streets are narrow and
graveled. Shade trees are so numerous that in places the houses are obscured.
DEAM ARBORETUM, east end of South St., has 600 forest trees of both native
and foreign varieties, 60,000 specimens of plant life, and 100 varieties of wild
flowers. Charles C. Deam, owner of the arboretum, is the author of *Trees of
Indiana* and other nature books.

Left from Bluffton on State 116 to the WELLS COUNTY STATE FOREST
AND GAME PRESERVE (*adm. free; shelter house, picnic grounds*), 23.7 *m.,*
an 850-acre tract including a nursery for evergreen trees, pens for raising
young pheasant and quail, and a display of wild life.

BERNE, 86.4 *m.* (825 alt., 2,075 pop.), was founded in 1852 by
Mennonite immigrants from Berne, Switzerland, and a Swiss accent is
still noticeable among the citizens. There is an unusually large Mennonite congregation here. In the center of town is the MENNONITE
BOOK CONCERN, the national official bookstore and publishing company for the Mennonite General Conference. Starting in 1882 as a
bookstore in a one-story frame building, the enterprise was made a
church institution two years later, and became the Mennonite Book
Concern in 1893. More than 200 Sunday schools are supplied with religious books and pamphlets by this publishing house. It is the sole
publisher and distributor for the Mennonite faith in the United States
and Canada.

In GENEVA, 91.2 *m.* (841 alt., 966 pop.), a rural community, is the
GENE STRATTON PORTER HOUSE (*adm.* 25¢), a 14-room cedar log
house, one-half block L. of the highway at the southern edge of town.
The novelist lived here with her husband and daughter, and found
time to romanticize the adjacent swampland that Hoosier farmers had
regarded only as a bug- and snake-infested menace to health. At
Geneva, Mrs. Porter wrote *The Girl of the Limberlost, The Song of
the Cardinal,* and *Freckles.* Limberlost Swamp, the setting of these
stories, was originally called the Loblolly but was named Limberlost
after a hunter, 'Limber Jim' McDowell, who was lost in its fastnesses
for three days, evading his companions whom he mistook for hostile Indians. Mrs. Porter built her home here in 1893 and remained until
1913, when the swamp was drained and denuded of its trees. She then
moved to Rome City, in Noble County (*see Tour* 14), and built another cabin. The Porters later moved to California where Mrs. Porter
died ·in an automobile accident in 1924.

PORTLAND, 102.2 *m.* (909 alt., 6,362 pop.), Jay County seat, is
known for its cement stave silos, and for the overalls, shirts, and
jackets manufactured here and sold largely by chain stores. The SITE
OF THE BIRTHPLACE OF ELWOOD HAYNES (1857–1925), inventor of the

first successful clutch-driven automobile (see Tour 17b), is marked at High and Commerce Streets.

In BLUFF POINT, 108.3 m. (993 alt., 25 pop.), is the THAD BIESEL TURKEY FARM (visitors welcome), established in 1918. Biesel raises between 1,200 and 1,400 turkeys annually for market distribution. The birds are shipped alive by motor trucks; the principal market is Dayton, Ohio.

The spire of the Randolph County Courthouse breaks the sky line long before WINCHESTER, 120.2 m. (1,087 alt., 5,303 pop.), a grain and livestock shipping center, is reached. The highway passes through the center of the busy shopping district bounding the courthouse square, and on through residential sections where well-kept lawns are shaded by tall elms.

At the Randolph County Fairgrounds in the northwestern part of the city are the REMAINS OF THE FUDGE MOUNDS. These old earthworks, excavated in 1931, and flattened, once enclosed 31 acres. In the center was a mound nine feet high and elliptical in form, in which skeletons, spear points, and copper bracelets were found. There are still several unexcavated mounds in the neighborhood.

Winchester is at the junction with State 32 (see Tour 6).

LYNN, 129.3 m. (1,162 alt., 1,014 pop.), is at the junction with US 36 (see Tour 7).

FOUNTAIN CITY, 135.8 m. (1,093 alt., 491 pop.), is famous in Indiana history as the 'grand central station' of the Underground Railroad, the road to freedom for fugitive slaves. The town, incorporated as Newport in 1834, was renamed Fountain City upon the discovery of an underground lake from which water rises automatically to the surface if pipes are driven into the ground.

The LEVI COFFIN HOUSE, east side of North Main St., a modest two-story brick residence built flush with the sidewalk, is in good condition and has undergone few alterations. It is estimated that between 1827 and 1847 at least 2,000 slaves were sheltered here on their way to Canada and freedom. Levi Coffin and his wife, the latter affectionately known as 'Aunt Katie,' took care of the fugitives and helped them to finish their journey in safety. The name, Underground Railroad, was originated by a frustrated slave-hunter from Kentucky who remarked that 'they must have an underground railroad running hereabouts, and Levi Coffin must be the president of it.' According to a well-established tradition, Eliza Harris, heroine of Uncle Tom's Cabin, was sheltered in Levi Coffin's home for several days after she had made the dramatic crossing of the Ohio River by leaping from one cake of ice to another, carrying her child and pursued by bloodhounds.

Three principal lines of the Underground Railroad, from main crossing points on the Ohio River, converged at this place. They ran from Cincinnati, Madison, and Jeffersonville to Fountain City. There were 'depots' along these routes at intervals of about 15 or 20 miles. The 'schedule' was operated only during the night. Levi Coffin in his memoirs explained the details of the system as follows:

The roads were always in running order, the connections were good, the conductors active and zealous, and there was no lack of passengers. Seldom a week passed without our receiving passengers by this mysterious road. We found it necessary to always be prepared to receive such company and properly care for them. We knew not what night or hour of the night we would be aroused by a gentle rap at the door. That was a signal announcing the arrival of a train of the Underground Railway, for the locomotive did not whistle or make any unnecessary noise. I have often been awakened by this signal, and sprang out of bed and opened the door. Outside in the cold or the rain, there would be a two-horse wagon loaded with fugitives, perhaps the greater part of them women and children. I would invite them in a low tone to come in, and they would follow me into the darkened house without a word, for we knew not who might be watching or listening. When they were all safely inside and the door fastened, I would cover the windows, strike a light and build a good fire. By this time my wife would be up and preparing victuals for them, and in a short time the cold and hungry fugitives would be made comfortable. I would accompany the conductor of the train to the stable and care for the horses that had, perhaps, been driven 25 or 30 miles that night through the rain and cold. The fugitives would rest on pallets before the fire the rest of the night. Frequently wagon loads of passengers from the different lines have met at our house, having no previous knowledge of each other. The companies varied in number from two or three to seventeen.

Newport (Fountain City) was a Quaker settlement in which most of the residents were ardent Abolitionists, and other families besides the Coffins aided the slaves in escaping. Many slaves were given work until they could be sent north, but some made permanent homes here and have descendants living in the community at the present time.

Coffin's activities were often investigated but no legal action was ever taken against him. He was proscribed by his church but was afterward reinstated. In 1847 he moved to Cincinnati, where he continued his antislavery work on a much larger scale. In 1864 he went to England and organized a Freedman's Aid Society, which sent money and clothing to the United States. He was a delegate to the International Anti-Slavery Conference at Paris in 1867.

RICHMOND, 145.1 m. (954.1 alt., 35,147 pop.) (see Tour 8a), is at the junction with US 40 (see Tour 8a) and US 35 (see Tour 17).

The SMITH-ESTEB MEMORIAL HOSPITAL, 152.1 m., a sanatorium (R) for tubercular patients, was given to Wayne County with 100 acres of land, by Mr. and Mrs. David Esteb.

At 156.6 m. is a boulder (R) bearing the notation that a half mile east of the spot is the site of the BIRTHPLACE OF JOAQUIN MILLER, 'the Poet of the Sierras.' The brick house in which the poet was born has long since been razed and nothing remains to mark the spot. Although Joaquin (Cincinnatus Heine) Miller (1841–1913) was a native of Indiana, he was taken to frontier Oregon in 1854.

LIBERTY, 159.2 m. (980 alt., 1,496 pop.), a leisurely town of comfortable old houses on tree-lined streets, is in a region of long swelling hills given over to farming. There are three grain elevators in the town, but little other industry.

The rambling two-story house on the SITE OF THE BURNSIDE HOUSE, Seminary and Fairground Sts., was remodeled from the original structure. Ambrose Burnside lived here from shortly after his birth in 1824 until 1843 when he entered the United States Military Academy. He served as a lieutenant during the Mexican War. In the Civil War he was raised to the rank of major general, succeeded McClellan in command of the Army of the Potomac, and met disaster at the Battle of Fredericksburg. After the war he was governor of Rhode Island for three terms, and United States senator from that State between 1874 and his death in 1881.

At the intersection of US 27 and State 44 is the UNION COUNTY COURTHOUSE built in 1890 of hand cut stone. In the COURTHOUSE MUSEUM (*adm. free*) is a collection of Indian relics.

1. Right from Liberty on State 44 to the junction with a graveled road, 1.6 *m.;* R. on this road to the SITE OF THE BIRTHPLACE OF MRS. ALICE GRAY, 2.6 *m.,* the 'Little Orphant Annie' of James Whitcomb Riley's poem. The site is now a vegetable garden across from a gravel pit.

2. Right from Liberty on State 101 is ROSEBURGH, 3.5 *m.,* a hamlet; R. from Roseburgh on a dirt road and over a covered bridge, and L. through Quakertown, constantly bearing L. until an iron bridge is crossed, is (R) the SITE OF COCKEFAIR MILL, 7.5 *m.,* the first woolen mill west of the Allegheny Mountains. It was built by Elisha Cockefair in 1818, and was at one time one of the most famous mills in the country. In 1930 it was given by the Cockefair heirs to Henry Ford, who had it removed to his Pioneer Village in Dearborn, Michigan.

At 160.8 *m.* is a stone marker designating the site as near the BIRTHPLACE OF AMBROSE BURNSIDE.

WEST COLLEGE CORNER, 167.3 *m.* (1,042 alt., 454 pop.), is the sister town of College Corner, Ohio.

Within the town US 27 crosses the Ohio Line, six miles northwest of Oxford, Ohio (*see Ohio Guide*).

✓✓✓

Tour 14

(Sturgis, Michigan)—Huntington—Marion—Anderson—Junction US 36; State 9.
Michigan Line to junction with US 36, 133.5 *m.*

Paved roadbed throughout.
The Pennsylvania R.R. roughly parallels the route between the Michigan Line and Rome City; the Cleveland, Cincinnati, Chicago & St. Louis R.R. roughly parallels it southward from Marion to the junction with US 36.
Accommodations of all kinds at short intervals.

State 9, running north and south through eastern Indiana, traverses an area as rich in legends of the past as it is in present productivity. Along this route are the tamarack swamps that were sanctuaries for bands of horse thieves and murderers nearly a century ago; the Limberlost cabin made famous by Gene Stratton Porter; and the scene of some of Hoosierdom's most vigorous political squabbles. Johnny Appleseed, eccentric wanderer of the early nineteenth century, planted many of the apple orchards still found throughout the northern portion of the tour, which is dotted with dozens of small lakes and summer resorts. Farther south, where the countryside tapers off into gently rolling farm land with well-ordered, cultivated fields on both sides of the highway, are the cities of the gas belt. This district, after the discovery of vast quantities of natural gas in 1886, was transformed almost overnight from an agricultural area to a bustling factory center. Because it was cheaper to let gas street lights burn all day than to hire someone to turn them on and off, the cities were lighted day and night by gas; and great flambeaux (flaming torches of natural gas) were to be seen everywhere. Almost as suddenly as it came the gas boom died out when the fuel supply was exhausted, but nearly all the cities of the region retain an essentially industrial character.

State 9 crosses the INDIANA LINE, 0 *m.*, 3 miles south of Sturgis, Michigan.

On the edge of the village of Howe is (L) the HOWE SCHOOL (*visitors welcome, guide furnished*), 2.1 *m.*, founded in 1884 with funds provided in the will of John B. Howe, a leading citizen of the community. A widely known military school offering grammar school and college preparatory courses for boys between the ages of 8 and 18, Howe has 14 buildings grouped around a parade ground set in the midst of a shaded 40-acre campus. Howe Hall is a three-story brick building with a pyramidal tower and dormers, resembling Magdalen College, Oxford, England. Knickerbocker Hall is a buff brick structure of the English collegiate design. In the center of the campus is St. James Chapel, a Tudor Gothic stone structure similar in design to the Eton College chapel in England. The interior has carved oak woodwork and a hammer-beamed roof support. Here the cadet corps—some 100 boys—attends daily vesper services. A military parade is held every Sunday afternoon.

HOWE, 2.6 *m.* (880 alt., 810 pop.), a quiet little farming town of sedate old houses and sweeping terraces, was platted in 1834 on the site of a Potawatomi village called Mongoquinong (white squaw). According to early settlers, the western part of the community was once a vast apple orchard that had been planted by Indians and French traders with seeds supplied by Johnny Appleseed (*see Folklore and Folkways*). For years these trees flourished on the banks of Pigeon River.

Originally the seat of LaGrange County and named Lima, Howe was renamed in 1884 to honor the founder of the Howe School. While the county seat, the settlement was the scene of much political activity.

During the presidential campaign of 1840 the Whigs held a demonstration in honor of 'Tippecanoe and Tyler Too,' and 800 men—many of them Democrats—gathered to hear the speeches. One man became ill and some friends bathed his head with whisky, the pioneer remedy for most ailments. The Whigs then conceived the idea of dousing the heads of all the Democrats present in whisky and baptizing them into the true Whig faith. So with mugs of whisky as baptismal founts the Whigs segregated the Democrats and proceeded to wash away their political sins.

Near Howe are several lakes (*accommodations for vacationists*) where the fishing is good.

In LAGRANGE, 8.1 *m.* (913 alt., 1,814 pop.) (*see Tour* 1), is the junction with US 20 (*see Tour* 1).

At 13.6 *m.* is the junction with a graveled road.

> Right on this road to OLIVER LAKE (*hotel, cottages, and bathing beach on north shore*), 1 *m.*, the largest of the many lakes in LaGrange County. Bass, bluegills, perch, sunfish, and crappies are plentiful. LIMBERLOST CAMPS, INC., formerly called the Wainwright Band and Orchestra Camp, occupies 80 acres on the east side of the lake. Founded in 1926, this camp offers instruction in band and orchestral work to 300 boys during the summer months. Public concerts are given every Friday evening and Sunday afternoon during the camp season.

WOLCOTTVILLE, 17.1 *m.* (957 alt., 612 pop.), is a prosperous trade and vacation center on the LaGrange-Noble County line in the midst of the lake region. The town's slogan is 'Twenty Lakes, Twenty Minutes.' It was settled more than a century ago, and grew up around pioneer industries established by George Wolcott, a Connecticut Yankee: a gristmill, sawmill, a tan yard, and distillery. Before the construction of the Grand Rapids and Indiana Railroad, Wolcottville was an important station on the Fort Wayne-Sturgis stage route.

South of Wolcottville is a fertile area that was once a dense tamarack swamp, the resort of a notorious gang of horse thieves and counterfeiters known as 'Blacklegs,' who operated in Noble County and throughout northeastern Indiana during the late 1840's and early '50's. The words tamarack and 'Blacklegs' were associated with terrorism in the minds of the early settlers; finally the State legislature passed an act authorizing the formation of several companies of 'Regulators,' whose duty it was to apprehend horse thieves and felons. When members of the gang were arrested it was discovered that several prominent citizens of the county were leaders of the 'Blacklegs.' Years after the gang was broken up a Noble County farmer discovered a secret basement under the stable of his farm, used by the 'Blacklegs' to hide stolen horses.

According to tradition, an early resident of Noble County was 'the meanest man in the world.' No names and dates are available, but the story has remained in circulation through several generations. A man grew tired of his wife and divorced her. She was unable to earn a living and was sent to the county poor asylum; in the meantime, her former husband remarried. At intervals throughout the year the poor asylum held a public paupers' sale when inmates of the institution were sold to the highest bidder and farmed out to work for the people who bought them. They were virtually slaves, receiving nothing but a meager living. This woman was put up for sale at a paupers' auction and her former husband, in the market for a woman to do the heavy housework that his new wife refused to do, purchased her.

On a hillside (R) is the KNEIPP SANATORIUM (Roman Catholic), 18.8 *m.*, a group of tile-roofed red brick buildings with Gothic towers. This hospital and home of the Sisters of the Most Precious Blood occupies the site of an apple and plum orchard planted by Johnny Appleseed. Here, also, is the site of the French ghost town of North-port, platted in 1838 by Francis Comparet. The town was once an important trading post, but with the growth of Rome City, it gradually declined.

SYLVAN LAKE, 19 *m.*, a 1,200-acre artificial lake (L), whose water level is above the roadway, was built in 1837 as a feeder for a pro-posed Michigan and Erie Canal to connect with the Wabash and Erie Canal at Fort Wayne. The projected waterway was never completed and the lake now serves as Rome City's principal resort attraction. Parts of the unfinished feeder canal can still be seen in the neighbor-hood. Two hotels and cottages around the lake provide ample accom-modations. From Sylvan Lake, the highway makes a wide sweeping curve and climbs into Rome City.

ROME CITY, 19.4 *m.* (920 alt., 300 pop.), a resort village, was founded as the result of construction activities begun in 1837, and named by the Irish workers who built a dam across the tributary of the Elkhart River, thus forming Sylvan Lake.

Both French and Irish workers were employed on the dam, and there were frequent disagreements between them. The superintendent of construction decided to divide his forces; he sent the Irish workers to the south end of the dam and kept the French at the north end—Northport—where there were relatively good accommodations. The buildings at the south end of the dam, across the river from where Rome City now stands, consisted of a few rough shacks and a tool house. The Irish demanded better living quarters. This precipitated a fight, the superintendent leading the French workers against the Irish. After receiving a bad beating the Irish were told to 'do as the Romans do.' With ready wit, the Irish called their rude camp Rome, and when Rome City was platted on the site of the camp in 1839, it was given its present name. In and near Rome City there are several medicinal mineral springs that have valuable curative properties but are not highly exploited.

At 20.4 *m.* is the junction with a graveled road leading L.

Left on this road to LIMBERLOST, 1.5 *m.* (*adm.* 25¢ *and* 10¢, *guide furnished*), the last home in Indiana of the novelist Gene Stratton Porter (1868–1924). On the south shore of Sylvan Lake and surrounded by heavy woods, the entrance to the 150-acre estate is marked by two stone posts topped with large carved stone owls. Limberlost Cabin, named by Mrs. Porter after her earlier home in the Limberlost region at Geneva (*see Tour* 13), is constructed of red-cedar logs from Wisconsin and is roofed with California redwood; the interior paneling is of local wild cherry. The foundation, chimneys, and porches are of stone. Among the furnishings are rare etchings, valuable pottery, and watercolors. The north wall of the living room is dominated by a large plate-glass window, commanding a view of the lake. Imbedded in the masonry of the huge open fireplace at the east wall are many curious little stones shaped like Indian heads, collected in Mexico by Mrs. Porter. Next to the dining room is the conservatory; here Mrs. Porter carried on experiments in botany and grew rare flowers.

Surrounding Limberlost Cabin is WILDFLOWER WOODS, a sanctuary for birds, butterflies, moths, and every flower, tree, shrub, and vine native to northern Indiana. There are about 1,500 varieties of flowers, ferns, and trees. Under tall trees, over which wild grapevines hang in tangled masses, grow more than a dozen of the rarest orchids to be found in Indiana. The only formal planning done by Mrs. Porter in Wildflower Woods was the segregation of flowers of the same color into separate beds laid out parallel with the rail fence that marks the western boundary of the sanctuary.

At 22.5 *m.* is the junction with US 6 (*see Tour* 3), with which State 9 unites for 2.8 miles westward. State 9 then turns south.

ALBION, 29.2 *m.* (915 alt., 1,234 pop.), is the seat of Noble County, a distinction gained not without struggle. The first courthouse and jail of Noble County were built in Augusta, a small village two miles west. When the courthouse was destroyed by fire in 1843 the county seat was moved to Port Mitchell, three miles southwest of Augusta. This was unsatisfactory to most of the residents of the county, and the State legislature provided for an election to select a new county seat. Four towns—Ligonier, Rochester, Northport, and Springfield—entered the race, together with a nebulous settlement designated on the map of the county as 'the Center.' It took a year and three elections to settle the county-seat question. Finally 'the Center' won, and its name was changed to Albion. Some of the towns taking part in this county-seat war are only a memory today.

Before the Civil War nearly all the residents of Noble County were opposed to slavery, and 'passengers' on the Underground Railroad (*see Tour* 13) passed through the county regularly on their way to the Canadian border. The section of the Railroad between Albion and Kendallville was run by a three-man committee, with a fourth as 'station agent, conductor, engineer, and flagman.'

As early as 1844 Albion was on the mail route running from Wolf Lake on the Goshen Road, thence to Lisbon on the Lima Road. These roads were mere paths through the woods, and during the winter months and after heavy rains travel was difficult. Carriers rode horses as a rule, but tradition has it that one, John Hall, preferred a gentle bull.

MERRIAM, 37.2 *m.* (880 alt., 87 pop.) (*see Tour* 15), is at the junction with US 33 (*see Tour* 15).

At 41.4 *m.* is the junction with State 102.

Left on State 102 to the TRI-LAKES STATE FISH HATCHERY, 1.6 *m.*, maintained by the State Department of Conservation, which supplies thousands of game fish annually to Indiana streams. More than 750 cottages dot the wooded hills surrounding the three lakes (*fishing, swimming, and dancing*). The Y.M.C.A. camp of Muncie is on Round Lake. Cedar Lake, the largest of the three, covers 143 acres, and is surrounded by a wide sandy beach. All three lakes were created by glacial action.

In COLUMBIA CITY, 47.4 *m.* (839 alt., 4,219 pop.) (*see Tour 4*), is the junction with US 30 (*see Tour 4*).

At 49.7 *m.* the road crosses a low plateau comprising about 300 acres of land. Indians and early settlers called this area the Island. Bounded on the north by a high bluff along the Eel River, on the west and south by Mud Creek and swampland, and on the east by swamps, the Island was used by the Miami as a place of refuge. Here they could defend themselves against enemies. They believed that should a white man ever ride across the Island on a white horse, disaster would certainly follow. The Miami had more reason to fear the Potawatomi, who were pushing down from the northwest. Eel River was the dividing line between the territories claimed by the two tribes. At one time the Potawatomi nearly succeeded in dislodging the Miami from the Island, but in the end they were defeated when Little Turtle, the Miami chief (*see Tour 4*), led reinforcements against the Potawatomi. After this Little Turtle kept the Island strongly garrisoned.

HUNTINGTON, 67.4 *m.* (736 alt., 13,903 pop.) (*see Tour 5a*), is at the junction with US 24 (*see Tour 5*).

MOUNT ETNA, 78.7 *m.* (740 alt., 139 pop.), is a drowsy hamlet on an elevation above the Salamonie River, founded in 1839 and supposedly named after Mount Etna in Sicily.

At 86.6 *m.* is the junction with a graveled road.

Right on this road is the MIAMI INDIAN BAPTIST CHURCH, 5.5 *m.*, a small, one-room frame structure (R) in which Indian converts formerly worshiped. Among the Indian names on the tombstones in the cemetery at the rear of the church is that of Chief Meshingomesia, last chief of the Miami in Indiana; several of his wives lie buried beside him.

MARION, 92.6 *m.* (852 alt., 26,767 pop.), seat of Grant County, is a busy industrial city. Once known as the Queen City of the gas belt, Marion became a boom town with the discovery of gas and oil in the 1880's and experienced a few decades of great prosperity. When the gas supply was exhausted the city went through a period of economic decline.

Martin Boots, John Ballinger, and David Branson settled here in 1826. With the formation of Grant County in 1831, land donated by Boots and Branson was selected for the county seat and the town—named after General Francis Marion, cavalry officer in the American Revolution—was laid out. By 1850 the courthouse square was surrounded by small businesses and stores; a newspaper had been established and a two-story frame house no longer excited comment. After the Civil War the tempo of growth increased, and with the coming of the railroad in 1867 business and commerce became stable.

Prior to January 1887, Marion was predominately an agricultural town, but with the discovery of natural gas it was rapidly transformed into a noisy industrial city. Manufacturers were attracted by the cheap fuel and glass factories; paper mills, ironworks, and rolling mills were built in the booming city. By 1890 the population had increased to 9,000. But this growth was short-lived, for the supply of gas failed. Then oil was discovered and the boom was revived for a few months, only to be abruptly deflated when the oil wells went dry. The population decreased by 6,000 and Marion began to revert to its original status as a trade center. In 1905, however, $100,000 was raised by popular subscription to bring industries to the city. At the present time (1941) Marion has 45 factories, manufacturing radios and furniture; foundry, glass, paper, and food products; electrical, wire and cable appliances.

Marion covers an area of five square miles. Three State highways pass through the city, and four railroads and ten bus lines provide transportation. The municipal airport is accredited by the United States Department of Commerce. The local street railway is municipally owned and operated.

M. Clifford Townsend, former governor of Indiana, is a resident of Marion. Willis Van Devanter (1859–1941), justice of the Supreme Court of the United States, was born in Marion.

In MATTER PARK (*picnic grounds, zoo, swimming pool*), on the northwest edge of the city, is the Memorial Hall Museum which contains an old cabin and memorabilia of pioneer days. Hundreds of people visit the cabin annually in August when Grant County observes an Old Folks' Day. The museum is maintained by the Lions Club.

MARION MEMORIAL COLISEUM (L), a community hall and the center of Marion school athletics, is dedicated to Grant County war veterans. Adjoining the building is a football gridiron and a half-mile running track.

MARION COLLEGE (L), at the south edge of the city, is a Wesleyan Methodist institution, offering instruction in arts and sciences, teacher training, music, and theology. The college occupies the former campus and four brick buildings of the Marion Normal Institute, and has specialized in normal school instruction since 1890. About 350 students are now (1941) enrolled. Intercollegiate athletics are not permitted, social life is restricted, and the use of tobacco by students is prohibited.

In Marion is the southern junction with the Slocum Trail (*see Tour 5a*).

Left from Marion on State 21 is the VETERANS' ADMINISTRATION FACILITY (*visitors welcome*), 1.5 *m.*, a $5,000,000 Government hospital (L) of 94 buildings. About 1,500 World War veterans suffering from mental and nervous diseases are cared for here. On the grounds is the grave of Barnabas Vandeventer, soldier of the American Revolution, who died at the age of 103 years, 10 months, and 9 days.

At 98.1 *m.* is the junction with US 35 (*see Tour 17*).

At 102.1 *m.* is the junction with State 26.

Left on State 26 is FAIRMOUNT, 1 *m.* (852 alt., 2,382 pop.), and the WESLEYAN CAMP MEETING GROUNDS, site of State and National conferences of the Methodist church. A large cannery is the principal industry of Fairmount.

At 112.1 *m.* on the main route is the junction with State 28.

Right on State 28 is ELWOOD, 9.3 *m.* (862 alt., 10,913 pop.), an industrial community in the heart of Indiana's tomato-growing district. Elwood is the birthplace of Wendell L. Willkie (b.1892), Republican nominee for President in 1940 and former president of the Commonwealth and Southern Corporation. It was also the home of James J. Davis, now United States senator from Pennsylvania, who was active in the development of the Loyal Order of Moose and was Secretary of Labor under Presidents Harding, Coolidge, and Hoover.

Willkie, the only native Hoosier ever nominated for the presidency, graduated from the city high school and lived in Elwood until his 27th year. His mother was the first woman admitted to the Indiana bar; his father, also a lawyer, practiced in Elwood from 1893 to 1927.

A crowd estimated at from 100,000 to 200,000 gathered at Elwood on August 17, 1940, to hear Willkie's speech accepting the presidential nomination. He carried Indiana by about 25,000 votes, but lost the election to President Roosevelt.

A flourishing factory town in the days of the natural-gas boom, Elwood today is largely dependent on the agriculture of the surrounding area for its economic welfare. It is a long, narrow city, sprawling out east and west along the highway, and its residential sections are marked by broad, unevenly paved streets and towering shade trees. The business district is surprisingly large for a city of Elwood's size, but most of the buildings are time-worn relics of the 1890's. Busiest season is midsummer, when the many canning factories in the area are going full blast. The annual Tomato Festival, held late in July or early in August, includes pageants, parades, a street carnival, and the selection of a Tomato Queen.

The American Sheet and Tin Plate Company plant, first successfully operated tin plate mill in the United States and formerly one of the largest, was closed (probably permanently) in 1937, as was the MacBeth-Evans Glass Company plant, first in America to produce optical glass. A new industry is the NATIONAL TRAILER CORPORATION PLANT (*visitors welcome*), manufacturing house trailers.

ALEXANDRIA, 113.5 *m.* (855 alt., 4,801 pop.), is widely known for its rock-wool industry. The JOHNS-MANVILLE COMPANY PLANT, (*open by permission, obtainable at office*) was the first rock-wool insulation factory in the world. The first man to realize the possibilities of rock-wool, the late Charles C. Hill, lived in Alexandria. The rare argillaceous limestone, essential to the manufacture of rock-wool, is found in abundance here; Mud Creek is underlaid with an almost inexhaustible supply of the substance. The product is capable of withstanding extremes in temperatures ranging from 40° below zero to 1,600° above. Widely used in industry and as insulation for residences, it is also valuable for acoustical purposes in the motion-picture industry. Rock-wool is produced by melting the raw material and passing it through a blast of cold air; it then disintegrates into a mass of fluffy material, generally white, which is a tangled assortment of very thin glass fibers and small glass beads or 'shot.'

ANDERSON, 125.5 *m.* (892 alt., 41,572 pop.) (*see Tour 6*), is at the junction with State 32 (*see Tour 6*).

On the east (L) side of the highway from Anderson to PENDLETON (850 alt., 1,681 pop.) (*see Tour 7*) stretches a huge glacial esker, a mass of gravel and boulders, from 10 to 40 feet in height and 150 to 450 feet wide. This heap of glacial deposit continues for nearly four miles in an unbroken ridge. Between this esker and the highway is the bed of a glacial river, which formed beneath the ice sheet and cut a channel almost directly across present drainage courses.

At 133.5 *m.* is the junction with US 36 (*see Tour* 7).

ィィ

Tour 15

(Niles, Michigan) — South Bend — Mishawaka — Elkhart — Goshen — Fort Wayne; US 33.
Michigan Line to Fort Wayne, 88.2 *m.*

Two- to four-lane concrete roadbed except for short stretches of brick.
Route roughly paralleled by the New York Central Railroad between South Bend and Ligonier.
Accommodations of all kinds at short intervals.

Routed between two great industrial centers, this tour runs through a peaceful, flat countryside planted chiefly in corn, wheat, and oats. In this fertile region live members of the Mennonite and Amish denominations, noted for their strict moral discipline and prosperous farms. Eastward is a region dotted with small lakes, few of them visible from the highway. For many miles US 33 closely follows an old Indian trail, passing the sites of several Indian villages along the Eel River, a main arena in the American conquest of the Northwest. Little Turtle, greatest of the Miami leaders, was born in the Eel River Valley, and four battles were fought along the banks of the river.

US 33 crosses the MICHIGAN LINE, 0 *m.*, five miles south of Niles, Michigan. Between this point and South Bend the highway is united with US 31 (*see Tour* 16).

In SOUTH BEND, 6 *m.* (723 alt., 101,268 pop.) (*see South Bend*), are the junction with US 20 (*see Tour* 1) and the southern junction with US 31 (*see Tour* 16).

Here US 33 turns east to parallel the St. Joseph River, passing Lincoln Park, Battel Park, Merrifield Park, and many stately houses and landscaped lawns.

MISHAWAKA, 10.5 *m.* (742 alt., 28,298 pop.), is almost equally divided by the river, and has two business areas — one on each side of the St. Joseph — with one- and two-story buildings, old and in many instances weather-beaten. In the residential districts, however, the houses are neat and clean, and stand on wide, well-paved, and tree-shaded streets. Most of the people are factory workers of moderate means.

The MISHAWAKA WOOLEN AND RUBBER MANUFACTURING COMPANY PLANT (*obtain permission at office*), a subsidiary of the United States Rubber Company, is the city's largest industry. Here are manufactured felt and rubber boots, galoshes, raincoats, and woolen yard goods. About 5,000 persons are employed and the pay roll in peak years has reached $5,000,000.

Mishawaka also has meat packing, foundry equipment, conveyor, power transmission, structural steel, and heavy machinery manufacturing plants.

The MISHAWAKA GUN CLUB PRESERVE (*camping facilities, trap-shooting range*), in the northeastern part of the city at the confluence of Willow Creek and the St. Joseph River, consists of 20 acres set aside for the propagation of game fish, animals, and birds.

There is a BELGIAN COMMUNITY of about 6,000 persons in the southwestern section of the city. The homes here are models of sturdy neatness, and every foot of ground around the houses is utilized. The fenced-in yards are bright with flowers in season and at the rear of almost every house is a meticulously kept vegetable garden.

Most of these people came in 1919 and 1920, after the World War. They are hard-working, thrifty, and honest, and virtually all became American citizens as quickly as possible. An interesting early development was the formation of a 'home circle' to provide wholesome recreation for young people. By 1934 payments for a $25,000 clubhouse were completed. Although membership in the organization, called Broedernkring (Brother Circle), is limited to men and boys, women and girls often take part in its activities, which include athletics, dramatics, cards, billiards, bowling, and archery. Thus the problem of recreation was solved for a group that did not feel quite at home in a strange land. The community's traditional Thanksgiving carnival is one of the city's outstanding seasonal events.

According to local legend, Mishawaka was named for a beautiful Indian princess of that name, daughter of Elkhart, chief of a band of Shawnee who came to this territory before 1800. Mishawaka's hand was sought in marriage by Grey Wolf, a Potawatomi chief, and an unknown white trapper called by the Indians 'Dead Shot.' The Potawatomi were the strongest tribe in this part of the country and, desiring their favor and protection, Chief Elkhart urged Princess Mishawaka to accept Grey Wolf. Her heart, however, leaned to the white man and, encouraged by her mother, she declared in favor of Dead Shot.

The Potawatomi then declared war on Elkhart's band and in the fighting Grey Wolf captured the princess and dragged her into the forest where he offered her the alternative of marriage or death. The white trapper, suspecting what would happen, searched and found the struggling pair. His shot wounded Grey Wolf slightly and a terrific hand-to-hand encounter followed. Seeing that Dead Shot was about to master him, Grey Wolf slipped from the grasp of the white man and buried his knife in the princess' breast, then turned to Dead Shot and met his death. Dead Shot carried Princess Mishawaka to his camp and nursed her for many weeks. She finally regained her health and they were married. A bronze marker in Lincoln Park states that she was buried near this spot when she died in 1818 at the age of 32.

In ELKHART, 21.5 m. (778 alt., 33,434 pop.) (see Tour 1), is the junction with US 20 (see Tour 1).

DUNLAP, 25.5 m. (778 alt., 250 pop.), an elongated village strung out along US 33, is a residential community for Elkhart workers.

The KUNDERD GLADIOLUS FARM (visitors welcome), 27.9 m., is a 175-acre tract (R) used mainly for raising gladioli. Thousands of dollars' worth of flowers and bulbs are prepared annually for the market, and many new varieties of gladioli have been developed on this farm.

GOSHEN, 31.1 m. (797 alt., 11,375 pop.), a prosperous agricultural town, bears the unmistakable stamp of its large Mennonite population. Its industries include cabinet and veneer factories, and a plant manufacturing waterproof bags.

The ELKHART COUNTY COURTHOUSE, a red brick structure built in 1868, occupies a shady spot in the center of the city. A large statue of Neptune on his sea horse forms a fountain in a pool in the courthouse yard.

The SITE OF OLD FORT BEANE, a refuge for white settlers in early Indian troubles, is marked by a stone tablet just south of the high school.

GOSHEN COLLEGE, College Ave., 1.7 m. miles south of the courthouse, occupies a 20-acre campus and has seven brick buildings representing an investment of $250,000. The annual average enrollment is 350; courses are offered in theology, liberal arts, and teacher training. This coeducational institution, the only four-year college of the Mennonite Church in the Nation, evolved from the Elkhart Academy, founded in 1894. In 1903 the city of Goshen offered $10,000 for building purposes and the academy was reorganized as a junior college. A four-year curriculum was adopted in 1909. After a critical period in the early 1920's—when the school had four presidents in as many years—Goshen College was closed for a year and reorganized.

In the Administration Building is the book collection (1,800 volumes) of the Mennonite Historical Society. The other buildings of the college include a science hall, dormitories, and a gymnasium. The original building, East Hall (1903), is now an apartment house for faculty members.

The story of Goshen College is meshed with the history of the Mennonites and Amish in Indiana. Members of these denominations form a large part of the population of Elkhart County. The Amish, attracted by the fertile soil, arrived in 1841, and the Mennonites two years later, only eleven years after the first followers of the doctrines of Menno Simons reached the United States. Now, as in 1536 when Simons urged Christians to emulate Christ in a life of self-denial, the Mennonites stress simplicity in worship, church organization, and private life, although the discipline is less strict than in the old days. Liberalization, however, has not brought music or liturgy to the denomination's services. Mennonites are conscientious objectors to war, and though some of them hold minor public offices, few take any interest in politics. Alcoholic beverages are taboo and plain clothing is worn by most members. Students at the college are not permitted to use tobacco or attend motion picture shows.

The Amish cling more closely to the old ways. Originally a part of the main body of the Mennonite Church, they broke away in 1620 under the leadership of Jacob Amman, who thought the parent church was becoming too liberal. Emigrating from Switzerland to the United States early in the eighteenth century, they settled in Pennsylvania and gradually pushed westward.

As outward signs of unworldliness, Amish men wear long hair and beards. Their clothing is plain, fastened with hooks and eyes, and their black hats are broad-rimmed and flat. They do not wear neckties or suspenders. The women wear straight, black bonnets without ruffles, and skirts fastened to a close-fitting basque. The skirt is partly covered by a straight apron gathered to a band around the waist. Around the shoulders is a three-cornered cape, the two ends of which cross in front. The entire dress is without trimmings or buttons.

The Amish do not buy insurance, but give mutually in case of loss. They have no musical instruments in the home or church, no telephones, radios, or automobiles. They do not attend theaters or places of public amusement. Their homes are comfortably but simply furnished and, as a rule, have no shades or curtains on the windows. Infrequently curtains of plain white material and homemade carpets of a somber color are included in the home furnishings.

Amish men seem to select instinctively the best land in a community and their farms are usually large and profitable. Modern machinery is not in wide use, although the ban against using mechanical equipment has been relaxed somewhat in recent years.

Church buildings, according to the Amish faith, are evidences of worldly vanity, and services in German are consequently held in homes. Hymns are sung, but only the melodies, harmony being considered worldly. After a long sermon, the noon meal is eaten and services resumed in the afternoon. All social and educational life revolves around religious interests.

Like the Mennonites, the Amish do not take oaths, refuse to bear arms in war, and do not hold major political offices. In recent years the sect has lost many of the younger generation to the more liberal Mennonites, and in Elkhart County the Mennonite group is much the larger.

BENTON, 38.5 *m.* (845 alt., 140 pop.), on the bank of the Elkhart River, was platted in 1832 and named for Senator Thomas H. Benton of Missouri. The first white settlers found the Potawatomi village of

Aubenaube in this vicinity. Chief O-nox-see and his people were friendly and often visited the cabins of the whites.

LIGONIER, 49.6 *m.* (893 alt., 2,178 pop.), trade center of a rich dairy and poultry section, is bordered on one side by the Elkhart River, along whose tree-lined banks are neat houses and parks. Wide, paved streets, white-pillared houses fronting on large lawns, and brick business buildings give the community an atmosphere of prosperity. Many of Ligonier's early settlers were Jews, and a proportionately large percentage of the present population is Jewish.

In PRENTICE PARK, along the river, is the grave of Nathaniel Prentice, a Revolutionary War soldier. Born in Connecticut in 1764, Prentice became an officer's servant at the age of 12, and as soon as he was large enough to bear arms enlisted as a regular. He took part in several battles, was at West Point when Major André was executed, and at Valley Forge with Washington. Prentice was captured by the British and held on the prison ship *Jersey.* Taken to Jamaica, he was liberated after an exchange of prisoners. The date of his coming to Noble County is not known, but he, his wife, and five children for many years lived on a farm about three miles south of Cromwell, a town near here. He died there on January 23, 1839.

At 50.4 *m.* is the junction with US 6 (*see Tour* 3).

KIMMELL, 55.4 *m.* (880 alt., 300 pop.), is a shipping center for the large crops of onions produced in the neighborhood. In 1936 Andrew W. Milnar, of Kimmell, was crowned monarch of the onion growers by the Onion Growers Association Convention at Kalamazoo, Michigan. Milnar grew 1,471 bushels on one acre of land.

Southeast of Kimmell, the route passes through a flat area of muck land, one of the finest onion-growing sections in the northern United States. The region is dotted with lakes.

WOLFLAKE, 60.8 *m.* (888 alt., 250 pop.), was so named because at the time of its founding in 1832 wolves roamed about a small lake at the western edge of the settlement.

In MERRIAM, 65.6 *m.* (880 alt., 87 pop.), is the UNCLE SAM STORE, evidence of the credence the community gives to the story that the GRAVE OF SAMUEL WILSON in the Merriam cemetery is that of the original 'Uncle Sam.' The fact that a monument has been erected in Oakwood Cemetery at Troy, New York, next to the grave of the Samuel Wilson who lent his nickname to the United States, fails to disturb the community's belief in its own tradition. Strangely, the story told in 1928 by the then 93-year-old son of Merriam's 'Uncle Sam' corresponds with the history of New York's Samuel Wilson.

The Samuel Wilson who was the original Uncle Sam conducted a meat-packing business at Troy, New York, in the War of 1812. In checking and marking the packages delivered to the Army through an arrangement with Elbert Anderson, a government contractor, Samuel Wilson affixed the initials E. A.—U. S., the U. S. because he was familiarly known as Uncle Sam. His initials on government supplies and the circumstance of their corresponding with the initials of the United

States prompted the soldiers to call the government 'Uncle Sam.' The newspapers picked up the nickname and soon afterward the cartoonists created the personality.

Merriam is at the junction with State 9 (*see Tour* 14).

CHURUBUSCO (pronounced Chur-a-bus′ko), 73.2 *m.* (890 alt., 1,122 pop.), a rural center, is named for a Mexican town at which American forces won a battle in the Mexican War.

At 76.7 *m.* is the junction with blacktop Carroll Road.

Left on this road is the old EEL RIVER BAPTIST CHURCH, 0.3 *m.*, in the hamlet of Heller's Corner. The brick church and its adjacent cedar- and maple-shaded cemetery mark the site of one of the several defeats Little Turtle inflicted upon American expeditionary armies (*see Fort Wayne*). Here Colonel John Hardin's 570 militiamen fled from Little Turtle's trap without firing a shot, but 30 regulars fought until only 8 of them survived.

At 83.9 *m.* is the junction with US 30 (*see Tour* 4), which coincides with US 33 to Fort Wayne.

FORT WAYNE, 88.2 *m.* (779 alt., 118,410 pop.) (*see Fort Wayne*). In Fort Wayne are the junctions with US 24 (*see Tour* 5), US 27 (*see Tour* 13), and US 30 (*see Tour* 4).

✐✐✐

Tour 16

(Niles, Mich.)—South Bend—Indianapolis—Jeffersonville—(Louisville, Ky.); US 31.
Michigan Line to Kentucky Line, 259.7 *m.*

Two-lane concrete highway throughout, except for four-lane stretches north of South Bend and Indianapolis.
Route paralleled by Michigan Central R.R. between Michigan Line and South Bend; by New York Central and St. Louis R.R. between South Bend and Kokomo; by Indiana R.R. (electric) between Indianapolis and Seymour; and by Pennsylvania R.R. between Indianapolis and Louisville.
Accommodations of all kinds at short intervals.

US 31 is one of the principal north-south highways of the Middle West, carrying a heavy traffic load from the Canadian Line in northern Michigan to the Gulf of Mexico at Mobile, Alabama. In Indiana it passes through several principal cities and in its long course traverses every variety of Hoosier topography—the level, endless stretches in the north; the gently rolling land of the Tipton Till plain in central Indiana; and the hills of the far south, which become gradually steeper and more rocky as the route nears the Ohio River. On this tour are South Bend, an important manufacturing center and home of the University of Notre Dame; Kokomo, where one of the Nation's first successful 'horseless carriages' was built; Indianapolis, the State capital; and Jeffersonville, a former center of steamboat commerce on the Ohio.

Section a. MICHIGAN LINE to INDIANAPOLIS, 143.2 m.

Throughout this section dairy farms are frequent, and over large areas Dutch, Swedes, and Hungarians, who call themselves 'knee farmers,' raise truck produce. Near the Michigan Line is one of the two principal mint-growing areas in the United States, and farther south the highway passes mile after mile of broad cornfields. In addition to these fertile farm lands, this section passes Culver Military Academy, a famous school for boys; Rochester, winter home of Cole Brothers-Clyde Beatty Circus; and the site of several Indian villages.

US 31 crosses the MICHIGAN LINE, 0 m., 5 miles south of Niles, Michigan.

Between the Michigan-Indiana Line and South Bend, the highway passes through an almost unbroken lane of fruit and vegetable stands.

ROSELAND, 3 m. (730 alt., 782 pop.), a residential suburb of South Bend, is a restful retreat of clean and well-kept bungalows. It was named for the thousands of wild rose bushes that formerly grew in this area.

At 3.8 m. is a tree-bordered lane (R) leading to St. Mary's College (visitors welcome), a Roman Catholic institution of higher learning for girls. The buff brick buildings on the campus include LeMans Hall, housing offices, classrooms, chapel, and dormitories; Holy Cross Hall, a classroom structure; and an assembly hall, gymnasium, infirmary, and the convent chapel. The Loretto Chapel is a reproduction of the Santa Casa, or the Holy House of Loretto, which tradition asserts was the house of Jesus, Mary, and Joseph.

In 1855, in response to a request from Father Sorin, president and founder of the University of Notre Dame, Sister Angela (Eliza Maria Gillespie) led 25 nuns from the Bertrand Mission in Bertrand, Michigan, to this site to establish an academy. Aided by citizens of South Bend and vicinity, the institution grew rapidly. St. Mary's now owns 1,680 acres of land, has 225 teachers and women in religious training, and an enrollment of 621 students (1939-40).

Visible from the highway (L), just south of St. Mary's College, are the gold dome and spired campus buildings of the UNIVERSITY OF NOTRE DAME, one of the leading Roman Catholic educational institutions in the United States (see South Bend).

SOUTH BEND, 6 m. (723 alt., 101,268 pop.) (see South Bend).

In South Bend is the junction with US 20 (see Tour 1) and the southern junction with US 33 (see Tour 15).

At 10 m. is the junction with the Johnson Road, once considered the northern Indiana Line. The 1805 act of Congress which separated

Indiana and Michigan, was misunderstood by local surveyors. After many years of dispute, which included executive action by the President of the United States, and acts of the Congress and the State legislature, the line was moved 10 miles north to its present location.

LAKEVILLE, 16.5 *m.* (856 alt., 567 pop.), a summer resort and year-round trading center, was named for the chain of small lakes in the vicinity.

Left from Lakeville on the Lake Trail to RIDDLE LAKE (*dance hall, swimming beach, boats for rent*), 1.5 *m.*, a 40-acre lake lying in a gradually sloping basin. The water is exceptionally clear and free of weed and marsh growth. The surrounding woods are popular for outings.

At 22.2 *m.* is the junction with US 6 (*see Tour* 3).

PLYMOUTH, 29.5 *m.* (794 alt., 5,713 pop.) (*see Tour* 4), is at the junction with US 30 (*see Tour* 4).

ARGOS, 37.6 *m.* (828 alt., 1,190 pop.), a prosperous dairy-farming community, was named by Schuyler Colfax, Vice President of the United States in the Grant administration. Stately maple trees shade its business area and residential section. In its early days the town was a stagecoach station on the old Michigan Road (US 31 in this section).

Right from Argos on State 10 to CULVER MILITARY ACADEMY (*visitors apply at administration building*), 9 *m.*, its buildings and campus lying along the shore of 1,800-acre LAKE MAXINKUCKEE, whose waters are often dotted with the white sails of the academy's boats. The academy's 21 buildings of English collegiate design include 6 fire-proof barracks, an administration building, a riding hall, and a gymnasium. Founded in 1894 by Henry Harrison Culver, St. Louis stove manufacturer, the academy enrolls approximately 550 boys between the ages of 13 and 18. The regular military course is four years, with an optional junior college course of two years. The War Department maintains a Reserve Officers' Training Corps at the school.

Opposite the entrance to the military academy is the CULVER BIRD SANCTUARY (*do not build fires*), 120 acres of wooded land used by the Woodcraft Camp of the Culver Military Academy for studying trees, birds, and wild life. Nearly all kinds of native Indiana birds, including game birds, are found on the reserve.

At 10 *m.* is the junction with State 17; L. here to CULVER, 10.5 *m.* (748 alt., 1,605 pop.), a resort town of wide shaded streets and attractive houses, named for the founder of the military academy.

On the south bank (L) of the TIPPECANOE RIVER, 46.8 *m.*, is the SITE OF CHIPPEWANUNG INDIAN VILLAGE, one of the last of the Potawatomi villages in Indiana. Here conferences were held that resulted in two treaties between the U. S. Indian commissioners and the Potawatomi in 1832, by which the Indians relinquished, with a few minor exceptions, all their lands in Indiana. Succeeding treaties signed here brought about the removal to Kansas of all the Potawatomi in 1838 (*see Tour* 4).

ROCHESTER, 49.6 *m.* (770 alt., 3,835 pop.), seat of Fulton County and a popular resort town on Lake Manitou, has an air of sociability acquired through years of playing host to thousands of vacation visitors. The town was founded in 1831 as a central trading post in an area containing many Indian villages.

In COLE BROTHERS-CLYDE BEATTY CIRCUS WINTER HEADQUARTERS (*visitors welcome*), north end of Erie St., a $500,000 menagerie of wild animals is housed and trained during the winter.

Left from Rochester on State 14 to LAKE MANITOU (*cabins, hotels, golf course, parks; good fishing*), 1.1 *m.*, dotted with six tree-covered islands and bounded by an irregular shore. According to an ancient Chippewa legend, three monster devilfish that lived in Lake Huron, near the islands of Manitoulin, passed through the straits to Lake Michigan and through that lake to its southern tip. Thence they traveled overland to Lake Manitou, cutting a swath 60 feet wide and destroying every living thing. Arriving at the lake, the terrible creatures began destroying all the fish. They even drove the wild game away, for when the buffalo, elk, deer, and other animals came to the lake to drink, fearsome serpentine tentacles shot out and dragged them beneath the surface of the murky water. In despair, the tribes prayed to the good spirit, Manitou, to exterminate the monsters. Their prayers were answered and the Chippewa, out of gratitude for their deliverance, named the lake for the Great Spirit.

The only FEDERAL FISH HATCHERY (*open to public*) in Indiana is on the west shore of the lake.

MEXICO, 67.3 *m.* (789 alt., 510 pop.), was in its early days a bustling stagecoach stop between Indianapolis and Michigan City. Rough field-stone porches mark many of the houses in this village, which is inhabited largely by German Baptists.

EEL RIVER, crossed at 68.1 *m.*, was called Kenapocomoco (snake fish) by the Miami Indians, and L'Anguille by the French. Along this river lived one of the principal bands of the Miami nation—the Eel River Miami. Little Turtle's village was near the source of the river in Whitley County and he presided also over the village of Kenapocomaqua (*see Tour* 5), a few miles downstream from this point.

PERU, 72.7 *m.* (658 alt., 12,432 pop.) (*see Tour* 5), is at the junction with US 24 (*see Tour* 5), with which US 31 coincides for 2 miles.

KOKOMO, 93.3 *m.* (828 alt., 33,795 pop.), an industrial city and seat of Howard County, was laid out in 1844. The building of a railroad through the community in 1853 and the discovery of natural gas in 1886 brought many factories. Like most manufacturing centers its tempo is lively and it gives the impression of being a larger city than it actually is. Kokomo produces iron, steel, brass, farm machinery, automobile parts, radios, stoves, furnaces, canned goods, women's clothing, and many other articles.

At the entrance of PIONEER CEMETERY, intersection of Wildcat Creek and Purdue St., is a MONUMENT TO KOKOMOKO, the Miami chief for whom the city was named. In the cemetery are buried many of Howard County's pioneers and Civil War soldiers.

In the KOKOMO CITY PARK, east end of Deffenbaugh St., are a SULPHUR SPRING, a SYCAMORE TREE that measures 59 feet in circumference at its base, and, in the small building near the picnic grounds, the mounted form of what is said to have been the LARGEST STEER RAISED IN INDIANA, a shorthorn Hereford. It weighed 4,470 pounds, was 6 feet tall, and measured 16 feet, 10 inches from the tip of its nose to the tip of its tail.

KOKOMO JUNIOR COLLEGE, 508 W. Taylor St., is housed in two buildings—an administration building and a chemistry building—in·a residential section. Founded in 1932, the college is a privately owned venture offering instruction in liberal arts and pre-professional training. About 50 students are enrolled (1941). In 1936 the college was about to close because of lack of funds, but the students conducted a campaign that saved it.

Among the city's distinguished sons are General T. J. Harrison, Civil War leader; Richard Bennett, actor; Tod Sloan, jockey; and Elwood Haynes (1857–1925), inventor and builder of the first mechanically successful spark-ignition automobile. An undertaking establishment, Washington and Mulberry Sts., occupies the SITE OF THE ELWOOD HAYNES HOME. Haynes conducted his experiments in the back room of a gas office, but the first automobile was assembled in the RIVERSIDE MACHINE SHOP, on Main St. just south of Wildcat Creek. Haynes conceived the idea of a self-propelled vehicle in 1892. He experimented with electricity, steam, and finally with gasoline and a single-cylinder upright marine engine. When the chassis was completed, the motor was installed, and the first successful test was made on July 4, 1894 (see Tour 17b). Haynes gave his 'horseless carriage' to the Smithsonian Institution in 1910.

In Kokomo is the junction with US 35 (see Tour 17).

South of Kokomo the level countryside is used chiefly to raise tomatoes and other farm produce. WESTFIELD, 123.8 m. (950 alt., 709 pop.), founded in 1834 by Quakers, came to be known as the 'north central station' of the Underground Railroad in the period just before the Civil War. The town was considered the fugitive slave-hunter's 'last hope,' for when a slave got this far north he was reasonably safe from capture.

In Westfield is the junction with State 32 (see Tour 6).

At 134.8 m. is the junction with 75th Street, on the outskirts of Indianapolis.

Left on 75th Street is (L) the INDIANA SCHOOL FOR THE BLIND (visiting hours 9–3:30 Mon.-Sat.), 0.8 m., founded in 1846 by legislative act. Buildings on the 60-acre tract of lawns, a stream and lake, include a boys' unit, girls' unit, main building, music hall, industrial building, powerhouse, and dormitory. Loudspeakers are mounted on the tower of the main building. Besides grade and high school courses, the curriculum also includes handicrafts and music. Among the school's many amusement and recreation devices is a roller skating rink, an unusual feature in a school for the blind.

INDIANAPOLIS, 143.2 m. (750 alt., 386,972 pop.) (see Indianapolis).

Indianapolis is at the junction with US 36 (see Tour 7), US 40 (see Tour 8), US 52 (see Tour 18), State 37 (see Tour 19), State 34 (see Tour 8A), and State 29 (see Tour 17A).

Section b. *INDIANAPOLIS to KENTUCKY LINE,* 116.5 *m.*

Immediately south of Indianapolis the route passes through level country that is one of Indiana's foremost tomato-producing regions. The terrain gradually becomes more rolling, and ends in the hilly section of southern Indiana. For most of the distance the highway is level and comparatively free from curves.

GREENWOOD, 10.2 *m.* (814 alt., 2,499 pop.), is an industrial town with its business district chiefly along the highway that runs north and south through its center. The principal industries are an automobile-parts factory and a large canning company. Many of the inhabitants are employed in the car shops of the Big Four Railroad in Beech Grove, near Indianapolis.

FRANKLIN, 21 *m.* (733 alt., 6,264 pop.), a tree-shaded college town, is the seat of Johnson County and shipping point for an area producing large quantities of grain and tomatoes. It has several manufacturing establishments, making automobile parts, porch furniture, wearing apparel, and foodstuffs, but is primarily a trading center for the surrounding countryside. The business district is built around the courthouse square, occupied by a stone-trimmed brick courthouse constructed in 1883. Nearly two-thirds of Franklin's 1,500 families own their homes, and the residential districts contain comfortable frame houses with wide lawns and tall maple, elm, and oak trees.

Normally peaceful, Franklin takes on an air of hectic activity from August to October, when the tomato canning season is in full swing. Temporary workers are imported from southern Indiana and Kentucky to help pick and pack the vegetables, and they are housed wherever they can find room—in cheap hotels, empty dwellings, shacks, and even boxcars. These migratory workers constitute a serious problem for the county, since wages are low and many of them remain in or near Franklin after the canning season ends.

In the basement of the courthouse is the JOHNSON COUNTY MUSEUM (*open Sat.* 2–5; *free*), containing a collection of pioneer relics and other curios, including a bone-handled knife more than 300 years old, a Dutch Bible printed in 1651, and a fan spotted with what is said to be the blood of Abraham Lincoln. According to the story, the fan belonged to a woman who was seated in the President's box at the Ford Theater on the night of his assassination, and her dress and the fan were spattered with blood from his wound.

FRANKLIN COLLEGE, six blocks east (L) of the courthouse on East Monroe St., was founded in 1834 as the Indiana Baptist Manual Labor Institute. The institute became coeducational—the first Indiana college to do so—during a period of financial stress in 1842. The present name was adopted the following year and four-year courses in the liberal arts were offered. So many students volunteered for the Union Army during the Civil War that the college was forced to suspend operation for several years. On the eight-acre campus are six

Highways and Byways

ON THE HIGHWAY

Photograph by courtesy of Farm Security Administr

MARTIN COUNTY COURTHOUSE, SHOALS

ST. MEINRAD'S ABBEY, SPENCER COUNTY

FRENCH LICK SPRINGS HOTEL

tograph by Edgar C. Schmid

NOTRE DAME'S FOUR HORSEMEN AND SEVEN MULES (1924)

BASKETBALL—MOST POPULAR OF INDIANA SPORTS

Photograph by Grubbs and Sie

HORSERACING AT AN ANNUAL FAIR NEAR WASHINGTON

START OF INTERNATIONAL 500-MILE RACE, INDIANAPOLIS

OLD WHITEWATER CANAL LOCK AT METAMORA

INTERIOR OF KENNEDY COVERED BRIDGE NEAR RUSHVILLE

Photograph by Henley

POST OFFICE AT SANTA CLAUS

REMAINS OF CONNOR'S MILL, GRANT COUNTY
Near this spot was fought the battle of the
Mississinewa, last Indian battle on Indiana soil

MAIN STREET ON SATURDAY NIGHT

Photograph by courtesy of Life M

plain red brick buildings. The Main Building (begun 1843) houses offices, auditorium, and classrooms. There is a library of 29,000 volumes, a women's dormitory, a gymnasium, a science hall, and a heating plant. The enrollment (1939–40) was 367. Students are permitted much academic freedom and outstanding students are excused from regular class attendance.

PIONEER PARK (*adm. free; picnicking facilities, playground; swimming pool, adm.* 25¢), three blocks south of the courthouse, is a well-landscaped park (L) on the banks of Youngs Creek.

At the southern edge of Franklin is the INDIANA MASONIC HOME (R), consisting of 14 brick buildings on 320 acres of grounds. The home is for the aged and needy members of the Indiana lodge, as well as orphans and widows of deceased members. All are completely cared for, and children are provided with grade and high school training. The home shelters about 250 adults and an equal number of children.

EDINBURG, 31 *m.* (674 alt., 2,466 pop.), a brisk country town (L), has a canning factory, a large veneer mill, and a furniture factory. The ROTH MUSEUM (*free*), housed in the Railway Express Office, 105 Walnut St., contains memorabilia of Edinburg's early days, including old lamps, utensils, tools, and many curios and oddities.

COLUMBUS, 42.1 *m.* (627 alt., 11,738 pop.), seat of Bartholomew County, is a farming center and a manufacturing city. Because of this dual economy, Columbus has been less affected by depressions than many other communities of similar size. It has a large business district, stretching north along both Jackson (US 31) and Washington Streets, five blocks from the old courthouse square, site of the early town center.

The principal industries are a large automobile accessory plant, a Diesel engine plant, two tanneries, a shirt and overall factory, and a fork- and hoe-handle company. Columbus has benefited physically from these industries, since company officials have built many new and expensive residences in the northern section of the city. Fine houses, however, are not confined to this section but are found in any part of the city, with the exception of a small slum area 'across the tracks' and in the White River bottom lands. This collection of makeshift cabins is known locally as 'Death Valley.'

The site of Columbus was settled by General John Tipton, John Lindsay, and Luke Bonesteel, each of whom purchased land here in 1820 and built cabins along the east bank of the White River. The tiny settlement was called Tiptonia in honor of General Tipton who, in 1821, offered to donate 30 acres of his holdings for the county seat, if the new town was named after him. The county commissioners agreed and accepted the land, whereupon they promptly named the county seat Columbus. The indignant general left shortly thereafter to settle in northern Indiana. The new county seat did not fare well in its early days. Owing to the low swampy site, malaria caused frequent deaths among the residents, and this condition was not remedied for many years; as late as 1840 a portion of the town square was covered with water.

Some of the prominent men who have lived in Columbus are Kent Cooper, head of the Associated Press; William G. Irwin, National Chairman (1938) of the United States Chamber of Commerce; and Ken Maynard, hero of many Western movie thrillers.

At 17th Street and Central Avenue are the main offices and several plants of the NOBLITT-SPARKS INDUSTRIES, INC. (*visitors welcome*), manufacturing automobile heaters, mufflers, jacks, hub caps, and other parts. This unit covers two blocks and with another Noblitt-Sparks division, the ARVIN RADIO PLANT (*visitors welcome*), Maple Ave. and 14th St., employs between 800 and 1,000 persons. Noblitt-Sparks Industries, Inc., operate branch factories in Greenwood, Franklin, and Seymour.

The CUMMINS DIESEL ENGINE COMPANY PLANT (*visitors welcome*), Fifth and Wilson Sts., manufactures Diesel engines for locomotives, marine, truck, and, recently, passenger car use. In 1931 a racing car powered by a Diesel engine built in this plant completed the full distance in the annual 500-mile race at Indianapolis without a single stop. It averaged slightly more than 86 miles per hour and consumed 31 gallons of low-cost fuel oil for the entire run. This was the only car ever to travel the 500 miles of the Speedway race without a stop.

DONNER PARK (*camping facilities, shelter house*), between 19th and 22nd Sts., a 22-acre forested tract in the northwest part of town, is the larger of two municipal parks.

The COLUMBUS GOLF COURSE (*open to public; 35¢ weekdays, 75¢ Sun. and holidays*), 17th St. and Hawcreek Ave., is a well-kept, municipally owned nine-hole course.

William G. Irwin's SUNKEN GARDENS (*visitors welcome*), Fifth St. and LaFayette Ave., occupy three-quarters of a city square and are rich in multicolored flowers and rare collections. Several of the water fountains were brought from Vienna, and the coping of the garden's rock wall was found in the ruins of an Italian city once buried in lava. In the west end of the garden is a sundial made in England in 1699.

At the west end of Third Street is TIPTON KNOLL, now occupied by the Kollmeyer home. On this site General John Tipton, hero of Tipton's Island (*see below*) and Tippecanoe (*see Tour* 18), built his cabin in 1820.

Columbus is at the junction with State 46 (*see Tour* 9).

ROCKFORD, 60.6 *m.* (577 alt., 75 pop.), a suburb of Seymour, is at the junction with the Yellow Band Trail.

Left on the Yellow Band Trail (Riley Highway) around the bend of WHITE RIVER, 1.5 *m.*, to an INDIAN MOUND on the grounds of a pleasure resort known as POLLEY'S CAMP, an unusually well-formed conical mound in a good state of preservation. Excavation has proved that it was used for ceremonial and burial purposes. Upstream from the mound is the SITE OF THE BATTLE OF TIPTON ISLAND, 2 *m.* Here on March 19, 1813, Tipton and 29 soldiers drove the Indians from the island into the river in a lively 20-minute skirmish, avenging the killing and wounding of a party of white men by marauding Indians. Bathers and pleasure-seekers still search the river for rifles lost by the fleeing Indians.

SEYMOUR, 63 *m.* (614 alt., 8,620 pop.) (*see Tour* 10), is at the junction with US 50 (*see Tour* 10), with which US 31 unites eastward for three miles.

AUSTIN, 81.9 *m.* (537 alt., 650 pop.), is the canning center of Indiana. At the little town's northern limits is the main plant of the MORGAN PACKING COMPANY (*visitors admitted*). This company cans and markets $10,000,000 worth of produce yearly, including corn, tomatoes, beans, and nearly every type of vegetable. Branches scattered throughout the State pack tomato pulp into five-gallon cans and ship it to Austin to be converted into ketchup. In Austin are the company's printing shop with 28 presses for printing labels, and a factory for making truck bodies; during the canning season 3,000 persons, many of them from Kentucky and neighboring Indiana communities, are employed here. The AMERICAN CAN COMPANY (*obtain permission at office*) has a large plant that keeps the cannery supplied with cans; they are sent to the cannery through chutes from the adjoining building.

SCOTTSBURG, 86.3 *m.* (568 alt., 2,189 pop.) (*see Tour* 11), is at the junction with State 56 (*see Tour* 11).

Between Scottsburg and the Ohio River, the highway, with scarcely a rise in its level surface, follows the floor of a wide valley, on either side of which are the distant 'knobs,' a picturesque region of tumbled wooded hills.

PIGEON ROOST MEMORIAL, 91 *m.*, is (L) a shaft of Indiana limestone erected in memory of a group of settlers massacred by the Indians. Shortly before dusk on September 3, 1812, a wandering band of Indians, mostly Shawnee and a few Delaware, swooped down on Pigeon Roost, a three-year-old settlement, attacking all points simultaneously. In a little more than an hour, between sunset and twilight, they killed 3 men, 5 women, and 16 children, scalping and mutilating the bodies and throwing them into the burning houses. Only one house, that of William Collings, was left standing. Collings, an expert rifleman, engaged the Indians, killed three of them and made it possible for several of the white settlers to escape. The attack has been ascribed to resentment over the Battle of Tippecanoe (*see Tour* 18) and to the excitement of the War of 1812. It has also been said that there were local causes, such as the theft of a white elk belonging to the Indians, the cheating of an Indian in a horse trade, and a transaction by which some furs were obtained at a very low figure in exchange for whisky. The monument marks the site of the single grave in which all the victims were buried.

CLARK COUNTY STATE FOREST (*picnicking grounds, shelter houses, fishing*), 95 *m.*, is a 5,400-acre tract of forested hills, used for experimenting with native Indiana trees. Four stream-fed artificial lakes within the forest are stocked with game fish. The administration building and a nursery are at the entrance to the grounds.

For 10 miles south of HENRYVILLE, 96.5 *m.* (485 alt., 400 pop.), the highway runs through Clark's Grant, 149,000 acres of land given to George Rogers Clark and his soldiers for military services (*see Vincennes*).

SPEED, 105.6 *m.* (478 alt., 800 pop.), was named for W. S. Speed, cement manufacturer who founded the cement factory, sole industry of the town. The 136 houses, the store, the community center, and the bank are built of concrete and are company-owned.

SELLERSBURG, 106.7 *m.* (460 alt., 1,121 pop.), is a residential town. Many of the houses are built of concrete, an influence exerted by the cement industry at Speed, where the majority of the town's residents are employed.

US 31 forks at Sellersburg. The right fork, US 31W, goes to New Albany; the left fork, US 31E—over which this tour continues—goes to JEFFERSONVILLE, 115.5 *m.* (454 alt., 11,493 pop.) (*see Tour 11A*). Here is the junction with State 62 (*see Tour 11A*).

At 116.5 *m.* US 31 crosses the KENTUCKY LINE into the northern edge of downtown Louisville, Kentucky (*see Kentucky Guide*), by way of the Louisville Municipal Bridge (*toll* 35¢) over the Ohio River.

ⲓⲓⲓ

Tour 17

Michigan City—Logansport—Burlington—Kokomo—Muncie—Richmond—(Eaton, Ohio); US 35.
Michigan City to Ohio Line, 211.9 *m.*

Roadbed chiefly concrete and high-type bituminous; short stretches of oil mat. Route roughly paralleled by the New York Central & St. Louis R.R. between Michigan City and La Porte; by the Pennsylvania R.R. between Winamac and Logansport; by the New York Central & St. Louis R.R. between Kokomo and Jonesboro; by the Chesapeake & Ohio R.R. between Jonesboro and the Ohio Line; and by the Pennsylvania R.R. between Matthews and Muncie.
Hotels in larger cities; tourist camps at short intervals.

US 35 follows a wandering course across northern and central Indiana, passing through extremely diversified farming country and through a number of industrial cities. At the northern end of the route is an area specializing in apples, grapes, mint, onions, potatoes, and truck vegetables; elsewhere the chief crops are corn, wheat, oats, hay, and vegetables. Throughout the tour the terrain is level or gently rolling, and the farmhouses and buildings are well kept and comparatively prosperous in appearance. Although none of the cities are large, they are busy manufacturing and trading centers. Included on the route are Michigan City, a popular resort town that attracts many Chicago vacationers to its Lake Michigan beaches; La Porte, a clean and attractive city that manufactures a wide variety of products; Logansport, called the City of Bridges, chiefly an agricultural center; Kokomo, with its many foundries and factories; Muncie, made famous as 'Middletown' in two recent sociological studies; and Richmond, a beautiful city with a large Quaker population.

Section a. MICHIGAN CITY to BURLINGTON, 98.9 m.

Between Michigan City and Burlington, US 35 follows in part the old Michigan Road, one of the most heavily traveled north and south routes in Indiana during the early days. In the northern part the highway passes through level to slightly rolling country, its sandy soil adapted to the growing of mint and onions. Between Logansport and Burlington the route traverses level corn and wheat lands, one of the State's best agricultural regions.

MICHIGAN CITY, 0 m. (621 alt., 26,476 pop.) (see Tour 2), is at the junction with US 12 (see Tour 2).

US 35, branching southeast from Michigan City across a sandy, prairie-like moraine, coincides with US 20 (see Tour 1) for one mile.

At 10.1 m. (R) is PINE LAKE (fishing and boating), about one mile long and three-quarters of a mile wide, one of the many lakes about La Porte.

LA PORTE, 12.7 m. (815 alt., 16,180 pop.), seat of La Porte County, is a pleasant, bustling manufacturing city, surprisingly clean for an industrial center. The red sandstone tower of the La Porte County Courthouse rises above the public square, surrounded on all sides by wide, shaded residential streets. Nine lakes are clustered to the north and west of the town, two of them within the city limits.

La Porte has played a prominent part in the development of industry, agriculture, and transportation in northern Indiana. It was founded in 1830, at the time when the Michigan Road was being built. Situated at a point where the great forests of early Indiana met the open prairies of the north, it was called La Porte (Fr., the door) by the early French settlers. Through La Porte passed all the commerce between central and southern Indiana and the lake regions of Indiana, Illinois, and Michigan.

The diversity of La Porte's manufactured products is unusual for so small a city. Steel-tube furniture, florists' supplies, boilers, lingerie, pianos, conveyors, farm implements, saxophones, meat-slicing machines, cough drops, and baby carriages are among the products of the city's 37 industries, which employ about 3,500 workers.

Outstanding among the manufacturing plants is the ALLIS-CHALMERS PLANT, 1001 Lincoln Way, manufacturers of road-building machinery, farm implements and tractors. This concern employs 1,600 men and has a plant capacity of 60 combines a week. The LA PORTE-DANIELS WOOLEN MILLS, Fox and Water Sts., was established in 1863 and is now one of the largest woolen mills west of New England. Using 15,000 pounds of wool daily, it has 20 sets of cards, 136 broad looms, and 10,860 spindles.

The INTERLAKEN EXPERIMENTAL SCHOOL, founded in La Porte in 1907 by Dr. Edward A. Rumely, was the first school in this section of the country to introduce vocational training. In 1911 the school was moved from La Porte to the shores of Silver Lake near the village of Rolling Prairie (*see Tour* 1). During the first World War, school activities lagged and the property was turned over to the Government for use as a training camp. It was purchased in 1925 by the Order of the Holy Cross, University of Notre Dame, and turned into a novitiate, an institution in which young men who desire to become priests or brothers of that order can take one year of preparatory training before entering a seminary.

In the basement of the courthouse is a PIONEER LOG CABIN (*open 9-5 daily; free*), constructed by the local chapter of the Daughters of the American Revolution and furnished by the La Porte County Historical Society. Articles within the cabin include a rope bed, a Kentucky squirrel rifle used in 1833, an 1834 clock with mechanism of wood, a bed warmer, a coffee mill, two fireplace bellows, and numerous other articles used by Hoosier pioneers.

The walls of the RUMELY HOTEL LOBBY, Michigan and Jefferson Sts., are decorated with MURALS painted by Robert W. Grafton in 1913, depicting the evolution of industry and agriculture.

The PUBLIC LIBRARY, Maple and Indiana Aves., houses the LA PORTE COUNTY MUSEUM (*open Thurs. & Sat. afternoons; free*), which contains mounted specimens of birds and animals, pioneer tools and implements, and a collection of 900 firearms of various periods.

In the western part of La Porte is STONE LAKE (*bathing, boating, picnicking*), with SOLDIERS' MEMORIAL PARK, containing the Municipal Bathing Beach, on its banks.

CLEAR LAKE (*boating, fishing, picnicking facilities*), in the northeastern section of the city, is a pear-shaped body of water in a densely wooded setting. At the north end of the lake is FOX MEMORIAL PARK, a 30-acre tract of landscaped woodland. One half of the cost of the park was donated by the five sons of Mr. and Mrs. Samuel Fox, early settlers of La Porte, to carry out their mother's desire to found a park for the city. A shelter of neoclassic design is near a hill at the edge of the lake, and in a natural amphitheater is a bandstand. The park also has a sand beach, dance pavilion, and playground.

Right from La Porte on Lincoln Way (State 2) to the junction with Andrew Ave. at the southwest edge of town, 1 *m.;* L. on Andrew Ave. to a stone marker (R) at the SITE OF THE OLD DOOR VILLAGE FORT, 4 *m.* Fear of an attack by Chief Black Hawk and the Sauk Indians led to the erection of this fort by white settlers in 1832. The fort consisted·of a trench, earthworks, a palisade, and two blockhouses.

KINGSBURY, 18.9 *m.* (758 alt., 250 pop.), a quiet town laid out a century ago, has truck gardens and cow pastures between the white frame houses of its main street. The Wabash Railroad runs through the north end of the town and the Grand Trunk Railroad through the south end, and large amounts of grain are shipped from the elevators that are located at these crossings.

At 19.5 *m.* is the junction with US 6 (*see Tour* 3), which unites southeastward with US 35 for five miles.

In this section the route traverses level country that produces onions, peppermint, and many grain crops.

At 28.2 *m.* is the junction with a graveled road.

Right on this road is the OLD LIBBY PRISON (*free*), 1.5 *m.* This building (L), formerly a tobacco warehouse in Richmond, Virginia, was converted into a prison by the Confederates during 1863–4. In 1893 it was carefully dismantled, removed to the World's Columbian Exposition at Chicago, and used as a museum. When the exhibit failed financially, the structure was sold to Senator Charles Danielson, who removed it to his farm and converted it into a barn, 129 feet in length and 60 feet wide. The interior is constructed of the original huge timbers of the prison, which are placed close together and some of the partitions are fastened with large wooden pins. Dates and names of many Union prisoners are cut into the uprights and beams.

At 31.1 *m.* US 35 crosses US 30 (*see Tour* 4) on an overpass. In this vicinity are large-scale truck farms operated principally by Polish, Hungarian, and Lithuanian farmers.

At 36.1 *m.* is the junction with State 8.

Right on State 8 to the KANKAKEE GAME PRESERVE (*adm. free; fishing permitted, hunting and trapping prohibited*), 6 *m.*, a 2,300-acre tract along the Kankakee River (*see Tour* 4) that was donated to the State in 1927 by the farmers of Starke and La Porte Counties, who owned portions of this swamp. Although the land is too low and wet for cultivation, it is ideal for wild life and is stocked with ring-necked pheasants, waterfowl, prairie chickens, quail, and several varieties of fur-bearing animals.

In KNOX, 37.6 *m.* (702 alt., 2,165 pop.), seat of Starke County, there are Poles, Syrians, Italians, Swedes, Bohemians, Belgians, French, and Germans, who farm the surrounding countryside. Many of them have come from Chicago, Gary, and South Bend, where they worked in the steel and automobile industries and saved their money to buy land and become mint and onion growers.

Knox is a quiet country town during the week, but on Saturdays the streets echo with greeting and conversation in a half dozen different tongues. Slavs, Italians, Scandinavians, and other nationalities mingle on the streets and in the stores, laying in their supplies for the coming week. On the courthouse square the shoppers gradually gravitate into little sidewalk groups of their own nationalities, laughing, joking, and exchanging gossip while they keep a watchful eye on their children.

Within the CITY PARK (*picnic area, tennis courts*) along the Yellow River is the KNOX FISH HATCHERY (*visitors welcome*), a privately owned commercial hatchery used to propagate bluegills and bass for restocking purposes.

BASS LAKE (*cottages, hotels, restaurants, bathing beaches, dance pavilions, tourist camps*), 44.2 *m.*, is a popular fishing resort (L), so named because of the former abundance of black bass in its waters. Its store of black bass is now depleted but silver bass, bluegills, yellow or ringed perch, and wall-eyed pike are still plentiful. Busses make daily stops here from near-by towns.

At 44.7 *m.* is the junction with State 10.

Left on State 10 along the wooded shores of the lake to the junction with a blacktop road, 2.5 *m.*; L. on this road is (R) the BASS LAKE FISH HATCHERY (*guides*), 3.5 *m.*, belonging to the Indiana Department of Conservation. This is the largest and most productive of Indiana's fish hatcheries.

At 51.2 *m.* is the entrance (L) to the WINAMAC RECREATIONAL DEMONSTRATION AREA (*adm. free*), under the direction of the National Park Service, United States Department of the Interior, co-operating with the State of Indiana. The 6,150-acre tract is being developed for recreational and reforestation purposes. A picnic area (*shelter house*) borders on the Kankakee River, two group camps are available for outing organizations, and a fire tower affords an excellent view of the area.

WINAMAC, 54.9 *m.* (695 alt., 1,835 pop.), seat of Pulaski County, is an active trading center on the sluggish, tree-fringed Tippecanoe River. Founded in 1835, it was named for Chief Winamac, a Potawatomi warrior who fought in the Battle of Tippecanoe (*see Tour 18b*). The site on which Winamac now stands, once a Miami village, was ceded by the Miami to the Potawatomi in 1818 and became Government property in 1832. In the CITY PARK are tennis courts, an artesian well, and a suspension bridge. On the Tippecanoe River is a BATHING BEACH.

At 78 *m.* is the junction with US 24 (*see Tour 5*), which unites with US 30 to LOGANSPORT, 79.9 *m.* (607 alt., 20,177 pop.) (*see Tour 5b*).

In Logansport is the junction with State 25 (*see Tour 5b*).

SYCAMORE LANE, 90.1 *m.*, is a tunnel of foliage formed by a 400-foot row of tall sycamore trees on each side of the roadway, which narrows here to about 20 feet. According to legend, the road, formerly an Indian trail, was built of sycamore poles laid side by side. It is said that the poles sprouted on each end, took root, and developed into the present lane.

BURLINGTON, 98.9 *m.* (750 alt., 615 pop.), built on a hill south of Wildcat Creek, was founded in 1832 and named for Chief Burlington of the Wyandotte Indians who lived in this vicinity for many years. Shady, tree-lined streets, neat houses, and a progressive spirit mark this village, which serves as the social and trading center of a fertile agricultural region. Burlington was formerly a stagecoach and tavern stop on the Michigan Road. A tollgate at the south edge of the village charged 10¢ for the passage of a vehicle.

In Burlington is the junction with State 29 (*see Tour 17A*).

Section b. BURLINGTON to OHIO LINE, 113 m.

This section of the route traverses level to gently rolling country, used for dairy farming and the raising of corn, wheat, tomatoes, and soybeans. Pumpkin Vine Pike, famous as the road on which Elwood Haynes made the test run with one of America's first mechanically successful automobiles, is near the beginning of this section. Midway on the route is Muncie, the *Middletown* of the widely discussed books by Robert S. and Helen M. Lynd (*see Muncie*). Farther east is the site of Buckongehelastown, an Indian village where Tecumseh and the Prophet planned the Indians' last stand against white penetration of Indiana.

KOKOMO, 14 m. (838 alt., 33,795 pop.) (*see Tour 16a*), is at the junction with US 31 (*see Tour 16*).

At 17.4 m. is the junction with Pumpkin Vine Pike.

Right on Pumpkin Vine Pike to the ELWOOD HAYNES MONUMENT, 1 m. (L), erected in honor of the builder of America's first mechanically successful spark-ignition automobile. The car, built in Kokomo, was towed behind a horse-drawn carriage to this spot on July 4, 1894. After final adjustments were made, it was ready for its test run. In Haynes's own words, 'It [the car] moved off at once at a speed of about seven miles per hour and was driven about one and one-half miles into the country. It was then turned around and ran all the way back into the city [Kokomo] without making a single stop.'

A short time before his death Haynes conducted an informal tour over Pumpkin Vine Pike and pointed out where incidents of interest occurred in the course of that historic drive. One of these places, a slight incline in the road, had prompted Elmer Apperson, who accompanied Haynes as chauffeur on the test run, to ask, 'I wonder if the little devil can make the hill?' Haynes said that he thought it could. He laughed gleefully as he told how the machine laboriously pounded its way over the gentle rise. As they approached Kokomo they met a bevy of young girls on bicycles who fluttered off the road like frightened chickens at the sight of the strange new monster.

GREENTOWN, 23.5 m. (840 alt., 1,060 pop.), is a typical Hoosier rural town with low buildings, wide streets, and many shade trees. It was founded in 1848 and named for Chief Green of the Miami Indians. Many descendants of the early English, German, Scotch, and Dutch settlers still live on land deeded to their ancestors by the United States Government.

At 38.7 m. is the junction with State 9 (*see Tour 14*).

JONESBORO, 41.1 m. (817 alt., 1,791 pop.), now a trading center with an electrical wire and cable factory as its main industry, was once a town of considerable distinction. Platted on the west bank of the Mississinewa River in 1837 by Obadiah Jones, the town once vied with Marion (*see Tour 14*) for the Grant County seat of government. The KNIGHTS OF PYTHIAS BUILDING, a three-story structure across the street from the post office, is said to have been the largest building between Indianapolis and Fort Wayne when it was built in 1866. On its stage on the third floor, popular traveling stock companies played for many years to capacity crowds, attracted as much by the size of the building as by the performances. Immediately east of the Knights of Pythias Building is the site of the former TRACY TAVERN, built in 1856 and for many years a stopping place for stagecoach passengers. Between 1872 and 1895 this tavern was the scene of many checker tournaments in which most of the skilled checker players of Indiana, Ohio, and Illinois competed. Known as the Cleeland House from 1861 until 1872, and then as the McKeever Hotel, it was closed as a tavern in 1895 and used as a store for secondhand furniture until 1934, when it was remodeled into apartments.

Left from Jonesboro on State 22 is GAS CITY, 1.2 *m.* (847 alt., 3,488 pop.), an industrial town and trading center with an exciting economic past. From a crossroads hamlet at the time of the discovery of natural gas in the region in 1887, it grew in four years to a city of 6,000 population. Following the exhaustion of the gas supply in 1891, the mushroom town for a time held part of its growth, then gradually dropped to its present status. A veteran of the gas boom is the OWENS-ILLINOIS GLASS COMPANY PLANT, the town's principal industry.

UPLAND, 9.2 *m.* (901 alt., 900 pop.), is a small manufacturing center and college town. It was platted with the coming of the railroad in 1867 and was for a time a brisk sawmill town. Many of the early settlers were Quakers, who banded together to boycott the community's first saloon, called 'The Snake Hole.' The natural gas boom of the 1890's brought window-glass and fruit-jar factories to the town, but these industries no longer operate. Today retail stores, a foundry, and a glove factory give employment to the residents.

TAYLOR UNIVERSITY is a United Brethren coeducational college that moved to Upland from Fort Wayne in 1893. In addition to the four main buildings on its 10-acre campus, there are a number of small cottages built by former President Reed for 'those students who commit the unpardonable sin of getting married before completing their education.' About 350 students are enrolled. The institution offers courses in arts and sciences, teacher training, theology, and music.

At 44.2 *m.* on the main route is the junction with a graveled road.

Right on this road to the junction with another graveled road, 1 *m.;* L. here to LAKE GALATIA (*camping ground, fishing*), 1.3 *m.*, surrounded by a bog that makes it impossible to fish from the shore. A SPIRITUALIST TOWN, on the west shore, was platted, according to legend, under the supervision of spirits, who even suggested the names of the streets. In 1854 rappings, writings, and other supernatural manifestations were reported on the farm of William Chamness. Soon Chamness's home became a rallying place for adherents of spiritualism. A sawmill and several houses were built by the believers, and a town was laid out and named Galatia. The town never prospered, and after several years it declined.

The skeleton of an unusually large mastodon unearthed a half mile south of this lake is now in the Smithsonian Institution. Its tusks measure 15 feet, its forehead 3 feet, 9 inches across, and it stands 11 feet high at the shoulders. The skeleton of a smaller mastodon, found a short distance west of the lake, is on display at the American Museum of Natural History, New York City.

MATTHEWS, 51.1 *m.* (882 alt., 468 pop.), a rural village, has grown but little since its founding in 1833 when it boasted a gristmill, sawmill, blacksmith shop, and general store. A small canning factory is its only industry.

MUNCIE, 68 *m.* (949 alt., 49,720 pop.) (*see Muncie*).
Muncie is at the junction with State 32 (*see Tour 6*).

Left from Muncie on Burlington Drive to the marker on the SITE OF
BUCKONGEHELASTOWN, 3.6 *m.*, on a hilltop (R). The site is locally known as
Old Town Hill. Buckongehelas, a chief of the Delaware, was with Little Turtle
in his battles with General St. Clair and General Wayne (*see History*); he was
one of the signers of the Treaty of Greenville, August 3, 1795. Ten years earlier
he had attended a peace conference near the present site of Cincinnati for
the purpose of meeting General George Rogers Clark, whom he admired. After
discovering General Clark, he arose, saluted him, and addressed him in these
words: 'Not as a king but as a warrior, I, Buckongehelas, address you. You
are the head of a great nation, as I am of mine. To the Great Spirit I give
thanks for having preserved us till this day when we have the opportunity
of speaking together. Three weeks are gone since I assigned the hatchet into
the hands of my kings. Since that time I have ceased to war and have now
come to this council fire with my chiefs, our women and children, to promote
the work of peace . . . Brother, General Clark, again as a warrior I tell you I
am glad to see you and thank the Spirit above who on this morning has
brought us together.'

Buckongehelas died in 1804, about a year before the famous Shawnee
brothers, Tecumseh and the Prophet, came here and began organizing a hostile
Indian confederacy that General Harrison destroyed six years later in the
Battle of Tippecanoe (*see Tour 18b*). The brothers came to Buckongehelastown
from a Shawnee village near Greenville, Ohio, where jealousy of the older
chiefs had made them unwelcome. The Prophet had been a drunkard until
one day, as he later explained it, he fell over in a drunken stupor and 'dreamed'
a new religion. He said that he had been in the spirit world, and as a result
of a vision he constructed a new religion that was a curious mixture of Indian
and Christian doctrines. While the Prophet preached his religion, his brother
Tecumseh was busy organizing the Indians for a determined stand against
further white penetration of Indian lands.

One of the principal doctrines of the Prophet's new religion was that the
Indians should abandon all things connected with the white man's civilization
and return to the ways of their forefathers. He felt that the Moravian mission
established near Anderson by John P. Kluge in 1801 for the conversion of
Indians to Christianity (*see Tour 6*) would hinder his plans. With a band
of warriors painted in black and red, he attacked the mission on several
occasions and burned Indian converts at the stake, denouncing them as witches.
Because of these activities, the mission was closed. When William Henry Harrison, governor of Indiana Territory, learned of these depredations, he warned
the Delaware to desist and challenged the powers of the Prophet, saying:
'Who is this pretended prophet who dares speak in the name of the Great
Creator? If God has really employed him, He doubtless has authorized him
to perform miracles. If he is really a prophet, ask him to cause the sun to
stand still—the moon to alter its course—the rivers to cease to flow—or the
dead to arise from their graves. If he does these things, you may then believe
that he has been sent from God.'

Governor Harrison's challenge proved to be a steppingstone to greater
power for the Prophet. He had learned in some way that an eclipse of the
sun was to take place about noon on June 16, 1806, and boldly announced
that on this day he would cause darkness to come over the sun, as proof of
his supernatural powers. When the day and hour of the eclipse arrived and
the earth was shrouded in twilight, he shouted to his gathering: 'Behold!
Did I not prophesy truly?'

This made a great impression on the Indians, and from that day until the
Battle of Tippecanoe the Prophet's power grew tremendously. His keen and
scheming mind, coupled with his dramatic leadership, made him the undisputed
head of a large following and a powerful enemy of white civilization. The
Prophet and his brother Tecumseh returned to Greenville, soon after this

'miracle,' and remained there until 1808, when they came to the Wabash River near the mouth of the Tippecanoe. Here they resumed their organization of the Indian confederacy.

BLOUNTSVILLE, 81 *m.* (1,066 alt., 169 pop.), is a dilapidated rural hamlet on a small crest, its cluster of drab, unpainted houses contrasting sharply with the surrounding countryside.

At 83 *m.* is the junction with US 36 (*see Tour* 7).

ECONOMY, 92 *m.* (1,093 alt., 251 pop.), stands on a high hill overlooking fertile farming country. Considering the place and name as appropriate, in April 1936 Dr. James R. King began in Economy an unusual experiment in co-operative medical care, called the Economy Mutual Health Association. He attends the families of Economy at a yearly fee of $16 per family. His services include medical attention, medicine, and minor surgery, but do not include hospital and X-ray treatment; there is an extra charge of $10 for maternity cases.

RICHMOND, 108 *m.* (954 alt., 35,147 pop.) (*see Tour* 8*a*), is at the junction with US 40 (*see Tour* 8) and US 27 (*see Tour* 13).

East of Richmond, US 35 coincides for three miles with US 40 and then branches southeastward, crossing the OHIO LINE at 113 *m.*, 11 miles west of Eaton, Ohio (*see Ohio Guide*).

ꜰꜰ

Tour 17A

Burlington—Kirklin—Indianapolis—Shelbyville—Greensburg—Madison—(Milton, Ky.); State 29.
Burlington to Kentucky Line, 152 *m.*

High type bituminous to junction with State 28; concrete to Versailles; oil mat to Madison.
The Cleveland, Cincinnati, Chicago, and St. Louis R.R. parallels the route between Zionsville and Greensburg.
Accommodations at intervals; hotels chiefly in cities.

This route, away from the main arteries of Hoosier traffic, wanders through farming country that is quiet and serene, and the highway is comparatively free from the billboards, eating places, and filling stations that mar the attractiveness of more heavily traveled highways. It is one of the oldest roads in the State, for the right-of-way now followed by State 29 was acquired by Indiana in 1826, when the Potawatomi ceded a tract of land 100 feet wide extending from Lake Michigan to the Ohio River. The highway cut through the wilderness in the next 12 years was known as the Michigan Road, and over it passed settlers in oxcarts and huge wagons, on horseback, or on foot. Taverns were built every few miles, stagecoach lines established, and for years the Michigan Road was Indiana's most important north-south thoroughfare.

Today highway signs reading 'Old Michigan Road' are almost the only reminder of the days when this route was an important link with the northwest. Tractors, combines, and other modern farm machines are used extensively on the level land along the highway, and well-kept farmsteads dot the landscape. As the route approaches the Ohio River, however, the terrain becomes more hilly, and thickly wooded areas appear frequently. Here the population thins out into sporadic little groups of farms and farming settlements, where corn and to-bacco are the chief crops. Folk songs and square dances flourish at Saturday gatherings, but during the rest of the week life is placid. The residents spend much of their time roaming the hills in search of game, which is fairly abundant, fishing along the streams, or loafing around the stoves in the country stores.

In BURLINGTON, 0 *m.* (750 alt., 615 pop.) (*see Tour 17a*), State 29 proceeds south from its junction with US 35 (*see Tour 17*).

At 8 *m.* is the junction with a graveled road.

Left on this road to a ROOKERY OF HERONS (*visitors welcome*), 2 *m.*, a grove (R) in which blue herons roost and mate between April and September. As many as 10 nests are often built in one tree, 50 or more feet above the ground. Since the birds feed in the surrounding swamps during the day, early morning and late afternoon hours are best for visiting the rookery.

MICHIGANTOWN, 10.5 *m.* (867 alt., 417 pop.), founded in 1830, derived its name from the Michigan Road. Once a stage stop and a thriving trade center, Michigantown's chances of developing into a city dwindled as the importance of the Michigan Road declined. To-day (1941) it is a cluster of houses built around a few retail stores and a grain elevator.

At 13 *m.* is the junction with paved State 28.

Right on State 28 is FRANKFORT, 6 *m.* (855 alt., 13,706 pop.), seat of Clinton County and the center of a diversified farming and apple-growing region. Clinton County was organized in 1830 and named for DeWitt Clinton, governor of New York and 'father of the Erie Canal,' who was thus honored by early Indiana settlers in the canal boom days. The county seat was named for Frankfurt am Main, Germany, home of the grandfather of the Pence brothers, who owned the land on which the city stands.

America's entry into the Spanish-American War was announced at Frank-fort by the booming of a homemade cannon, constructed from a bored-out locomotive axle. Clinton County quickly raised a group of volunteers, who arrived at the State Fairgrounds in Indianapolis, to find the gates locked and the grounds deserted. The detachment climbed over the fence and took pos-session of the exposition grounds, and were later enrolled in the volunteer infantry.

Frankfort's sky line is dominated by the clock tower of the 60-year-old courthouse and the 6-story home-office building of an insurance company. Local industries include meat packing, enameling of sheet metal, and the manufacture of brass fittings. The city is at the junction of The New York Central, Pennsylvania, and Monon Railroads, which maintain repair shops here.

KIRKLIN, 19.9 *m.* (918 alt., 712 pop.), a rural village with a red brick business section, was named for Nathan Kirklin who had bought all the land near here in 1828 when it seemed likely that a proposed State road would intersect the Michigan Road at this point. His deductions were correct, and he built a tavern at the crossroads and founded the town.

At 31 *m.* is the junction with State 32 (*see Tour* 6), and at 37.2 *m.* is the junction with State 334.

> Right on State 334 to ZIONSVILLE, 1.3 *m.* (880 alt., 1,314 pop.), an agricultural center. In DEPOT PARK, between First and Second Streets, a stone marker indicates the site where Abraham Lincoln spoke on February 11, 1861. Lincoln, speaking from the rear platform of a special train en route to Washington for his first inauguration, said: 'I would like to spend more time here, but there is an event to take place in Washington which cannot start until I get there.'

State 29 continues through productive farm land that gradually changes to a country-estate region on the rolling land around the White River, as the route nears Indianapolis.

INDIANAPOLIS, 51.1 *m.* (750 alt., 386,972 pop.) (*see Indianapolis*).

Indianapolis is at the junction with US 31 (*see Tour* 16), US 36 (*see Tour* 7), US 40 (*see Tour* 8), US 52 (*see Tour* 18), State 37 (*see Tour* 19), and State 34 (*see Tour* 8A).

NEW BETHEL, 60.1 *m.* (800 alt., 500 pop.), a pleasant, prosperous farming community stretching along the highway, is the scene of the annual Marion County Fair.

At 67.1 *m.* is the junction with a blacktop road.

> Right on this road are the RED MILLS (*open*), 5 *m.*, a large water-powered flour- and gristmill on the banks of Sugar Creek (R). The mill, housed in a large red building, has been in constant operation since 1820. It is powered by 2 turbines of 35 horsepower each.

SHELBYVILLE, 78.2 *m.* (766 alt., 10,791 pop.), seat of Shelby County, lies in the midst of Indiana's richest corn belt. The county has for many years produced some of the Nation's finest seed corn. The town—platted in 1822 and named for the first governor of Kentucky—is an active and prosperous community with wide, paved and shaded streets and fine residences. Ten furniture factories provide the principal source of employment for the inhabitants.

Shelbyville was the home of Thomas A. Hendricks (1819–85), former Vice President of the United States and governor of Indiana, and of Charles Major (1856–1913), author of *When Knighthood Was in Flower, Dorothy Vernon of Haddon Hall, The Bears of Blue River,* and other historical romances and books of pioneer life. Major's home, two blocks south of Blue River, was torn down after his death.

The SHELBY COUNTY COURTHOUSE, a modern steel and concrete structure faced with Indiana limestone, was begun in 1936 with the aid of a PWA grant.

At 79.2 *m.* is a STONE MARKER (L) commemorating the completion, on July 4, 1834, of the first railroad in Indiana. The rails were of wood, to which strap iron was nailed. The mile-and-a-half line was built for a steam railroad, but when the owner, Judge W. J. Peasley, was unable to secure a locomotive, he hired a farmer to hitch his horse to the single passenger coach. The marker erroneously states that this experimental stretch of the proposed Lawrenceburg and Indianapolis Railroad was the first railroad west of the Alleghenies, but it was preceded by the Lexington and Ohio, another horse-drawn line.

GREENSBURG, 98.9 *m.* (950 alt., 6,065 pop.) (*see Tour* 9), is at the junction with State 46 (*see Tour* 9) with which State 29 unites for four miles.

OSGOOD, 118 *m.* (991 alt., 1,198 pop.), is the second largest town in Ripley County. A stone quarry and a factory making wooden plugs —used chiefly in the ends of rolls of paper—are the principal industries; farm trade is Osgood's chief source of business.

At 123.1 *m.* is the junction with US 50 (*see Tour* 10), with which State 29 unites to VERSAILLES, 124.1 *m.* (1,000 alt., 582 pop.) (*see Tour* 10).

At 150.1 *m.* there is an excellent view of Madison, lying several hundred feet below, and the Ohio River winding its way through a forest-fringed valley. From here the highway descends sharply into Madison.

In MADISON, 151.1 *m.* (550 alt., 6,923 pop.) (*see Tour* 11), is the junction with State 56 (*see Tour* 11).

At 152 *m.* State 29 crosses the KENTUCKY LINE, 1.2 miles north of Milton, Kentucky (*see Kentucky Guide*), by way of the Madison-Milton Bridge (50¢ *toll for automobile and four passengers; 5¢ each additional passenger*) across the Ohio River.

↑↑

Tour 18

(Cincinnati, Ohio)—Brookville—Indianapolis—LaFayette—Kentland —(Sheldon, Illinois); US 52.

Ohio Line¹ to Illinois Line, 198.7 *m.*

Roadbed concrete throughout; two to four lanes.

The Cleveland, Cincinnati, Chicago & St. Louis R.R. parallels the route between the Ohio Line and Metamora and between Indianapolis and Earl Park; and the Baltimore & Ohio R.R. parallels the route between Rushville and Indianapolis. Accommodations of all kinds at intervals; hotels chiefly in cities.

US 52 runs diagonally across the State from southeast to northwest, traversing first broken, hilly terrain, then typical rolling Indiana farm country, and finally extremely flat prairie land. It passes through two widely separated regions that were particularly important in the early history of Indiana—the beautiful valley of the Whitewater River, near the Ohio Line; and the Wabash Valley in the vicinity of LaFayette, far to the north and west. The broad and fertile Whitewater River basin was, in the years following Indiana's admission to the Union, the most thickly populated section of the State; and to Brookville, now a sleepy town of many memories, gravitated a group of lawyers who played a dominant role in Indiana politics for 25 years. From their ranks came one of the State's first two United States senators and every governor between 1825 and 1840, as well as later senators, representatives, and other important officials. At one time all the members of the State supreme court were men who had practiced law in Brookville. The building of Whitewater Canal, an ambitious project along the banks of the river and a vital part of the Mammoth Internal Improvement Program begun in 1836, was due largely to the influence of this group.

LaFayette, now the seat of Purdue University, was another populous center in pioneer times. Near by is the site of Fort Ouiatenon, said by some authorities to have been the first permanent white settlement in present-day Indiana. The fort, built about 1720 by the French and occupied at various times by French, British, and American troops as well as by Indians of the Wea tribe, was destroyed in 1791. On the opposite side of LaFayette is Battleground, where William Henry Harrison's militia, in the Battle of Tippecanoe (1811), defeated the disgruntled Indians who had rallied around Tecumseh and the Prophet to halt the white advance into their hunting grounds.

Section a. OHIO LINE to INDIANAPOLIS, 90 m.

This region is given over largely to stock-raising, although large grain crops are grown in the fertile river valleys. The highway follows the route of the Whitewater Canal for more than 30 miles, and its remains or restored sections are visible at many points. On the route are West Harrison, last town in Indiana visited by General Morgan during his Civil War raid; Oldenburg, with one of the largest Roman Catholic ecclesiastical communities in Indiana; and Rushville, a trading center in the heart of a rich agricultural area.

Twenty-one miles northwest of Cincinnati, Ohio, US 52 turns right from Harrison Avenue, the main street of Harrison, Ohio, into State Street, the main street of West Harrison, Indiana. The highway is for several blocks the State boundary line and is half in Ohio and half in Indiana; westbound travelers are in Ohio and eastbound in Indiana.

WEST HARRISON, 0 *m.* (520 alt., 311 pop.), established in 1813, was the last town raided by General John Hunt Morgan and his Confederate cavalry during their Civil War foray into Indiana (*see Corydon*). After a brief stay on July 13, 1863, with headquarters in the AMERICAN HOTEL (L) on Harrison Ave., the Confederate raider and his men rode down State Street and passed into Ohio. A MARKER at the intersection of US 52 and State Street designates the point at which Morgan left Indiana.

West Harrison's OLDEST HOUSE, State St. and Broadway, is a two-story frame structure built at an undetermined date prior to 1812. The occupants of this house fed many of Morgan's raiders shortly after noon on the day of the raid, as did other residents of West Harrison; they then fed the pursuing Union forces under the command of General Edward Hobson soon after dark of the same day. For the most part, West Harrison's residents gave food to Morgan's men because they were afraid to refuse, but they fed General Hobson's men joyfully, welcoming them as saviors of the town.

On State Street at the southern edge of West Harrison is (R) the two-story red brick BARNEY SIMONSON HOUSE (*private*). At a granary adjacent to this house Morgan's men fed more than 1,500 horses.

Near the present bridge over the Whitewater River are the tumbled-down ABUTMENTS of the bridge Morgan burned as he entered West Harrison. Hobson's forces, arriving six hours later, saw a long line of gray-clad cavalry (Morgan's rear guard) riding eastward toward Ohio; but the Union soldiers, because the bridge had been destroyed, were unable to cross the river until the next morning. They continued the pursuit into Ohio; Morgan lost several hundred men at Buffington Island in the Ohio River and narrowly escaped capture at Blennerhassett Island and at the Muskingum River. With a remnant of his forces, Morgan was finally captured on July 26 near Salineville, Ohio. He was imprisoned in the Ohio Penitentiary at Columbus, but dug his way out four months later and escaped to the South. He was killed in action at Greenville, Tennessee, on September 4, 1864.

Four days before Morgan invaded Indiana, General Lee had been defeated at Gettysburg, and Vicksburg had fallen to General Grant. Morgan's five-day raid in Indiana was a bold attempt by a daring leader to retrieve a lost cause; it destroyed $500,000 worth of property and gave the State its only first-hand taste of the Civil War.

South and west from West Harrison is a narrow, winding, paved county road, formerly State 46. It was over this route that Morgan and his men rode into West Harrison from Logan, and the course of his flight is marked by boulders with inscribed bronze plaques.

DOVER, 8.7 *m.* (535 alt., 150 pop.), was settled early in the nineteenth century by Irish Roman Catholics, who were joined later by French and German Catholic immigrants. One of the oldest Roman Catholic parishes in

Indiana is at NEW ALSACE, 12 *m*. (640 alt., 100 pop.), where St. Paul's Church (R), a red brick structure built in 1837, still stands.

SUNMAN, 16.5 *m*. (1,016 alt., 352 pop.), is a quiet village of wide streets and freshly painted houses.

For 31 miles northwest of West Harrison, the highway parallels the winding Whitewater River, along the banks of which are remnants of the Whitewater Canal. In 1836 Indiana embarked on its Mammoth Internal Improvement Program of turnpike, canal, and railroad construction. The Whitewater Canal between Cambridge City (*see Tour 8a*) and the Ohio River was given precedence over other projects, and by December 1838 Indiana's part of the canal was completed from West Harrison about 20 miles northwest. By this time, however, the program had bankrupted the State and all work ceased until 1842. Then a private company took over the canal, completing it to Brookville in 1843, to Connersville in 1845, and to Cambridge City a year later. Floods in 1847 and 1848—the valley was too steep to hold the canal—caused damage estimated at nearly $200,000. In 1865 the Whitewater Valley Railroad was built, paralleling the canal and completely outmoding it as a means of transportation. Several parts of the canal have since been restored for use as water power.

At 3 *m*. is the junction with State 46 (*see Tour 9*).

NEW TRENTON, 6 *m*. (600 alt., 165 pop.), was a village of some importance during the pioneer period, and its taverns were popular with the workers who built the Whitewater Canal. The Manwarring Tavern, a two-story brick structure (L) at the only side street connecting with the highway, was built in 1810. The proprietor, Thomas Manwarring, dispensed liquors through the week, and on Sundays preached to the assembled pioneers from the steps of the tavern.

At 17.6 *m*. is the Little Cedar Baptist Church, the first Baptist church in Indiana and one of the earliest in the Mississippi Valley. Built in 1812, this simple brick building with a gable roof contains a gallery supported by hand-hewn ash columns. In front of the pulpit, which is large, high, and plain, is a charcoal hearth that served to heat the church. Several generations of boys have carved initials and names on the high-backed seats, and time has given the interior woodwork a rich brown color. To the west of the church, on a high point, is the old graveyard, filled with sunken and, for the most part, nameless graves. Since the Civil War, only occasional services have been held in the church, which is now owned by the Brookville Historical Society.

BROOKVILLE, 20.6 *m*. (646 alt., 2,194 pop.), seat of Franklin County, is the trading center for a small agricultural region. A quiet town with a number of century-old houses and buildings, Brookville has no industries today; but when the State was young it was one of Indiana's most important towns.

Selecting as a likely site a ridge between forks of the Whitewater River and surrounded by wooded hills, Amos Butler and Jesse Brooks Thomas had a town platted here in 1808. They called it Brooksville, in honor of Thomas's mother, whose maiden name was Brooks; but when Franklin County was organized three years later the name was shortened to Brookville. The county soon became one of the most populous in Indiana; its industries included meat-packing houses, cotton and woolen mills, distilleries, and scores of grist-, flour-, and sawmills.

To Brookville, center of all this activity, came a little group of men, most of them lawyers, whose individual and collective brilliance was to outshine that of any other group in the State. Among them were James Noble, United States senator from 1816 to his death in 1831; James Brown Ray, governor from 1825 to 1831; Noah Noble, governor from 1831 to 1837; David Wallace, father of General Lew Wallace and governor from 1837 to 1840; Robert Hanna, who succeeded James Noble as United States senator; Isaac Blackford, Stephen Stephens, and James McKinney, justices of the State supreme court; and John Test, representative from Indiana in the 18th, 19th, and 21st Congresses.

Jesse Brooks Thomas, leaving the town he had helped to found a few years after it was established, became a United States senator from Illinois. He was in large measure responsible for the famed Missouri Compromise of 1820, for he re-introduced the bill after it had been rejected once by the Senate, and offered the amendment providing that no territory north of 36° 30′ should be admitted into the Union as a slave State. This was the form in which the Compromise was finally adopted.

The HERMITAGE (*private*), end of Eighth St., was formerly the home of J. Ottis Adams (1851–1927), one of the 'Hoosier Group' of painters (*see Arts and Crafts*). Set among trees at a bend of the east fork of Whitewater River, this frame structure, built in 1817 by Amos Butler, has been restored and dormer windows have been placed in the attic. A wide, long porch runs across the façade.

On Seventh Street are the WHITEWATER CANAL LOCKS and the WATER-POWERED PAPER MILL of the company that owns the water rights of the Whitewater Canal, restored for water power between Laurel and Brookville. This was the second dry-roll paper mill west of the Alleghenies; its product was used for printing books at New Harmony during the period of Robert Owen's social experiment there (*see New Harmony*).

A government land office occupied the PIONEER HARDWARE STORE building (L), 700 block Main St., between 1823 and 1825. Directly across the street is the GENERAL HANNA HOUSE, built in 1818 and now used for an insurance office and a barbershop. Robert Hanna was the first United States marshal for Indiana Territory and was appointed United States senator in 1831 to fill the unexpired term of James Noble.

The GOVERNOR RAY RESIDENCE (*private*), 210 East Tenth St., a two-story frame house with a lean-to kitchen at the rear, was built during James Brown Ray's campaign for governor in 1825. The ornate

Palladian window in the side of the second story almost caused Ray's defeat when a picture of it was published in an Indianapolis news-paper and the opposition campaigned on the issue that Ray was a ...an of extravagant habits.

Ray, who served two terms as governor, was elected as the candidate of the Internal Improvement faction, but broke with his supporters over the building of the Wabash and Erie Canal. He pointed out to the legislature the many obvious advantages of railroads over canals, and prophesied that Indianapolis would someday be a great railroad center with lines radiating in all directions like the spokes of a wheel. The proponents of a canal system, however, were too strong, and Ray's political career was wrecked on this issue. A lover of flourish and display, he always signed his name in hotel registers, 'J. Brown Ray, Governor of Indiana and Commander-in-Chief of the Army and Navy thereof.'

On the southwest corner of Tenth and Main Streets is the HOUSE OF JOHN TEST, a congressman from Indiana. In this house Esther Test, the congressman's daughter, became the wife of David Wallace. Their son, Lew Wallace (*see Tour 8A*), Civil War soldier and author of *Ben-Hur*, was born in 1827 in their home on Third Street. The SITE OF THE BIRTHPLACE OF LEW WALLACE, at the rear of the Roman Catholic school, is marked.

The SITE OF THE HACKLEMAN CABIN, in which was born General Pleasant A. Hackleman, the only Indiana general killed in the Civil War, is just south of town. The cabin was moved to the Rushville Memorial Park. A MONUMENT to the general's memory stands in the Brookville courthouse yard.

BOUNDARY HILL, 21.1 *m.*, received its name because at one time the frontier of white settlement in Indiana was a line extending from here to Fort Recovery, Ohio, and Carrollton, Kentucky. The line was fixed by the Treaty of Greenville, signed in 1795 (*see History*).

For eight miles west of Brookville the highway is paralleled by the restored path of the WHITEWATER CANAL (L). A railroad, its bed the old TOWPATH, parallels the canal.

METAMORA, 28.6 *m.* (676 alt., 250 pop.), one block L. of the rerouted highway, is an old farming community with much of the detached and self-sufficient quality of a New England village. When the Whitewater Canal was in full operation a number of mills and factories were located here, and there is still a WATER-POWERED GRIST MILL at the western edge of the village.

The WHITEWATER CANAL AQUEDUCT is a wooden channel carrying the full flow of the canal across Duck Creek. This shed-like structure, built in 1848, is 80 feet long and 16 feet above the bed of Duck Creek. It has a flood gate in the center of the span and a sidewalk for pedestrians.

At 28.9 *m.* is the junction with State 229 (oil mat).

Left on this highway is OLDENBURG, 10 *m*. (990 alt., 533 pop.), founded by German immigrants in 1837 and now one of the State's outstanding Roman Catholic communities. Its spired places of worship and religious education, set among hills and valleys, are alternately seen and lost to sight as the winding, rolling highway approaches the village. The CONVENT OF THE IMMACULATE CONCEPTION (R) is the mother home of more than 900 Sisters of St. Francis, who have charge of Catholic academies in six States. Directly across the street is the CHURCH OF THE HOLY FAMILY with its steeple rising 187 feet. The church is a brick structure built in 1861–2 near the old stone church that replaced the original log structure. Father Rudolph, the first pastor, is buried under the church.

The OLDENBURG FRANCISCAN MONASTERY is beside the church. In the monastery's House of Theology brown-robed students with white, knotted rope belts complete the last four years of a 13-year course that fits them for priesthood in the Order of St. Francis.

Oldenburg was formerly a brick manufacturing center, and its once busy factories produced the bricks that were used to build the church, convent, and monastery. Today there are no industries; many of the townspeople work in furniture factories at near-by Batesville (*see Tour 9*).

1. Left from Oldenburg on a graveled road to the SHRINE OF THE SORROWFUL MOTHER, 1 *m*., bearing a striking resemblance to the wayside shrines so common in the Bavarian Alps and the Austrian Tyrol. It is built of brick with an ornamental frame pediment resting on two wooden columns. Behind a grill is a group of wood carvings that depicts the body of Christ resting on the knees of His grief-stricken Mother at the foot of the Cross. The group rests on the base of the stone in which are imbedded a fragment of a cleft rock from Calvary, another from the temple ruins of Baalbek, and one from the Colosseum of Rome. The carving was saved, according to tradition, by a pious Alsatian family who feared that their church might be sacked during the French Revolution, and was brought to America by a descendant of the family. The identity of its designer and the date of execution are not known. Every year, usually on the third Sunday in September, a field mass is celebrated before the shrine.

2. Right from Oldenburg on the graveled Hamburg Road to an 80-acre VIRGIN FOREST, 3 *m*. No timber has ever been cut from this tract, owned by Elizabeth Meyers, whose family originally purchased it from the government. Ancient trees, five or six feet in diameter, cover the area.

At 30.9 *m*. on the main route is a junction with State 121 (oil mat).

Right on State 121, 2.5 *m*., to MIDWAY FARM (L), the name in large letters on the sloping roof of a barn. A short distance through the fields is DERBYSHIRE FALLS, where the water, tumbling over a 40-foot limestone precipice, has created an enormous cavern under and directly behind the falls.

As the highway turns into the town of LAUREL, 5 *m*. (725 alt., 533 pop.), it passes a vacant lot (L) where once stood the Somerset Tavern, on the SITE OF SOMERSET. Somerset was founded 20 years before Laurel, in 1816. From the tavern, in that year, Jacob Whetzel blazed the Whetzel Trace through 60 miles of primeval forest—now three and a half counties—to the White River south of Indianapolis. Later he cut out a roadway along the trace and sold the land bordering it to friends in the East. When the trace was subsequently surveyed it was found that the pioneer woodsman had varied but four degrees from due west in the entire undertaking.

Laurel was founded by James Conwell who named it for Laurel, Delaware. Originally a farming community, it became a mill town and shipping center during the canal period. With the decline of water transportation came a boom in the stone industry. And now, since there are no industries, many of the townspeople have again turned to farming, while others are employed in Connersville.

Just off Washington Street (R) is an OLD STONE BARN, a massive roofless skeleton—a monument to Laurel's 'stone age' when quarrying was a lively industry. The walls of the old stone barn mark the SITE OF THE WHITEWATER CANAL BASIN from which the produce of the surrounding countryside was formerly shipped to the Ohio River. During the stone-quarrying period 80 horses were stabled in the barn. Adjacent to it and built of the same roughly cut stone stands the LAUREL JAIL, a low one-room structure with one tiny window and a dark, dank interior.

The LAUREL ACADEMY BUILDING, Main and Pearl Sts., erected in 1837, is now unused, except for occasional lodge meetings. The CONWELL GENERAL STORE BUILDING, Main and Franklin Sts., built by the town's founder in 1833, is now a hotel. The WHITEHALL TAVERN, Baltimore and Franklin Sts., stands on a hill beside REMAINS OF THE CANAL AND TOWPATH. The tavern was unusual in the roistering days of the old waterway in that its proprietor, Squire Clements, served no alcoholic beverages. The structure is well preserved, its terraced lawn surrounded by an old stone retaining wall.

The two-story brick BIRTHPLACE OF CHARLES MURRAY, motion picture comedian, is at Washington and Baltimore Sts. Here the actor lived until he was 12 years old, charging pins for admission to shows he staged in a barn that stood behind the house. In the COLTER HOUSE, SW. corner of Conwell and LaFayette Sts., Oliver Wendell Holmes got a drink of water when he visited the graves of his friends, the poets Byron Forceythe Willson and his wife, Elizabeth Conwell Smith Willson (*see New Albany*), in Laurel Cemetery. The Willsons had lived in the home of James Russell Lowell in Cambridge, Massachusetts, and had been friends and neighbors of Holmes. The BIRTHPLACE OF MRS. ELIZABETH WILLSON is a rambling brick dwelling at the corner of Church Street and Colter Hill.

An INDIAN MOUND, rising 150 feet above the valley, crowns LAUREL HILL at the northern edge of town. Atop the mound is a bandstand overlooking a landscape that Meredith Nicholson, Indiana author, described as 'one of the loveliest in Indiana.'

ELMHURST, 16 *m.*, set far back (L) on a 40-acre wooded tract, is a stately white brick mansion that has had a variety of owners. In 1831, Oliver Hampton Smith (1794–1859), U. S. senator (1837–43), built a 4-room house that forms the central part of the present structure of 40 rooms. He sold it seven years later to Caleb Blood Smith (1808–84), who was Secretary of the Interior in President Lincoln's Cabinet. Samuel Parker (1805–59), who served a term in the House of Representatives, bought the property from Smith in 1842, and it remained in the Parker family until 1881, when it was purchased by James N. Huston (1849–1927). Huston was chairman of the State Republican Committee during Benjamin Harrison's successful campaign for the presidency, and Harrison visited Elmhurst several times to discuss campaign strategy. After his election he appointed Huston Treasurer of the United States.

Elmhurst's next two owners were Dr. A. W. Daum and Dr. William J. Porter, each of whom operated a sanatorium here. It was purchased for a summer home in 1906 by George B. Markle, but three years later he turned it over to Miss Isabel Cressler and Miss Caroline Sumner, who founded the Elmhurst School for Girls; the school was moved to New England in 1925. The final venture, Pennton Military Institute, was housed in Elmhurst during the school year of 1927–8. At present (1941) the mansion, unoccupied except for a caretaker, is owned by a group of Connersville businessmen.

There are several remarkable trees on the Elmhurst tract. The 'Elmhurst elm,' 95 feet high and 16 feet in circumference, is believed to be 300 years old. Near by are a fine specimen of *Catalpa speciosa,* 8 feet in circumference, and a magnificent beech tree 100 feet high.

CONNERSVILLE, 16.2 *m.* (832 alt., 12,898 pop.), seat of Fayette County, has factories that produce toys, blowers, auto bodies, refrigerators, and furniture. The Auburn, Cord, and Duesenberg motor cars were formerly manufactured in this community. John Conner (1780–1826), the town's founder, was kidnapped by Indians when a boy and grew to manhood in their care. A shrewd, self-educated man, he was one of the most enterprising settlers in this section of the country. Licensed to trade with the Indians for furs in 1801, he established a fur-trading post in 1808 on the present site of Connersville. He was interpreter and guide for General William Henry Harrison in the War of 1812, founded Connersville in 1813, and was elected the first sheriff. A wealthy landowner, he also owned and operated the first gristmill, the first sawmill, the first tavern, and the first store in what is now Fayette County. Conner, one of the nine commissioners who selected Indianapolis as the State capital in 1820, died in 1826 while a member of the Indiana House of Representatives.

Connersville's first industrial boost came from the Whitewater Canal, a restored section of which is now used by the local light and power company to generate electricity. Behind the Palace Hotel, Fourth and Central Aves., is the old structure that served as the OFFICE OF THE CANAL COMPANY, organized at the time the canal was extended from Brookville to Connersville. This building, Greek revival in design with supporting pillars, was later known as the Portia Vance Hanson mansion. It is now a dog and cat hospital.

ANDERSONVILLE, 38.9 m. (900 alt., 165 pop.), marks a change of landscape. Eastward the country is hilly; westward it is level to gently rolling. Between Andersonville and Rushville US 52 follows the route of the first plank road in Rush County.

At 47.4 m. is the junction with the graveled Wilson Pike.

Right on this road, 2.5 m., to a small MONUMENT TO BLUE BULL (R), famous sire of trotting horses, just inside the Wilson farm fence. Under the monument is buried the horse that sired 60 record-making trotting horses, and whose daughters produced 173 well-known trotters. Rush County has long been known for its fast harness horses.

RUSHVILLE, 49 m. (956 alt., 5,960 pop.), seat of Rush County, is the center of rich farming country, notable in the State for corn and hog raising. Founded in 1822, the town and county were named for Benjamin F. Rush, physician and philanthropist, Revolutionary War soldier, and signer of the Declaration of Independence.

The WATSON HOUSE (private), 805 N. Main St., is the home of James E. Watson, a representative and senator from Indiana for 35 years and Rushville's best-known resident. A powerful figure in State and National politics for years, he completed his last term in the United States Senate in March 1933. His reminiscences, As I Knew Them, published in 1936, are filled with history, anecdote, and humor.

In MEMORIAL PARK is the reconstructed HACKLEMAN LOG CABIN, moved from Brookville, in which was born General Pleasant A. Hackleman, who practiced law in Rushville.

On a GLACIAL BOULDER, NE. corner of the courthouse square, is a plaque honoring William B. Laughlin. Dr. Laughlin studied law, medicine, and surveying at Jefferson College in Philadelphia. He came to Indiana in 1816, and was a member of the legislature that created Rush County, after which he surveyed the county and named it. He donated the land on which Rushville is located, named the town, built the first house, established the first school, and was its first teacher. At the southwest corner of Third and Morgan Streets is the SITE OF THE LAUGHLIN ACADEMY, first in the county, which Dr. Laughlin opened in 1828 in a two-story log house. This pioneer institution offered a course of study in the classics.

MORRISTOWN, 64 m. (847 alt., 665 pop.), has a large CANNING FACTORY (R) at its western edge. In the latter part of August, farmers' wagons heaped high with sweet corn form long lines beside the factory, awaiting their turn at the unloading platform.

At 65 m. is the bridge over BLUE RIVER, a stream made familiar to children by the book, *The Bears of Blue River*, by Charles Major of Shelbyville (*see Tour 17A*).

Left along Blue River on a graveled road is the FREEPORT SUMMER RESORT, 2 m. (*cottages, boating, and swimming*).

FOUNTAINTOWN, 69 m. (844 alt., 210 pop.), is a village with no industries, its inhabitants chiefly retired farmers.

Right from Fountaintown on State 9, a paved road, to an OIL PUMPING STATION (*visitors welcome*), 1 m., one of several spaced at 45-mile intervals across Indiana by means of which crude oil is piped, rather than shipped, from the Southwest to Buffalo, New York, for refining. The pipe line is laid 20 inches deep, and occasionally farmers 'tap in' and enjoy the benefits (until stopped) of a little oil well on their own farm. The station is on a well-kept 25-acre site with modern brick residences for the employees, an orchard, and vegetable and flower gardens.

CARROLLTON, 71.1 m. (830 alt., 89 pop.), a village with a church, several stores, and a blacksmith shop, has been immortalized in James Whitcomb Riley's poem, 'The Little Town o' Tailholt.' The community, founded in 1854, has had several names. Its post office was successively known as Kinder, Carrollton, and Finley, while the Baltimore & Ohio Railroad named its station at this point Reedville. Bewildered by this wealth of names, the people of the neighborhood took to calling the place 'Tailholt,' and the publication of Riley's poem made this name official as far as the residents of the village are concerned.

At 79 m. is the MARION COUNTY INFIRMARY (R), known as Julietta. The first Marion County infirmary was established in a two-room log cabin on a farm west of Indianapolis in 1832, and it remained at this location, in three successive buildings, for 106 years. Meanwhile Marion County established a hospital for the incurably insane at Julietta. In 1938 the Julietta patients were transferred to the Central State Hospital for the Insane in western Indianapolis, and the Julietta establishment became the Marion County Infirmary.

Right on the graveled County Line Road that borders the infirmary, 0.5 m., to a junction with a dirt road; R. on this road to a GERMAN SETTLE-MENT, 2 m., founded in 1828 by Carl Leopold Albert von Bonge, a Prussian nobleman banished from his country for political activity. In the settlement's German Lutheran Church of Zion, services are still conducted in German on the first Sunday in each month.

INDIANAPOLIS, 90 m. (750 alt., 386,972 pop.) (*see Indianapolis*). Indianapolis is at the junction with US 31 (*see Tour 16*), US 36 (*see Tour* 7), US 40 (*see Tour* 8), State 29 (*see Tour* 17*A*), State 37 (*see Tour* 19), and State 34 (*see Tour* 8*A*).

Section b. *INDIANAPOLIS to ILLINOIS STATE LINE,* 108.7 m.

Between Indianapolis and the Illinois Line the route passes the locale of the Battle of Tippecanoe and one of the first French trading posts in Indiana. In this flat, intensively cultivated region, corn, oats, and wheat are grown in great quantities. The landscape gradually changes from the typical tree-rimmed Indiana scene to corn-growing prairie country.

The highway crosses WHITE RIVER at 2.8 m. and skirts the western edge of THOMAS TAGGART RIVERSIDE PARK (*see Indianapolis*), largest of Indianapolis' recreational centers. In the park and visible from the highway (R) is the $500,000 UNITED STATES VETERANS' HOSPITAL, a branch of the Veterans' Administration Facility.

At 4.7 m. is the HOOSIER AIRPORT (L), one of the several privately operated airports about the State capital.

FLACKVILLE, 5.4 m. (825 alt., 140 pop.), named for Joseph Flack, first owner of the land, was once a tollgate station on the old LaFayette Pike. A gasoline station at the junction with a projection of Indianapolis's 30th St. is on the SITE OF THE LAFAYETTE PIKE TOLL-GATE.

TRADERS POINT, 12.8 m. (830 alt., 50 pop.), was so named because in the early days an Indian trading post was located one mile west of here. Many fine estates lie in the rough wooded area around the village.

LEBANON, 28.7 m. (900 alt., 6,529 pop.), is the seat of Boone County, noted for the excellence of its farms. The town was so named because its surrounding forests reminded one of its founders of the Biblical Cedars of Lebanon. The huge COURTHOUSE PILLARS, each three stories high and weighing 50 tons, are among the largest hand-hewn limestone monoliths in the United States.

The RALSTON HOUSE (*private*), 520 N. Meridian St., was the home of Samuel M. Ralston (1857–1925), governor of Indiana and United States senator, one of the State's most beloved executives. A school-teacher and a lawyer before entering public office, he is remembered for his aid to the State's schools and universities, his promotion of State parks, and his sponsorship of the Dixie Highway.

In MEMORIAL PARK, on the north side of Lebanon, is a pioneer two-room LOG CABIN removed from a near-by farm and reconstructed by the local chapter of the Daughters of the American Revolution. Outfitted with pioneer furniture and relics, it is used as a D.A.R. chapter house.

Lebanon is at the junction with State 32 (*see Tour* 6).

At 35.6 m. is the junction with State 47 (oil mat).

Left on State 47 to THORNTOWN, 2 *m.* (840 alt., 1,226 pop.), rich in Indian history and known until 1828 as the Thorntown Indian Reservation. There was an Indian village here as early as 1719, called Keewaskee (place of thorns), and so the white settlement that replaced it was named Thorntown. Jesuit missionaries established a trading post in Keewaskee and made the village a religious center for the Indians. Between 1818 and 1828 the site was one of the principal Indian reservations west of Pittsburgh. In 1828 the Indians were removed to a reservation near Logansport and the following year Thorntown was platted by Cornelius Westfall, who purchased the land from the Government at $4 an acre.

The MILLS MEMORIAL FOUNTAIN, in the center of the principal street intersection, is a gift to the town from its most distinguished son, the late General Anson Mills. General Mills, a 'fighting Quaker,' served with distinction in the Civil War and in western campaigns against the Indians. After his retirement from the Army, he invented and manufactured the Mills Woven Cartridge Belt, used by the armed forces of many countries. Before his retirement from business in 1905, General Mills had amassed a fortune of $1,300,000. He died in 1924.

The WILLIAM ROSS SANATORIUM, 59.7 *m.*, is a 40-bed hospital (L), fully equipped for the diagnosis and treatment of tuberculosis. This institution, the gift of Mr. and Mrs. David Linn Ross to Tippecanoe County, is on a wooded 60-acre tract. The three-story brick building flanked by two-story wings is of Georgian Colonial style.

At 61.7 *m.* the route proceeds straight ahead on US 52B, the business route to LaFayette.

US 52, for through-traffic and trucks, turns R. here to bypass the city and rejoins US 52B at 67.9 *m.*

LAFAYETTE, 63.7 *m.* (540 alt., 28,798 pop.), seat of Tippecanoe County, was named in 1824 by its founder, William Digby, for the Marquis de LaFayette. Digby purchased the site of LaFayette for $1.25 an acre; a year later he sold the tract to Samuel Sargent for $240, reserving a small portion of land for ferry landings on the Wabash River. Sargent, in turn, sold some of the lots and at his death his heirs donated the remainder to the county with the provision that LaFayette become the permanent county seat.

Before the advent of railroads, LaFayette was a shipping center for many years. Produce was brought to the town in wagons from the surrounding country, and sent from there to market on the steamboats of the Wabash River and the canal boats of the Wabash and Erie Canal.

Local industries manufacture automotive gears and tools, sponge rubber products, safes and locks, electrical appliances, building blocks, soybean oil, and wire goods, and now (1941) employ about 1,600 workers.

COLUMBIAN PARK (R), in the eastern part of town, is a 35-acre municipal park with lakes, bridges, recreation facilities, and one of the largest zoos in Indiana.

On the slope leading down to the Wabash River is the TIPPECANOE COUNTY COURTHOUSE, a three-story square limestone structure built in 1882. A STATUE OF LAFAYETTE, NE. corner of the treeless courthouse lawn, is one of the early works of Lorado Taft (1860–1937). For many years it was generally forgotten that he had designed the statue. When the noted sculptor was reminded of the commission by a Purdue University professor, he wrote: 'The LaFayette [statue] was about the first order I had in Chicago as I arrived there with high hopes—and little else—the first day of 1886. It was a copy of Bartholdi's "LaFayette" in New York City that was required of me and one tiny photograph of that figure was all that was given me for data. I wonder at the temerity of youth, but I had to have the money and that supplies unlimited courage.'

Near the statue is the point from which a balloon ascended, on August 17, 1859, carrying the first airmail flown in the United States—23 circulars and 123 letters locked in a mail bag and addressed to New York City. The balloon failed to reach its destination by a wide margin; it landed at Crawfordsville, 27 miles south, and the mail completed its journey by train.

A business building, 622 Main St., stands on the SITE OF THE HOME OF GENERAL JOSEPH REYNOLDS, West Point classmate of General U. S. Grant. A bronze tablet relates how Grant was visiting Reynolds's home in LaFayette in 1861 just after he had been offered the commission of colonel of the Twenty-First Illinois Regiment by Governor Richard Yates. Grant had resigned his commission in the United States Army in 1854, and, at this time, was clerking in his father's leather store in Galena, Illinois. Discussing with Reynolds the offer of a colonel's commission, Grant said he was not capable of commanding a regiment of 1,000 men; he felt that he had been out of the service too long to hold so responsible a position. He said, however, that he would accept a commission as captain, and was about to wire Governor Yates rejecting his offer.

At this moment William F. Reynolds, Joseph's older brother and a railroad president, came into the house. When told of Grant's decision to reject a colonel's commission he said: 'Young man, you have been trained at the Government school and at public expense, and if you don't know how to command, who does? To whom are we to look in such times of peril—can't you accept? You have got to. What's a thousand men? I give orders to that many myself, and a railroad is not so much different from an army. Give me that telegraph blank. I will write your answer.' Reynolds wrote an acceptance and Grant signed it, thus beginning the military career that carried him to the command of the Union armies.

At 658 Main Street is the TIPPECANOE COUNTY HISTORICAL MUSEUM and the LAFAYETTE ART MUSEUM (*open 12–5 weekdays*). Among the exhibits in the Historical Museum are Tippecanoe battlefield mementoes, including a large wooden bowl made by the Indians; a Fort Ouiatenon collection that includes some Jesuit crosses; pioneer articles, dresses, and wedding gowns; mahogany furniture brought to this part of the country over the Wabash and Erie Canal; portraits by George Winter of Frances Slocum, Joseph Barron, and Francis Godfroy, last war chief of the Miami Indians; and the genealogy of the Marquis de LaFayette on 11 illuminated parchments. The Art Museum holds monthly exhibits of the work of Tippecanoe County artists from October to June.

In the ANN ELLSWORTH HOUSE, 7th and South Sts., the words for the first telegraph message sent by Samuel F. B. Morse, the inventor, were chosen. Morse had promised Miss Ellsworth the honor of sending the first words when his invention was perfected. Upon completion of the telegraph line between Baltimore and Washington in 1844, the inventor informed her that he was ready, and she sent him the message, 'What hath God wrought?'

The ROSS GEAR AND TOOL COMPANY PLANT (*visitors welcome*), 7th and Heath Sts., manufactures steering gears for all kinds of motor vehicles, including road graders, farm tractors, fire apparatus, and boats.

LaFayette is at the junction with State 25 (*see Tour 5b*).

1. Right from LaFayette on Ninth Street (Davis Ferry Road, paved) to REMAINS OF THE WABASH AND ERIE CANAL, 0.7 *m*. The piling that formed the base of the turn-bridge still stands in the center of the turn basin.

An INDIAN MOUND, 2 *m*., on the Priest Farm, is visible (R). A number of points, arrowheads, and celts have been taken from this mound.

BATTLEGROUND, 7 *m*. (584 alt., 506 pop.), now headquarters of the Northern Indiana Methodist Conference, was the scene of the Battle of Tippecanoe (*see History*). The BATTLEFIELD (*open*) on Burnett's Creek at the edge of town is a State and National park, a memorial to the soldiers of William Henry Harrison's command who lost their lives here on November 7, 1811. The triangular 16-acre park, enclosed by a high iron fence, precisely outlines the field of battle. (James Whitcomb Riley was shown around this historic spot, and all the circumstances of the battle were related to him by distinguished persons acting as guides. When asked if he had any questions, Riley is said to have replied, in the whimsical manner that so endeared him to the American people, 'How in the devil did the Indians get over that iron fence?') A 92-foot MONUMENT, with a life-size statue of General Harrison on one side, is near the northern entrance. Near by is a large, glass-encased pictorial map and a detailed account of the conflict between General Harrison's forces and the Indians led by the Prophet, brother of Tecumseh (*see Tour 17b*). The course of the battle, positions of the several units taking part, the points from which the Indian attacks were launched, and where casualties occurred are clearly shown.

The Battle of Tippecanoe, although a decisive defeat for the Indians, settled none of the problems that caused the conflict. The frontier was still unsafe, and Indian depredations against white settlers increased. However, Tippecanoe contributed to the prestige of General Harrison, and he went into the White House exactly 30 years later on the campaign slogan of 'Tippecanoe and Tyler Too.'

Tecumseh and his brother, the Prophet, were born in Ohio. Their father was a Shawnee warrior and their mother a Creek. Laulewasikaw (the man with the loud voice) later became known as the Prophet, and urged a return to the simple life—the golden age of the Indians when whisky-drinking and other habits acquired from the white man were unknown. Tecumseh (the-wild-cat-that-leaps-upon-its-prey, or the-shooting-star) planned a great Indian confederacy to include all tribes between the Great Lakes and the Gulf, the Alleghenies and the Rockies. Such a confederacy would, he believed, stop the piecemeal cessions of Indian lands to the Government. The teachings of the Prophet fitted in with Tecumseh's organizational plans, and 'what was at first a simple religious revival soon became a political agitation.'

In 1808 Tecumseh and the Prophet established a village on the Wabash

River at the mouth of Tippecanoe River. Prophet's Town soon became a thriving village; intoxicants were prohibited, crops were planted, and the village grew in size. When reports of closer co-operation between the British in Canada and Tecumseh and the Prophet in Prophet's Town reached Governor Harrison, he summoned Tecumseh to Vincennes.

Their conference lasted two weeks. Both parties expressed a desire for peace, but nothing was settled. A difficult situation was made worse when the Fort Wayne land cessions deprived the Indians of their last great hunting grounds in Indiana. Indian tribes rapidly joined Tecumseh's confederacy. After two more meetings with Harrison at Vincennes, Tecumseh proposed a truce while he visited Southern tribes, after which he planned to see President Madison in an effort to solve completely the difficulties existing between the two peoples.

Harrison then prepared to march on Prophet's Town. An army of 900 men, composed of 24 companies of regulars, militia, and Indians was organized. On November 6, within a few hundred yards of Prophet's Town, Harrison was met by Indians who asked for a peace council. He agreed, preferring to postpone his attack until the next morning. Camp was made for the night on Burnett's Creek about a mile from the Indian village. The troops built camp fires, and during the cold, rainy night slept on their arms, guarded by 100 sentries. Knowing that he might be attacked in the early morning, Harrison awoke about 4 A.M. and prepared to arouse his force. A single rifle shot followed by war cries and a volley of shots warned the whites that they must defend themselves. Fighting desperately, often hand-to-hand, it was only after daylight that the Indians were driven into a near-by swamp. Harrison's losses were heavy; 61 officers and men were killed and 127 seriously wounded. The Indian casualties were small. The next morning a body of mounted troops rode to Prophet's Town, now deserted, and burned the village.

The Prophet made a grave mistake by launching the attack on Harrison during Tecumseh's absence. He had told the Indians that they would be protected against the white man's bullets by his magic charms, which he brewed in a pot over the fire. After the battle, in an effort to justify his course of action, he blamed his squaw; she had broken the spell by touching the pot, thus causing the Indians' defeat. Prophet's Town was soon rebuilt, and, despite his loss of prestige, the Prophet came back to the village. Tecumseh returned from his Southern trip and expressed the opinion that had he been at Prophet's Town the attack on Harrison's force would not have occurred. Tecumseh agreed with the British that the Indians must be united before any general uprising should take place.

Left from Battleground on the Prophet's Rock Road is PROPHET'S ROCK, 1 *m.*, a stony elevation (R) from which the Prophet roared exhortations to the Indians he sent into battle. Over the intervening treetops the stone shaft marking the historic conflict is clearly visible. A marker has been placed at the base of the elevation.

2. Left from LaFayette on paved State 25 is WESTPOINT, 10.5 *m.* (626 alt., 300 pop.), a farm trading center on a knoll (L). Platted in 1833, the town is midway between LaFayette and Attica (*see Tour 20*), and was a place for eating and change of horses in stagecoach days.

ODELL, 15.5 *m.* (600 alt., 200 pop.), was named for Major John W. O'Dell, a soldier of the War of 1812 and the Black Hawk War. A settlement, O'Dell's Corners, sprang up soon after his arrival here in 1831. When a post office was established in 1871, the name was shortened to its present form.

At 16.5 *m.* is a junction with State 28; right on State 28 to ATTICA, 26 *m.* (550 alt., 3,760 pop.) (*see Tour 20a*), at the junction with US 41 (*see Tour 20*).

The main route, US 52B, crosses the Wabash River into WEST LAFAYETTE, 65.5 *m.* (545 alt., 6,270 pop.), home of PURDUE UNIVERSITY, an institution offering instruction in science, pharmacy, agriculture, engineering, and home economics to approximately 8,000 students (1941). The university, founded in 1874, owes its origin and academic specialization to the provisions of the Morrill Land-Grant Act of 1862, offering Federal lands to States for the founding of schools of agriculture and mechanic arts. The school receives both State and Federal funds, and bears the name of John Purdue, a LaFayette businessman who, with other Tippecanoe County citizens, offered $200,000 to establish the school on its present site. The GRAVE OF JOHN PURDUE is on the 115-acre campus (L), on Northwestern Avenue.

Other university holdings include 2,665 acres of farm and forest land used for instruction and experimental work in agriculture, an airport, and a housing project. Purdue carries on State-wide extension work in engineering and agriculture. A staff of 240 performs such diverse duties as building and testing strips of roadway, sampling soils, assisting county agricultural agents, organizing farm youths' clubs, or writing agricultural bulletins. The university also offers short courses, institutes, and meetings. Two-thirds of the resident students are citizens of Indiana; 43 other States and 17 foreign countries were (1939–40) represented in the student body.

Many of the academic buildings on the main campus are of red brick trimmed with stone. Administration and general purpose buildings include the EXECUTIVE BUILDING (1936); FOWLER HALL (1902), the auditorium; the LIBRARY (1913, 1933), housing 140,000 volumes; the MEMORIAL GYMNASIUM (1908) for women; PURDUE MEMORIAL UNION BUILDING (1928), which contains the studios of the university radio station, WBAA, and is the social center of the campus; and seven dormitories housing 400 men and a like number of women. Seven co-operative houses for men and three for women afford many students an opportunity to defray expenses by group living. About a fourth of the students are women.

Among the engineering buildings are HEAVILON HALL (1895), with a clock tower rising above the level, park-like campus, and separate structures for mechanical, chemical, and electrical engineering. In the LOCOMOTIVE MUSEUM are railway engines dating from 1858 to the present. The 224-acre PURDUE AIRPORT, first university airport in the country, provides hangar space for 15 planes, a weather bureau, three aeronautical laboratories, machine shop, classrooms, and office. This department of the university equipped the late Amelia Earhart's 'Flying Laboratory' plane.

The agricultural buildings include those housing the divisions of horticulture, agricultural chemistry, and poultry husbandry, many barns, greenhouses, and a livestock-judging pavilion. The departments of home economics, pharmacy, and education are each housed in separate buildings. Nearing completion (1941) are additional dormitories, a Hall of Music Auditorium to seat 6,200 persons, and a chemical and metallurgical engineering building.

The FIELDHOUSE AND GYMNASIUM for men, Northwestern Avenue, is a vast structure of red brick walls and glass block windows, erected in 1938. Behind it is the ROSS-ADE STADIUM, named for two Purdue alumni, David E. Ross (b.1871), LaFayette manufacturer, and George Ade, novelist and playwright (*see Tour 5b*).

A row of fraternity and sorority houses (R) overlooks the Wabash River. In this area also is the 143-acre PURDUE HOUSING RESEARCH CAMPUS, which contains several small houses, each designed and built for less than $5,000 by the Purdue Research Foundation to determine the architectural features and construction materials best suited to moderate-priced one-family dwellings.

1. Right from West LaFayette on paved State 43 is the INDIANA STATE SOLDIERS' HOME (*open*), 3 *m*. Beautifully situated on a 187-acre bluff overlooking the Wabash River with winding tree-bordered roadways leading up to it, the home has the military neatness and appearance of an army post. The community is complete in itself from hospital to commissary. The buildings range from barracks-like structures to snug cottages grouped around a landscaped oval on which an illuminated 20-foot fountain plays at night. The cottages were built by the several counties of the State for their veterans; maintenance is by the State and Federal Governments. The home is administered from the COLONEL'S MANSION (the superintendent of the institution is called 'the colonel' by the inhabitants). The colonel is the supreme authority of the 'village' and banishment is his weapon of extreme punishment. Founded in 1886 by the Grand Army of the Republic for the care of veterans of the Civil War, the home was taken over by the State in 1895 and subsequently expanded to provide for veterans of all wars, their wives, their widows, and army nurses.

2. Left from West LaFayette on the winding, tree-bordered South River Road (graveled) to the SITE OF FORT OUIATENON, 4 *m*. A blockhouse (L), erected in 1930, marks the site of the fort over which waved the flags of three nations. The reconstructed blockhouse is about 400 feet from the Wabash River and commands a good view in all directions. On one side, where the Indians grew their maize, corn is still cultivated. Along the river are summer vacation cottages.

The Ouiatenons, a tribe of Indians belonging to the Miami confederacy, came to this locality sometime prior to 1718, after having lived in central Wisconsin and at Fort St. Louis, on the Illinois River. La Salle, in an effort to protect the French fur trade in the Ohio and Wabash Valleys against the British and their Indian allies, the Iroquois, had organized a confederacy of Indians with headquarters at Fort St. Louis. Between 1671 and 1683 the Indiana tribes had emigrated to La Salle's headquarters, and the State was virtually depopulated. After La Salle's assassination the Indians returned to Indiana, the Ouiatenons coming to the Wabash.

In 1718 Ouiatenon (Ouia or Wea-town), situated on a hill on the north bank of the Wabash River four miles below the present site of LaFayette, was composed of five contiguous Indian villages and several miles of fields in which maize, melons, and pumpkins were cultivated. More than 1,000 warriors, their squaws, and children lived here. Lavishly painted, they played and danced incessantly. The reconstructed blockhouse now stands on the site of their fort.

Here the French established a fortified trading post—a dozen cabins surrounded by a stockade—in 1719 or 1720. It was an ideal spot for both trading post and Indian village. Near by were forests in which game was plentiful; the fertile soil was excellent for the primitive agricultural methods of the Indians; the Wea River, close by, provided fish in large quantities. Easy water transportation to the Great Lakes and to the Ohio River was a factor of importance to the French traders.

A garrison under the command of Sieur Dubuisson was established in 1720. He was succeeded by François Morgane, Sieur de Vincennes, who remained in command for several years. He founded Post Vincennes in 1732 or 1733, and was killed a few years later by hostile Chickasaw, who were allied with the

British. Grants of land were not made to settlers, and as a consequence Ouiatenon had only a small white population. The French, however, considered the post important from a military standpoint. For the next few decades—until the close of the French and Indian War—the post was constantly garrisoned against attempts by the British to obtain a foothold in the Ohio Valley.

With the surrender of Montreal in 1760, Canada and the Old Northwest became British territory and the French posts on the Wabash became British garrisons. In June 1763, during Pontiac's War, the British garrison at Ouiatenon was captured by Indians. By 1767 Ouiatenon was primarily an Indian rendezvous, although white fur traders still lived here. When the tribes decided to stop the advance of the white settlers into their hunting grounds, the meeting was held at Ouiatenon. Indian depredation against the whites followed, and, in order to stop what might develop into a large-scale Indian war, General Charles Scott received orders to destroy the Wea villages along the Wabash. In June 1791 an expedition of 800 cavalrymen rode into the Wabash country and destroyed Ouiatenon and Kethtippecanunk, sometimes called Upper Ouiatenon, which was located at the mouth of the Tippecanoe River. A second expedition against the Wabash Indians in August of the same year destroyed Kenapocomaqua, the Eel River village near the present site of Logansport, and completed the destruction of Ouiatenon and Kethtippecanunk. Kethtippecanunk, later rebuilt and called Prophet's Town (*see above*), became the headquarters of the Wabash Indians. Ouiatenon was never rebuilt.

At 67.9 *m.* is the junction with US 52, now the route.

MONTMORENCI, 73.7 *m.* (629 alt., 213 pop.), is a trading center for many fine surrounding farms, among them the 3,000-acre farm of Henry W. Marshall, LaFayette publisher and politician.

At 80.4 *m.* is CHESALONCHI PARK (R) (Ind.: beautiful spot), a part of the Benton County Fairgrounds when Dan Patch, one of the greatest harness race horses of all time, was trained here from 1898 to 1902. The track is still used for the training of harness horses.

Left from the park on State 352 (oil mat) is OXFORD, 2 *m.* (736 alt., 863 pop.), where in December 1896 Dan Patch was foaled on a manure pile back of KELLY'S LIVERY STABLE. The legend, 'Home of Dan Patch—1:55' is painted in large letters on the sloping stable roof. Dan Patch was destined to make the town famous. The bay colt, out of Zellica by Joe Patchen, of the famous Patchen stock, was long-legged and ungainly, with white feet and a white star on his forehead. Dan Messner, his owner, was disappointed by the colt's awkward appearance but, under the training of John Wattles, Dan Patch attained grace and a great reaching stride. A model of pacing form, he broke his own world's record for the mile many times, and, when 10 years old, paced that distance behind a windshield at the Minnesota State Fair in 1 minute, 55 seconds. This record stood until 1938 when it was equalled by Billy Direct without a windshield. Dan Patch changed hands several times, his last owner, M. W. Savage, of Minneapolis, paying $60,000 for him.

Oxford was, at one time, the seat of Benton County; the courthouse stood on the present site of the bandstand in TOWN PARK. A refreshment stand and a swimming pool, in ACADEMY PARK (L) occupy the site of an academy built in 1866.

FOWLER, 90.7 *m.* (796 alt., 1,903 pop.), seat of Benton County, is an attractive town with trees lining its downtown streets. The old-fashioned red brick courthouse at the eastern edge of the town is set among large, beautiful trees, apparently veterans of the virgin forest. The Benton Review Shop, a printing establishment specializing in catalogues and high school and college yearbooks, is the leading industry.

At 94.7 *m.* is a junction with US 41 (*see Tour* 20), which unites with US 52 for 10 miles.

EARL PARK, 97.9 *m.* (800 alt., 507 pop.) (*see Tour* 20*a*).

In KENTLAND, 104.7 *m.* (730 alt., 1,608 pop.) (*see Tour* 5*b*), is the northern junction with US 41 and a junction with US 24 (*see Tour* 5), which unites with US 52 to the Illinois Line at EFFNER, 108.7 *m.* (706 alt., 20 pop.), sometimes called State Line, two miles east of Sheldon, Illinois (*see Illinois Guide*).

↑↑

Tour 19

Indianapolis — Martinsville — Bedford — Paoli — Sulphur; State 37. 123.5 *m.*

Roadbed is high type bituminous and concrete throughout.
Route roughly paralleled by the Chicago, Indianapolis & Louisville (Monon) R.R. between Bloomington and Paoli.
Accommodations of all kinds at frequent intervals.

This route, extending from central to southern Indiana, first traverses rolling farm land, which gives way to high wooded bluffs and broad green valleys along the White River; orchards dot the hillsides of the limestone-quarrying region; and in the southern section is densely wooded knob country. Along the route are the Morgan-Monroe County State Forest, Spring Mill State Park, and a part of the proposed Hoosier National Forest.

INDIANAPOLIS, 0 *m.* (750 alt., 386,972 pop.) (*see Indianapolis*).

Indianapolis is at the junction with US 31 (*see Tour* 16), US 36 (*see Tour* 7), US 40 (*see Tour* 8), US 52 (*see Tour* 18), State 29 (*see Tour* 17*A*), and State 34 (*see Tour* 8*A*).

WAVERLY, 16 *m.* (650 alt., 100 pop.), lies between the highway and the White River (R). Founded in 1837, when the old Central Canal, a branch of the Wabash and Erie Canal, was being constructed, Waverly is a town of antiquated frame houses, most of them occupied by farmers. In early days the economic life centered about a large gristmill, a sawmill, and a woolen mill. At night, when the Irish canal workers gathered at the saloon, Waverly was a lively spot. It was the terminus of the Whetzel Trace (*see Tour* 18*a*), cut through 60 miles of wilderness from the east by Jacob Whetzel. Over this route came a majority of the early settlers of central Indiana. The dirt road that forms Waverly's one street is a part of the old trace.

At 23 *m.* is the junction with a graveled road.

Right on this road and across the White River to the junction with another graveled road, 3 *m.; L.* on this road to another junction, 4.2 *m.; L.* across a covered bridge spanning White Lick Creek is BROOKLYN, 4.5 *m.* (658 alt., 485 pop.), a thriving community of well-kept residences. Drain tile and brick are manufactured by Brooklyn's two plants; an almost inexhaustible mound of excellent fire clay, at the south edge of the village, provides the raw material.

BETHANY PARK (*cabins, boating, fishing, swimming*), south of Brooklyn, is maintained by the Christian Church of Indiana. West of the park is LAKE JEWELL, created by draining a swamp and erecting a dam.

GOLD CREEK, in the hills west of the park, was the scene of a gold rush in the early 1900's. An English engineer made an analysis of the waters of the creek and his report pictured the place as a second Klondike. A company was hurriedly formed and a prospectus circulated. Three million shares, par value $1, were offered to the public, no one person being permitted to purchase more than 200 shares. Prospectors rushed to the creek and sluiced its waters for 'pay dirt'; but 25¢ proved to be an exceptional return for a day's work and the gold rush came to a sudden end.

Right (west) from Bethany Park on a graveled road, 1.9 *m.*, is TANAGER HILL (*private*) and the LINK ASTRONOMICAL OBSERVATORY (*open by appointment; free*). Tanager Hill, the summer home of Dr. Goethe Link, Indianapolis surgeon, is at the head of Gold Creek on the edge of a glacial shelf overlooking a valley more than 300 feet below the observatory. In the twin-domed observatory building are a 5⅛-inch Zeiss triple glass refractor and a reflecting telescope with a polar axis 124 inches long resting upon concrete piers built on bedrock. The optical tube, made of Lynite, a duralumin alloy, was the first to be made of that metal. The glass mounted in the instrument is the result of a long series of experiments made by the Corning Glass Works in conjunction with the California Institute of Technology. The observatory is owned by the Goethe and Helen Link Foundation and supported by an endowment. A resident astronomer co-operates with the department of astronomy at Indiana University.

The aquarium and conservatory (R) of the GRASSY FORK FISHERIES (*open* 6:30 A.M.-6:30 P.M. *daily; free*), 27 *m.*, is one of the largest goldfish-breeding establishments in the United States. The 615 ponds, covering 275 acres, and the 216 hatching tanks are so terraced as to be continuously fed by the many springs on the 1,500-acre farm. Fifty million goldfish are hatched annually and sold in all parts of the world. The corporation's aquatic plants department grows more than 60 varieties of water lilies, as well as perennials, marsh and bog plants, and shallow water flowers for pools and rock gardens.

MARTINSVILLE, 29 *m.* (597 alt., 5,009 pop.), spreads out from a shaded public square around the red-painted brick courthouse built in 1859. The town is called the 'Artesian City' because of its therapeutic artesian waters, accidentally discovered many years ago when prospectors were drilling for gas. This water is now piped to several sanatoria treating arthritis, rheumatism, and kindred ailments. According to old-timers, the curative properties of the water were discovered when a broken-down race horse, retired to pasture, drank of an artesian well and was rejuvenated, later winning many races for his owner.

Martinsville was the boyhood home of two former Indiana governors,

Emmett Branch and Paul V. McNutt. Branch, born in Martinsville in 1874, served several terms as State representative, and was elected lieutenant governor in 1920. Succeeding Warren T. McCray as governor on April 30, 1924, Branch served until January 1, 1925. He died in Martinsville on February 23, 1932.

Paul V. McNutt was born in Franklin in 1891, and at the age of eight came to Martinsville, where his father opened a law office. After graduating from Indiana University and Harvard Law School he became dean of the Indiana University School of Law in 1925. He served as governor of Indiana from 1933 to 1937, was later named United States High Commissioner to the Philippines, and is now (1941) administrator of the Federal Security Agency.

Martinsville's factory district, along the railroad tracks south and west of the square, includes three grain mills and elevators, sawmills, a bucket factory, a factory making hickory rustic furniture, and two brick plants.

LOOKOUT POINT, a high hill at the north end of Patterson St., affords an excellent view of Martinsville and the White River Valley. This hill was once an Indian camp site and signal tower along the old Delaware trail.

Martinsville is at the junction with State 39 (*see Tour 19A*).

For two miles south from Martinsville the route is over a new concrete road built above the bottom land to escape the quick-rising flood waters of Indian Creek; it then twists into the hills, and at 38 *m.* passes the entrance (L) of the MORGAN-MONROE COUNTY STATE FOREST (*adm. free; shelter houses, picnic areas*). This rugged forest preserve of more than 13,000 acres was, before 1929, occupied by farmers attempting to scratch an existence by cultivating the hillsides and gullies. The timber was badly damaged by recurring forest fires, and the entire area was tax delinquent. Using mature and defective timber obtained from improvement cuttings, the administration buildings and barns were built by members of the Civilian Conservation Corps, which maintains a camp on the preserve. Moose, elk, and deer are enclosed in corrals, and wild game is carefully protected. Six artificial lakes, the largest 70 acres in area, have been completed. Connecting all developments are blacktop or stone roads; there are also fire lanes for the protection of the timber, which is oak, hickory, walnut, maple, and tulip poplar, ranging in age from 10 to 75 years. Reforestation has been so successful that the forest has been accepted as the experimental area for the Central States Experimental Station at Columbus, Ohio.

The highway curves through a rock-sided valley to CASCADE PARK (*adm. free; playground, swimming pool, picnic area*), 49 *m.*, owned by the adjacent city of Bloomington. In the 300-acre park are many high cliffs, deep ravines, and small waterfalls.

In BLOOMINGTON, 50.5 *m.* (753 alt., 20,870 pop.) (*see Tour 9*), is the junction with State 46 (*see Tour 9*). South of Bloomington the route enters a limestone region, a country of tumbled hills and many sink holes. General farming, dairying, and fruit growing—all on a small scale—are carried on in this area.

HARRODSBURG, 61 *m.* (516 alt., 400 pop.), a century-old village formerly called New Gene, lies (R) on the old Bedford Road a short distance from the main route. The town is the center for a number of small stone quarries.

OOLITIC, 69.5 *m.* (650 alt., 1,186 pop.), is almost an island of houses and streets on a hill surrounded by quarries and the Salt Creek bottoms. Named for the oölitic texture of its limestone, the town grew steadily when the building-stone business flourished and reached its peak in 1924. Since then, Oolitic and its building-stone industry have gradually declined. At the north edge of the town are the QUARRIES (*obtain permit at office*) of the Indiana Limestone Corporation. Near by are the scabbling and stacking yards of the same company, where in prosperous times huge blocks of stone were stacked 50 to 75 feet high, awaiting movement to the mills.

Right from Oolitic on paved State 54 is AVOCA, 2 *m.* (543 alt., 500 pop.), a quiet village built on the slopes of a hill. The AVOCA STATE FISH HATCHERY (*open 7–7 daily; free; guide*) is (L) one of six hatcheries operated by the State Department of Conservation for the propagation of game fish. On the hatchery grounds is the 'Doc' BRIDWELL HOUSE, built in the early 1840's. This rambling two-story Colonial-style house, framed with 4-by-4 and 8-by-8 yellow poplar beams secured by hickory pins, was used as a hotel and store as well as the home of 'Doc' Bridwell. It is now (1941) the residence of the hatchery superintendent. One hundred yards southwest of the old home is COLD WATER SPRING, which in pioneer days furnished power for a gristmill and a distillery. Traces of the old mill race still remain. The spring now supplies water for the hatchery pools and for the Bridwell house.

BEDFORD, 73.5 *m.* (703 alt., 12,514 pop.) (*see Tour* 10), is at the junction with US 50 (*see Tour* 10), with which State 37 unites southward to the White River bridge, 77 *m.*

The RED CROSS FARM, 78.5 *m.*, now privately owned, once belonged to the American Red Cross, having been bequeathed to that organization by Dr. Joseph Gardner, a Bedford physician. Clara Barton, founder of the Red Cross, used the LOG HOUSE (L), now a tourist tavern, as a part-time residence in the 1880's. Ownership of the farm reverted to the Gardner family when the Red Cross failed to live up to certain provisions of the bequest.

At 83.5 *m.* is the junction with State 60, an oil mat highway.

Left on State 60 is MITCHELL, 0.5 *m.* (685 alt., 3,393 pop.), a sprawling little city of wide main streets lined with old one- and two-story brick business buildings. A cement plant is the chief industry. Settlers took up land near the site of Mitchell as early as 1813, but not until after the Louisville, New Albany, and Salem Railroad (now the Monon) extended its line through Lawrence County nearly 40 years later was a town platted. After 1856, when the Ohio and Mississippi Railroad (now the Baltimore & Ohio) crossed the earlier line at this point, the town began to develop rapidly. It was named for O. M. Mitchell, construction engineer for the O. and M. and later a general in the Union Army.

SPRING MILL STATE PARK (*adm.* 10¢; *hotel, meals, picnicking and camping areas*), 2.5 *m.*, is a 1,978-acre area (L) established by the State

Department of Conservation in 1927 on land formerly occupied by Piankeshaw, Shawnee, and Delaware Indians. Part of it is virgin forest containing some of the largest trees in Indiana, and during the spring and summer nearly every variety of wild flower and bird indigenous to Indiana is found in the park.

Samuel Jackson, a Canadian, received a grant of land in this region from the United States Government as a reward for services in the War of 1812, and he built a gristmill operated by water piped from a cave through hollowed-out poplar logs. In 1816 he sold his claim to Thomas and Cuthbert Bullitt, who quarried limestone near by and constructed a three-story mill building that still stands (1941). Around this mill, one of the best in southern Indiana in its time, a village soon grew up; a distillery and tavern were established, and a boatyard furnished flatboats that carried meat, grain, and whisky to the New Orleans market. Part of the land now in the park was bought in 1860 by George Donaldson, a native of Scotland, who carefully preserved the forested area known today as Donaldson's Woods.

In the northwest section of the park is the PIONEER VILLAGE. On the main street, about 1,200 feet long, are a hat shop, tavern, cobbler shop, stillhouse, loom house, and a pottery plant, all reconstructed of logs. Log houses of long-dead Spring Mill villagers have been rebuilt and furnished with the household goods of a century ago. Formal gardens and wide sweeping lawns adjoin some of the old residences. Through the village sparkles a small stream, carried by an overhead flume to the MILL, in which an overshot water wheel and wooden gears creak ponderously, operating stone burrs that grind corn. Water also furnishes power for the slash mill where a saw slowly slips back and forth through large logs. Articles used on backwoods farms and in homes are exhibited on the second and third floors of the mill.

Other attractions of the park include marked hiking trails; an 80-room hotel overlooking an artificial lake; DONALDSON'S CAVE with long, narrow punts (*boat trip* 10¢) on its underground river in which swim blind fish; and TWIN CAVES (*boat trip* 10¢) where a river flows briefly in the open between two caverns. Such caves are a part of the complicated limestone drainage system underlying the cavern region of Indiana and Kentucky.

ORLEANS, 88.8 *m.* (639 alt., 1,428 pop.), an orchard and dairy center, has a large co-operative creamery as its principal industry. Founded in March 1815, two months after General Jackson's victory at New Orleans—from which it got its name—Orleans is the oldest town in Orange County. Almost nine-tenths of its present population are direct descendants of the early settlers of this region.

The highway crosses LOST RIVER, 92.8 *m.*, an elusive stream occupying underground and surface channels by turns, depending upon the amount of rainfall. East and west of the highway, the river is a surface stream, but here the depressed bed is often dry.

PAOLI, 96.5 *m.* (638 alt., 2,218 pop.) (*see Tour 12*), is at the junction with US 150 (*see Tour 12*) and State 56 (*see Tour 11*).

At 101.8 *m.* is the ORANGE COUNTY FIRE TOWER (*visitors welcome*), 100 yards (L). Miles of densely forested hills and valleys are visible from the tower, one of a score erected and maintained by the State Department of Conservation as a preliminary step in the development of the Hoosier National Forest. An area of 545,000 acres in Orange County and other counties reaching from Bloomington to the Ohio River constitute the Purchase Unit of the forest. Of this area 84 per cent is now timberland or is returning to timberland; the remainder is eroded or has lost so much top soil that it is useless for farming. The purpose of this national forest is to build up a future supply of timber from Indiana hardwoods, and to provide for the protection and propagation of wild life and for public recreational areas.

ENGLISH, 113.7 *m.* (530 alt., 757 pop.), lying in a deep valley and on the slopes of undulating hills, was platted in 1839. At the time of the Civil War it was still only a cluster of cabins and a store; its real development dates from 1893 when it became the county seat. The courthouse, built of native stone and red brick, overlooks the southern part of the community from Courthouse Hill. Water from 11 springs on the hills surrounding English flows by gravity to the mains and circulates constantly. A bronze STATUE OF WILLIAM HAYDEN ENGLISH (*see Tour* 11), for whom the town was named, is in a small park at the western edge of the town.

The country in this vicinity is rough and heavily wooded and has not been affected greatly by modern civilization. There are many small cabins and shacks, built on the hillsides along the winding road, and corn, tobacco, and vegetables are grown in small patches in clearings. Not only is the absence of automobiles noticeable, but also the absence of the horse and buggy, for here the horse, minus the buggy, is the chief means of transportation. During the hunting season men and boys, carrying long-barreled guns of ancient vintage, roam the fields and forest in search of small game. Life here differs but little from the days when Indiana was a wilderness.

SULPHUR, 123.5 *m.* (800 alt., 27 pop.) (*see Tour* 11*A*), is at the junction with State 62 (*see Tour* 11*A*), the southern terminus of the route.

↗↗↗

Tour 19A

Martinsville—Spencer—Worthington—Bicknell—Vincennes; State 39 and State 67. 83.4 *m.*

Concrete roadbed throughout.
Indianapolis-Vincennes Division of Pennsylvania R.R. roughly parallels entire route.
Accommodations at frequent intervals; hotels in larger cities.

Generally following the winding course of the west fork of White River, this route runs through heavily wooded country, dipping into valleys planted almost wholly in corn, and climbing hills where outcroppings of limestone and sandstone form steep cliffs. Set in the heart of this rugged area is a 25-mile stretch of flat land, formerly a vast marsh, that has been converted by the use of drainage ditches into one of the State's most productive agricultural regions. Farther south is a rolling section where the farm lands are interspersed with the tipples and dumps of coal mines. Here most of the people show traces of their European ancestry; customs and holidays retain the flavor of the Scottish, French, Italian, Polish, or Greek villages from which many of the residents migrated. On the route are a number of sleepy towns that have seen more prosperous days. Many of them boomed during the canal-building period 100 years ago, and others were thriving mining communities until they were caught in the coal industry's slump, which has left thousands unemployed.

State 39 branches west (R) from State 37 (*see Tour* 19) at MARTINSVILLE, 0 *m.* (597 alt., 5,009 pop.) (*see Tour* 19).

At the west end of the WHITE RIVER BRIDGE, 1 *m.*, is the junction (L) with State 67, now the route. Southwestward for 17 miles State 67 has been relocated to avoid grade crossings and sharp curves. Abandoned sections of the old blacktop road twist back and forth on both sides of the new concrete highway.

WHITAKER, 11.2 *m.* (653 alt., 25 pop.), is a sawmill hamlet with huge stacks of rough lumber along the highway.

> Right from Whitaker on a graveled road to the junction with another graveled road, 3.5 *m.*; L. on this road is PORTER'S CAVE (*adm. free*), 5.2 *m.*, approximately 100 yards (L). The mouth of the cave is high up on a stone bluff, and from it flows a stream to form a cascade below the entrance to the cave. Numerous cold water springs that emerge from rocky sides of the cavern form a creek that flows through its entire length. In this cave, which is between 10 and 18 feet high and 10 to 30 feet wide, are many stalactite and stalagmite formations. It is possible to enter the cave at this entrance and emerge at another opening about three-quarters of a mile north.

GOSPORT, 16.1 *m.* (595 alt., 729 pop.), is a quiet village (L) directly on the Ten O'Clock Line, established by the terms of a treaty between William Henry Harrison and the Indians at Fort Wayne in 1809 (*see History*). Platted in 1829, Gosport was once a prominent shipping point for the flatboat trade that flourished on the White River; a large pork-slaughtering house also carried on a great volume of business here. The village subsequently declined and is now largely residential.

The White River, which marks the Owen-Monroe County Line at the southeast edge of Gosport, is crossed on a bridge, half of steel girders and half of the wooden covered type. Each half was built according to the preferences of the county in which it stands.

> Left from Gosport on old State 67 is ROMONA, 4.4 *m.* (577 alt., 91 pop.), a sprawling cluster of dilapidated one-story structures that house quarry workers. Here is the ROMONA QUARRY (*visitors welcome*) of the Ingalls Stone Company, one of the largest limestone quarries in Indiana.
> An eccentric old bachelor named Adam Brinton laid out this village in 1819 and called it Brintonville, hoping that it would become the county seat. Intending to get rich from the sale of lots, Brinton hired a minister of ques-

tionable repute to run up the price at the auction. The people of the surrounding country, aware of this scheme, refused to bid, so the lots were undeveloped for years until the price became reasonable.

At 17.1 *m.* on State 67 is the junction with a graveled road.

Right on this road is 45-acre HOLLYBROOK LAKE (*adm. free; 10¢ per day to fish from bank; boats $1.25 per day; cabins*), 0.5 *m.*, a privately owned lake encircled by shady hillsides, and popular for swimming and fishing.

SPENCER, 24.7 *m.* (577 alt., 2,375 pop.) (*see Tour 9*), is at the junction with State 46 (*see Tour 9*).

FREEDOM, 33.6 *m.* (534 alt., 300 pop.), a languid village, gives ample evidence of the fact that it is more than a century old. One hundred yards from the highway (L) is a COVERED BRIDGE.

At 41.8 *m.* are junctions with two graveled roads, 60 feet apart.

1. Left on the first road to the junction with a country lane, 0.5 *m.;* R. on this lane to the DEVIL'S TEA TABLE ROCK, 0.7 *m.*, on a high hill (L) overlooking a railroad and the cornfields of the White River bottom lands. This rock, which closely resembles a gigantic table, has long been a landmark. According to tradition, its broad, flat top was used as a lookout point by the Indians for centuries. All over the rock are carved the names of six or seven generations of residents of the vicinity and the names of many visitors, with dates ranging over a period of 120 years.

2. Left on the second road, which turns sharply L., is the SITE OF OLD POINT COMMERCE, 0.2 *m.* A two-story red brick house and a half-dozen small decrepit frame dwellings on a hilltop overlooking the old bed of White River (now a cornfield) are all that remain of Point Commerce. The town reached the zenith of its importance just prior to the heyday of canal transportation in Indiana.
Immediately after the passage of the Internal Improvement Bill of 1836, it was decided that the two canals provided for by the bill should be joined at the mouth of the Eel River. Realizing the possibilities of this site, the Allison brothers of Spencer bought the land in 1836 and laid out Point Commerce. A flourishing little town, with a population of 500 in 1848, it was a receiving point for merchandise from eastern markets and in turn shipped about 15 boatloads of produce every year. But it dwindled and was finally pushed into oblivion by the routing of the Wabash and Erie Canal through near-by Worthington. The river, which formerly came to the foot of the hill on which Point Commerce was situated, is now about a quarter of a mile east of this point.

WORTHINGTON, 42.7 *m.* (520 alt., 1,729 pop.), which owes its existence to the building of the Wabash and Erie Canal, suffered a setback with the abandonment of canal shipping. The Indianapolis and Vincennes R.R. (now the Pennsylvania R.R.) rescued the town from oblivion and it has drifted along as a small residential community.

WORTHINGTON CITY PARK (*camping grounds*), at the north end of town, formerly contained a mammoth sycamore tree, cut down several years ago, that measured 43 feet 3 inches in circumference at the base and stood 150 feet high. A limb of this tree, on display in the park, is larger than the trunks of most trees in Indiana.

SWITZ CITY, 49 *m.* (527 alt., 405 pop.), is a sprawling crossroad village on a slight elevation in otherwise flat farming country. Many of the villagers are employed in the near-by strip-mining coal fields.

Right from Switz City on paved State 54 is LINTON, 5.8 *m.* (530 alt., 6,263 pop.), a mining town in one of the most productive coal fields in Indiana. Linton reflects the rugged character of the inhabitants, who work hard all week in the mines and play hard at Saturday night dances in the Moose Hall and the Knights of Pythias Hall. The atmosphere is one of rough congeniality and friendliness. The mines have attracted a mixed population of Scots, Poles, Hungarians, and French, who have mingled with the original German and English strains. The town is compactly arranged with old red brick buildings crowding the downtown street corners. Although the largest community in Greene County, Linton is not the county seat, and so lacks the spacious public square of the typical southern Indiana small city. There are some pretentious residential streets, but coal mines come up to the very doors of the city. Behind the high school, in the northern part of town, great spoil banks rear up beyond the athletic field.

Right from Linton on a rock road to the junction with a country road, 0.7 *m.;* R. on this road, 1.1 *m.*, to a group of stripper hills (L); L. over a footpath across the hills to the CENTER OF POPULATION OF THE UNITED STATES (1930 census), 1.4 *m.*, designated by a tapering monument about six feet high of lacquered coal mounted on a concrete base. The term 'center of population,' as used by the Bureau of the Census, is that point which may be considered as the center of gravity of the United States. In other words, it is the pivot point at which the United States would 'balance,' assuming that all individuals were of equal weight. This center is thus affected not only by the numbers of persons at different points in the country, but also by the distance of each individual from the center. For 160 years the center of population in the United States has been moving gradually westward; since 1890 it has been in Indiana.

LYONS, 53.2 *m.* (516 alt., 794 pop.), a trading center, holds an annual fair on the last three days of the third week in September. All kinds of stock, agricultural products, needlework, and baking and canning specimens are on display.

WESTPHALIA, 63.8 *m.* (461 alt., 200 pop.), like most German communities, is meticulously clean and wholesome in appearance, with a pronounced atmosphere of comfortable well-being. The village is an offspring of the older German village of Freelandville, six miles west. The social life of the community centers around the only church, the German Evangelical Lutheran, which stands on a grassy knoll (R) at the northwestern end of the village.

EDWARDSPORT, 68.2 *m.* (456 alt., 850 pop.), lies (L) between the highway and the White River on a slight elevation. It was for many years a prominent flatboat landing place and owes its present site to that fact. The tall chimneys of a POWER PLANT (*visitors welcome; guides*) of the Indiana Public Service Company can be seen from any point in town. Here water from the White River and coal from near-by strip mines are used to generate electric power for many cities of southwestern Indiana.

BICKNELL, 73 *m.* (489 alt., 5,110 pop.), is surrounded by coal mines. The miners dwell at the outskirts of town in boxlike frame structures, many of them painted in solid reds, greens, and yellows. The streets are narrow and for the most part dingy, typical of most coal-mining towns. The first local mine was dug in 1875; others soon followed and Bicknell grew with the industry. At the peak of production in 1926, 14 mines were listed in the Bicknell field; today (1941) 8 mines are in operation. About 25 per cent of Bicknell's population is foreign-born, or of foreign-born stock, including Scottish, English, French, Italians, a few Bulgarians, Belgians, Lithuanians, Poles, and Greeks.

The Scots, most of whom reside in the northwestern part of Bicknell, are probably the most homogeneous group. They are a thrifty, industrious people proud of their membership in the Presbyterian Church and the Clan Cameron. 'Bobbie' Burns's birthday (January 25) and New Year's, or 'Rugmanae,' are occasions for hilarious gatherings. Scottish ballads are sung and bagpipes accompany participants in the Highland fling. Shortbread, Scotch buns, and fruit dumplings are washed down with ginger wine, and the celebrants revert temporarily to the pleasures and customs of their native land.

Ernest P. Bicknell (1862–1930), a descendant of the founder of the town and former national vice chairman of the American Red Cross, spent the early years of his life on a farm near by. At various times Bicknell directed Red Cross activities in Europe, Asia, and North and South America. At the time of his death he was in charge of the Red Cross insular operations.

Left from Bicknell on Main Street to a junction with a paved road, 2.3 *m.;* R. on this road to RAGSDALE, 3.3 *m.* (490 alt., 54 pop.), a straggly little settlement of miners who are employed at the large coal mine near by.

Left from Ragsdale on a blacktop and coal road is the AMERICAN No. 1 MINE (*not open to public*), 3.9 *m.,* one of the largest and best-known deep coal mines in Indiana. This mine has four times held the world's record for tonnage of coal hoisted in one eight-hour day. The last record set by the mine was on June 5, 1926, when 7,157 tons were hoisted. Today the average daily output of 3,300 tons is surpassed by better-equipped mines. Employment has decreased from about 1,100 men at peak production to some 400 at the present time (1941).

BRUCEVILLE, 77.5 *m.* (504 alt., 700 pop.), is a placid hilltop town, first settled by Major William Bruce in 1805. Fear of hostile Indians led to the building of a fort on the Bruce farm, and the founding of Bruceville in 1811. It subsequently became a flourishing village, but with the development of towns that were more advantageously situated, it was forced into the background. It enjoyed a transitory revival in 1914, when a coal mine was sunk near the town. Stimulated by the employment of between 300 and 400 men, the community reveled in a newly acquired prosperity—but not for long. After an explosion in 1919 the mine was worked for brief periods and then abandoned in 1923. Many Bruceville residents moved to other localities and several of the houses were torn down and taken away. The community consequently returned to its present status of an agricultural village.

State 550 (Bruceville's Main Street) winds up the hill through the town, past its little business block to the old Christian Church (L). Just behind this church is the old BRUCE HOUSE (*adm. frce*), a one-story red brick house of four rooms on the corner of Washington and Back Streets. Completed in 1811 by Major William Bruce, it was originally a large two-story structure, but the upper portion was torn away by a storm many years ago. In this house Major Bruce reared his family of 25 children and kept a tavern where travelers rested overnight before dashing for the Vincennes land office at daybreak. Here, in 1844, came a tall, gaunt stranger accompanied by Judge Abner T. Ellis, of Vincennes (*see Vincennes*). After eating a hearty supper, about 'early candle-lighting time,' they were escorted by their host one block north to an old schoolhouse that stood opposite the present Christian Church, in the middle of a GROVE OF WALNUT TREES. Here the stranger, a young Illinois lawyer named Abraham Lincoln, made a speech in behalf of Henry Clay, Whig candidate for the presidency. The meeting had hardly begun when a large group of Democrats, who also had a meeting scheduled, appeared on the scene. For a time it seemed that bloodshed could not be avoided, but the riot was finally quelled; whereupon Lincoln, who had sat calmly waiting until the trouble was over, resumed his speech. Lincoln slept in the Bruce home that night and continued his trip the next morning.

The old Bruce home is unoccupied, but is still furnished much as it was when Lincoln spent the night there almost a century ago.

At 81.3 *m.* is the junction with US 41 (*see Tour* 20), with which State 67 unites to VINCENNES, 83.4 *m.* (422 alt., 18,228 pop.) (*see Vincennes*).

In Vincennes are junctions with US 41 (*see Tour* 20), US 50 (*see Tour* 10), and US 150 (*see Tour* 12).

↑↑

Tour 20

(Chicago, Ill.)—Hammond—Kentland—Terre Haute—Vincennes—Evansville—(Henderson, Ky.); US 41.
Illinois Line to Kentucky Line, 282.6 *m.*

Concrete roadbed, two- to four-lane, throughout.
Route paralleled by New York Central R.R. between Hammond and Kentland; by Chicago, Attica & Southern R.R. between Attica and Sterling; and by Chicago & Eastern Illinois R.R. between Terre Haute and Evansville.
Accommodations of all kinds at frequent intervals.

A direct route from Michigan to Florida, US 41 is heavily traveled by tourists and businessmen from Chicago, Milwaukee, and other Northern cities. It runs almost due north and south through Indiana, skirting the western border of the State for its entire length, and passing through several important cities. To the north is Hammond, one of the busy, smoky cities of the Calumet. Southward are Terre Haute, long an industrial center and the birthplace of Eugene Debs, Theodore Dreiser, and Paul Dresser; and Evansville, trade outlet since 1820 for southern Indiana. For many miles the route roughly parallels the Wabash River, traversing country through which William Henry Harrison, Indian fighter and President of the United States, marched with his militia on their way to meet the forces of Tecumseh and the Prophet at the Battle of Tippecanoe. Near Terre Haute, midway through the State, is the site of Fort Harrison, successfully defended against a large force of Indians during the War of 1812 by 50 soldiers led by Captain Zachary Taylor, also destined to become President.

Section a. ILLINOIS LINE to TERRE HAUTE, 172 m.

After leaving the highly populated region of the Calumet cities, US 41 abruptly enters a prairie devoted to corn growing and dairy farming. Nearly every foot of the rich black soil is under cultivation, and even the meadows, in which herds of beef cattle graze during the summer months, are almost entirely free from trees, wildflowers, and vines. Farther south the land becomes less level, and in this region is Turkey Run State Park, a wild and rugged area of deep canyons, winding streams, and timberland.

US 41 crosses the ILLINOIS LINE, 0 m., at the Chicago city limits.

HAMMOND, 6.4 m. (598 alt., 70,184 pop.) (see Hammond).

Hammond is at the junction with US 12 (see Tour 2) and US 20 (see Tour 1).

South of Hammond, US 41 passes through a region of intensive truck farming. Large crops of garden produce are raised here by hard-working Dutch landowners.

MUNSTER, 10.3 m. (616 alt., 1,751 pop.) (see Tour 3), is at the junction with US 6 (see Tour 3) with which US 41 unites eastward for two miles to HIGHLAND (650 alt., 2,723 pop.) (see Tour 3).

At 17 m. is the junction with US 30 (see Tour 4).

The route continues south on a busy, four-lane concrete highway to SAINT JOHN, 19.8 m. (702 alt., 383 pop.), a community of Catholic farmers.

At 26 m. is the junction with a concrete road.

> Left on this road is CEDAR LAKE, 1.5 m. (695 alt., 500 pop.), a summer resort on a forest-rimmed lake (hotel, cabins, boats for rent) of the same name. From a high bluff on its eastern shore, near the public bathing beach, is a view of the entire lake and the village on the opposite shore, with the Franciscan monastery, formerly a clubhouse, in the background.

CUMBERLAND LODGE (open), 37.1 m., is an old hunting lodge (R) built by a Lord Parker, an Englishman, when houses in this region were few and taverns fewer. The lodge stands at the edge of what was once the desolate Kankakee Marsh, which abounded in wild game.

SUMAVA RESORTS (pronounced Soom'uh-vuh), 40.7 *m.* (636 alt., 70 pop.), with its mile-long water front on the wooded Kankakee River, is a popular recreational center.

LAKE VILLAGE, 42.8 *m.* (660 alt., 250 pop.), was so named because before the site was reclaimed by artificial drainage it was swampy wasteland. The surrounding region is excellent for farming, and raising milk goats is one of the principal occupations.

MOROCCO, 56.4 *m.* (653 alt., 1,151 pop.), is a quiet farming town in a region that was known years ago as Beaver Prairie because its streams teemed with beavers.

At 62.5 *m.* is the junction with State 16, a paved road.

Left on State 16 is BROOK, 3.5 *m.* (653 alt., 888 pop.), home of the Hess Manufacturing Company, makers of cosmetics. The industry began here when a local druggist started to concoct witch hazel lotion in copper clothes boilers on an old kitchen stove. The factory still occupies a small building, but modern equipment has increased the daily output to over 20,000 packages.

HAZELDEN (*private*), 5 *m.*, home of George Ade, Indiana author and humorist (*see Tour 5b*), is set in spacious lawns and gardens. The rambling building with its high gabled roof resembles an English manor house.

KENTLAND, 69.5 *m.* (680 alt., 1,608 pop.) (*see Tour 5b*), is at the junction with US 24 (*see Tour 5*) and US 52 (*see Tour 18*), with which US 41 unites south and southwest for 10 miles.

EARL PARK, 76.1 *m.* (660 alt., 507 pop.), is an attractive town of wide streets shaded by rows of towering maple trees. At the southwestern edge of town is a MONUMENT TO EDWARD C. SUMNER, one-time cattle baron who owned 35,000 acres of land near by. PARISH GROVE, near the monument, is named for Chief Parish, a Kickapoo who, according to legend, fell to his death from one of the giant trees.

At 79.2 *m.* is the southern junction with US 52, which continues southwest; US 41 turns due south.

BOSWELL, 88.7 *m.* (756 alt., 877 pop.), a busy town catering to tourists and truckers, is the only settlement on a 25-mile stretch of US 41.

CARBONDALE, 100.3 *m.* (756 alt., 50 pop.), is on the route followed by General William Henry Harrison when he marched his army to the Battle of Tippecanoe (*see Tour 18b*). According to local tradition, the sound of Harrison's marching army may still be heard on the trail, the shouts of the men and the sound of bugles and drums growing in volume as the phantom army approaches, and then fading as the ghostly files pass into the quiet night.

At 105.7 *m.* is the junction with a graveled road.

Left on this road is KRAMER, 3.2 *m.* (750 alt., 1,200 pop.), the home of the MUDLAVIA HOTEL AND RESORT. The therapeutic properties of the soil in this neighborhood were accidentally discovered by John Story, an early settler. While digging on his land, he noticed that the rheumatism with which he had been afflicted for years had suddenly left him. All the rheumatics of the community applied themselves industriously to the ditch-digging cure with equally gratifying results. It remained for H. L. Kramer, for whom the town was named, to realize the commercial possibilities of the site. He built a resort hotel and called it the Fountain of Youth. The hotel was leveled by fire in 1920 and not rebuilt until 1934. In the intervening years the little town languished and its population scattered. Now it is slowly regaining its former proportions.

At 106.3 *m.* on the main route is a junction with State 28, a concrete road.

Right on State 28 is WILLIAMSPORT, 1 *m.* (668 alt., 1,222 pop.), seat of Warren County since 1828. Reputedly named for General William Henry Harrison, who owned land on this site, the town was nicknamed 'Side Cut City' during the Wabash and Erie Canal days. A local subscription of $16,000 made it possible to dig a 'spur' of the canal to the town, thereby ushering in a boom for the merchants. In 1856, the Wabash Railroad reached the town and the population shifted back from the rise along the river, still known as Old Town.

Cannon from the Civil War stand on the lawn before the domed WARREN COUNTY COURTHOUSE, the fourth erected in Williamsport. The first two burned to the ground, and the third, built in the early '70's, was torn down to make room for the present structure in 1907. South of the business district, in the rear of the municipal light plant, are the WILLIAMSPORT FALLS, where Fall Creek drops over a 55-foot sandstone ledge. From the falls a mile-long canyon, fringed with sandstone cliffs, leads eastward to the Wabash River. A well-preserved STONE HOUSE (*private*), originally built as a tavern in 1853, stands on Old Town Hill; it is a two-story structure with huge recessed doorways and shutters on the first floor windows.

At 107.6 *m.* on US 41 is the junction with a blacktop road.

Left on this road is INDEPENDENCE, 5.5 *m.* (521 alt., 178 pop.), a peaceful village on the banks of the Wabash River. Here lived Zachariah Cicot (1781–1850), a French-Indian trader and scout for General William Henry Harrison's expeditionary army. Son of a French father and a Potawatomi mother, Cicot became one of the leaders of his tribe, stoutly hostile to Tecumseh and the Prophet, whom he considered tools of the British. Tecumseh banished Cicot from all the tribes of the Indian confederacy, including his own, just at the time General Harrison was planning his expedition. Remembering Cicot's former services as a scout and informer, the General called him to guide the army from Vincennes to the Prophet's town at Tippecanoe.

Before his expulsion from the tribes Cicot had fallen in love with a Kickapoo girl whose English name was Kate, and the two lovers continued to meet. At their last tryst, Kate told Cicot of a planned Indian ambuscade of Harrison's troops. Thus informed, he was able to guide Harrison's army safely around the ambush. Kate's act of treachery was discovered and by decree of the council she was drowned in a near-by pond. Later, Cicot married Pecequat, daughter of Chief Perig, and founded the town of Independence in 1832 on ground given him by the Government for his services. He died in 1850 and is buried in the INDEPENDENCE CEMETERY, a short distance northwest of the town.

At 107.9 *m.* US 41 crosses the Wabash River, Indiana's largest waterway, and one of vital importance in the early settlement of the Midlands.

ATTICA, 108.3 *m.* (550 alt., 3,760 pop.), is a compact and attractive trading town with a business section that is crowded daily with shoppers and farmers from the surrounding countryside. Its wide streets, shaded by great trees, its neat houses and clean, closely grouped business buildings give the town a prosperous air. The principal industries are the manufacture of overalls, steel castings, and brick. The HARRI-

SON STEEL CASTINGS COMPANY PLANT (*open*), manufacturing railroad car couplers, is the town's largest factory, and employs about 450 men.

There was a famous Potawatomi settlement here. In a great war council held at the SITE OF THE TECUMSEH COUNCIL OAK, 206 Perry St., Tecumseh and chiefs of the Kickapoo, Potawatomi, and the Winnebago laid the foundations for the Indian military alliance crushed by General Harrison at the Battle of Tippecanoe (*see Tour 18b*). In 1866 the tree was felled to obtain timber for the FRANK MERRICK HOUSE on Jackson Street. Also on the site of Attica lived Topenebee, chief of the Potawatomi, who fought in the unsuccessful Indian defense of Ouiatenon and in the Indian defeat at Fallen Timbers (*see Fort Wayne*). Topenebee was one of the signers of the Treaty of Greenville in 1795.

Attica grew into a town in the late 1840's with the extension of the Wabash and Erie Canal. Competition between the stagecoach companies and canal transportation companies brought about the construction of docks and additional warehouses and stables. REMAINS OF THE STONE STEPS leading down to the old canal boat landings are at the foot of Main Street.

Early in the operation of the canal, Attica and Covington (*see Tour 8A*) fought a 'canal war.' Edward A. Hannegan (*see Tour 8A*), later a United States senator and minister to Prussia, led an invading mob of 300 indignant Covington citizens into Attica to protest that Attica was hoarding the canal water supply. They opened the Attica floodgates at Jackson and Washington Streets and, in the fight that ensued, Hannegan knocked Zeke McDonald, leader of the defending Atticans, into the canal. McDonald made it a point to visit Covington soon afterward and search out his assailant. He met Hannegan on the street and, explaining that he had sworn to whip the man who had pushed him into the canal, gave the future statesman a beating.

Attica's most prominent citizen was Dr. John Evans (1814–97). As a young physician he predicted to friends that, before he died, he would build a city, found a college, govern a State, serve in the United States Senate, and amass a fortune. His friends expressed concern for his mental health, but Dr. Evans came little short of attaining the ambitious schedule he set for himself. In 1842 he was elected to the Indiana legislature, introduced a bill that brought about the establishment of the Central Hospital for the Insane at Indianapolis, and became the institution's first superintendent. He took a leading part with Orrington Lunt in the founding of Northwestern University in 1854, selecting Evanston (named for him), Illinois, as the site. In 1862 President Lincoln made him Territorial Governor of Colorado. Upon his resignation from this office in 1865 the Territory of Colorado sought admission to the Union as a State and elected him to the United States Senate. President Johnson denied the petition for statehood and Dr. Evans failed to serve in the Senate. At Denver, he founded the Colorado Seminary, now the University of Denver, gave $200,000 to the school at the outset, and later settled upon it a large endowment. For

full measure, he built a railroad in Colorado and became its president.
Attica is at the junction with State 28 (*see Tour* 18).

STERLING, 121.5 *m.* (605 alt., 350 pop.), a cluster of gasoline stations and tree-shaded homes strung along both sides of US 41 at its
intersection with State 34 (*see Tour* 8A), is a suburb of Veedersburg
(*see Tour* 8A).

At 138 *m.* is (L) JUNGLE PARK (*hotel, cabins, meals; adm. on race
days* 75¢, *grandstand* 50¢ *additional*), featuring a half-mile asphalt
automobile race track. Races, with an average of 35 cars participating,
are held once each month during the summer.

At 138.6 *m.* is the junction with State 47 (paved).

Left on State 47 to TURKEY RUN STATE PARK (*adm.* 10¢; *lodge,
camping, picnicking; nature study guides*), 1.7 *m.*, 1,300 acres of virgin timberland cut through by deep canyons, gorges, and winding streams. Geologic
formations that antedate the glacial period, and many native species of trees,
shrubs, flowers, birds, and wild life make the park especially interesting. The
yew tree, rare in the Middle West, grows profusely at Turkey Run. It was
this park, unsurpassed by any in the State for beauty, that inspired the
State's present conservation program. The park was named for the great flocks
of wild turkey once common to the region. Foot and bridle paths cover the
park, passing along the cliffs, through gorges, over a swinging bridge, and
into groves of giant trees.

SUGAR CREEK winds through the park, affording bathing, canoeing, and
fishing. A LOG CHURCH, built in 1871 on Brisley Ridge in Sugar Creek Township and later abandoned, was moved to the western part of the park in 1923,
and is used each Sunday throughout the summer for services. Near the eastern
edge is the LUSK HOMESTEAD, a two-story red brick structure built in 1841
when utility and permanence were the required qualities in a residence. It is a
seven-room house with a gabled roof, a louvered cupola, and a two-story
portico. With the exception of the glass (there are 15 panes in each of the
eight front windows) and a small amount of wrought iron, the entire house
was built from materials produced on the Lusk estate.

Captain Salmon Lusk was given 1,000 acres by the Government as a reward
for military service and it was here that John Lusk was born, lived all his
life, and acquired a reputation for eccentricity. After the deaths of his parents,
John Lusk lived alone for 35 years until his death in 1915. A recluse with
strong likes and dislikes, fearful and suspicious of people, he was especially
apprehensive of members of the Masonic order, believing they planned to
poison him. His love for the forest in which he lived and his repeated refusals
to sell it for large sums of money offered by timber interests saved it for
the State. The Indiana Department of Conservation purchased the estate in
1919, four years after John Lusk's death.

At 140.1 *m.* on the main route is the junction with a graveled road.

Right on this road is ANNAPOLIS, 0.5 *m.* (642 alt., 120 pop.), a village
that was formerly the home of Joseph G. Cannon (1836–1926), for eight
years Speaker of the House of Representatives.

A MONUMENT TO ALFRED AND RHODA HADLEY, 140.8 *m.*, Quakers
who conducted an Underground Railroad station near here, stands in a
grove (L).

ROCKVILLE, 146.8 *m.* (678 alt., 2,208 pop.) (*see Tour* 7b), is at
the junction with US 36 (*see Tour* 7).

Between Rockville and Terre Haute US 41 passes through a shaft-mining coal country. The grimed dwellings of miners straggle along the highway and cluster into towns on the side roads of this region. At 158.2 *m.* is the junction with paved State 163.

Right on State 163 is CLINTON, 1.2 *m.* (494 alt., 7,092 pop.), a coal-mining town platted on the west bank of the Wabash River in 1829 and named for DeWitt Clinton (1769–1828), governor of New York. Many of Clinton's inhabitants are coal miners, the majority of them foreign born; Italians, residing in the northwest section of town, predominate. The largest industry, aside from coal mining, is an overall factory.

At 2.7 *m.* is a 'Y' intersection; L. here to a sharp turn, 4 *m.* and a junction with a graveled road; R. to the KRECKLER HOME, 4.1 *m.* (*open*), the residence of two Indiana governors, James Whitcomb and Claude Mathews, grandfather and father respectively of the present owner. Erected in 1840, the house is Georgian in design with a two-story portico. Originally it had 16 rooms; these have been reduced to 8, and the weatherboarding has been covered with stucco. A large picture over the dining-room fireplace is made from a combination of daguerreotypes and shows the United States Senate being addressed on March 7, 1850, by Daniel Webster. In the group are Calhoun, Clay, and Whitcomb, the latter serving in the Senate after his term as governor of Indiana. The picture is colored in ink and is said to be one of three such in the United States. The other two are in Independence Hall, Philadelphia, and in the Boston Library. There is also a huge gilt-framed mirror that hung in the reception room of the historic St. Louis Hotel in New Orleans. Among other pieces of interest is a canopied bed made about 1669.

In ROSELAWN MEMORIAL PARK, 166.9 *m.*, a cemetery (R), vesper services are conducted each Sunday evening in July and August from the TOWER OF MEMORIES. This chimes tower, one of the few in Indiana, is a 50-foot octagonal shaft of limestone with bronze trim. Hundreds of cars park about the tower during the services and the concert that follows. The sunrise service held here each Easter morning is attended by thousands.

NORTH TERRE HAUTE, 167.7 *m.* (495 alt., 800 pop.), is a coal-mining town. On the banks of Otter Creek, one mile east of the town, are the FOUNDATIONS OF THE MARKLE MILL, destroyed by fire in 1938. The mill was built in 1816, the year Indiana was admitted to the Union, and around it grew Vigo County's first settlement. The old ledger of Abraham Markle, the builder of the mill and a major in the American Army in the War of 1812, is a prized possession of the Hansel family, present (1941) owners of the site. During the turbulent years preceding the Civil War, the mill was a busy place, serving also as an Underground Railroad station for fugitive slaves.

At 169.4 *m.* is the junction with the Fort Harrison Road.

Right on this road is the ELKS' FORT HARRISON COUNTRY CLUB, 1.5 *m.*, on the site of old Fort Harrison, the stockade built in 1811 by General William Henry Harrison in his campaign against the Indian confederacy. Built on a bend in the Wabash River, the old fort commanded an unobstructed view of more than a mile in both directions.

Long before white settlers invaded Indiana, the Wea, a powerful tribe of the Miami, occupied this territory. Here, according to tradition, the allied forces of the Miami and Illinois Indians defeated the Iroquois in a great battle, driving the eastern tribes forever from western soil.

All of General Harrison's official orders issued from this place designated it as Camp Batelle des Illinois. General Harrison and his troops, numbering slightly more than 1,000 men, arrived at the site in October 1811, and began construction of a fort. The large open space, where the Elks' golf course now lies, was the drill ground. All through October the General drilled his army, hoping to impress the Indians into a peaceful settlement. The completed fort was about 150 feet square; at each corner were two-story, 20-foot block-houses, built of logs, with the upper story projecting. Between the blockhouses were barracks and on the east side was a large gate, protected by bastions and palisades, and a trench about four feet deep. On Sunday, October 27, the troops assembled in front of the fort, and Major Joseph Hamilton Daviess, killed ten days later in the Battle of Tippecanoe, christened the stronghold Fort Harrison. The army left the fort on Tuesday, October 29, fought the Battle of Tippecanoe on November 7, and returned to the fort November 15. A small permanent garrison was established and in June 1812 the 27-year-old Captain Zachary Taylor was placed in command.

Part of the British strategy in the War of 1812 was to capture Fort Harrison and deprive the United States of control of the Indians in this region. Accordingly, about 600 Indians attacked the post on the night of September 4, 1812. More than half of the 50 defending soldiers were ill with fever and Captain Taylor himself was convalescing and hardly fit for duty. But the little garrison held off the attacking Indians all night long, filling in with temporary breastworks the opening left in their fortification when a blockhouse burned. At dawn, the Indians abandoned the attack. All the livestock was killed or driven away, nearly all the provisions were lost, and the garrison was in great distress when relieved four days later. Both Harrison, who built the fort, and Taylor, who so ably defended it; later became Presidents of the United States.

In TERRE HAUTE, 172 m. (541 alt., 62,693 pop.) (see Terre Haute), are junctions with US 40 (see Tour 8), State 46 (see Tour 9), and US 150 (see Tour 12), which unites southward with US 41 for 56 miles.

Section b. TERRE HAUTE to KENTUCKY LINE, 110.6 m.

South of Terre Haute are gently rolling hills; although pastoral in appearance, the region contains the richest coal deposits in Indiana. Between Vincennes, once the capital of the Northwest Territory, and Evansville, fifth largest city in the State, peaches and cantaloupes are grown extensively. During the late summer heavy trucks, burdened with melons, rumble along the highways to the northern markets.

At 3.7 m. is a junction (R) with the Blocksom Road (dirt), the first westward road south of the Municipal Airport.

Right on the Blocksom Road 2.8 m. to the entrance of the FEDERAL PRISON, which lies between State 63 and the Wabash River. This prison, erected in 1939-40 at a cost of approximately $3,000,000, is located on a 1,200-acre tract and has a main group of 19 buildings, besides a sewage disposal plant, a garage, and a private residence for prison officials. The institute accommodates between 700 and 1,000 inmates, about 90 per cent of whom are persons from other institutions who have not committed crimes of violence and are nearing time of release.

The most advanced ideas in penology are put into practice here. There is no lockstepping and prisoners are treated with consideration and fairness. Rules of the institution are intended to contribute to the rehabilitation of the inmate and to restore him to society as a potentially useful citizen. An important factor in the selection of this site for the prison was the adaptability of the soil to truck gardening. A large portion of the vegetables necessary to feed the prisoners is raised here; poultry furnish eggs and meat and a thoroughbred dairy herd is maintained. Thus, the outdoor activities give the men an opportunity to acquire habits of industry and to leave the prison in good health.

At 13.5 *m.* is the junction with State 246, an improved road.

Right on State 246 to a junction with State 63 in MIDDLETOWN, 6 *m.* (512 alt., 175 pop.); L. here on State 63 to FAIRBANKS, 10 *m.* (530 alt., 100 pop.), named for a Lieutenant Fairbanks, who, with most of his command, was slain near here early in September 1812, by attacking Indians. Right from Fairbanks on the Old River Road is the SITE OF THE FAIRBANKS MASSACRE, 12.5 *m.* Only three of the soldiers convoying a wagonload of supplies from Vincennes to Captain Zachary Taylor at Fort Harrison escaped the massacre. General Harrison had dispatched the supplies after Captain Taylor had advised him by messenger of the Fort Harrison battle and of the plight of the garrison. Lieutenant Fairbanks's sword, found later at the scene of the battle, is in the State Historical Museum at Indianapolis.

Oil wells have been drilled in the country around Fairbanks and many pumps may be seen on near-by farms.

FARMERSBURG, 14.5 *m.* (595 alt., 1,005 pop.), is an appropriately named trading center, its population being made up almost entirely of farmers and retired farmers.

At 18.5 *m.* is the junction with State 48, a blacktop road.

Left on State 48 is HYMERA, 4.8 *m.* (496 alt., 1,298 pop.), once a prosperous coal-mining town and a stronghold of Methodism in its early days. Immediately after the discovery of extensive coal deposits in the neighborhood in 1870, the town was platted and named Pittsburg. When John Badders, the postmaster, discovered that another town in Indiana had previously been named Pittsburg, he changed the name to High Mary, for his unusually tall adopted daughter, Mary. Later the new name was shortened to Hymera. At the town's western limits is a life-sized STATUE OF NATHAN HINKLE (R), Revolutionary War soldier who died in Hymera in 1848 at the age of 99.

At 7.5 *m.* is SHAKAMAK STATE PARK (*adm.* 10¢; *cabins* $2.50 *per day,* $10 *per week; camping and picnicking grounds; foot and bridle paths*). Established in 1929 and covering 1,021 acres of woodland, the park was named for a near-by stream that the Indians called Shakamak (river of the long fish), for the eels in it. SHAKAMAK LAKE (*fishing, boating, bathing*), in the center of the park, has a 5-mile shore line and is 57 acres in area. A SHAFT COAL MINE is kept open for inspection by park visitors. Other features of the park are a WILD LIFE EXHIBIT of deer, elk, buffalo, birds, and waterfowl, and a GROUP CAMP where 4-H Club members and other youth groups enjoy outings.

SHELBURN, 19 *m.* (541 alt., 1,606 pop.), is a typical Indiana coal-mining town, its central section a compact arrangement of business establishments and its residential sections composed of scattered miners' cottages. The town was founded in 1818, but its real growth began in 1868 with the sinking of the first coal mine in the district. The mine that launched Shelburn was at the time the only one between Terre Haute and Vincennes. At the peak of its mining history, 12 large coal mines were in operation near here.

At 21 *m.* the route crosses MORRISON CREEK, where Lieutenant Morrison and four of his men were killed by Indians on May 13, 1815.

Lieutenant Morrison, en route to Fort Harrison with 16 soldiers, was guided by an Indian, Little Eyes. Despite the warning of Little Eyes, one of the party had shot a deer shortly before sundown, and the Indian deserted, fearing that the noise of the shooting would bring down upon the party an attack by Potawatomi whom he knew to be in the neighborhood. Simulating the grunting of pigs to cover their approach, the Indians crept upon the campers, killing Lieutenant Morrison and three of his men instantly. Another soldier was slain a moment later in a near-by hazel thicket. The surviving soldiers escaped and made their way safely back to Fort Knox. This was the last encounter between Indians and white men in this vicinity.

SULLIVAN, 26 *m.* (539 alt., 5,077 pop.), a progressive coal-mining and agricultural center, was platted in 1842 so that the Sullivan County seat might be moved from Merom to the more central location. The townspeople depend almost entirely upon coal mining for employment.

One of the worst disasters in Indiana mining history occurred at the CITY COAL MINE, a mile west of Sullivan, on February 21, 1925. Only four of 55 men buried in the mine by a gas explosion were rescued. Impeded by the deadly after-damp, rescue crews worked for two days before the 51 bodies were removed to the surface.

SULLIVAN CITY PARK (*ovens, tables, playground facilities*) is on South Main Street.

Sullivan is the home town of Will H. Hays, the movie czar, who still considers it his home and speaks of it as 'a typical small town in the valley of democracy, where the people have their feet on the ground and their eyes on the stars.' Hays resigned the postmaster-generalship under President Harding in 1922 to become president of the Motion Picture Producers and Distributors of America. The sign, 'Hays & Hays, Attorneys,' has hung continuously for 65 years in front of the firm that Will H. Hays and his father formerly directed.

At 28.8 *m.* is a junction with State 54.

Right on State 54 to MEROM, 9 *m.* (445 alt., 499 pop.), pronounced 'Meer'um' (high ground along the waters). Overlooking miles of beautiful countryside from its position on the highest bluff of the Wabash River, Merom was named for the highest lake along the Jordan River, the scene of Joshua's battle with the assembled kings. For 25 years, until 1842, Merom was the county seat of Sullivan County, a busy shipping point and the headquarters of a fleet of Wabash River flatboats.

In 1849 UNION CHRISTIAN COLLEGE, a school of liberal arts, was established in the south part of town. Closed in 1924, the college was reopened in 1936 by the Congregational-Christian Church and the Chicago Theological Seminary as Merom Institute. Ministerial students, pastors, and lay church leaders assemble each summer for training in rural church problems. During the year, a community education program is conducted, and institute leaders and townspeople co-operate in the management of a community laundry, maple-sugar camp, book club, folk games, and other vocational and recreational activities.

The main building, approached along an avenue of trees, was completed in 1860. Combined Romanesque and Gothic in design, the structure contains a spiral stairway leading into an observation tower 300 feet above the Wabash River. The stairway is believed to have been built by Francis Costigan, architect of the Lanier Mansion in Madison (*see Tour 12a*). A 40-room brick dormitory, built in 1861, was destroyed by fire in 1939.

For nearly three-quarters of a century the college was a center of learning, preparing students for the teaching profession and for the ministry of the Christian Church. The college was closed for a time during the Civil War, while the majority of its students fought in the Union Army. Dr. Nickolas Summerbel, first president of the college and a chaplain in the Union Army, was a crusader against the Knights of the Golden Circle (*see Tour 5a*). Wilbur Glen Voliva, overseer of Zion City, near Chicago, from 1907 to 1939, is a graduate of Merom.

In MEROM PARK, atop the bluff, the Merom Chautauqua has been held each year between August 15 and 30 since 1903. At the height of the Chautauqua's popularity it attracted seasonal attendances of more than 50,000 persons. Included among its noted speakers were William Jennings Bryan and 'Billy' Sunday.

PAUL LINDSAY ISLAND, a 33-acre island in the Wabash River just below Merom Bluff's highest point, is a part of the town, incorporated after the Civil War so that the town authorities could police it. During the war the island had been a rendezvous for a bandit gang led by Paul Lindsay. Vigilantes finally raided the gang stronghold, but what happened to Lindsay has never been revealed.

Several of General Harrison's soldiers are buried in MEROM CEMETERY.

Just west of the cemetery is a three-acre wheat field, the SITE OF FORT AZATLAN, credited by archeologists to the Tennessee-Cumberland variant of the Mound Builders. Precipitous slopes guarded the ancient fort on three sides, and accounts written 75 years ago relate that the southeastern and level side was protected from attack by an earthen wall. The site has been extensively cultivated since 1903, and farmers have uncovered numerous skeletons, fragments of dishes made of shells mixed with clay, and a variety of implements indicative of two periods, the Stone Age and the era of the American Indian.

Right from Merom on State 63 to the junction with the Mann Cemetery Road (dirt), 1.1 *m.;* L. here across the prairie to other MOUNDS, also under cultivation and to MANN CEMETERY (R), 4.4 *m.* Here are buried two of General Harrison's soldiers, Kentuckians who carried an old family feud into the army and killed each other on the way to the Battle of Tippecanoe.

At 4.7 *m.* is (L) the SITE OF OLD FORT TURMAN (Tierman), an outpost from which General Harrison issued regimental orders on his northward march.

At 5.3 *m.* is the junction with the Graysville Road. Right on the Graysville Road to a junction at 5.4 *m.;* R. here to a bridge over Big Springs, branch of Turman Creek, 5.6 *m.;* 50 yards L. of the bridge is the BIG SPRING, where General Harrison's expeditionary army camped the night of September 29, 1811. It was at this spring that the two soldiers from Kentucky slew each other. The waters of the spring are caught now in a moss-covered brick enclosure.

At 30.2 *m.* US 41 crosses BUSSERON CREEK, named for Francis Busseron, one of the judges of the old Northwest Territory. In the vicinity of the bridge the stream flows between high wooded banks.

CARLISLE, 35.3 *m.* (482 alt., 874 pop.), is one of the oldest towns in Indiana. Settled in 1803 on ground the Government granted Samuel Ledgerwood for services in negotiating an Indian treaty, the town was platted shortly after the close of the War of 1812. Until its mines were worked out, Carlisle was an important coal-mining center.

In the old CARLISLE CEMETERY at the northwestern edge of town a small granite stone marks the grave of 'Handy' Handley, a Revolutionary War soldier who was with Washington when he crossed the

Delaware. Handley is said to have been one of the guards selected by Washington to maintain the campfires throughout the night before the Battle of Trenton, a maneuver that deceived the British and paved the way for the successful surprise attack. Also buried in the Carlisle Cemetery are James L. Scott, first chief justice of Indiana Territory; and John W. Davis, first Indiana speaker of the House of Representatives and United States minister to China.

Under an old elm tree, 36.6 *m.*, known as the TREATY TREE (L), Samuel Ledgerwood, founder of Carlisle, negotiated the treaty that gave the Government additional lands in this section. The trunk of the aged landmark is 25 feet in circumference and some of its branches are as large as ordinary trees.

OAKTOWN, 41.6 *m.* (478 alt., 793 pop.), formerly known as Oak Station, is a shipping center for the highly productive fruit and farming area that surrounds it. Melons, peaches, apples, and sweet potatoes are the major crops. Oil and gas have been discovered in the neighborhood and there are now (1941) 10 oil and gas wells about Oaktown.

Right from Oaktown on graveled Washout Road, to the junction with another graveled road, 0.8 *m.*; L. here to the junction with a third graveled road, 2.8 *m.*; R. here to the old SPRINKLE HOUSE, 3.9 *m.*, a two-story residence built on the SITE OF SHAKERTOWN, of brick salvaged from the old Shaker Meeting House.

Founded in 1804, the religious colony disintegrated in the 1870's, a victim of its religious and economic dogmas and, finally, of an epidemic of fever. Its citizens were members of the United Society of Believers in Christ's Second Appearance and were called Shakers because of the shaking motion they affected in their worship. They pooled the profits of their labor in a common fund, the converts turned their property over to the organization, and marriage was forbidden. Many of the younger members of the community left.

Because the Shakers were a benevolent sect and penniless widows and orphans could find a safe refuge by joining their society, the colony became a haven for the unfortunate. For a number of years after its establishment on the 2,000-acre tract that is still known as Shaker Prairie, the colony operated a distillery, a gristmill, and a sawmill on Busseron Creek. Its members farmed and raised stock, taking the produce along a road they built to the Wabash and then down the river in flatboats to New Orleans. In 1820 they built a three-story, 25-room brick community house with 60 windows, 21 fireplaces, and two kitchens (one for the women and one for the men). In the basement were two dungeons, one for male and one for female offenders. The rafters, sills, and other heavy timbers were of burr oak while the casings and doors were of the finest black walnut. Six massive doors of walnut were hung by heavy five-foot hinges. The locks were of brass, the keys weighing three pounds each. On the south side of the building were the large letters 'C. H.' and 'D. H.' forged of iron and signifying 'church house' and 'dwelling house.'

In 1821 the Shakers built the meeting house across the road from the big church and dwelling house. Believed to be a frame structure, it was discovered when it was torn down in 1875 to have brick walls between all the studding. It is of these bricks that the old Sprinkle House is made. The meeting house was so constructed that the ceiling between the first and second floors could be moved up and down by a windlass in the attic. Benches in the meeting house were arranged along two opposite walls, the men sitting on one side and the women on the other, facing each other. Services started when a group arose and formed a circle. A tune was struck up and the Shakers began to rock back and forth with the music. Then they would march, keeping time with quick, outward movements of their arms, palms upward. As the music stopped, their arms fell to their sides and they retired to the benches. A brother would speak and the shaking dance would be resumed with the hymn that followed.

At 52.5 *m.* on the main route is the junction with the Fort Knox Road.

Right on this road to the SITE OF OLD FORT KNOX, 1.1 *m.*, built in 1788 on the high wooded knoll that slopes gradually for 100 yards to the bank of the Wabash River. From the site of the old fort there is an excellent view of the Wabash. To the north a wide bend in the river is backed by the wooded slopes of Robeson's Hills. Built by Major John F. Hamtramck, then commandant at Vincennes, and named for General Henry Knox, first United States Secretary of War, the old fort was the scene of the assembly of troops that General William Henry Harrison commanded at the Battle of Tippecanoe. Captain Zachary Taylor was in command at Fort Knox at the time of the mobilization.

At 53.6 *m.* is the junction with State 67 (*see Tour 19A*), which coincides with US 41 to VINCENNES, 56.1 *m.* (442 alt., 18,228 pop.) (*see Vincennes*).

Vincennes is at the junction with US 50–150 (*see Tours 10 and 12*) and State 67 (*see Tour 19A*).

Right from Vincennes at the south end of Sixth Street on the Cathlinette Road; this road is along the ROUTE OF CLARK'S ADVANCE to the capture of Vincennes (*see Vincennes*). At intervals along the road are markers with accounts of the historic march. The inscriptions were taken from the journal of Major Joseph Bowman, one of Clark's trusted officers.

At 7 *m.* is the junction with a paved road; R. on this road to CLARK'S FERRY, 11 *m.* (25¢ *one way; 35¢ round trip*), which crosses to St. Francisville, Illinois. The ferry is operated night and day from the point where Clark and his men crossed the river, and saves approximately five miles over the Vincennes Bridge route into southeastern Illinois.

At 65.3 *m.* are the DESHEE FARMS, INC., (R) a co-operative agricultural experiment, sponsored by the Farm Security Administration, that embraces some 2,700 acres of rich lowlands along the little creek that is called the River Deshee. This co-operative association consists of 35 families (1941) that have been removed from impoverished farm lands of southern Indiana and selected according to their character and reputation. The Government has invested in land, buildings, stock, and machinery for the association and is recovering its investment as the project liquidates itself. A diversified crop program insures against a general failure and promotes better farming practice. Wheat, corn, and potatoes, poultry and poultry products, dairy and beef cattle, and hogs are marketed by the association and the earning is distributed to the heads of the families of the community. Throughout the year, the workers are given a 15¢ per hour advance against this annual share. Each family is given a house, usually consisting of about five rooms. Each member of the association has one vote and all business is conducted by a board of five directors, elected by the members. The farms are all under the supervision of one farm manager, who is responsible only to the directors and who assigns each resident to the job for which he is best suited. There are two community houses, one at either end of the farms, for community business meetings and recreation.

HAZELTON, 69.6 m. (430 alt., 516 pop.), is the trading center for one of the best cantaloupe-producing regions in the Middle West. Settlement of the town on a high hill on the south bank of White River began shortly after Jarvis Hazelton, a hunter, built his camp here in 1807. In its early days, when it boasted a number of sawmills and gristmills, Hazelton was port of call for small White River freight boats. In the flood of 1937, it was one of the first towns stricken. More than a week before the flood reached dangerous proportions along the Ohio River, Hazelton was hemmed in by the backwaters of White River. Because of its elevation, little damage was done and by the time the Ohio River towns were being inundated the crisis here had passed.

South of Hazelton the country is delightfully rugged, the highway winding gracefully through heavily wooded hills.

PATOKA, 76.1 m. (427 alt., 569 pop.), on the banks of the Patoka (Ind.: logs on the bottom) River, is surrounded by a rim of low hills, its tranquillity undisturbed by the heavy motor traffic that speeds through it. Once a center for grist- and sawmills, distilleries, and cooper shops, the town is a shipping center today for the grains, fruits, cantaloupes, watermelons, tomatoes, and sweet potatoes grown in the vicinity.

Settled in 1789 and platted in 1813, Patoka was in its early history an important stop on the Vincennes-Evansville stagecoach line. The RELAY STATION AND TAVERN, built in 1839, is now an abandoned, gray, weatherboarded building (L), three doors south of the Chicago and Eastern Illinois Railroad crossing.

PRINCETON, 80.1 m. (483 alt., 7,786 pop.) (see Tour 11), is at the junction with State 64 (see Tour 11).

At 87.1 m. is a five-foot limestone monument (R) marking the SITE OF OLD FORT BRANCH, built in 1811. The stockade stood about a half mile west of the marker. Just a little farther off the highway is the town of FORT BRANCH (451 alt., 1,552 pop.), named for the pioneer outpost.

The EVANSVILLE MUNICIPAL AIRPORT (visitors welcome), 102.1 m. (L), is a completely equipped 254-acre field. There is a 2,000,000 candle-power beacon and an auxiliary code beacon that flashes the letters EV (Evansville).

At 104.8 m. is the northern junction with State 62 (see Tour 11A), which unites with US 41 for three miles.

In EVANSVILLE, 107.8 m. (383 alt., 97,062 pop.) (see Evansville), is the junction with State 66 (see Tour 11B) and the southern junction with State 62 (see Tour 11A).

DADE PARK RACE COURSE, 110.3 m., was built in 1922 and designed after the historic track at Saratoga, New York. Every August running races are held on the one-and-an-eighth-mile saddle horse course. Since the park area is Kentucky territory, the Kentucky Racing Commission has authority over the races. The north bank of the Ohio River is ordinarily considered the boundary line between the two States, but Kentucky claims the Dade Park site on the ground that the Ohio River ran to the north of it until Green River, flowing into the Ohio just above the place, finally cut a new channel to the south early in the 1800's. The site was south of the Ohio River, Kentucky argued, at the time of the Kentucky and Northwest Territory land grants when the boundary between the two States was fixed as the low-water mark on the north side of the river. After many court battles in which Indiana contended that the present river should govern, the United States Supreme Court upheld Kentucky's claim.

At 110.6 *m.* US 41 crosses the Ohio River (*toll bridge; 35¢ for car and passengers*), six miles north of Henderson, Kentucky (*see Kentucky Guide*).

PART IV
Appendices

Chronology

1609	Northwest country granted to Virginia by charter.
1679	La Salle and party of 28 men camp near present site of South Bend; first known white men in Indiana.
1680	Father Allouez discovers Wea village on St. Joseph River in northern Indiana.
1681	La Salle holds council with Indians at Council Oak, on present site of South Bend.
1720	French build fort at Ouiatenon, near present site of LaFayette.
1722	French build Fort Miami on present site of Fort Wayne.
1732–3	Late in 1732 or early in 1733 François Morgane de Vincennes builds a stockade fort on present site of Vincennes.
1749	Beginning of extant records in Vincennes Roman Catholic Church, first church in Indiana.
1760	British take Montreal and French relinquish all claim to the western country, including Indiana. Ouiatenon and Fort Miami become British posts.
1763	February 10. Treaty of Paris signed, ending Seven Years' War and French and Indian War. King George sets aside region west of Alleghenies as an Indian reserve.
	May. Pontiac leads Indian tribes in war against frontier in Ohio Valley and beyond. Fort Miami captured.
	June 1. Indians capture and destroy post at Ouiatenon.
1765	George Croghan, Indian agent for British, makes treaties of conciliation with Indiana Indians.
1774	'Quebec Act' places all lands in northwest country under jurisdiction of British province of Quebec.
1777	Governor Henry Hamilton of province of Quebec sends Lieutenant Governor Edward Abbott from Detroit to rebuild stockades on Wabash River and to incite Indians against Virginian settlements.
1778	George Rogers Clark, major in command at Harrodsburg in 1777, takes charge of Kaskaskia operations as lieutenant colonel.
	July 4–5. Clark captures Kaskaskia.
	July. Father Pierre Gibault, representing Clark, induces people of Vincennes to swear allegiance to United States. Fort Sackville is occupied by Americans.
	December 17. British recapture Vincennes.
	Virginia organizes all lands northwest of the Ohio River as Illinois County.
1779	February 24. Clark retakes Vincennes.

February 25. Hamilton surrenders Fort Sackville; name changed to Fort Patrick Henry.

June. Civil and criminal court jurisdiction organized at Kaskaskia by John Todd, Jr., of Virginia, county lieutenant.

1779–80   Virginia legislature presents 150,000 acres of land in Indiana to Colonel Clark and his regiment.

1781   Don Pierro, Spanish commander of St. Louis, captures British post of St. Joseph, laying basis for Spanish claim to all territory northwest of Ohio River.

1784   Virginia conveys territory northwest of the Ohio River to United States.

1787   Congress passes ordinance providing for government of 'Territory Northwest of the River Ohio.'

General Harmar places Major Hamtramck in command of garrison at Vincennes; fort rebuilt and named Fort Knox.

Arthur St. Clair elected governor of Northwest Territory by Congress.

1790   Knox County, embracing all of Indiana and parts of Ohio, Michigan, Illinois, and Wisconsin, organized by Winthrop Sargent, secretary of Northwest Territory.

October. Harmar destroys Indian villages along Maumee River. Part of his force, under Colonel John Hardin, is annihilated by Little Turtle's Indians.

1791   June 1–3. General Charles Scott, with 800 men, destroys Indian villages of Ouiatenon, near present site of LaFayette, and Kethtippecanunk, at mouth of Tippecanoe River.

August. Colonel James Wilkinson destroys Eel River Indian village, near present site of Logansport.

November 4. Army under General St. Clair defeated by Miami Indians led by Little Turtle near Fort Recovery, Ohio.

1792   April. General Anthony Wayne succeeds St. Clair as commander of army in West.

September 27. Brigadier General Rufus Putnam concludes treaty of peace with Indians at Vincennes.

1794   August 20. General Wayne defeats Indians at Battle of Fallen Timbers, fought near Defiance, Ohio, breaking up Miami Confederacy.

October 22. Fort near junction of St. Joseph and St. Mary's Rivers completed on site of English fort built in 1764. Named Fort Wayne.

1795   Treaty of Greenville signed, opening half of Ohio and small strip of land in eastern Indiana for settlement.

1798   A Baptist church, first Protestant church in Indiana, organized at Owen's Creek in Knox County.

1800   May 7. Act of Congress approved dividing Northwest Territory; Ohio split off; Indiana Territory, with Vincennes the capital, established.

May 13. William Henry Harrison appointed governor of Indiana Territory. Territory population 5,641.

1801   January 10. Harrison arrives at Vincennes.

Clark County created out of part of Knox County.

1802   Harrison concludes first of treaties with Indians designed to extinguish all Indian titles in Indiana.

1803   Swiss colonists settle in Switzerland County and introduce grape culture into Indiana.

1804   March 26. U. S. land office established at Vincennes.

July 4. First issue of *Indiana Gazette,* later called *Western Sun,* first newspaper in Indiana, appears in Vincennes.

August 27. By Vincennes treaty, Delaware and Piankeshaw Indians cede to U. S. the region between Wabash and Ohio Rivers and south of road from Vincennes to falls of the Ohio.

September 11. Electorate of Territory votes for representative form of government in place of government by governor and judges.

1805   January 3. First Territorial election.

January 11. Michigan Territory is organized out of part of Indiana Territory.

February 1. Territorial legislature convenes for first time.

August 21. Treaty signed at Grouseland, near Vincennes, gives U. S. title to Indian lands in eastern Indiana.

1806   Vincennes University established by act of Territorial legislature.

1807   Laws of Indiana published at Vincennes.

1808   December 8. Harrison County is organized; Corydon laid out as seat of government. (Courthouse built 1811–12.)

1809   February 9. Illinois Territory organized.

September 30. Fort Wayne Treaty is ratified, whereby Governor Harrison, for $10,000 and a small annuity, buys 3,000,000 acres of land between Wabash and east fork of White River.

1810   August 20. Harrison and Tecumseh hold a council at Vincennes. Territory population, 24,520.

1811   General William Henry Harrison defeats Indians led by the Prophet, Tecumseh's brother, at Battle of Tippecanoe.

1812   June. War with England begins.

July 14. Little Turtle, leader of Miami Confederacy, dies.

September 3. White settlers at Pigeon Roost in Scott County massacred.

September 4–5. Night attack by Indians on Fort Harrison repelled by garrison under Captain Zachary Taylor.

September 5–12. Fort Wayne besieged by British and Indians. Relieved Sept. 12 by General Harrison.

December 17–18. Miami Indians defeated in battle fought on banks of Mississinewa River in Grant County. Last battle fought in Indiana.

1813   March 11. Territorial capital moved from Vincennes to Corydon. (Courthouse used as Territorial and State Capitol, 1813–25.)

October 5. General Harrison defeats Tecumseh and British at Battle of Thames, near Detroit. Tecumseh slain.

1814   September. Farmers and Mechanics Bank at Madison and Bank of Vincennes are chartered.

1815   Rappites settle at New Harmony.

1816   June 29. State Constitution adopted by convention held at Corydon.

August 5. First State election. Jonathan Jennings elected governor.

October 25. Terre Haute platted.

November 4. First State General Assembly convenes at Corydon.

November 8. James Noble and Waller Taylor chosen first U. S. senators from Indiana (seated December 12). William Hendricks, representative (seated December 2).

December 11. Indiana is formally admitted into Union as a State. Lincoln family move into Indiana; Abraham seven years old.

1817   First Medical Society in State organized by physicians of Vincennes.

1818   By Treaty of St. Mary's, Governor Jennings purchases from Wea, Miami, Potawatomi, and Delaware Indians most of central Indiana lying south of Wabash River.

1820   February 26. First permanent settler comes to present site of Indianapolis.

June 7. Present site of Indianapolis chosen as capital.

Legislature passes acts establishing State Seminary at Bloomington and incorporating Madison Academy.

First stage line in State established between Vincennes and Louisville.

Population (U. S. Census), 147,178.

1821   January. Capital site accepted by legislature; capital named Indianapolis.

October 9. First sale of town lots in Indianapolis.

1823   Alexis Coquillard establishes fur-trading post at present site of South Bend.

First theatrical performance in Indianapolis.

1824   April 10. U. S. mail stage, between Vincennes and Louisville, begins operation.

Indiana Seminary opens at Bloomington.

1825   State capital, moved from Corydon, established in Indianapolis.

Robert Owen launches New Harmony experiment.

1826   Treaty signed by State and Potawatomi Indians whereby land is ceded to State to build Michigan Road from Lake Michigan to Ohio River.

First free school, first free kindergarten, and first coeducational school in U. S. established in New Harmony. 'Boatload of Knowledge' arrives at New Harmony.

Treaty of Wabash signed, whereby Indians cede most of lands lying north and west of Wabash River to United States.

1827   Presbyterians establish Hanover College, first denominational college in Indiana.

Survey of National Road across Indiana completed.

Congress grants land to State for building Wabash and Erie Canal.

1828   Stage route established between Madison and Indianapolis.

First Democratic Convention in State held in Indianapolis.

1829   Indiana Colonization Society founded at Indianapolis for purpose of sending Negroes to Liberia.

1830   Lincoln family moves from Spencer County to Illinois.

State Historical Society organized at Indianapolis.

Work on Michigan Road begun.

Population, 343,031.

1831   Underground Railroad begins operations in Indiana at Cabin Creek, in Randolph County.

1832   Construction of Wabash and Erie Canal begins at Fort Wayne.

Black Hawk's War arouses sentiment against Indians; agitation starts for their removal from State.

1833   Wabash College opens at Crawfordsville; founded in 1832 as Wabash Manual Labor College and Teachers' Seminary.

1834   Legislature establishes State Bank of Indiana.

Bishop Bruté arrives in Vincennes, now a Catholic diocese.

First railroad track in Indiana, one mile long, laid at Shelbyville.

1835   Capitol building at Indianapolis completed.

1836   Legislature passes Mammoth Internal Improvement Bill appropriating $13,000,000 for internal improvements.

McGuffey readers begin to circulate in Indiana.

Excavation of Whitewater Canal begins (completed to Cambridge City in 1846).

1837   First coal is mined near Cannelton for river steamers.

Indiana Asbury University, now DePauw University, opens at Greencastle.

Indiana Baptist Manual Labor Institute, now Franklin College, opened.

1838   Potawatomi Indians escorted from State by military force.

Indiana University founded. (State Seminary chartered 1820; opened 1824; became Indiana College 1828.)

Indiana goes bankrupt.

1839   Henry Ward Beecher becomes pastor of Second Presbyterian Church in Indianapolis.

1840   William Henry Harrison elected President of the United States.

St. Mary-of-the-Woods founded in Terre Haute.

Population, 685,866.

1842   University of Notre Dame founded at South Bend; chartered 1844.

1843   July 4. Wabash and Erie Canal formally opened at Fort Wayne.

1844   Whig Convention held in Indianapolis.

1846   Married women given right to make wills.

Common school convention held in Indianapolis, the beginning of movement for free schools.

1847   October 1. First steam train arrives in Indianapolis from Madison.

State Hospital for Insane and School for Blind erected.

Electorate votes for free public school system for Indiana.

Quakers establish coeducational boarding school in Richmond, which became Earlham College in 1859.

1848   First meeting of Indiana Education Society held in Indianapolis.

1849   Electorate votes for constitutional convention.

James Whitcomb Riley born in Greenfield, Indiana.

1850   Constitutional Convention held in Indianapolis from October 7, 1850, to February 10, 1851.

State School for Deaf established.

Population, 988,416.

1851   February 14. State Board of Agriculture established.

New State constitution ratified by electorate.

1852   New school law creates tax-supported public school system for Indiana.

Studebaker Brothers come to South Bend.

October 20. First State Fair opens in Indianapolis.

1853   Wabash and Erie Canal completed.

First Union Station in United States built in Indianapolis.

1854   Convention of women meets in Indianapolis to demand political rights.

First big coal mine opened in Sullivan County.

Monon Railroad, connecting New Albany and Michigan City, completed.

1855   Northwestern Christian University, now Butler University, chartered in 1850, opens in Indianapolis.

Eugene V. Debs, labor leader and Socialist, born in Terre Haute.

1856   E. C. Atkins begins manufacturing saws in Indianapolis.

Oliver P. Morton nominated for governor on Republican ticket, first act of Republican party in Indiana.

Headquarters of U. S. Geological Survey moved from New Harmony to Washington, D. C.

1857   St. Meinrad's College, in Spencer County, opens.

1858   Indiana Academy of Science organized in Indianapolis.

1859   Minerva Club, first women's club in America with constitution and by-laws, founded at New Harmony.

First mail delivered by air carried by balloon from LaFayette to Crawfordsville.

1860   Indiana Republican delegates at Wigwam convention in Chicago help nominate Abraham Lincoln for President.

Population, 1,350,428.

1861   Oliver P. Morton becomes governor of Indiana.

Abraham Lincoln visits Indianapolis en route to Washington.

April 16. Governor Morton issues call for six regiments of soldiers, in response to Lincoln's appeal to put down rebellion in South.

1862   Knights of the Golden Circle become active in Indiana.

1863   General John Morgan and Confederate troops raid southern Indiana July 8–13.

1864   First streetcars in State begin operating in Indianapolis.

1865   April 30. Lincoln's body lies in state in capitol building at Indianapolis.

Legislation enacted enabling Negroes to testify in court.

Petroleum discovered at Terre Haute.

1866 National convention of Grand Army of the Republic held at Indianapolis.

1867 Indiana University opens its doors to women and receives State funds for its support.

1868 James Oliver, of South Bend, invents chilled-steel plow.

1869 Indianapolis *News* founded by John Holliday.

Legislation enacted admitting Negro children to public schools on same basis as white children.

State department of geology established.

1870 Indiana State Teachers College opens at Terre Haute.

Population, 1,680,637.

1871 Theodore Dreiser, novelist, born in Terre Haute.

Edward Eggleston's *The Hoosier Schoolmaster* published.

1872 State grange of Indiana organized.

1873 Office of county superintendent of schools created.

Woman's Prison established at Indianapolis.

First belt railroad in United States built around Indianapolis.

Purdue University, chartered in 1862, opens at LaFayette.

1874 Rose Polytechnic Institute founded at Terre Haute.

1878 Knights of Labor become active in Indiana.

1879 Legislation enacted providing for mine inspection and safety.

1880 September 28. Cornerstone of new statehouse is laid at Indianapolis (completed 1888).

General Lew Wallace's book *Ben-Hur* published.

Population, 1,978,301.

1881 Conference at Terre Haute launches American Federation of Labor.

State board of health established.

1883 May Wright Sewall founds Art Association of Indianapolis.

'The Old Swimmin' Hole,' by James Whitcomb Riley, published.

1885 Indianapolis Conference of Indiana trade unions organizes first State Federation of Labor in United States.

1886 Natural-gas well comes in at Portland.

1888 Benjamin Harrison becomes President of United States.

1889 Standard Oil Company builds world's largest refinery at Whiting.

First oil well in State drilled on farm of D. A. Beyson, near Keystone, Wells County.

1890 United Mine Workers are organized and become powerful in Indiana.

Population, 2,192,404.

1893 Eugene V. Debs organizes American Railway Union, first industrial union in American labor history.

Inland Steel Corp. moves its mills to Calumet region.

1894 Elwood Haynes runs self-propelled vehicle at speed of six to eight miles per hour.

Debs leads Pullman strike at Chicago; is imprisoned for contempt of court.

1897   First compulsory education law passed.

Legislation passed requiring inspection of manufacturing plants for sanitation and safety.

United Mine Workers call coal strike.

1898   Indiana regiments mustered into service for duty in Spanish-American War.

January 1. First interurban car runs from Anderson to Alexandria—the beginning of a network that covered the State and extended to Chicago, Louisville, and into Ohio.

Eugene V. Debs founds Social Democratic party.

1899   Booth Tarkington's *The Gentleman from Indiana* published.

1900   Debs nominated for President at convention of Social Democratic party held in Indianapolis.

Meredith Nicholson's *The Hoosiers* published.

Population, 2,516,462.

1901   Compulsory education law amended to compel children from 7 to 16 years of age to attend school throughout school year.

At convention in Indianapolis all Socialist elements are united into Socialist party of United States.

1902   George Ade's *Fables in Slang* begin to appear.

1904   September. Largest interurban terminal station in United States opened at Indianapolis.

Debs polls 402,312 votes for President.

December 31. Kin Hubbard's (Frank McKinney Hubbard) first 'Abe Martin' cartoon appears in Indianapolis *News*.

1905   United States Steel Corporation builds its largest plant in Calumet region. Gary founded.

1907   High schools become part of State public school system.

1910   Population, 2,700,876.

1911   Legislation passed making employers responsible for industrial safety.

First 500-mile race held at Indianapolis Motor Speedway.

1914   State Workmen's Compensation Act passed.

1915   Little Theater Society of Indiana organized, with George Ade as president.

Indiana Historical Bureau established.

1916   First State primary election held.

Centennial Exposition held.

James Whitcomb Riley dies.

1917   Governor appoints members of local draft boards as United States enters the World War.

Registration of men between ages of 21 and 31 for selective service.

1918   Registration of men between ages of 18 and 45 for selective service.

During World War 130,670 Indianians serve in armed forces of Nation.

1919   Nation-wide steel and coal strikes affect thousands in Indiana.

1920   Debs, in prison for opposing the draft, polls 915,302 votes for President.

Life of John Marshall, by Albert J. Beveridge, wins Pulitzer Prize.

Population, 2,930,390.

1921   December 23. President Harding frees Debs.

1925   Trial of D. C. Stevenson for murder results in startling exposé of corrupt role Ku Klux Klan played in Indiana politics.

An American Tragedy, by Theodore Dreiser, published.

1926   J. Arthur MacLean excavates a mound on Albee farm in Sullivan County, first scientific archeological excavation in State.

Archeological Section of Indiana Historical Society formed.

October 20. Eugene V. Debs dies.

1928   Indianapolis *Times* receives Pulitzer Prize for campaign against Ku Klux Klan.

Albert J. Beveridge's *Life of Abraham Lincoln* published posthumously.

1930   Population, 3,238,503.

1931   Indianapolis *News* receives Pulitzer Prize for advocating tax reforms.

1932   Full effects of Nation-wide depression felt in Indiana. Dozens of banks fail; thousands unemployed; mining and quarrying industries in state of collapse; farm prices dropping.

1933   Governor Paul V. McNutt signs act reorganizing State government.

1935   July 22–3. General strike at Terre Haute.

1936   Legislature passes social security and unemployment compensation acts.

State Department of Public Welfare established.

1937   Steel and automobile workers strike under CIO leadership.

Governor Clifford Townsend inaugurates the 'Indiana Plan' of adjusting labor disputes by contract.

Ohio River Valley devastated by worst flood in modern history. Property damage estimated at $500,000,000.

1940   Wendell Willkie nominated for President by Republican party; polls more than 22,000,000 votes and carries Indiana, but is defeated by President Roosevelt.

Population, 3,427,796.

Bibliography

GENERAL INFORMATION

American Automobile Association. *Northeastern Tour Book*. Washington, D. C., 1939. 656 p., illus., maps. See p. 46–67. Issued annually.

Indiana. Executive Dept. Division of Accounting and Statistics. *Statistical Report, State of Indiana*. Indianapolis, issued annually, 1924 to date.
——*Year Book of the State of Indiana*. Indianapolis, issued annually, 1917 to date. Includes reports of State departments.

Indiana. Highway Commission. *Official Indiana Highway Map*. Indianapolis, issued annually.

DESCRIPTION AND TRAVEL

Boswell, Jessie P. *Historical Markers and Public Memorials in Indiana*. 3d ed. Indianapolis, Indiana Historical Bureau, 1929. 106 p., illus. (Indiana History Bulletin v. 6, Extra no. 1).

Brennan, George A. *The Wonders of the Dunes*. Indianapolis, Bobbs-Merrill, 1923. 362 p., front., plates, port., maps.

Cobb, Irvin S. *Indiana*. With illustrations by John T. McCutcheon. New York, Doran, 1924. 52 p. incl. front., plates. (Cobb's America Guyed Books.)

Daughters of the American Revolution. Corydon, Indiana, Hoosier Elm Chapter. *Historic Corydon*. Corydon, Ind., 1929. 39 p., illus.

Dreiser, Theodore. 'Indiana: Her Soil and Light.' (In Gruening, Ernest, ed. *These United States*. 2d series. New York, Boni & Liveright, 1924. p. 264–76.)

Fretageot, Nora. *Historic New Harmony: A Guide*. 3d ed. 1934. 66 p., illus. (incl. ports., plan, facsims.).

Gutermuth, C. R. *Where to Go in Indiana: Official Indiana Lake Guide*. Indianapolis, Indiana Dept. of Conservation, 1938. 56 p.

Indiana. Dept. of Conservation. Division of Geology. *Guide to Indiana Caverns*. Indianapolis, 1939. 16 p., mimeo.

Indiana. Dept. of Conservation. Historical booklets and leaflets on the State Parks and Memorials.

Indiana Writers' Project of the Work Projects Administration. *The Calumet Region Historical Guide*. Gary, Garman Printing Co., 1939. 271 p., front., illus., maps, bibl.

Lindley, Harlow, ed. *Indiana as Seen by Early Travelers . . . Prior to 1830*. Indianapolis, Indiana Historical Commission, 1916. 596 p. (Indiana Historical Collections. v. 3.)

Lockridge, Ross Franklin. *The Old Fauntleroy Home*. Published for the New Harmony Memorial Commission, 1939. 219 p., front., illus., plates.

Nicholson, Meredith. *The Provincial American and Other Papers*. Boston and New York, Houghton Mifflin, 1912. 236 p.

——*The Valley of Democracy*. 4th ed. New York, Scribner, 1919. 284 p., front., plates. Essays dealing with the Middle West.

Simpich, Frederick. 'Indiana Journey.' *National Geographic Magazine*, Sept. 1936. v. 70: 267–320, illus., color plates.

Southwestern Indiana Civic Association. *The Lincoln Country of Southwestern Indiana*. Evansville, Ind., Koenemann-Riehl & Co., printers, 1935. 46 p., illus. (incl. port., map).

Vincennes Fortnightly Club. *Historic Vincennes*. 7th ed. Vincennes, 1939. 40 p.

Wilson, William E. *The Wabash*. New York, Farrar & Rinehart, 1940. 339 p., illus., bibl., index.

GEOLOGY AND PALEONTOLOGY

Blatchley, Willis Stanley. 'A Century of Geology in Indiana.' (In Indiana Academy of Science. *Proceedings*, 1916. p. 89–177.)

——'Indiana Caves and Their Fauna.' (In Indiana. Dept. of Geology and Natural History. *Annual Report*, 1896. p. 121–212.)

Fowke, Gerard. *The Evolution of the Ohio River*. Indianapolis, The Hollenbeck Press, 1933. 273 p., illus. (maps), bibl.

Harris, John A., and Ralph E. Esarey. *The Devonian Formations of Indiana. Part II: Structural Conditions*. Indianapolis, Indiana Dept. of Conservation. Div. of Geology, 1940. 32 p. incl. maps (part in pocket), charts, diagrs. (Part I to be published later.)

Indiana Academy of Science. *Proceedings*. Indianapolis, issued annually, 1891 to date.

Indiana. Dept. of Conservation. Division of Geology. *Handbook of Indiana Geology*, by W. N. Logan, R. R. Cumings, C. A. Malott, S. S. Visher, W. M. Tucker, J. R. Reeves . . . Indianapolis, 1922. 1,120 p., illus., fold. plates (incl. maps, diagrs.), tables, diagrs. (Pub. no. 21).

Indiana. Division of Geology. *Annual Report*. (Under various titles, these reports appeared occasionally from 1838 to 1869, and annually from 1869 to date. Since 1917 the reports have appeared in the *Year Book of the State of Indiana*.)

Leverett, Frank, and Frank B. Taylor. *The Pleistocene of Indiana and Michigan* . . . Washington, Government Printing Office, 1915. 529 p., illus., plates, maps (part fold., part in pocket), fold. tables, fold. diagrs., bibl. (United States Geological Survey Monographs, no. 53.)

Logan, William Newton. *Geological Conditions in the Oil Fields of Southwestern Indiana*. Indianapolis, 1924. 125 p., illus., tables, diagrs. (Indiana Dept. of Conservation. Div. of Geology. Pub. no. 42.)

——*The Geology of the Deep Wells of Indiana*. Indianapolis, 1926. 540 p., maps, tables. (Indiana Dept. of Conservation. Div. of Geology. Pub. no. 55.)

Logan, William Newton. *Outlines of Indiana Geology*. Des Moines, Iowa, Geological Publishing Co., 1923. (Reprinted from *The Pan-American Geologist*, v. 40. Sept. 1923, p. 111–40.)

——*The Sub-Surface Strata of Indiana*. Fort Wayne, Fort Wayne Printing Co., 1931. 790 p., incl. illus., maps, tables, bibl. (Indiana Dept. of Conservation. Div. of Geology. Pub. no. 108.)

Moodie, Roy L. *The Geological History of the Vertebrates of Indiana*. Indianapolis, W. B. Burford Printing Co., 1929. 115 p. incl. front., illus., maps, tables, diagrs. (Indiana Dept. of Conservation. Div. of Geology. Pub. no. 90.)

PLANT AND ANIMAL LIFE

Allyn, William P. 'Representative Animal Life in Indiana.' *Teachers College Journal*, Indiana State Teachers College, v. 6, no. 2, Nov. 1934. p. 95–125, illus.

Blatchley, Willis Stanley. *The Fishes of Indiana*. Indianapolis, Nature Publishing Co., 1938. 121 p., illus.

Butler, Amos William. 'The Birds of Indiana.' (In Indiana. Dept. of Geology and Natural Resources. *Annual Report, 1897*. p. 515–r1187 incl. illus., pl. XXI–XXV.)

Deam, Charles C. *Flora of Indiana*. Indianapolis, Wm. B. Burford Printing Co., 1940. 1236 p. incl. illus., plates, maps.

——*Grasses of Indiana*. With illus. and an article, 'The Grass Plant,' by Paul Weatherwax. Indianapolis, 1929. 356 p., illus. (incl. maps), diagrs., bibl. (Indiana Dept. of Conservation. Pub. no. 82.)

——*Shrubs of Indiana*. 2d ed. Indianapolis, 1932. 380 p. incl. illus., maps. (Indiana Dept. of Conservation. Pub. no. 44.)

——*Trees of Indiana*. 2d rev. ed. Fort Wayne, Fort Wayne Printing Co., 1931. 326 p. incl. illus., maps, tables. (Indiana Dept. of Conservation. Pub. no. 13.)

Lyon, Marcus Ward, Jr. *Mammals of Indiana*. Notre Dame, Ind., The University Press, 1936. 384 p., illus., maps, bibl. (Reprinted from *The American Midland Naturalist*, v. 17, no. 1, p. 1–384, Jan. 1936.)

Peattie, Donald Culross. *Flora of the Indiana Dunes . . .* Chicago, Field Museum of Natural History, 1930. 432 p., illus., fold. map.

Sheaffer, Frank E. *Some Insect Pests and Plant Diseases of Indiana*. Indianapolis, 1930. 99 p., illus. (Indiana Dept. of Conservation. Div. of Entomology. Pub. no. 103.)

RESOURCES AND THEIR CONSERVATION

Fix, Gordon F. *Mineral Resources of Indiana*. Indianapolis, Indiana Dept. of Conservation. Div. of Geology, 1938. 17 p., map.

Harrell, Marshall. *Ground Water in Indiana*. Indianapolis, 1935. 505 p., maps, tables, mimeo. (Indiana Dept. of Conservation. Pub. no. 133.)

Indiana. Dept. of Conservation. Division of Engineering. *Surface Water Supply of Indiana*. Indianapolis, Wm. B. Burford Printing Co., 1928. 158 p., map, tables. (Pub. no. 72.)

Indiana. Dept. of Conservation. [Publications.] Indianapolis, 1919 to date.

Indiana. Division of Geology. *Oil and Gas Developments in Indiana.* Issued annually by the Department of Conservation, Indianapolis.

Logan, William Newton. *Petroleum and Natural Gas in Indiana.* Fort Wayne, Fort Wayne Printing Co., 1920. 279 p., illus., maps (part fold.), diagrs. (part fold.). (Indiana Dept. of Conservation. Div. of Geology. Pub. no. 8.)

Loughlin, Gerald Francis. *Indiana Oölitic Limestone.* Washington, 1929. 202 p., illus., plates, tables. (U. S. Geological Survey Bulletin 811-C.)

Visher, Stephen Sargent. *Economic Geography of Indiana.* New York, Appleton, 1923. 225 p., double front (map), illus., diagrs.

Whitlach, George Isaac. *The Clay Resources of Indiana.* Indianapolis, Wm. B. Burford Printing Co., 1933. 298 p. incl. illus., map, tables, diagrs., bibl. (Indiana Dept. of Conservation. Div. of Geology. Pub. no. 123.)

ARCHEOLOGY AND INDIANS

Barce, Elmore. *The Land of the Miamis.* Fowler, Ind., Benton Review Shop, 1922. 422 p., col. front., plates, ports., maps, bibl.

Beckwith, Hiram W. *The Illinois and Indiana Indians.* Chicago, Fergus Printing Company, 1884. 183 p. (Fergus Historical Series, no. 27.)

Dunn, Jacob Piatt. *True Indian Stories, with Glossary of Indiana Indian Names.* Indianapolis, Sentinel Printing Co., 1908. 320 p., illus. (incl. maps), col. ports. (incl. front.).

Guernsey, Elam Y. *Indiana, the Influence of the Indian upon Its History—with Indian and French Names for Natural and Cultural Locations* [map]. Indianapolis, 1933. (Indiana Dept. of Conservation. Pub. no. 122.)

Hodge, Frederick Webb, ed. *Handbook of American Indians, North of Mexico.* Washington, Government Printing Office, 1912. 2 v., illus. (incl. ports.), fold. map. (Smithsonian Inst. Bureau of Am. Ethnology. Bulletin 30.)

Indiana Historical Society. *Prehistory Research Series.* Indianapolis, 1937 to date. Deals with Indiana archeology and with linguistic and anthropological studies of the Indians.

Kappler, Charles J. *Indian Affairs; Laws and Treaties.* Washington, Government Printing Office, 1904. 2 v.

Lilly, Eli. *Prehistoric Antiquities of Indiana* . . . Indianapolis, Indiana Historical Society, 1937. 293 p., illus. Contains a bibliography on Indiana archeology.

McDonald, Daniel. *Removal of the Pottawattomie Indians from Northern Indiana.* Plymouth, Ind., D. McDonald & Co., printers, 1899. 59 p., front., illus., plates, ports.

Moorehead, Warren King. *The Stone Age in North America; an Archeological Encyclopedia* . . . Boston and New York, Houghton Mifflin, 1910. 2 v., col. fronts., illus., plates, bibl.

————*Stone Ornaments Used by Indians in the United States and Canada* . . . Andover, Mass., Andover Press, 1917. 448 p., illus., plates, fold. map.

Oskison, John M. *Tecumseh and His Times*. New York, C. P. Putnam's Sons, 1938. 244 p., front. (port.).

Royce, Charles C. 'Cessions of Land by Indian Tribes to the United States: illustrated by those in the state of Indiana.' (In U. S. Bureau of American Ethnology. *First Annual Report, 1879–80*. Washington, 1881. p. 247–62, fold. map.)

Shetrone, Henry Clyde. *The Mound-Builders* . . . New York, London, Appleton, 1930. 508 p., col. front., illus. (incl. facsim.), maps, bibl.

Skinner, Alanson. *The Mascoutens or Prairie Potawatomi Indians*. Milwaukee, Wis., Pub. by order of the Board of Trustees, 1924–27. 421 p., plates (incl. ports.), diagrs. (Bulletin of the Public museum of the city of Milwaukee, v. 6.)

Trowbridge, C. C. *Meearmeear Traditions*, edited by Vernon Kinietz. Ann Arbor, University of Michigan Press, 1938. 103 p., illus., bibl. (Occasional Contributions from the Museum of Anthropology of the University of Michigan. no. 7.)

————*Shawnese Traditions*, edited by Vernon Kinietz and Erminie W. Voegelin. Ann Arbor, University of Michigan Press, 1939. 93 p. (Occasional Contributions from the Museum of Anthropology of the University of Michigan. no. 9.)

Winger, Otho. *The Last of the Miamis*. North Manchester, Ind., 1935. 38 p., illus. (incl. ports.).

————*The Lost Sister among the Miamis*. Elgin, Ill., The Elgin Press, 1936. 143 p., incl. front., illus. (incl. ports., maps). The story of Frances Slocum (1773–1847), a white girl kidnapped by Indians.

————*The Potawatomi Indians*. Elgin, Ill., The Elgin Press, 1939. 159 p. incl. front., illus. (incl. maps), ports.

Young, Calvin M. *Little Turtle, the Great Chief of the Miami Indian Nation* . . . Indianapolis, Sentinel Printing Co., 1917. 249 p., front. (port.), illus. (incl. ports.), bibl.

HISTORY

General

Ball, Timothy H. *Northwestern Indiana from 1800 to 1900*. Chicago, Donohue & Hennebury, 1900. 570 p., front. (port), illus., fold. map.

Chambers, David Laurance. *Indiana, A Hoosier History, Based on the Mural Paintings of Thomas Hart Benton*. Indianapolis, Bobbs-Merrill, 1933. 47 p., illus. The mural paintings represented Indiana at the Chicago Exposition.

Cottman, George S., and Max R. Hyman. *Centennial History and Handbook of Indiana* . . . by George S. Cottman . . . *A Survey of the State by Counties* . . . by Max R. Hyman. Indianapolis, M. R. Hyman, 1915. 464 p., illus. (incl. ports., maps, facsims.).

Dunn, Jacob Piatt. *Greater Indianapolis*. Chicago, Lewis Publishing Co., 1910. 2 v., illus., ports., maps.

————*Indiana and Indianans, a History of Aboriginal and Territorial Indiana and the Century of Statehood*. Chicago and New York, Am. Historical Soc., 1919. 5 v., front., illus. (incl. maps, facsims.), ports. Includes authoritative material on the word 'Hoosier.'

Esarey, Logan. *A History of Indiana.* 3rd ed. Fort Wayne, Hoosier Press, 1924. 2 v., illus. (incl. maps).

Indiana. Historical Bureau. *Indiana Historical Collections.* Indianapolis, 1916 to date.

————*Indiana History Bulletin.* Indianapolis, issued monthly 1923 to date.

Indiana Historical Society. *Publications.* Indianapolis, 1895 to date.

Indiana Magazine of History. Bloomington, Ind., Indiana University Department of History, issued quarterly 1905 to date.

Indiana Review, Pictorial, Political, Historical. Indianapolis, Bookwalter-Ball-Greathouse Printing Co., 1938. 382 p., illus., ports., map, tables.

Indiana State Teachers' Association. History Section. *Readings in Indiana History* . . . Bloomington, Indiana Univ., 1914. 470 p., illus.

Kemper, General William Harrison. *Medical History of the State of Indiana.* Chicago, American Medical Association Press, 1911. 393 p. incl. front., illus., ports.

Kettleborough, Charles, ed. *Constitution Making in Indiana; A Source Book of Constitutional Documents.* Indianapolis, Indiana Historical Commission, 1916–30. 3 v. (Indiana Historical Collections.)

Levering, Mrs. Julia Henderson. *Historic Indiana* . . . Centennial ed., rev. and enl. New York and London, Putnam, 1916. 565 p., front., plates, ports., map, facsim., bibl.

Monks, Leander J., ed. *Courts and Lawyers of Indiana.* Indianapolis, Federal Publishing Co., Inc., 1916. 3 v., fronts., plates, ports., maps.

Pence, George, and Nellie C. Armstrong. *Indiana Boundaries, Territory, State, and County.* Indianapolis, Indiana Historical Bureau, 1933. 883 p., illus. (maps). (Indiana Historical Collections. v. 19.)

Roll, Charles. *Indiana, One Hundred and Fifty Years of American Development* . . . Chicago and New York, Lewis Publishing Co., 1931. 5 v., front. (v. 2), illus., plates, ports., maps, facsims.

Early Period

Baldwin, James. *In My Youth.* Indianapolis, Bobbs-Merrill, 1914. 493 p. A fictional account of life and manners in the early days of the Middle West.

Bartlett, Charles H., and Richard H. Lyon. *LaSalle in the Valley of the St. Joseph* . . . South Bend, Tribune Printing Co., 1899. 118 p. incl. illus., ports., front., plates, map.

Bond, Beverly W. *The Civilization of the Old Northwest; a Study of Political, Social, and Economic Development,* 1788–1812. New York, Macmillan, 1934. 534 p.

Clark, George Rogers. *The Capture of Old Vincennes; the Original Narratives of George Rogers Clark and of His Opponent Gov. Henry Hamilton.* Edited with introduction and notes by Milo M. Quaife. Indianapolis, Bobbs-Merrill, 1927. 231 p., port. (incl. front.), maps, facsim.

Cockrum, William M. *History of the Underground Railroad.* Oakland City, Ind., Press of J. W. Cockrum Printing Co., 1915. 328 p., front., illus. (map), plates, ports.

Cockrum, William M. *Pioneer History of Indiana*. Oakland City, Ind., Press of Oakland City Journal, 1907. 638 p. incl. front. (port.).

Cox, Sandford. *Recollections of the Early Settlement of the Wabash Valley*. LaFayette, Courier Steam Book and Job Printing House, 1860. 160 p.

Craig, Oscar J. *Ouiatenon; a Study in Indiana History*. Indianapolis, Bowen-Merrill, 1893. 32 p. (Indiana Historical Soc. *Publications,* v. 2, no. 8.) An account of a trading post near the present site of LaFayette.

Dillon, John B. *A History of Indiana* . . . 2d ed. Indianapolis, Bingham & Doughty, 1859. 637 p., front., plates, port., fold. maps.

Dunn, Jacob Piatt, ed. 'Documents Relating to the French Settlements on the Wabash.' (In Indiana Historical Soc. *Publications*. Indianapolis, 1894. v. 2, p. 403–42.)

Dunn, Jacob Piatt. *Indiana; a Redemption from Slavery*. New and enl. ed. Boston and New York. Houghton Mifflin & Co., 1905. 506 p., front (double map). (American Commonwealths, v.,12.)

English, William Hayden. *Conquest of the Country Northwest of the River Ohio*, 1778–1783; *and Life of Gen. George Rogers Clark*. Indianapolis and Kansas City, Bowen-Merrill, 1896. 2 v., front., illus., plates, ports., maps, facsims.

Hall, Baynard Rush. *The New Purchase; or, Seven and a Half Years in the Far West,* by Robert Carlton, Esq. (Baynard Rush Hall). Indiana Centennial ed., edited by James Albert Woodburn. Princeton, Princeton Univ. Press, 1916. 522 p., front., plates, ports., map. 1st ed., New York, 1843. An account of pioneer life in Bloomington.

Indiana. Adjutant General's Office. *Indiana in the Mexican War*. Indianapolis, Wm. B. Burford, printer, 1908. 496 p., illus., port., tables.

Indiana Daughters of the American Revolution. *Roster of Soldiers and Patriots of the American Revolution Buried in Indiana,* compiled and edited by Mrs. Roscoe C. O'Byrne. Brookville, Ind., 1938. 407 p., ports.

Indiana. Governor. *Messages and Letters* [*1800–1825*], edited by Logan Esarey. Indianapolis, Indiana Historical Commission, 1922–4. 3 v. (Indiana Historical Collections, v. 7, 9, and 12.)

Lockwood, George B., and Charles A. Prosser. *The New Harmony Movement,* by George B. Lockwood, with the collaboration of Charles A. Prosser in the preparation of the educational chapters. New York, Appleton, 1905. 404 p., front., plates, ports., facsims., bibl. An account of the communal experiments of Robert Owen and George Rapp.

Ogg, Frederic Austin. *The Old Northwest; a Chronicle of the Ohio Valley and Beyond*. New Haven, Yale Univ. Press, 1921. 220 p., col. front., fold. map, bibl. (The Chronicles of America Series, Allen Johnson, ed. v. 19.)

Smith, Oliver H. *Early Indiana Trials; and Sketches*. Cincinnati, Moore, Wilstach, Keys & Co., printers, 1858. 640 p., front. (port.).

U. S. Dept. of State. *The Territorial Papers of the United States*. Compiled and edited by Clarence Edwin Carter. Washington, U. S. Government Printing Office, 1934–   . Vol. 2–3 on Northwest Territory; Vol. 7–8 on Indiana Territory.

Wilson, George Robert. *Early Indiana Trails and Surveys*. Indianapolis, C. E. Pauley & Co., 1919. p. 349–457, illus. (maps). (Indiana Historical Soc. Pub. v. 6, no. 3.)

Later Period

Indiana. Adjutant General's Office. *Indiana in the War of the Rebellion*. Official report of W. H. H. Terrell, adjutant general. Indianapolis, 1869. 8 v.
——*Record of Indiana Volunteers in the Spanish-American War 1898–1899*. Issued by authority of the 61st General Assembly of Indiana. Indianapolis, Wm. B. Burford, printer, 1900. 368 p., illus. (incl. front.), tables.
Indiana Federation of Clubs. *History, Indiana Federation of Clubs*. Compiled by Grace Gates Courtney, edited by Arcada Stark Balz. Fort Wayne, Fort Wayne Printing Co., 1939. 587 p., front., illus., ports., facsim.
Indiana. Historical Bureau. *Indiana World War Records: Indiana Book of Merit*, comp. by Harry A. Rider. Indianapolis, Indiana Historical Bureau, 1932. 827 p., ports.
Indiana. Historical Commission. *Indiana World War Records: Gold Star Honor Roll*. Fort Wayne, Fort Wayne Printing Co., 1921. 750 p., ports.
Lemcke, J. A. *Reminiscences of An Indianian*. Indianapolis, The Hollenbeck Press, 1905. 224 p., front. (port.).
[Merrill, Catharine.] *The Soldier of Indiana in the War for the Union*. Indianapolis, Merrill and Co., 1866–9. 2 v., front., port., maps.
Pratt, Mrs. Sarah Smith. *The Old Crop in Indiana*. Indianapolis, Pratt Poster Co., 1928. 272 p., front., illus. An account of Nineteenth-century Hoosier life.
Trissal, Francis Marion. *Public Men of Indiana, A Political History*. v. 1, 1860–1890; v. 2, 1890–1920. Hammond, Ind., W. B. Conkey Co., printer, 1922–3. 2 v., plates, ports., facsims.
Turpie, David. *Sketches of My Own Times*. Indianapolis, Bobbs-Merrill Co., 1903. 387 p.

BIOGRAPHY

Beveridge, Albert J. *Abraham Lincoln, 1809–1858*. Boston and New York, Houghton Mifflin, [1937]. 4 v., fronts. (ports.), bibl. (Standard Library ed. First pub. 1928.)
Bodley, Temple. *George Rogers Clark: His Life and Public Services*. Boston, Houghton Mifflin, 1926. 425 p., front., port., map, bibl.
Bowers, Claude G. *Beveridge and the Progressive Era*. Boston, Houghton Mifflin, 1932. 610 p., front., plates, ports., facsim., bibl.
——*The Life of John Worth Kern*. Indianapolis, The Hollenbeck Press, 1918. 475 p., front., illus., plates, ports.
Clarke, Grace Julian. *George W. Julian*. Indianapolis, Indiana Historical Commission, 1923. 456 p. (Indiana Historical Collections, v. 11.)
Cleaves, Freeman. *Old Tippecanoe, William Henry Harrison and His Time*. New York, Charles Scribner's Sons; London, Charles Scribner's Sons, ltd., 1939. 422 p., front., illus. (maps), plates, ports., facsim.

Coffin, Levi. *Reminiscences of Levi Coffin, the Reputed President of the Underground Railroad*. Cincinnati, Western Tract Society, 1876. 712 p., port. (incl. front.).

Coleman, McAlister. *Eugene V. Debs, a Man Unafraid*. New York, Greenberg, 1930. 345 p., front., plates, ports., bibl.

Dickey, Marcus. *The Maturity of James Whitcomb Riley*. Indianapolis, Bobbs-Merrill, 1922. 427 p., front., plates, ports.

——*The Youth of James Whitcomb Riley* . . . Indianapolis, Bobbs-Merrill, 1919. 425 p., front., plates, ports., facsims.

Dreiser, Theodore. *A History of Myself*. New York, Horace Liveright, 1931. 2 v. Vol. 1, 'Dawn'; vol. 2, 'Newspaper Days.'

Dye, Charity. *Some Torch Bearers in Indiana*. Indianapolis, printed by The Hollenbeck Press, 1917. 327 p., front., illus. (music).

Eggleston, George Cary. *The First of the Hoosiers; Reminiscences of Edward Eggleston* . . . Philadelphia, D. Biddle, 1903. 382 p., plates, ports., incl. front.

Foulke, William Dudley. *Life of Oliver P. Morton, Including His Important Speeches*. Indianapolis, Kansas City, Bowen-Merrill, 1899. 2 v., front. (port.).

Foulke, William Dudley, ed. *Lucius B. Swift*. Indianapolis, Pub. for the Society by Bobbs-Merrill Co., 1930. 153 p., ports. (Indiana Historical Society. *Publications*, v. 9.)

Godecker, Sister Mary Salesia. *Simon Bruté de Rémur, First Bishop of Vincennes*. St. Meinrad, Ind., St. Meinrad Historical Essays, 1931. 441 p., front., plates, ports., map, facsims., bibl.

Goebel, Mrs. Dorothy Burne. *William Henry Harrison; a Political Biography*. Indianapolis, 1926. 456 p., front., illus. (map), plates, port., bibl. (Indiana Historical Collections, v. 14 . . . Biographical Series, v. 2.)

Gresham, Mrs. Matilda. *Life of Walter Quintin Gresham, 1832–1895*. Chicago, Rand McNally, 1919. 2 v., fronts. (ports.).

James, James Alton. *The Life of George Rogers Clark*. Chicago, Univ. of Chicago Press, 1928. 534 p., front., plates, port., maps, facsim., bibl.

Kenworthy, Leonard S. *The Tall Sycamore of the Wabash, Daniel Wolsey Voorhees*. Boston, Bruce Humphries, 1936. 155 p., front. (port.), plates.

Leopold, Richard William. *Robert Dale Owen: a Biography*. Cambridge, Mass., Harvard University Press, 1940. 470 p., illus., bibl., index. (Harvard University Studies, v. 45.)

Lockridge, Ross F. *La Salle*. Yonkers-on-Hudson, New York, World Book Company, 1931. 312 p., incl. front., illus.

Marshall, Thomas Riley. *Recollections of Thomas R. Marshall, Vice-President and Hoosier Philosopher; a Hoosier Salad*. Indianapolis, Bobbs-Merrill, 1925. 397 p., front., plates, ports., facsims.

Pancoast, Elinor, and Anne E. Lincoln. *The Incorrigible Idealist, Robert Dale Owen in America*. Bloomington, Ind., Principia Press, 1940. 150 p., front. (port.), bibl.

Podmore, Frank. *Robert Owen; a Biography*. New York, Appleton, 1924. 688 p., front., plates, ports., facsims., bibl. First pub. in 2 v., London, 1906.

Tarbell, Ida M. *The Early Life of Abraham Lincoln*. New York, S. S. McClure, 1896. 240 p. incl. fronts., illus., ports.

――――*The Life of Elbert H. Gary: The Story of Steel*. New York, D. Appleton & Co., 1923. 361 p., front., illus.

Thomas, Charles Marion. *Thomas Riley Marshall, Hoosier Statesman*. Oxford, Ohio, The Mississippi Valley Press, 1939. 296 p., front. (port.).

Thompson, Charles N. *Sons of the Wilderness, John and William Conner*. Indianapolis, 1937. 283 p. incl. front., plates, ports., fold. maps, bibl. (Indiana Historical Soc. *Publications*, v. 12.) The story of two early settlers in Indiana.

Wallace, Lewis. *Lew Wallace, an Autobiography*. New York and London, Harper & Brothers, 1906. 2 v., fronts., illus., plates, ports., facsims.

Wiley, Harvey W. *An Autobiography*. Indianapolis, Bobbs-Merrill, 1930. 339 p., front., plates, ports.

Woodward, Walter C. *Timothy Nicholson, Master Quaker*. Richmond, Ind., The Nicholson Press, 1927. 252 p., front. (port.).

Woollen, William Wesley. *Biographical and Historical Sketches of Early Indiana*. ·Indianapolis, Hammond & Co., 1883. 568 p., front., ports.

GOVERNMENT AND POLITICS

Bradshaw, Wilfred. *Indiana Government in Brief,* prepared for the Hoosier Boys' State. Indianapolis, The American Legion, Department of Indiana. 64 p.

Feightner, Harold C. *Indiana County Government*. Indianapolis, Indiana Historical Bureau, 1932. p. 285–402. (Indiana History Bulletin, v. 9, no. 6.)

Indiana. Department of Public Welfare. *State Institutions of Indiana, 1940*. Indianapolis, Indiana Department of Public Welfare, 1940. 60 p., ·illus.

Indiana. Laws, Statutes, etc. *Baldwin's Indiana Statutes, Annotated, 1934*. Edited by William Edward Baldwin, V. Ed. Funk, and Wallace B. Heiser. Cleveland, Banks-Baldwin Law Publishing Co., 1934. 3746 p. With cumulative pocket supplement, 1935 to date.

――――*Burns' Annotated Indiana Statutes, 1933*. Edited by Harrison Burns. Indianapolis, Bobbs-Merrill, 1933–5. With annual cumulative pocket supplement, 1935 to date. 12 v.

Indiana League of Women Voters. *Indiana Voters' Handbook*. 5th ed. rev. by Virginia Mannon. Indianapolis, 1940. 184 p., illus., maps, diagr.

Indiana. Legislative Bureau. *Legislative Procedure in the General Assembly of the State of Indiana*. Indianapolis, Wm. B. Burford Printing Co., 1928. 100 p. incl. forms.

Indiana Taxpayers Association. *Cost of Government in Indiana*. v. 1–4. Published biennially by the Indiana Taxpayers Association, Indianapolis.

Rauch, John G., and Nellie C. Armstrong. *A Bibliography of the Laws of Indiana, 1788–1927*. Indianapolis, Indiana Historical Bureau, 1928. 77 p. (Indiana Historical Collections, v. 16.)

Seeds, Russel M. *History of the Republican Party of Indiana*. Indiana History Co., 1899. 578 p., illus., port.

Sikes, Pressly Spinks. *The State Government of Indiana*. Bloomington, Ind., Principia Press, 1937. 120 p., maps, diagrs., bibl.

Stoll, John B. *History of the Indiana Democracy, 1816–1916*. Indianapolis, 1917. 1090 p., ports.

Swank, Paul, Mathew M. Hamilton, and Herman O. Makey. *Living with Your Government in Indiana*. Fort Wayne, Educational Book Division, Fort Wayne Printing Co., 1939. 526 p. incl. illus., diagrs., forms.

Woodburn, James Albert. 'Party Politics in Indiana during the Civil War.' (In Am. Historical Assn. *Annual Report . . . for the Year of 1902*. Washington, 1903. v. 1, p. 223–51.)

AGRICULTURE

Kellar, Herbert Anthony, ed. *Solon Robinson, Pioneer and Agriculturist; Selected Writings*. Indianapolis, 1936. 2 v., front., illus., plates, ports., map, plans, facsim. (Indiana Historical Collections, v. 21.)

Latta, W. C. *Outline History of Indiana Agriculture*. LaFayette, LaFayette Printing Co., 1938. 372 p., illus., charts, maps.

Purdue University. Dept. of Agricultural Extension. [Publications.] La-Fayette.

——Agricultural Experiment Station. [Publications.] LaFayette.

INDUSTRY, COMMERCE, AND LABOR

Appleton, John B. *The Iron and Steel Industry of the Calumet District; a Study in Economic Geography*. Urbana, Ill., 1927. 133 p. incl. plates, fold. maps. (Univ. of Illinois Studies in the Social Sciences, v. 13, no. 2.)

Esarey, Logan. *State Banking in Indiana, 1814–1873*. Bloomington, Ind., 1912. p. 219–305, illus. (map). (Indiana University Studies, no. 15.)

Hagerty, James Edward. 'Early Financial History of Indiana.' Indianapolis, 1937. (In *Indiana History Bulletin*, v. 14, no. 10, p. 265–341.)

Indiana. Bureau of Industrial Hygiene. *Preliminary Industrial Hygiene Survey of Indiana Industries*. Indianapolis, Indiana State Board of Health, 1939. 162 p., illus., plates, map, tables (part fold.), diagrs., charts.

Indiana State Chamber of Commerce. *Directory of Indiana Manufacturers*. Indianapolis, 1940. 134 p.

Indiana University. *Indiana Business Studies*. Bloomington, Ind., 1924 to date.

Lockhart, Oliver C. 'Oölitic Limestone Industry of Indiana.' *Indiana University Bulletin*, Sept. 1910, v. 8: 71–110.

Starr, George W. *Industrial Development of Indiana*. Bloomington, Ind., School of Business Administration, Indiana University, 1937. 124 p., diagrs. (Indiana University Bureau of Business Research. Indiana Studies in Business.)

TRANSPORTATION

Benton, Elbert Jay. *The Wabash Trade Route in the Development of the Northwest.* Baltimore, 1903. 112 p. (Johns Hopkins Univ. Studies in History and Political Science, series 21, nos. 1–2.)

Blackburn, Glen A. 'Interurban Railroads in Indiana.' *Indiana Magazine of History,* Sept. and Dec. 1924, v. 20: 221–79, 400–464.

Burns, Lee. *The National Road in Indiana.* Indianapolis, 1919. p. 209–37, illus. (Indiana Historical Soc. *Publications,* v. 7, no. 4.)

Daniels, Wylie J. *The Village at the End of the Road, A Chapter in Early Indiana Railroad History.* Indianapolis, 1938. 112 p., illus. (plates). (Indiana Historical Society *Publications,* v. 13, no. 1.)

Esarey, Logan. 'Internal Improvements in Early Indiana.' Indianapolis, 1912. p. 47–158. (Indiana Historical Society *Publications,* v. 5, no. 2.)

Hargrave, Frank F. *A Pioneer Indiana Railroad: the Origin and Development of the Monon.* Indianapolis, Wm. B. Burford Printing Co., 1932. 229 p., front., plates, map, facsims., bibl.

Hulbert, Archer Butler. *The Ohio River.* New York and London, G. P. Putnam's Sons, 1906. 378 p., front., plates, ports., maps (fold.), plan.

Montgomery, Ethel L. *The Building of the Michigan Road.* LaFayette, 1902. Mimeographed.

Murphy, Maurice. 'Big Four Railroad in Indiana.' *Indiana Magazine of History,* June and Sept. 1925, v. 21: 109–273, illus. (plates).

SOCIAL AND ECONOMIC CONDITIONS

Indiana. Board of State Charities. *Indiana, A Century of Progress: A Study of the Development of Public Charities and Correction 1790–1915,* by Amos W. Butler. Indiana Reformatory Printing Trade School, 1916. 145 p., illus., port., plans.

Indiana. Department of Public Welfare. [Reports and Publications.] Indianapolis.

Klinger, John H., and Thomas G. Hutton. *Indiana and the Adult Offender.* Indianapolis, 1938. 104 p. incl. illus. (maps), tables, diagrs.

Lynd, Robert S., and Helen Merrell Lynd. *Middletown: a Study in Contemporary Culture.* With foreword by Clark Wissler. New York, Harcourt, Brace and Co., 1930. 550 p., incl. tables. Describes Muncie, Ind.

——*Middletown in Transition: a Study in Cultural Conflicts.* New York, Harcourt, Brace and Co., 1937. 604 p., diagrs. Describes Muncie seven years later.

Shaffer, Alice, Mary Wysor Keefer, and Sophonisba Breckinridge. *The Indiana Poor Law.* Chicago, The University of Chicago Press, 1936. 378 p. (Social Service monographs, no. 28.)

State Planning Board of Indiana. *Preliminary Report on the State Plan for Indiana.* Mimeographed. Indianapolis, 1934. 163 p., maps, charts.

U. S. Prison Industries Reorganization Administration. *The Prison Problem in Indiana.* Washington, U. S. Government Printing Office, 1938. 183 p. incl. tables.

Wilson, Helen. *Treatment of the Misdemeanant in Indiana, 1816–1936.* Chicago, University of Chicago Press, 1938. 113 p. (Social Service monographs.)

EDUCATION

Boone, Richard C. *A History of Education in Indiana.* New York, Appleton, 1892. 454 p.

Bourne, Randolph S. *The Gary Schools.* With intro. by William Wirt. Boston, New York, etc., Houghton Mifflin, 1916. 204 p., front., plates, bibl.

Cotton, Fassett A. *Education in Indiana (1793-1934).* Bluffton, Ind., Progress Publishing Co., 1934, 491 p., bibl.

Indiana. Department of Public Instruction. *School Laws of the State of Indiana.* Indianapolis, Wm. B. Burford Printing Co., 1939. 533 p.

Indiana. Education Survey Commission. *Public Education in Indiana.* New York, General Education Board, 1923. 304 p. incl. tables, diagrs., front., plates.

Indiana. Superintendent of Public Instruction. [Reports and Bulletins.] Indianapolis, 1843 to date.

Indiana University. School of Education. [Publications.] Bloomington, Ind.

Kennedy, Millard Fillmore. *Schoolmaster of Yesterday.* New York, Whittlesey House, 1940. 359 p. incl. illus., plate, front.

McDaniel, Ethel H. *Contributions of the Society of Friends to Education in Indiana.* Indianapolis, 1939. p. 117–223, illus. (plates). (Indiana Historical Society *Publications,* v. 13, no. 2.)

Thomas, John Hardin. 'The Academies of Indiana.' *Indiana Magazine of History.* Dec. 1914, v. 10: 331–58; March 1915, v. 11: 8–39.

RELIGION

Blanchard, Col. Charles. *History of the Catholic Church in Indiana.* Logansport, A. W. Bowen, 1898. 2 v., plates, ports.

Cauble, Commodore Wesley. *Disciples of Christ in Indiana; Achievements of a Century.* Indianapolis, Meigs Publishing Co., 1930. 305 p., plates (incl. ports.), bibl. Includes biographies.

Coleman, Christopher B. 'Some Religious Developments in Indiana.' *Indiana Magazine of History,* June 1909, v. 5: 57–71.

Edson, Hanford A. *Contributions to the Early History of the Presbyterian Church in Indiana . . .* Cincinnati, Indianapolis, etc., Winona Publishing Co., 1898. 281 p.

Harris, A. C. 'Quakerism in Indiana.' *The American Friend,* Oct. 29 to Nov. 19, 1896.

Holliday, Fernandez C. *Indiana Methodism.* Cincinnati, Hitchcock & Walson, 1873. 360 p., ports.

Stott, William T. *Indiana Baptist History,* 1798–1908. Franklin, Ind., 1908. 381 p., plates, ports., bibl.

Sweet, William Warren. *Circuit-Rider Days in Indiana.* Indianapolis, W. K. Stewart, 1916. 344 p., maps, bibl.

Winger, Otho. *History of the Church of the Brethren in Indiana.* Elgin, Ill., 1917. 479 p.

LITERATURE, JOURNALISM, AND PRINTING

Beeson, R. Katherine. *Literary Indiana*. Indianapolis, Bobbs-Merrill, 1925. 31 p., illus.

Butler, J. H. 'Indiana Newspapers, 1829–1860.' *Indiana Magazine of History,* Sept. 1926, v. 22: 297–333.

Cordell, Richard A. 'Limestone, Corn, and Literature; the Indiana Scene and Its Interpreters.' *Saturday Review of Literature,* Dec. 17, 1938.

Cottman, George S. 'Early Newspapers in Indiana.' *Indiana Magazine of History,* Sept. 1906, v. 2: 107–21.

Harrison, Henry, ed. *An Anthology of 48 Living Writers; Indiana Poets.* With foreword by E. Merrill Root. New York, H. Harrison, 1935. 160 p.

Holliday, Robert Cortes. *Booth Tarkington*. Garden City, N. Y., Double-day, Page & Co., 1918. 218 p., front. (port.), plates. Appraises Tarkington as an artist.

McMurtrie, Douglas Crawford. *Indiana Imprints, 1804–1849.* Indianapolis, Indiana Historical Society, 1937. p. 307–93. (Indiana Historical Society. *Publications,* v. 11, no. 5.)

Masters, Edgar Lee. 'James Whitcomb Riley.' *Century Magazine,* Oct. 1927. v. 114, no. 6, p. 704–15.

Nicholson, Meredith. *The Hoosiers*. New York and London, Macmillan, 1915. 296 p. First pub. 1900. Describes the literature and political and social history of Indiana.

Parker, Benjamin S., and Enos B. Heiney, compilers and editors. *Poets and Poetry of Indiana* . . . New York, Boston, etc., Silver, Burdette & Co., 1900. 464 p., front., ports. A collection of Indiana poetry, 1800–1900, with biographical notes.

Pattee, Fred Lewis. *The New American Literature, 1890–1930.* New York and London, Century, 1930. 507 p. Includes chapters on 'The Emergence of Indiana' and 'Theodore Dreiser.'

Rusk, Ralph Leslie. *Literature of the Middle Western Frontier*. New York, Columbia University Press, 1926. 2 v., 866 p.

Stillson, Blanche, and Dorothy Ritter Russo. *Abe Martin—Kin Hubbard.* Indianapolis, The Hoosier Book Shop, 1939. 39 p. incl. front. (port.), illus.

Venable, William Henry. *Beginnings of Literary Culture in the Ohio Valley: Historical and Biographical Sketches*. Cincinnati, R. Clarke & Co., 1891. 519 p.

Walker, Mary Alden. *The Beginnings of Printing in the State of Indiana*. Crawfordsville, R. E. Banta, 1934. 124 p., bibl.

ART AND ARCHITECTURE

Burke, Mrs. Robert E. *Handicrafts in Indiana*. Bloomington, Ind., 1940. 30 p., illus. (Bulletin of Extension Div., Indiana University, v. 25, no. 5.)

Burnet, Mrs. Mary O. *Art and Artists in Indiana.* New York, Century, 1921. 448 p., col. front., plates, ports., bibl. Describes painting and sculpture in Indiana from pioneer days.

Burns, Lee. *Early Architects and Builders in Indiana.* Indianapolis, 1935. p. 179–215. (Indiana Historical Soc. *Publications,* v. 11, no. 3.)

Forsyth, William. *Art in Indiana.* Indianapolis, H. Lieber Co., 1916. 39 p.

Indiana Artists' Club. *Biographical Directory of Indiana Artists,* compiled by Flora Lauter. Indianapolis, 1937. 38 p.

Indiana Federation of Art Clubs. *Art Guide to Indiana* . . . Compiled, organized and prepared by Mrs. H. B. Burnett . . . and Mrs. Robert E. Burke. Bloomington, 1931. 184 p., illus. (incl. map). (Bulletin of Extension Div., Indiana University. v. 16, no. 8.)

Johnston, Ella Bond. *A History of the Art Association of Richmond, Indiana.* Richmond, Ind., 1937. 48 p., front. (port.), plates.

Knox, Julia LeClerc. 'Pioneer Homesteads.' *Indiana Magazine of History,* Dec. 1924, v. 18: 371–80.

Peat, Wilbur D. 'Preliminary Notes on Early Indiana Portraits and Portrait Painters.' *Indiana History Bulletin,* v. 17, no. 2, Feb. 1940. p. 77–93.

Rabb, Kate Milner. *Indiana Coverlets and Coverlet Weavers.* Indianapolis, 1928. 45 p., illus. (plates). (Indiana Historical Soc. *Publications.* v. 8, no. 8.)

Shulz, Adolph R. 'The Story of the Brown County Art Colony.' *Indiana Magazine of History,* Dec. 1935. v. 31: 282–9.

MUSIC AND FOLK GAMES

Brewster, Paul G. *Ballads and Songs of Indiana.* Bloomington, Ind., 1940. 376 p., music. (Indiana University Publications, Folklore Series no. 1.)

Cregor, Gertrude. *Indiana Composers, Native and Adopted.* Bloomington, Indiana University, 1936. 51 p.

Dreiser, Theodore. 'My Brother Paul.' (In *Twelve Men.* New York, Boni & Liveright, 1919. p. 76–109.)

Wolford, Leah Jackson. *The Play-Party in Indiana; a Collection of Folk-Songs and Games* . . . Indianapolis, 1916. 120 p., illus. (music), diagrs., bibl. (Indiana Historical Collections.)

Index